CW01649119

OASIS
ARTISTS' STUDIOS IN HONG KONG Vol.2

Editor-in-chief	Victor Lai Ming-hoi
Conceptual Director	Carl Cheng Chi-ming
Contributors	Teresa Chan
	Carl Cheng
	Stephanie Cheung
	Alice Choi
	Livia B Garcia
	Ronny Leung
Sub-editor (English)	Jo Baker
Sub-editor (Chinese)	Miranda Li
Translator (Chinese to English)	Teresa Chan
	Stephanie Cheung
	Alice Choi
	Livia B Garcia
Assistant Editor	Yu Kei-kei
Photographer	Lumenvisum
Project Co-ordinators	Heidi Chan
	Quinny Li
Publisher	Peter Lau
Business Manager	Heidi Chan

Design and Retouching by AOMM Creative Limited
Colour management by Asia One Graphic Limited
Printing by Asia One Printing Limited

asiaone

Published by Asia One Product & Publishing Limited
aopp@asiaone.com.hk
www.asiaonebooks.com

First published in September 2008

ISBN 978-988-17041-6-0

This publication is sold on the understanding that the publisher, contributors and their employees are not responsible for the results of any actions, errors or omissions taken on the basis of information contained in this publication. The publisher, contributors and their employees expressly disclaim all and any liability to any person, whether a purchaser of the publication or not, in respect of any action or omission or the consequences of any action or omission by any such person, whether whole or partial, upon the whole or part of the contents of this publication.

Copyright ©2008 Asia One Product & Publishing Limited. All rights reserved. No part of this work, covered by the publisher's copyright may be reproduced in any form by any means, graphic, electronic or mechanical, including photocopying, recording, taping or information storage and retrieval, without the written permission of the publisher. Any unauthorised use of this publication will result in immediate legal proceedings.

OASIS

ARTISTS' STUDIOS IN HONG KONG Vol.2

Contents

The Freestyle Studio

Academic Essays

Appendix

Preface

The publication of the first volume of *Oasis: Artists' Studios in Hong Kong* in 2007 carried special meanings in the local art scene: first, it represented the local community's effort to compile an oral history of contemporary Hong Kong art. Academics and art practitioners have always lamented the lack of historical record. With little literature for public reference, promoting local art and culture has been a difficult task. By recording people's experiences through dialogue, oral history gives a vivid account of the current state of art making.

To avoid simple speculation, our crew visited artists in their studios and conversed with them. Firsthand information was then organised, analysed and reviewed. This is the best way to write history. Such a strenuous project should actually be embarked upon by the government or the academia. However, in the past 20 years there have been relatively few books on the history of Hong Kong art, which shows that the institutions concerned have little regard for the writing of its history. However, under the auspices of Peter Lau, the two volumes of *Oasis: Artists' Studios in Hong Kong* have come out as a blueprint. Capturing the true image of Hong Kong culture, this project is highly meaningful. Jerry Kwan, an artist covered in the first volume, died just months ago. In this case it seems that there is a particular urgency for the recording of our oral histories.

Another significance of the publication of *Oasis* is the exposition of creative work through interviews with, and reports on artists. Although the artists' works are only presented in words and pictures, as Tang Ying-chi, editor-in-chief of the first volume, noted: "With the studio open days, art itself has become less cold, untouchable and mysterious... letting the readers and the public know that the artists strive to carry on with the work of creation whilst earning a living. Some also participate in social affairs and take up social causes". Artists' studios are not only places where creative ideas are given shape, but also where artists realise their talent, assert their identity, struggle in the creative process and find refuge for their souls. Thus studios are a necessity for professional artists, instead of an alternative luxury as people thought in the past.

However, the ideal studio varies from artist to artist. Some, such as Wucius Wong and John Li Tung-keung, prefer an orderly space. Some, like Danny Lee Chin-fai, need the dynamism of chaos and the dramatic clash of scattered objects. Some crave solitude in an undisturbed world. Some enjoy company and interaction with their peers. Thus this volume of *Oasis* stretches the spatial concept of the studio and has been divided into three sections: the Studio Space, the Shared Studio and the Freestyle Studio.

The Studio Space explores the relationship between individual artists and their work spaces. Physical space has a direct impact on creative work. The indoor and outdoor settings – from historical buildings such as Pauline Lam Yuk-lin's at the Cattle Depot Artist Village or interiors like Yank Wong Yan-kwai's, which are filled with visual ornaments and music – all reflect individual characters. The Shared Studio is about the sharing of space, with artists who gain inspiration through interaction with their peers. Lee Chi-hoi and Kong Khong-chang construct a Hong Kong identity with comics; Tong Ng Kwun-lun and Celia Ko Tin-yan find resonance in the pairing of eastern and western media, abstraction and realism; Hong Chi-fun and Choi Yan-chi are partners in art and in life. Some artists, such as Cheung Chung-chu, Fung Ho-yin and Yung Sau-mui of the Hong Kong Open Printshop, and the young members of Ten O Four, work together because they share the same vision or commitment. The Freestyle Studio finds room for art in life. Homes or workshops are used as creative spaces and creativity furnishes these dwellings. 'Studios' of this kind include those of Kan Tai-keung, Chu Hing-wah and Yip Man-yam. Other artists in the section include scholar-artist Wan Qingli; Van Lau, who works in both Hong Kong and China; and So Yan-kei, Leung Mee-ping and Luke Ching Chin-wai whose studios vary according to their creative concepts.

The editorial direction of the present volume follows that of the first volume. Readers will gain a deeper understanding of the art scene and the social structure of Hong Kong between its lines and images. The difference lies in this volume's attempt to write an oral history of the artists and their works. The emphasis is on the interplay of their way of thinking and living, and the inspiration they gain in their studio. The photographs focus on the artists, the happenings and the objects in their studios. These snapshots reflect the various characters of the photographers and their models, and they aim to capture history in a spontaneous way.

The success of the first volume of *Oasis* has given us both encouragement and pressure. Encouraged by the positive response from the art field and the market, we have been propelled and pressured to do even better. Let me take this opportunity to thank the 36 artists and art groups who welcomed our visits and the contributors, Livia B Garcia, Teresa Chan, Ronny Leung, Stephanie Cheung and Alice Choi, who worked hard to meet pressing deadlines. Special thanks should be given to the photographers, Raymond Chan, Dick Chan, Leon Suen and Tse Ming-chong, who made it to every studio, and professors Frank Vigneron, Daniel Lau and Choi Yan-chi, who enrich the volume with their scholarly essays. Credit also goes to the team that strived for the quality of this publication: Carl Cheng, conceptual director; Yu Kei-kei, assistant editor; Mirandi Li and Jo Baker, sub-editors; and Heidi Chan and Quinny Li, project coordinators. Last but not least, I am grateful to Peter Lau, publisher of Asia One Product and Publishing Limited, whose generosity and support contribute greatly to the local art scene.

Victor Lai Ming-hoi
Editor-in-chief

The Studio Space

Wucius Wong

The Modest Way of a Master

By Teresa Chan

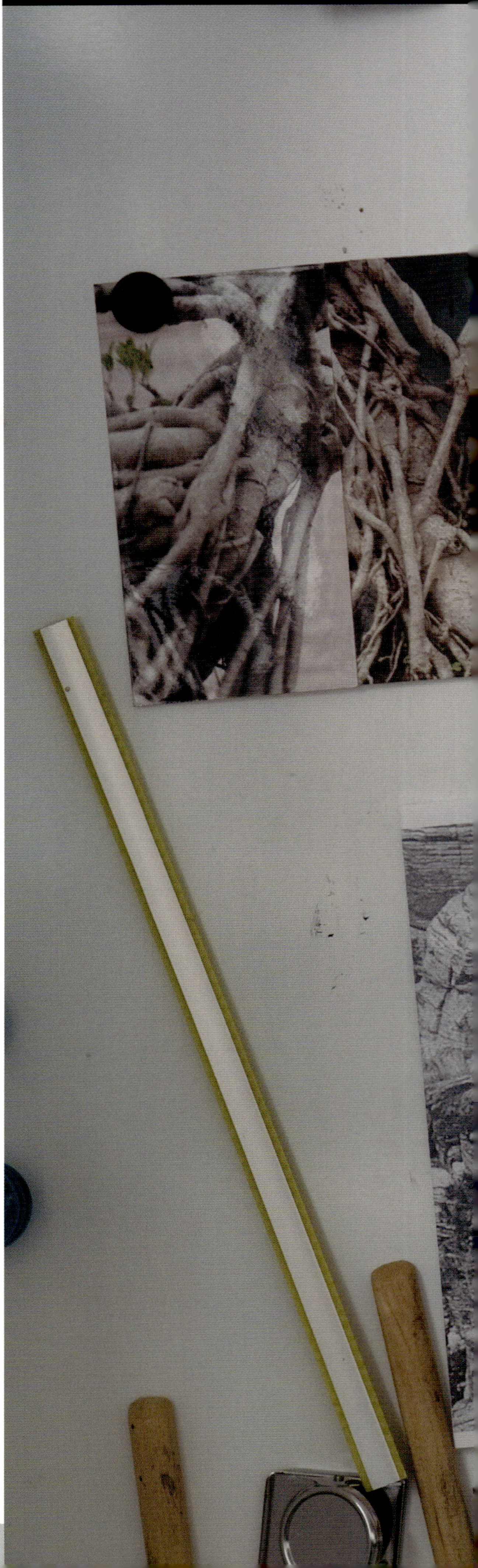

Wucius Wong was born Wong Chung-kee in Guangdong, China, in 1936. A literature lover since his early years, Wong later turned to study painting. He went to the United States for further studies in the 1960s and returned to Hong Kong in 1965 to work in the City Museum and Art Gallery, and teach in the School of Design at the Hong Kong Polytechnic. Wong left for the United States again in 1984 and stayed for more than 10 years before coming back to Hong Kong in 1996. He has been an active artist for decades and strives to find a new order between Eastern and Western art. His paintings are of a unique style that combines a structured layout with the sensation of Chinese ink painting. Wong was awarded the Emeritus Fellowship by the Hong Kong Arts Development Council for the year 1997-1998. He was awarded the Bronze Bauhinia Star in 2007 by the Hong Kong Special Administrative Region Government in recognition of his artistic achievement and his contribution to art education.

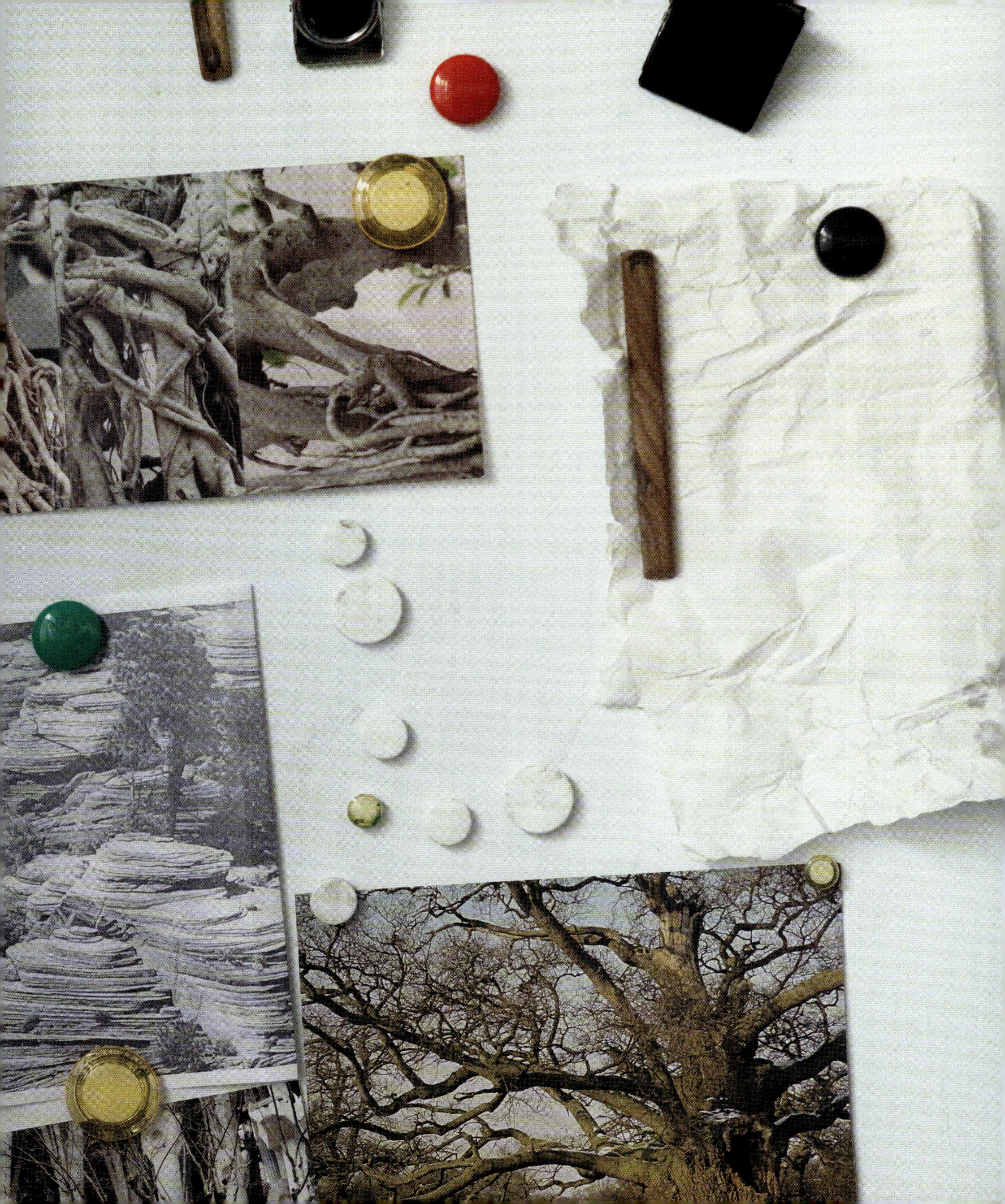

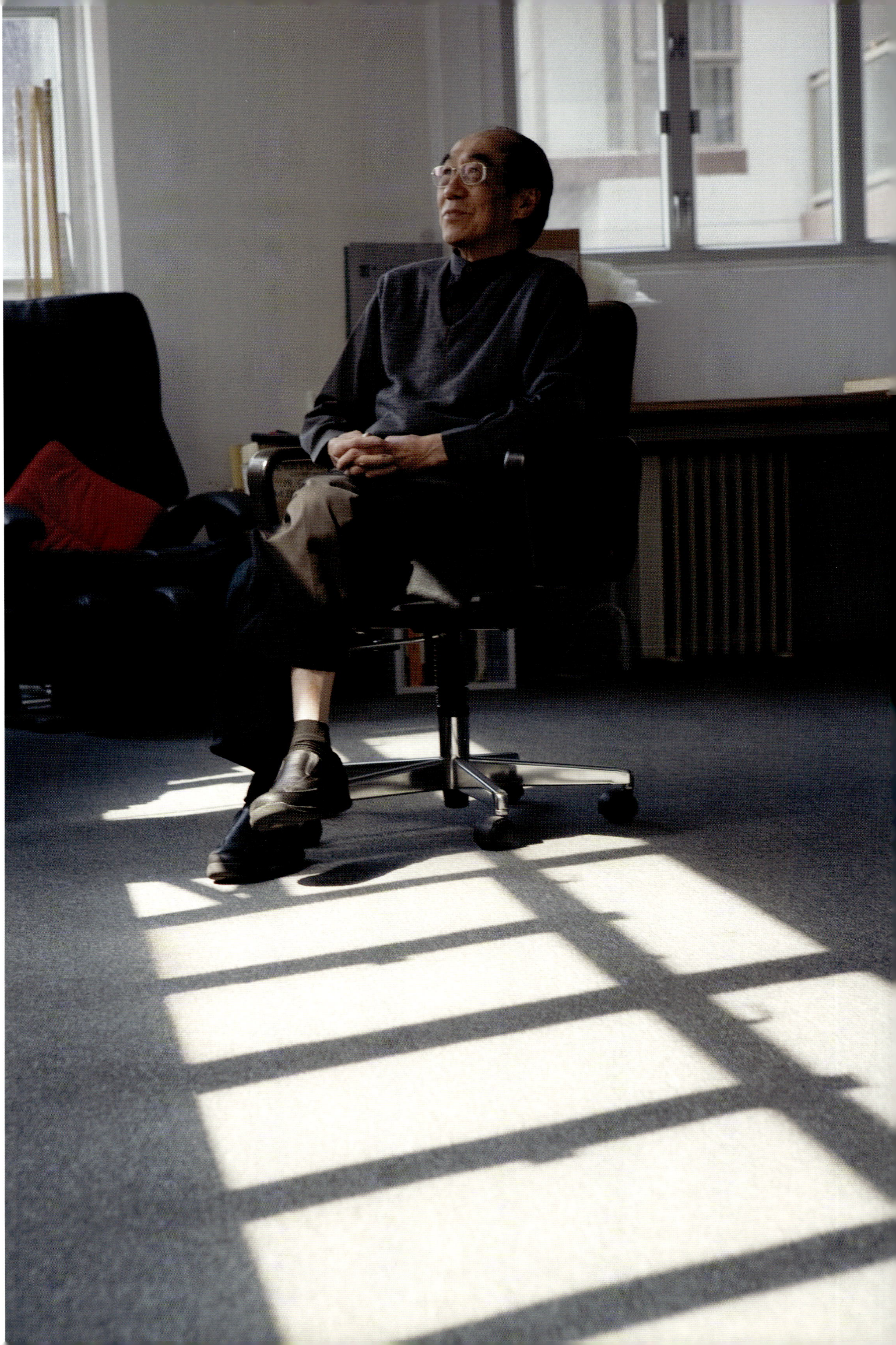

Serenity and sunlight provide Wucius Wong with inspiration for creativity and space for ideas

The name of Wucius Wong was no stranger to me before this interview. Wong is not only an experienced artist held in great respect by the art community, but he is also a core figure of the movement of new Chinese ink painting. In most of the articles I found in my research, the focus is on Wong's artistic explorations between East and West and his unique style of bringing Eastern and Western elements together in harmony. At the *East-West Crossroads*, the title of a major retrospective exhibition held for Wong at the end of 2006 to celebrate his 70th birthday, seems to be a clear and concise summary of his art career so far. I was thrilled to have the chance to meet such a renowned artist who is so knowledgeable about both Eastern and Western art.

The first impression I get is of a courteous and sincere gentleman, reminding me of some unique attributes found in Chinese scholars

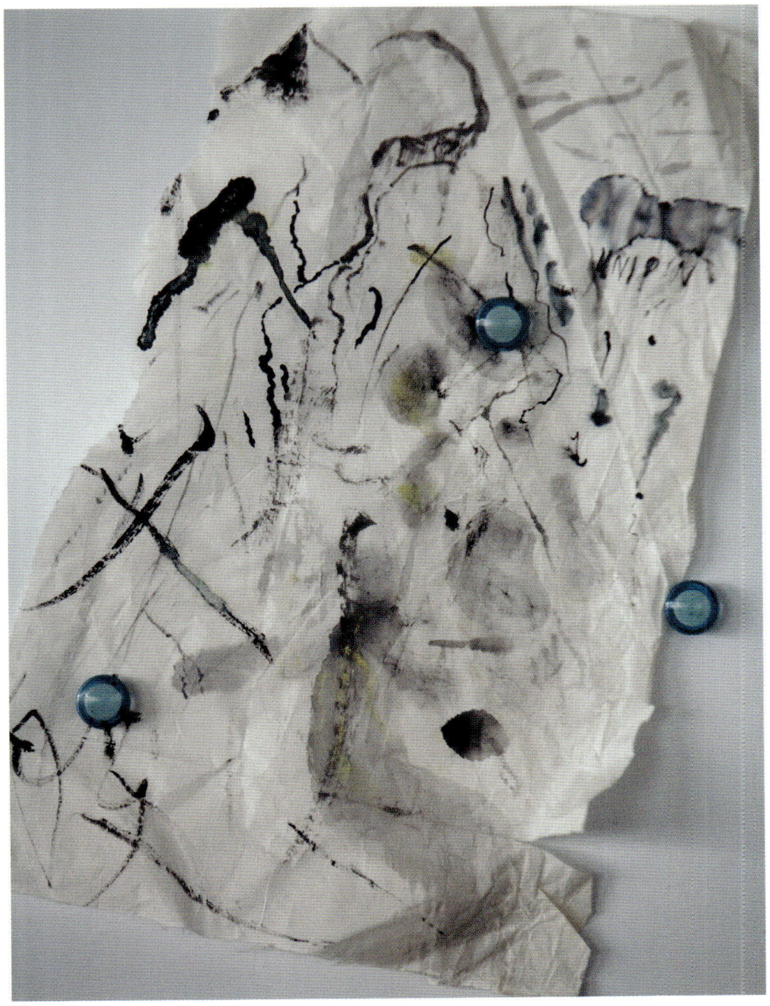

On the day of the interview, Wong greets us at the door of his studio. The first impression I get is of a courteous and sincere gentleman, reminding me of some unique attributes found in Chinese scholars. It seems that the years spent in the West have not left many marks on Wong's outer appearance. The studio is clean and well-lit, with a large working table in the centre of the room. Some low bookshelves run along the wall and on another small table are found paint brushes and other tools. Set up against the largest wall is a painting yet to be finished. The studio is comfortably spacious, probably because there are no unnecessary furniture items in it. When the morning sun comes in through a row of windows, special patterns are cast on the floor. If this space were to be described in the simplest way, I would use the word 'serenity'. I bring Wong a copy of the newly published *Oasis: Artists' Studios in Hong Kong* and he browses through the book, pointing out pictures of artists he knows. As the conversation continues we are brought back to the local art scene in the 1960s, the years in which Wong was a young artist.

At that time there was far less exhibition space in Hong Kong. According to Wong, if one wanted to hold an exhibition there were not many alternatives other than the British Council, the side chapel of St John Cathedral, the Consulate General of the United States or some major hotels. Works of art had limited opportunity to meet the public and the market was comparatively small. As it was not easy to make a living by just selling one's works, many artists had to find a job in addition to art making. Wong once wanted to be a poet and his cultural career started with writing. Apart from writing poems and essays, he also ran a literary magazine. However he considered his writing skills undeveloped and did not continue to lead a writer's life. He chose another language — visual art, to express what he thinks and feels.

Wong says that he was originally self-taught, and he benefited greatly from the teaching of according to HKMA's publication, it should be Lü Shoukun, a master of great attainment in Chinese ink painting with a broad artistic perspective. When Wong pursued further studies in the United States in the 1960s, not only did he have the chance to see painting and design in the Western world, but he had the opportunity to experience a way of logical thinking that is less predominant in Chinese society. Learning from both the East and the West, Wong has tried to blend the characteristics of the two sides in his artistic exploration.

For this merging of East and West he draws an analogy between his works and the city of Hong Kong. In his landscape ink paintings we can sometimes see lines incorporated in a grid structure, or the complete filling up of surfaces with colour and lines, as found in many Chinese ink paintings. Upon close examination of such a layout one finds, however, the flow and spirit of Chinese ink painting in between the dots and lines. This journey of seeking a balance point between East and West has already lasted for half a century. Looking back, Wong says that he has found too many intersection points and has yet to find the ideal balance.

Mountains and rivers are frequently portrayed in Wong's works. He considers them more a reflection of his own situation and feelings than a portrait of a particular mountain or river.

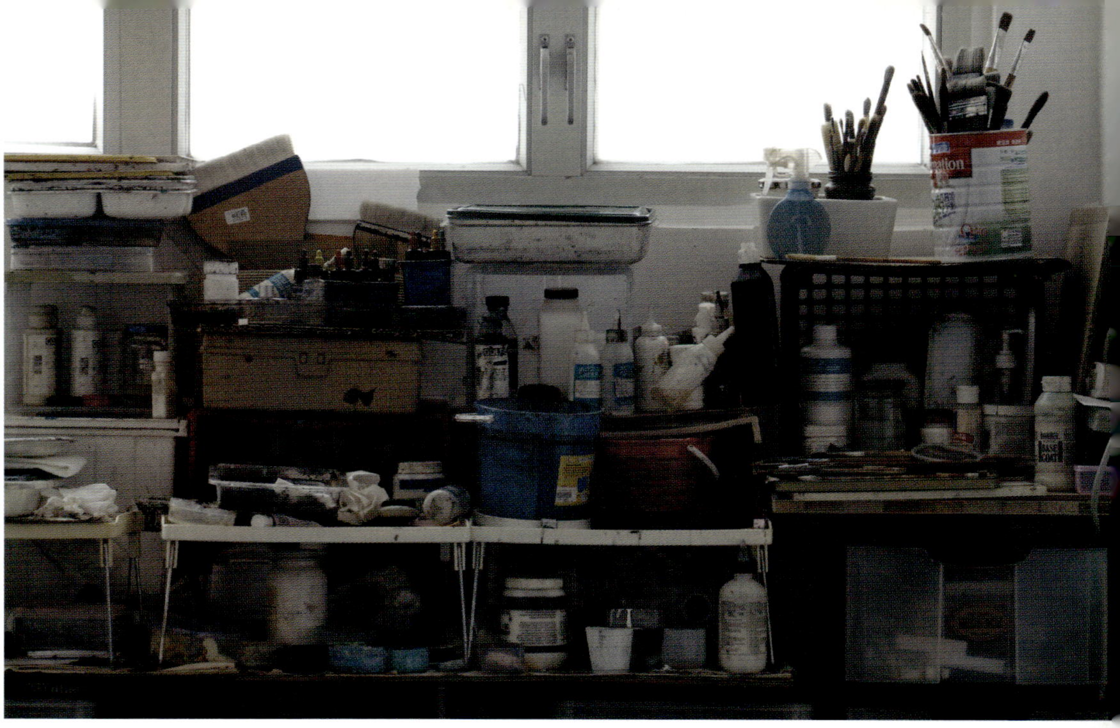

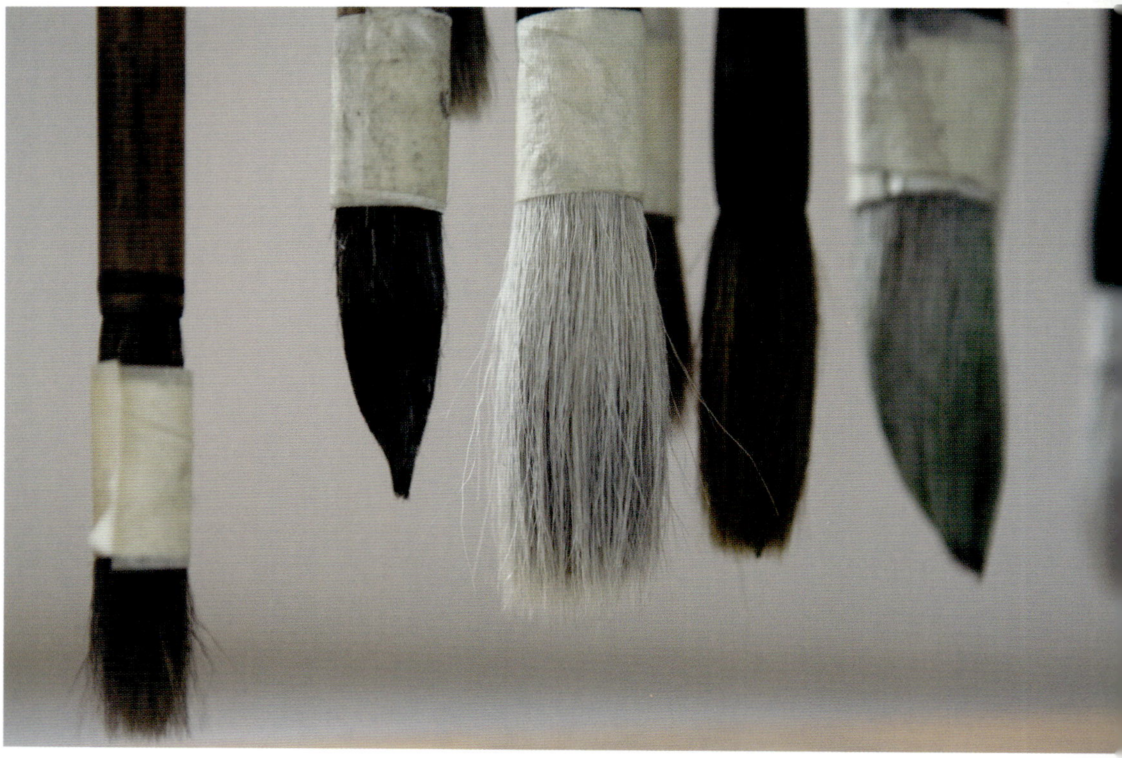

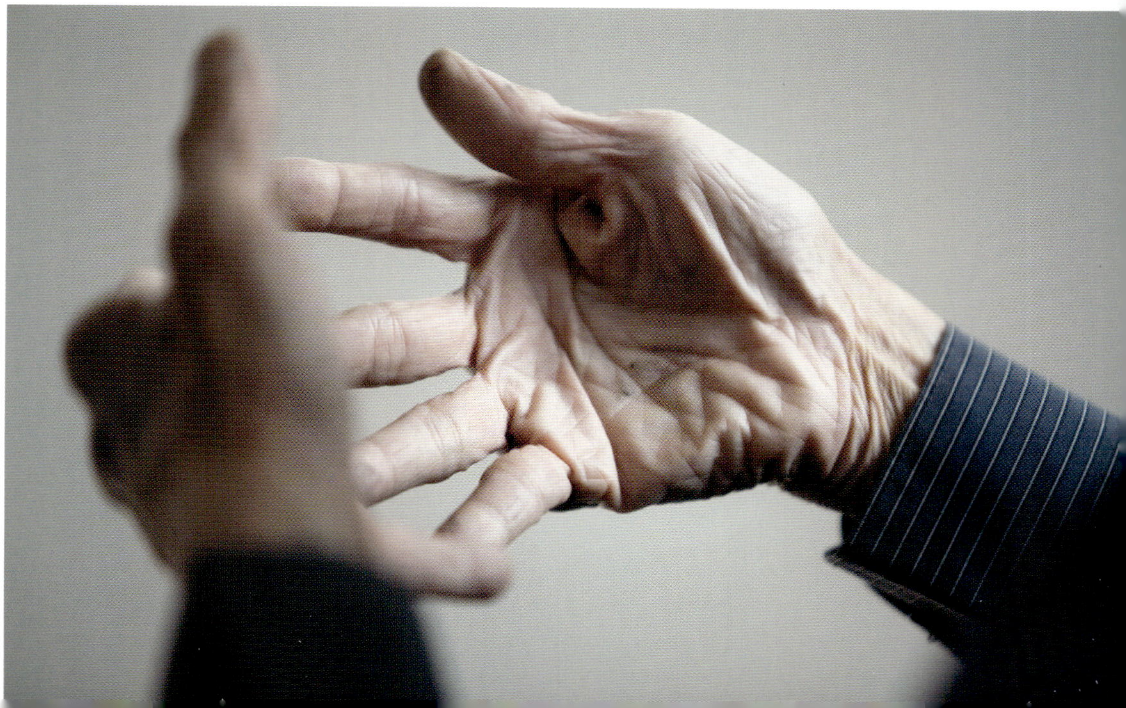

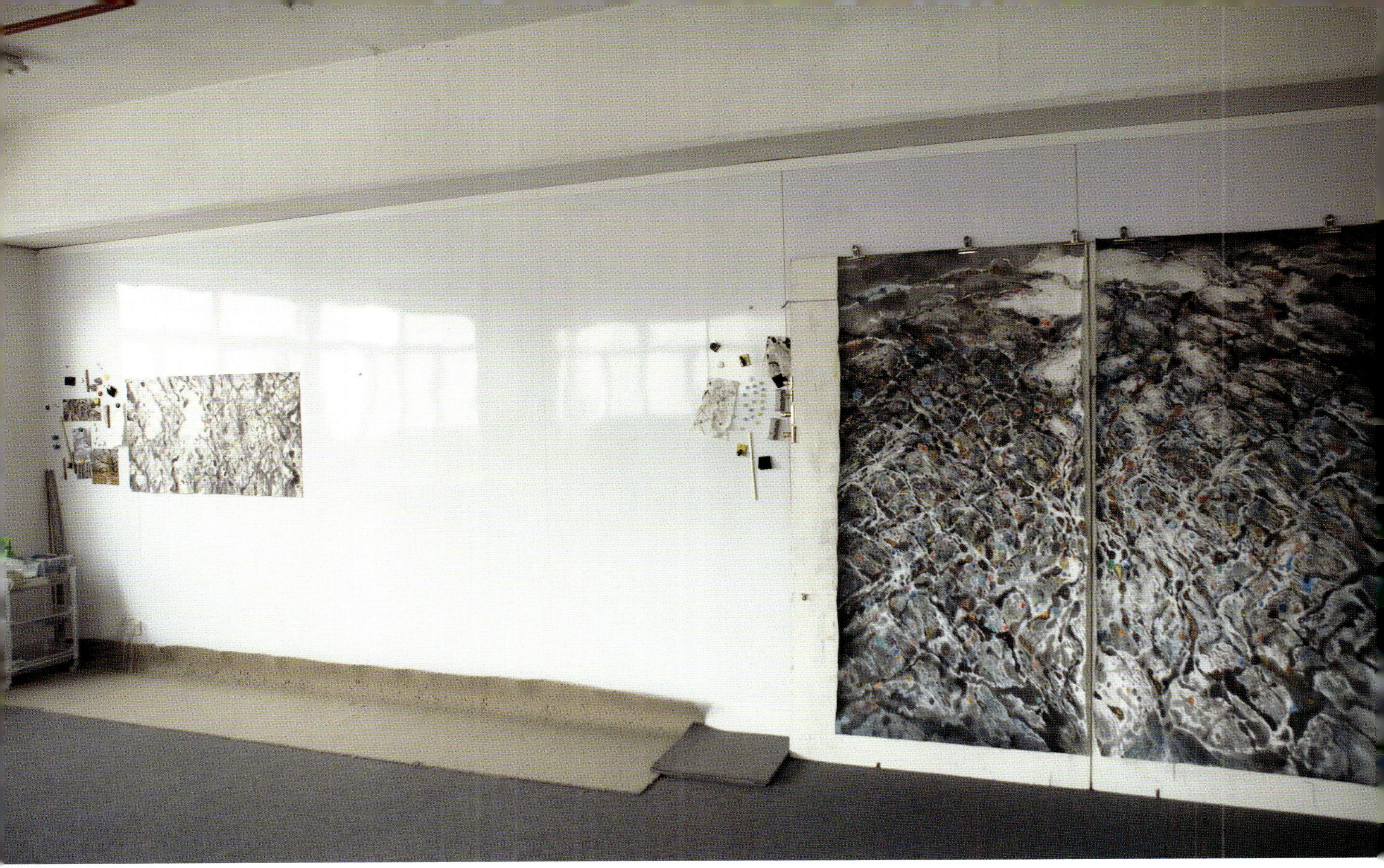

The unfinished painting on the wall is a continuation of dots and lines, and also a testimony of the flow of life

The single peak in his early works echoes the lonely journey of an artist, but it also reveals a determination to find the perfect combination of man and universe. In the years spent in the US, Wong often used rivers as a subject matter. Rivers reminds viewers of the passing of time and also the conditions of an artist far away from his homeland. Before the reunion of Hong Kong and China, Wong 'reunited' with the city and the subject of his paintings changed – to trees. Trees are connected to the land and grow only in soil, symbolising everybody's desire to seek a permanent home.

Wong says that his works draw references from his physical surroundings. When he lived in Hong Kong's Mid-level district, some of his works captured the change in space as skyscrapers kept growing. Now that he lives in the Southern district, the sea has become one of his many subjects. The Chinese poems Wong loves are also a constant source of inspiration. During our interview he quotes *A View of Taishan*, a poem by Du Fu[1], to illustrate how a reader can be emotionally touched by a poem and can in turn infuse the feelings into other works. He considers visual aesthetics to be the external side of an artwork, and a strong emotional base to be the core element.

Wong's works are known for their fine structure and grandeur. Talking about the painting process, he says that he sometimes makes a draft and enlarges it for the real-size painting. However, it is more common for him to allow the work to form bit by bit, without advance planning, following his own thoughts and feelings at the time.

Wong is generally categorised as a Chinese ink painter, and rarely is he associated with graphic design. Yet the artist has not only studied graphic design but taught and written books on the subject, and he is well recognised as a pioneer in design training in Hong Kong. As the variety of media used in art expands, design and fine arts may influence and even overlap. Are they two sides of a coin? What does Wong, a leading figure in both, think about this? He says that some people will use functionality to judge whether a work belongs to the field of art or design. However the differentiation of the two is never as distinct as black and white. For example portraiture has been an important genre in painting and it is functional; it records the face and bearing of the person portrayed. Many crafts and ornaments contain artistic as well as functional value. There are masterpieces in both art and design, and it is not necessary to put any of them in a higher position than the other.

When I first see the semi-finished painting on the wall as I enter the studio, the lively extension and movement of dots and lines on the surface makes me believe that it is an ink painting on paper. Not until Wong asks me to take a closer look do I find that it

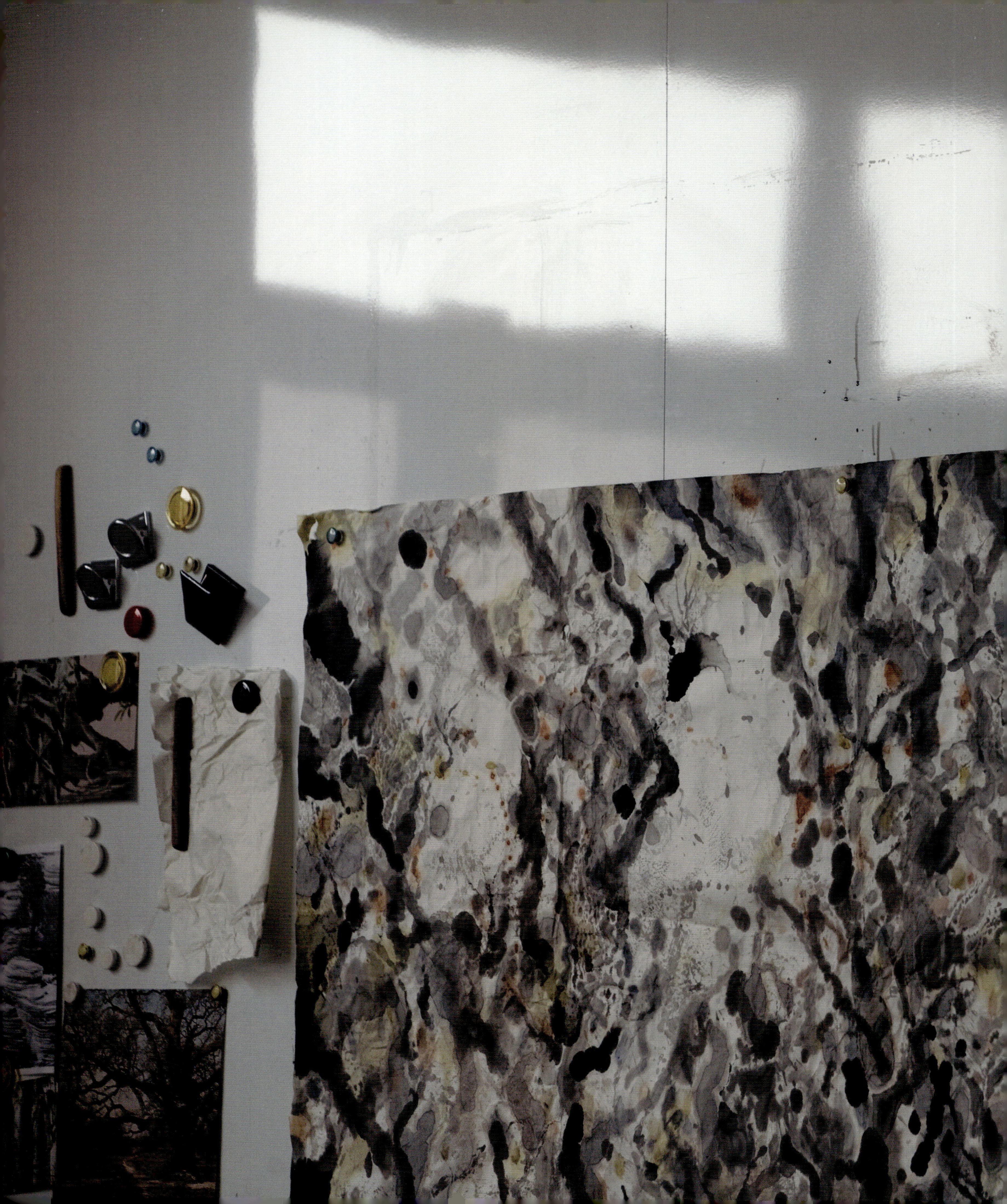

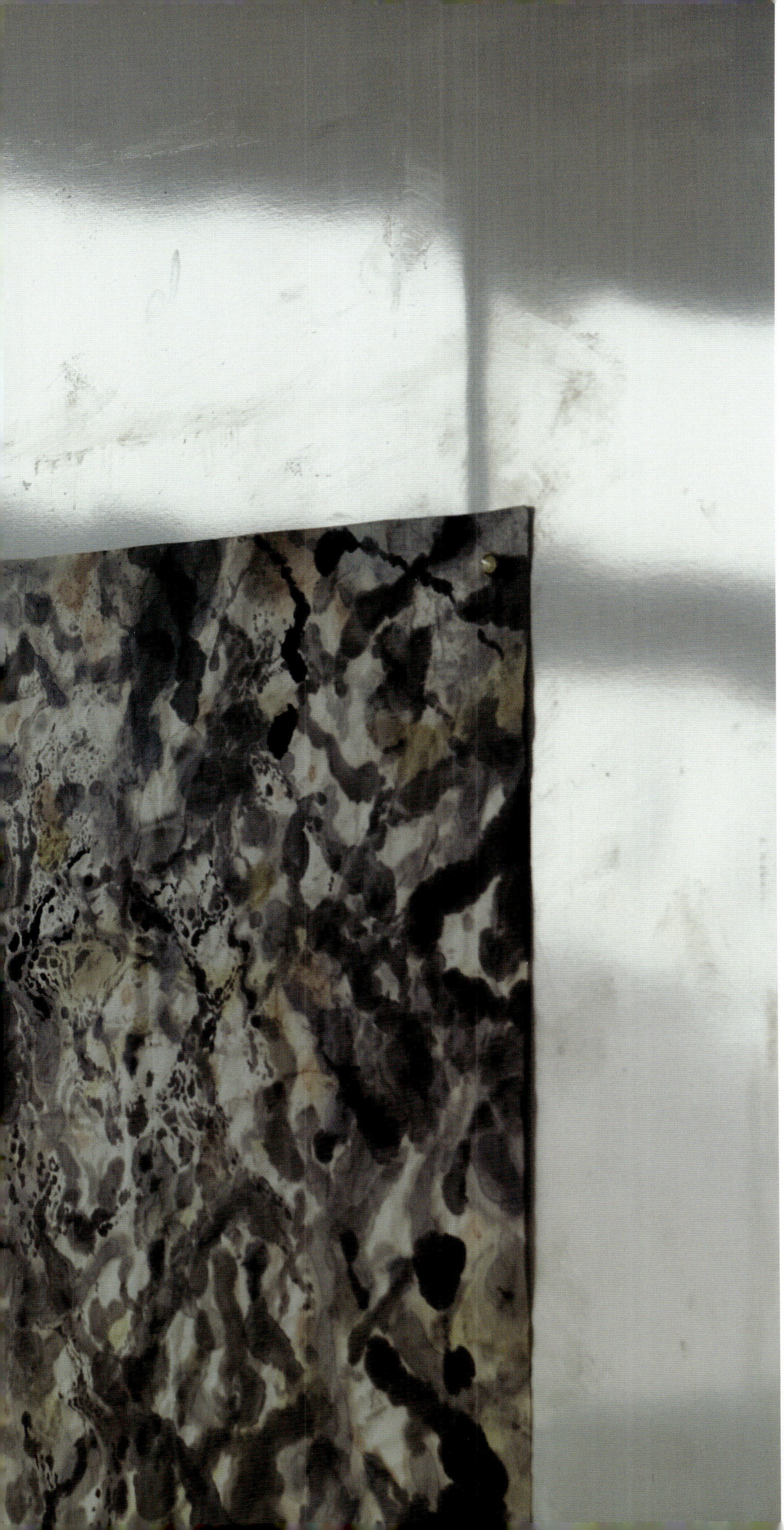

is a work of acrylic on canvas. Combining a western medium and the spirit of Chinese ink painting in one work is a task that can only be accomplished by an artist like Wong, who has a deep understanding of both Eastern and Western art.

Facing an ever-increasing variety of art media, has Wong ever been tempted to use media other than paint, during his long years of art making? He says that each medium has its own characteristics and, at the same time, shares some features with others; painting is a choice he made after careful consideration of his own abilities and time. Although devoted to one medium, Wong believes that "when walking in the company of other men, there must be one I can learn something from".[2] Therefore he won't resist other forms of media and art making, and has always been modest in learning from others and reviewing his own inadequacies.

When talking about art development in Hong Kong, Wong says that it has not developed along a straight line. Changes in the population profile have, to a certain extent, had an impact on shaping our art. For example, many Hong Kong people of the past generations are immigrants from southern China, and the Cantonese culture brought with them is revealed in the artworks of those decades. While artists of each generation will continue to have their own context, and Hong Kong has long been a meeting point of East and West, Wong believes that Chinese culture and tradition will still be passed on in our art. He hopes that all artists, no matter what media they use, will always bear in mind the diligence and patience highlighted in the traditional training of Chinese masters.

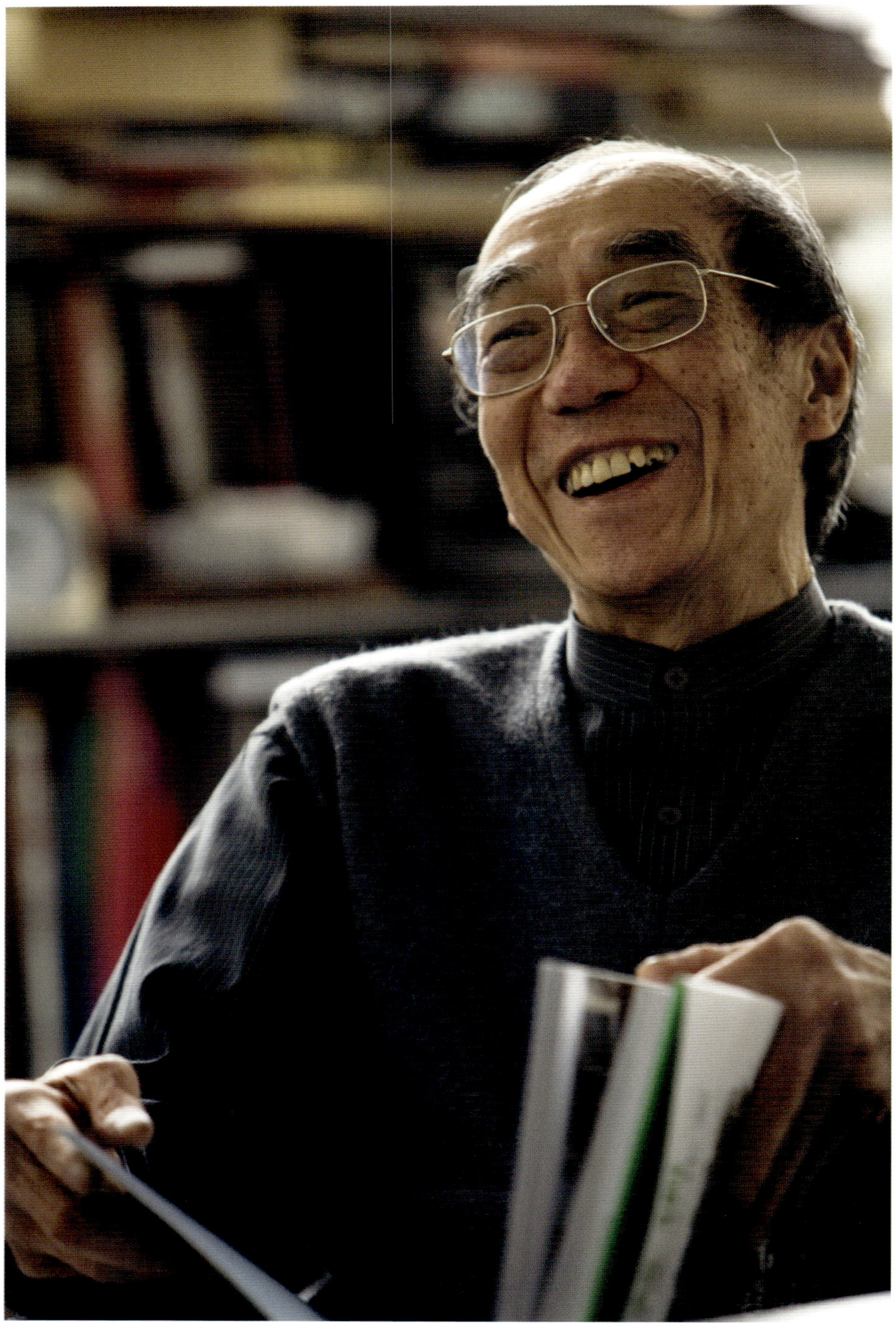

While our photographer snaps away, Wong and I talk about his studio. He now works four days a week in the studio and completes smaller works at home. Although a large studio facilitates the making of big works, artists should never allow limitations in space to strangle their creativity, he says. Countless masterpieces were produced under difficult circumstances.

Many people believe that artists are rather self-centred. However, Wong's words and his bearing have made me realise that no matter which field we are working in, we should keep our horizons open, and keep expanding our scope in order to make continuous progress. The poem, *A View of Taishan*, quoted by Wong exactly conveys this open attitude:

What shall I say of the Great Peak?
The ancient dukedoms are everywhere green,
Inspired and stirred by the breath of creation,
With the Twin Forces balancing day and night.
I bare my breasts toward opening clouds,
I strain my sight after birds flying home.
When shall I reach the top and hold
All mountains in a single glance.[3]

1. Translator's note: Du Fu (A D. 712-770) was a prominent Chinese poet of the Tang Dynasty.

2. Translator's note: A saying by Confucius, recorded in his Analects of Confucius. English translation from Analects of Confucius, translated by Li Po and Xia Yuhe, Beijing, 1994, 116.

3. English translation by Witter Bynner, http://afpc.asso.fr/wengu/wg/wengu.php?l=Tangshi&no=-1&auteur=Du_Fu [retrieved on 2.6.2008]

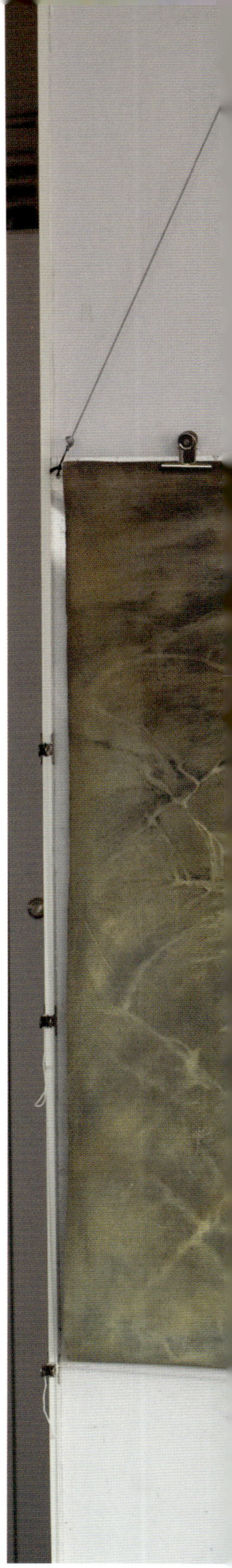

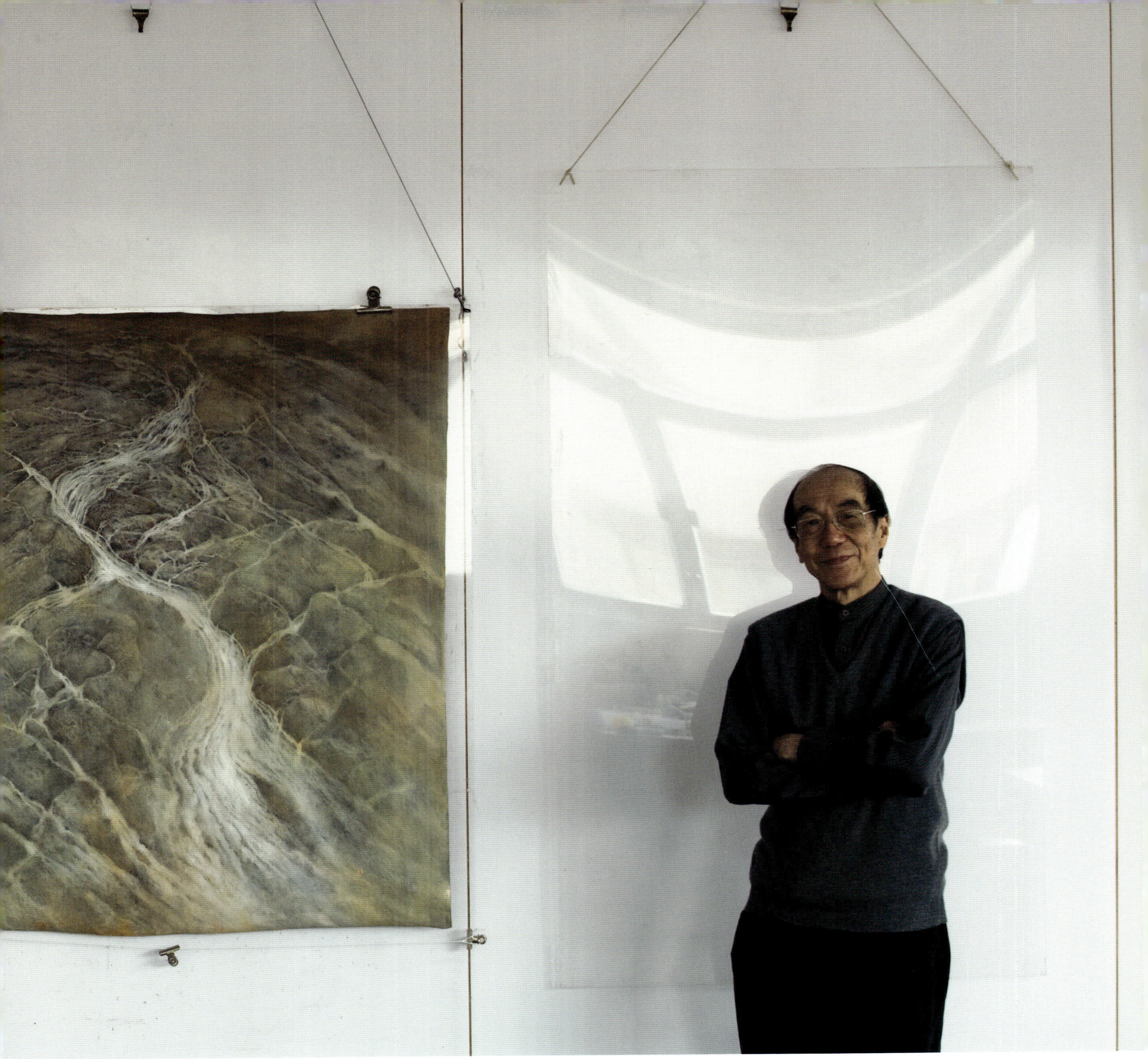

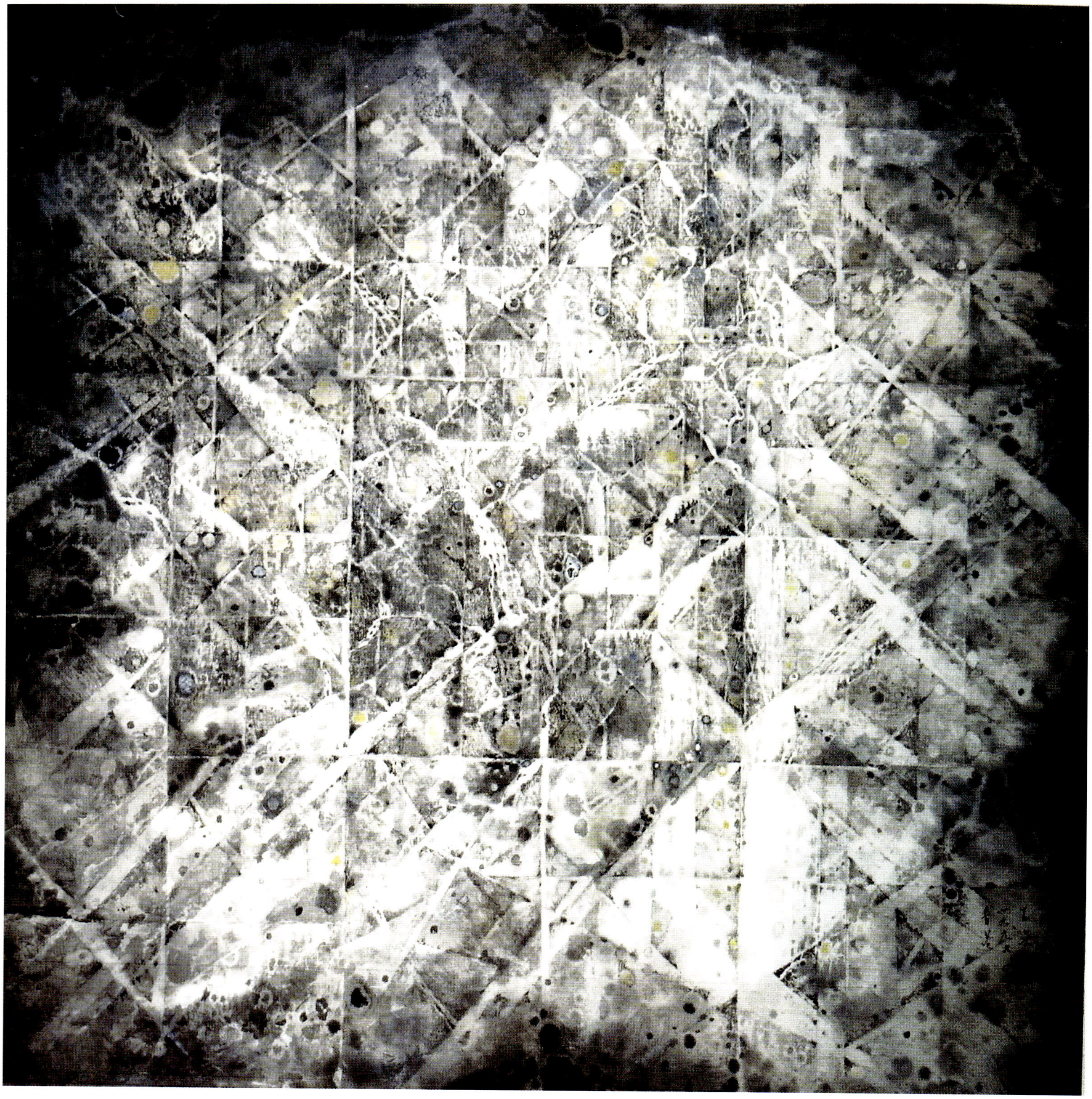

(Above) Superimposed Thoughts #5
Ink & colour on paper, 66x66 cm, 1997

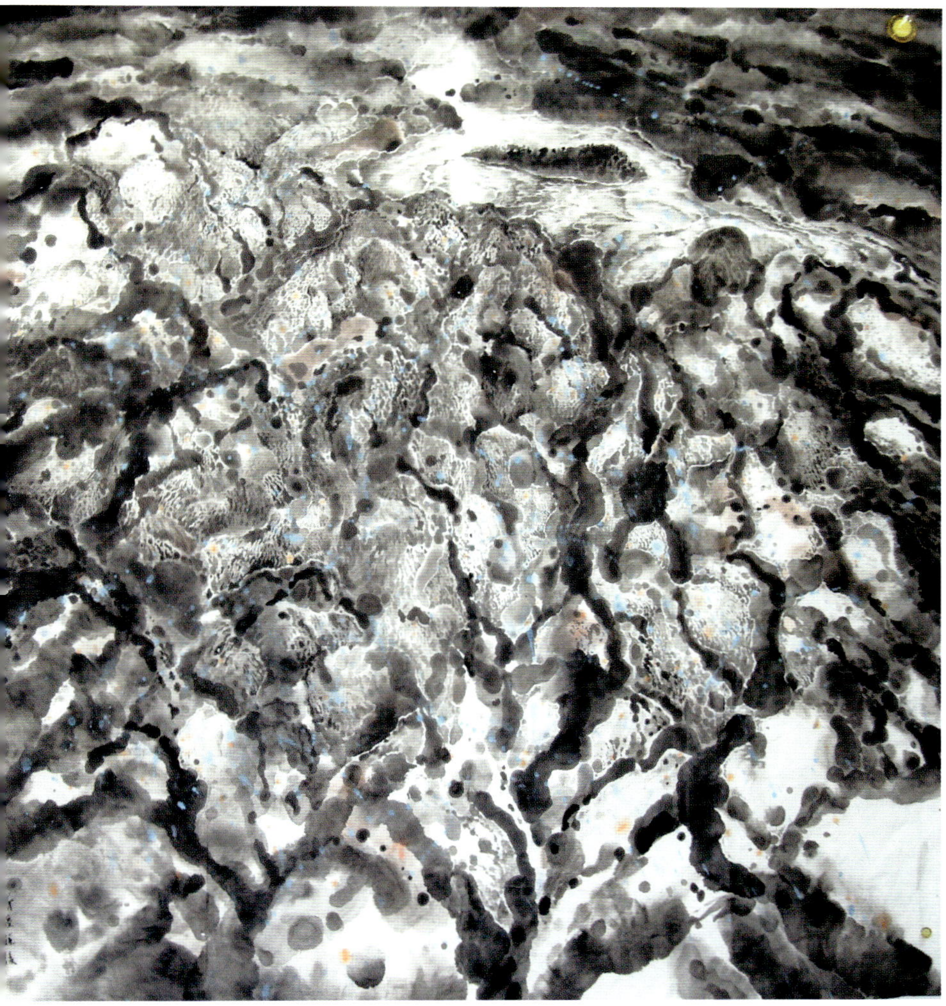

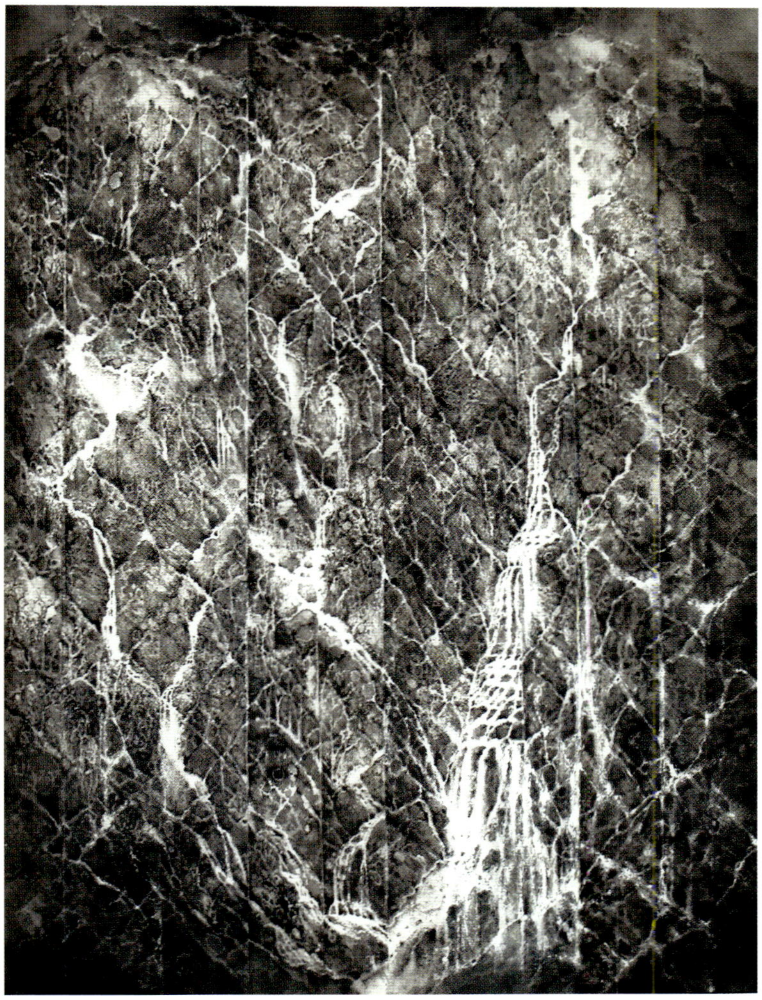

(Left) Xinjiang Impression
Ink & colour on paper, 137.5x137.5 cm, 2006

(Right) Lake Dream #2
Ink & colour on paper, 74x57 cm, 2002

Danny Lee Chin-fai

Reflective Reflections

By Stephanie Cheung

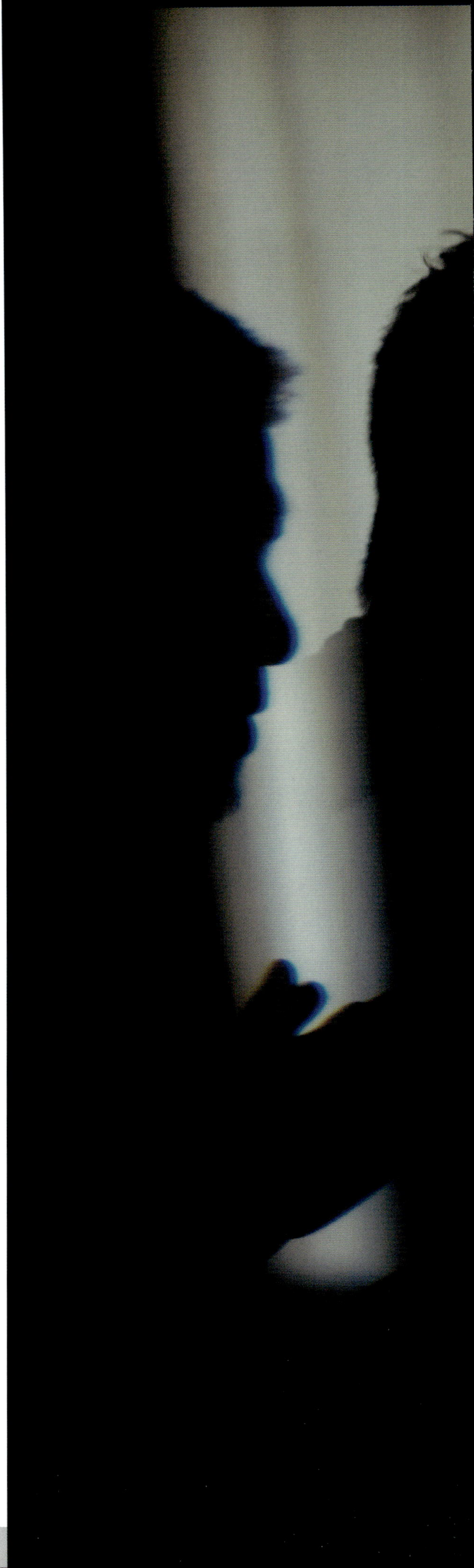

Danny Lee Chin-fai was born in Hong Kong. He has worked as a graphic, interior and advertising designer and is currently a full-time artist. In the early 1980s he started experimenting with copper carving and casting. Lee considers his work – which incorporates various materials – as 'installation sculpture'. He has taken part in numerous local and overseas exhibitions and has received many public art commissions. His works are collected by public organisations, corporations and individuals, and they have been selected for Hong Kong Art Biennials. He was awarded the first prize for sculpture in the New Life competition (organised by the Hong Kong Hospital Authority) and second prize for sculpture in the Olympic Art and Sport Contest 2000 (Hong Kong) (organised by the International Olympic Committee). He is the founding chairperson of Creative Sculptors Hong Kong. He also chairs the Hong Kong Visual Arts Society.

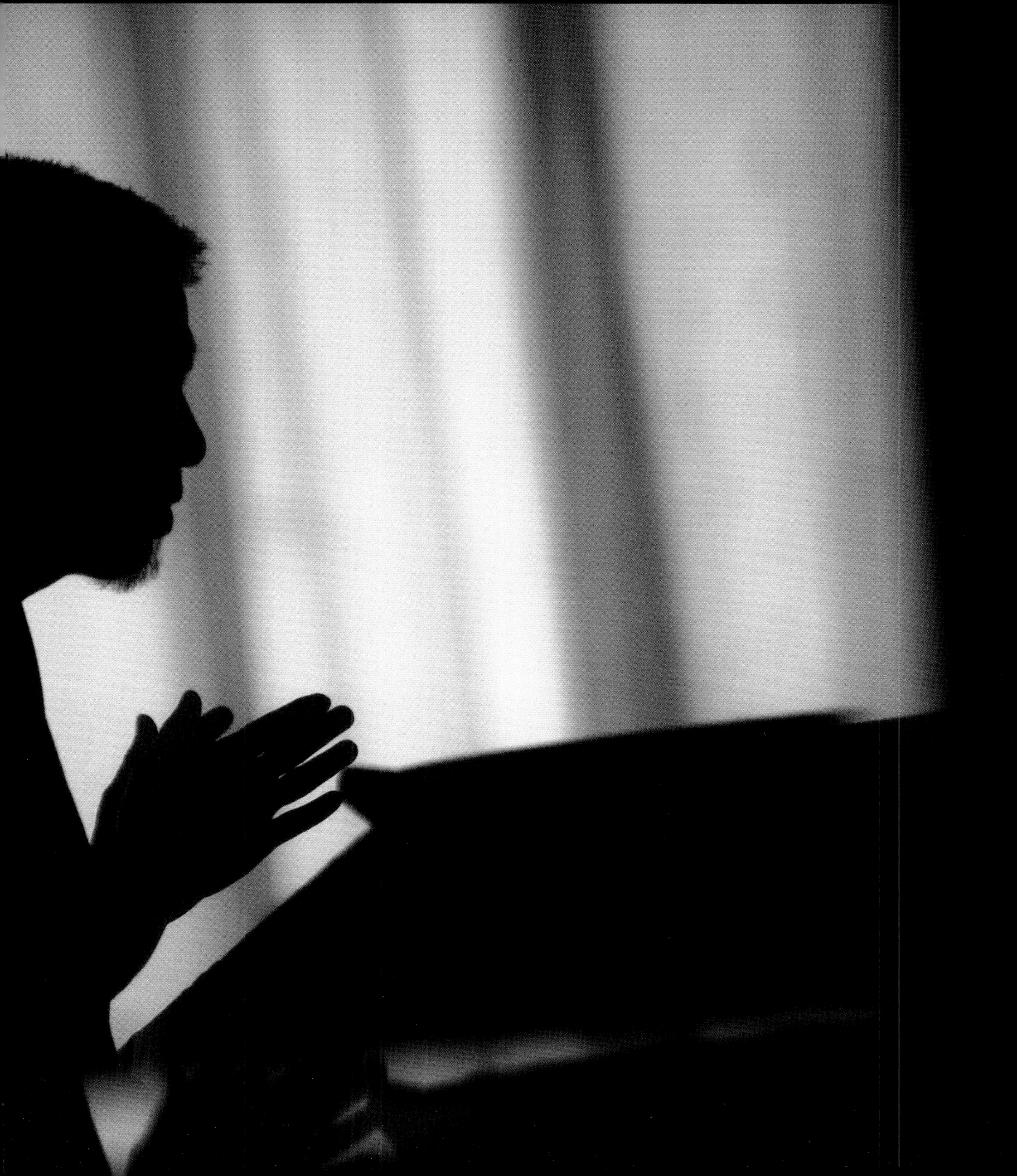

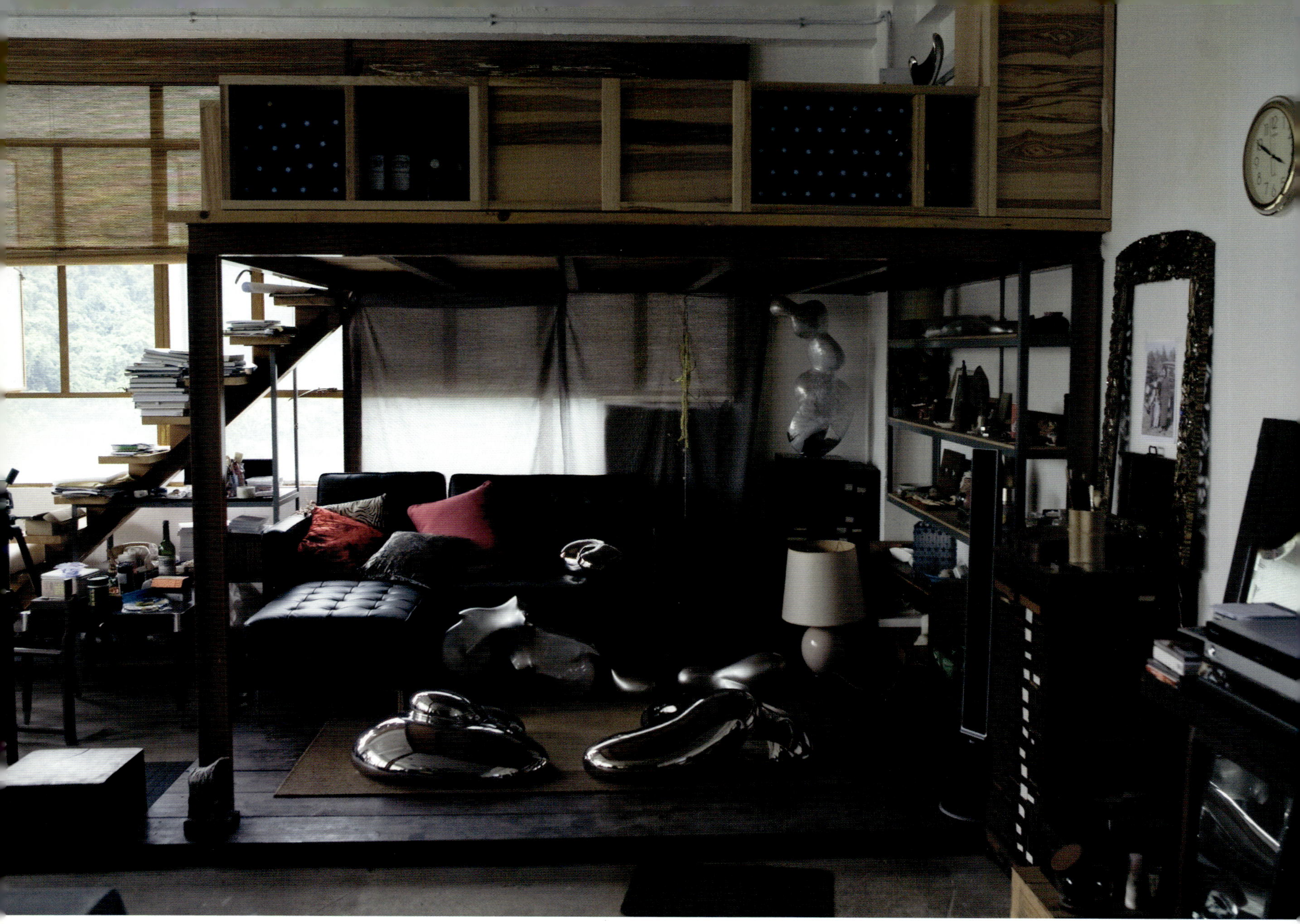

Solitary contemplation is Danny Lee Chin-fai's ideal way of creating art

Danny Lee Chin-fai has just moved into his studio in Fo Tan. His sculptures are here and there, many of them yet to be unwrapped. The sculptor's space, however, is getting into shape.

At the back of the studio the windows frame a view of verdant mountains. On the other side, shelves hold his small-scale works. A huge table occupies the centre space. Beside pens and papers, there is a pot of tea. Music flows through the room. In one corner a flight of steps leads to a cosy penthouse, and beneath it one can relax on a sofa.

"My friends drink so I have a stock of wine... The tables are tailor-made. They can be easily carted away," Lee says.

Lifting the drape, I see a neat, thoughtfully crafted table.

Like his studio, Lee's work involves a lot of thought. "When I started, I went to different directions. Eventually [the work] becomes more mature and art making is actually thinking," he explains. As the artist experiences life, he reflects upon it. To sculpt is to give shape to thought.

In Lee's oeuvre there is a series titled *Scenery* , which features drops of stainless steel that vary in size and shape. The series is inspired by water droplets, expressed in ink landscapes. The artist suggests that many people fix their eyes on distant vistas and overlook what is right in front of them; this is like neglecting the present for faraway dreams. The magnified droplets draw the viewers' attention to what is before their eyes. On the convex reflective surface, the viewers see almost everything. In the midst, they see themselves.

A variation on the *Scenery* series addresses the city. In *City • Landscape — Rock*, irregular shapes reminiscent of Futurist sculptures, represent automobiles and their emissions. Lee sees these as elements of the man-made landscape in cities. "The traffic is like a river," he explains. "I call the automobiles, parked on the road, 'rocks'. We need modern conveniences, but at the same time we are blocked by the 'rocks'." The reflective surfaces of these man-made rivers and rocks call for human reflection on the different sides of development.

Although he expresses his ideas through his work, Lee has no intention of imposing his beliefs on viewers. When he develops his art, he writes to record and organise his thoughts; these texts are just for himself. When he shows his works, he rarely talks about them in words. He reckons that viewers from different backgrounds see them differently and he appreciates every thoughtful interpretation.

In such a way Lee's works – shaped simply and without lengthy captions – find their way to various spots across the city. He has been commissioned to install a number at the Hong Kong International Airport. One is on the theme 'communication'. In a thoroughfare there is a row of stone blocks which sit at intervals. The top faces are polished; in closure the shiny surfaces form a rhythmic flow in the air, echoing the title, *Lineal Continuum*. Pedestrians can pass through the gaps and by doing so they 'interflow' with the work. They

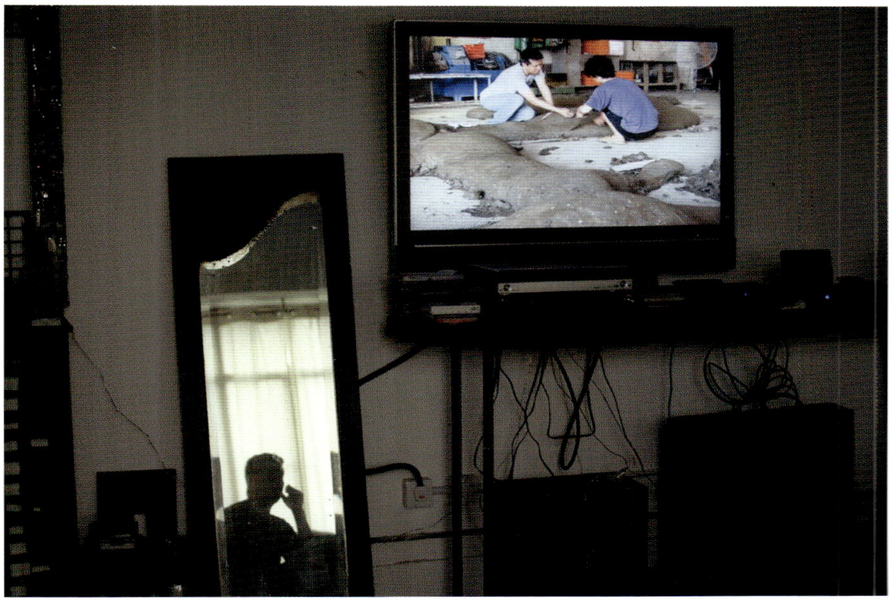

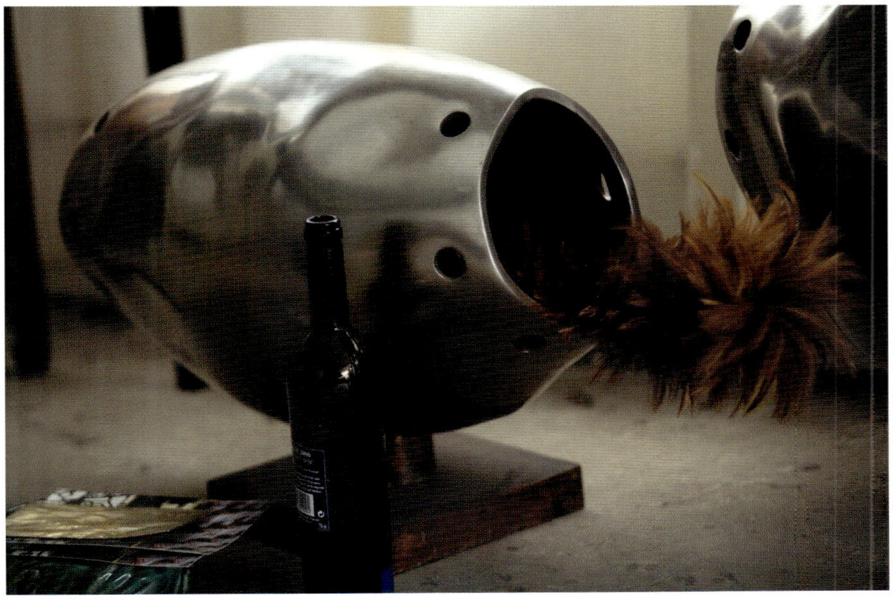

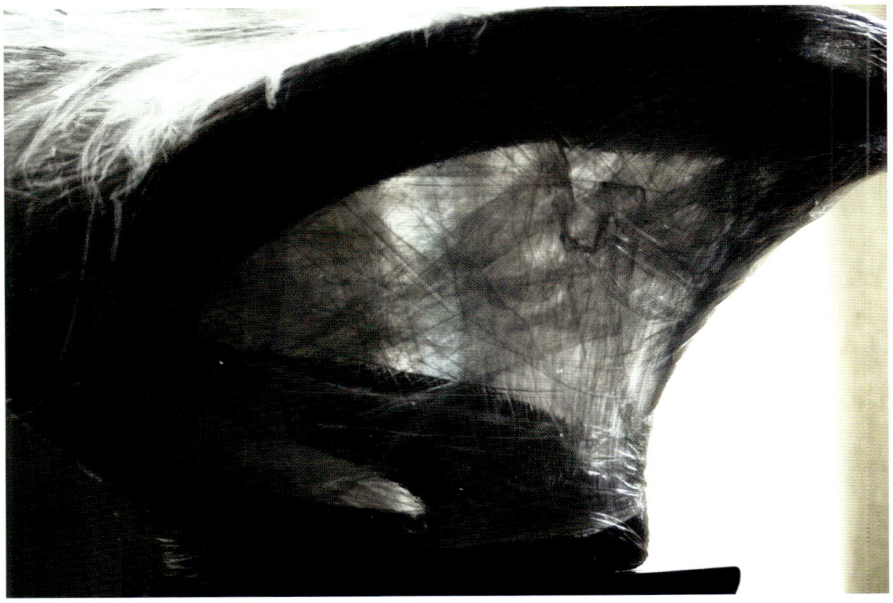

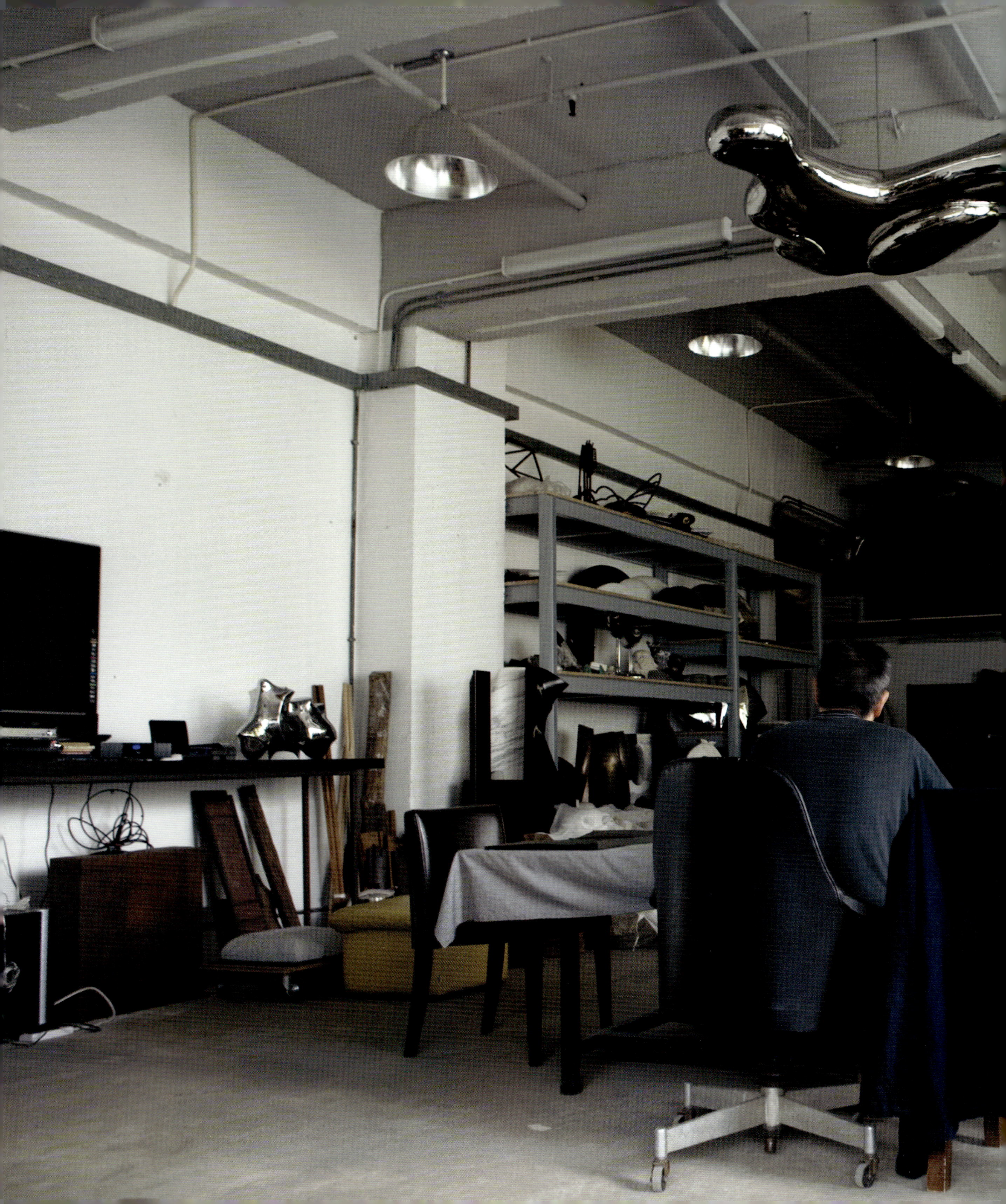

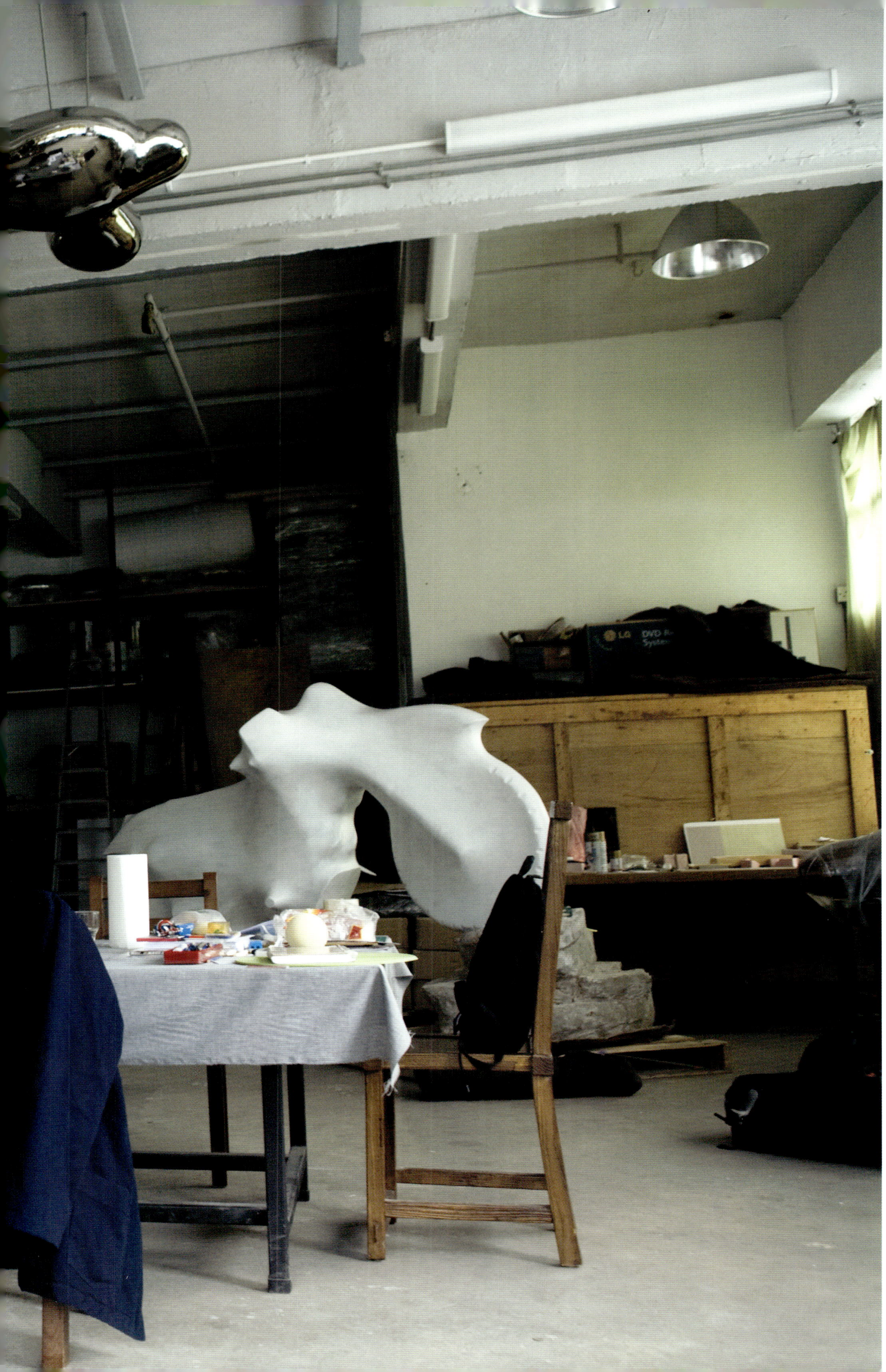

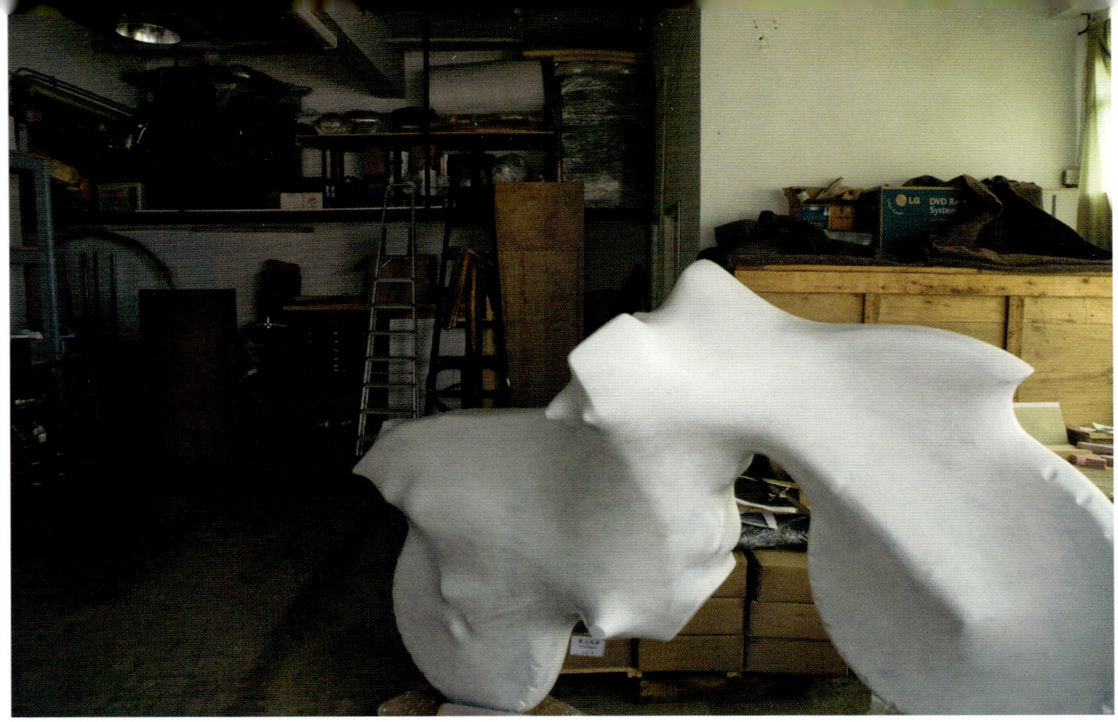

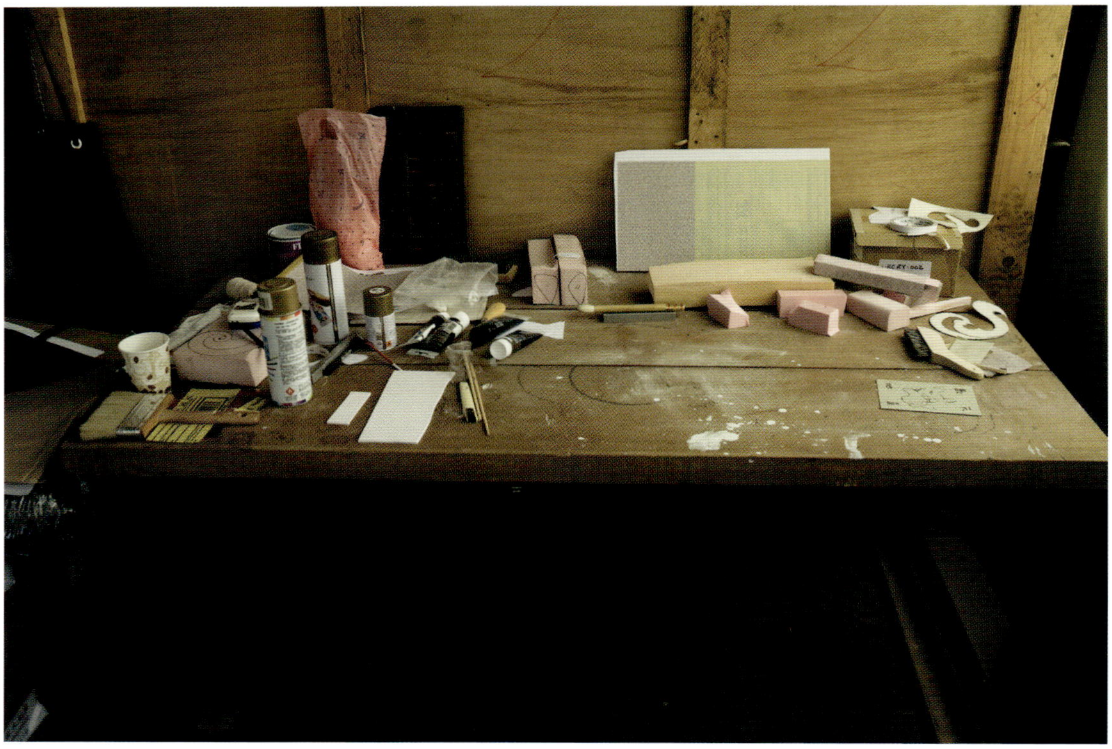

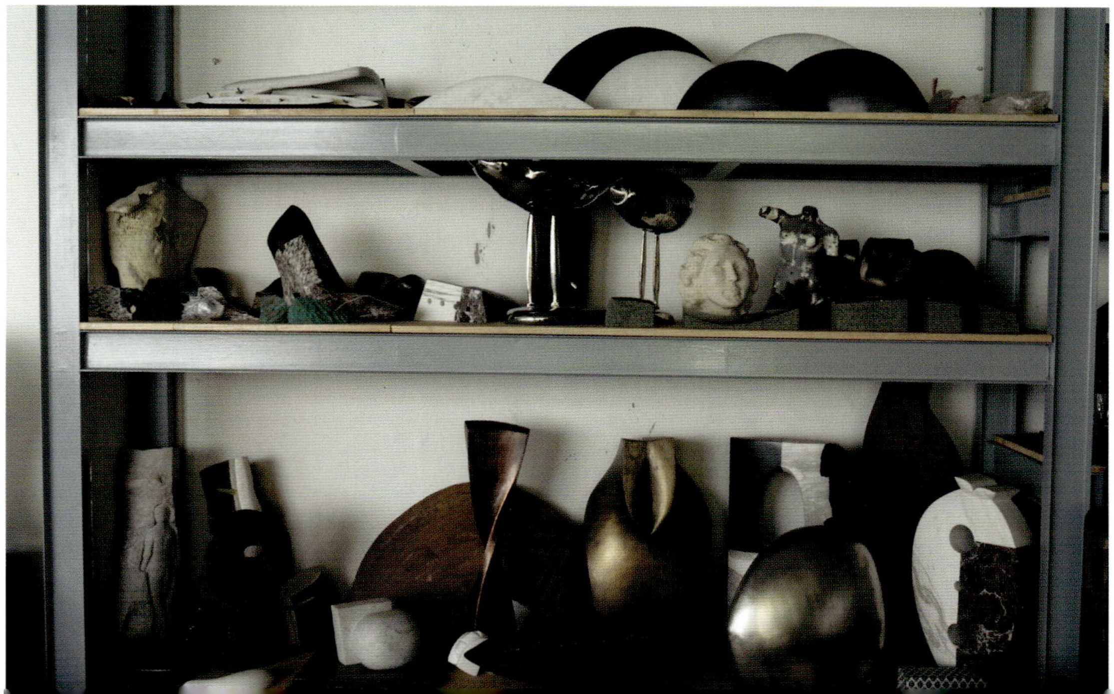

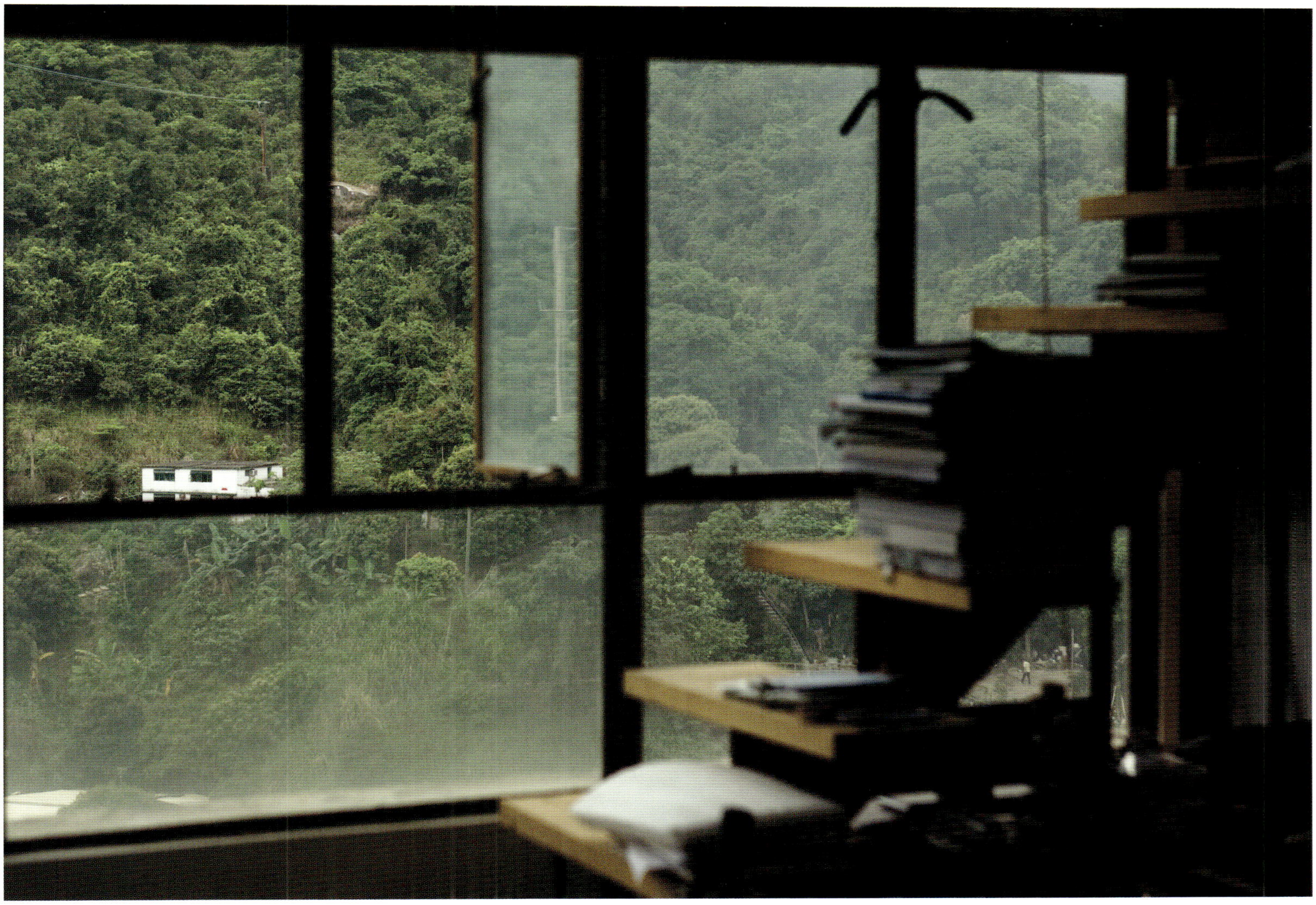

may form different ideas about the work. They may think about the notion of acquaintance. They may pass it without a thought. Or they may stop and take a picture with their loved ones, their union reflected in the masonic ribbon.

Lee calls his work 'installation sculpture'. Like the above example, it always interacts with the environment. He also likes to combine materials. In the early years of his career he experimented with a lot of materials and this has given him a rich vocabulary, enabling him to articulate his thoughts with eloquence.

Twenty years ago Lee started creating three-dimensional works while studying graphic design at the Hong Kong Polytechnic (now the Hong Kong Polytechnic University). After graduation he became a professional designer. While he worked in the fields of graphic design, interior design and advertising he kept on making sculptures. Eventually he realised that he was spending more and more time on the latter, so he decided to quit his job and devote himself to art.

A lot of adjustments were needed when Lee became a full-time artist. He remembers the host of a TV programme saying something inspirational: "Some may lament if they have to feed on a piece of bread," he remembers. "But if one appreciates the bread, the scenario is totally different." Lee believes that if one is truly committed, external constraints can always be overcome. One can always create space for oneself.

Lee started his artistic career at a little table. Years ago he lived in an old building in Wanchai and his table was in the kitchen where he could think quietly. When he was done with thinking, he made his sculptures in his roof-studio. However the old building did not have a lift and it was exhausting to move the heavy materials all the way up to the roof, so after working out his finances he rented an extra space on the ground floor of the same building. Besides working from his own place, he also used the studios at the Visual Arts Centre and a copper casting shop in Stone Nullah Street gave him 'technical support'.

Stone was frequently used in Lee's earlier work, but it was very difficult to find stone suppliers in Hong Kong. The artist ended up getting his stone from a tombstone

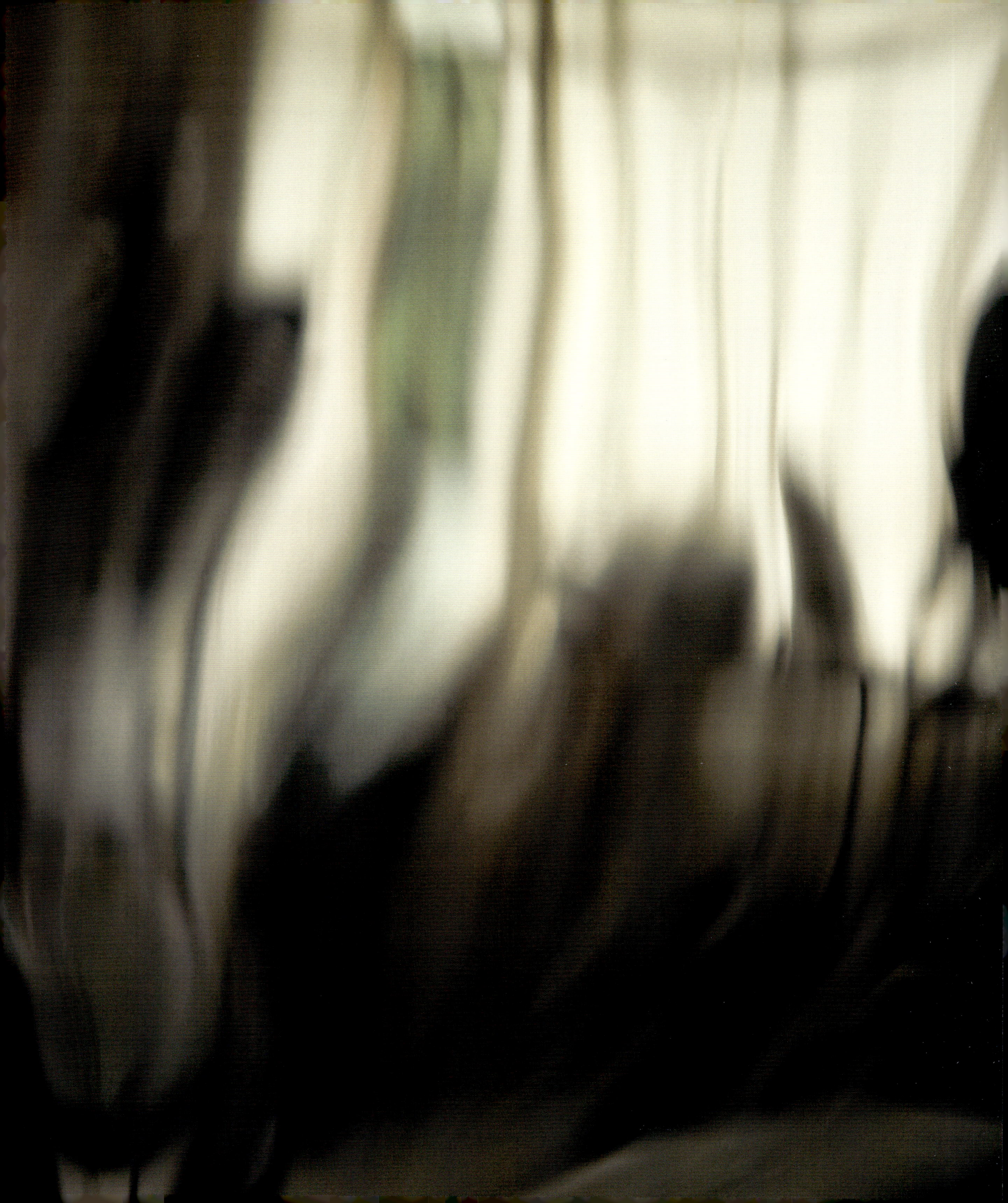

manufacturer that imported marble from Italy. Working at the site turned out to be a smart way of reducing transportation costs, but tombstone manufacturers are, of course, located near cemeteries. So for a while Lee's studio was right next to a cemetery. He went there daily with the workmen and left with them when the sun set. Since his tools were plugged in there he shared a portion of the electricity bills, and the skillful craftsmen were his 'technical consultants'.

As things piled up his studio, the artist needed more storage space. He first rented a small warehouse in To Kwa Wan. When it became full he got another in Yuen Long. Together with the items stored in his studio in Wan Chai, his things were literally all over the place. In order to put everything together he started looking for a larger space. His friends suggested artist villages like Oil Street and the Cattle Depot but though he liked the idea of having friends around, Lee knew he needed a place for solitary contemplation. The moment he opened the door of his current place in Fo Tan, he knew it was the one for him. Now it is where he thinks, writes, sketches and makes small pieces and his large-scale works are done in China where, in a spacious workshop, he drafts on the floor, makes models and sculpts.

Over a cup of tea, Lee shares his story: how he creates space for himself; how he shapes this place; how he tailors his tables. Like his work, these are all reflective.

In this studio, Lee wants to bring together his work and space. Close to the windows, there is an assemblage of iron bars and rear-view mirrors. It is called *Karma*, which drives the cycle of cause and effect. By reflecting the space behind as one looks forward, the mirrors unite the past and the future. To the artist, art making is his way of reflecting upon life. "In my work, people see themselves," he says. "They see what is good and bad. They see whether they are happy or sad... But true happiness is invisible here. One can only see it when one is above the clouds."

Directly above his work space there is a ceiling piece. It is in the shape of a cloud. We look up to it from below.

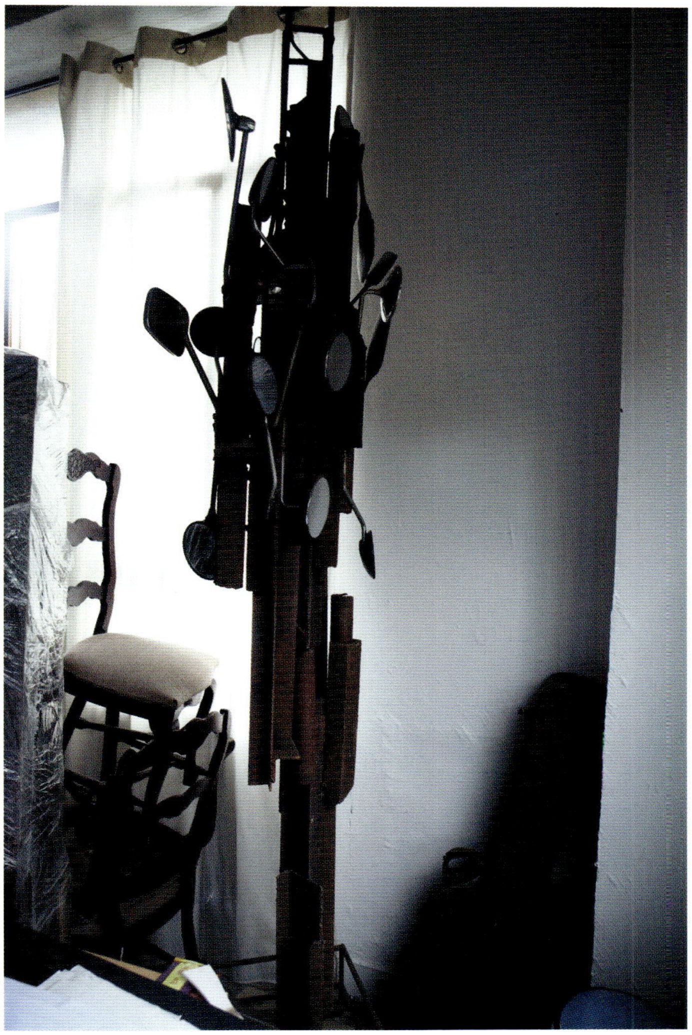

To artists, art making is a self-reflection and reminder of one's life

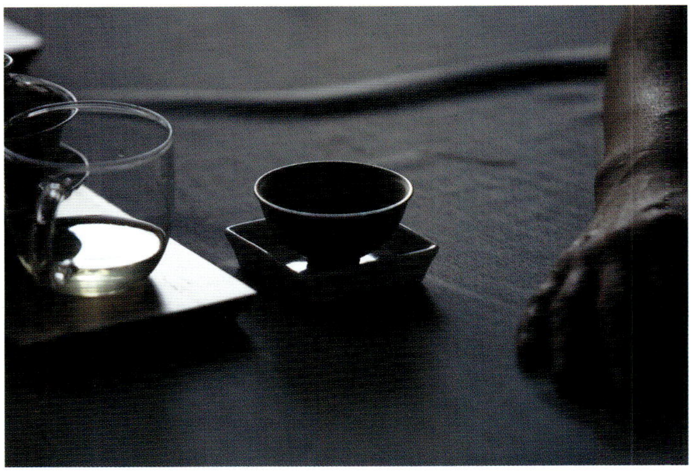

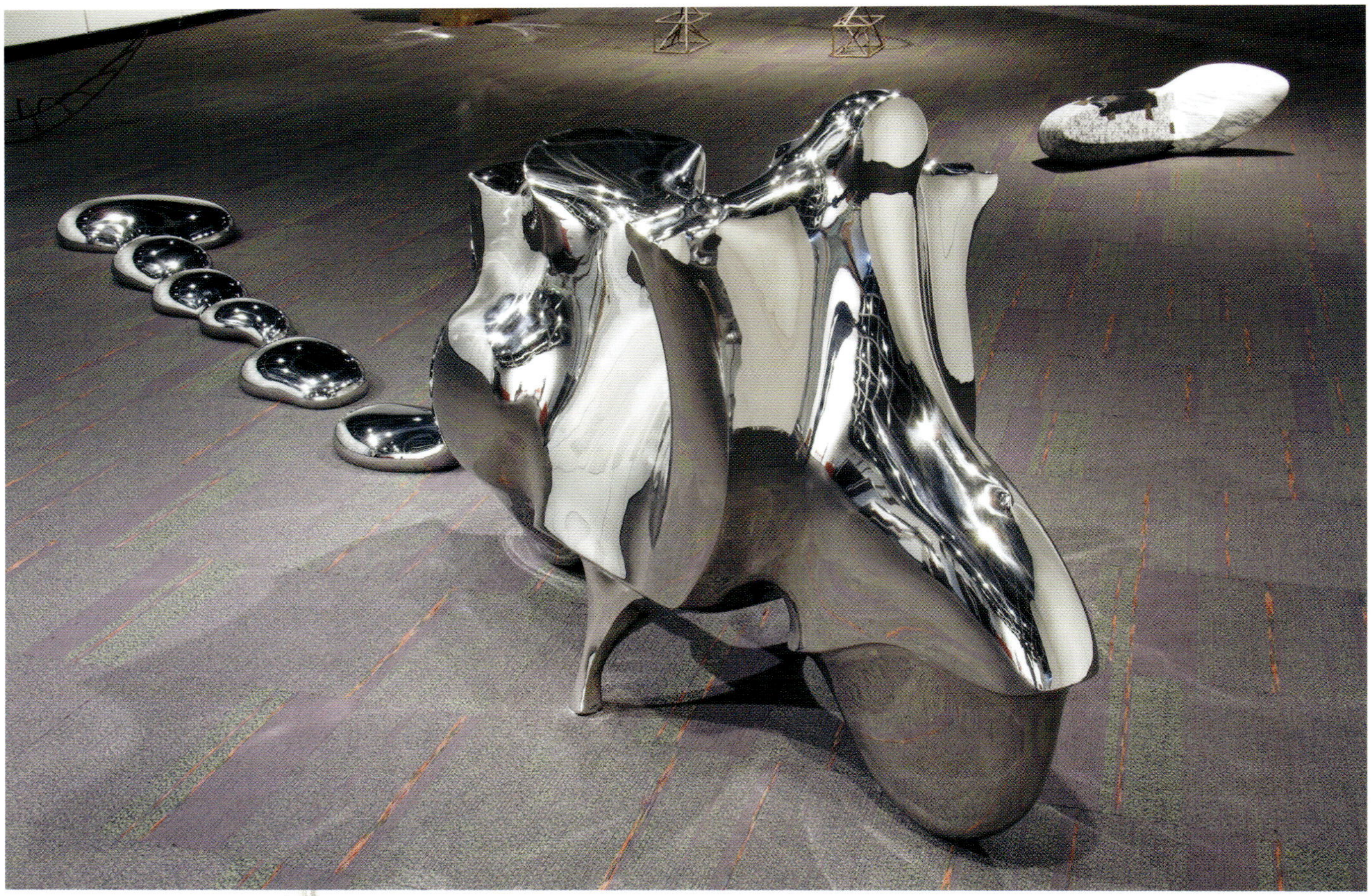

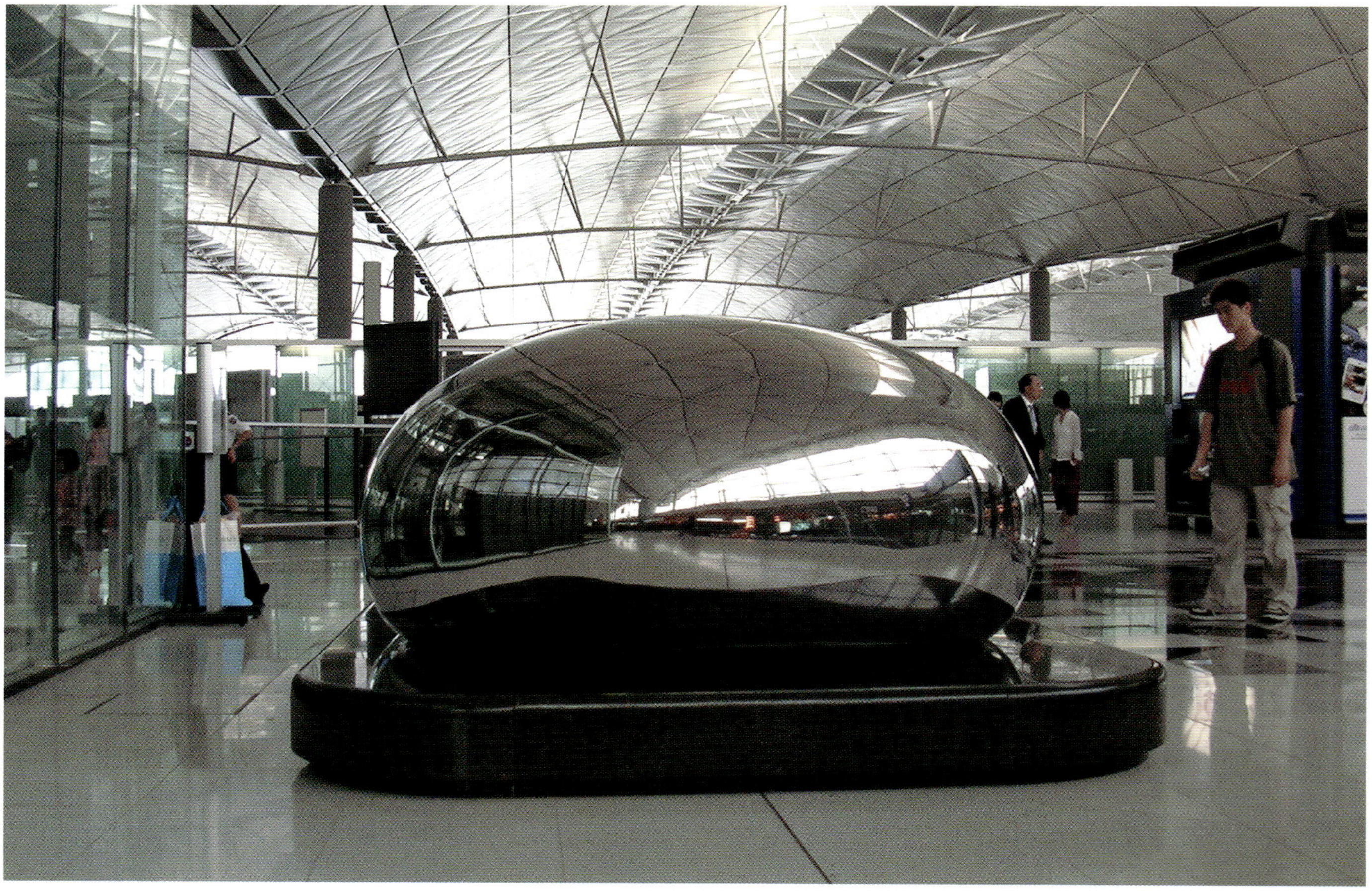

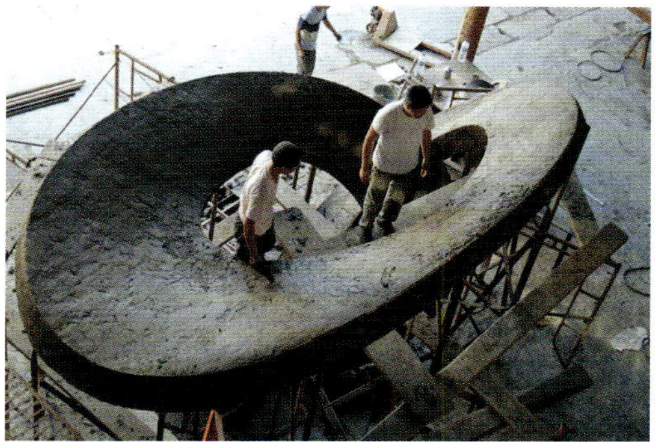

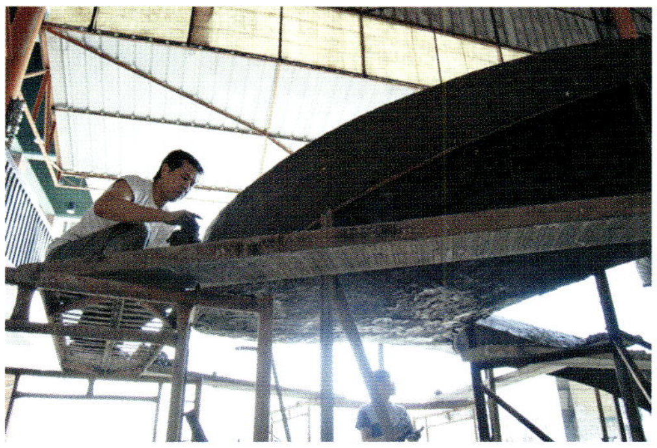

(Left page, above) City Landscape
Stainless steel, 550x70x120 cm, 2007

(Left page, bottom) Dew Drop
Stainless steel and black stone, 400x280x130 cm, 2005

(This page) Eternity
Bronze, 500x360x350 cm, 2007

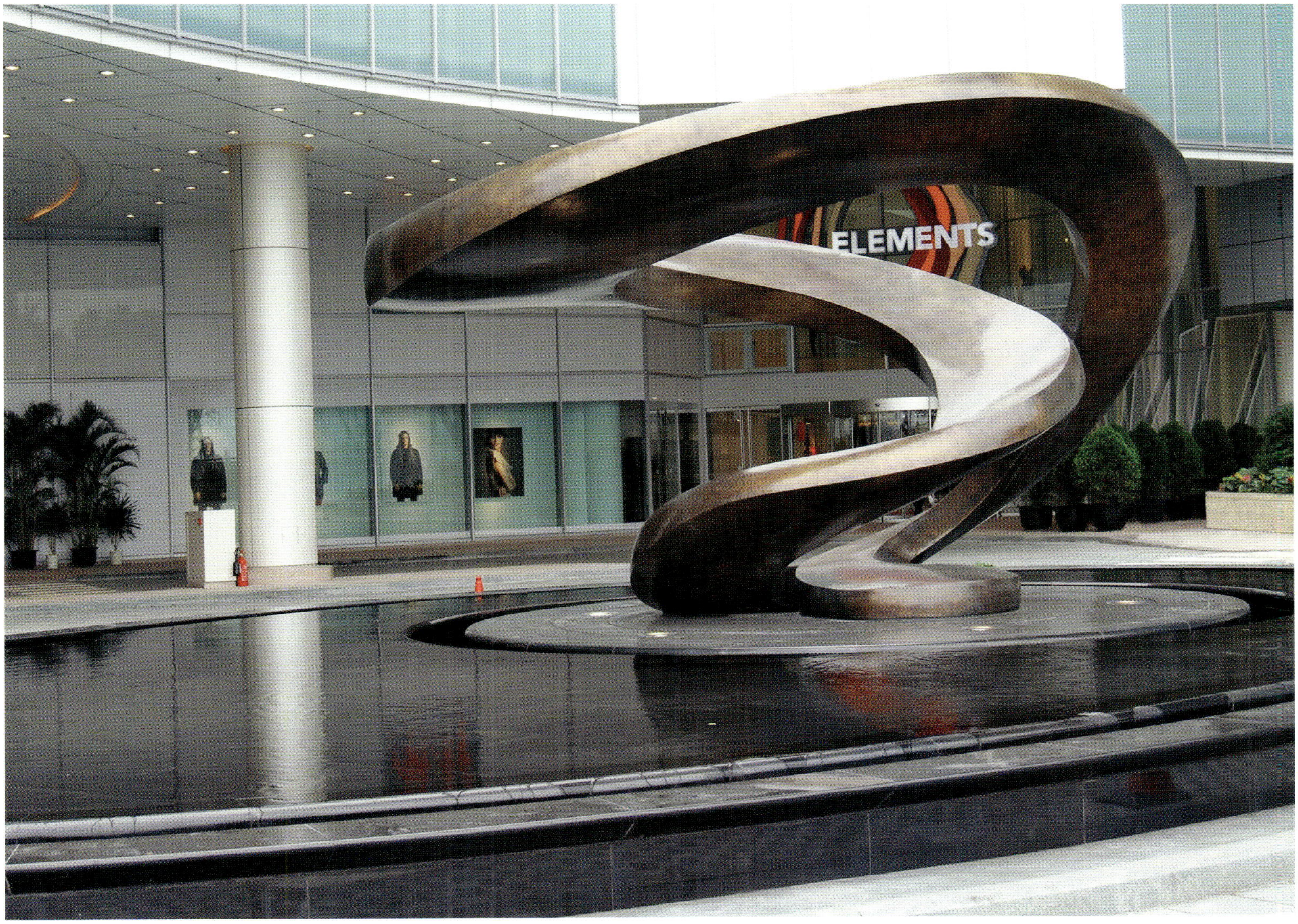

Jaffa Lam Laam

A Simple Heart

By Alice Choi

Jaffa Lam Laam obtained a Bachelor and Master's degree in fine arts in 1997 and 1999, and a postgraduate diploma in education from the Chinese University of Hong Kong (CUHK) in 2000. In recent years she has been focusing on site-specific sculptural installation and public art, using materials like wood, metal, glass, plastics, water and light. She now teaches at the Hong Kong Art School, and has founded the AiR Association Ltd, which actively participates in and promotes local and overseas art exchange. Lam has been chosen as artist-in-residence in establishments in the United States and Canada, and has exhibited around the world, including in Kenya, Bangladesh, New York, Auckland, Toronto, Macau, Paris, Singapore, Shanghai and Taiwan. Her works were selected for the Contemporary Hong Kong Art Biennial Exhibition in 1996 and again in the Hong Kong Art Biennial 2001, 2003 and 2005. She was also one of the highlighted artists in the Artists in the Neighbourhood Scheme II 2003 exhibition, and her works are collected by the Hong Kong Museum of Art, the Hong Kong Heritage Museum and the CUHK as well as by private collectors.

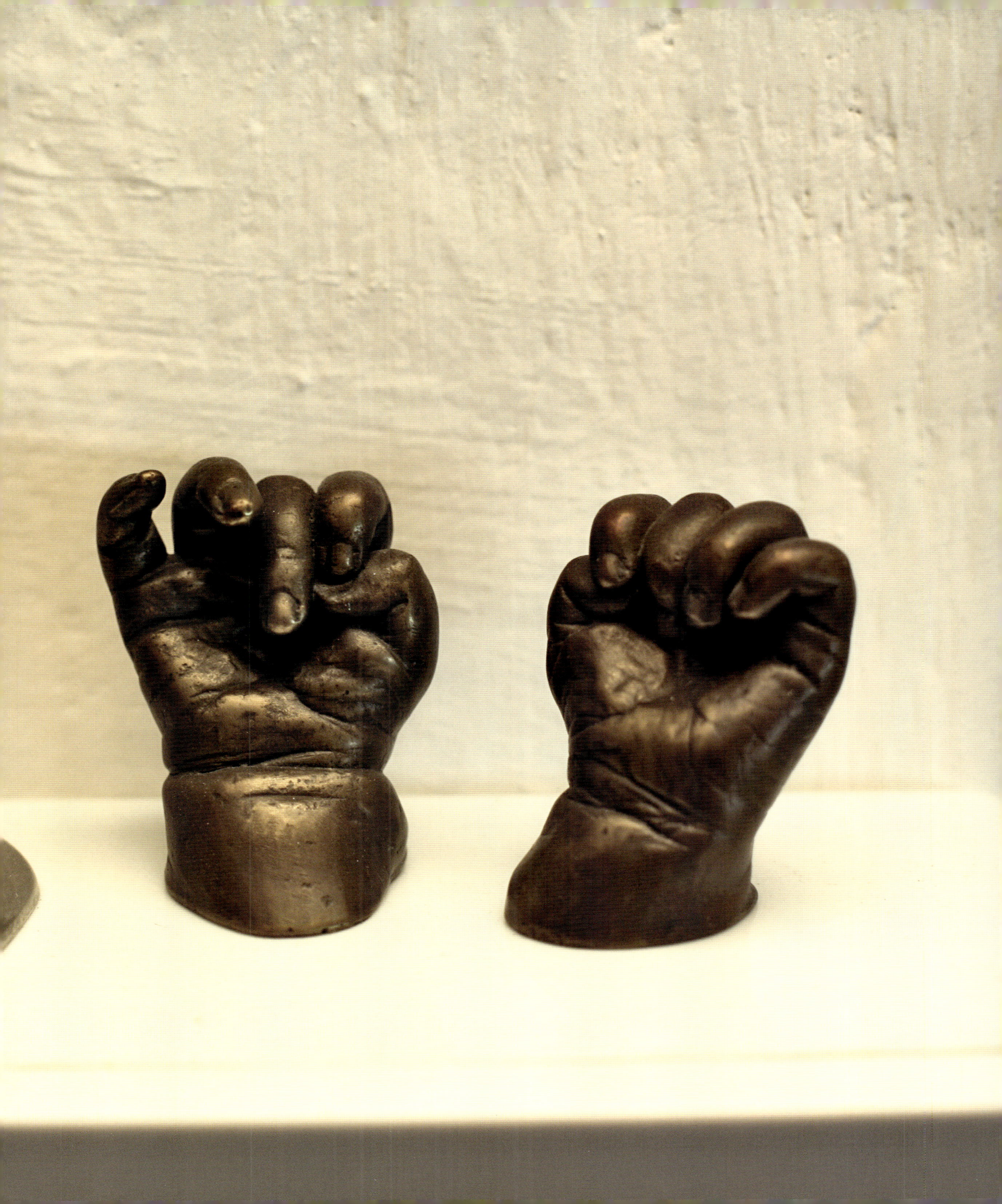

Jaffa Lam Laam is fortunate to have met inspiring mentors at pertinent stages of her life. Lam-Hong Yuk-wai, a secondary school art teacher, was her first tool of enlightenment. "Mrs Lam is a charismatic teacher. It was her who encouraged me to apply CUHK, and she was also the one who gave me the aspiration of becoming a secondary school art teacher," she recalls.

Afterwards Lam was admitted to the Department of Fine Arts at the CUHK. Being familiar with Chinese art, Lam was a bit uneasy when first exposed to the media in Western art, until she met her mentor Cheung Yee in her third year. Cheung Yee is an artist and educator who never gives up on his students. "I was not very confident at the time, yet he encouraged me, giving me faith and hope," she remembers. Cheung's artistic lifestyle was attractive to Lam, who liked the idea of having control over her lifestyle and pace, time and income. "The days of learning with Cheung were all about food and life!" she says. "However during those exchanges I learnt from him without being aware of it. He once said that the most important thing is not how to earn but how to spend money." Not only did Cheung give Lam knowledge and techniques; he gave her a dream.

Upon the completion of her Bachelor degree Lam moved on to postgraduate studies, where she met two fellow students – Luke Ching Chin-wai and Annie Wan Lai-kuen. To prepare herself for the role of secondary school art teacher she went for a postgraduate diploma in education, but during the course she realised that teaching was not her real dream after all.

During her seven years of study, her peers had established careers. "When I graduated I was working as a kindergarten teacher

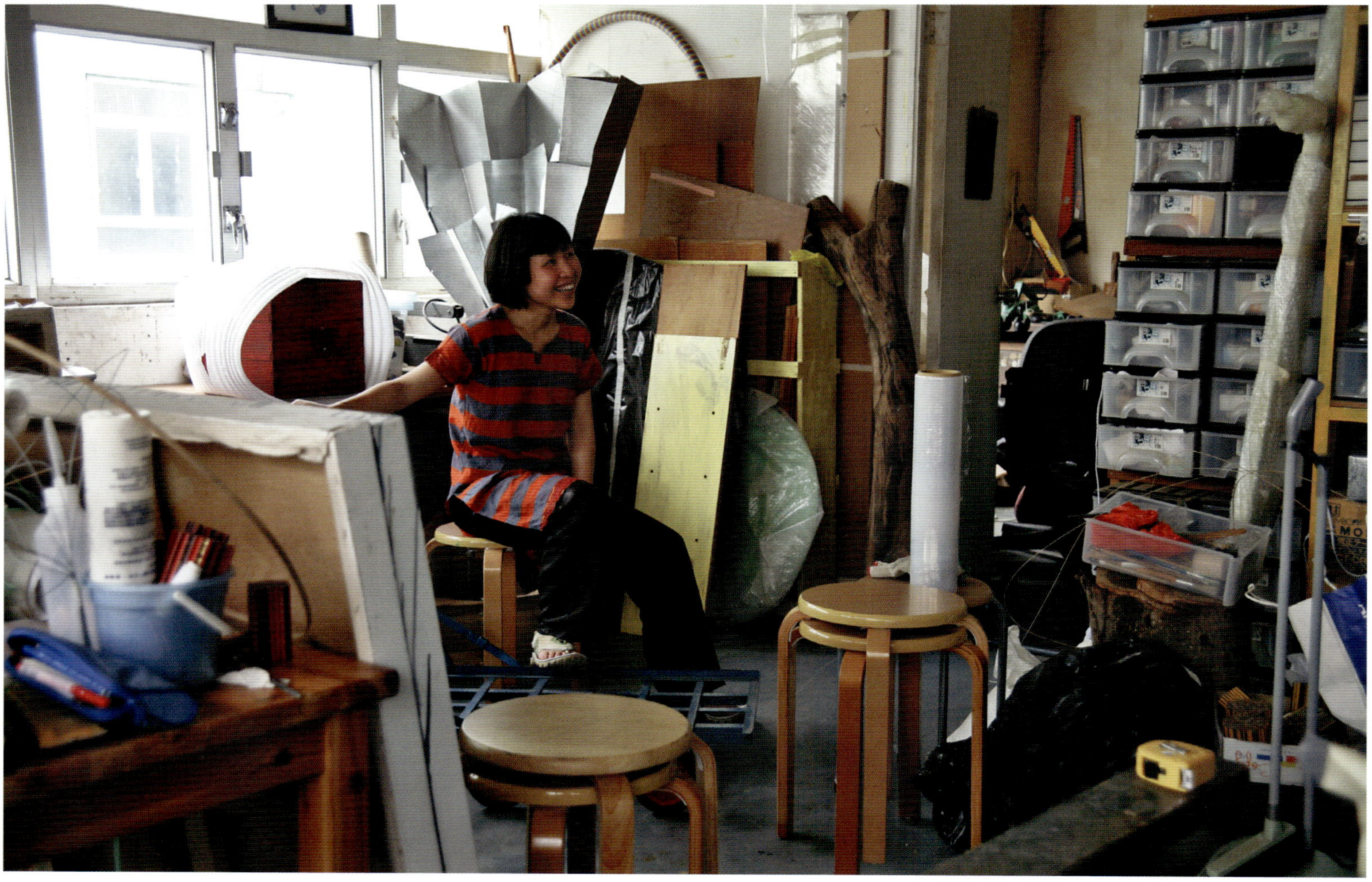

Sunlight and Jaffa Lam Laam's brilliant smile fill the room with the joy of art

with an income of only HK$8,000, while my peers were already earning several times that much," she recalls. "The price of a coffee in the coffee shop where we met was on the high side. Once a classmate seemed to realise my concern and bought me a drink at HK$35. I was grateful but felt a bit uneasy. Now my income is still not high but it's sufficient, and above all, it is the kind of lifestyle that I've chosen."

Lam makes an analogy between rumination and art making. As one's knowledge and experience accumulate in the art making process, they integrate for use. She does not believe that art is a talent for a select few but considers it an innate ability in all, and that what matters is how those abilities are drawn out. She believes that although techniques are important, encouragement from teachers is the key. In Lam's case she had been formally trained in Chinese painting and calligraphy, so when she moved to sculpture all the related skills and knowledge came by practice and experimentation. Still, it was not until she met her colleague Ho Siu-kee that she began to understand what sculpture really is.

Lam did not encounter the essence of art making until she started working. It was the thought process born of practice that enabled her to progress. "Assisting my teacher Kurt Chan Yuk-keung in a project enabled me to truly understand what he had meant by problem-solving skills," she says.

It is hard to tell that Lam originally practised calligraphy by just looking at her works. Her first attempt at conceptual art was related more to her rebellious nature. "Teachers used to say that it takes at least 30 years to excel in calligraphy. I could not agree with this view," she protests. "Life is short. How many 30 years do we have?" In 1996 a calligraphy work of Lam's was shortlisted by the Contemporary Hong Kong Art Biennial Exhibition. It was a piece of text adapted from a press release on the Tsing Ma Bridge, written in the 'black-tiger style' developed by Luo Shu-zhong (1898 – 1969), a calligrapher born in the late Qing Dynasty. She never thought that the piece would be selected; for her, writing calligraphy by drawing with ink was just a gimmick. She was very disappointed and became disillusioned with the medium. She has not picked up a calligraphy brush since.

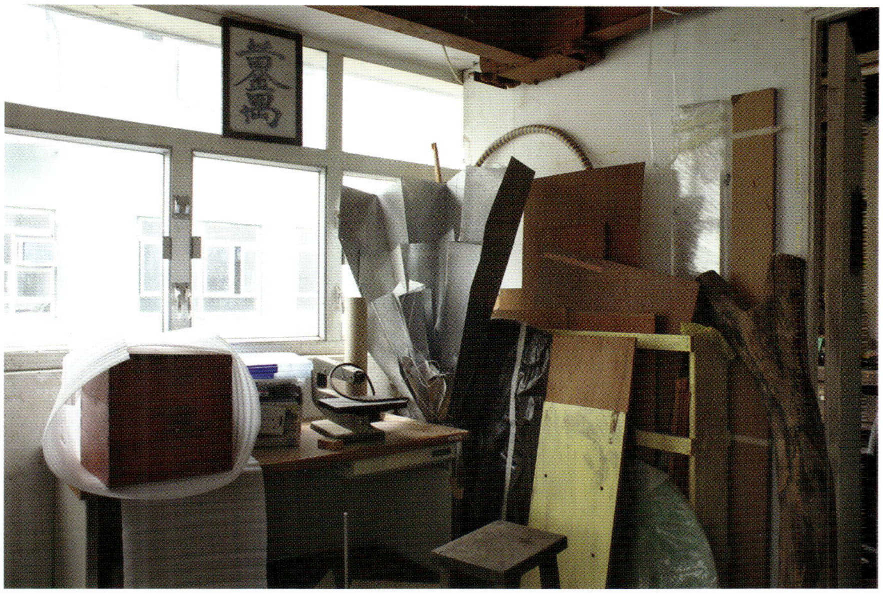

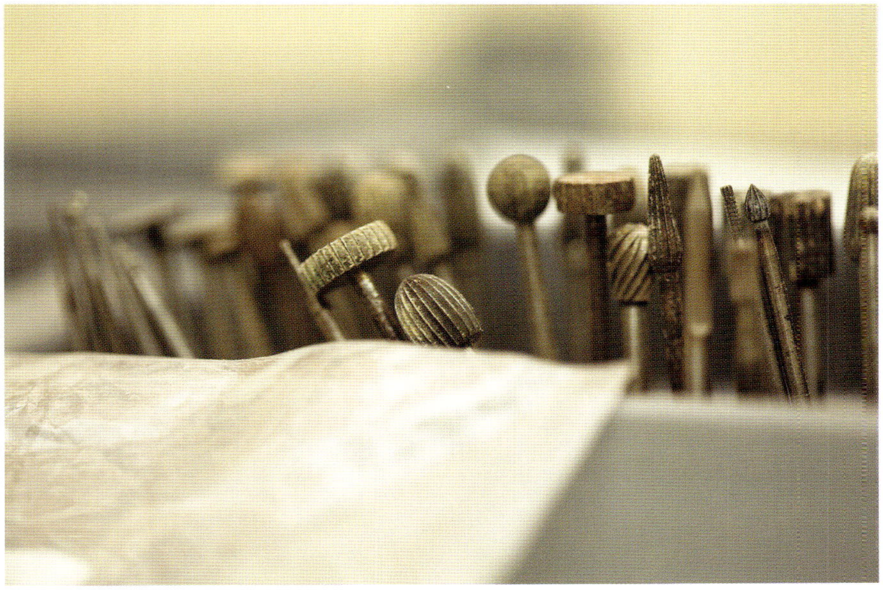

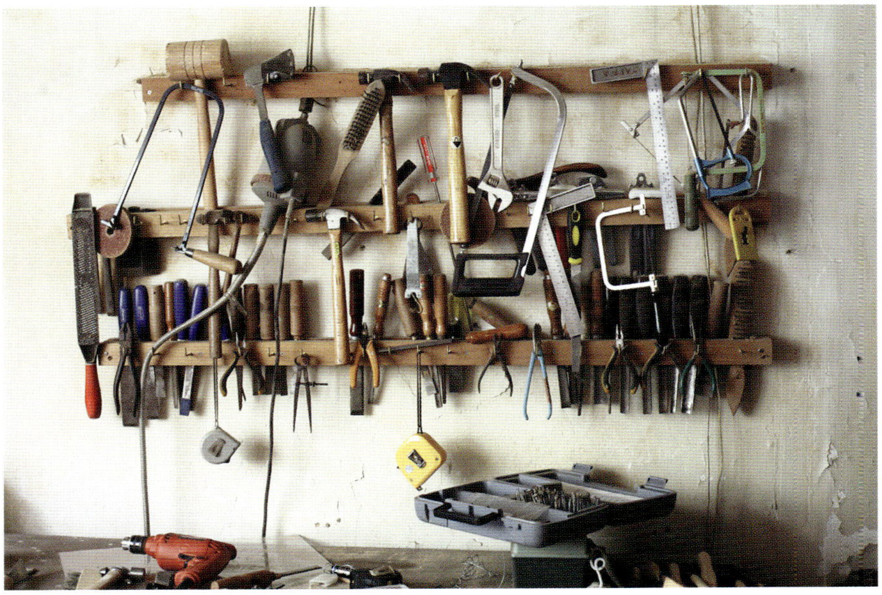

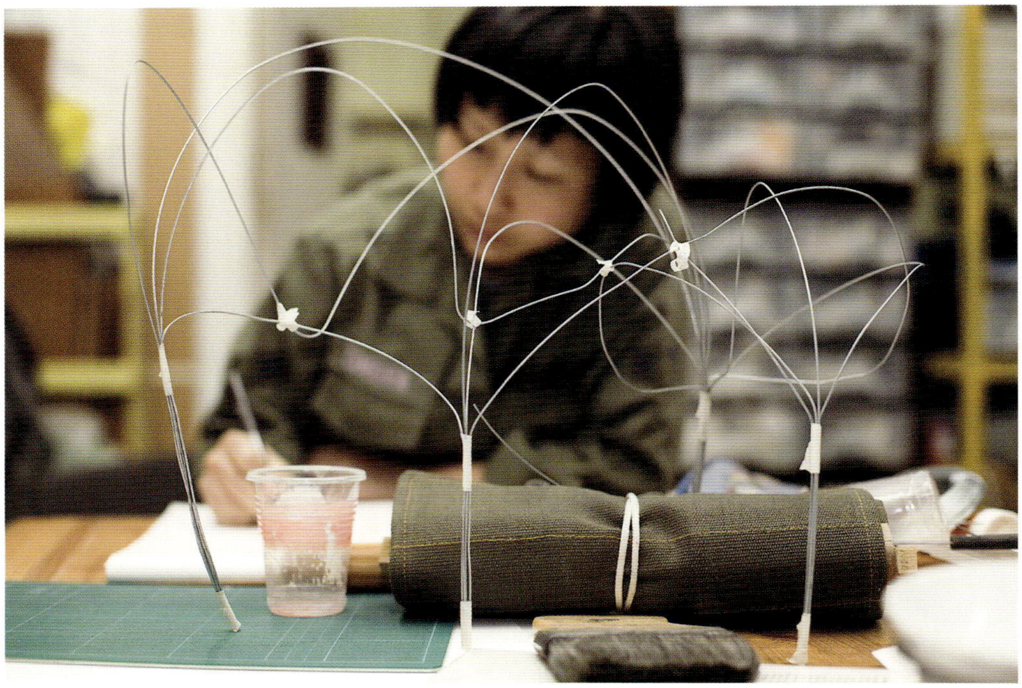

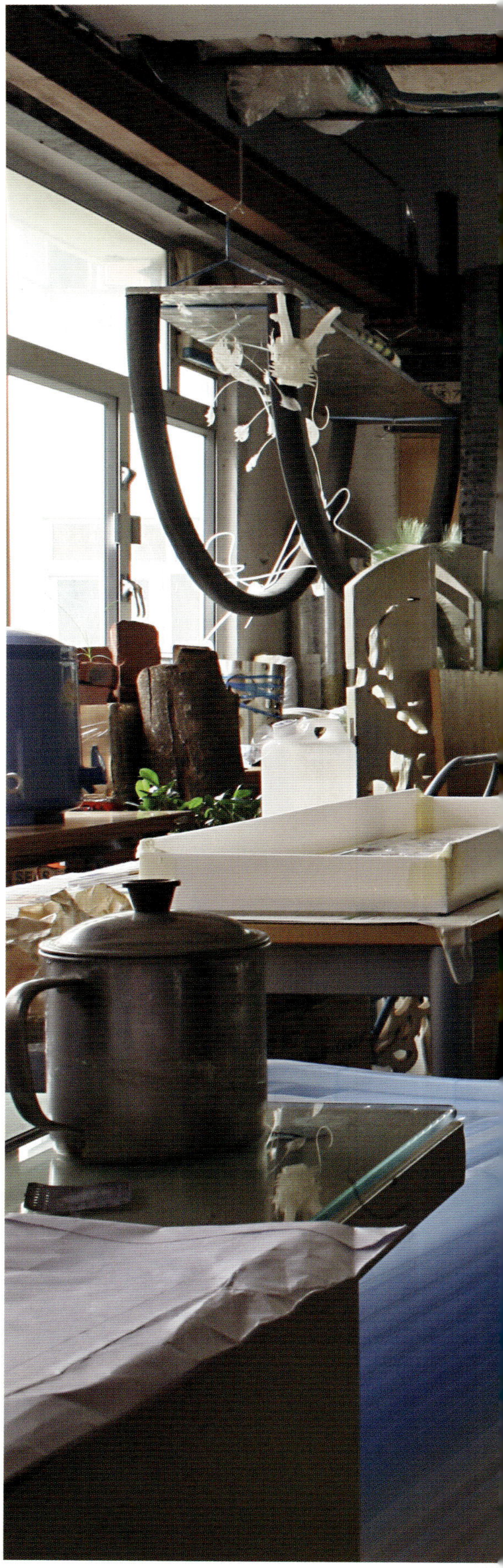

The year 2003 was a turning point for Lam's creative output. "Before 2003 my works were more personal, playful and smaller in size, bringing surprises to viewers," she says. The outbreak of Severe Acute Respiratory Syndrome (SARS) in 2003 changed a lot of lives, including Lam's. "Originally I planned to make a series of wooden toy trains and rails for the Artists in the Neighbourhood Scheme," she says. "Soon SARS broke out. I was terribly sad as I witnessed the development of the epidemic. I could not continue with my original idea." Eventually she turned the wood into four impressive sculptures, of which two, *To Someone Who Wants to Cry* and *To Someone Who Wants to Fly*, were selected by the Hong Kong Art Biennial Exhibition.

"Before 2003, I firmly believed in my feelings; almost all my works were related to my personal feelings," she confesses. "However since the outbreak of SARS I have realised that art is not limited to the personal level, but can transcend it to a broader social and universal context." Very often we learn more about life in adversity. SARS enabled Lam to strike a new balance between lightness and heaviness, the personal and the social.

On the days when she does not need to do studio work, Lam enjoys her leisure time like everybody else – by dressing up and going shopping. She deliberately spares time to relax. She thinks that it is not easy to be a full-time artist, but that doing it part-time would be even more difficult. "Art and life are inseparable. My whole life, from working and shopping to exercising and resting, are all related to art," she says.

Lam thinks that having a stable income is very important to one's development in art. "My life is very simple and I do not need much," she acknowledges. "However, I would feel very bad if I could not even sustain my basic lifestyle, and that would directly affect the quality of my life and work." Financial independence also helps. "I do not need to make art for money, nor to compromise with market tastes," she continues. "If others appreciate my works,

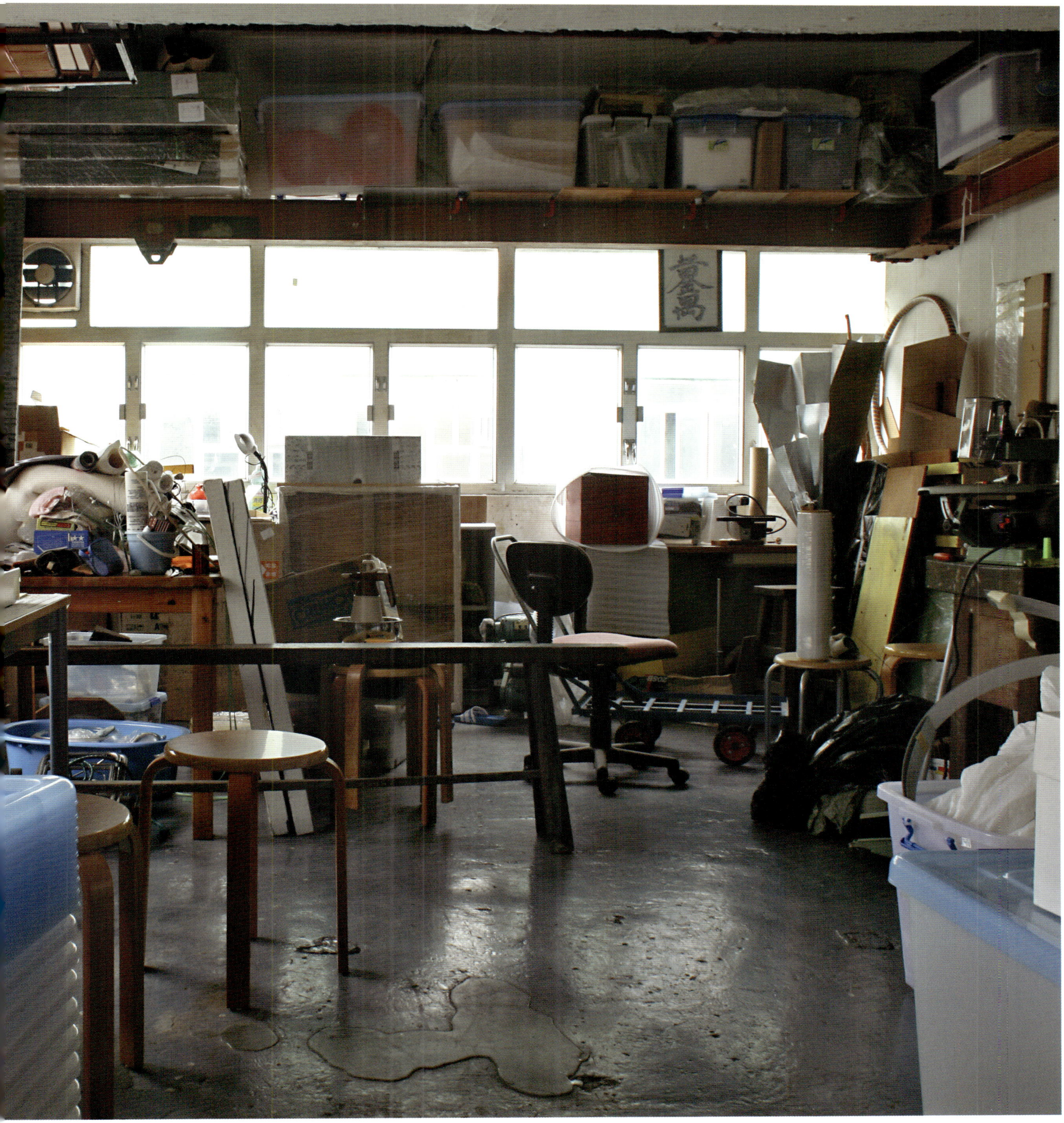

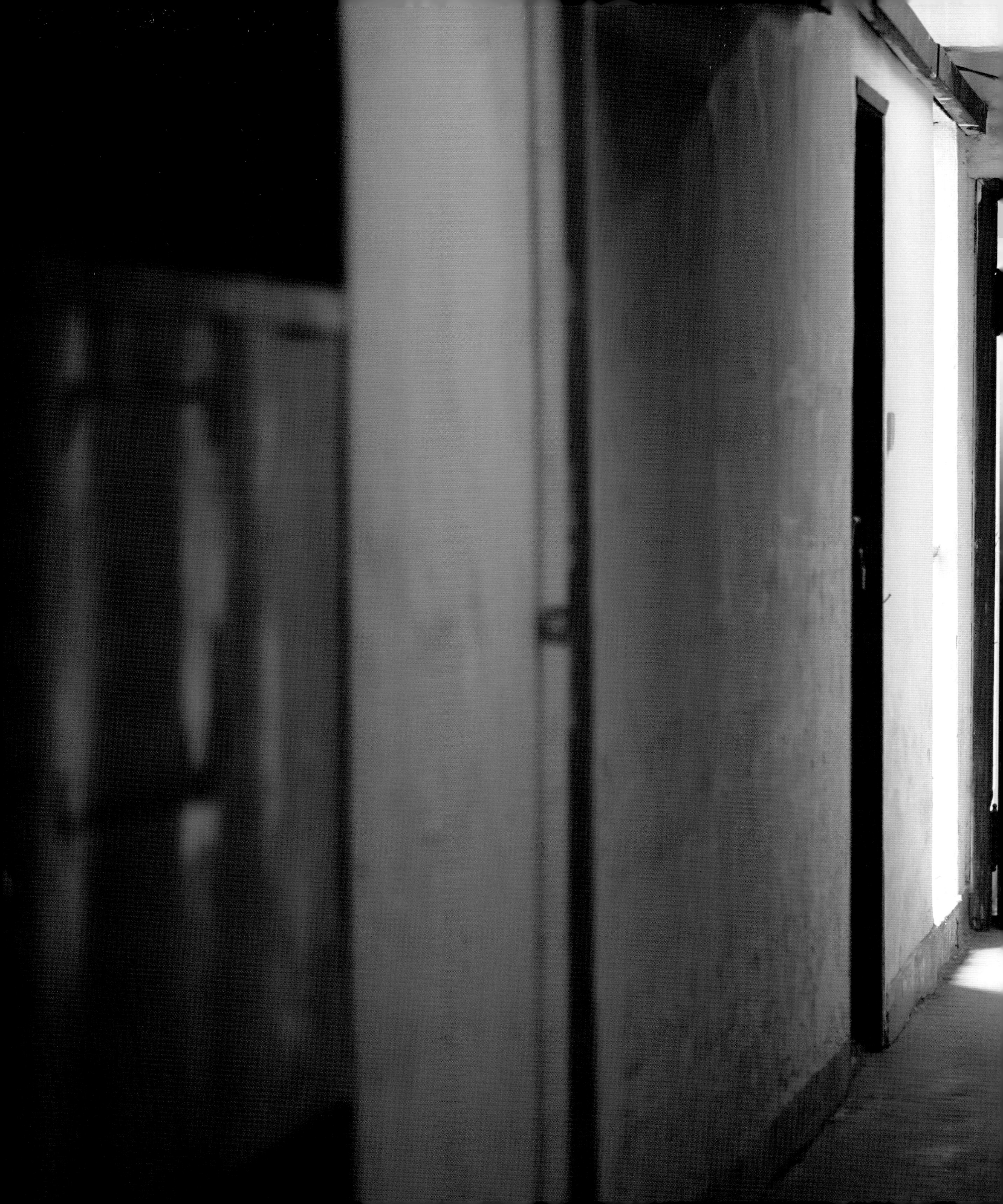

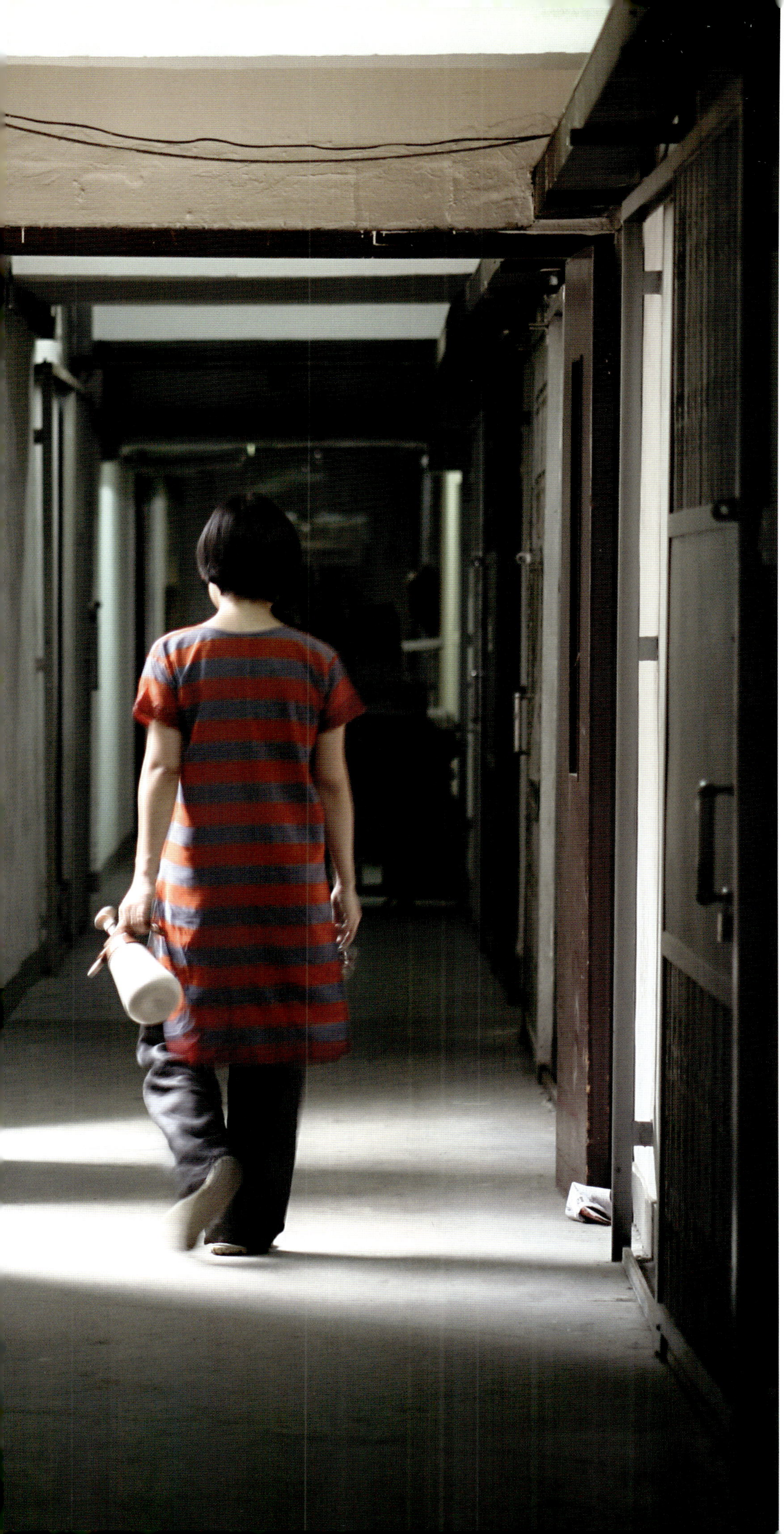

"I have realised that art is not limited to the personal level, but can transcend it to a broader social and universal context"

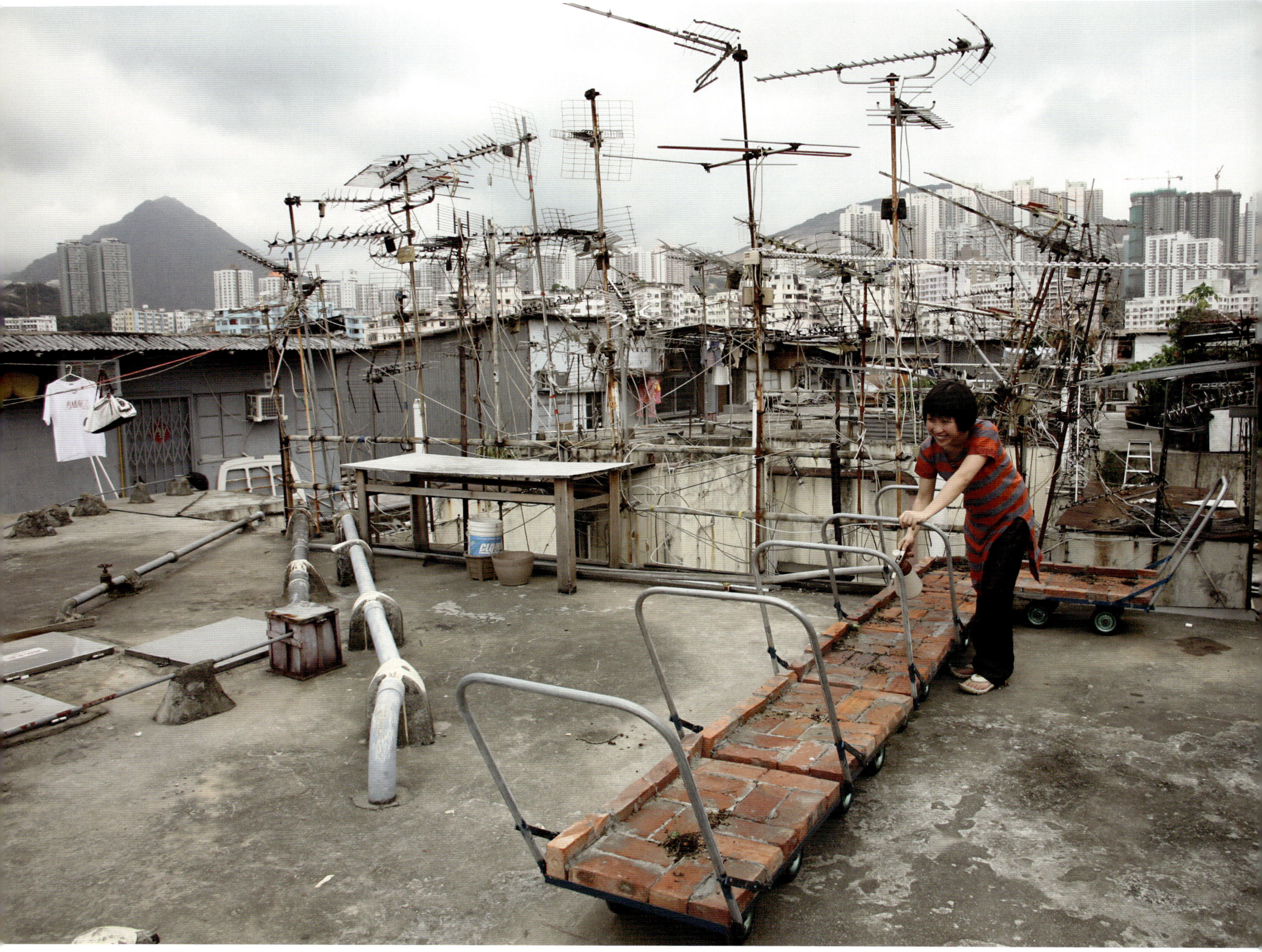

Her ideal studio would be self-owned, with a roof. It was on a roof that she remembers first marvelling at the delights of visual perception

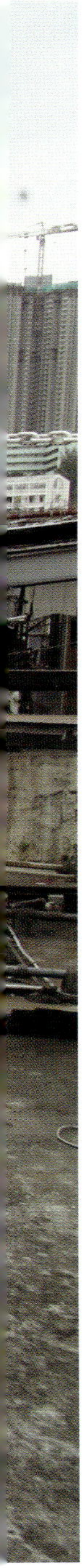

whether they collect them or not is not that important. I do not want to make art for the sake of money."

Even though Lam has her studio in Hong Kong, she participates actively in art projects overseas. "In Hong Kong there are too many responsibilities that are distracting. When I am away from this place I can put aside my work and responsibilities, and concentrate on my ideas and art making," she says.

"So far I am satisfied with all the works that I have done overseas. Perhaps the identity and attitude as a 'visitor', when you are away from home, makes it easier to get along and to be more tolerant of new friends. The cultural difference is also enriching. I am not fond of a particular place; it depends on whether a place has people or things in it that matter. The non-local experiences are ephemeral. It is contradictory that sometimes I long to have people around me, but at times the presence of a crowd makes me uneasy."

Lam's studio is very important to her and she particularly enjoys time alone there. She shares her studio space but she and her friend each have different schedules, so each can enjoy some quiet time in the studio alone. She rents this studio for two reasons: the kindness of the landlord and the room number of the studio. "The number of my studio is 1312," she says. "At first I was not aware of its meaning, but one day a carpenter from a local store delivered wood that I had ordered. He saw the room number 1312 and immediately associated it with a Chinese idiom describing a person's single-mindedness, something artists need in order to persist in their work. Years later I ordered wood from the same store and met the same carpenter. We smiled in silence. I guess we are both dedicated to our mission."

Her ideal studio would be self-owned, with a roof. It was on a roof that she remembers first marvelling at the delights of visual perception. "My family and I used to live on a roof when I was a kid," she says. "Many of our neighbours were southeast Asian and their clothes and bedding were colourful. On sunny days the colourful fabrics, together with the green plants on the roof, created such a beautiful picture. What a beautiful world!" It seems that a simple heart is the key to happiness.

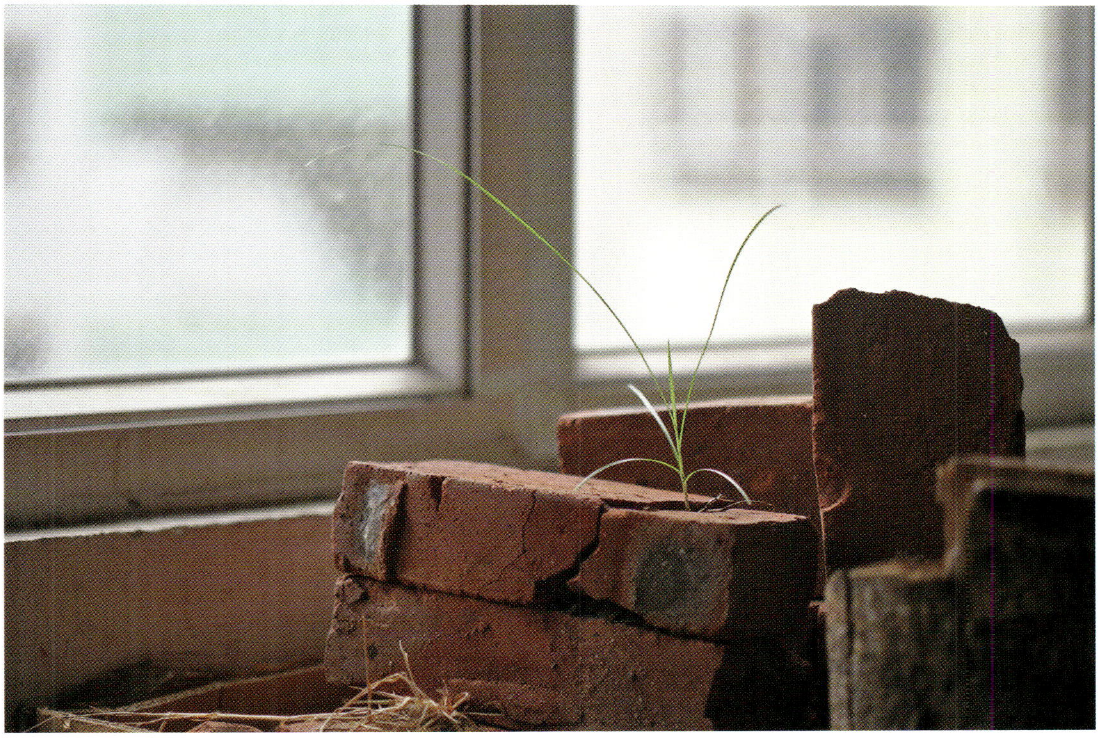

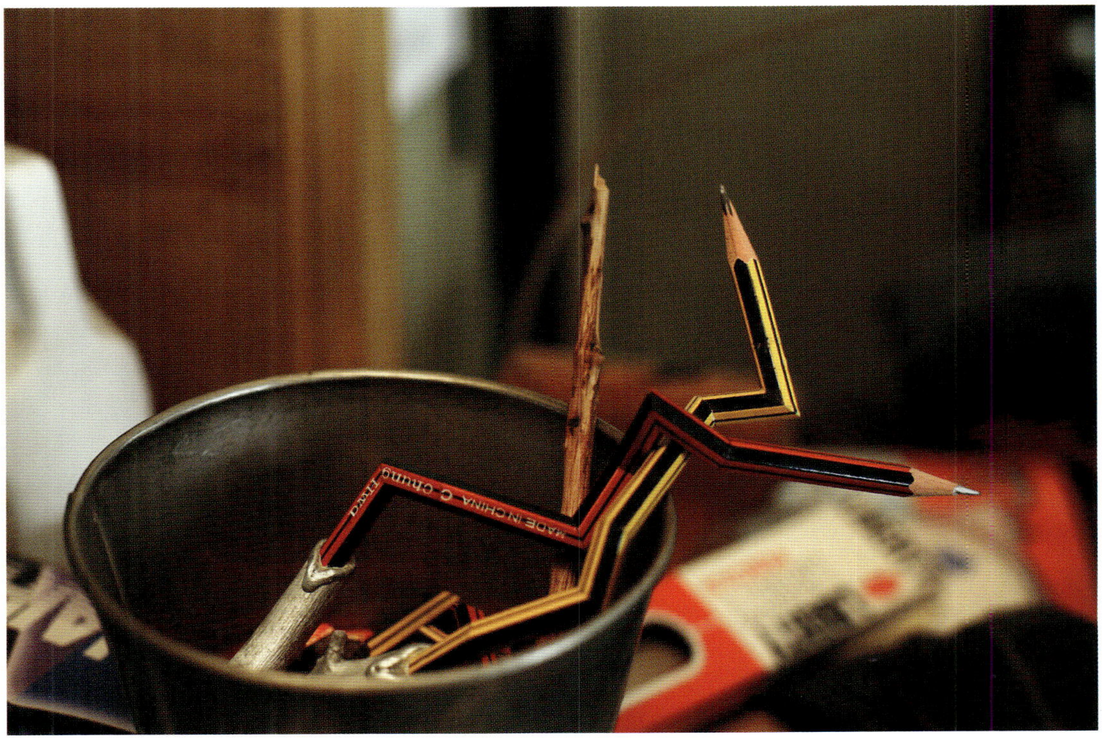

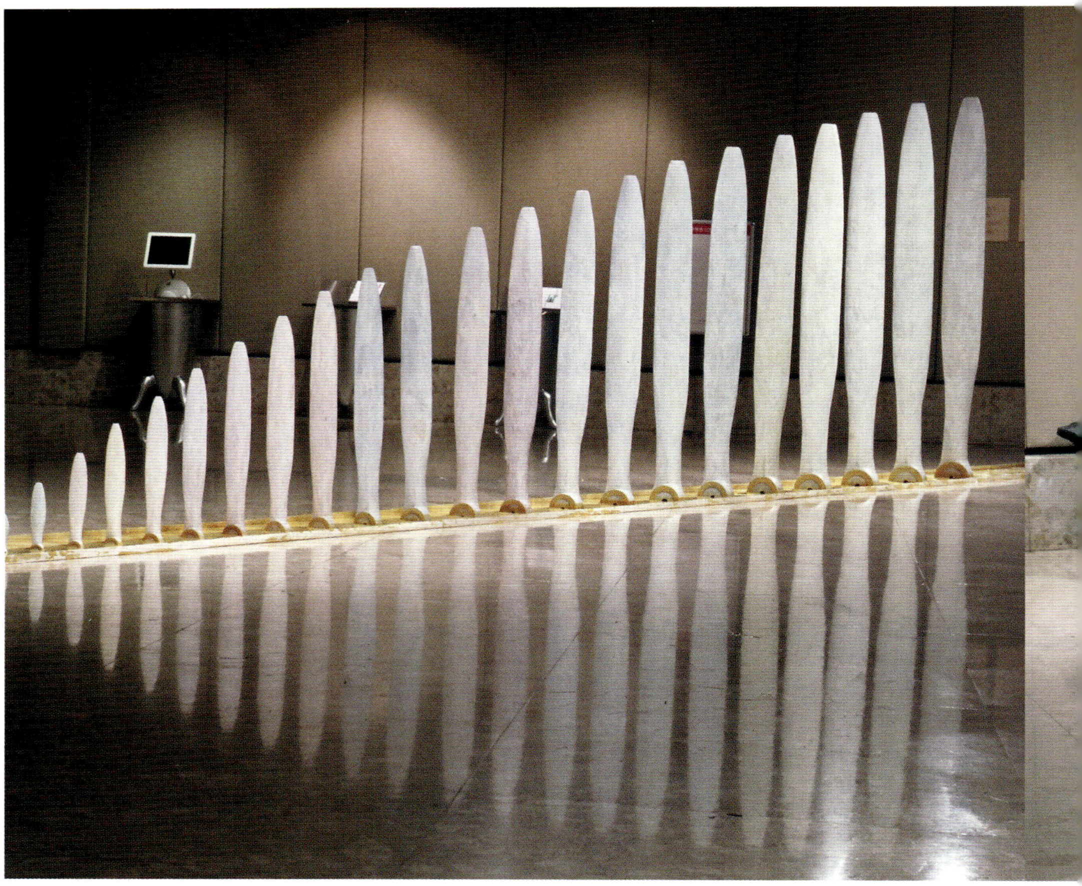

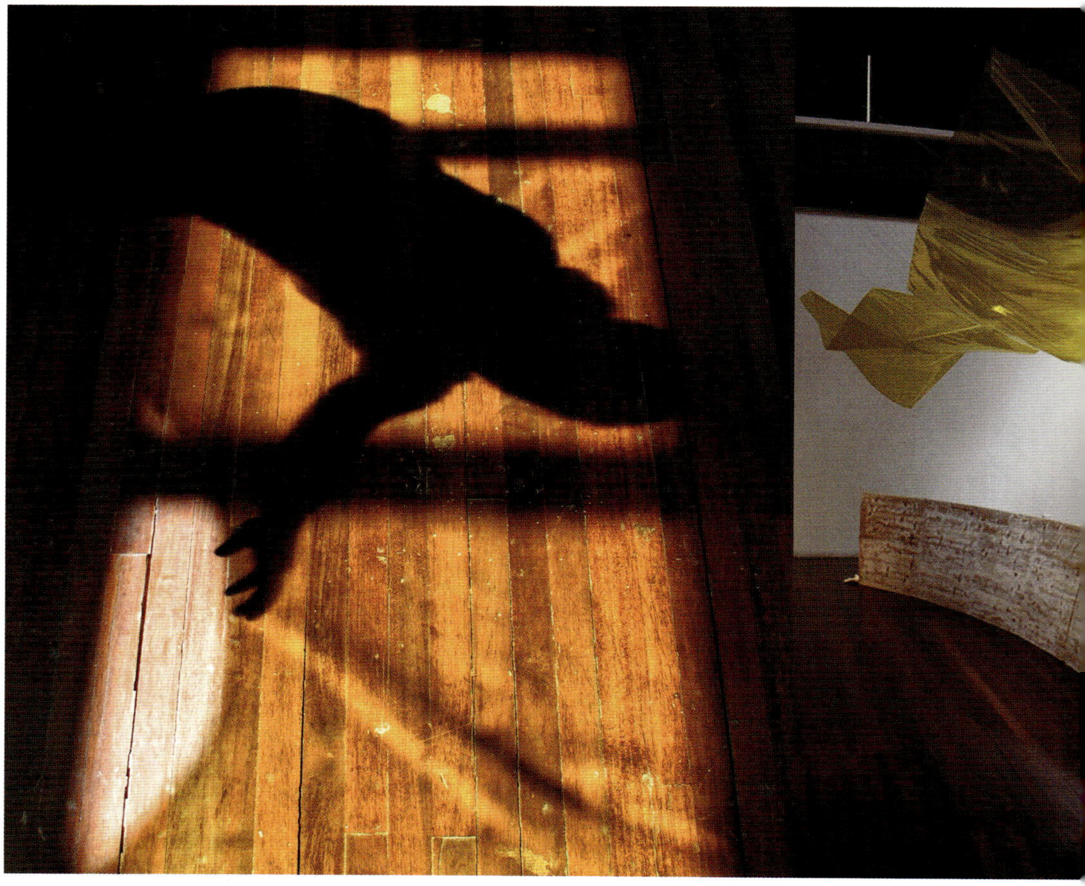

(Left above) To Someone Who Wants to Fly
Wood, water, ricepaper, bees wax, 2-200 cm
(from shortest to tallest), 2003

(Middle above) To Someone Who Wants to Hide
Wood, 800x130x60 cm, 2003

(Right above) To Someone Who Wants to Cry
Water, acrylic, wood, carpet
Sculpture: 290x30x31 cm (each)
Carpet: 142x25 cm, 2003

(Buttom) Shanghai Pottery Workshop Residency –
I Touched Those Light from the Sky.
Wood, ceramics, plastic sheet, 900x30x100 cm, 2004

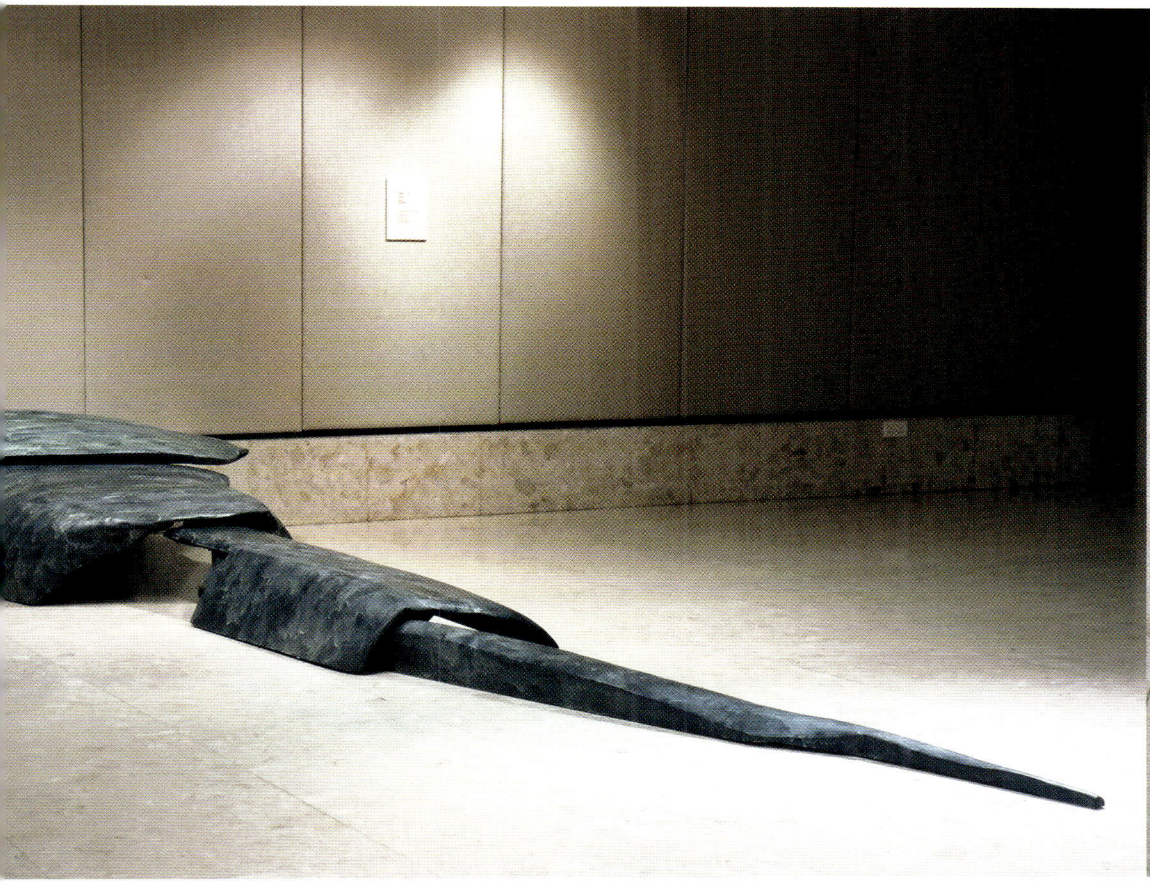

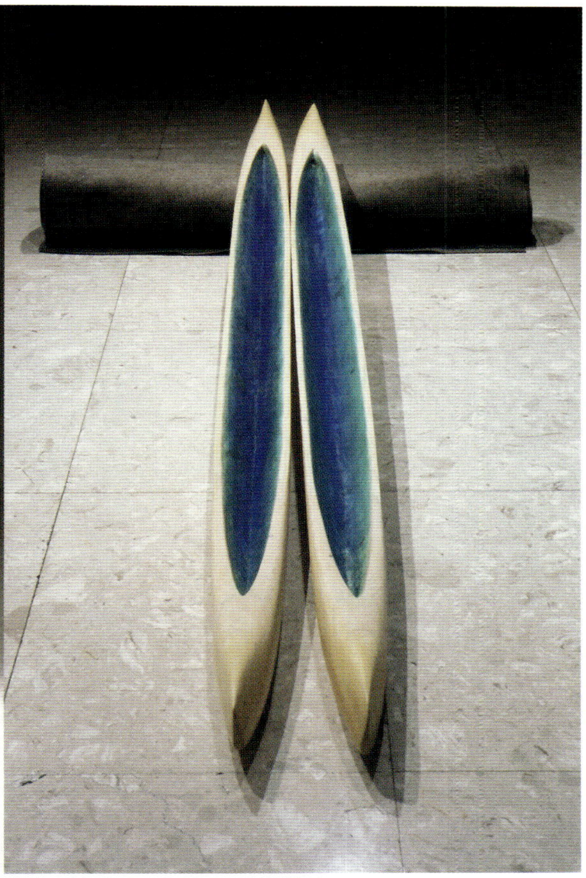

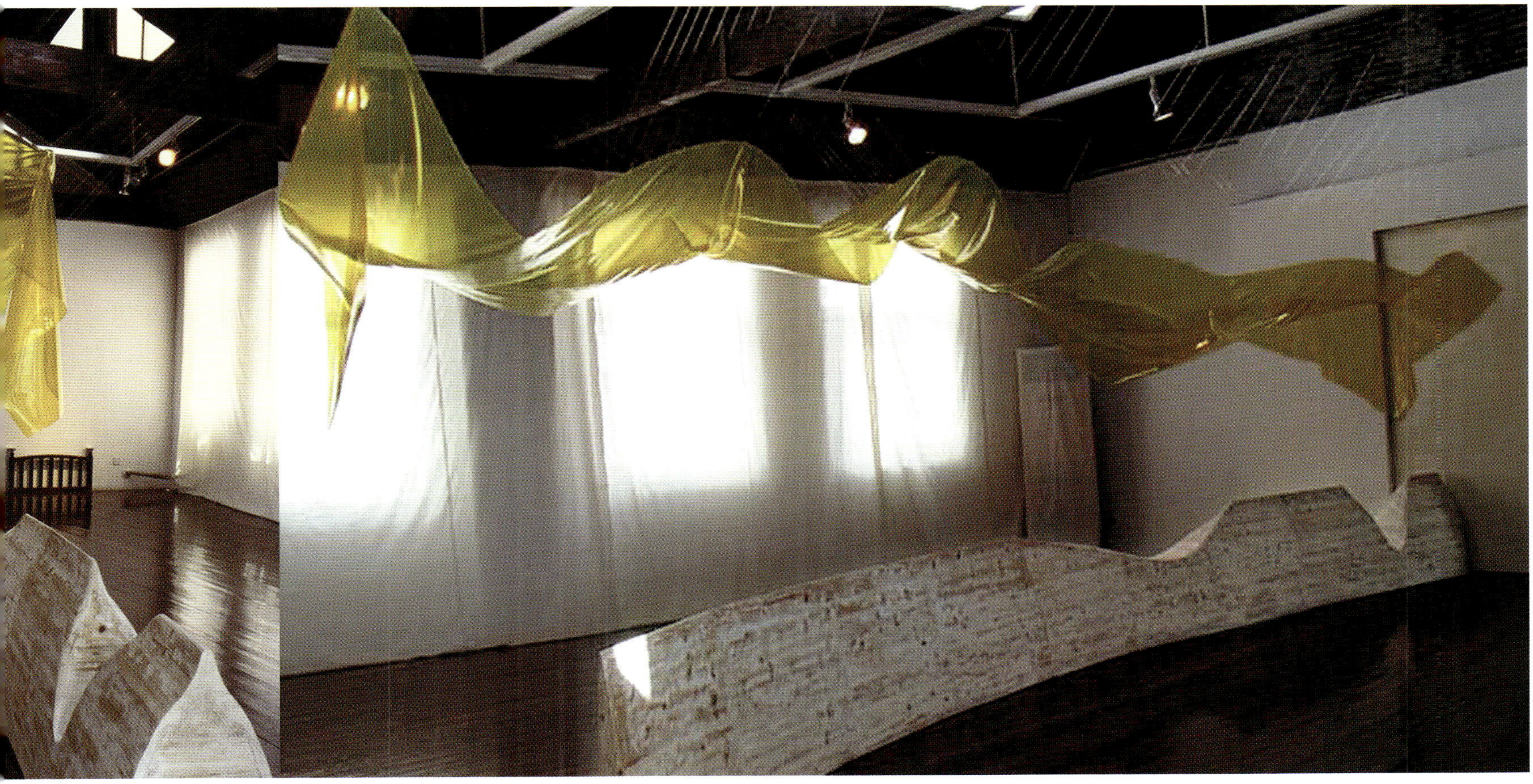

Ellen Pau

The Interior and Exterior of Images – Reflections of the Inner Self

By Livia B Garcia

Ellen Pau was born in Hong Kong. She was self-taught in art and has been a film artist, video artist, curator, art educator, director of music television programmes and administrator. Her full time profession is a radiographer. In 1995 she took part in the Gwangju Biennale in Korea, curated by Kim Hon Yee and Nam June Paik. Pau is one of the founders of a media art group, Videotage. She is also a curator of the Microwave International Media Art Festival. Pau has lectured at the University of Hong Kong, the Hong Kong Polytechnic University and the Hong Kong Academy for Performing Art and has taken part in many exhibitions both locally and overseas, including Munich, Berlin and Barcelona.

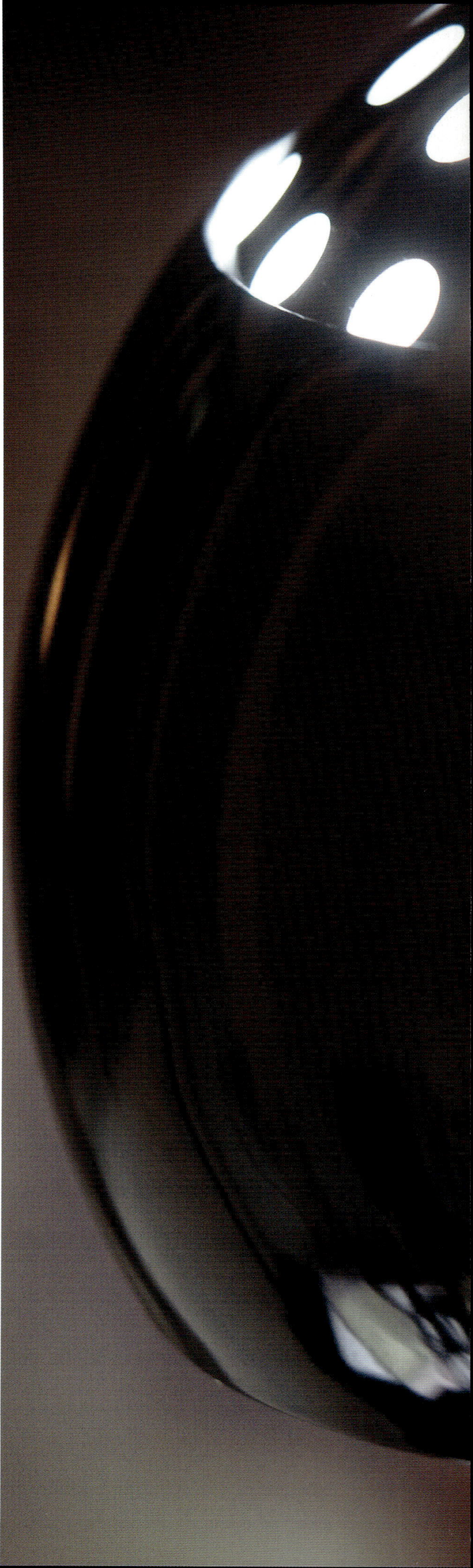

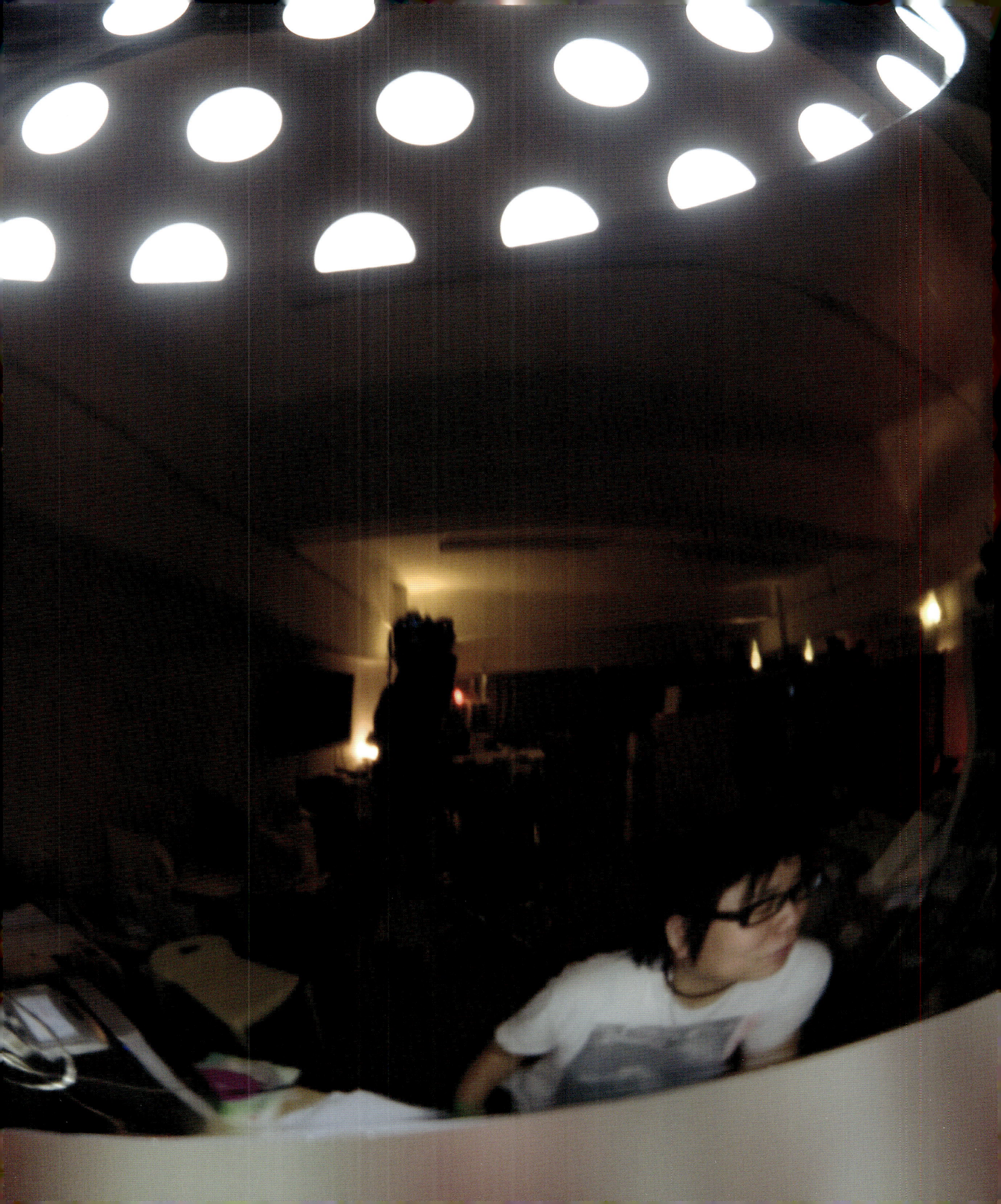

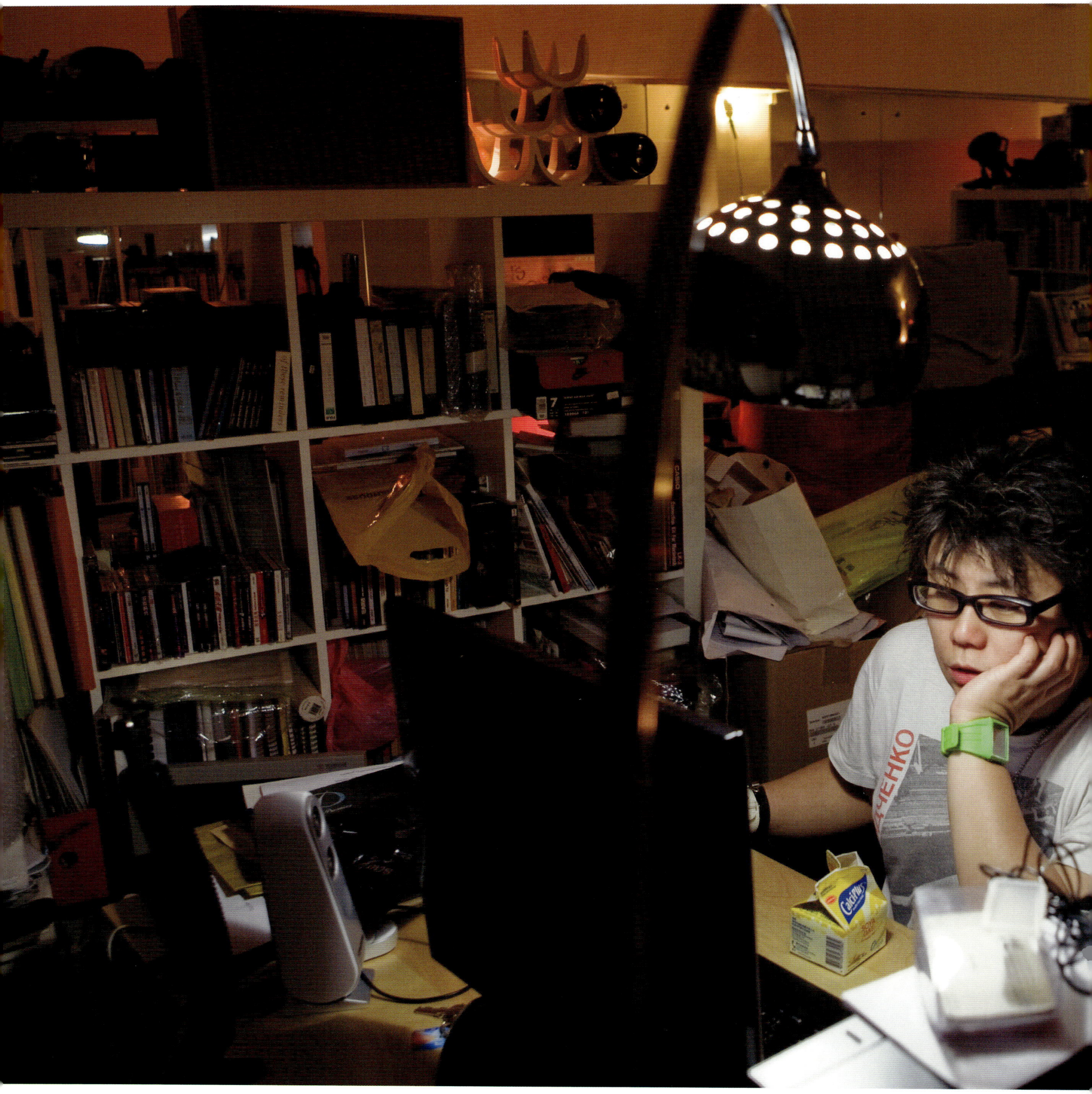

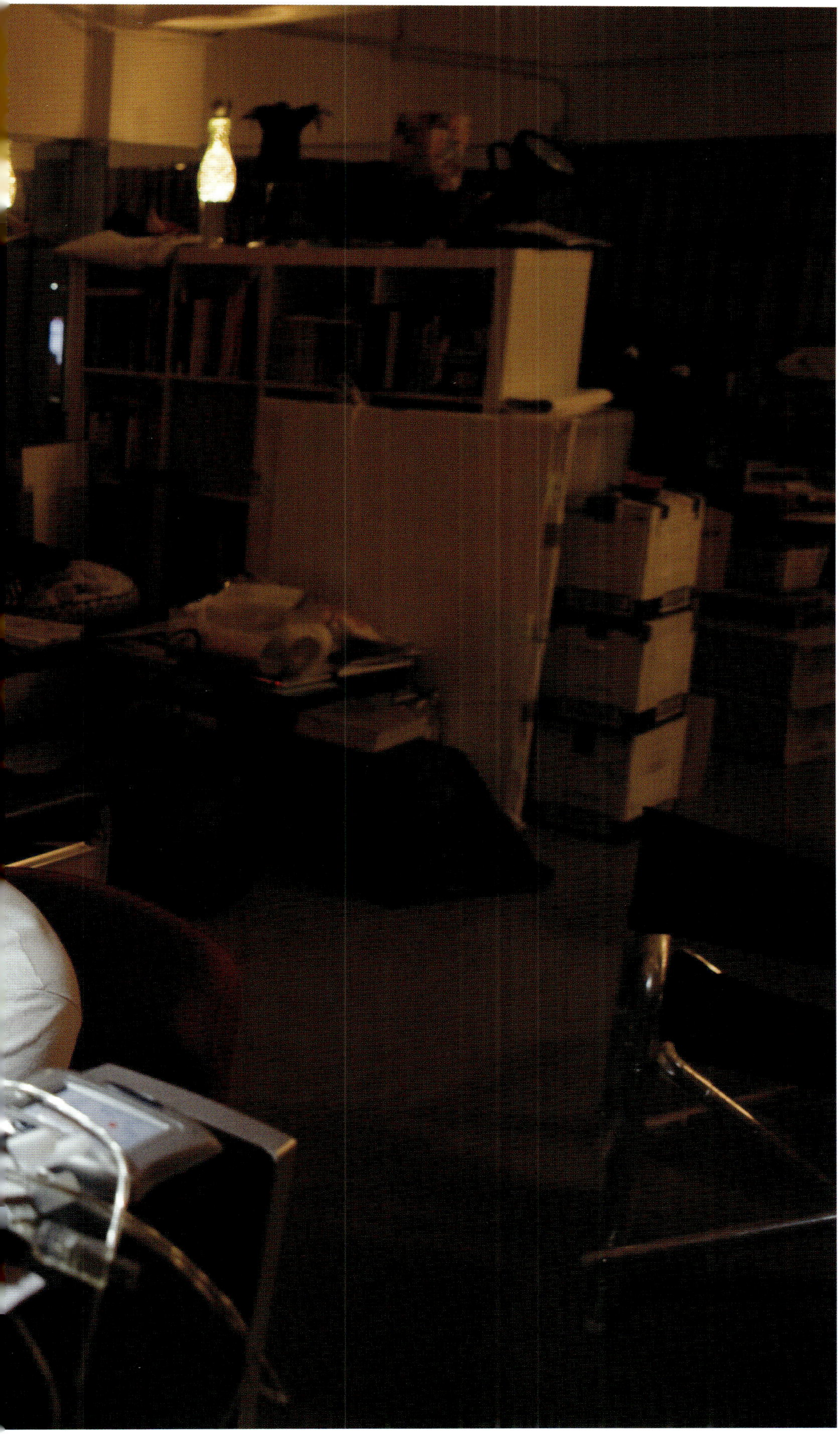

Before the interview I collected some information about Ellen Pau and I found that she is a 'self-taught' artist. Without any certificate, the road that she has had to travel may seem longer than that of other artists.

The main medium that Pau adopts is video. She says, "I started filming in Super-8 when I was studying for my diploma in radiography at the Hong Kong Polytechnic (now called the Hong Kong Polytechnic University) in the '80s. The first piece of work was *Gloves*. I had participated in some theatre productions as well as writing music critiques."

"Theatre, music and visual arts are very similar. Different threads actually tie many things in life, 'punk' music and 'punk' fashion is a good example. Apparently music is about an attitude to life. I paid much attention to the culture of the time but information technology was not all that well developed then so I had to rely on myself to discover the field. That's how I started to communicate with some overseas artists."

In 1986 Pau, Wong Chi-fai, May Fung and Comyn Mo jointly founded a media art group named Videotage. From their meetings at local cha chan ting (or tea houses) in the beginning to those at the Cattle Depot now, the group has consistently pushed forward local media art. They have archived and distributed works, and they have also curated shows and generated ideas on how to promote new products.

Now a professional radiographer, Pau says, "Radiography is about how to make use of X-rays to visualise images of human bodies, and how to analyse the objects that you see. We pay attention to the way they are structured, their colours, light, shadows and so on."

"If X-rays make individual human bodies visual then how do the lights seen by our eyes make humans and objects visual, and how also do lights help define the relationships between these objects? I am mostly interested in light, diagrams and structures."

Pau has also participated in the production of music television programmes. The Hong Kong singers she has worked with include Tat Ming Pair, Cass Pang and Faye Wong, among others. I asked her if she would drop

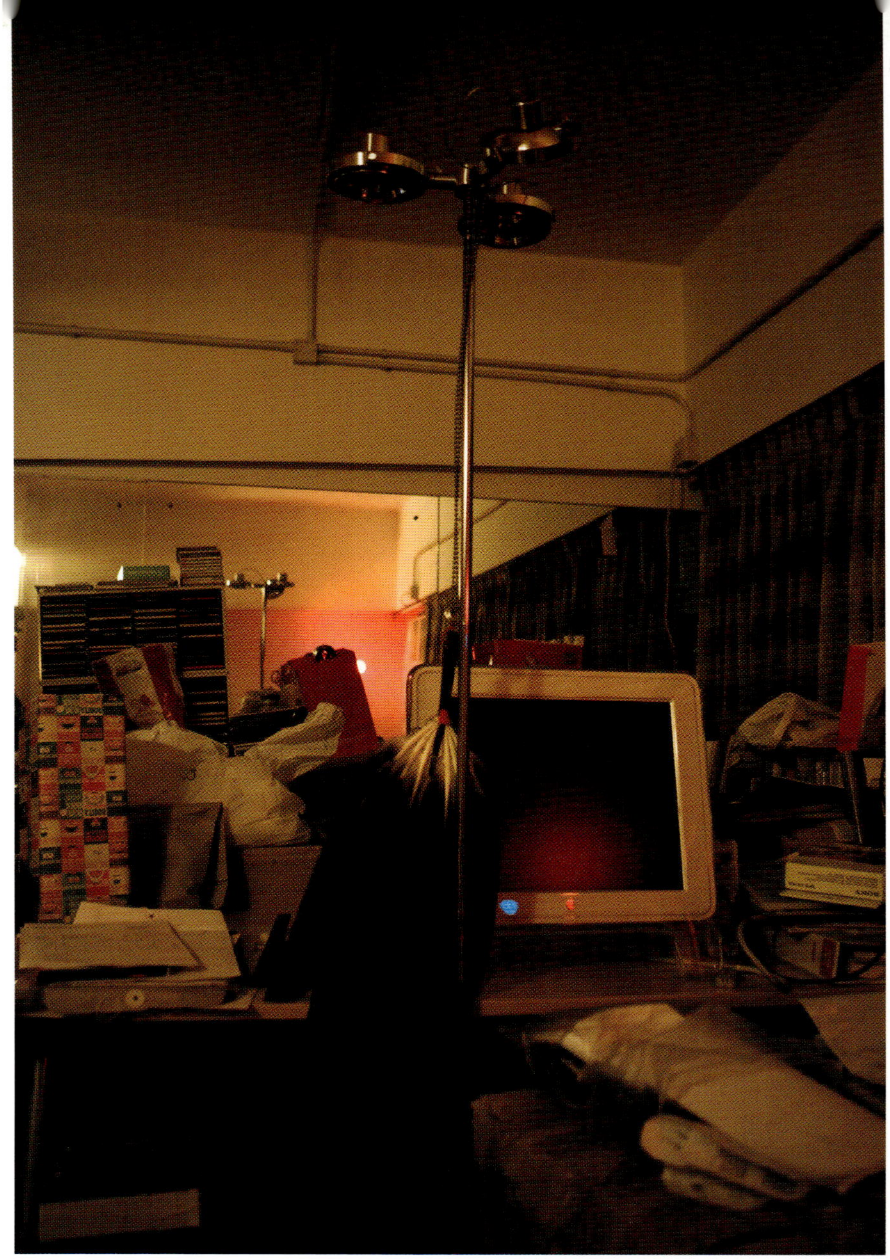

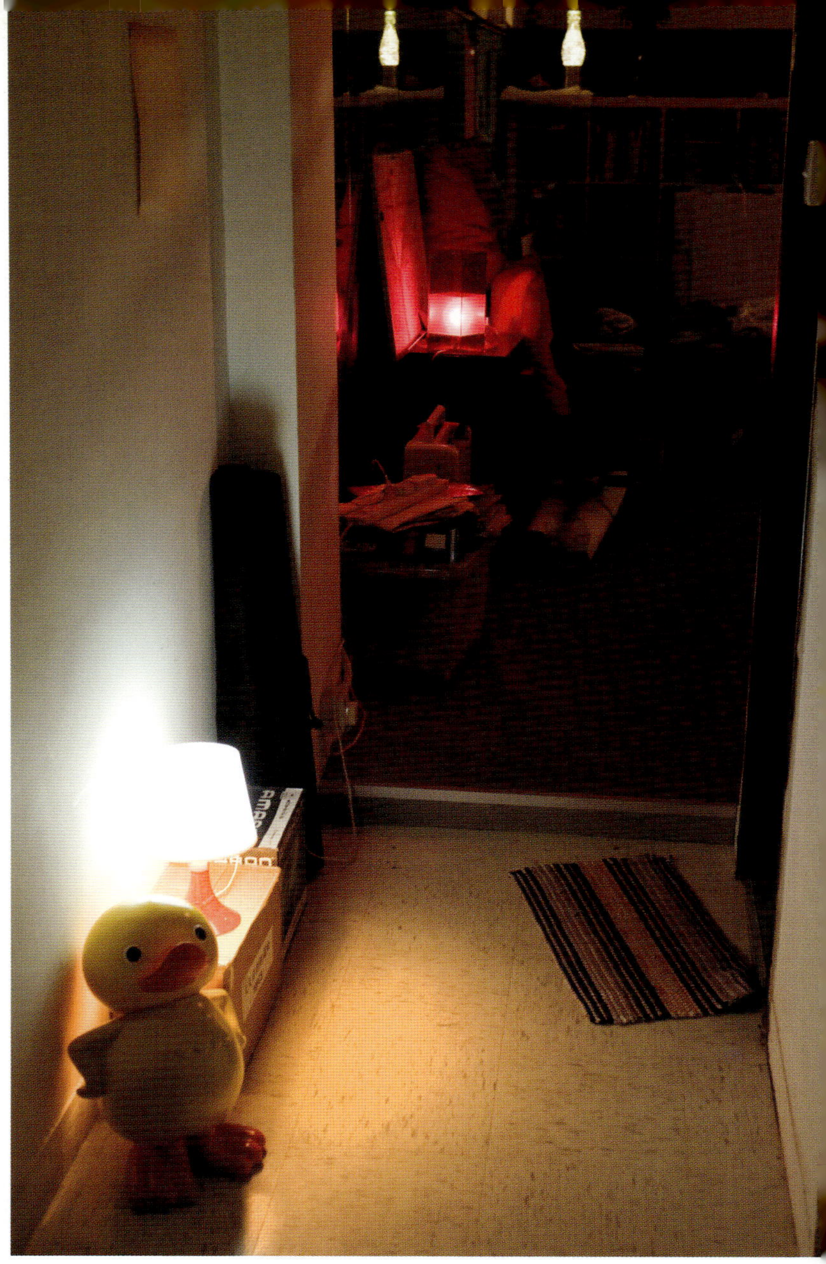

"Sometimes I see friends who are also in the art circle in the lift. That kind of emotional build-up and the connection between people is important"

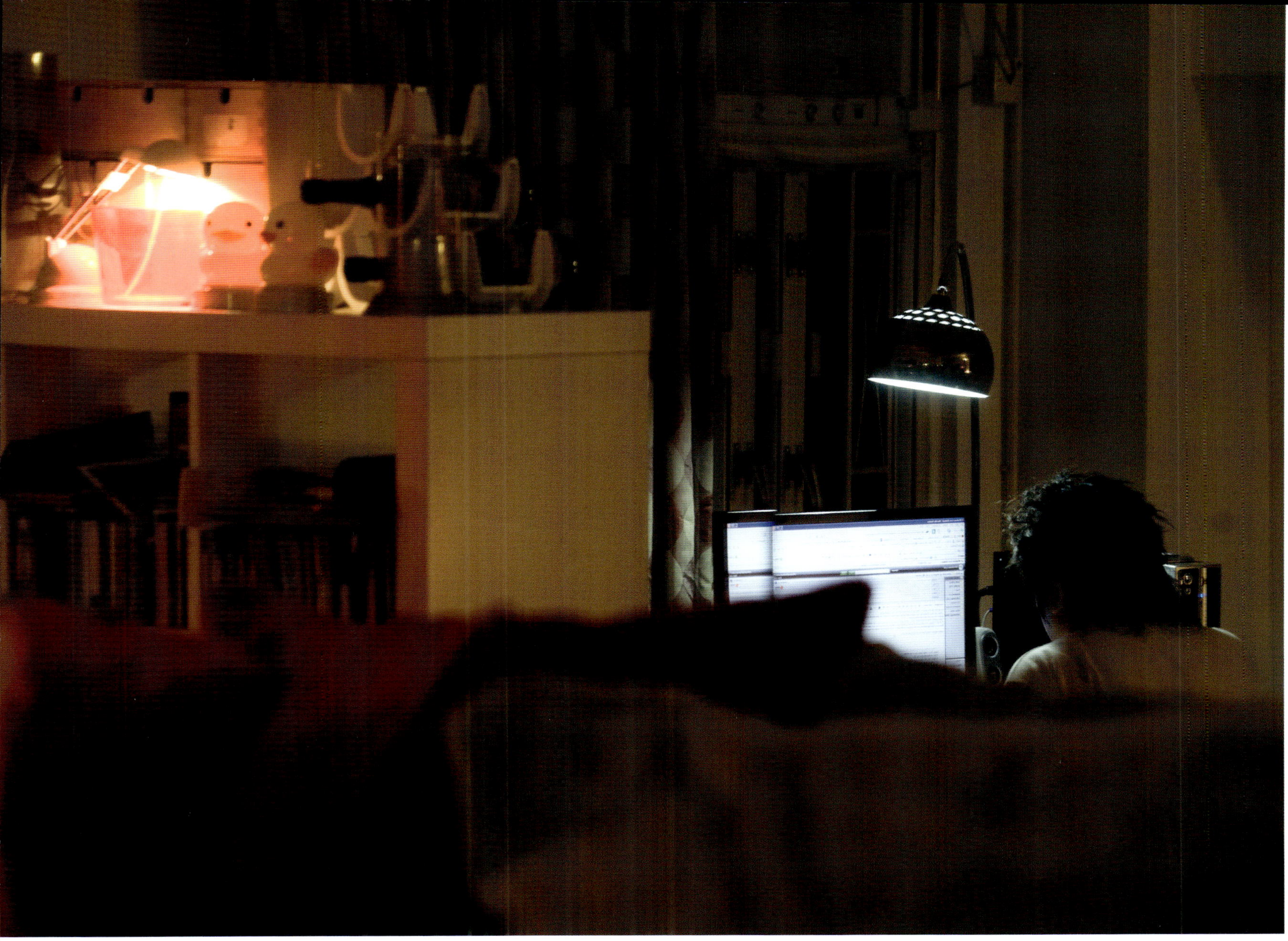

her career as a radiographer in hospitals and fully immerse herself into art making. "Well, I have pondered this before, but one still needs to solve the very practical problem of making a living and so one needs to work," she answers. "I can't think of any other job that could give me as much freedom to create and I quite enjoy my current work. It gives me chance to be in touch with the public on the frontline. I can feel the pulse of Hong Kong society."

Pau moved into her current studio in Fu Tak House in Wanchai in November 2005. "Quite a number of media artists have gathered here, forming a small cluster," she says. Her studio does not have a high ceiling. The whole setting appears in between that of an office and an art studio space. "I feel happy coming to work," she says. "Sometimes I see friends who are also in the art circle in the lift. That kind of emotional build-up and the connection between people is important."

"To me, it does not matter whether there is a high ceiling or wide space, although of course, a convenient location and cheap rent are very important. Here I can buy the materials and tools I need from the nearby shops anytime, which is very handy. Actually, my home is kind of like a studio, but it is lonely if I work there. It does not feel quite the same as it does here. I tend to be more focused, working back in the studio."

During the interview Pau mentions the importance of the ex-Government Supplies Depot in Oil Street, North Point, which had provided a point for artists to meet. She thinks that Oil Street was where the art circle started to grow. People nowadays come from a diverse background. Previously, artists were mostly trained overseas, but more locally trained artists have emerged in recent years. As to the various clusters of studios that have developed over these last few years, Pau thinks that there is a need for people to work together, so this is only a natural phenomena.

Pau's works have evolved around three main themes. The first is gender, the second is about the handing over of Hong Kong in 1997 and the third is the shape and formation of the city and its architecture. In 1992 Pau got offered a fellowship from the Asian Cultural Council to further her research in the States for nine months. During that time she was touched by the story of the relationship of two female Chinese opera singers Yam Kim-fei and Pak Shuet-sin, both on and off stage. It inspired her to make the work *Song of the Goddess*. The piece raises question of gender identity and the stage.

In the interview Pau also mentions *I Only Tell It to Strangers*, which she took to Denmark to exhibit. This video installation was set up inside a container. Among the materials used was a piece of rubber which was first applied to her back and then got peeled off. On this piece of rubber an image of the artist's back was projected. "The first viewer for each of my own works is myself," Pau says. "The work has to appeal to me. Artworks are not only to communicate; they can also be analytical and meaningful. Just like a poet, I detach myself from reality. Sometimes I use video images as reflections of my inner self to create dialogues." One of the many items on her schedule is the exhibition that she is curating at the Hong Kong Museum of Art in 2008. The show is called *Digit@logue of the Hong Kong Art: Open Dialogue*. She is also compiling a book about media art.

While we are discussing the medium of video, Pau explains, "This is a real-time media. You can 'play' with time. For example, you can slow down or repeat some of the images. There is still room to explore concepts with this media." During our discussion, Pau has referred to jargon such as 'video sculpture' and 'video installation'. I interpret them as: there are spaces both inside and outside the projection screen, we see one on the screen and the real world outside also forms another space, which artist can work on.

On her art path Pau has met a few important people including Danny Yung, founder of experimental theatre company 'Zuni Icosahedron'. She says she learnt from Yung what theatre is and how to perceive problems. Later, some important curators such as Oscar Ho and Johnson Chang introduced her works in exhibitions overseas. They are the ones who have given her the chance to face the world. It was from then on that Pau felt that her works should not be at a level that only serves her own criteria; they now truly represent Hong Kong abroad.

As someone who became an artist through self-teaching, what kinds of people does she think can become artists? "I think anyone can become an artist, as each person has his or her own characteristics," she says. "If you are willing to put time and effort into art, and if you can face yourself and your viewers, then you can be regarded as an artist."

"Similarly, everyone can enjoy art. I would encourage friends to look at art and not start

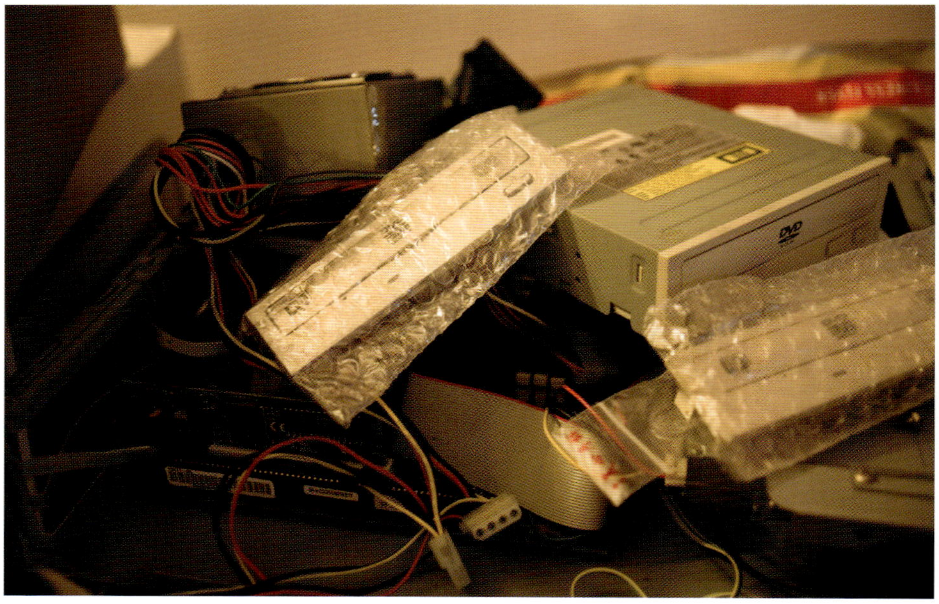

The profusion of audio-visual equipment makes this different from conventional studios, but equally create touching artworks

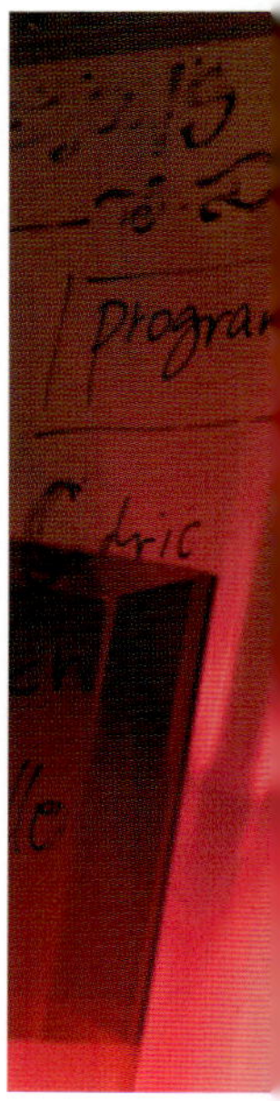

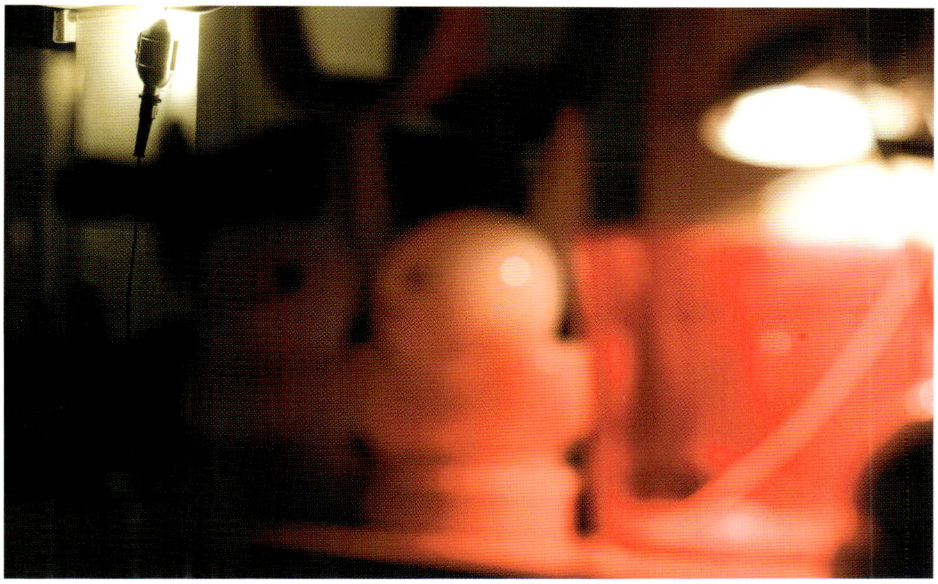

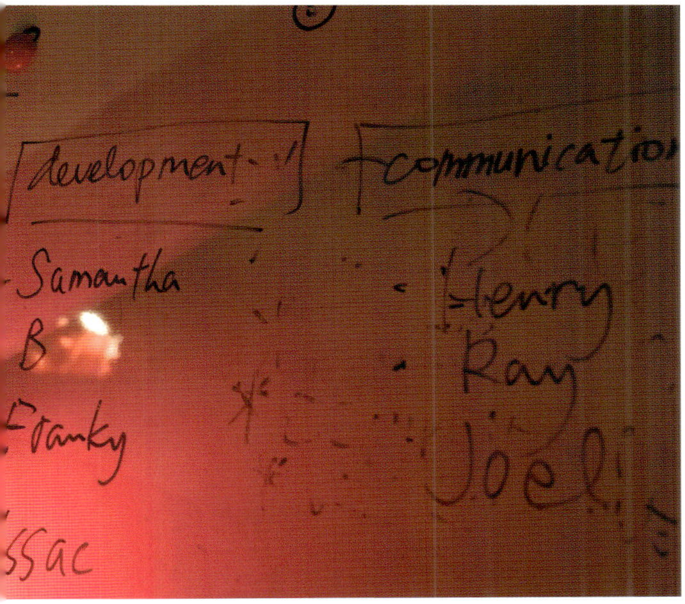
development
Samantha
Henry
Ray
Joel

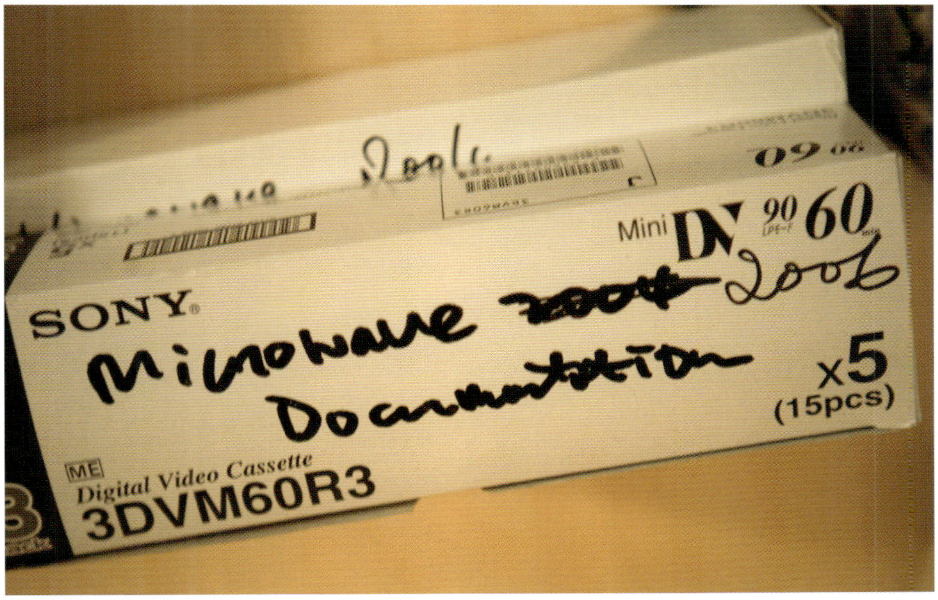
Mini DV 60
SONY
Microwave 2006
Documentation
x5
(15pcs)
Digital Video Cassette
3DVM60R3

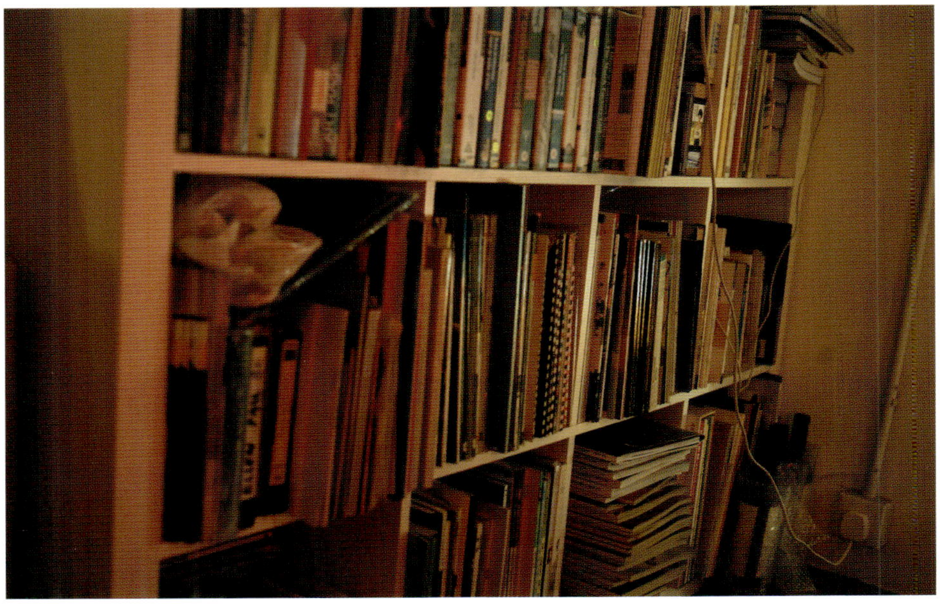

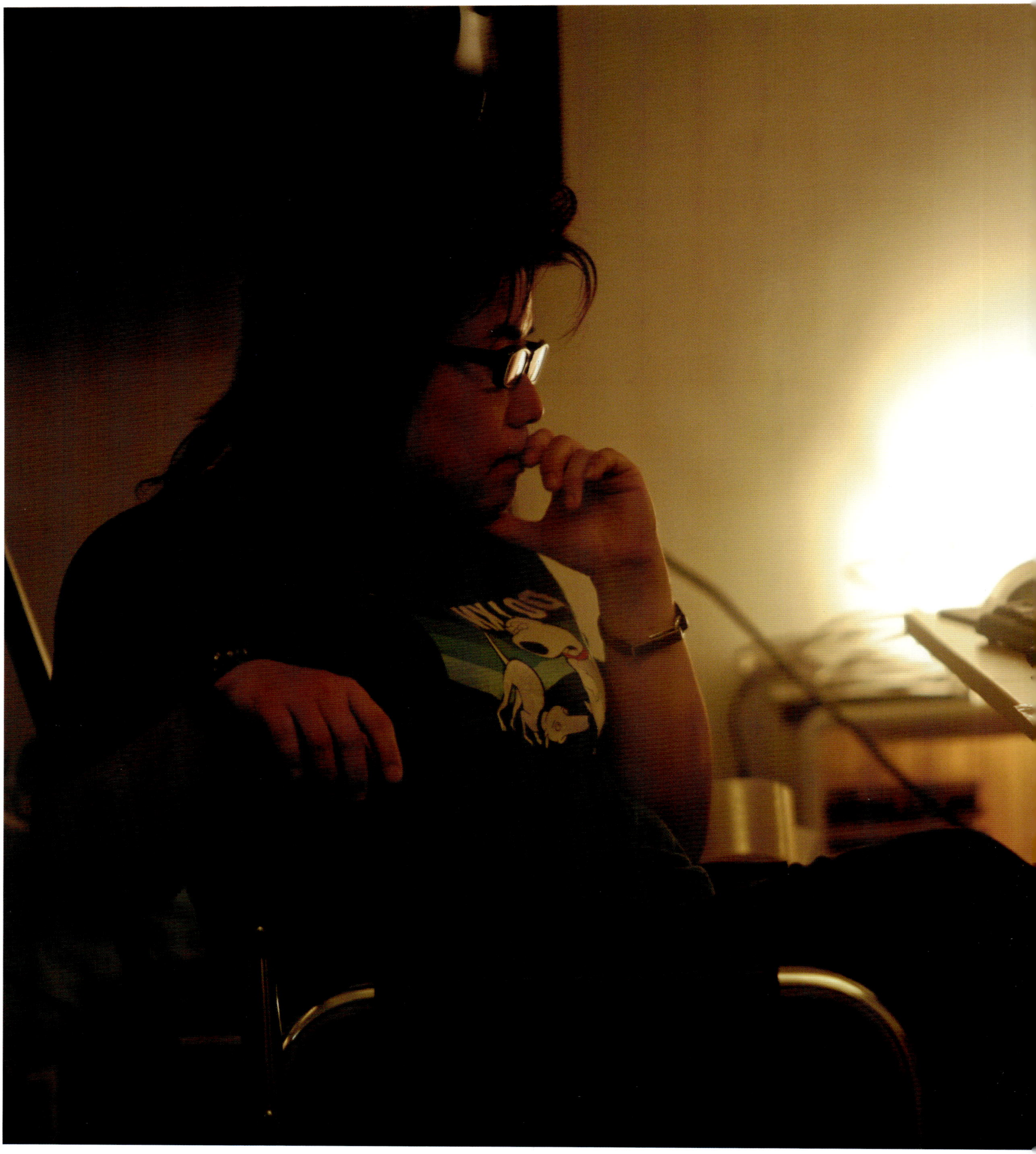

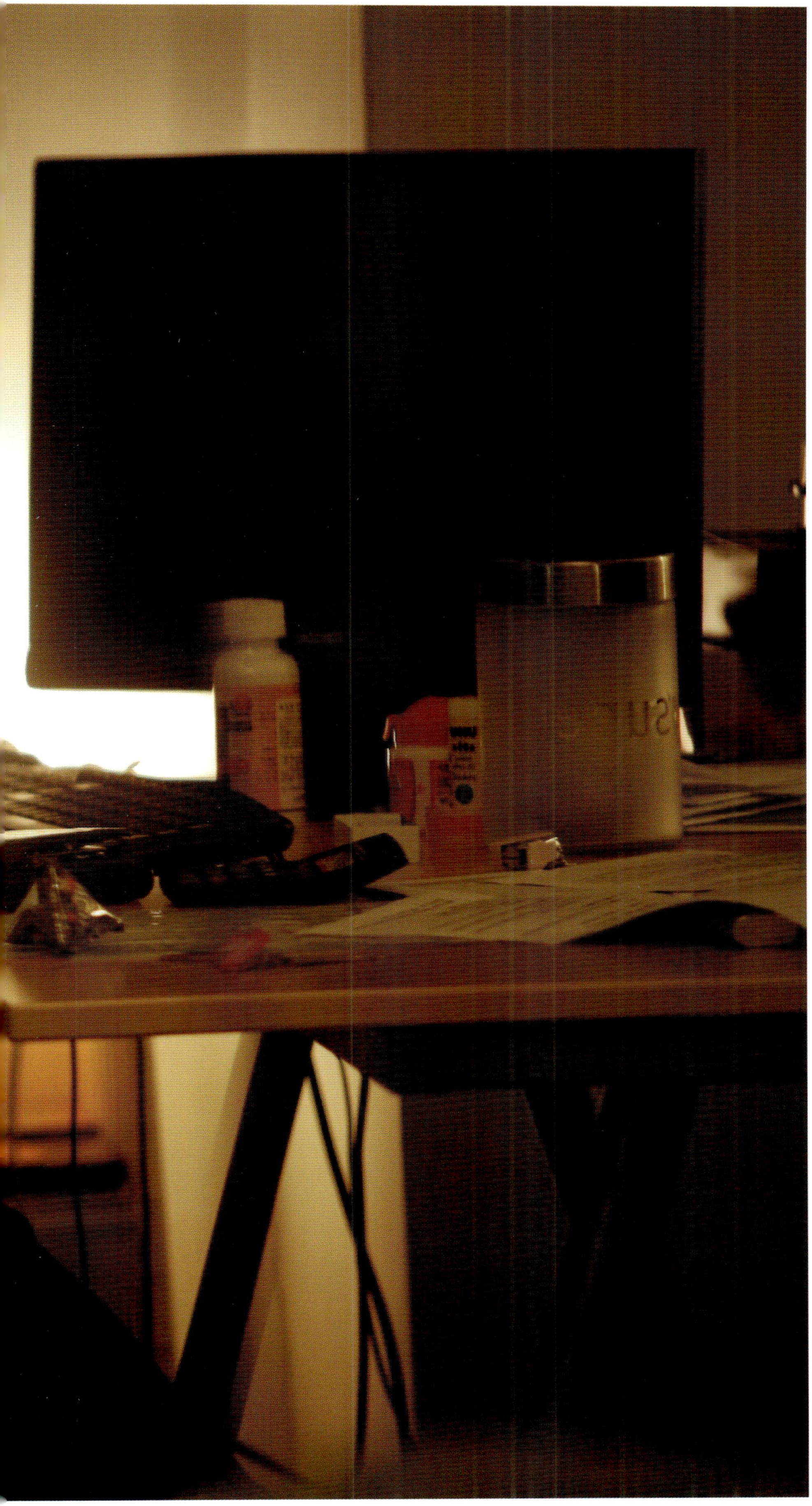

by worrying whether you can understand it or not. If you keep looking, asking and thinking then slowly you will develop a set of concepts about art. You will see the meaning of what you want to know and understand."

Pau thinks that traditional art training such as drawing, trains the coordination between the eyes and hands, as well as a sense for details. It is a technical rather than mental training. Training the mind not only includes seeking knowledge, but being attentive to the people and things around. One should be open on the outside for analysis and inside for criticism. In addition, she feels, you should maintain an individual attitude that doesn't just follow trends. Art reflects life and that's why Pau likes to read about art history, and problems faced by artists across the ages; a lot of artists have this kind of non-conforming attitude.

This now-friendly and talkative artist was apparently very shy when she was little "I like people but I also feel that it is difficult to communicate with people," she admits. "I was very lonely when I was studying in primary school. Very often I simply wanted to run away from people and hide... During breaks I would hide inside the washrooms."

"The fact that I had asthma didn't help the situation either... but on the other hand I also liked to face danger. My dream then was to become a frontline war reporter who would explore life and death, as well as revealing things first." A unique world of her own making; the eagerness to explore and the drive to discover: these are not things that a certificate alone can prove.

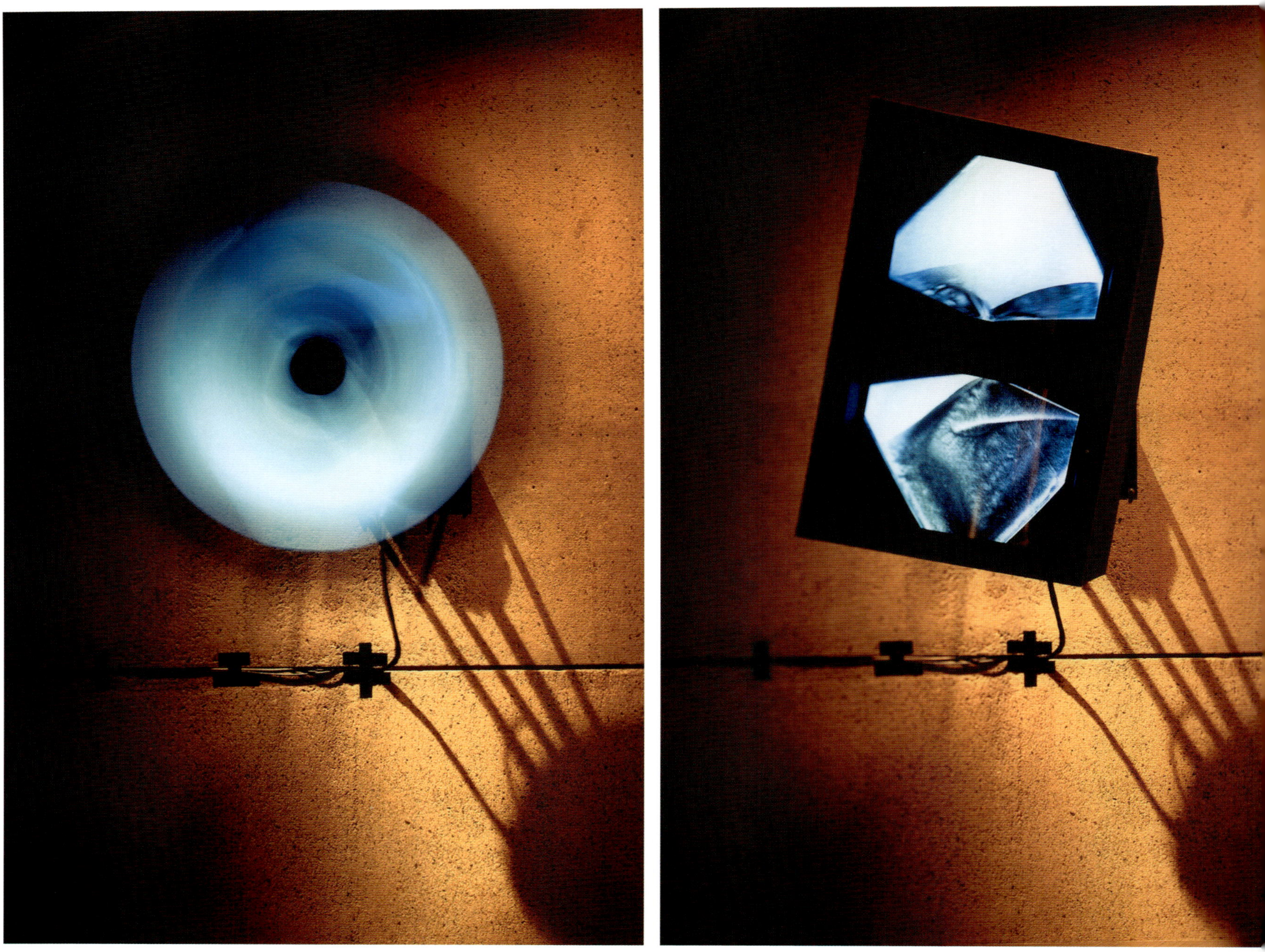

Drained IV (Series #4 of Drained)
Video installation, dimensions variable, 1996-97

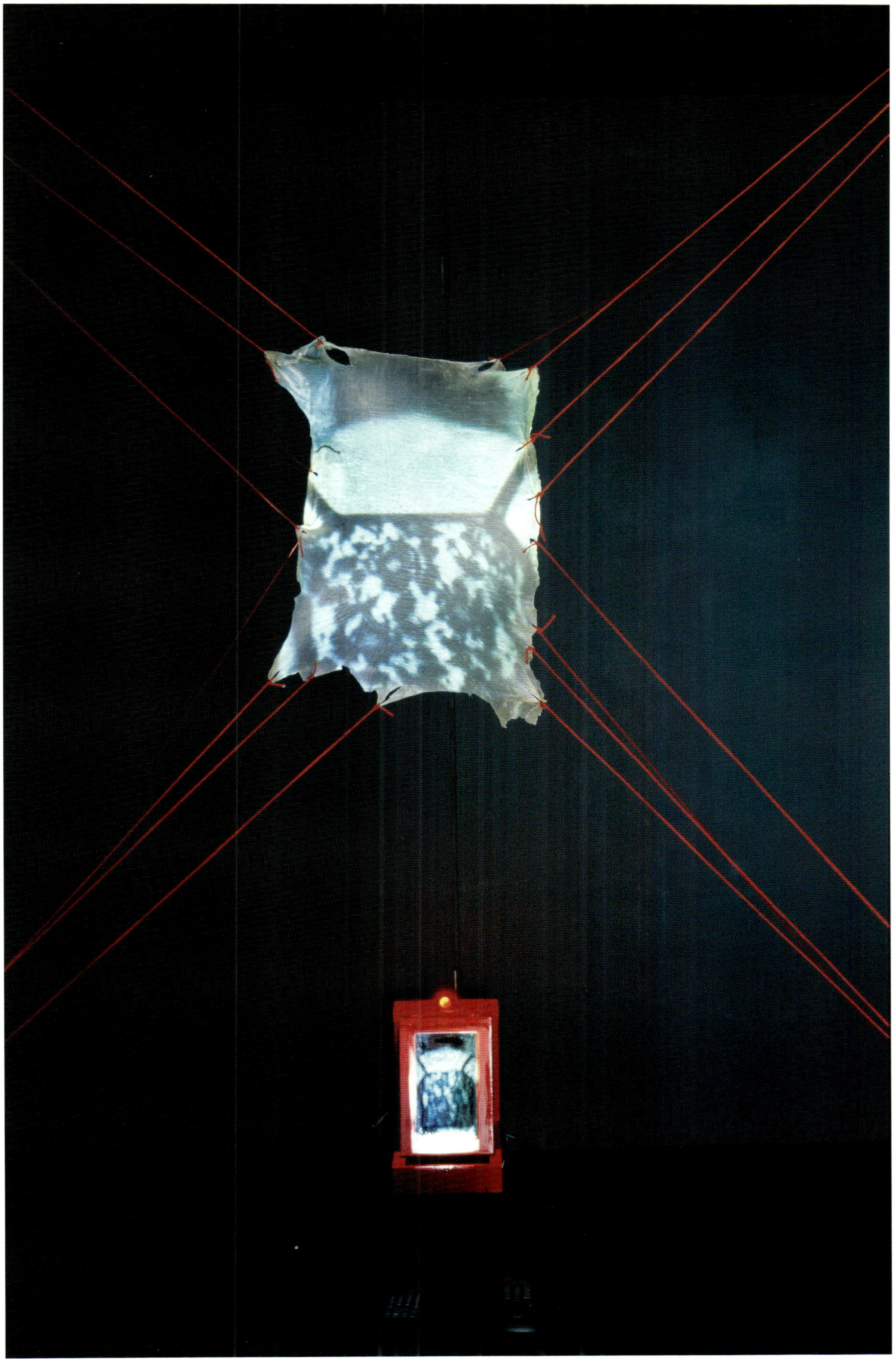

I Can Only Talk to Strangers
Video installation, dimensions variable, 1996

Ivy Ma

Collage as a Reflection of the Inner Self

By Teresa Chan

Ivy Ma attained her Bachelor of Fine Art with the Royal Melbourne Institute of Technology University in 2001. She was awarded a scholarship by the Hong Kong Arts Development Council in the same year to pursue her master's studies in Britain. She is a visual artist who employs a wide variety of media, and has participated in a number of local and international artist workshops and artist-in-residence projects. Her work was selected for the Hong Kong Art Biennial 2005 and is collected by the Hong Kong Heritage Museum. An active member of the local art community, Ma has also taken up art-related programme planning and teaching posts.

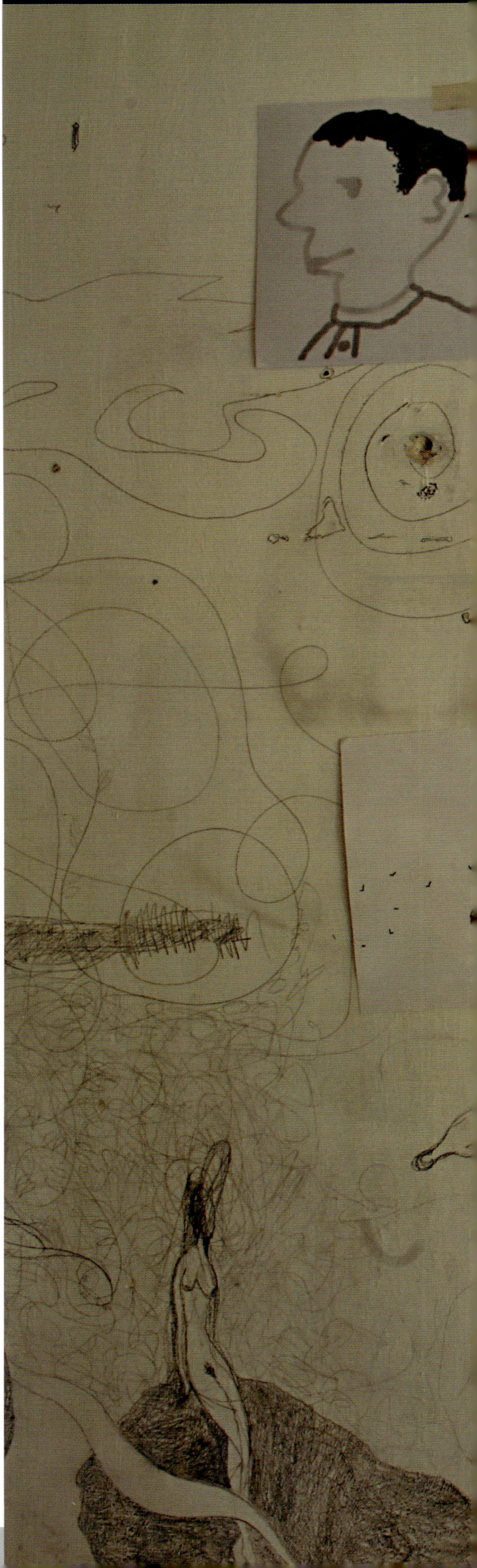

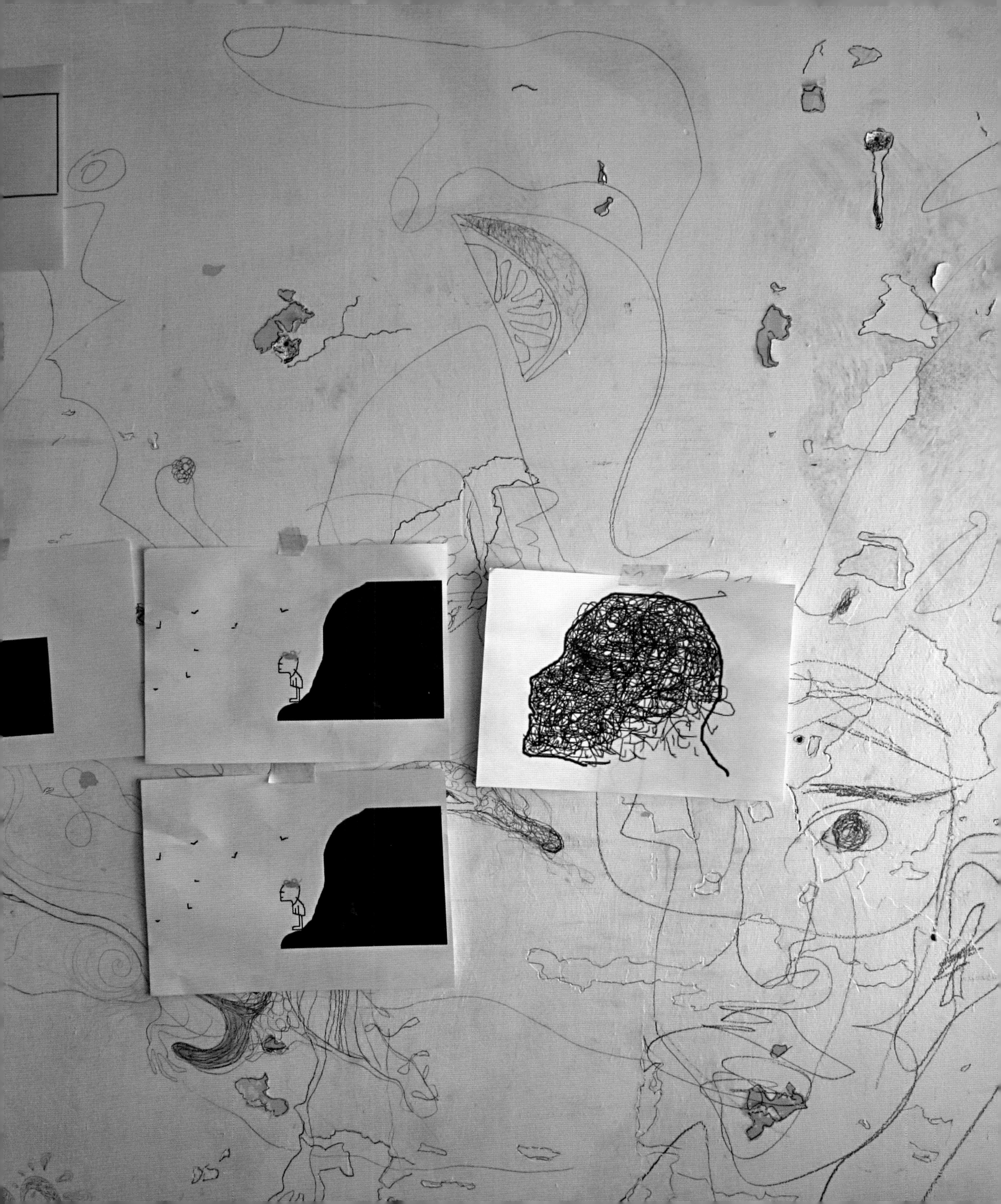

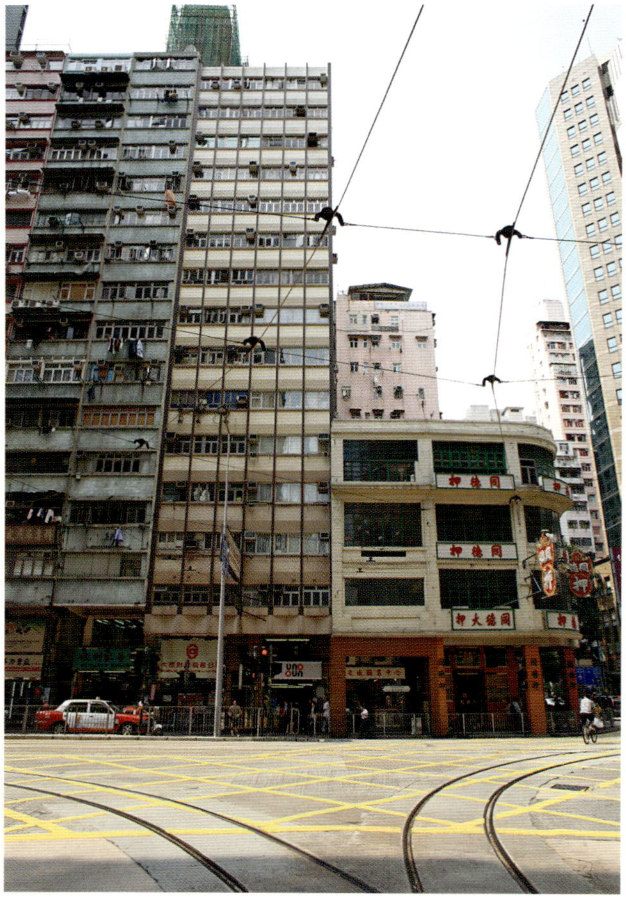

Working on the interview with Ivy Ma reminds me of my first link with her a few years ago. At that time I stood at a crossway, puzzling about a decision to be made about pursuing part-time studies in fine arts – something unrelated to my job. In the prospectus of that year is a short article by a graduate who shares her experience of taking the fine arts programme I was interested in, and like me, she had studied in other fields before fine arts. That was the first time I encountered the name of Ivy Ma. The next time I saw her name was after I enrolled in the programme. In a visit to the Para/Site Art Space with a class, I saw her works *Before the Disappearance of Rain* and *Before the Incarnation of Cloud*. I also learned that she continued making art after graduation and had become an active artist. In the following years there were a number of occasions on which I would come across Ma's works, but I never had the chance to know the artist herself until this interview, three years later.

Ma's studio is located on the eighth floor of a building in Wanchai. When I step into her studio, I have a special feeling that everything seems to slow down and becomes veiled by a shield of silence. I am not sure if it is caused by the interaction of the light at dusk with the colours of the studio, or a result of the hectic traffic flow outside being cut off by the studio door. In the space is a mood of solitary meditation.

Ma tells me that when she comes to the studio she does not have to spend the time in art making. Rather, she may experiment

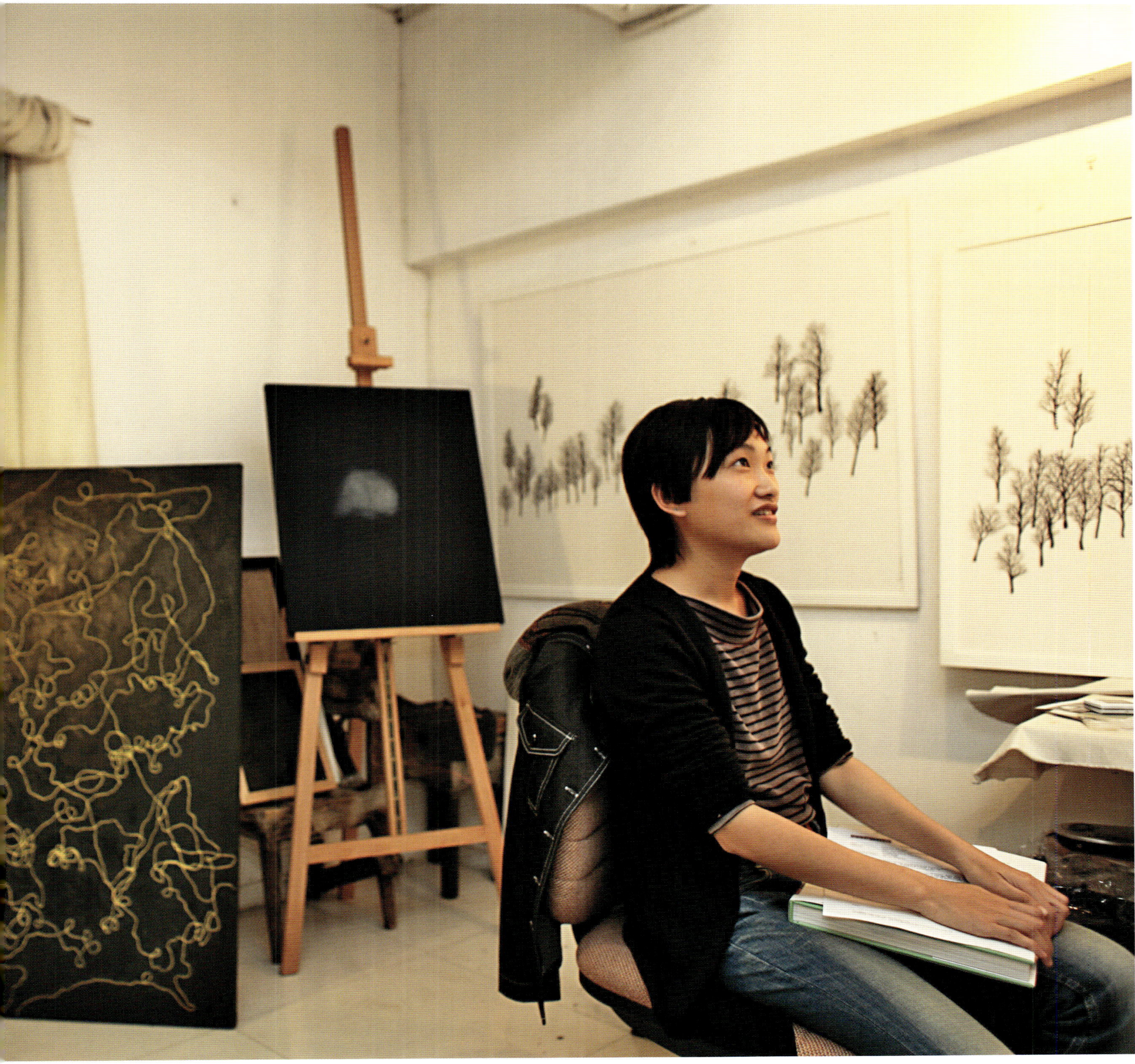

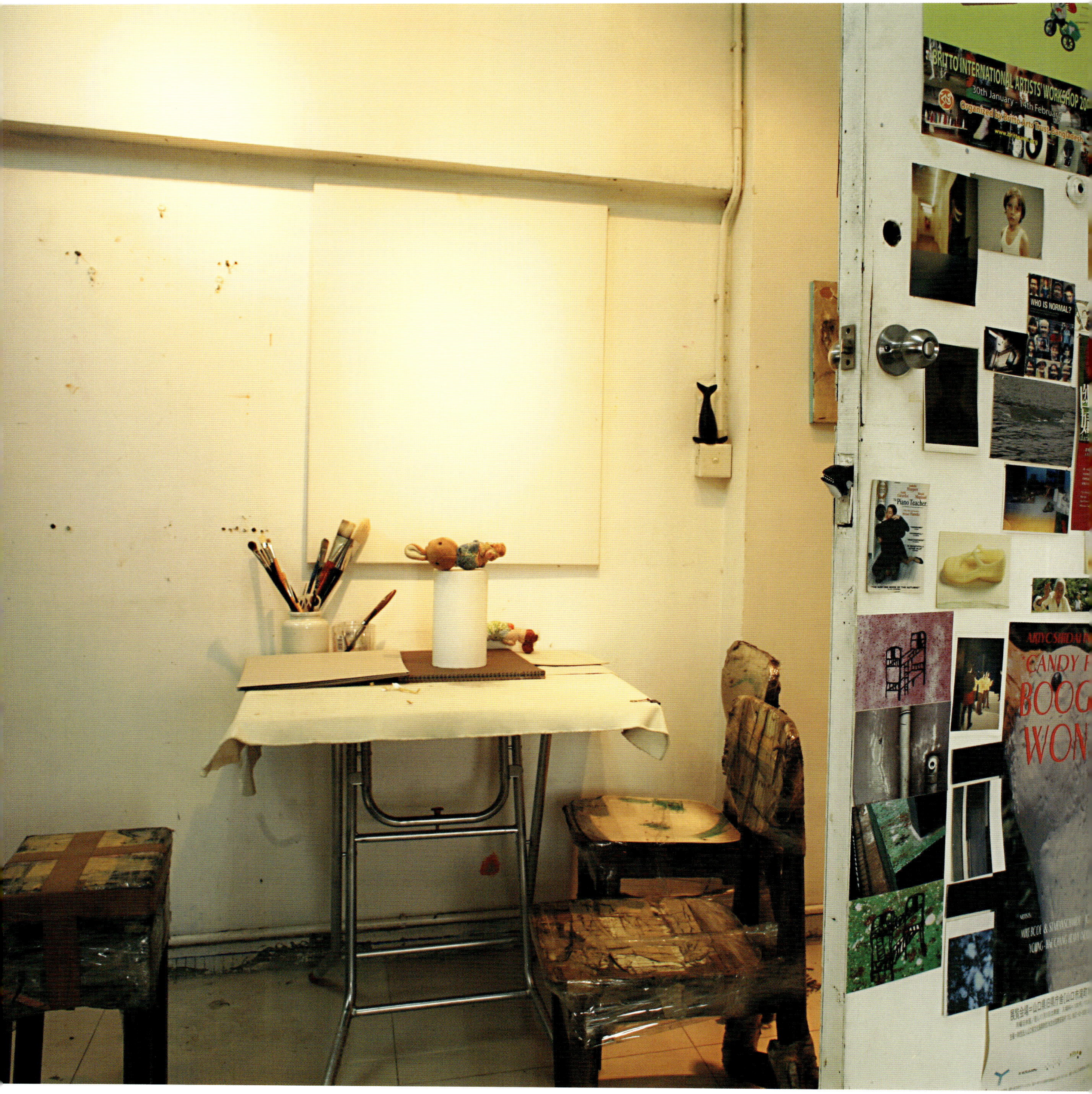
30th January - 14th Februar
WHO IS NORMAL?
Piano Teacher

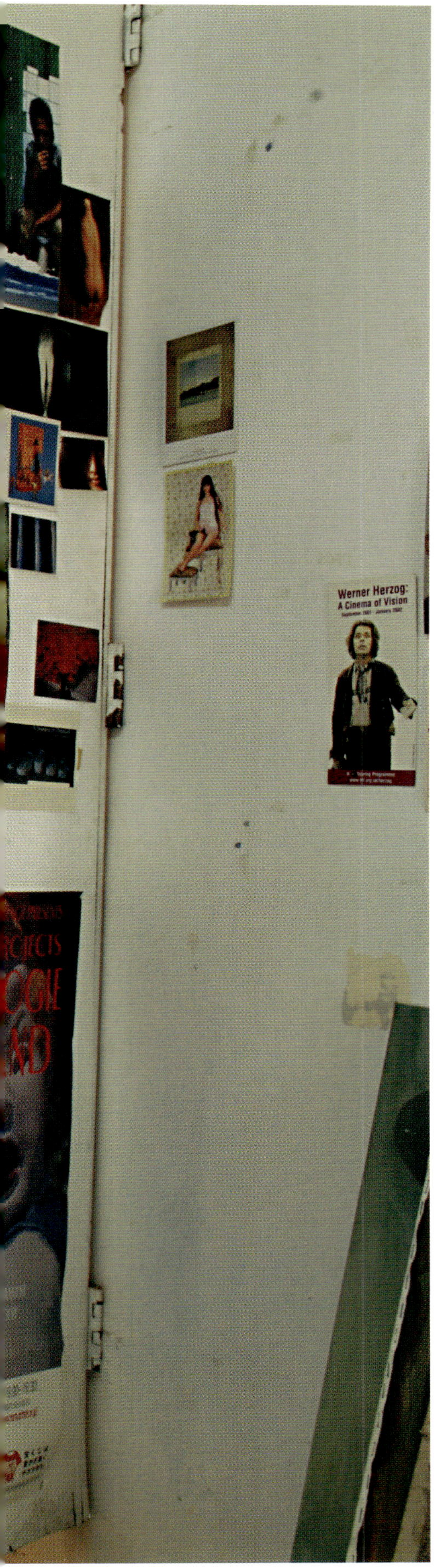

with ideas for her works, or just read and think in the living room. She shows me around the studio room, where, apart from materials, some two-dimensional works can be found on a table and the walls. Compared with the living room, this is a place with more traces of activity.

We sit down next to a small table in the living room and our conversation starts with Ma's entry into the world of art. As a child, she liked drawing and doodling just like any other kid. However, the starting point of her artistic journey can be traced back to a desire to make things with her hands. The world of art turned out to be the place where her dreams could come true.

When Ma was still a student she had no detailed plans for the future. After completing a degree course in information systems she worked in several web design and network development companies. A few years later she started to think about her own future. She asked herself, if one cannot conform to the pace and values of society, what should one continue to do in life? Ma believed that she could find the answer in art. She enrolled in a degree course in fine arts and started to seriously explore where art could take her.

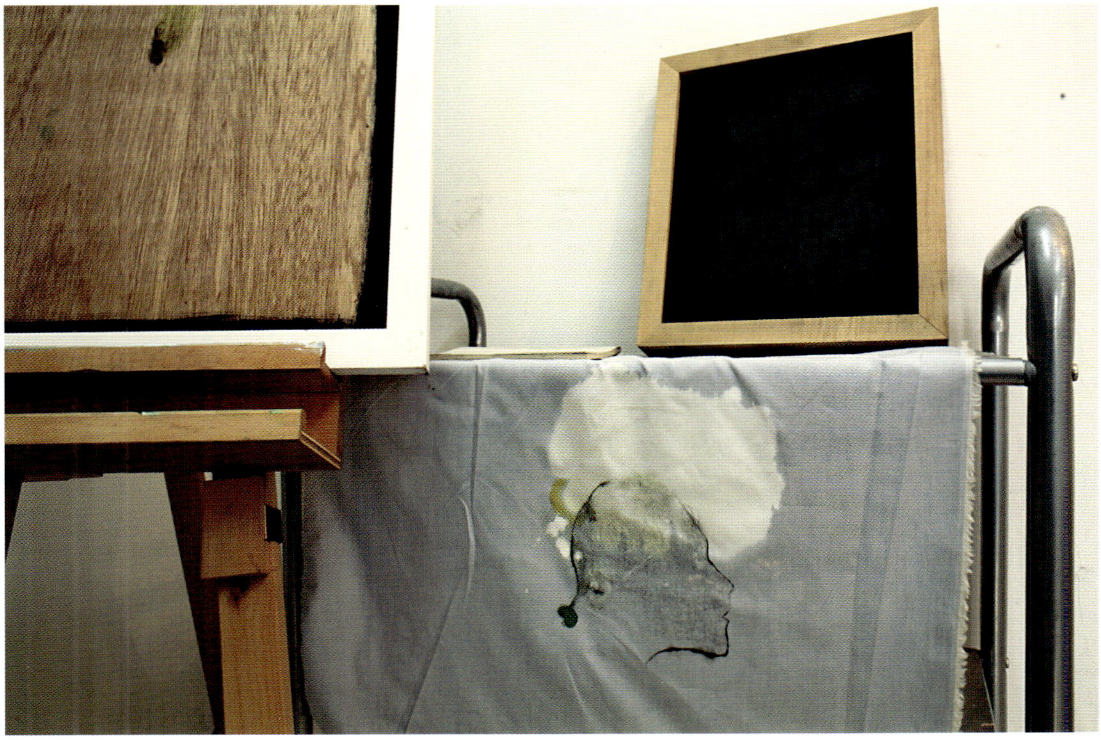

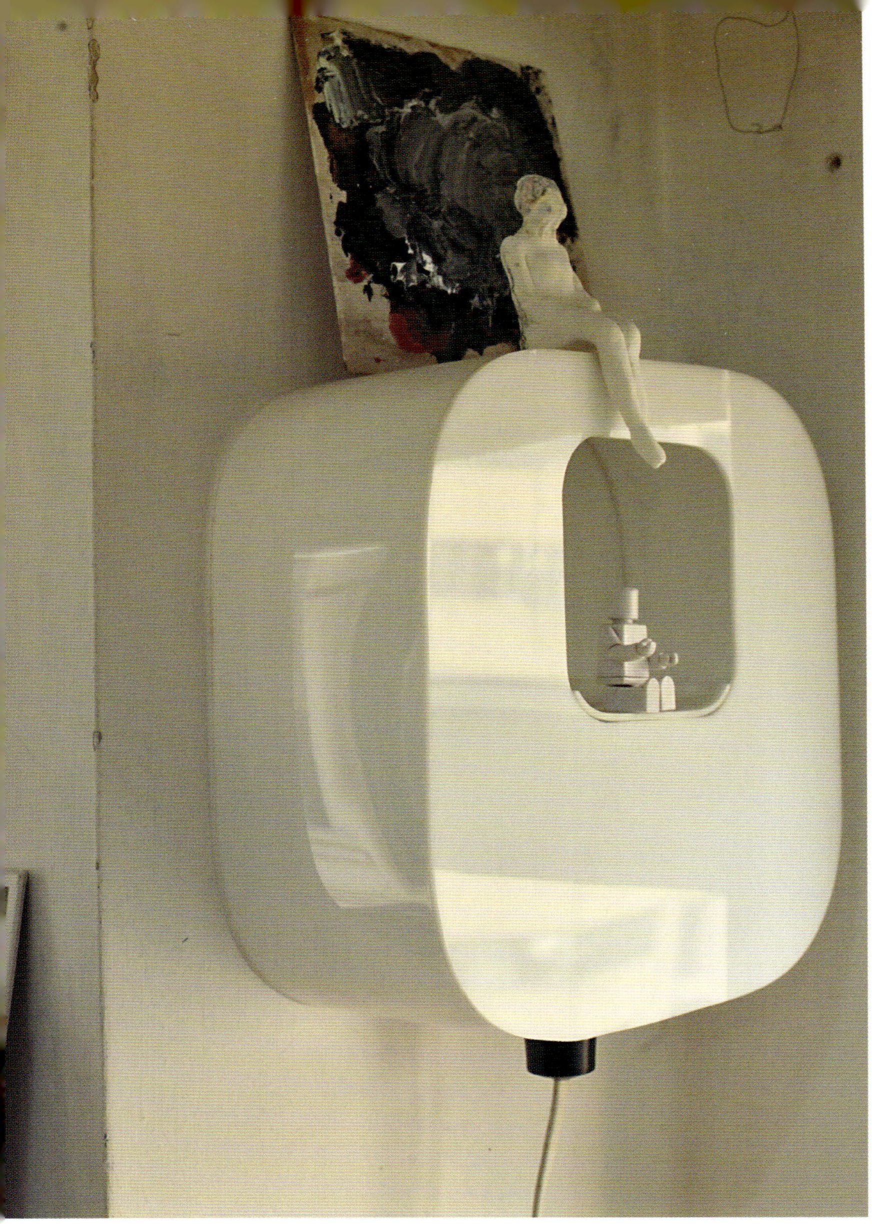

The studio is a place for experimentation

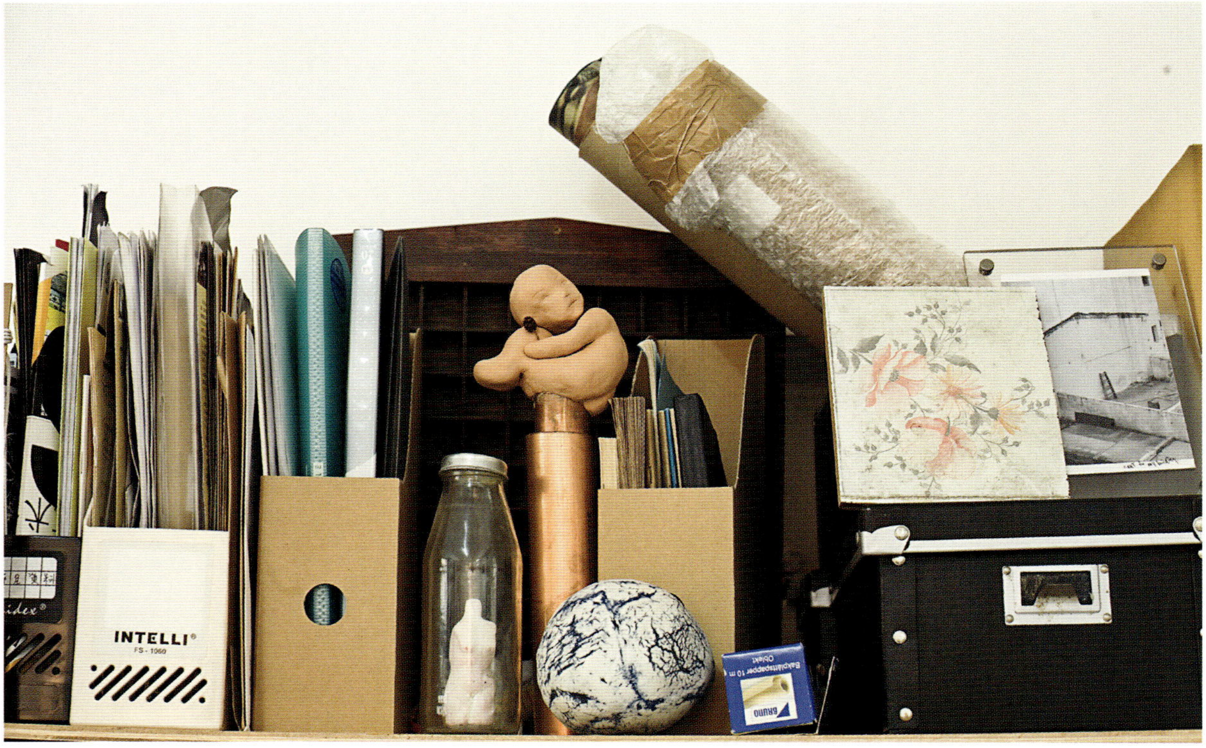

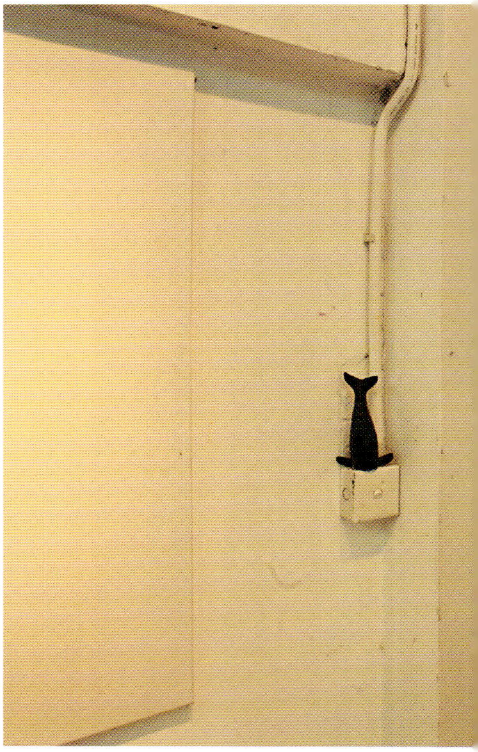

The programme took Ma to a wide world of art, spanning centuries. At the beginning of the course she was preoccupied with painting surface and she tried hard to create different layers and effects in her works. But she also found that what one can achieve in painting relies heavily on one's techniques. It was at this time she first came across collage and assemblage, the two media which would change her approach to art making. Ma admits that she loves doing collage and experimenting with a lot of materials in the process. During her explorations she spent a good deal of time looking for an object that could give the effect of brushstrokes before identifying the black hairpins she often used when she wore her hair long. The hairpins are an important element in her first installation work.

Ma's first installation was *Room of Memories*, shown in Macau's Old Ladies House (2001). A great number of fine hairpins are linked together to form a circle which casts a shadow on a wall behind, creating an illusionistic three-dimensional image in a real space. This work transferred her art from a semi two-dimensional plane to a three-dimensional space, and strengthened her studies and her exploration into materials. In the years to follow, Ma's works were mostly three-dimensional, both indoor and outdoor. Objects and video, as well as various natural and man-made materials (moulded, cut and assembled) have come to grow, change and transform in her art. She says she shifts a lot in her method of art making and her choice of materials. Whenever Ma is satisfied with a work (which she describes as "reaching a good point"), she cannot help but become anxious and begin to question if it has any room for further development. Perhaps this instability, caused by the uncertainty that comes with art making, has become her motivation to learn more and seek progress. Ma uses the metaphor of a sponge absorbing water to describe her years as a student artist, as she always wanted to know more. In the year of her graduation, she was awarded the Chevening Scholarship, which allowed her to take her master's studies in Feminist Theories and Practice in Visual Art at the University of Leeds. That was the first time Ma had not relied on a job to support her. She was then able to spend her days looking at art and making art, and this has widened her perspective. She chose a theory-based course because she believes a rich theoretical knowledge can provide artworks with fuller background and meanings, just like the layers in a painting.

After completing her studies, Ma returned to Hong Kong and took up the post of Art Administrator and Manager of 1a space – a non-profit making visual art organisation – going back to splitting her time between a job and art making. When asked if she ever wanted to become a full-time artist, Ma says that the good thing about having a job is that it prevents her from getting disconnected from society. A full-time artist may need to consider the market more for financial reasons, and may make very different decisions when producing art. Ma appreciates the advantages of having a job and she jokes that the type of artworks she makes will not attract high prices on the market.

Since her return to Hong Kong, Ma's art career has not been restricted to the city. She took part in a number of exchange programmes and artist-in-residence projects in 2005 and 2006, travelling to places from Bangladesh to Finland, and even the latters' Åland Archipelago, an unfamiliar place to many Hong Kong people. Going farther and seeing more, the artist transforms and grows with each journey. But Ma's sensitivity towards materials, space and her environment remains the same despite the changes in the appearance and scale of her works. The series of outdoor works

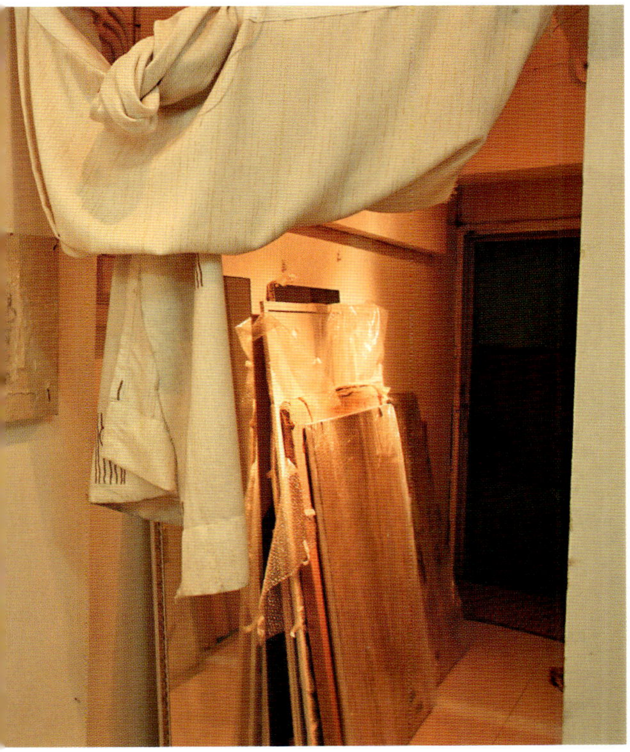

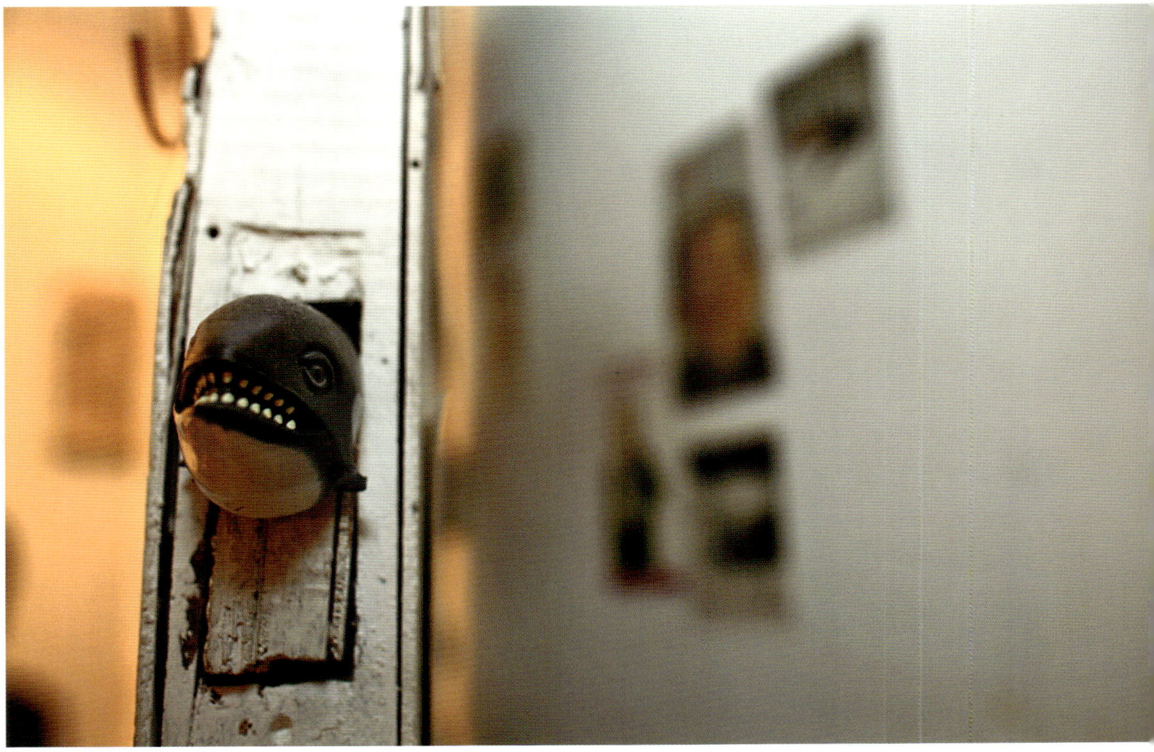

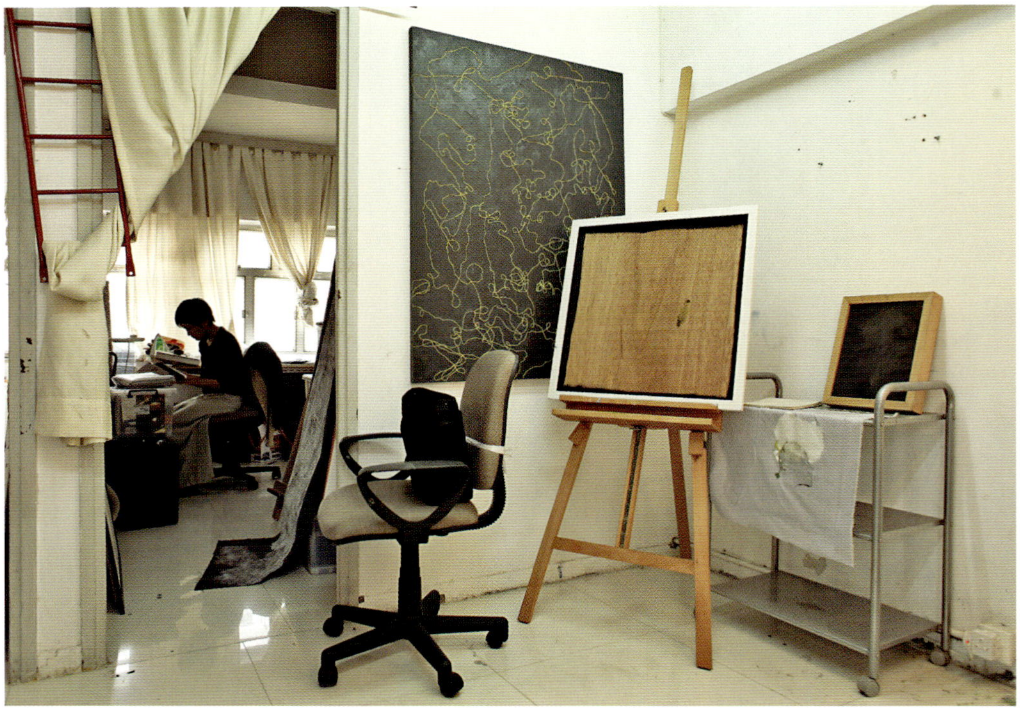

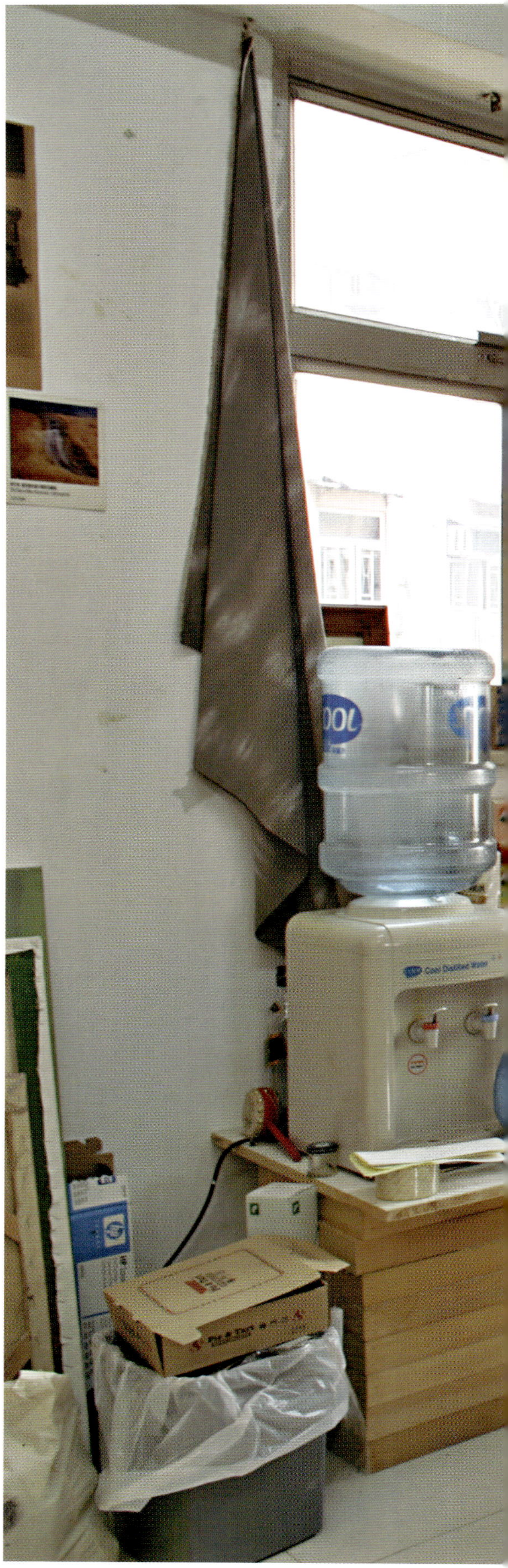

she completed in Helsinki, Finland, titled *Perception of Phenomenal Soundlessness*, with broken branches, a suitcase, a human body and a puppet doll set in a snow-covered world, is itself like a collage with nature as support. The special thing about this collage is that it is site-specific and will dissolve, eventually disappearing. In terms of both form and meaning, it goes beyond the collages on canvas that led Ma into a new area of creation years ago.

Ma's works seem to have a power that gets people to stop and think, and to make lost thoughts reappear. Ma considers visual elements and their effects important to a work of art, and she wants to continue re-examining the themes in her art making. Man's psychological status, female sensibilities, sex, disappearance, memories and the meeting of body and soul — these are themes that Ma repeatedly ponders. On the small table in the living room is a painting with trees depicted in simple black lines, scattered on a pure white background – a scene from Åland Archipelago.

Has Ma returned to painting? She says she loves painting but not the way that paint is used, so she still thinks about materials and space whenever she paints, trying to find alternatives to the two-dimensional plane.

At the end of the interview we talk about the programme both of us took. Ma says that a society's art development relies on the quality of its people, and this has everything to do with art education and training. Recently awarded the Lee Hysan Foundation Fellowship by the Asian Cultural Council, Ma will leave Hong Kong again in mid-2008 to further her studies in the United States. So, how will this new journey inspire and influence an artist with such a delicate sense of perception, and a mind that has the courage to break with convention? As someone who loves her art, I will patiently wait to see her future works. And in the days to come, whenever I make my own art or enjoy others' works, I think I will remember a line of Ma's: "It is a gift to have art in life."

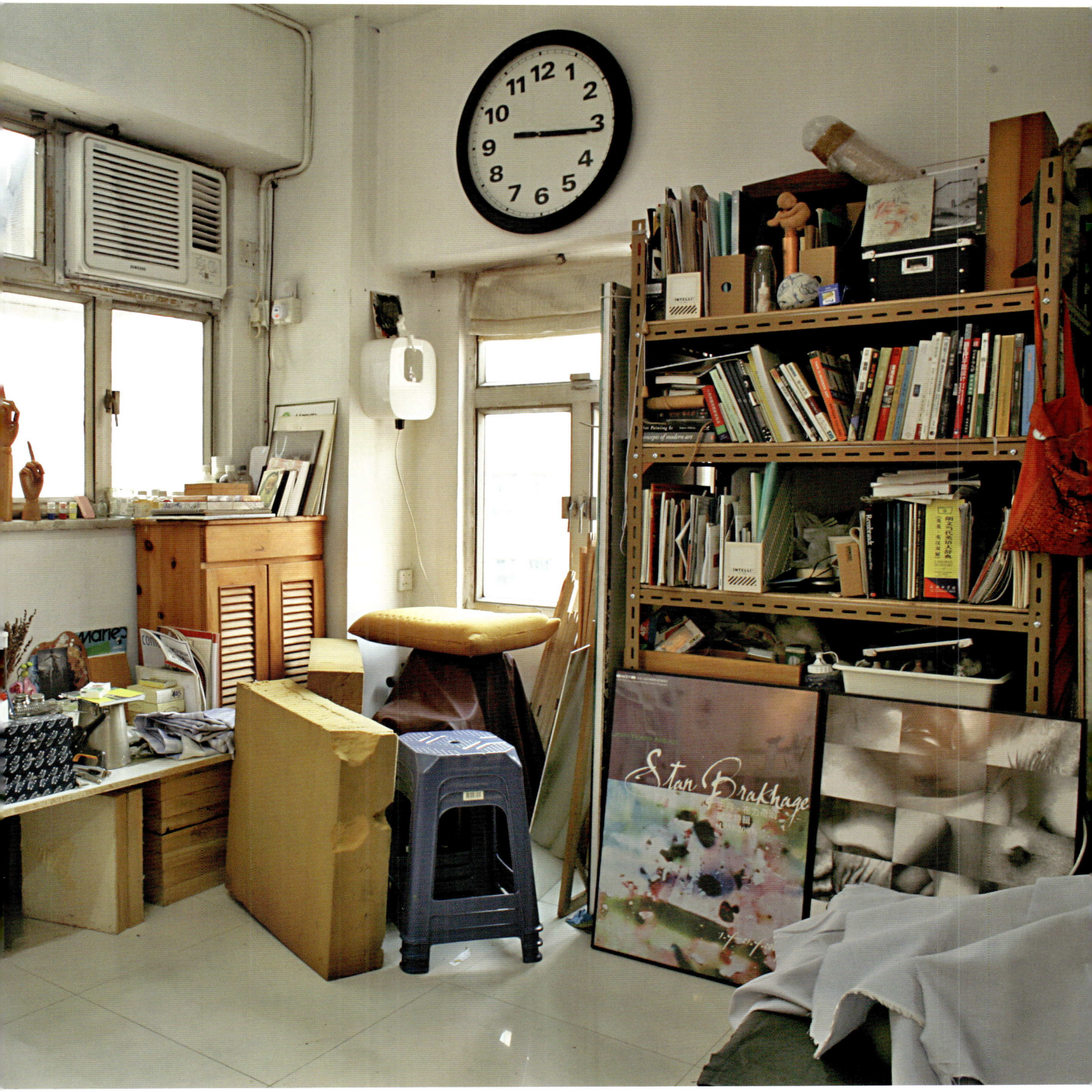
Stan Brakhage

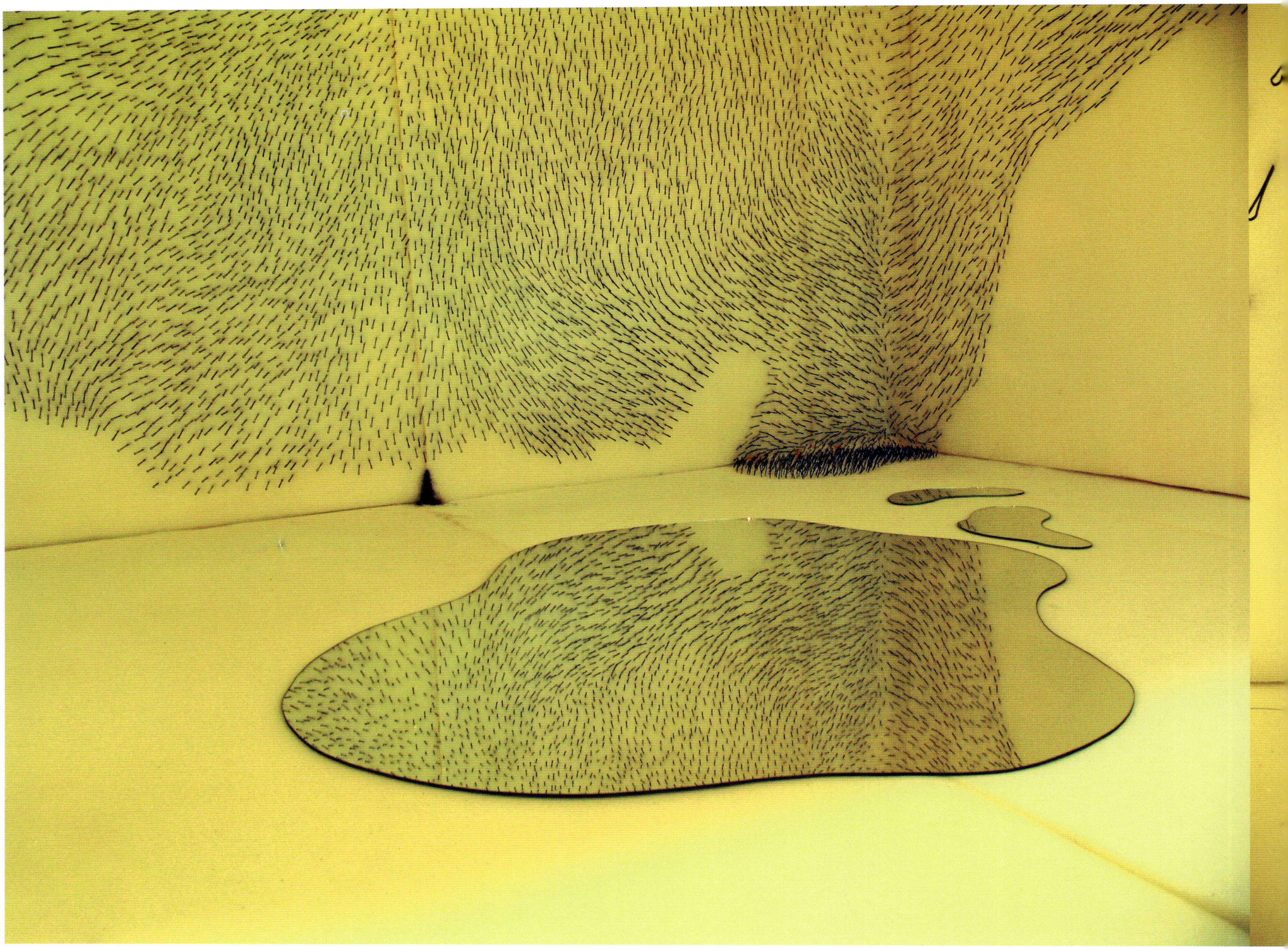

(Left) Before the Disappearance of Rain
Mixed-media installation, dimensions variable, 2005

(Middle) Before the Disappearance of Rain (detail)

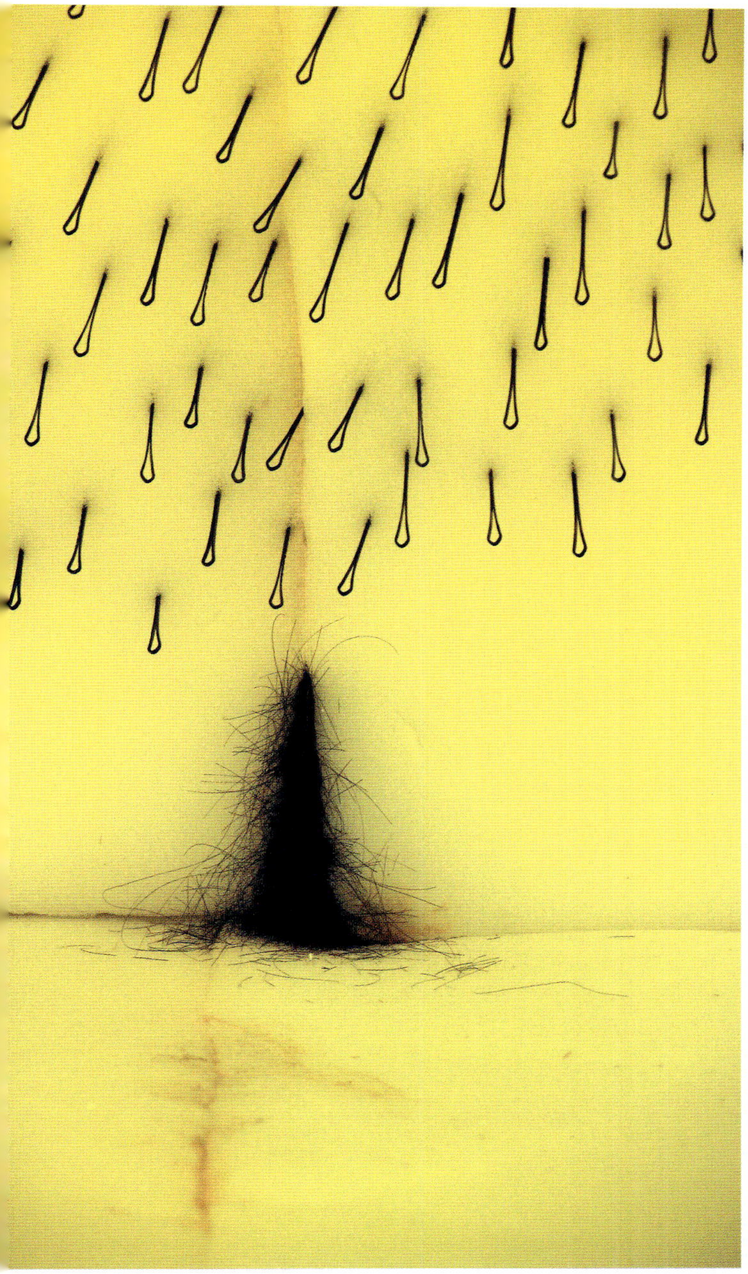

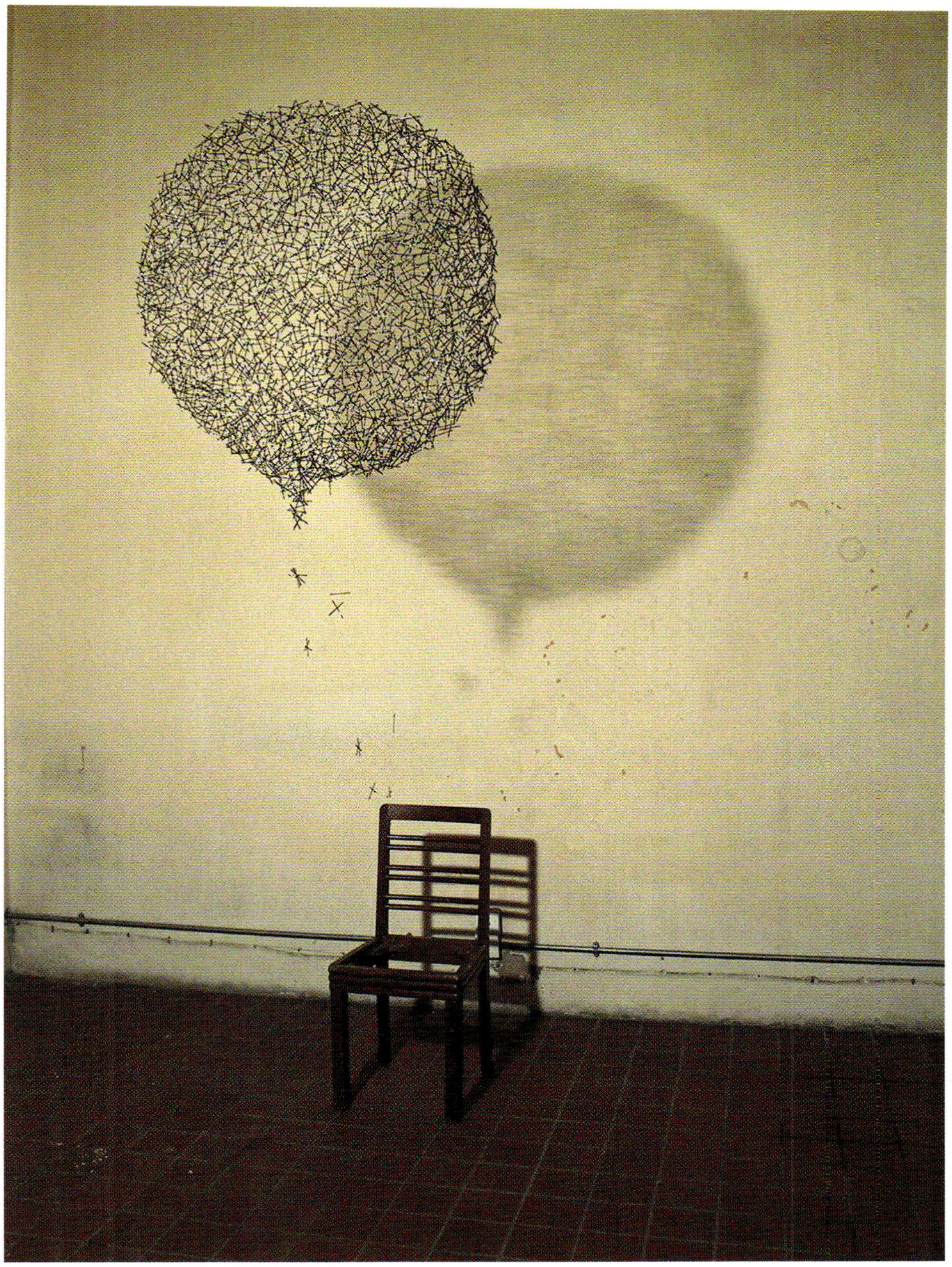

(Right) Room of Memories
Mixed-media installation, dimensions variable, 2001

Pauline Lam Yuk-lin

Creation Breeds Belief

By Alice Choi

Pauline Lam Yuk-lin obtained her Bachelor degree in fine arts and her postgraduate diploma in art education from the Chinese University of Hong Kong (CUHK). She received a certificate in computer arts and design from the University of Hong Kong's School of Professional and Continuing Education (HKU SPACE) and a Master's in fine art from the Royal Melbourne Institute of Technology University. Lam actively participates in art education and publication, exhibitions and competitions, and has received numerous awards. She has taught in the Department of Extramural Studies at the CUHK and is now teaching at the Department of Creative Arts and Physical Education at the Hong Kong Institute of Education. Before she joined the teaching profession she worked at a television station and an art gallery. She is one of the few active artists with a full-time job.

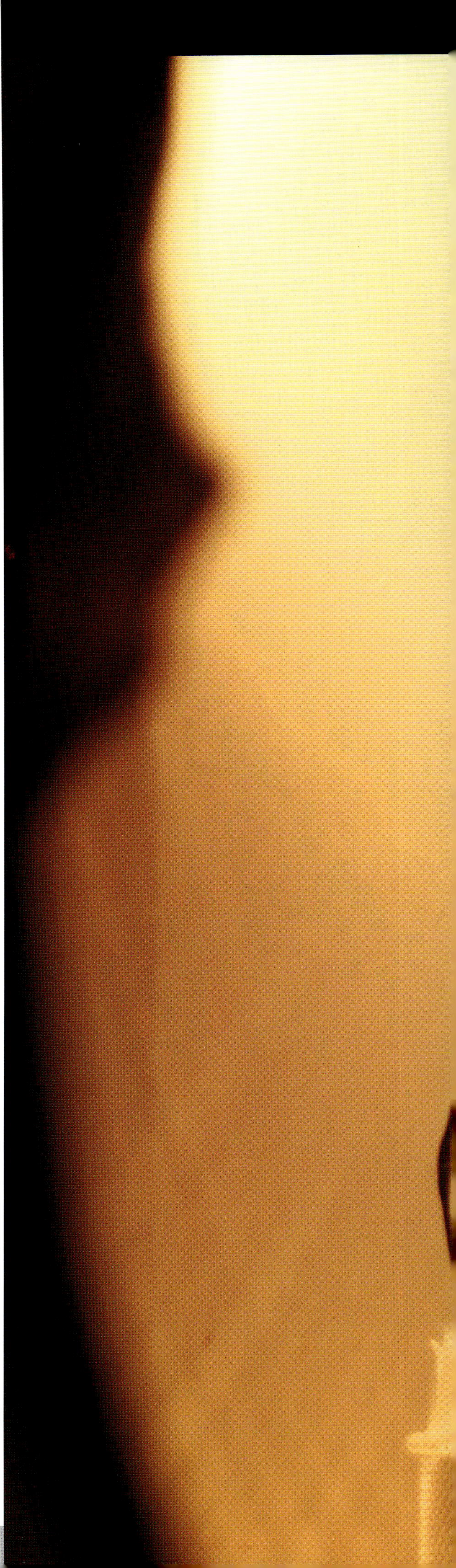

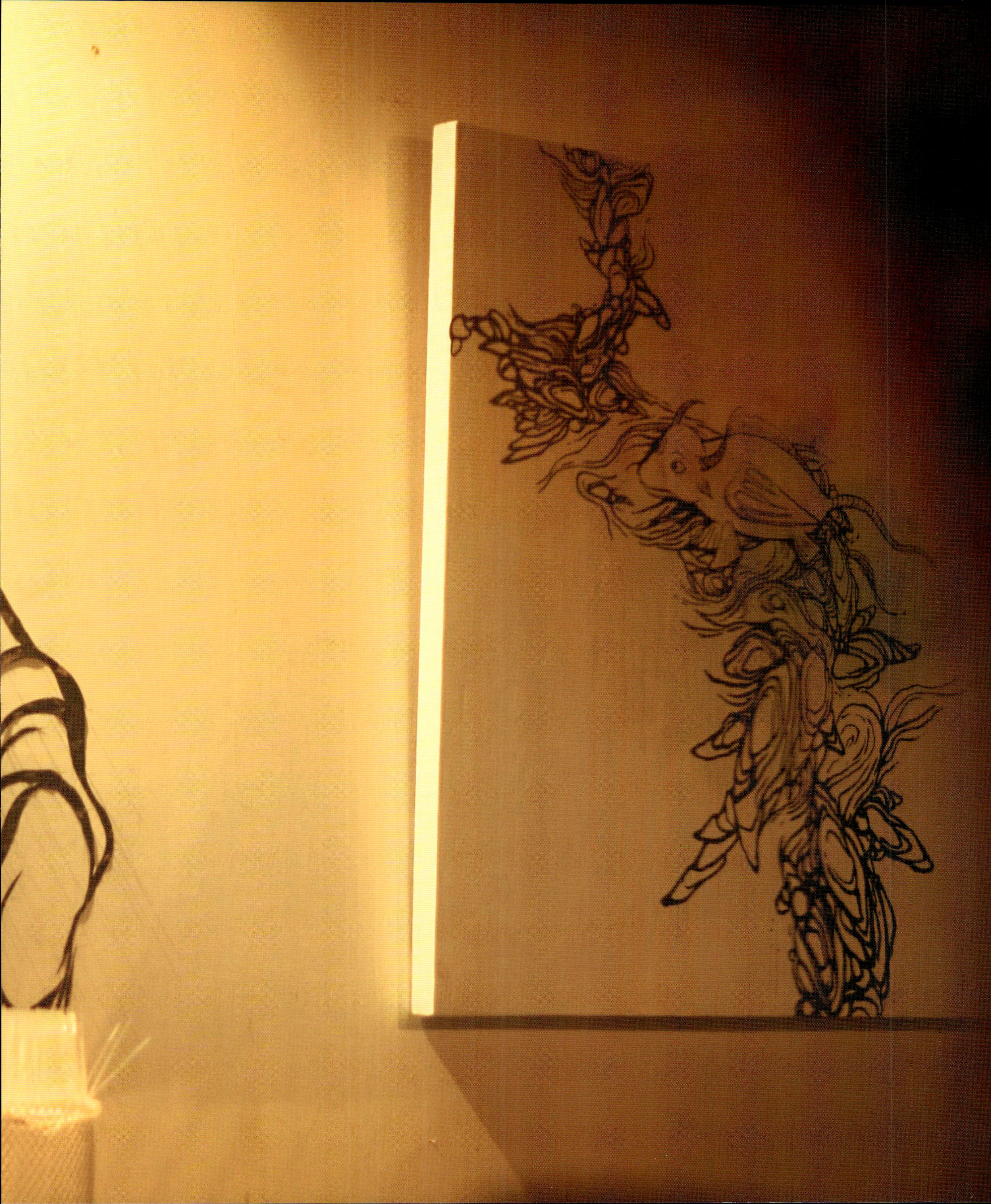

We have only 24 hours in a day. To squeeze time from a tight schedule to make art, there is little choice but to sacrifice one's sleep. Pauline Lam Yuk-lin only sleeps for two to three hours a day and she has been known to work through the night. Not until recent years has she realised the importance of health to the sustainability of an artistic career, and has begun to rest and do exercise to keep her body and spirits in good shape.

Lam enjoys teaching students of all ages. Teaching in the university environment is favourable to her research in art, and as university students are more mature, there is more interaction in the teaching and learning process, which brings insight to both students and teachers. In education, apart from the transmission of knowledge, Lam considers the elimination of doubt most important. She takes her work and life seriously. She values enlightening students but she is more concerned about their personal growth.

An artist's outlook on life is more or less reflected in his or her works. As an educator Lam aims to be a role model for her students. Her students not only learn art and professional tips from her, but also attitude. The subject matters for her artworks are often inspired by real-life situations. One of the most important principles in her exhibitions is the protection of her environment – to minimise damage to exhibition venues and to return them to their original state afterwards. "Threads are used in my work *Light Capturer* to represent beams of light through the windows, shining on plants made of stainless steel," she says. "Those threads were hinged on the rim of the windows without damaging the venue; not even a pin was used." In guiding students to prepare for exhibitions she always reminds them of this principle, not only for the sake of protecting the space, but more as a way of upholding artists' professionalism.

Her professional attitude brings her different exhibition opportunities – local and non-local, moving and static, public and private, on land and sea. Her works move from museum and gallery to shopping mall, bookshop, pier, ferry, railway, walled village, university and year-end market. To her, an exhibition venue is more important than a studio. "Some exhibition venues were explored by myself, while some were opportunities awarded from competitions,

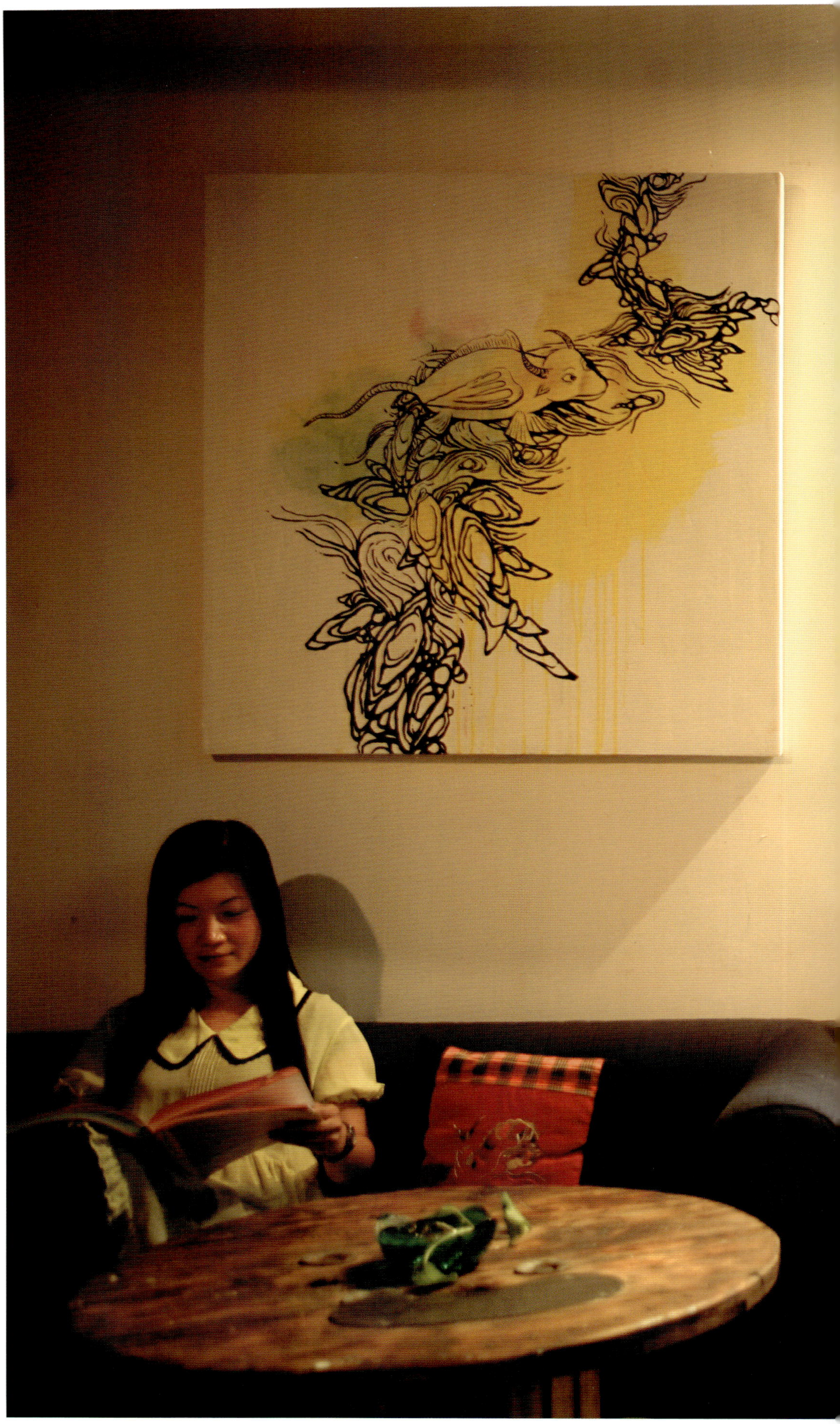

Happiness is pure interaction with art

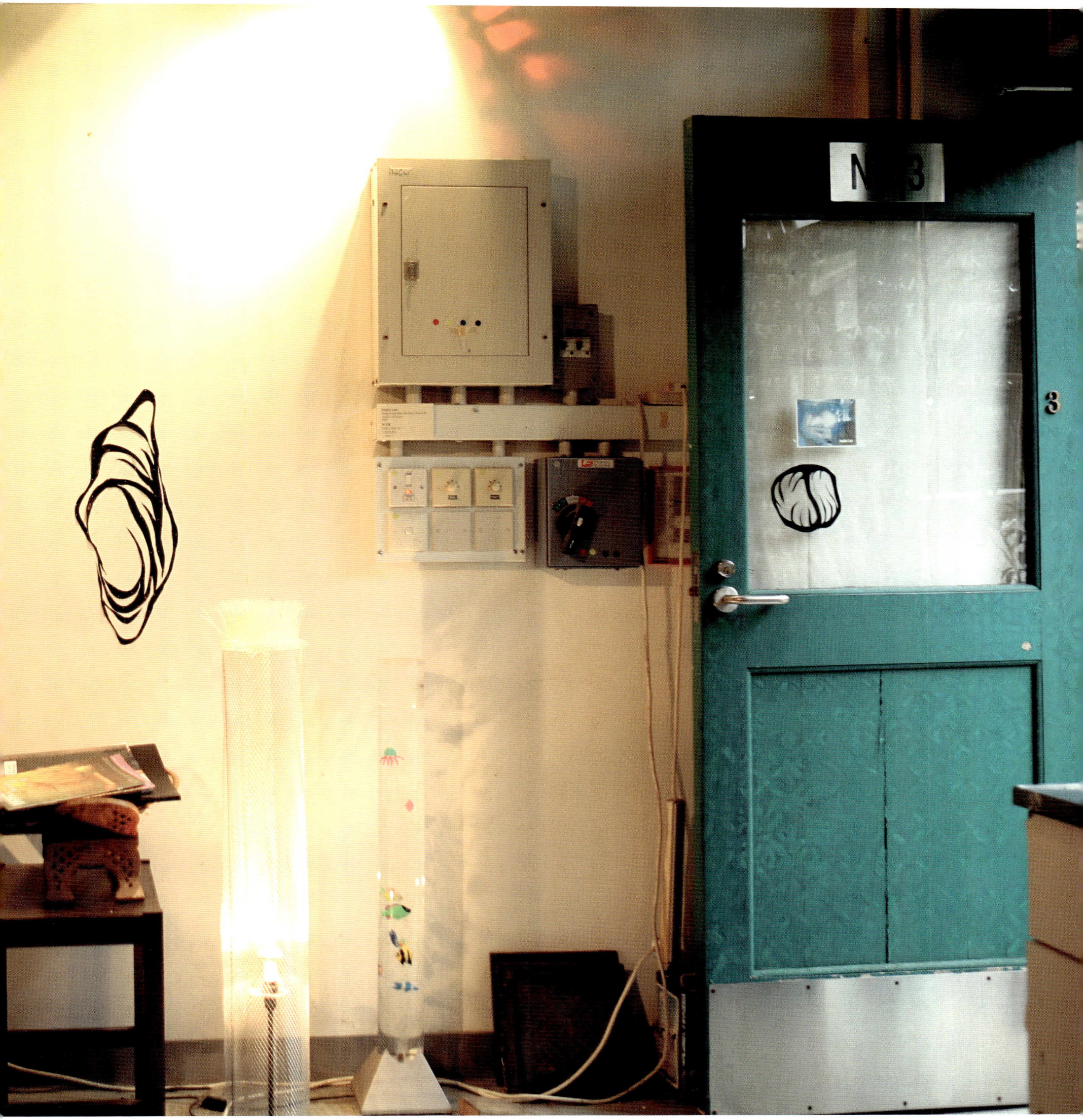
3

like *Drifting Sky*, exhibited at the VIP lounge of a triple deck ferry called *Xin Guo*," she says. "A good thing about competitions is that not only do your works get recognised, but very often you also have the opportunity to show them without going through the application procedures for venues. I was once invited by a curator to exhibit my work at the walled village, Kat Hing Wai. The curator considered my work suitable for the site and rented a village house to curate a show for me."

"These are all precious opportunities which give you great satisfaction. Above all, art is about communication and introspection, and to touch and influence other people's lives through art is more important than just exhibiting one's works."

Lam has earned numerous awards. "Competitions can be regarded as a good start for young artists, and commercial activities and art creation are not contradictory in nature,"

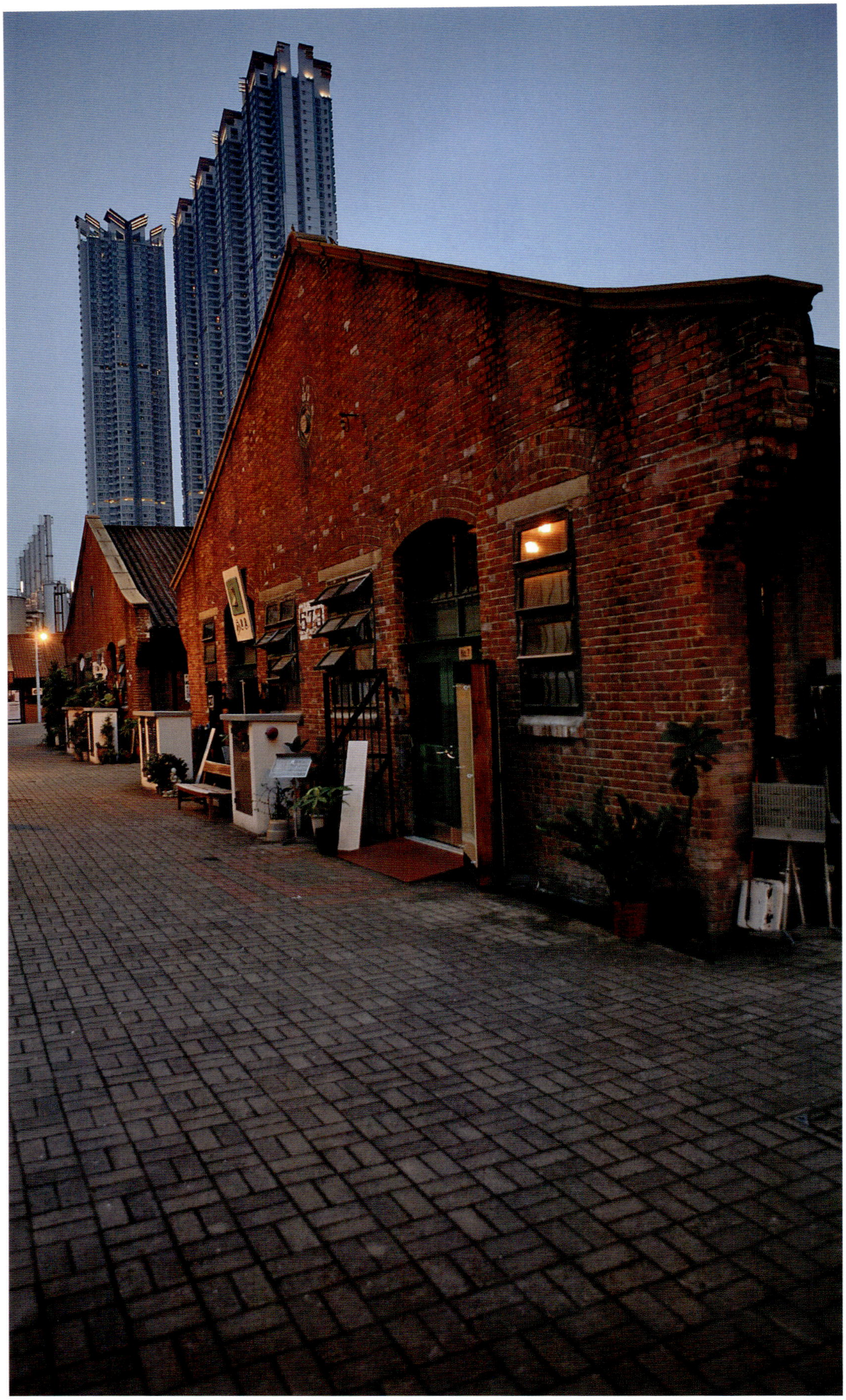

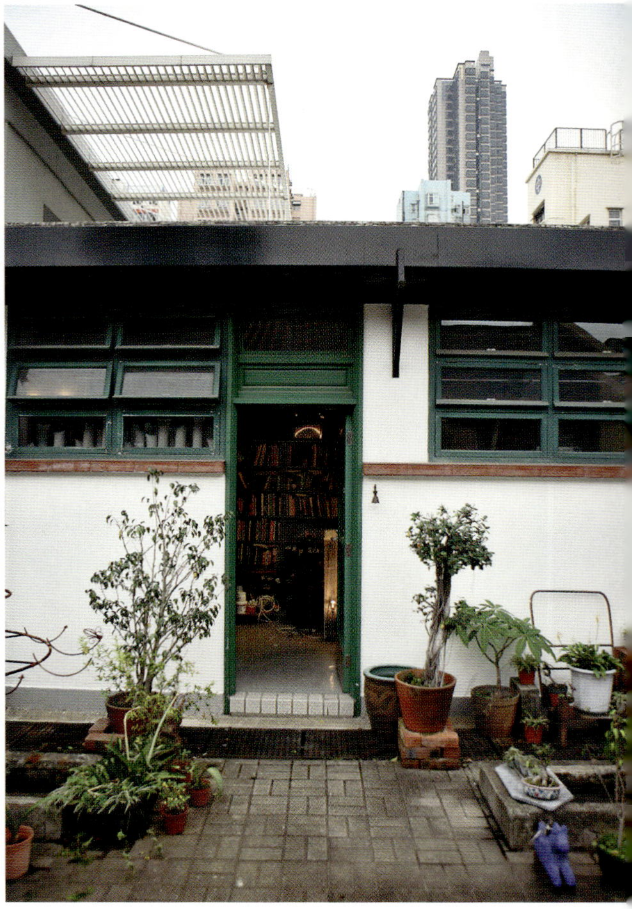

When the night falls, many people at Cattle Depot are still working she says. "Being recognised is certainly delightful, but it may not be a good thing when fame comes too soon. One has to work hard and examine one's works from time to time. Right now I am more mature, and I don't need to earn a living by selling my work. As long as my artworks are not limited by market value, I take it easy."

Teaching and making art are both important to Lam. Her studio is set up at the Cattle Depot Artist Village, and she once shared another studio with a former classmate at the Fotan Artists' Village. She worked between the two studios depending on her media and use of materials. Now she only uses the studio at the Cattle Depot. As art making is Lam's second career, her studio is her second home and safety is her main concern for her studio space, as she explains. "Fotan and the Cattle Depot each have their own characters. As a woman I am particularly concerned about safety. Fotan is more remote and turns quiet after dark. The space next to my old studio at Fotan was a warehouse where people rarely passed by. On the days when I worked late, I often chose to stay there overnight. The studio at the Cattle Depot is guarded so I feel more secure and can concentrate on my work."

Lam categorises her artistic development in different stages: *Test of Rebirth* from 1993 to 1995, *The New Renascent Bronze Age* from 1997 to 1998, *Cultivating Civilisation* from 2001 to 2005, *Book of Mountain and Sea – Hong Kong Version* since 2005. All are about the environment, civilisation and cultural identity. Yet she never stops exploring, and her methods have evolved into a variety of media and presentation methods, such as painting, sculpture, installation, interactive art and performance art. Among the various media she is particularly fond of installation, as she enjoys the challenge of working within the limitations of space. "Installation involves the experimentation

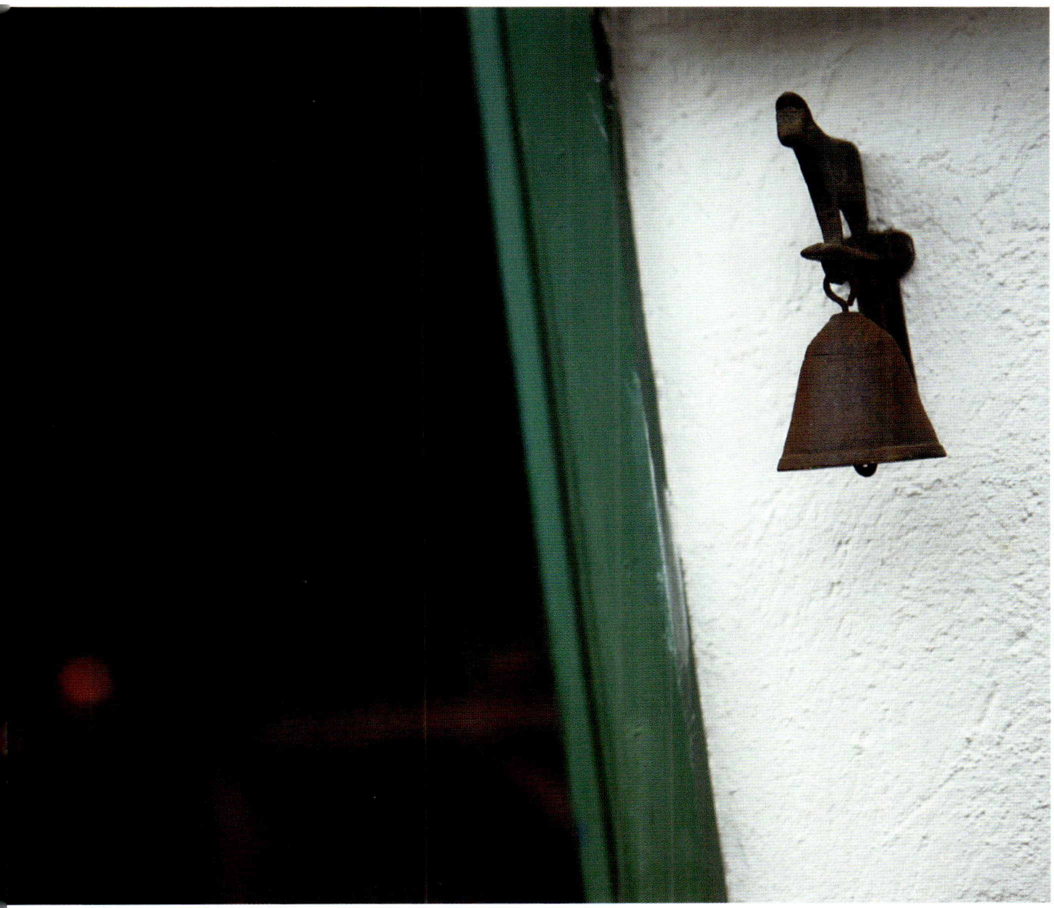

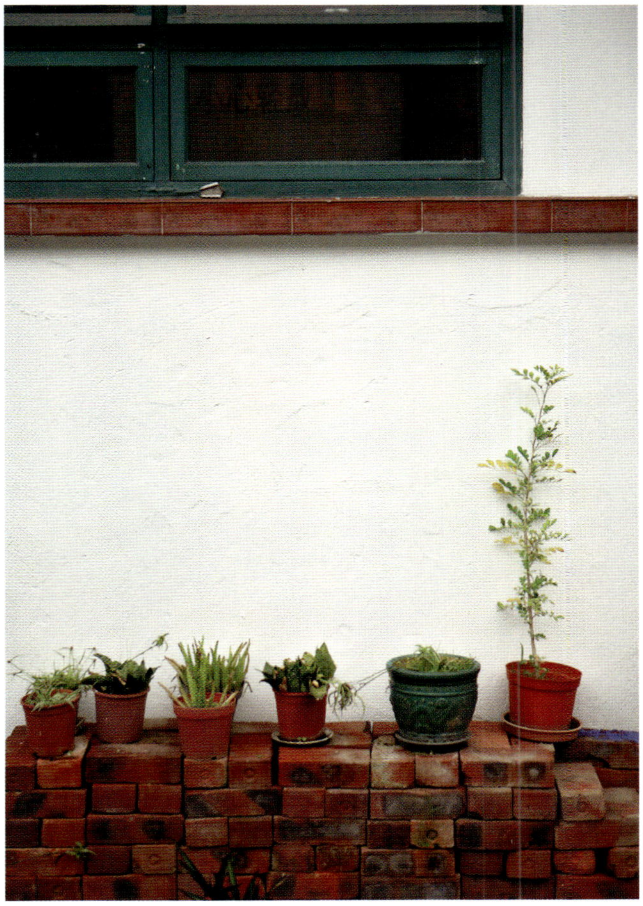

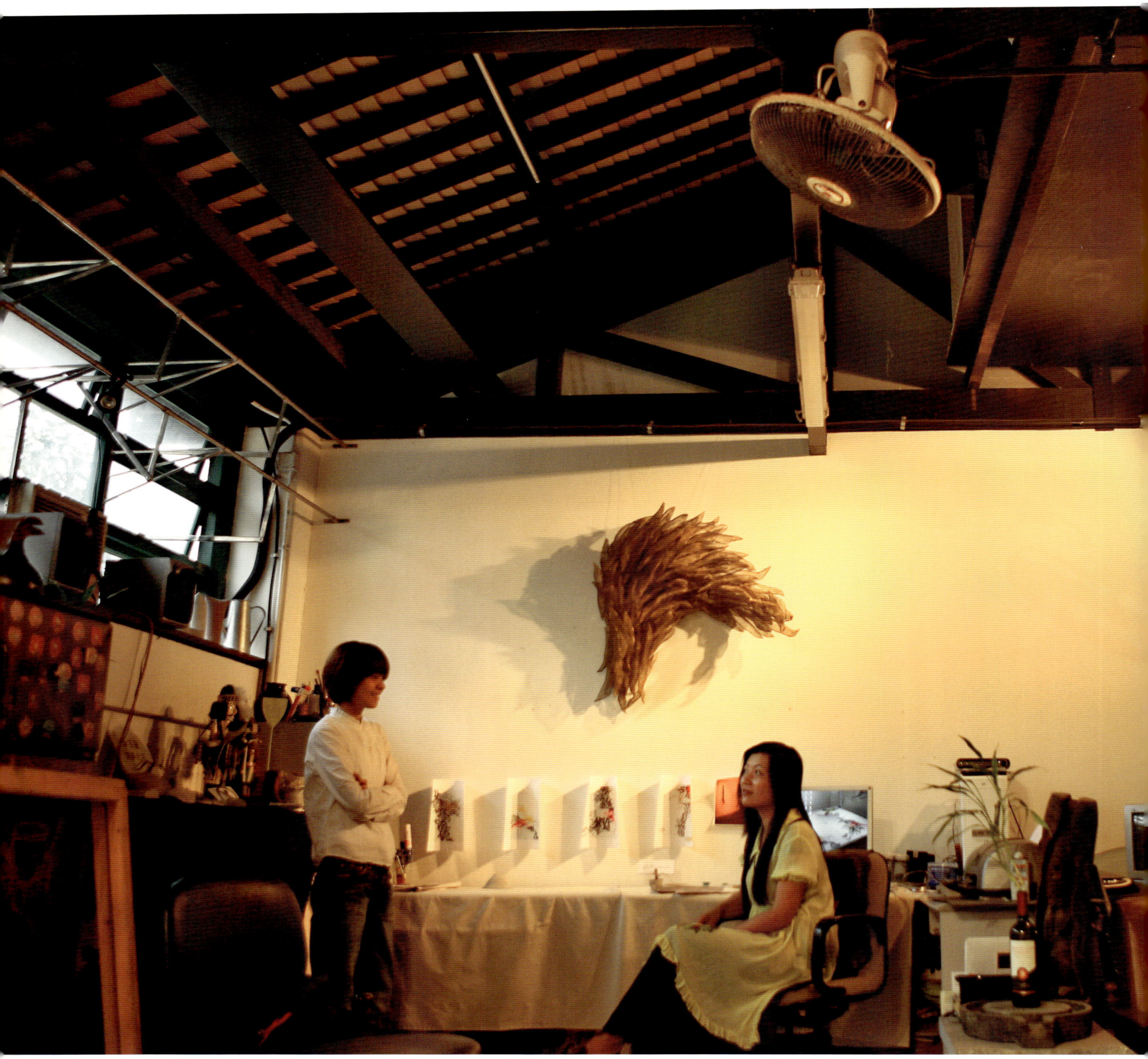

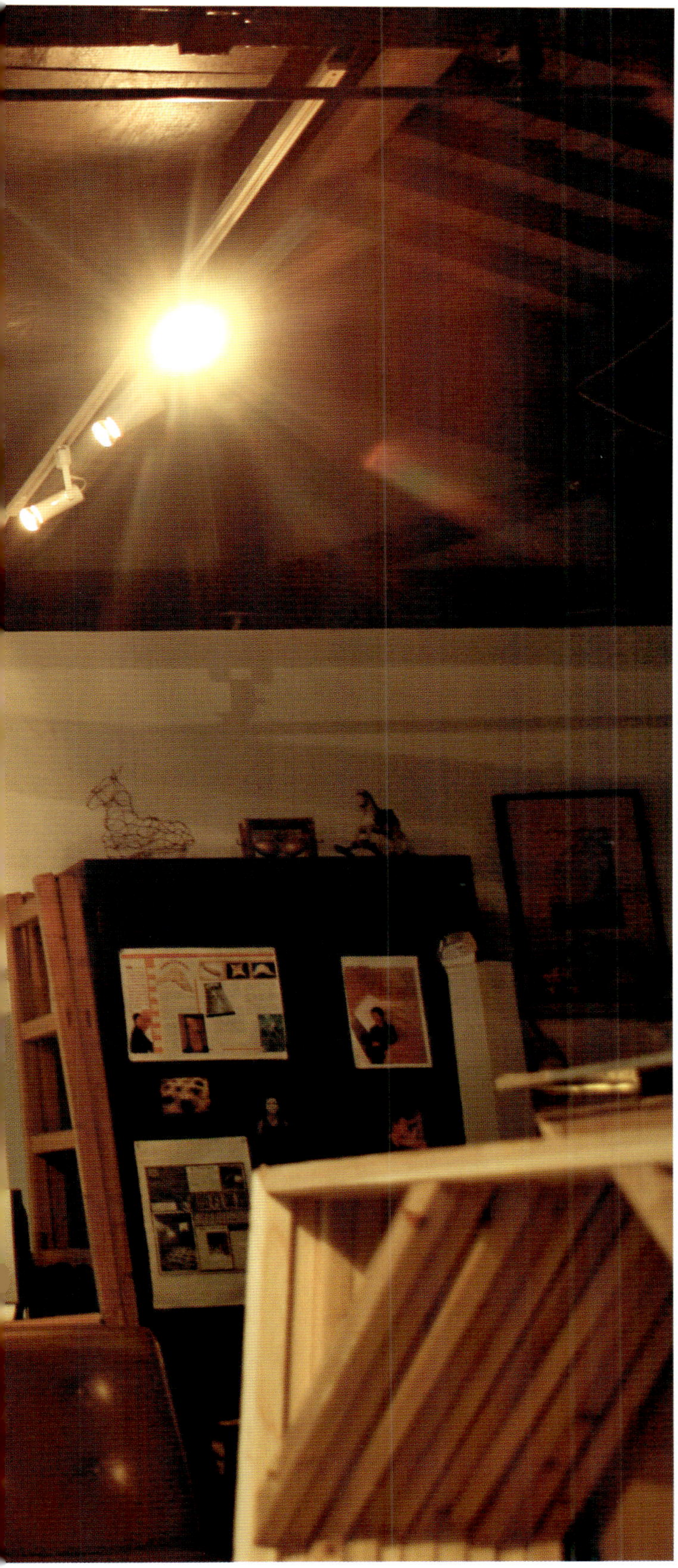

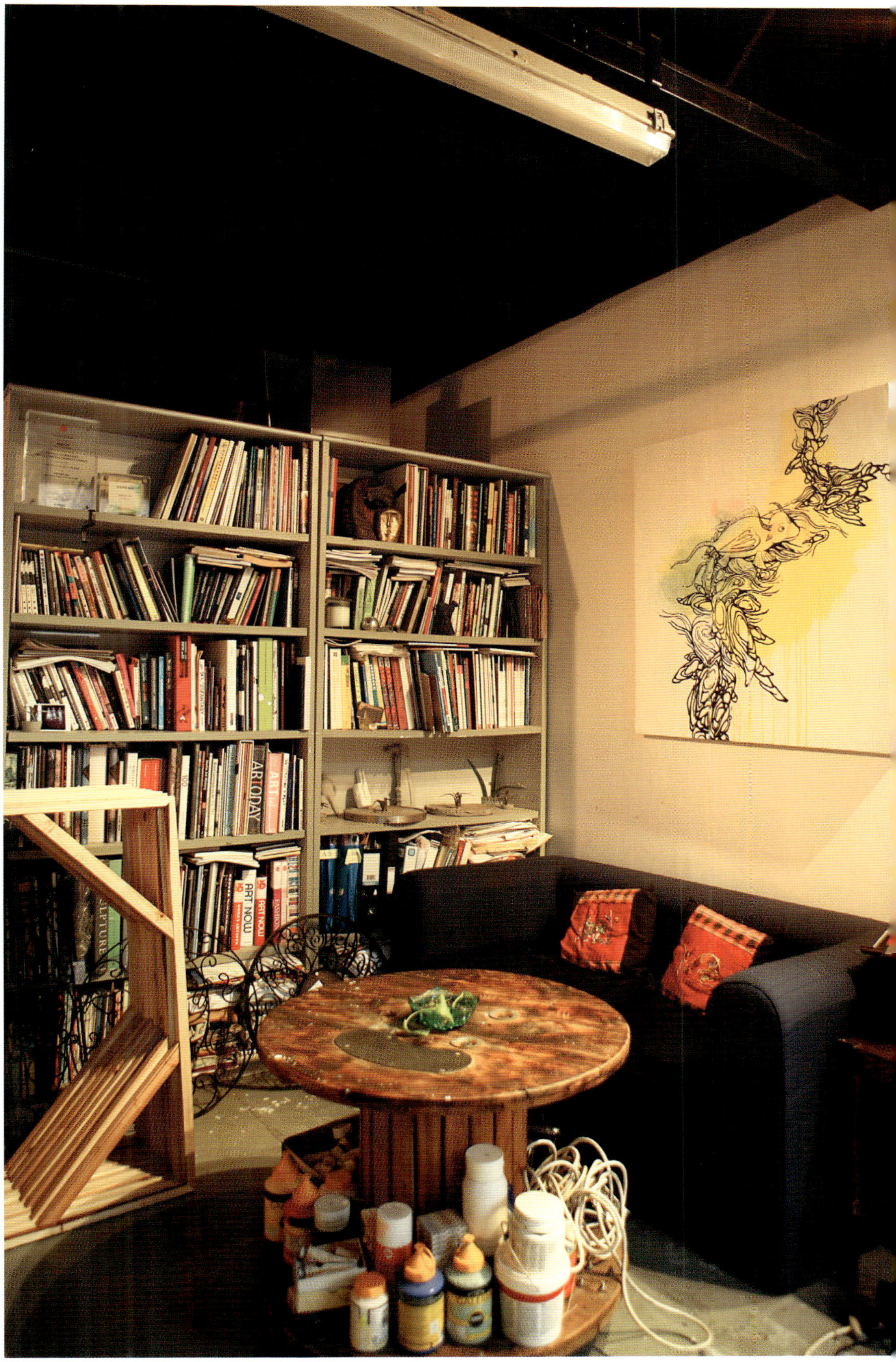

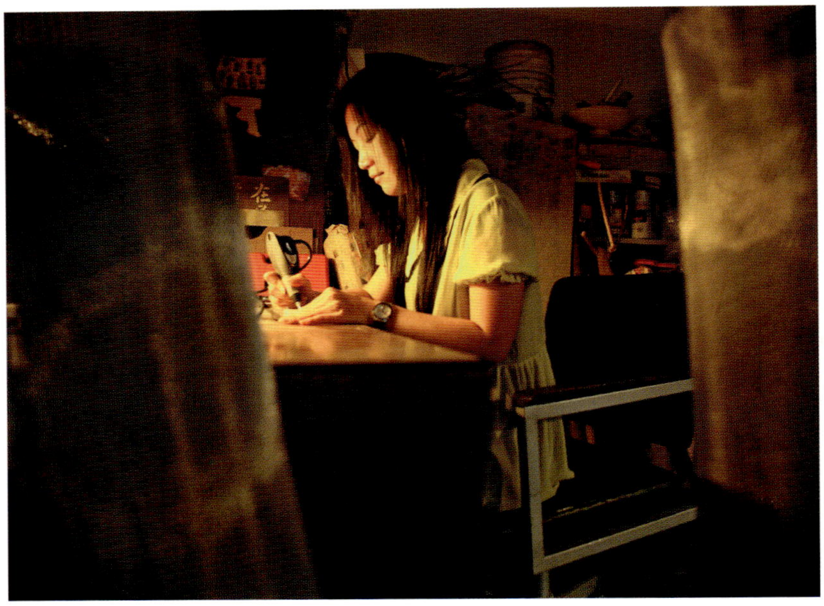

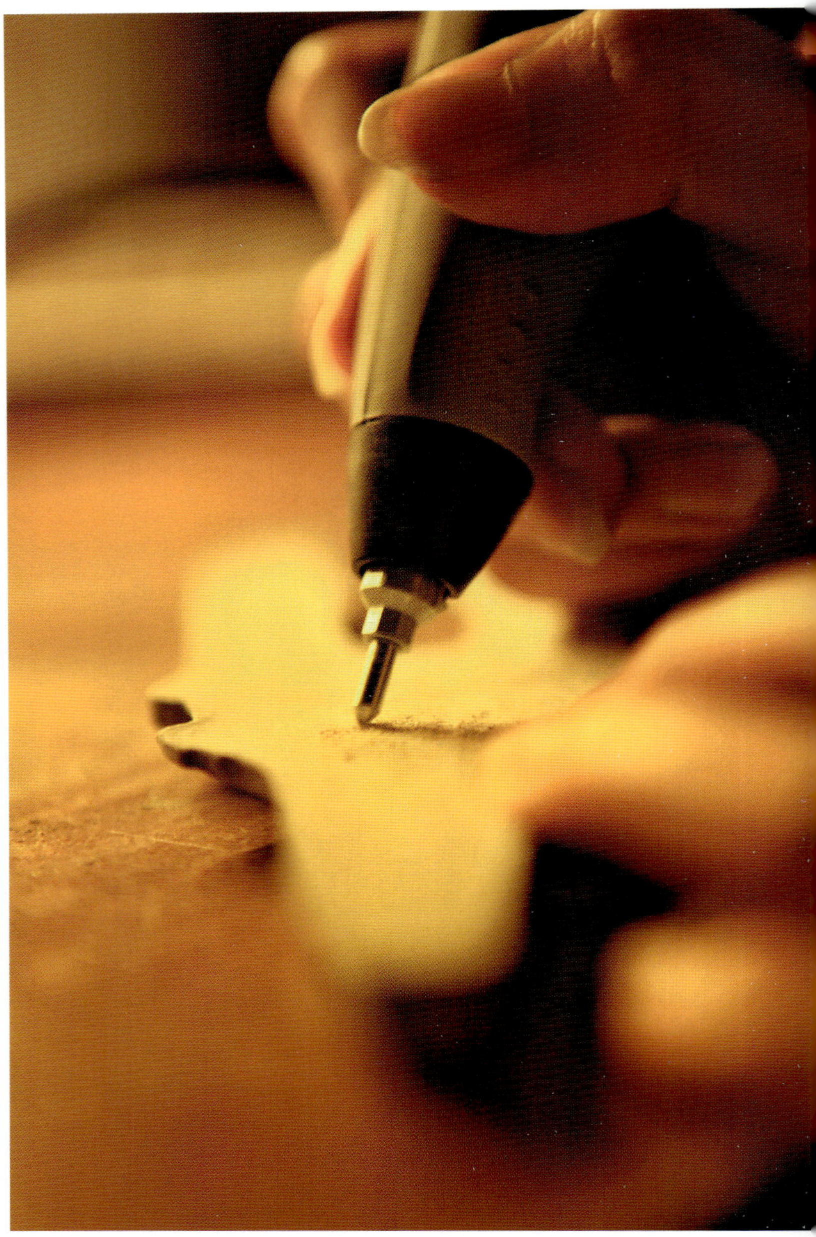

Artworks carry the marks of the artist's experience

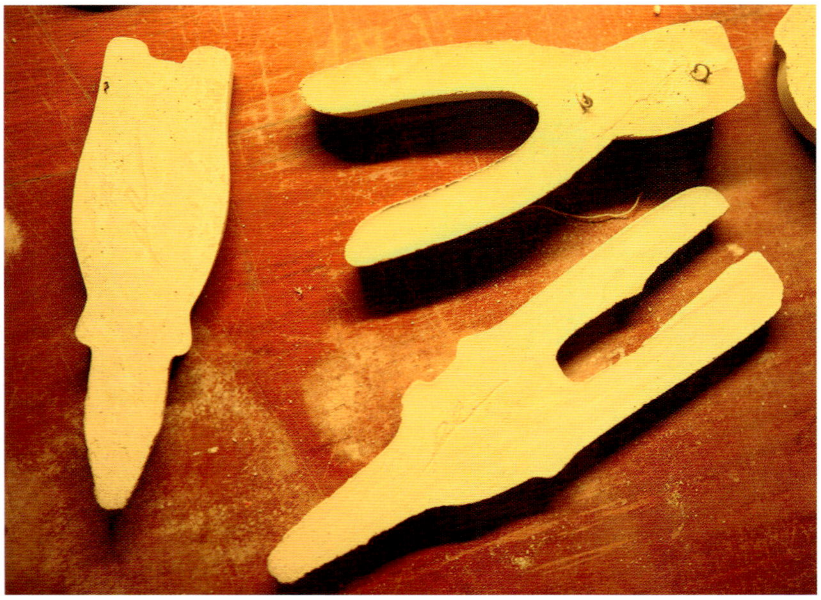

of different visual presentations, and the creative process is interrelated with space, in which a lot of immediate decisions need to be made," she says. "In particular, with site-specific installation artists have to work to maximise space. One has to integrate into the space but at the same time not damage the environment."

"The interaction between space and the artist is full of challenges, as in my work *Civilised Fossils* I and II. The former was hung in the air. In order not to damage the venue, first I had to install a 3X3 m reticular rack on the ceiling, after which each piece of work was hung from the ceiling by wire one by one. The latter, II, was presented on dark plinths; works were laid horizontally on the plinths as if they were artefacts. Even though the content of both works are the same, the different displays invite different readings."

Lam believes that materials themselves have their own implied meanings. She has used Chinese herbs, metal, concrete, stone, nylon, beef and plastic bags, and whether subtle or apparent, each has carried symbolic meaning and a unique visual language which gives life to the art. Recent works like *The Canopy is Cramming with Lemon* in 2005 conveyed a sense of political humour while *Chocolate Chandelier* and *Chocolate Rain*, exhibited in Time Square during the St Valentine's Day week in 2006, symbolised the ephemeral nature of modern attitudes to love, and also childhood fantasy. *Deletion Track* in 2007 recorded the artist bidding farewell by blowing on a statue made of chalk; *One Minute Prison* in 2008 was an interactive conceptual art piece that invited viewers to contemplate their wrongs by locking themselves inside a space for one minute. Through collective memories and universal experiences the artist connects with her viewers.

Life and art are inseparable to Lam. She is persistent in her art making, in both quality and quantity, and her output is comparable to a full-time artist. Her achievements are partly because of her talent, but they say more about her extraordinarily strong will, her professionalism, her respect for others and her principles at work. She is serious and diligent, and is conscientious about her work and art. She conducts herself virtuously and lives out the meaning of a Chinese idiom that says: you harvest what you cultivate.

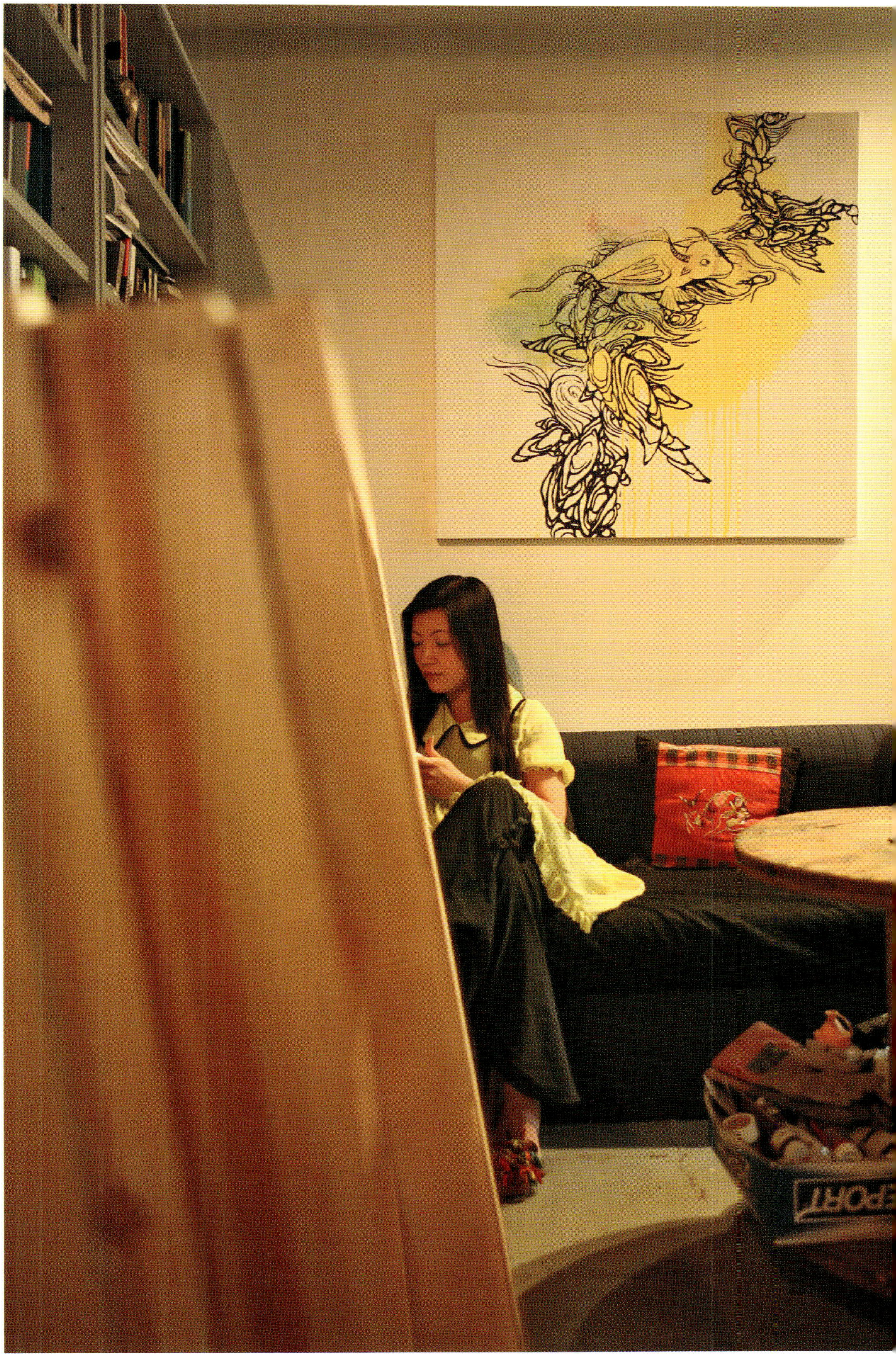

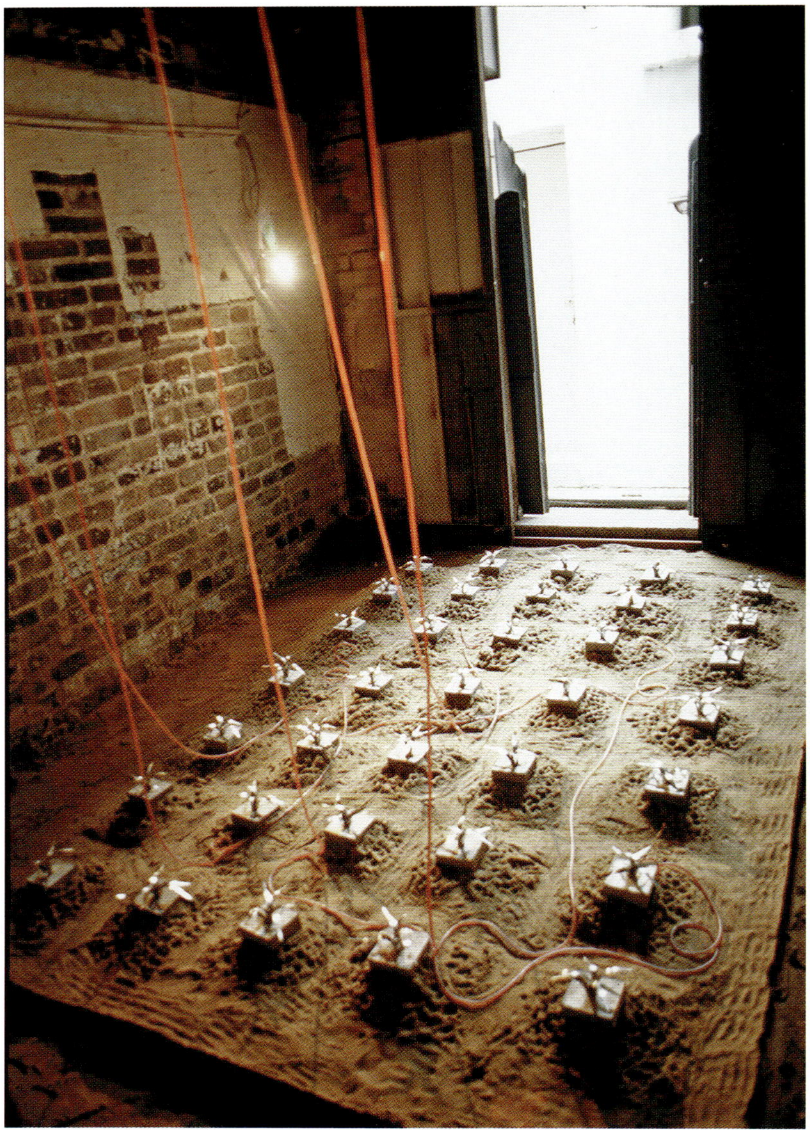

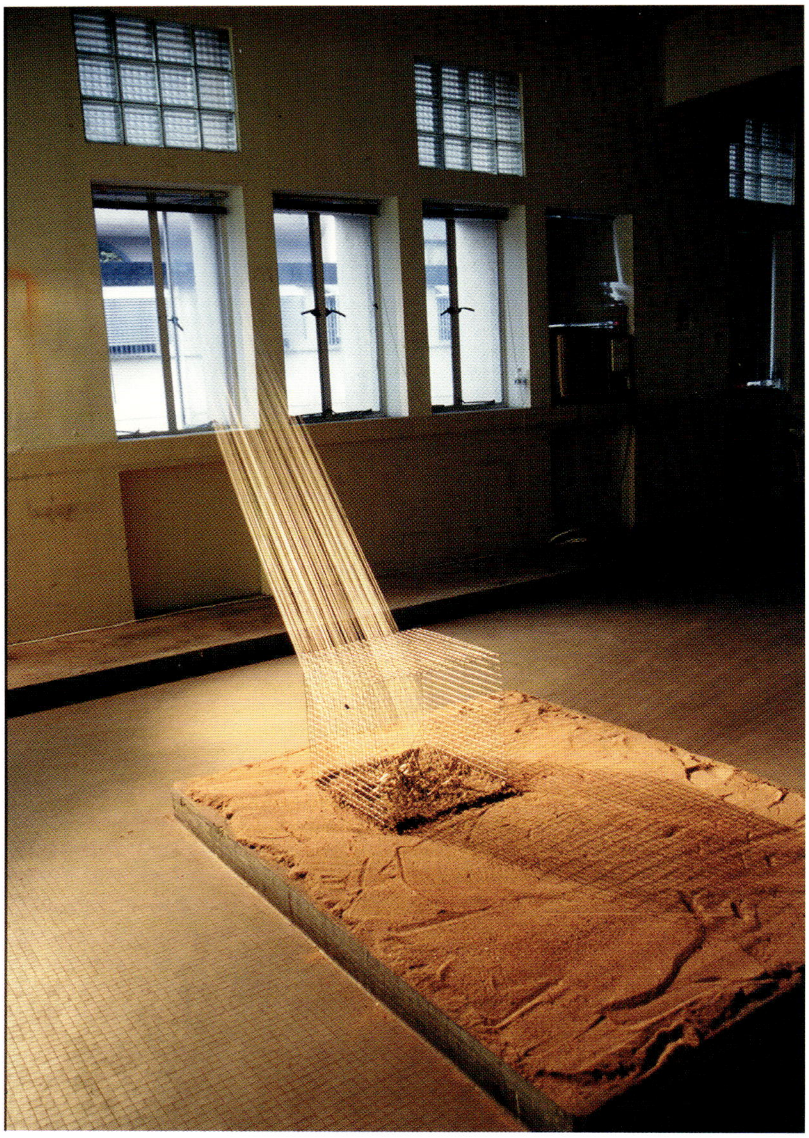

(Left) Cultivating Civilisation
Concrete, steel and other, the cottage house at Kat Hing Wai, Yuen Long, 2001

(Right) Light Capturer
Bronze, iron mesh and other, a room in Oil Street Artist Village, 1999

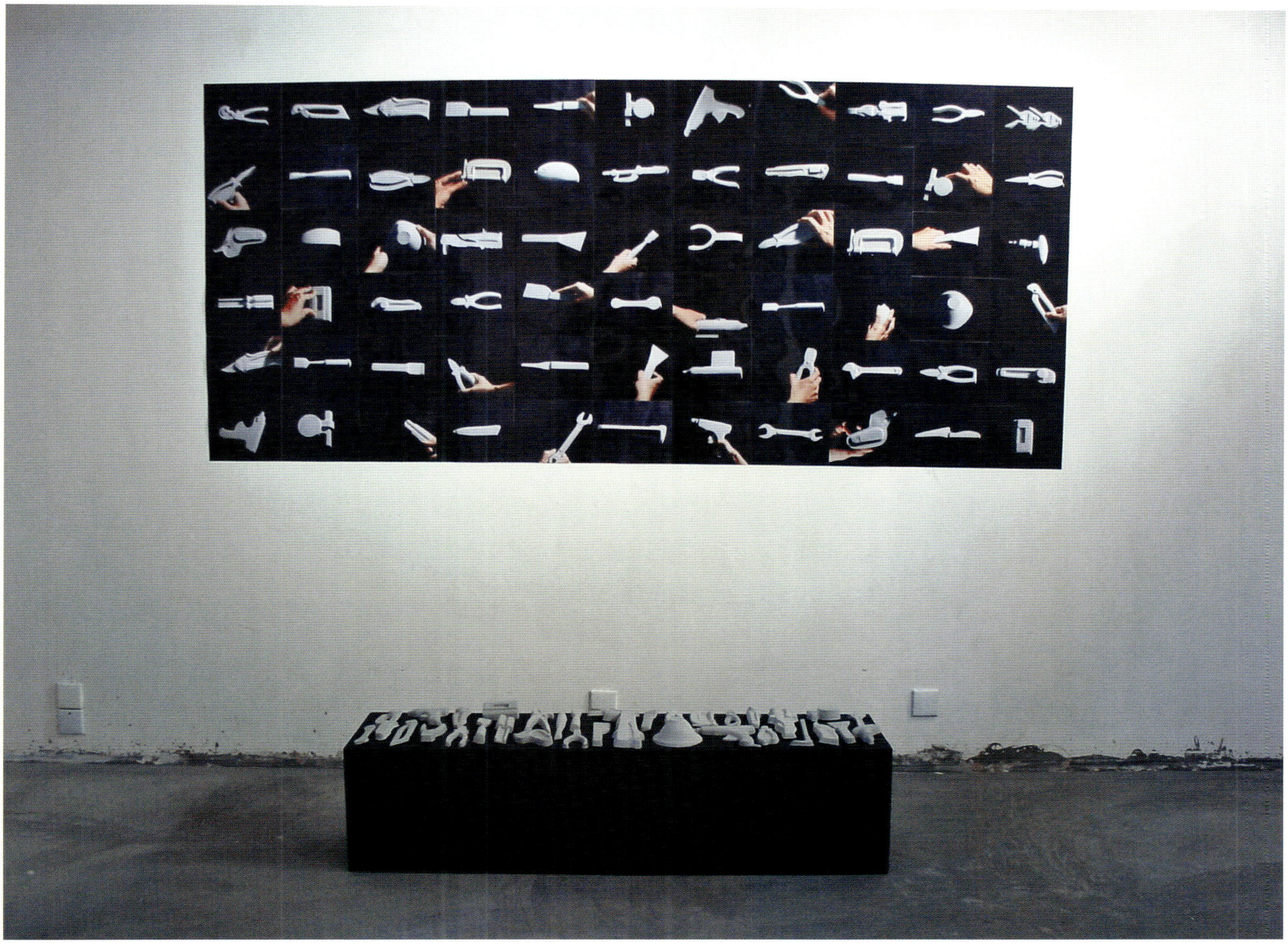

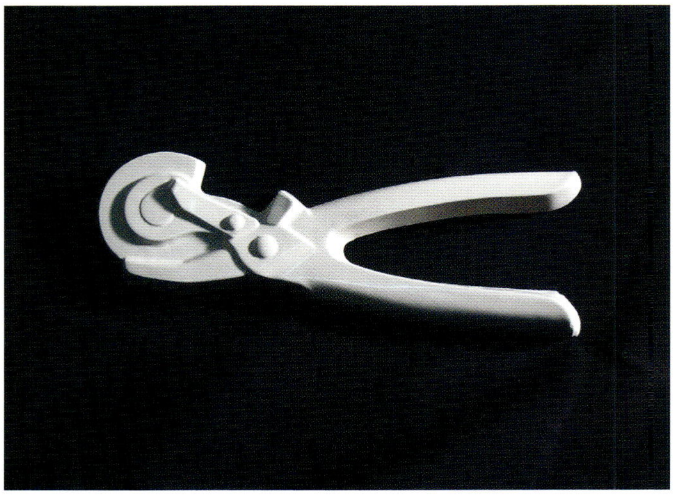

(Above) Civilised Fossils II
Concrete, 66 copies of 8R photos, dimensions variable, 2003
(Below) Civilised Fossils II (detail)

Yank Wong Yan-kwai

A Utopia of Purity and Freedom

By Alice Choi

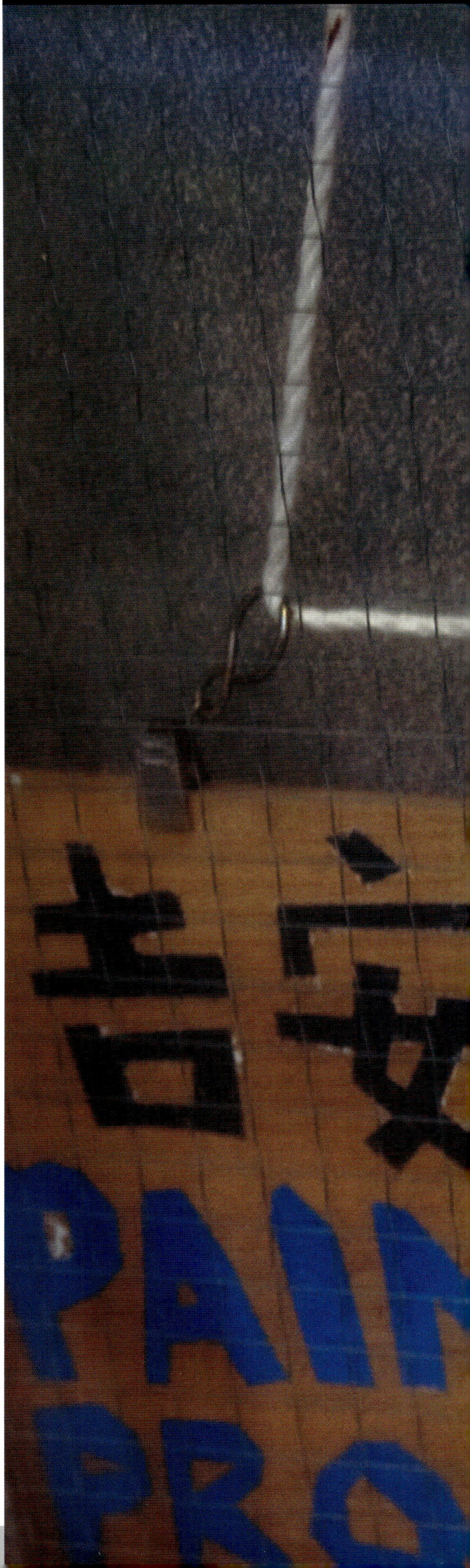

Yank Wong Yan-kwai started to learn Chinese painting when he was 12. In 1973 he went to France to further his studies in painting, first as a visiting student at the École Nationale des Beaux Arts, Poitiers, and then at the École Nationale Supérieure de Beaux Arts, Paris. He returned to Hong Kong in 1979 and became the art director of *City Magazine*. Art critics describe Wong as a Renaissance Man; he is not only an artist but a film art director and a blues guitarist. He does not favour (and is even a little against) bureaucracy and has his own definition of 'success'. In the 1990s, together with other artists, he established the Quart Society, a non-profit making art space. He teaches painting at local tertiary institutions and spends time painting with the mentally disabled, nurturing their potential by sharing his experience. He advocates freedom and enjoyment in painting.

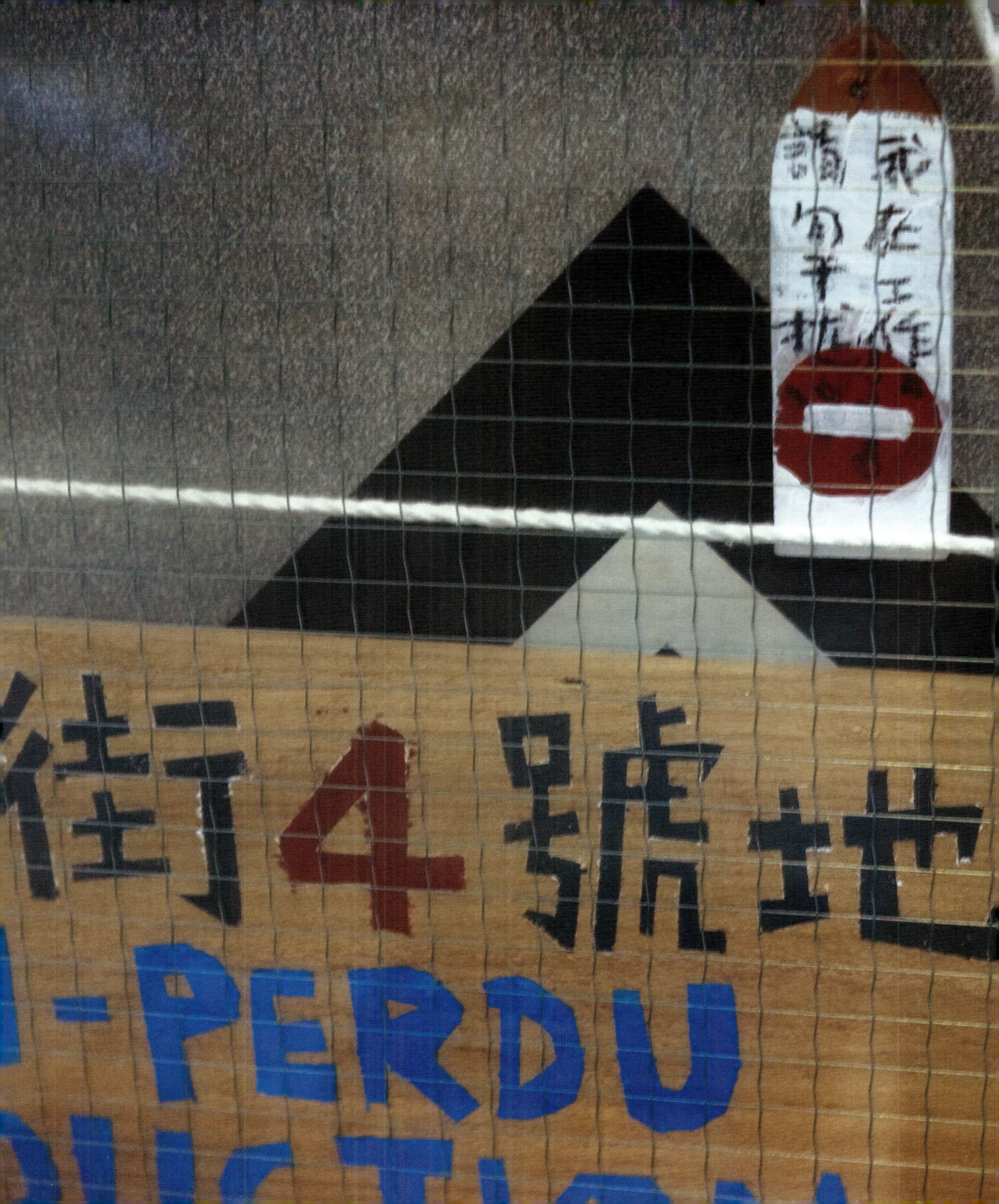
街4號地
PERDU

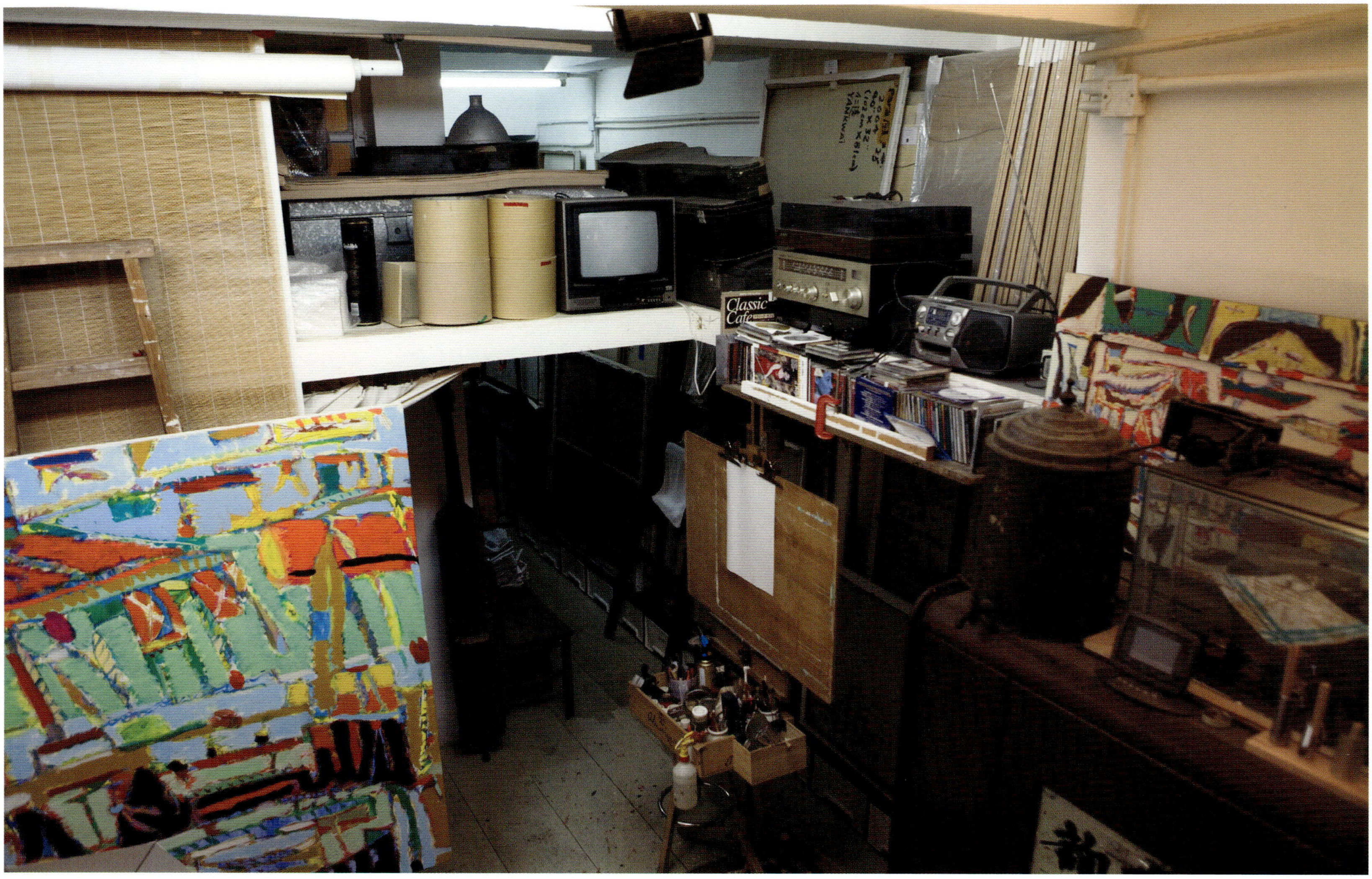

During our interview, Yank Wong Yan-kwai worked on making a musical instrument. Looking around his studio one sees that it is full of all sorts of instruments: hand-made guitars and string instruments made of garbage and ready-made materials like wooden wine boxes and pan lids. Even the painting brushes that he uses are not conventional, like cleaning brushes for babies' bottles.

Wong thinks that music and painting are interrelated. In the '90s he collaborated with the Hong Kong Sinfonietta, projecting different images of his paintings on a screen while the orchestra was performing. The images kept changing as the music developed. In 2005 he collaborated with the City Contemporary Dance Company in *Colour Fugue*, in which he was responsible for the visual effects. That time he did not show his paintings but kept to a limited palette, with lots of white and light grey. Erik Satie's music is his favourite, and is closest to his ideal art form.

Studios are very important to Wong. "To paint outdoors, one has limited freedom owing to limitations and compromises," he explains. "Nowadays when I am outside I only observe with my eyes. I always take along a digital camera and photograph whatever interests me. The only limitation of the digital camera is the shutter speed, which is relatively slower and less sensitive."

Wong's ideal studio is spacious with an abundance of natural light. He is very satisfied with his current studio space, as now his largest paintings are 68x68 inches and do not take up much space. On bright days he can paint in the courtyard outside to enjoy the natural light. "The current studio was found with little thought," he says. "I had to move out of my old studio and a friend working

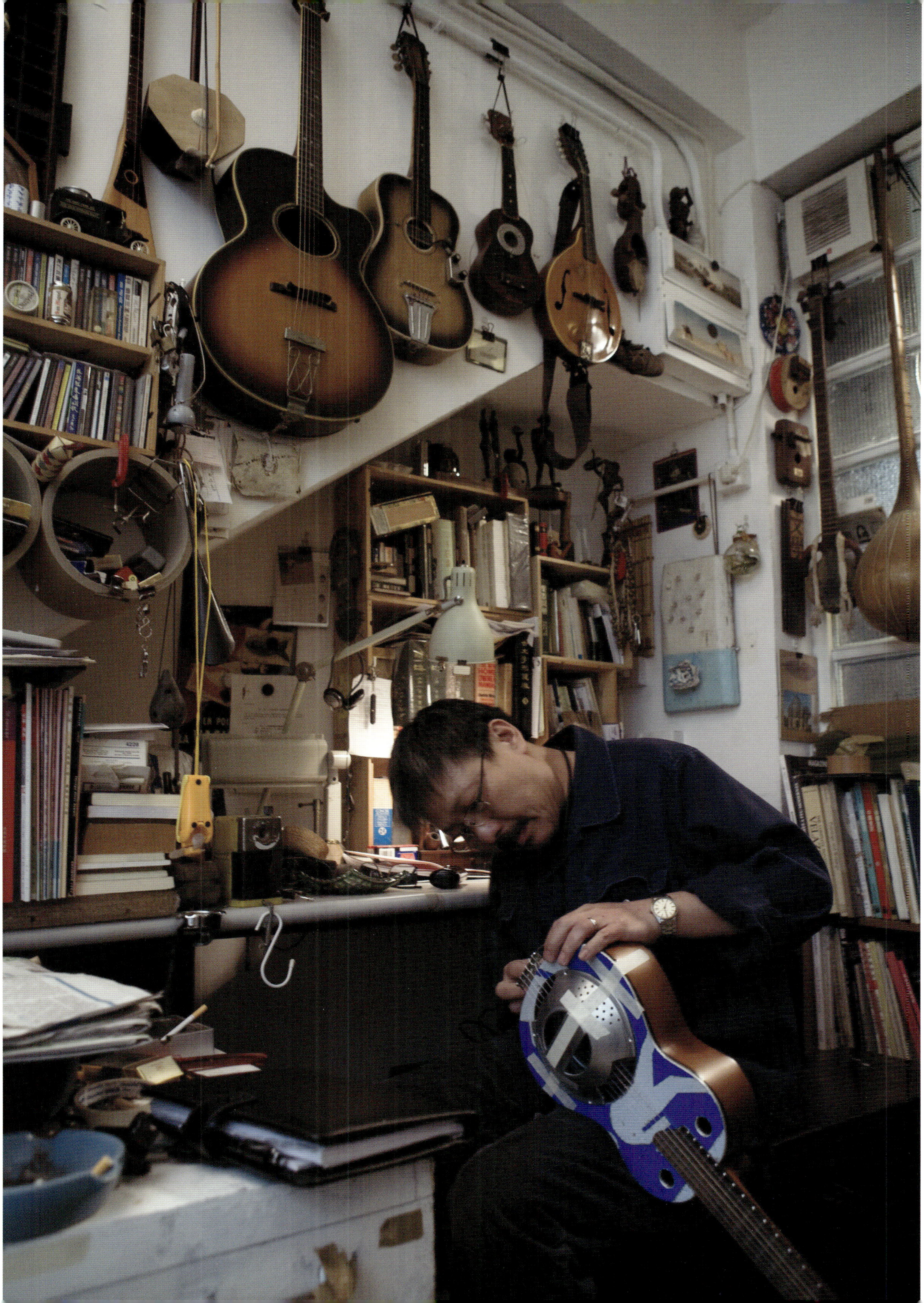

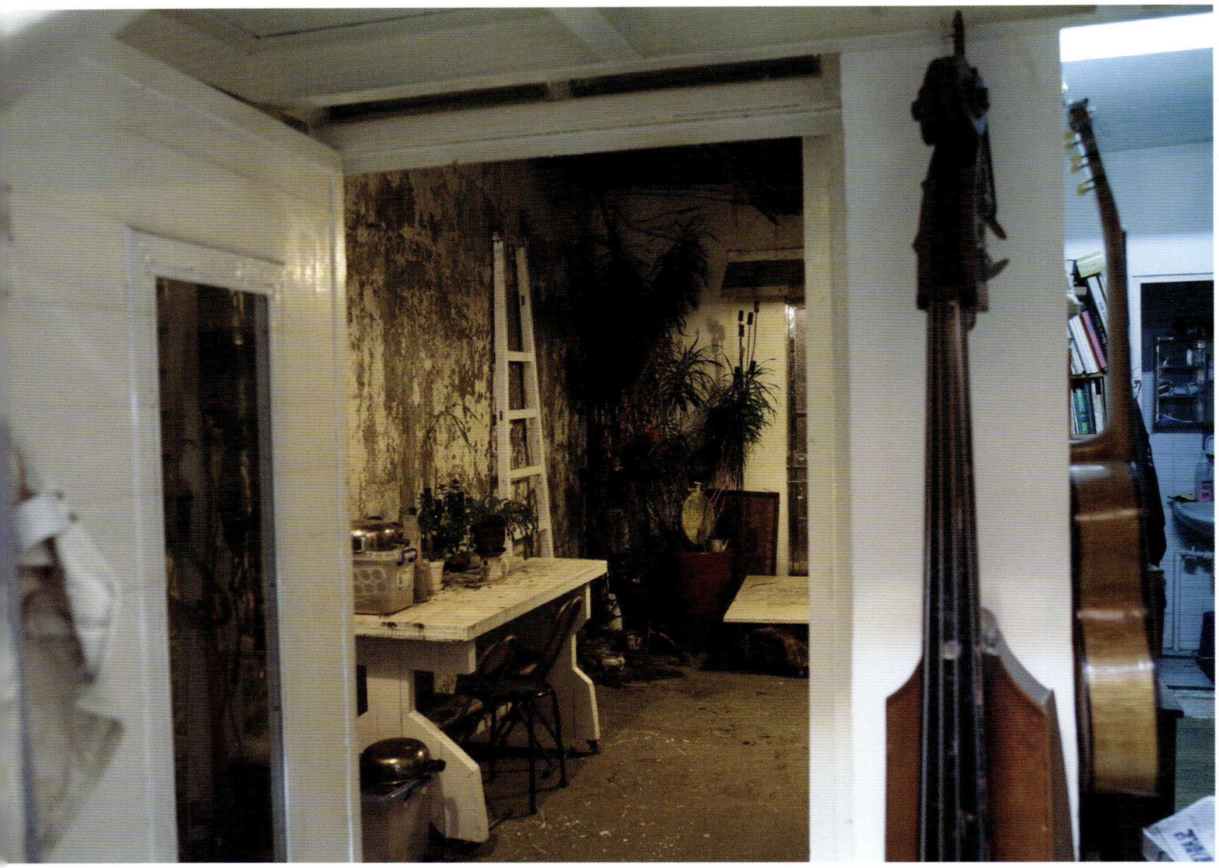

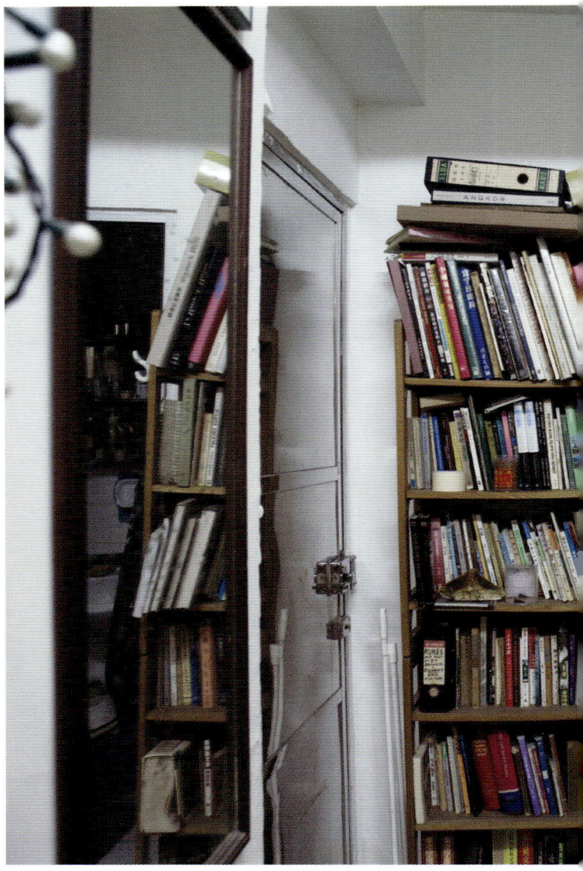

"One day I was painting what I saw through a skylight. Throughout the process I had to make a lot of choices. The light and shadow never stopped changing. In an instant I experienced a sense of freedom in painting and since then my direction has changed"

at a social service organisation told me that there was a vacant space nearby. On the day I came to look at the space I rented it without a second thought. I do not have plans to buy my own property; on the one hand the property prices are too high and on the other hand, renting is more flexible and I can relax without bearing the burden of a mortgage."

Wong's art education began with his training in Chinese painting through the imitation of his teacher's paintings. "Imitation is one of the learning methods, but not the only one," he explains. "The master and apprentice relationship in Chinese painting does not aim to open one's sense of sight. At most it is only the transmission of techniques."

In 1973 Wong went to France to further his studies. "Before I departed for France I flattered myself that I understood what painting was," he remembers. "Upon arrival, when I visited the museums, I could not comprehend modern and contemporary art at all! That day I sat at the far end of St Louis Island, facing the Seine, pondering what painting was, and realised that I had taken too many things for

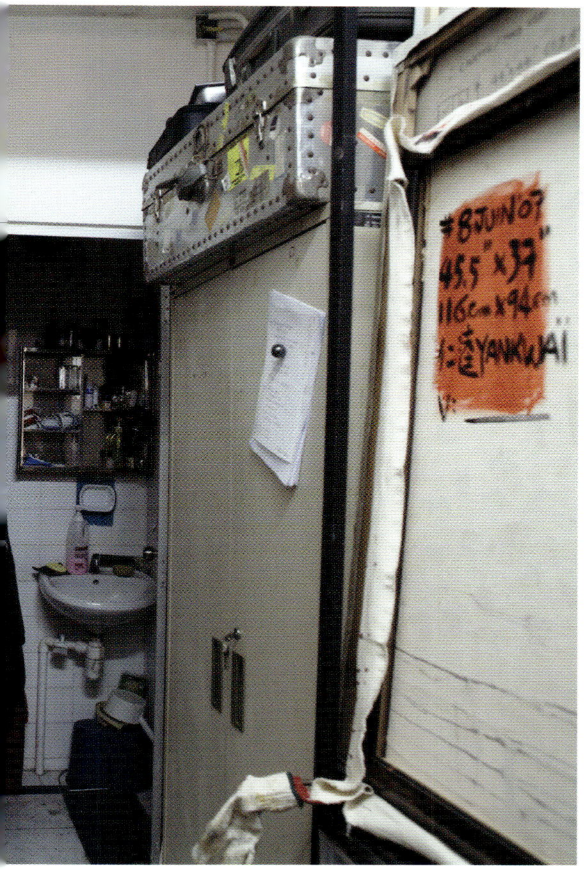

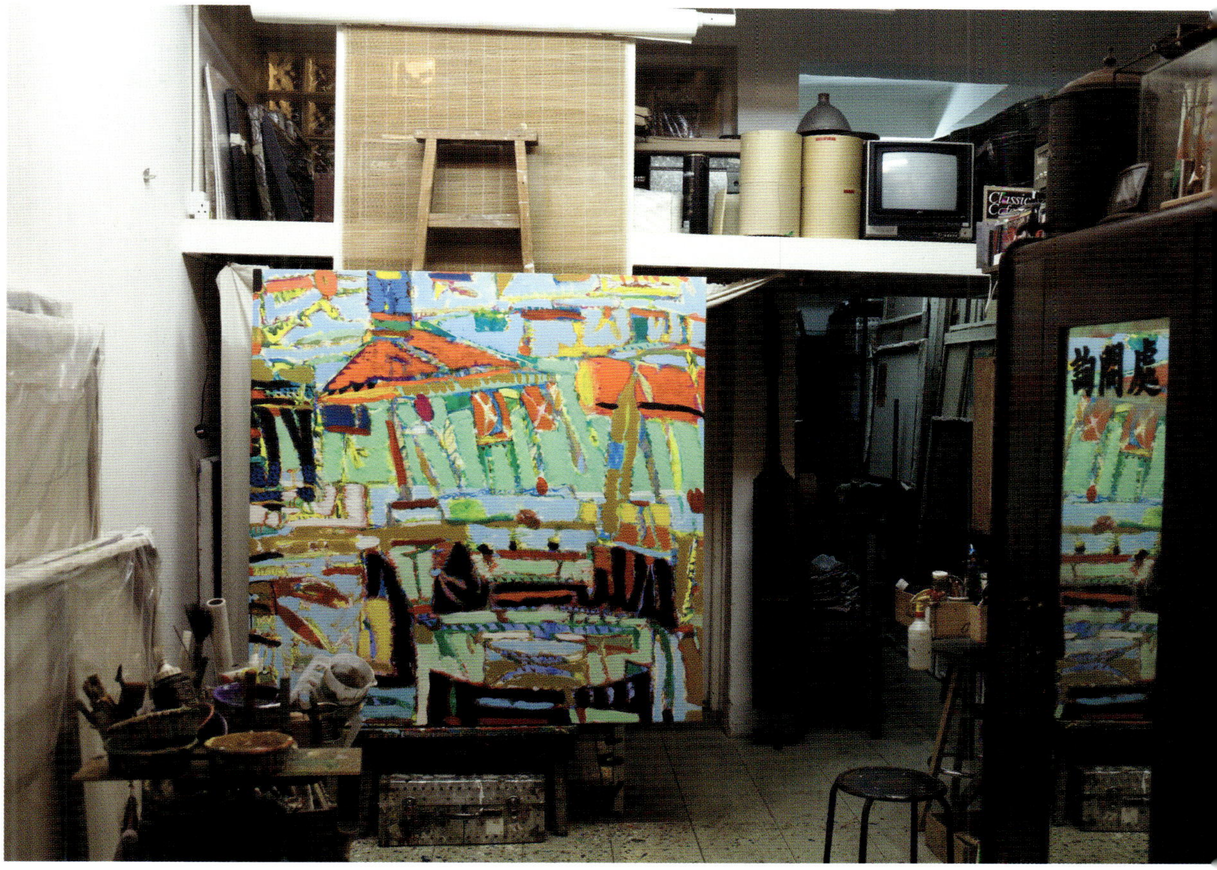

granted. Years later when my child was 10 I took her to the same spot and told her my stories."

But why France? To learn about art it is not necessary to go to France, but the place has different people and one will be stimulated by the different styles there. "The notion of genius is only a myth," Wong opines. "Every person has different talents. Education at art schools is for you to discover your potential. A foundation is essential, but there is no universal foundation suitable for all painters. We all have different skills and philosophies that suit us, so teaching with a student-oriented approach in accordance with students' aptitudes is important. When there is no better foundation, drawing is not a bad place to start."

Learning methods in France are liberal and student-oriented. "Students have to be proactive and have discussions with their professors," says Wong. The first year starts with drawing and students need the initiative to attend life drawing classes. At the end of the semester professors conduct an assessment to determine whether a student passes or not. "I worked very hard for a year and passed," says Wong. "Life drawing trained my observation skills, sketching in particular drilled my ability to master and determine, in the blink of an eye, which few lines are important."

For the first two years Wong's style tended to be more naturalistic due to his interest in Superrealism. However he started to get bored after a while. "One day I was painting what I saw through a skylight," he remembers. "Throughout the process I had to make a lot of choices. The light and shadow never stopped changing. In an instant I experienced a sense of freedom in painting and since then my direction has changed."

Starting from their second year, students in France have to find their own advisers. If accepted, the apprentices are allowed to go to their advisers' studios to paint. "My last adviser's studio was located in a deserted greenhouse inside a botanic garden," remembers Wong. "His style was very unique – he painted with brooms. I did not particularly adore his style so choosing him was solely because I liked the environment. That day I had walked in the snow for a long time to reach his studio."

"During that period I had frequent discussions with my adviser, but not until the day before I left France did he finally tell me that he wasn't actually that interested in my paintings, and he thought that there were other artists who were more suitable to be my advisers. However he had been touched by my sincerity and did not want to reject me after the long time I spent walking in the snow to find him."

Wong's intention is to paint what he imagines in order to make the invisible visible. It does not matter to him whether the painting is abstract or representational; after all, once you paint there is a form, but whether the form is recognisable and whether it signifies something, is another matter. "Colour itself is absolute. It does not carry any extended symbols or significance," Wong explains. "'Colour' has no 'intent'. I do not have exquisite taste in colours, I just use whichever is suitable. Many people have a misunderstanding that colour is equal to happiness. The world in reality is colourful, but that doesn't mean that the world is happy."

"Art is life," Wong continues. "French painter Paul Cézanne's paintings are pleasant and painterly. I don't want painting to be too distant from the public. Instead of gazing in awe, I would rather people have a closer look at what painting is about." Wassily Kandinsky, Marc Chagall and Willem de Kooning are Wong's favourite artists. In his mind, paintings by children under the age of six are also very close to the ideal. "Painting itself is clearer than any theory of art. Painting can be free of narratives, ornaments and concepts," he says.

If Wong has something to say he prefers to use other channels. He expresses political topics in magazine columns, for example, as he believes they can be better expressed in words. The same applies to his choice of media in the realm of visual art. "I once went to Mongolia. The local people told me that each family had a custom of painting on the door plank of one's yurt," he remembers." You can tell what sorts of people are living inside a yurt just by looking at the door plank."

"My paintings are very personal, but I don't mind people looking at them, nor do I care whether they understand or not. If possible, I prefer painting directly on the wall to painting

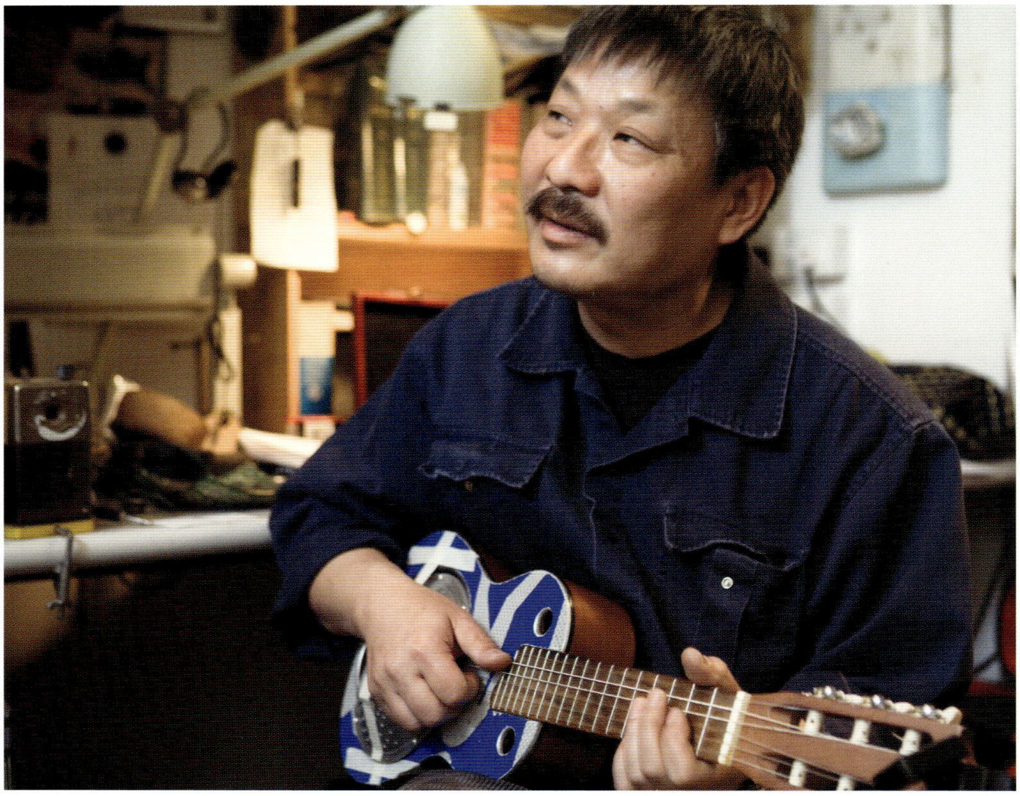

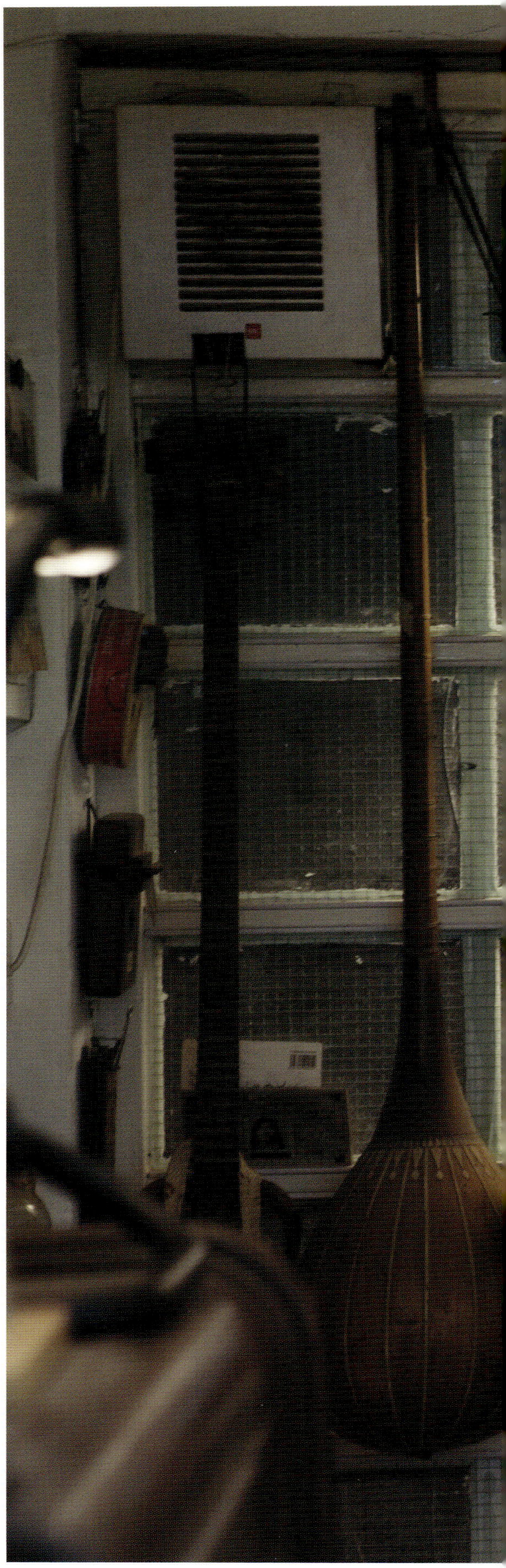

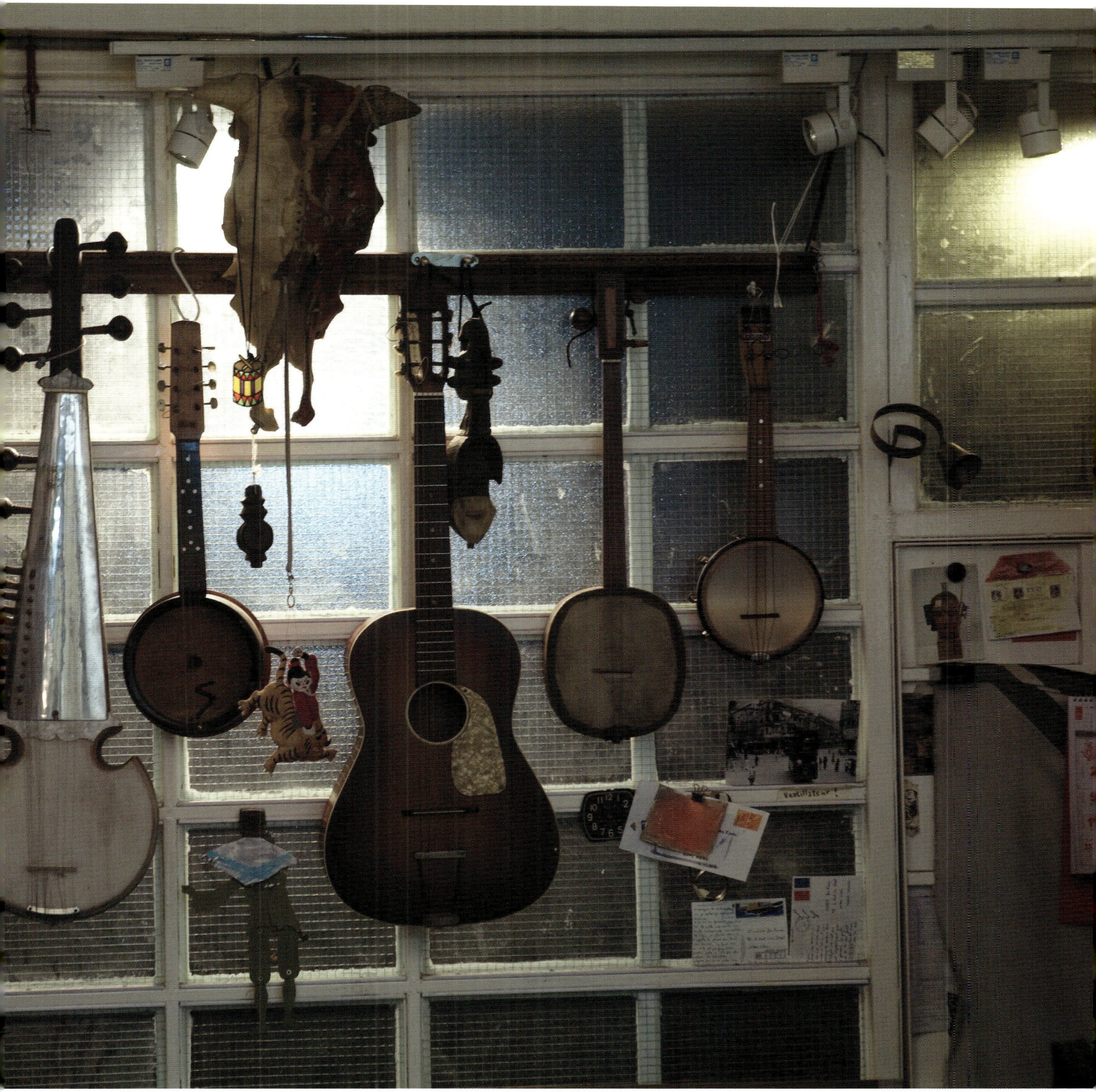

Instruments are more than pieces of wood – they are Yank Wong Yan-kwai's studio acquaintances

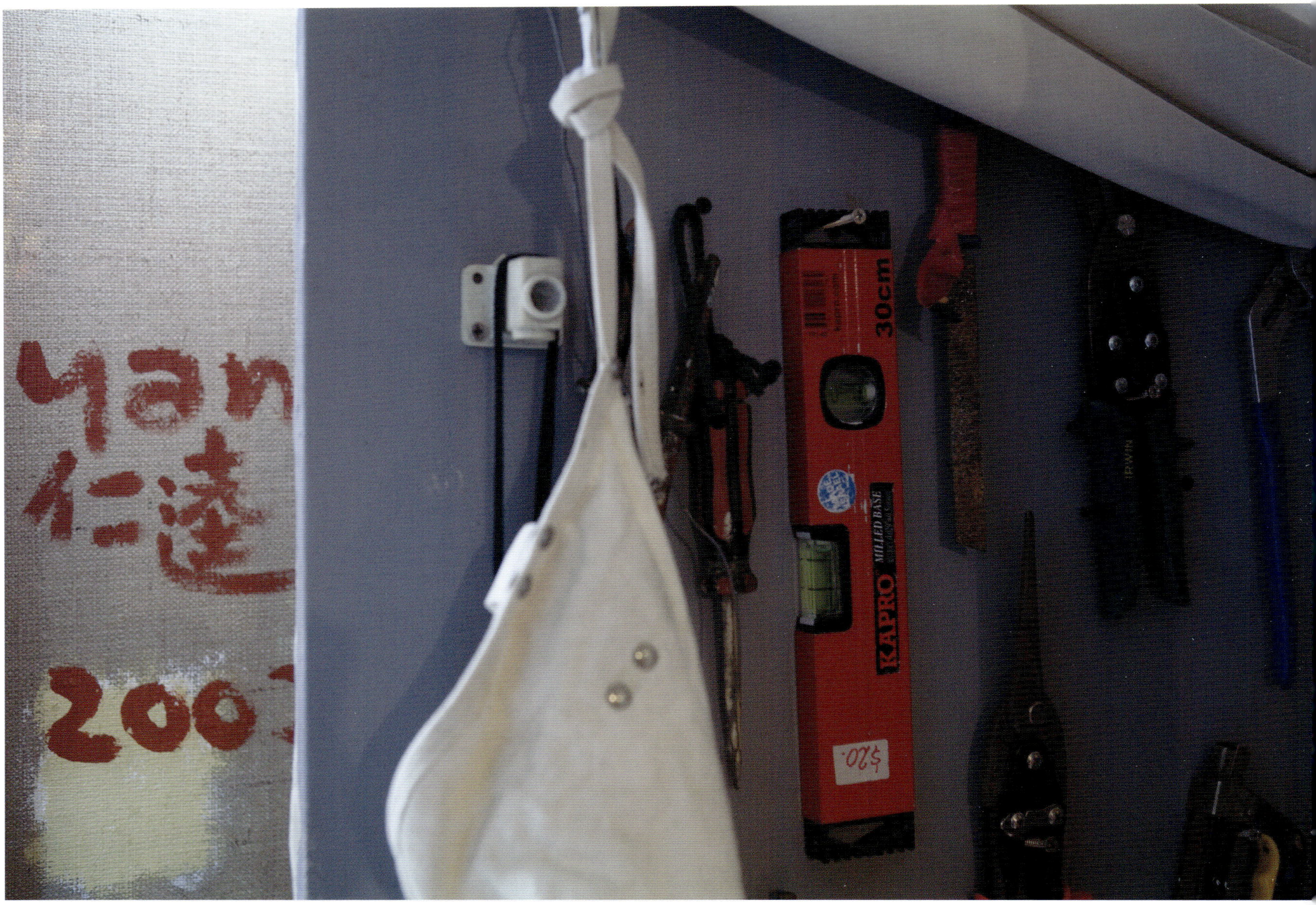
yan
仁達
30cm
KAPRO
MILLED BASE

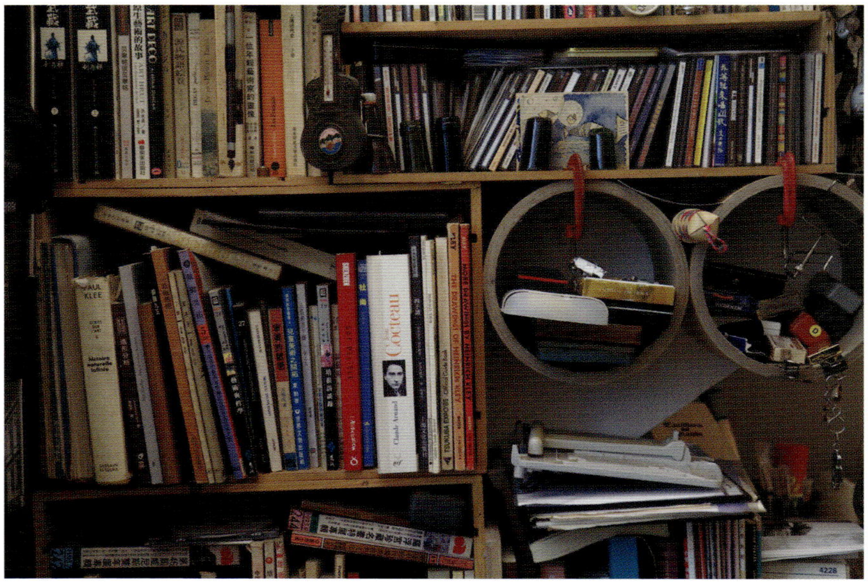
Cocteau

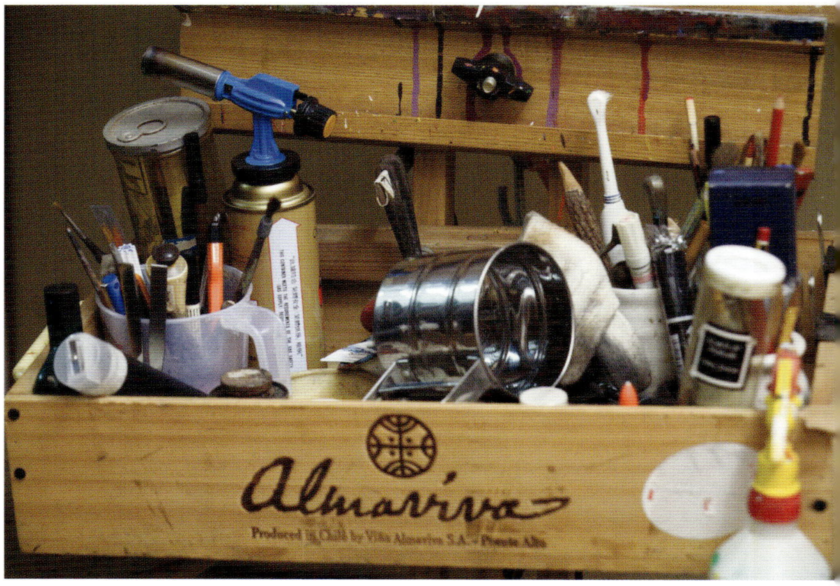
Almaviva

on canvas. Painting on canvas is my only compromise for the sake of easy transportation for exhibitions."

"Many people are doubtful about the way an artist knows his painting is finished," he says. "Once you put down the first stroke, you have disturbed the original equilibrium of the surface. From the beginning to the end, the surface is a draft. A painter has to keep adding strokes in pursuit of the state of equilibrium. Each stroke is to balance the previous one. In conclusion there is no such thing as a finished painting. There is only a moment when an artist does not want to add one more stroke."

"To know a person, look at what they do after work, not what they do at work"

Wong has different interpretations of the concepts of 'job' and 'career'. Painting and music are his career, and his career needs work to sustain it. For him, a job is a way of helping other people solve their problems while paying for his own lifestyle, allowing more freedom to develop his career without compromise. He has never taken requests from galleries. Trading artworks is a kind of commercial activity, but that is not his purpose for painting. Wong chooses the limitation of other jobs to gain freedom in his career. "To know a person, look at what they do after work," he says. "Not what they do at work."

Confucius said that a person should know their destiny by the age of 50. Yank Wong Yan-kwai seemed to have acknowledged his long ago, and within that he has found his freedom.

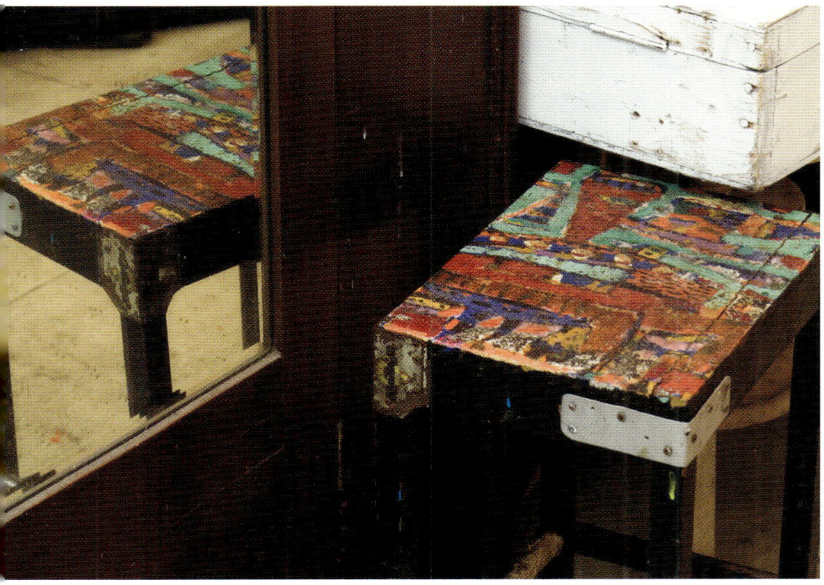

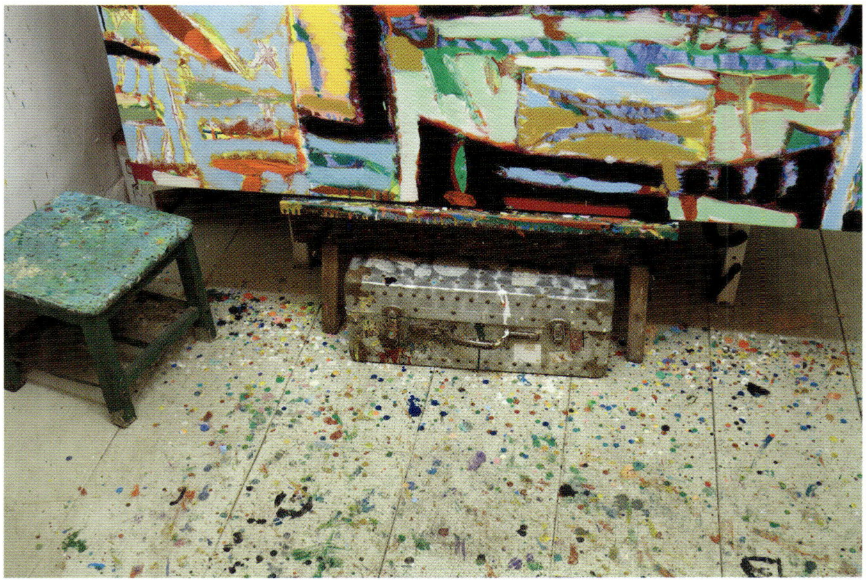

Despite the absence of 'mobile white', the floor is full of dancing colours

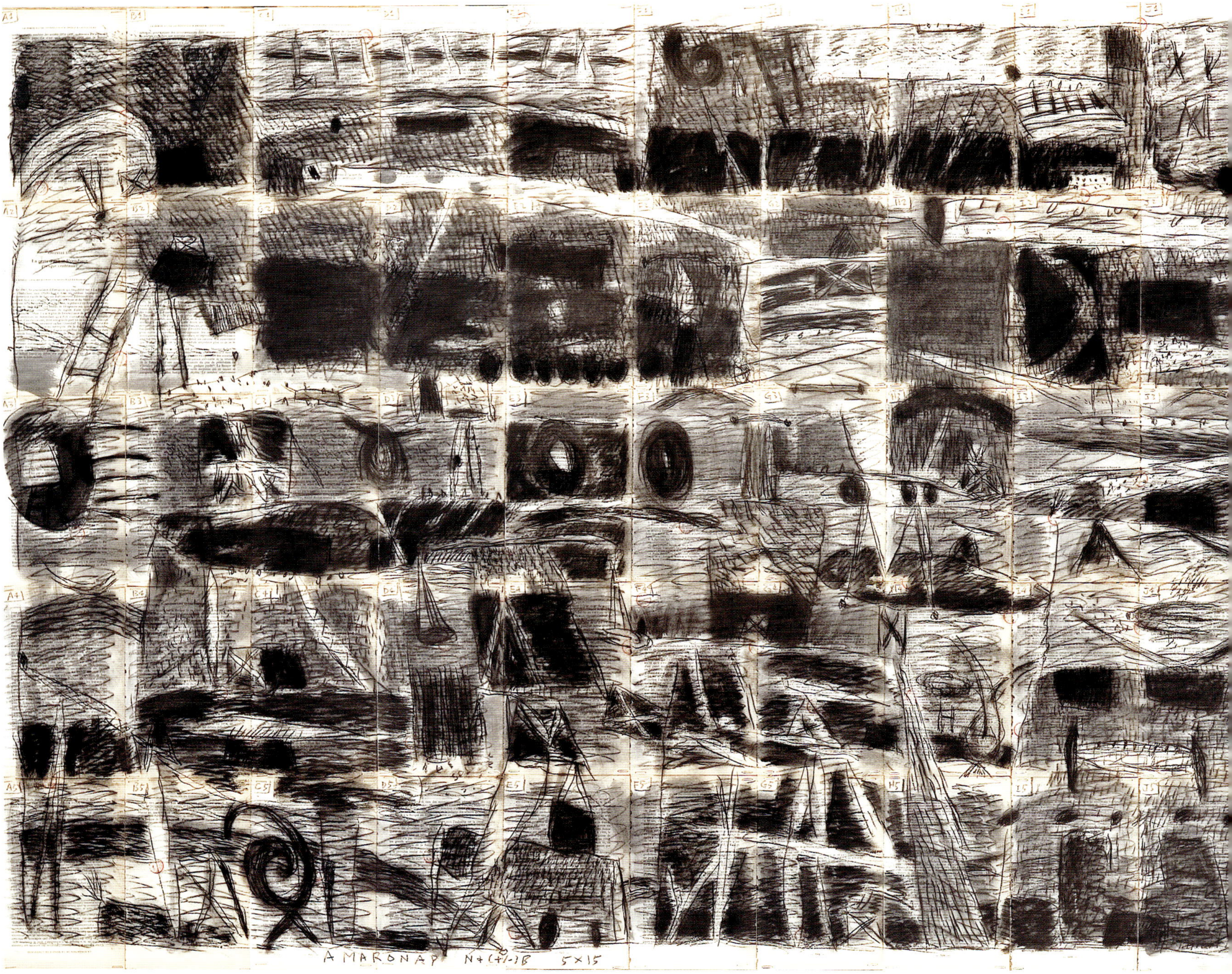

(Left) Amaronap/Old Book
Mixed-media on paper, 122x244 cm, 2007

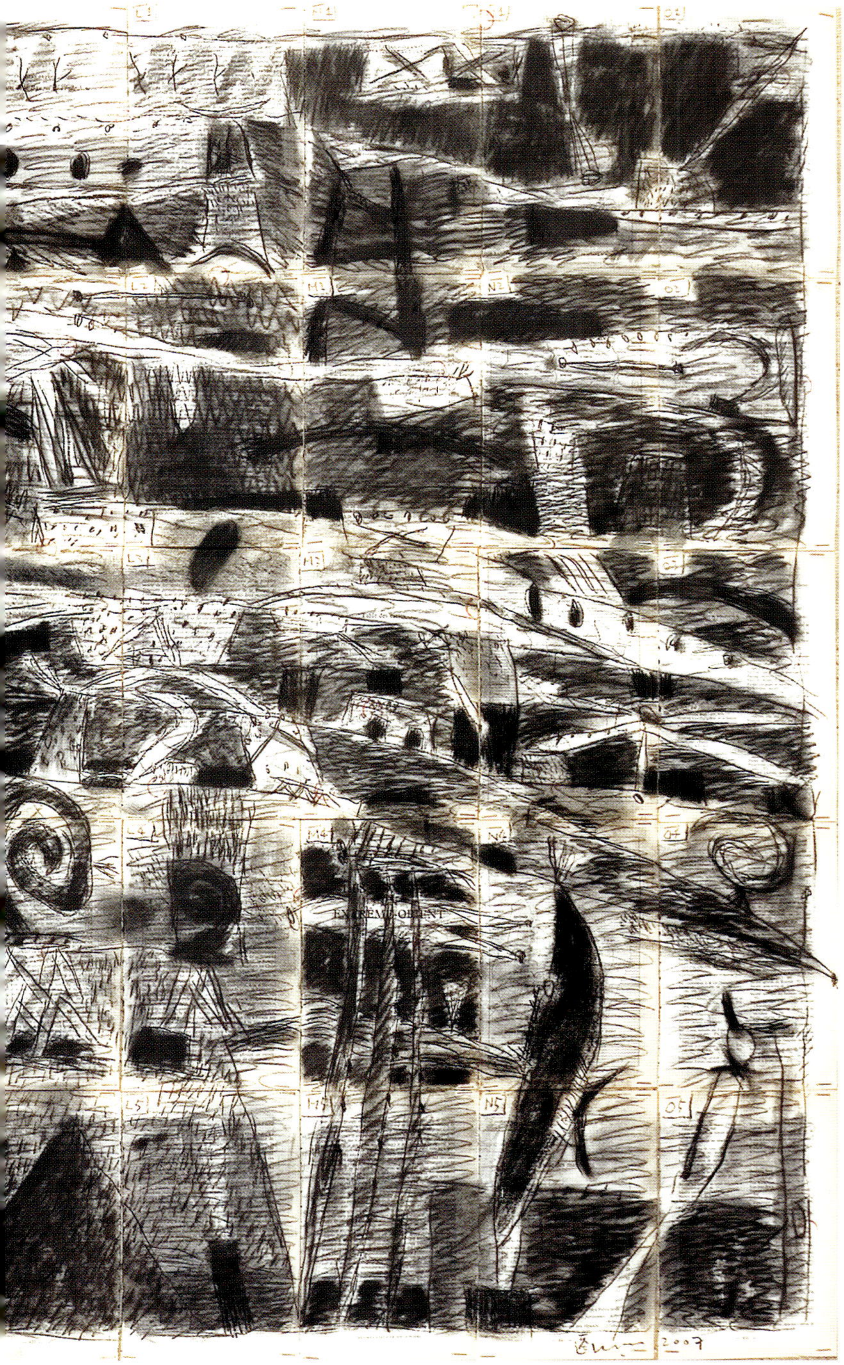

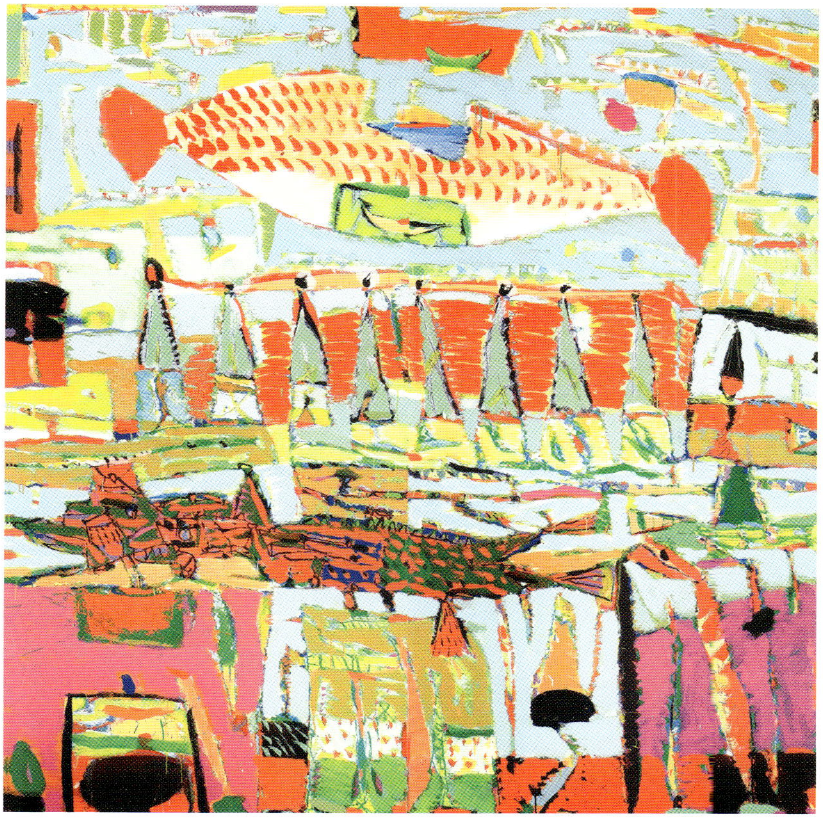

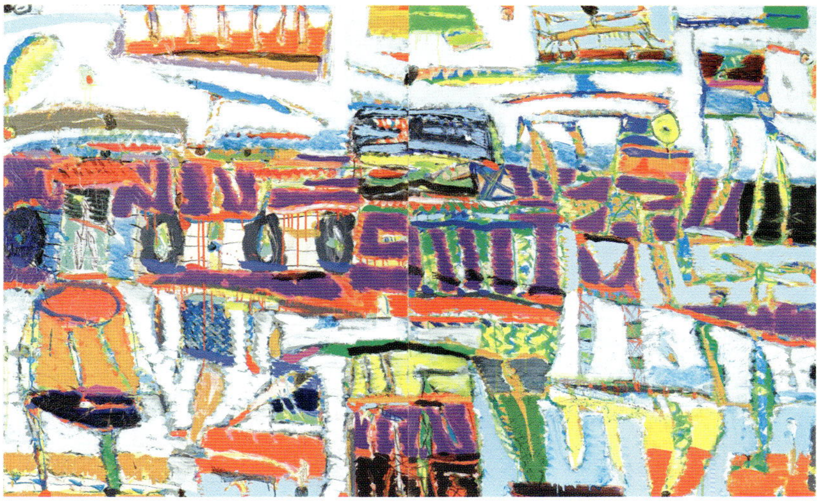

(Right above) Fond 2
Acrylic on canvas, 208x208 cm, 2006

(Right bottom) Scenary with Green-line
Acrylic on canvas,138 x224 cm, 2007

Denise Chen Hui-lien

Living as Her True Self

By Carl Cheng

Denise Chen Hui-lien is Taiwanese and moved to Hong Kong in 1989. She earned her BA in fine art and a Master in fine art, jointly offered by the Royal Melbourne Institute of Technology University (RMIT) and the Hong Kong Art School (HKAS) in 2001 and 2005 respectively, majoring in ceramics. Her works, which explore the extension, immediacy and transformation of materials, have a strong visual impact, and are collected by the Hong Kong Heritage Museum and private enthusiasts.

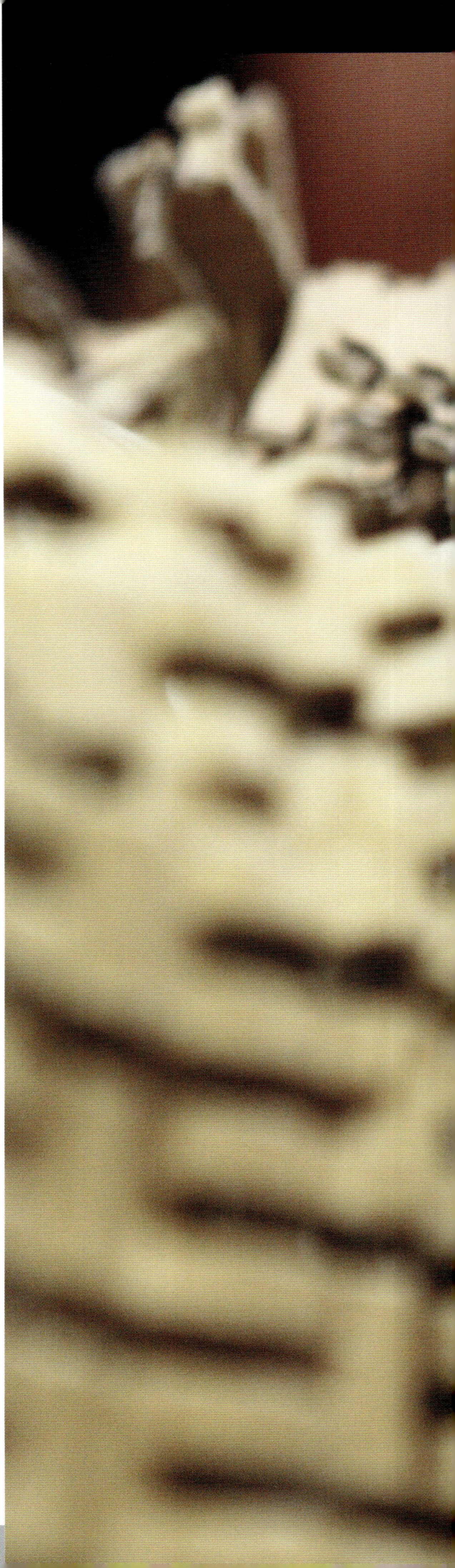

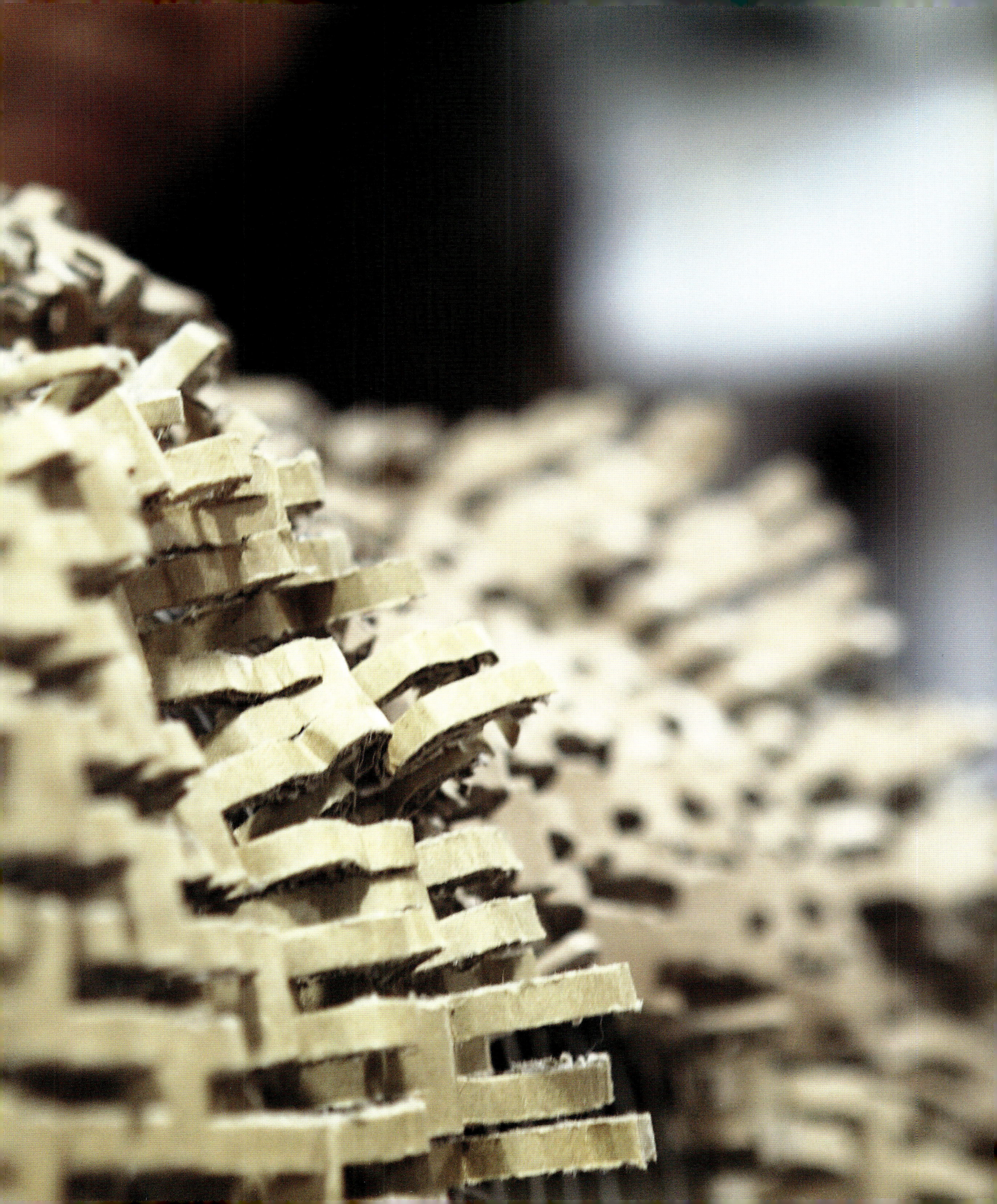

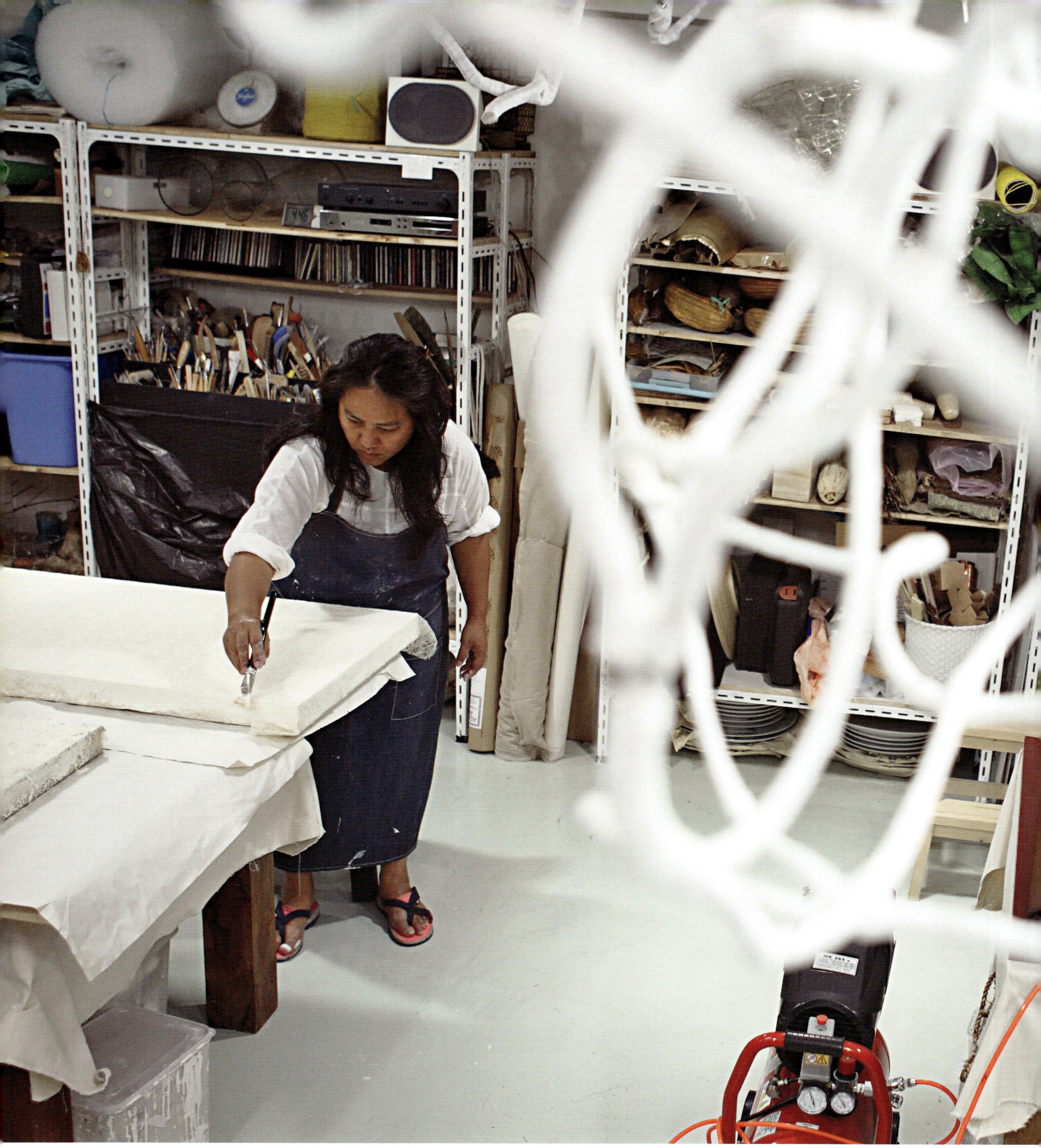

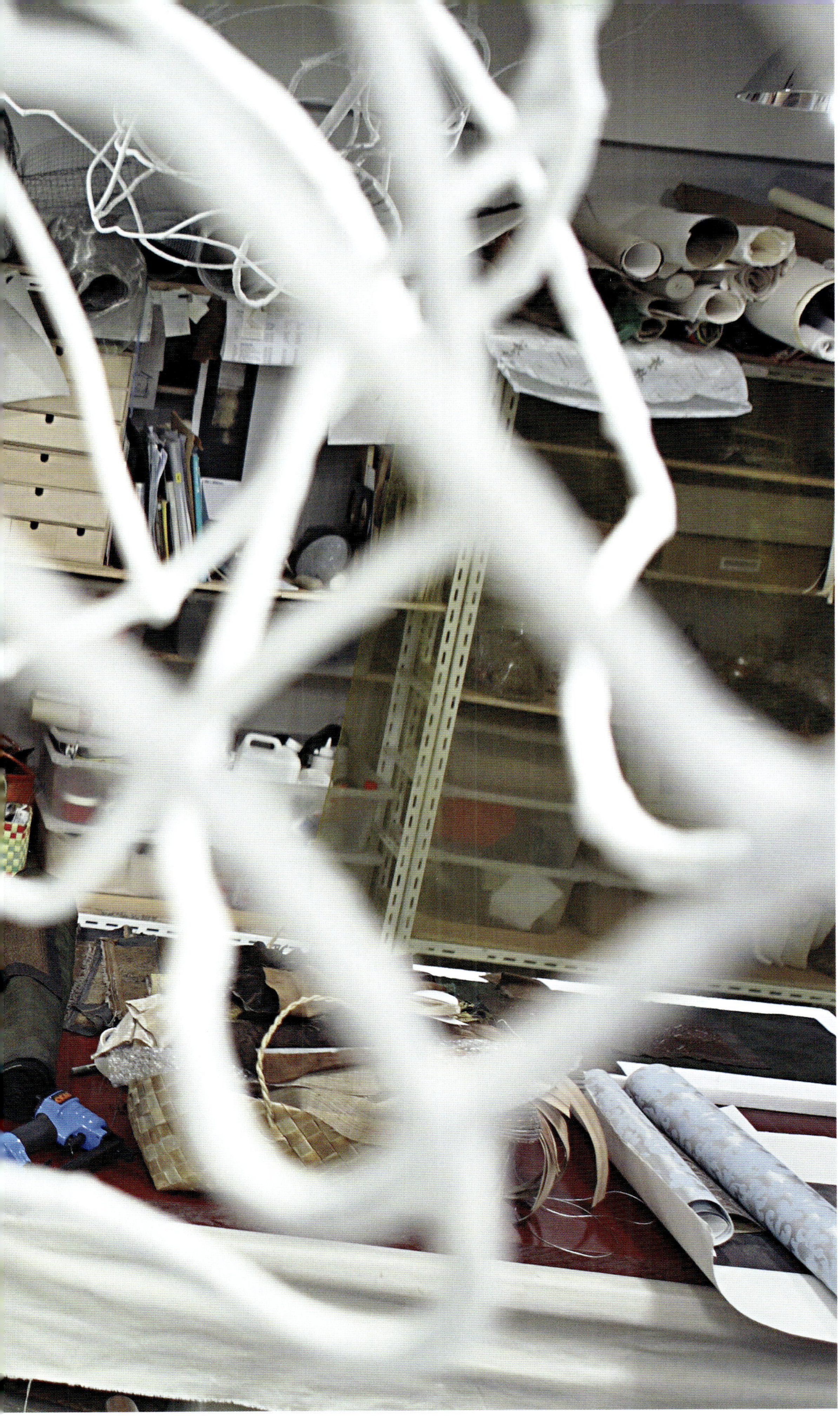

Directions in life may not always be clear, and they may sometimes even be confusing. Moving in a direction completely opposite to one's personality and aspirations will make one feel uneasy. Denise Chen Hui-lien from Taiwan felt this way. She had lived her life in discontent for years until she moved to Hong Kong, where she encountered fine art by chance and fell in love with it. Her life has since been full of excitement, enabling her to be her true self.

Chen belongs to the Paiwan tribe in southern Taiwan. Following her brothers' path in the medical profession, she was educated as a nurse while her brothers trained as doctors. However deep inside her heart she knew that the medical profession was not where her aspirations lay. In 1989 she followed her husband to Hong Kong. She found a part-time job as a gallery assistant in Central and learned ceramics at a nearby studio to kill time. Gradually her interest in ceramics developed, and several years later she realised that this was what she really loved to do. She soon took up the programme jointly offered by the RMIT and the HKAS, earning a Bachelor's degree and later a Master's degree in fine art. She is now pursuing her Doctorate degree.

The first thing that strikes me as I entered Chen's studio in Chai Wan is the open space and the book collection on a shelf more than 20 feet long. This shows how committed she is to her research and art. Talking about studios, Chen admits that the space was planned according to her basic needs. The size of the

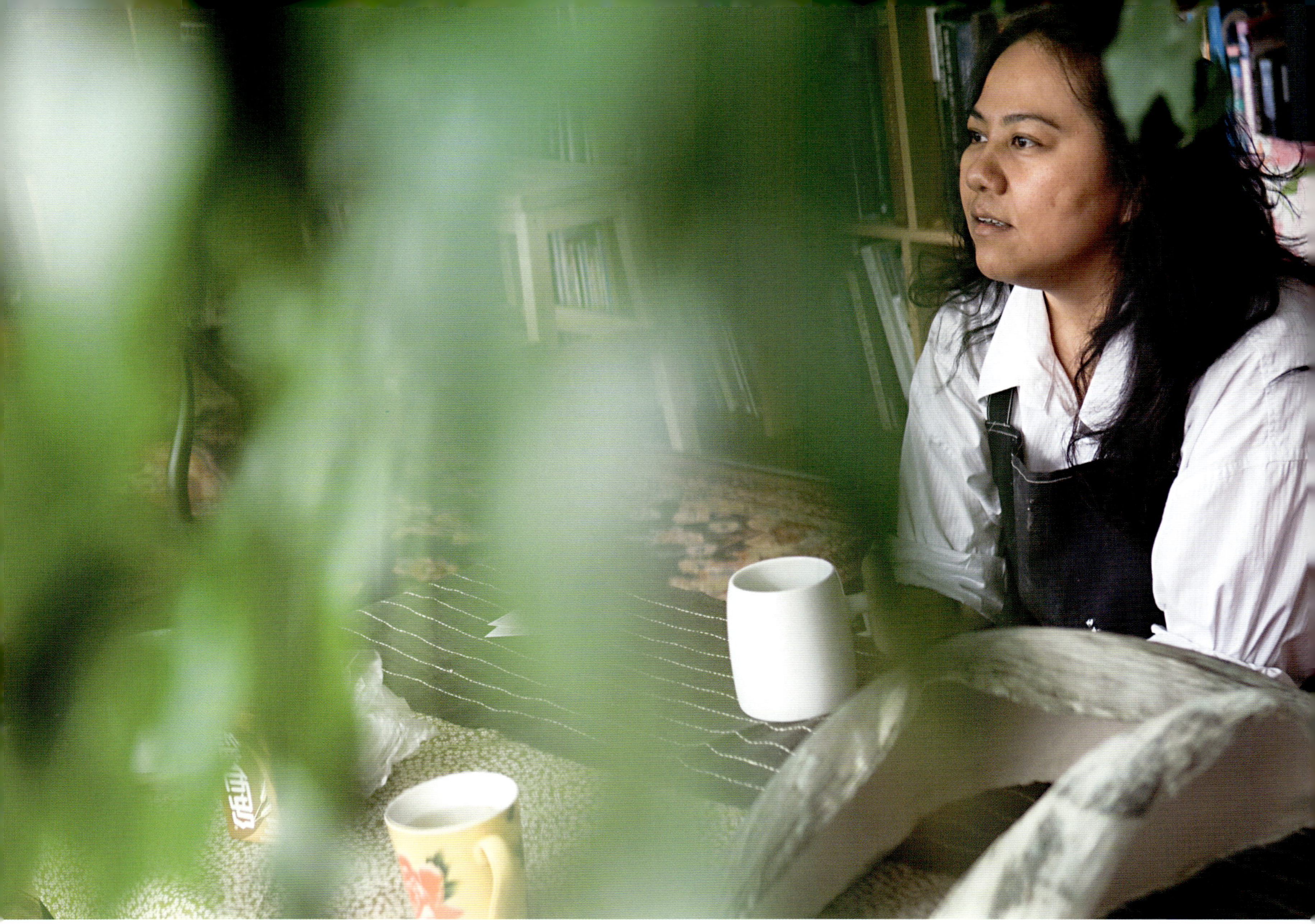

She is fascinated with the uncertainty of integrating familiar and unfamiliar materials

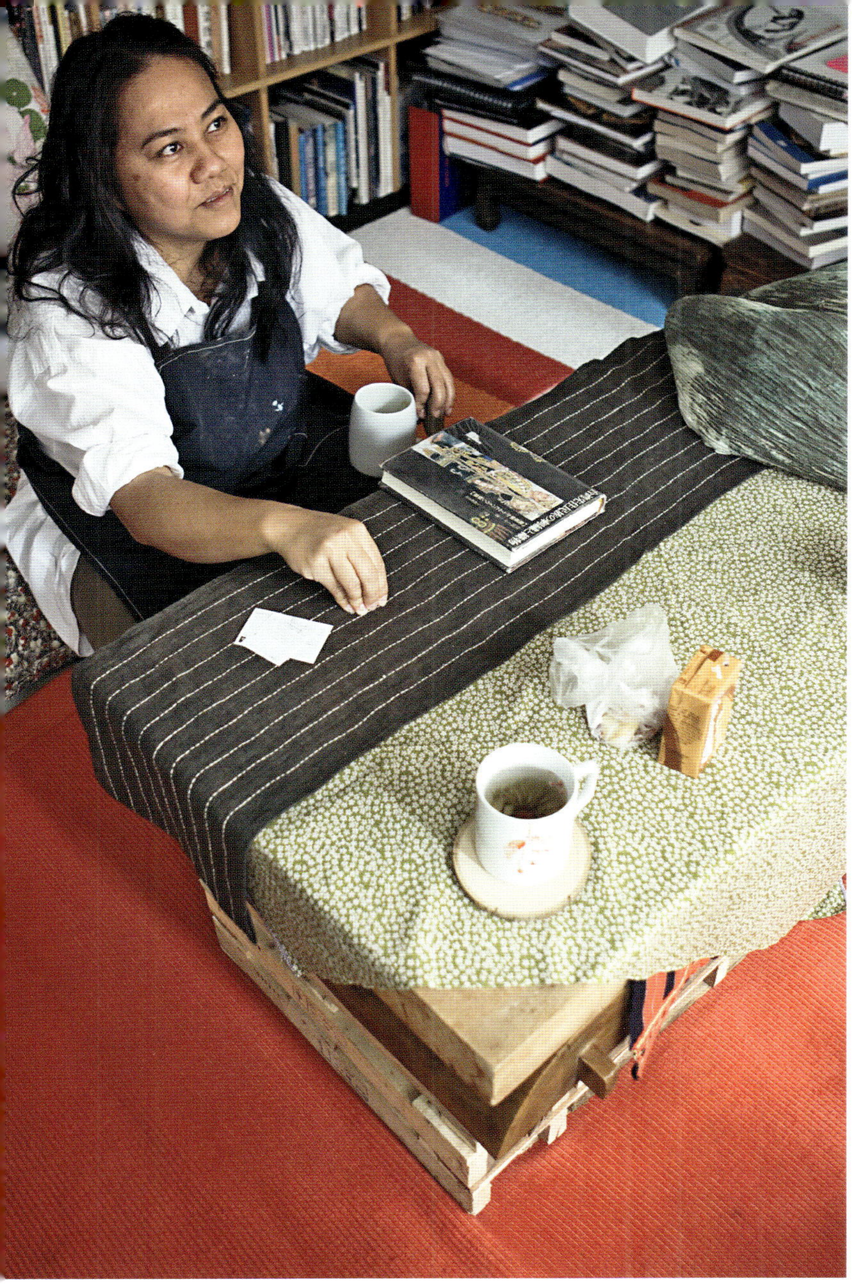

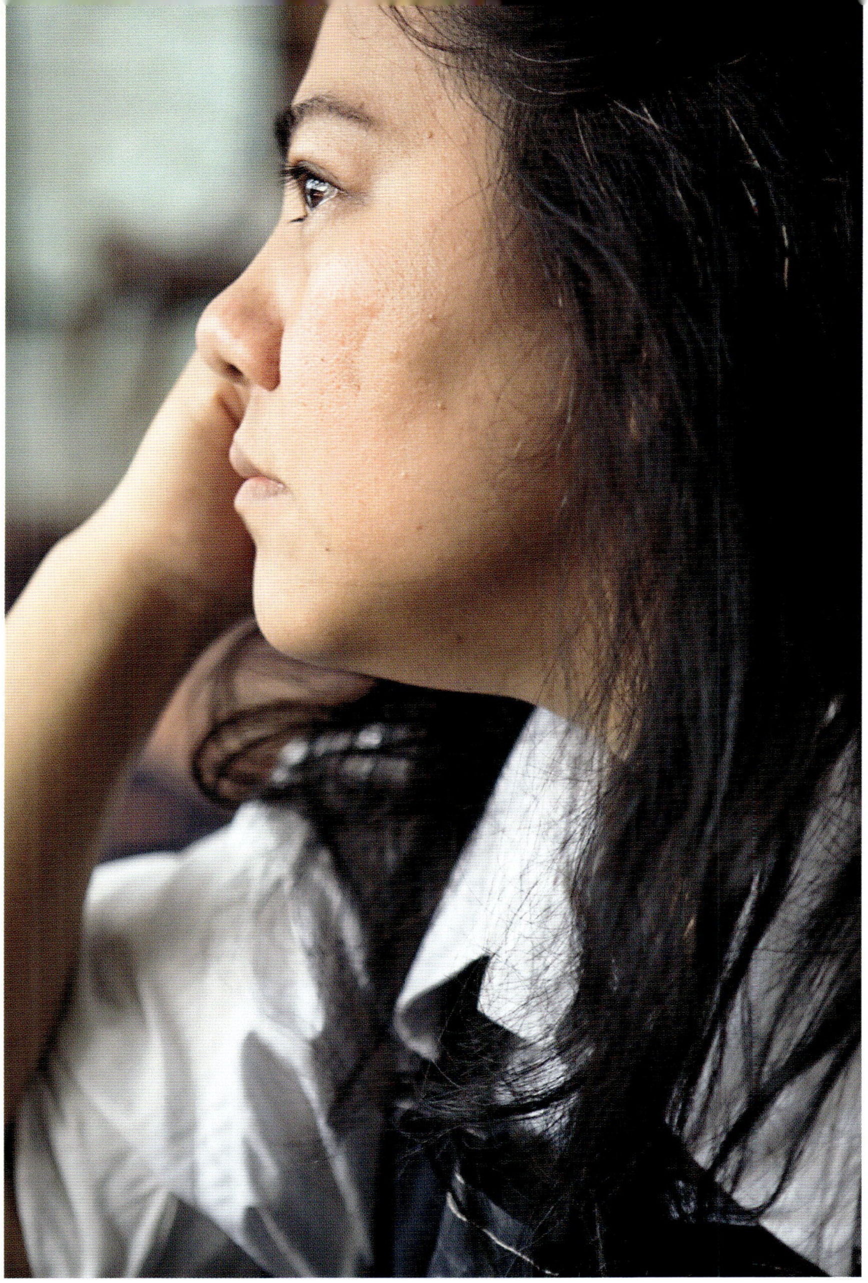

studio does not limit her art making. As she recalls, in the early days she only worked in a corner at her home in Discovery Bay, later in the garage and then the Hong Kong Visual Arts Centre. Her current studio is 2,000 sq-ft for the large-scale artworks she is commissioned to do, which supports the rent. In the past she could only create after working and studying, leaving her little time. Now she goes to her studio early every morning, spending time on her commissioned project first, and then focusing on her doctoral research and studio practice until late at night, without being aware of the passing of time.

Chen recalls the prolonged feeling of suppression she had when she did a non art-related job in the past. Even when she started to learn ceramics she was still very tense and reserved. It is art that has finally set her free. The state of being relaxed and free, for her, is irreplaceable. She therefore treasures every moment of making art, and feels content.

The turning point of Chen's artistic life was studying for her Bachelor's degree. Apart from learning, the encouragement she found among classmates was a great source of motivation. A Japanese classmate in particular has left a deep impression on her. Although in her fifties, the classmate was still full of the energy and vitality of youth. When Chen met her she was greatly encouraged and motivated. Unfortunately she lost contact with this classmate when she left for Guam.

Chen is very familiar with her medium – clay – yet there was also a point when she struggled with traditional constraints and could not move forward. For two years she deliberately used media other than clay, yet the mode of thinking from ceramics was still dominating her concept development; even though the finished products were not ceramic, the functional aspect of ceramics and its integration with other materials were still evident in her works. She is fascinated with the uncertainty of integrating familiar and unfamiliar materials. Contrasting materials, time, immediacy and transformation are often seen in Chen's works.

After discovering herself through art, Chen found the beauty in life. Her curiosity is like

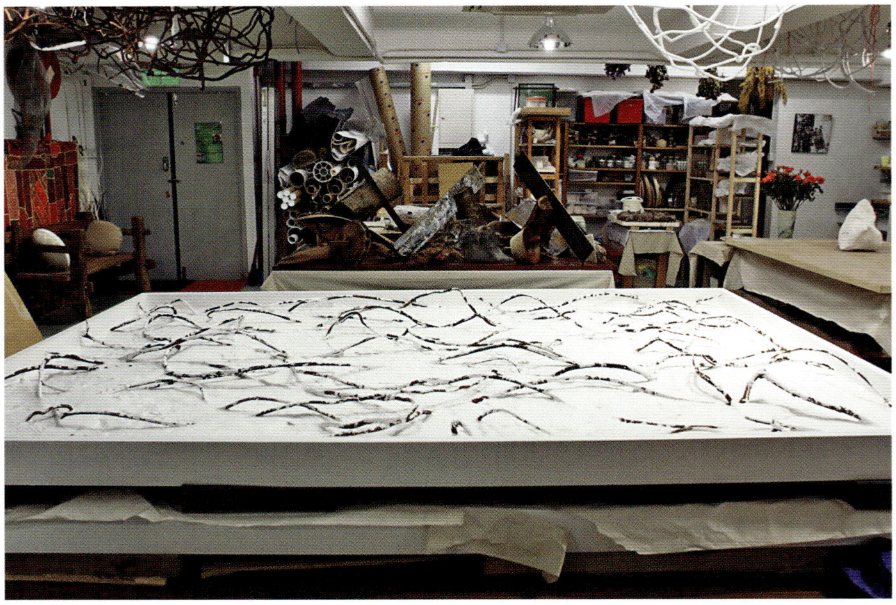

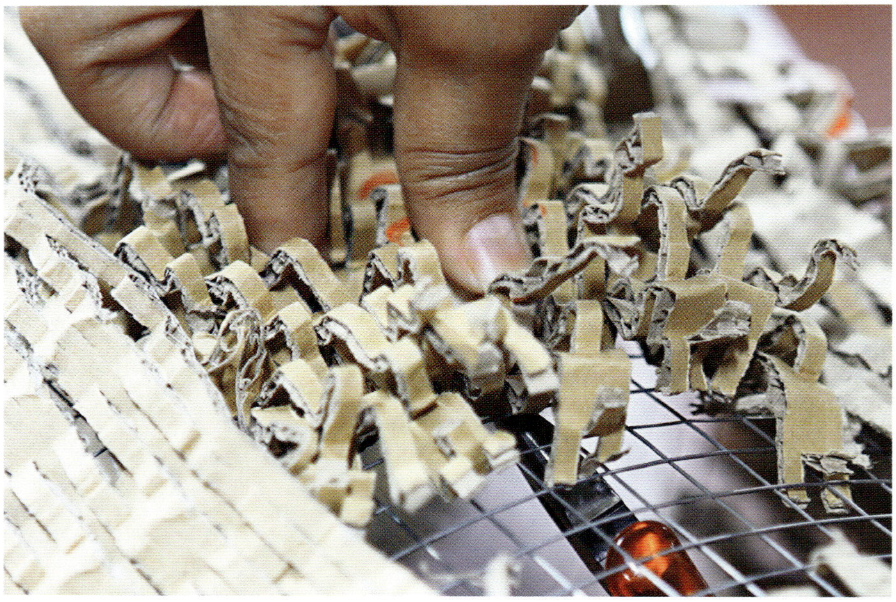

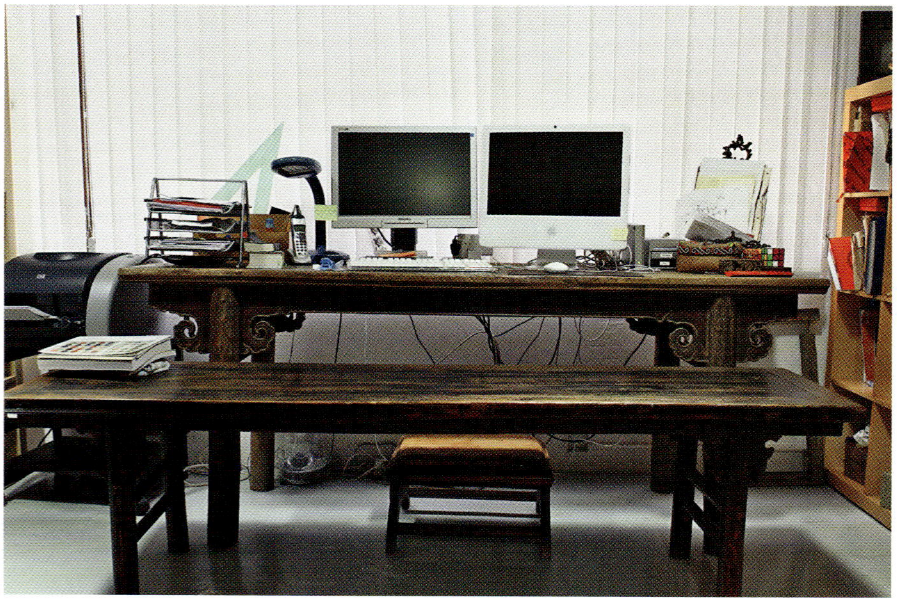

Art is a journey of self-discovery

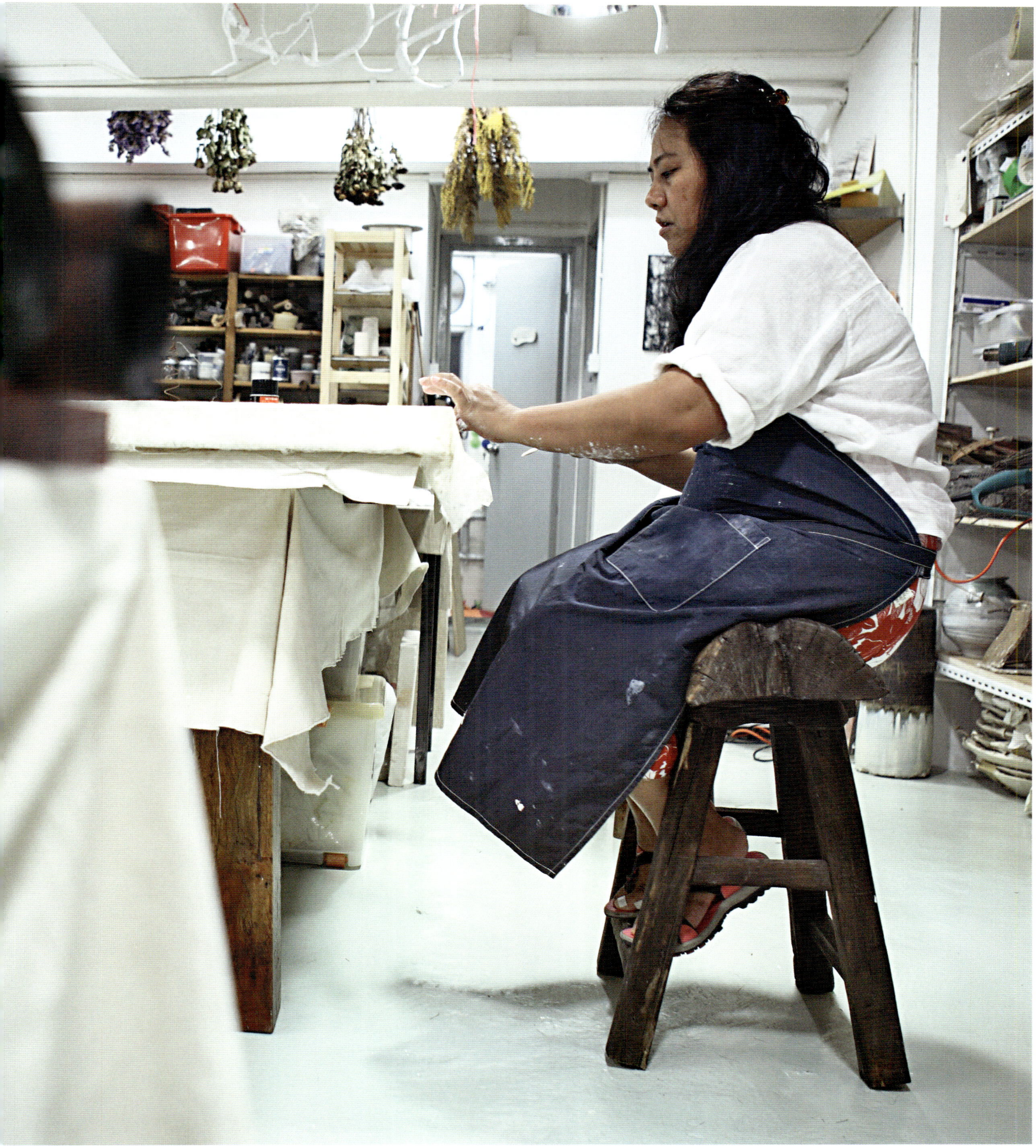

a newborn, pushing her to think, explore and travel back to her origins to discover the long history of art and culture of her tribe in Taiwan.

Chen has been deeply influenced by her grandmother and aunts, who are familiar with native tribal culture and art, and have a valuable collection of tribal art and handicrafts. When Chen was planning for her doctorate studies she decided to study the artistic value of Paiwan tattoos, costumes and decorative patterns, with a view to developing a body of works and gaining a deeper understanding of her origins.

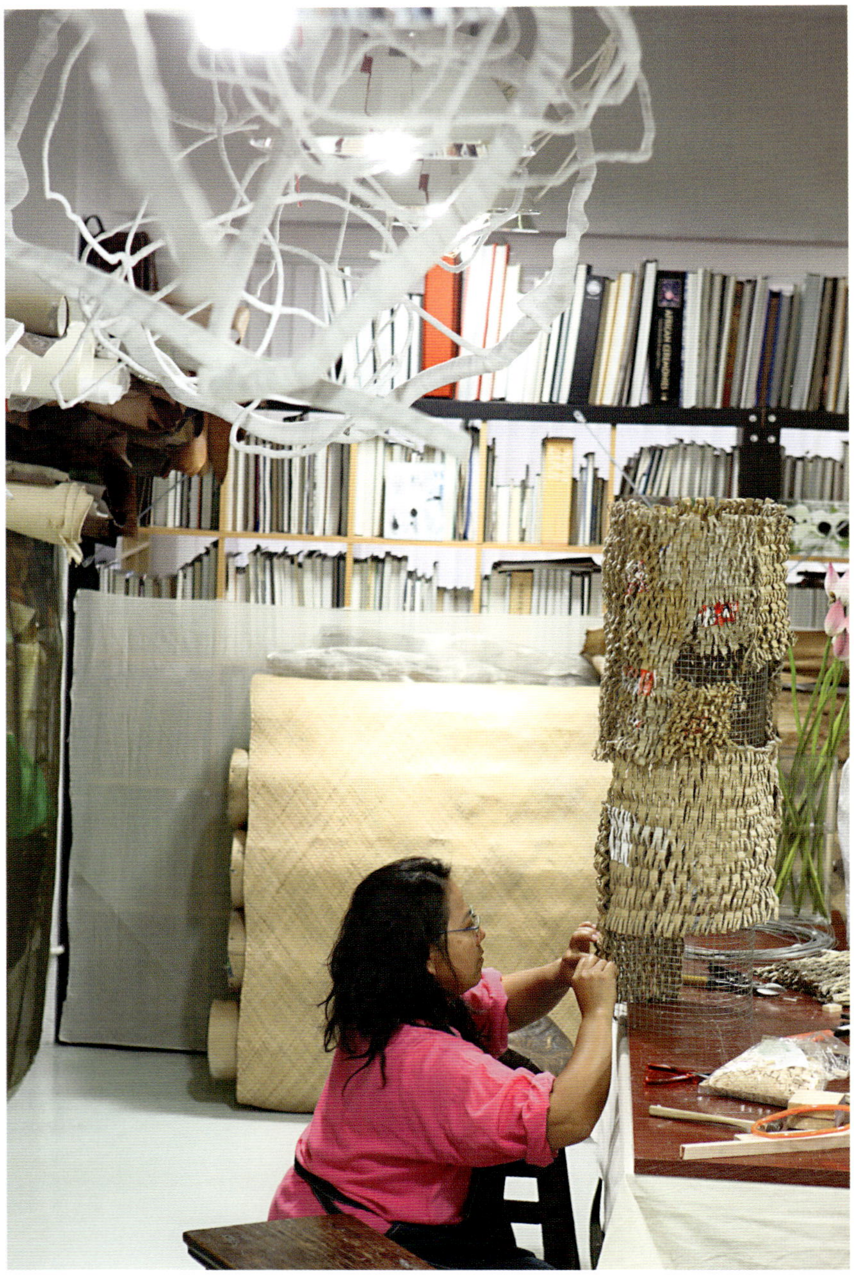

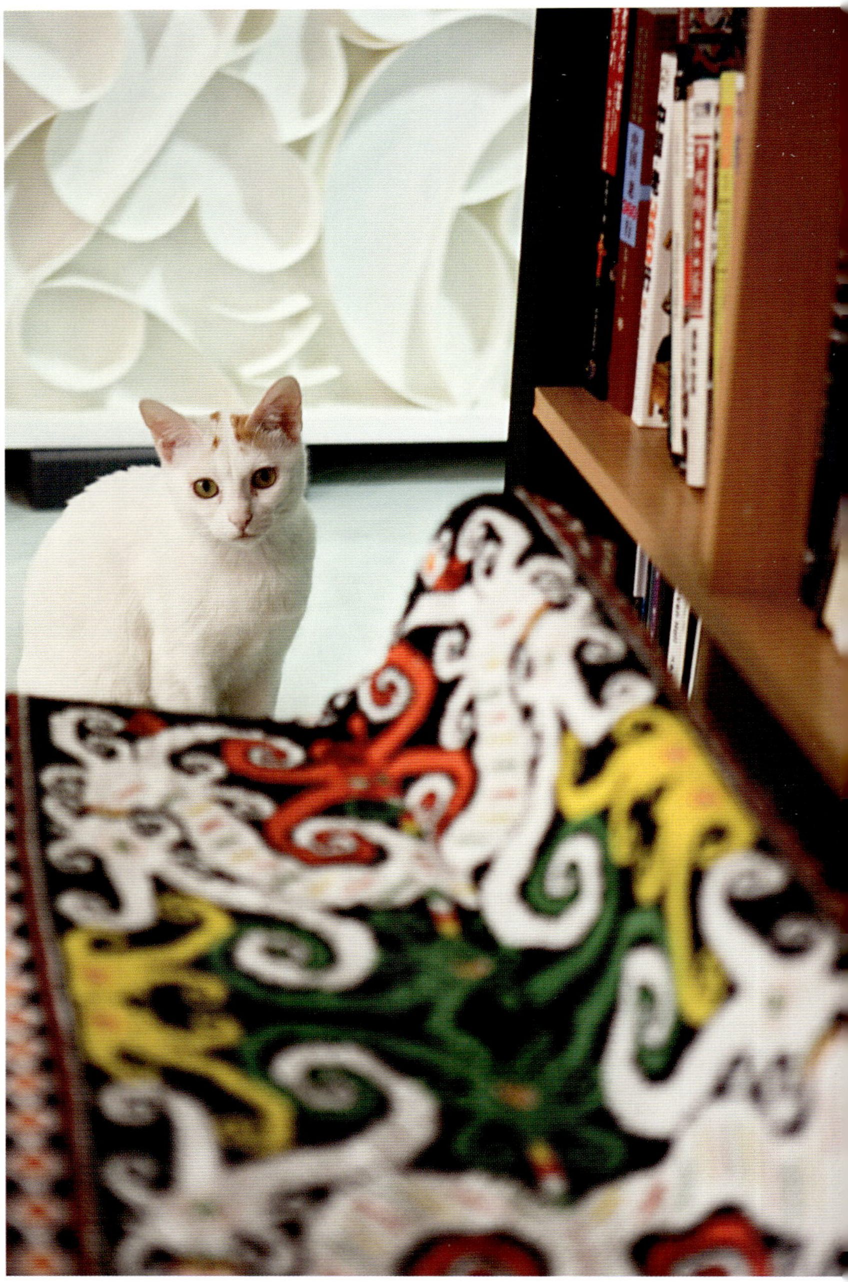

All along Chen has not been searching for herself deliberately, but has been taking things as they come. Her love for art has brought her commissions for two-dimensional, three-dimensional and ceramics projects. Work has kept her so busy that sometimes she needs to hire assistants. She finds her present life challenging but rewarding.

Chen has aspirations that extend beyond Hong Kong. She is living a comfortable life and has established her career, and has lots of friends in Hong Kong, yet her eyes are set on Taiwan. She hopes that one day when she finishes her DFA and has saved enough money, she can go back to her hometown to open a workshop, to continue her artwork and display Paiwan tribal art. Ideally she hopes to set up studios in both Taiwan and Hong Kong.

Art takes courage. The process takes time and energy, but self-discovery and a sense of fulfilment are more precious than any masterpiece.

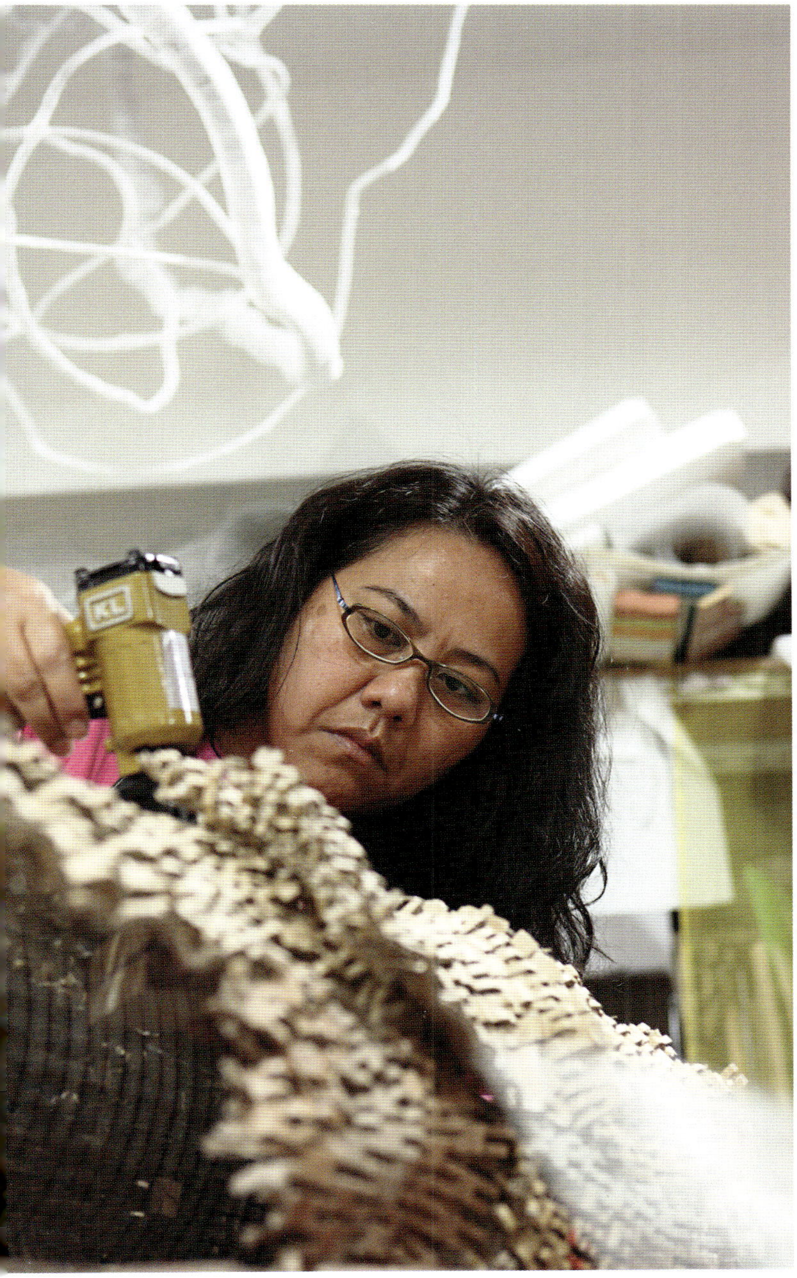

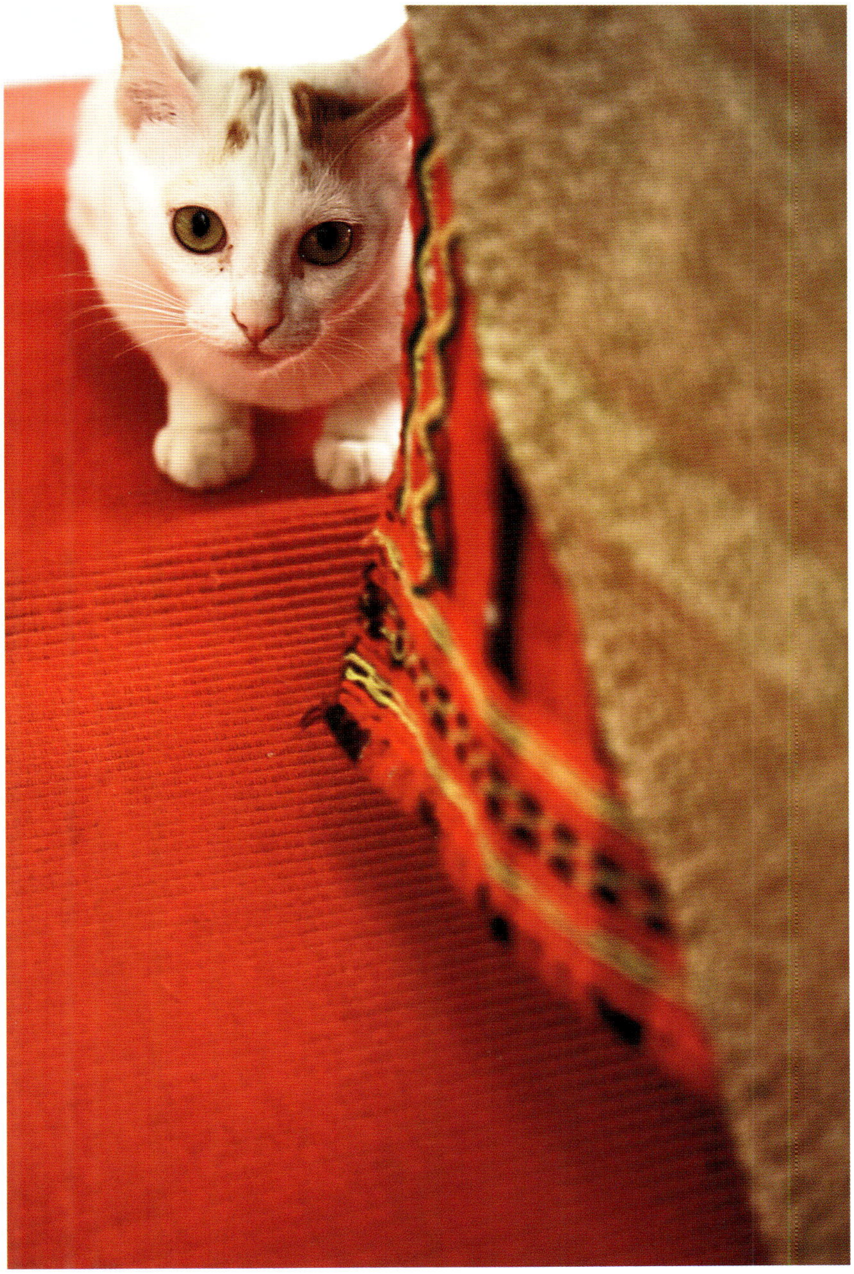

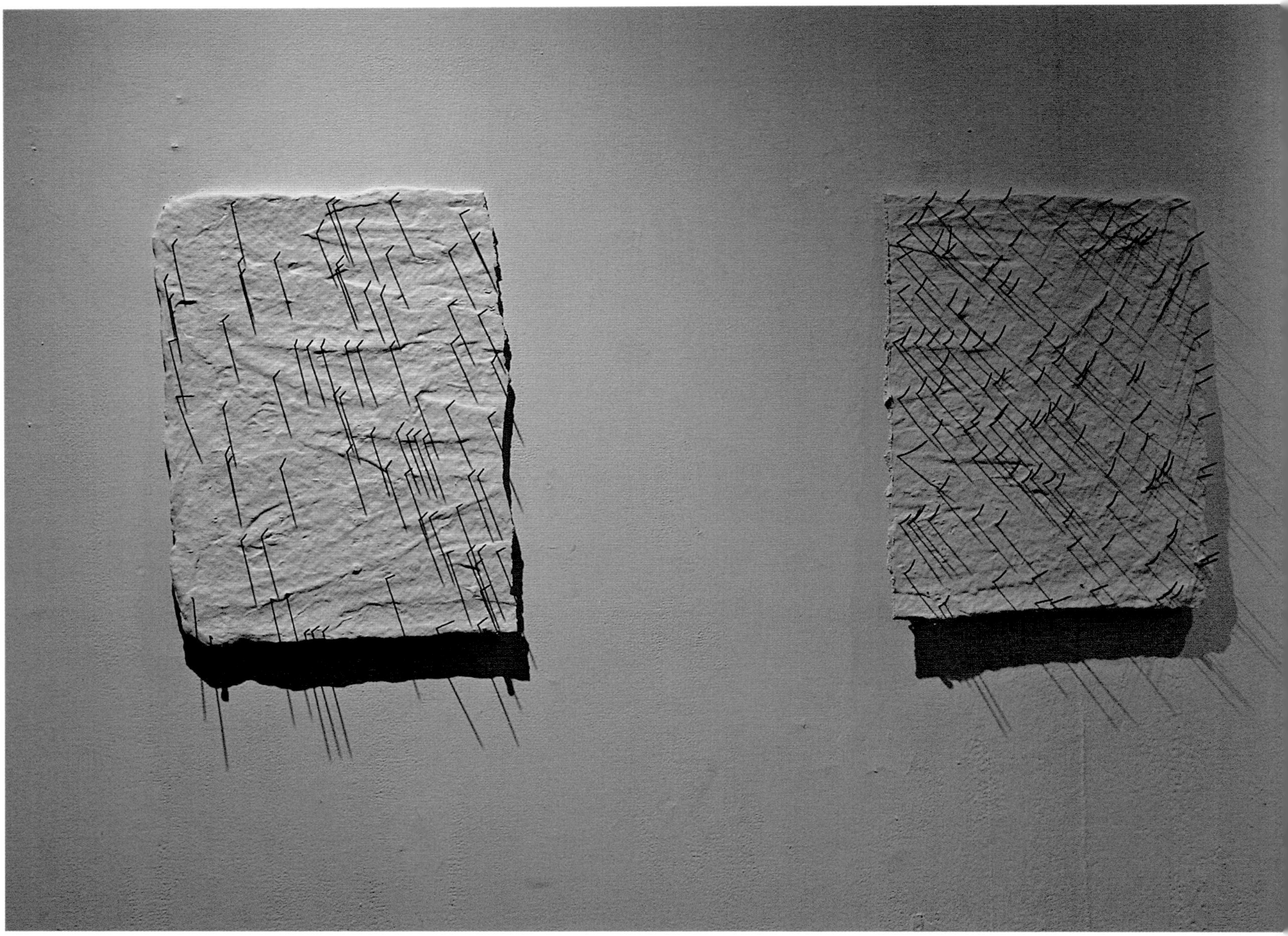

"Specimen No-3"
Bisqueware, porcelain and needle, 33x28x15 cm, 2007

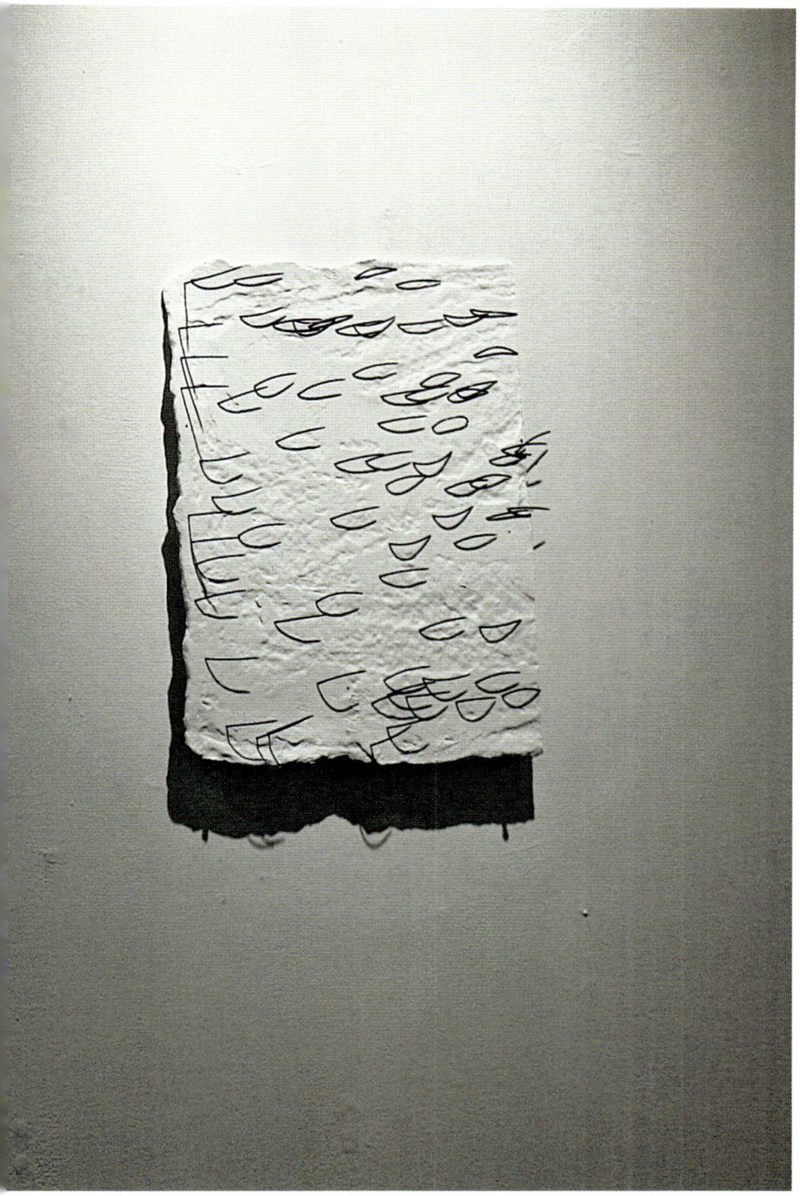

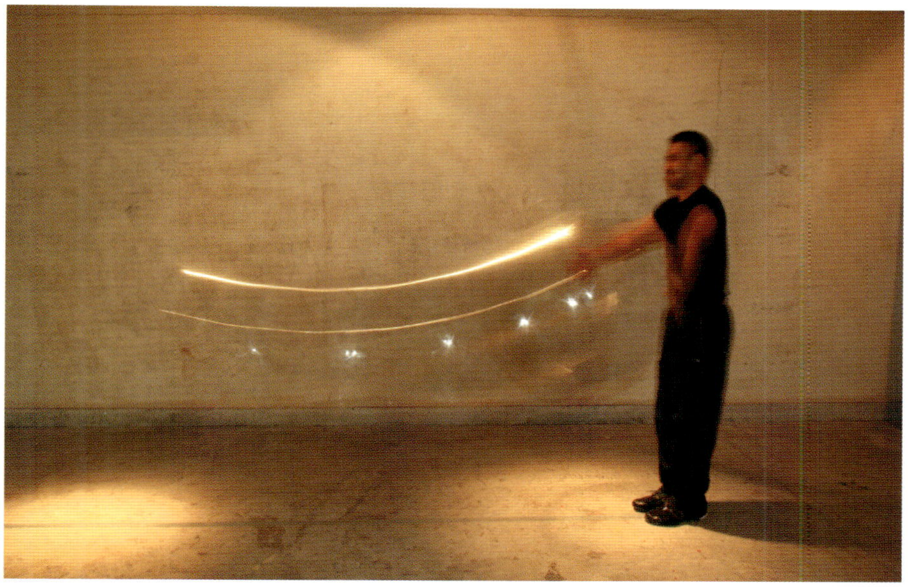

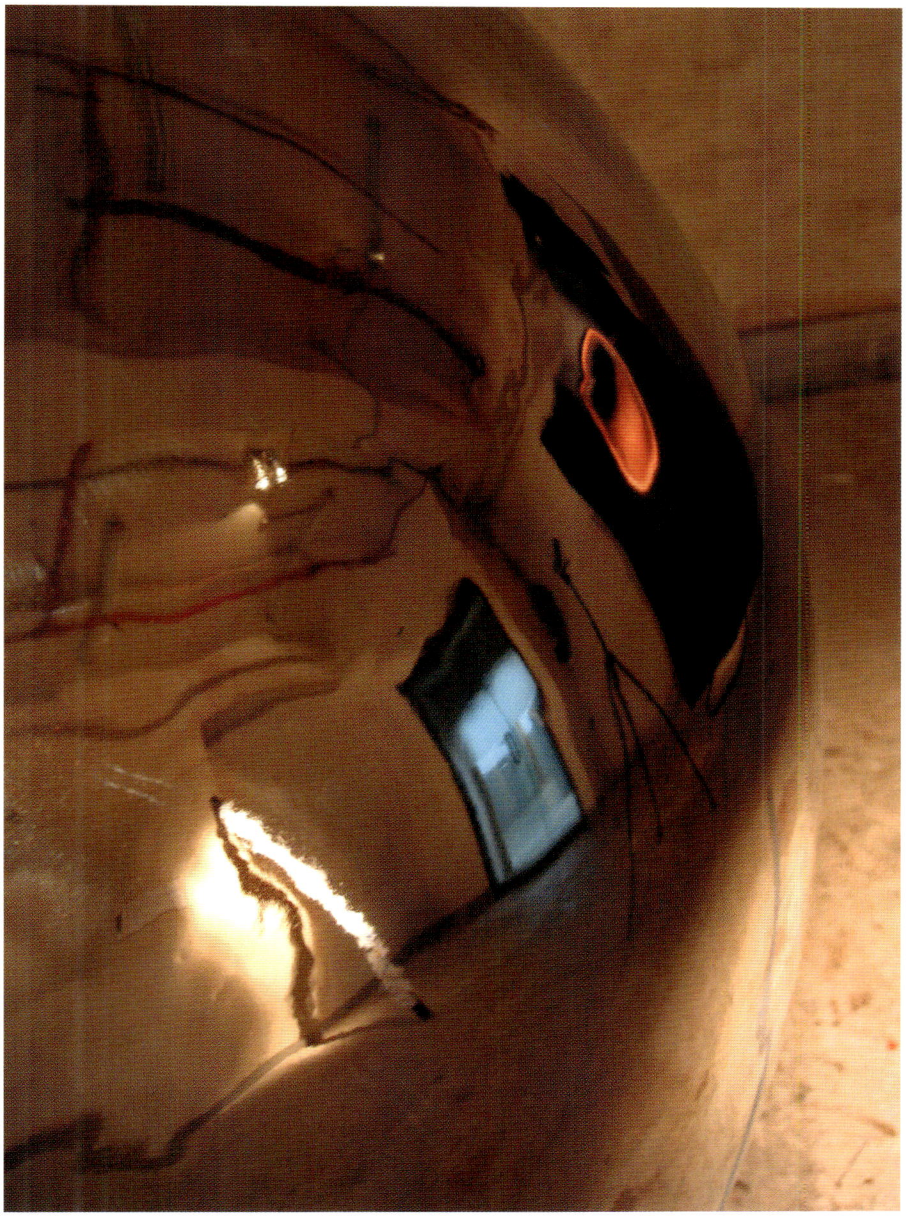

(Right above) "The Ultimate"
Metal ball and wire, 80x80 cm, 2005

(Right bottom) "The Ultimate" (detail)

Florence Yim Wai-wai

Igniting the Flame - A Dream Hunter

By Carl Cheng

Florence Yim Wai-wai is a ceramic artist and art educator. She graduated from the Department of Fine Arts of the Chinese University of Hong Kong (CUHK) in 1982, and obtained a higher certificate in studio ceramics from the former Hong Kong Polytechnic in 1991. From 1985 to 1993 she worked as an assistant curator at the Hong Kong Museum of Art. Later she established the Art Farm Children's Studio with her friends, and has been actively engaging in art education, art publishing and the promotion of ceramics since then. From 2002 to 2003 she was the chairperson of the Contemporary Ceramic Society (Hong Kong). From 2004 to 2007 she was an instructor and the course coordinator of the art specialist course in ceramics run by the Art Promotion Office. In 2007 she participated in the artist-in-residence programme at the Shigaraki Ceramic Cultural Park in Japan. Her ceramics explore the interrelationship of earth, the body and the soul. The forms of human organs and biochemical mechanisms appear frequently in her works. She uses mixed media, but ceramics remain her primary material. Her works are collected by the Hong Kong Museum of Art, the Hong Kong Heritage Museum and private collectors.

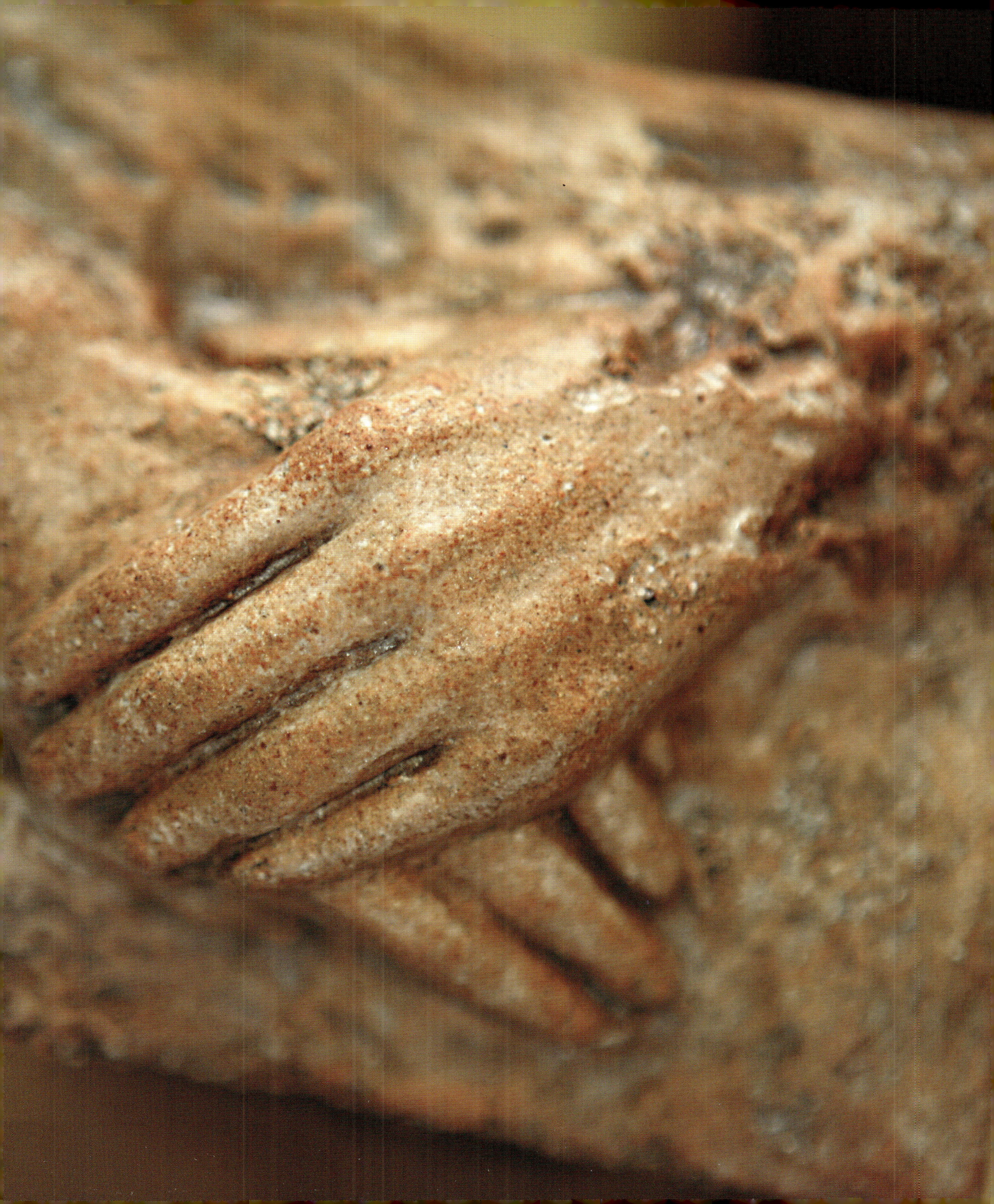

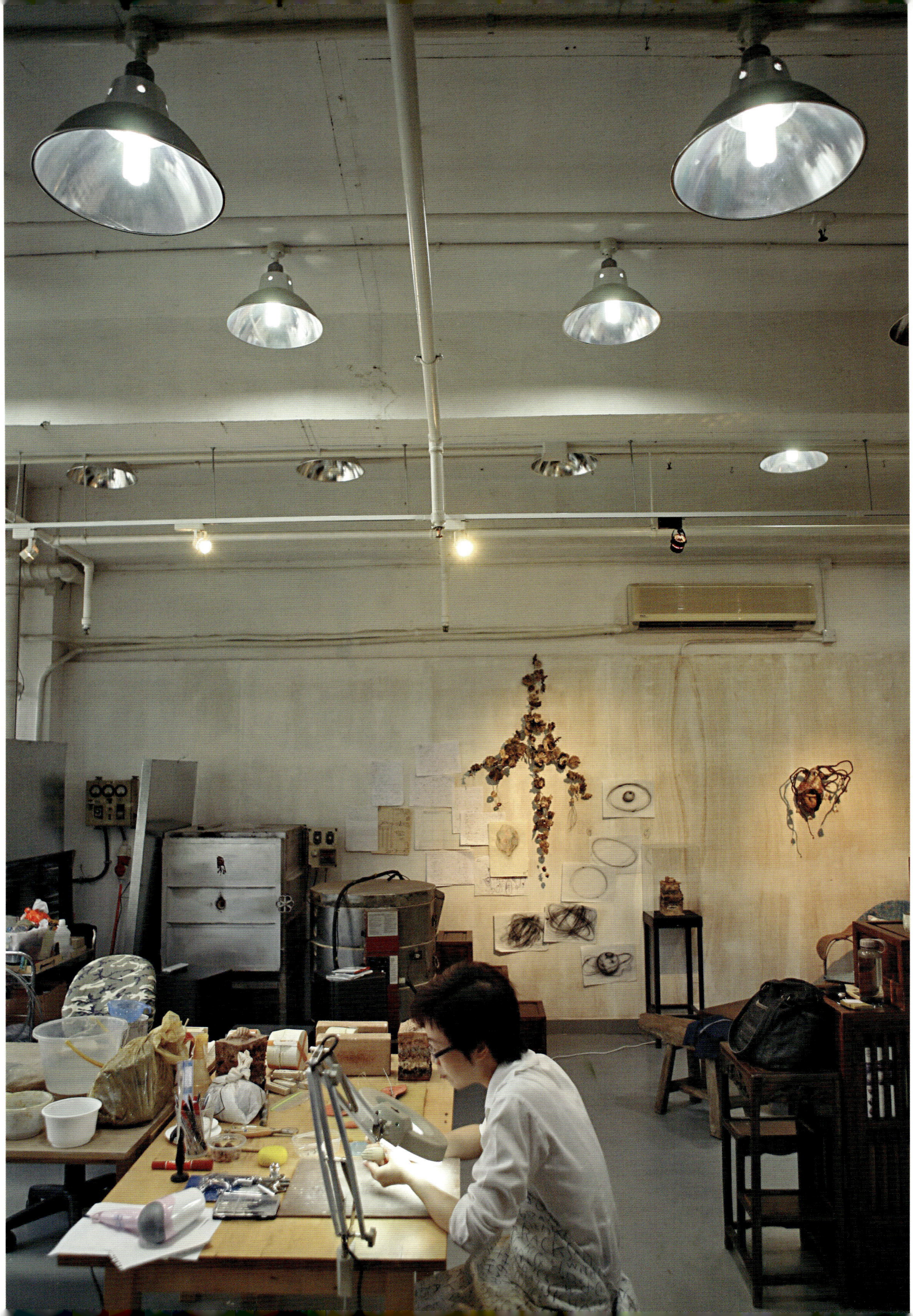

To realise one's dreams requires belief, will and courage. Fortunately there are still people in search of their dreams who have passion and strength. Life is delightful if you encounter people striving for a common goal. Ceramicist Yim Wai-wai is one dreamer in the promotion of art education.

Yim was an art-lover at a very young age. Her artistic talent was discovered by her teacher at St Catharine's School for Girls, which placed importance on art education. Deeply inspired by Reverend Joyce Bennett, who recognised the power of art to benefit ones mentality and potential, Yim chose art as her elective when she was studying in the science stream in secondary six, and was subsequently admitted to the Department of Fine Arts at the Chinese University of Hong Kong to further her studies. She firmly held on to her belief in the contribution of art education to human development.

On completion of her university education, she first started as a teaching assistant at the CUHK's department of fine arts, and afterwards as an assistant curator at the Hong Kong Museum of Art, specialising in art and education promotion. The series of educational experiences further established determination to promote art education. In 1994, together with her colleagues Chiu Kam-shing and Lee Yuen-wah, the Art Farm Children's Studio (Art Farm) came into existence. Art Farm aims to inspire children and youths by means of creative pedagogy, embedded in a holistic and integrated curriculum, and puts emphasis on self-understanding, cultural knowledge, creative thinking and aesthetic exploration. The team recruits many young artists to join their teaching force, opening up alternative art education outside the school curriculum.

Yim has taken on numerous activities in addition to her teaching, such as workshops, seminars, educational publications and guided exhibition tours, which often involve complicated and tedious logistics. As well as her busy schedule during the day, Yim insists on studio practice in her spare time, as she cannot imagine her life without art. Moreover, various curriculum designs flood her with inspiration, giving her endless energy and motivation in her own art practice.

Yim's early works involved mainly two-dimensional paintings and printmaking, but

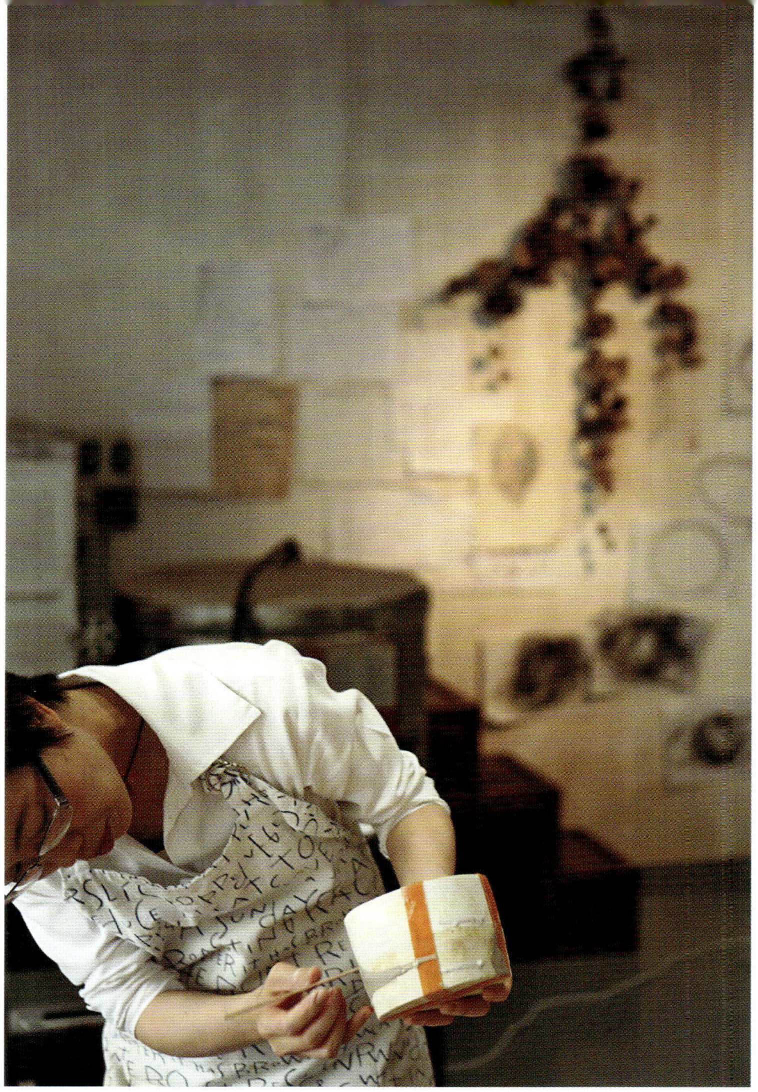

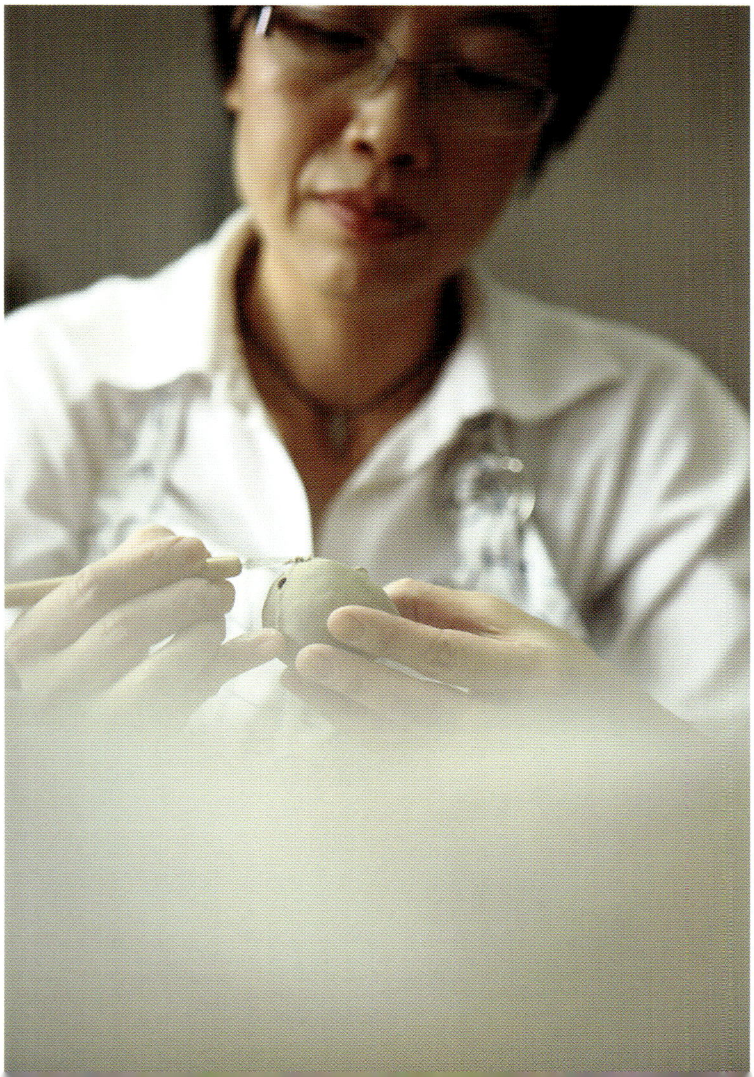

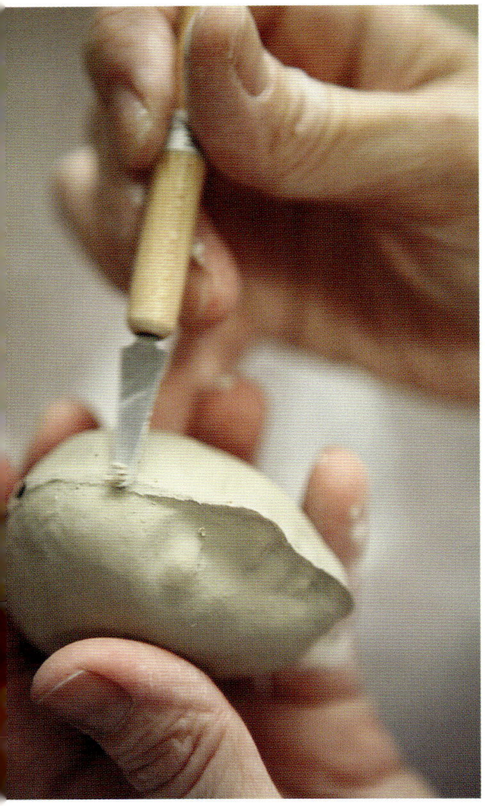

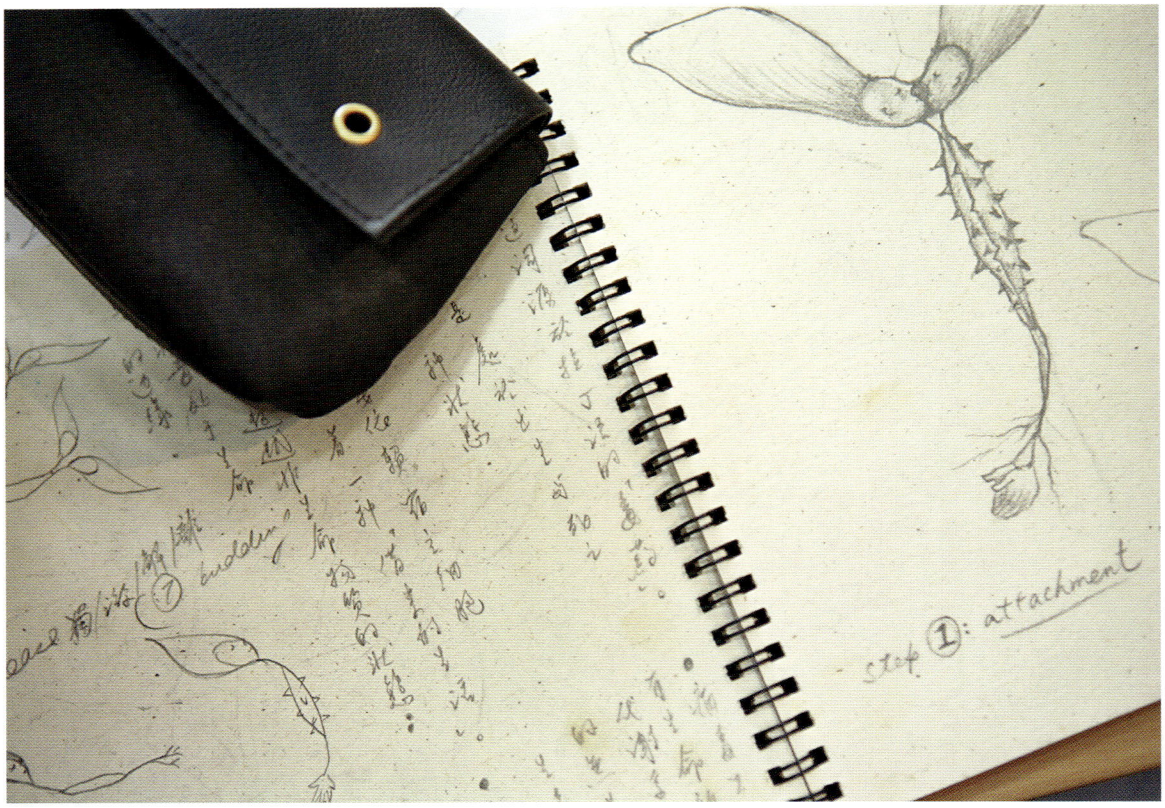

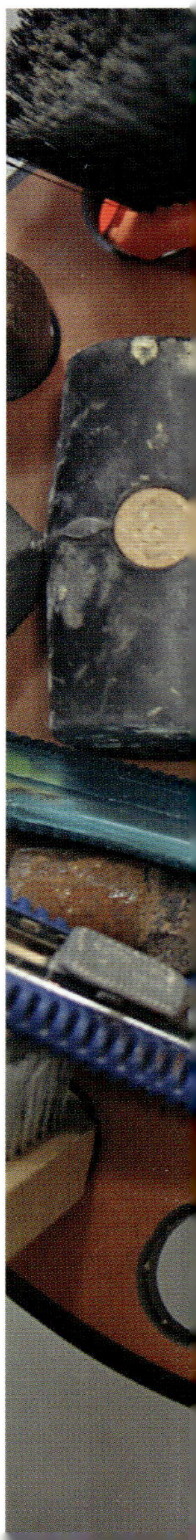

she was interested in other media as well. Later when she was studying for her higher certificate in studio ceramics from the former Hong Kong Polytechnic, she realised that she was even more interested in ceramics. Since then she has been creating with ceramics and mixed media. She says, "I have never restricted myself to clay, but it's just that when I am playing with the material, ideas emerge one after another. Time after time, traces left behind by firing have expressed my deepest feelings. I have never thought of putting ceramics aside."

In the past Yim used to make her art at Art Farm. Owing to limited space and class schedules she had to keep cleaning up for classes and could not concentrate on her own work. After the outbreak of the Severe Acute Respiratory Syndrome (SARS), when the prices of industrial buildings dropped dramatically, she bought her current studio in Chai Wan as storage space for her and her husband. Here she has greater private space to do large-scale work.

Yim jokes about the creative process. "Instead of the works which came about smoothly, I treasure the works which put me in dilemma during the creative process," she says. "Perhaps creative people love looking for enjoyment in hardship."

Yim admits that she has inherited her talents from her parents. Her mother was good at embroidering shoes, while her father was a dim sum master who loved making ornaments with common materials – which we would call mixed media nowadays. Growing up in such an environment, Yim developed an interest in observation, courage for creation and an eagerness for expression, which later became her principles for education. Thanks to Yim's training in science, she possesses both sentimental and logical elements as an artist. Influenced by her father's research in acupuncture and medical theory, Yim is also interested in anatomy, and she enjoys looking at the internal and external structure of human body from different perspectives, as well as the correlation between biochemical mechanisms and mental states – the connection between the physical and the spiritual. Being a Christian, she thinks that every detailed part of the human body is complicated and miraculous, and that nothing is accidental. She recalls, "Once I read an article in the *Hong Kong Economic Journal* about the

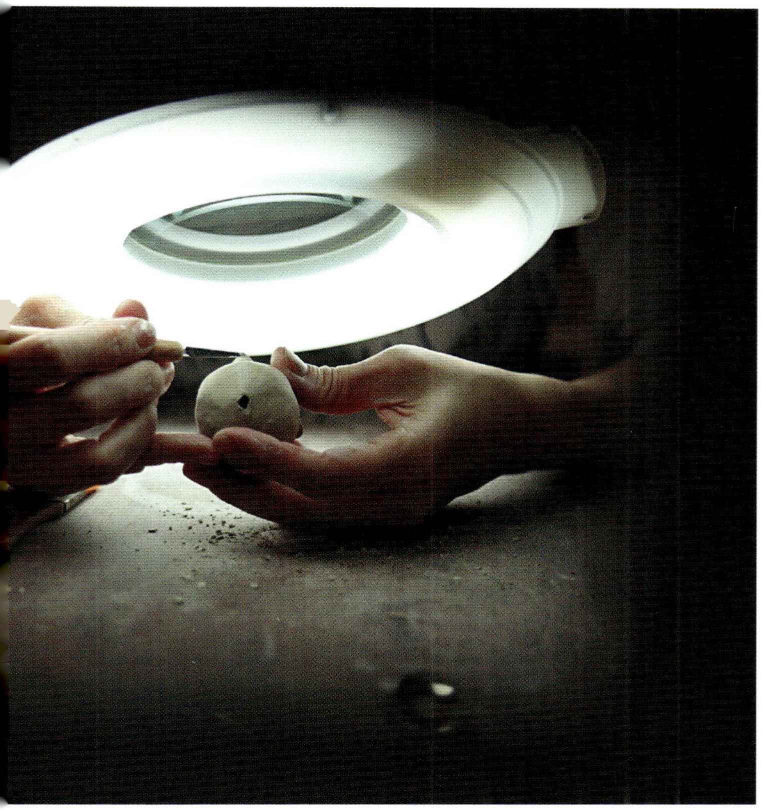

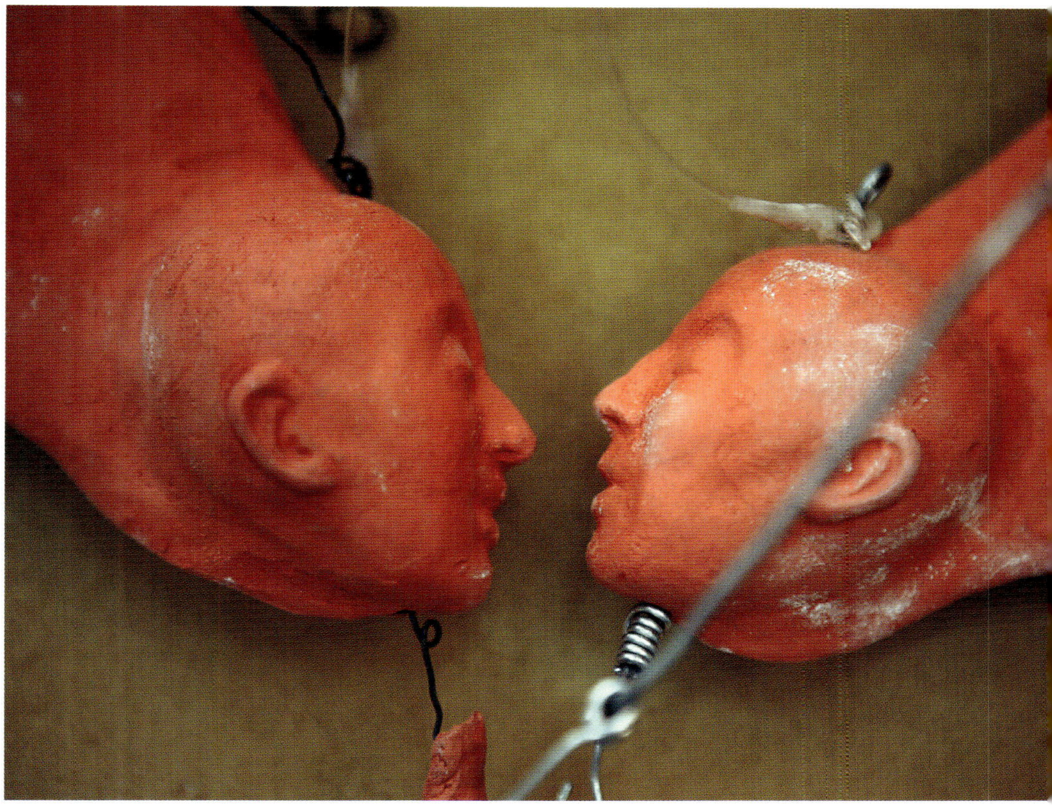

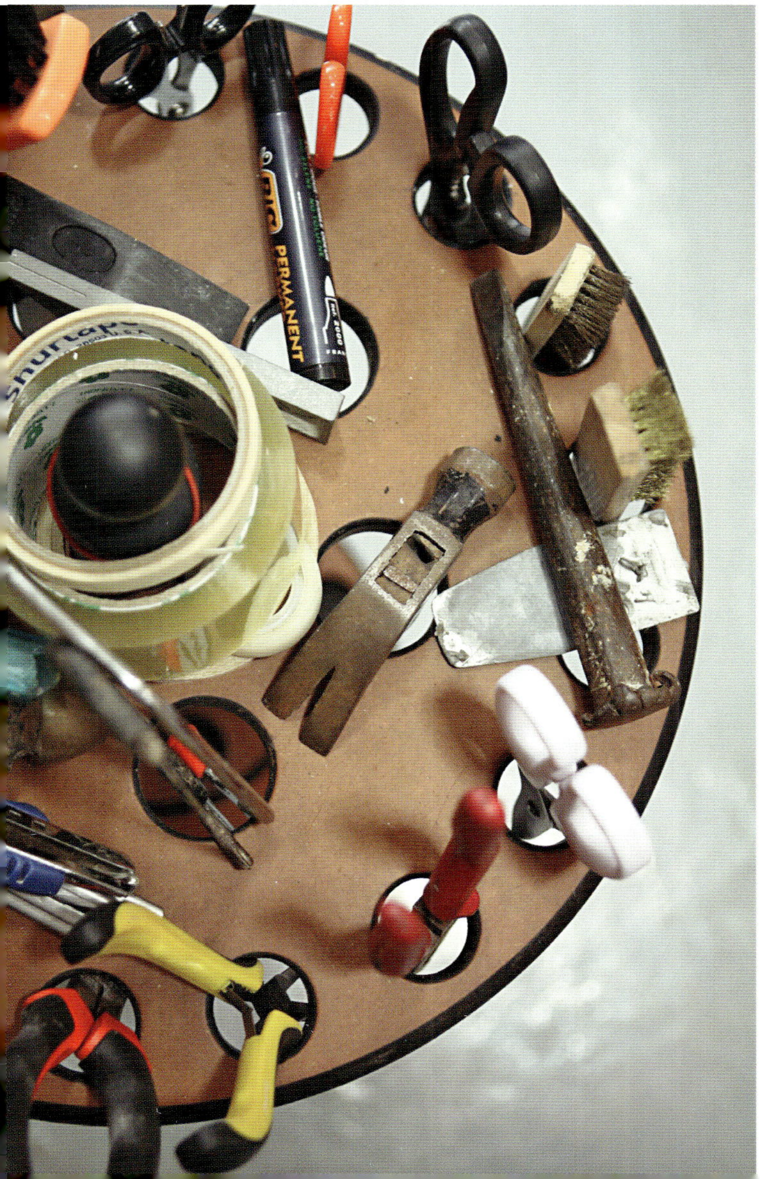

hippocampus of the human brain, which processes long-term memories. In an instant ideas came into my mind that urged me to represent them with art. Subsequently a series of works about human functions emerged."

Yim emphasises that art should react and respond to society, just as she teaches her students to develop their observation. She thinks that people in Hong Kong have been facing significant issues, like the return of sovereignty, financial crisis, SARS; no matter how calm they appear, their hearts are full of conflict. This state of hysteria is well portrayed with clay, since using a spiritual material like clay to represent organic forms carries another layer of symbolic meaning. She says, "Modern people have a common symptom of inconsistency between their body and soul. Sometimes when I look at this condition from a distance, I cannot help feeling the brutality within."

At present Yim takes time from teaching to enable concentration on her artworks. To expand her horizons, she just returned from a three-month artist-in-residence programme at the Shigaraki Ceramic Cultural Park in Japan. She admired the superior Japanese

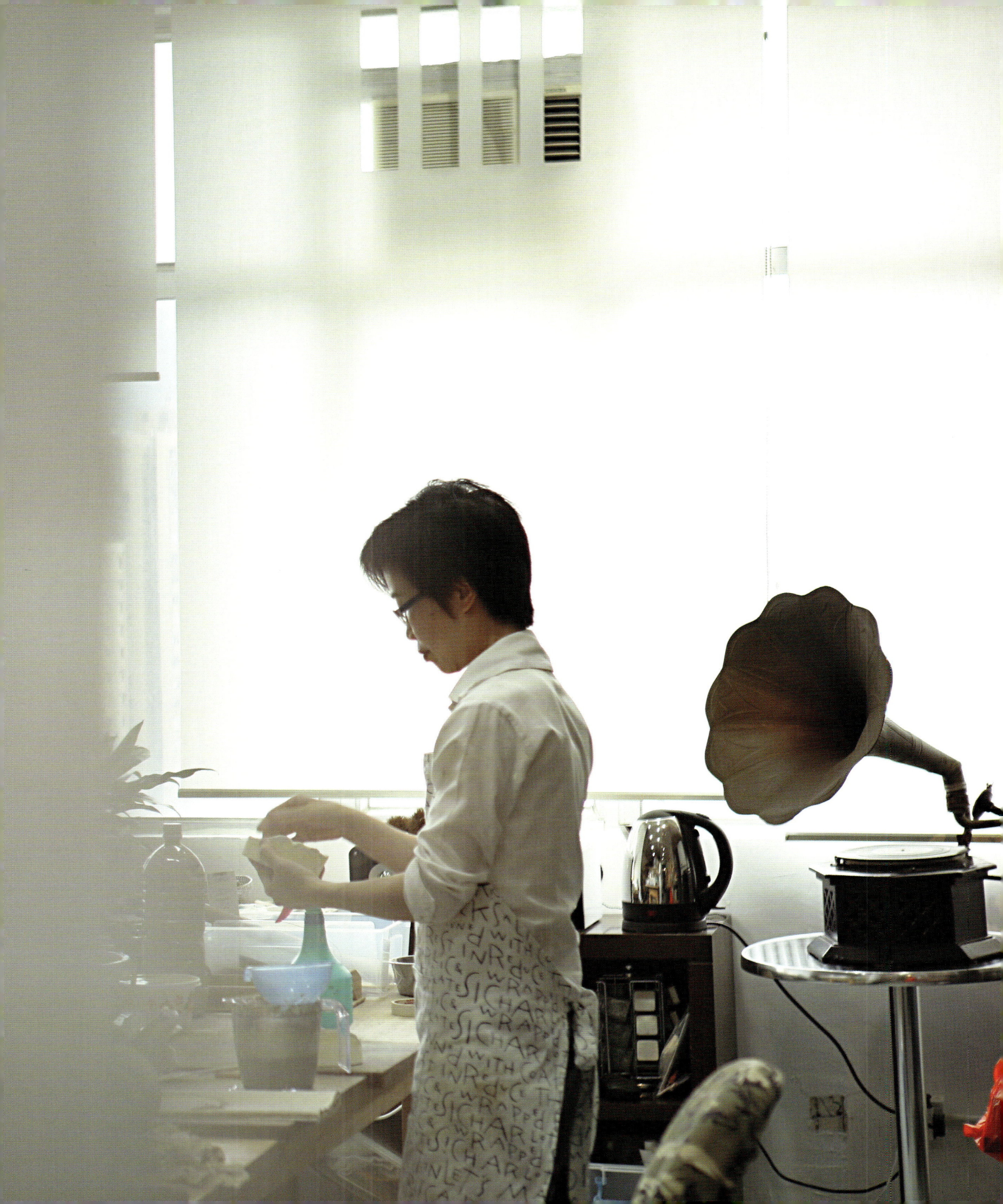

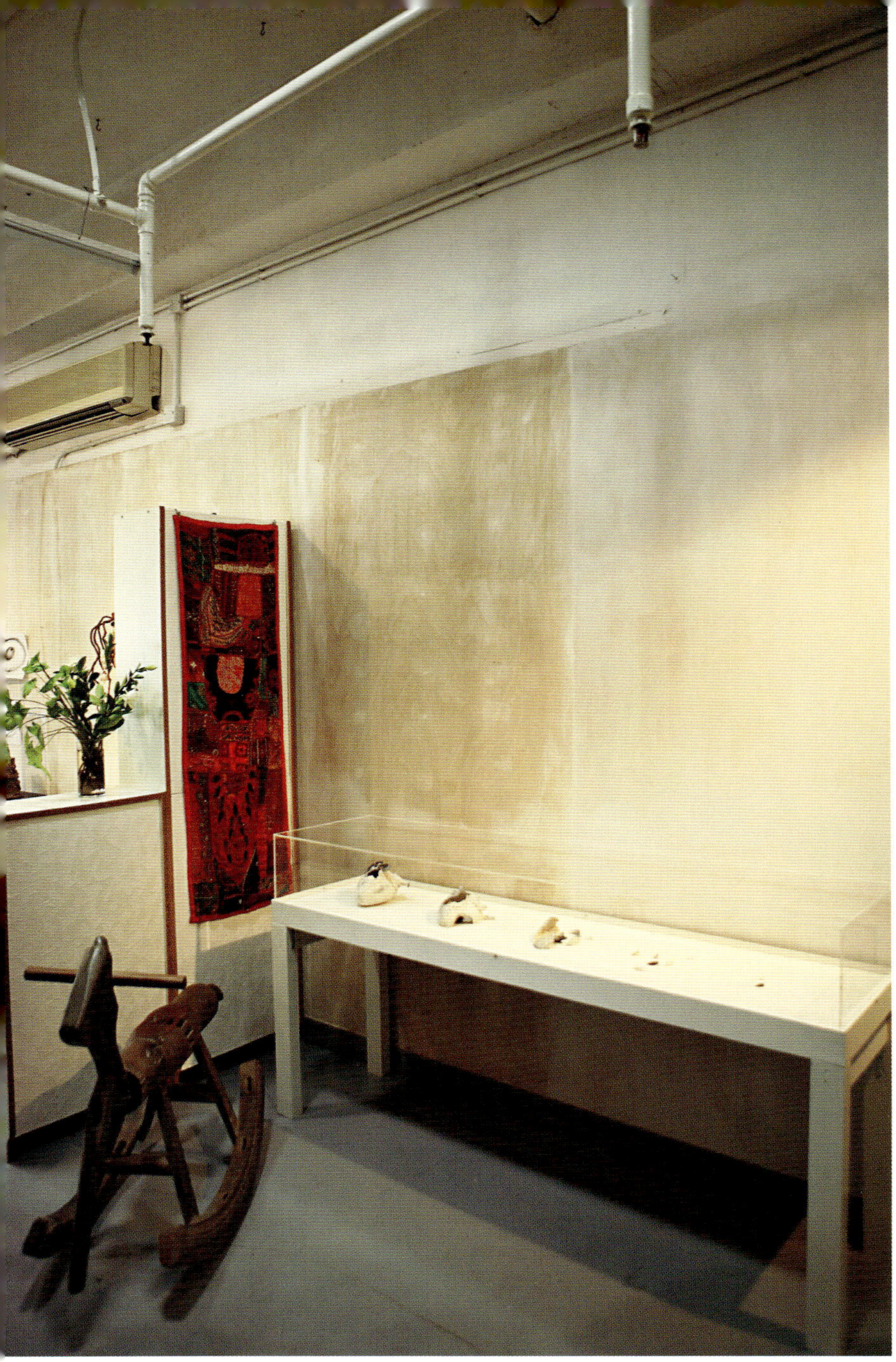

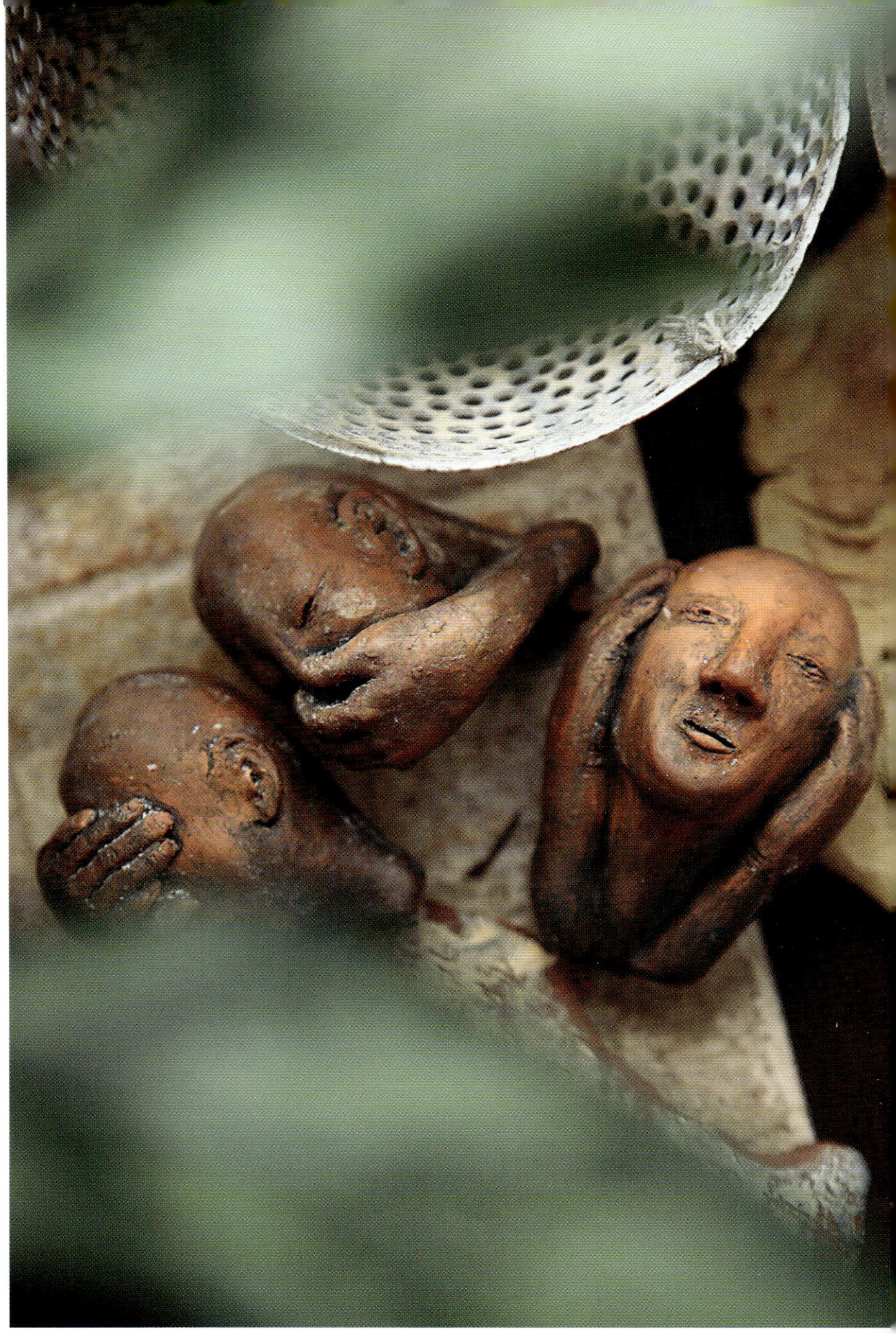

firing techniques, their focus on the texture of materials, their delicate sensitivity to colour and touch, their serious development of techniques and their unyielding persistence. She hopes that she can integrate what she has learned and apply that in her practice one day. After years of experience in ceramics, Yim still has the passion to learn. "The nature of clay and what we have in mind may not always be compatible," she says. "When one can tolerate the other and vice versa, the work will come out smoothly like a fish in the water; otherwise it can be an unbearable torture."

In such a utilitarian and shortsighted society, a dreamer with aspirations for art and education will not always have an easy path, but there are companions along the way. Yim has devoted herself wholeheartedly to art education for more than two decades, yet there is still a long way to go. Art and religion both have a different value system from the secular realm; they emphasise giving to receiving and a return that can be way beyond expectation. As it says in the Bible's Book of John, chapter 12 verse 24:

"If a seed of grain does not go into the earth and come to an end, it is still a seed and no more; but through its death it gives much fruit."

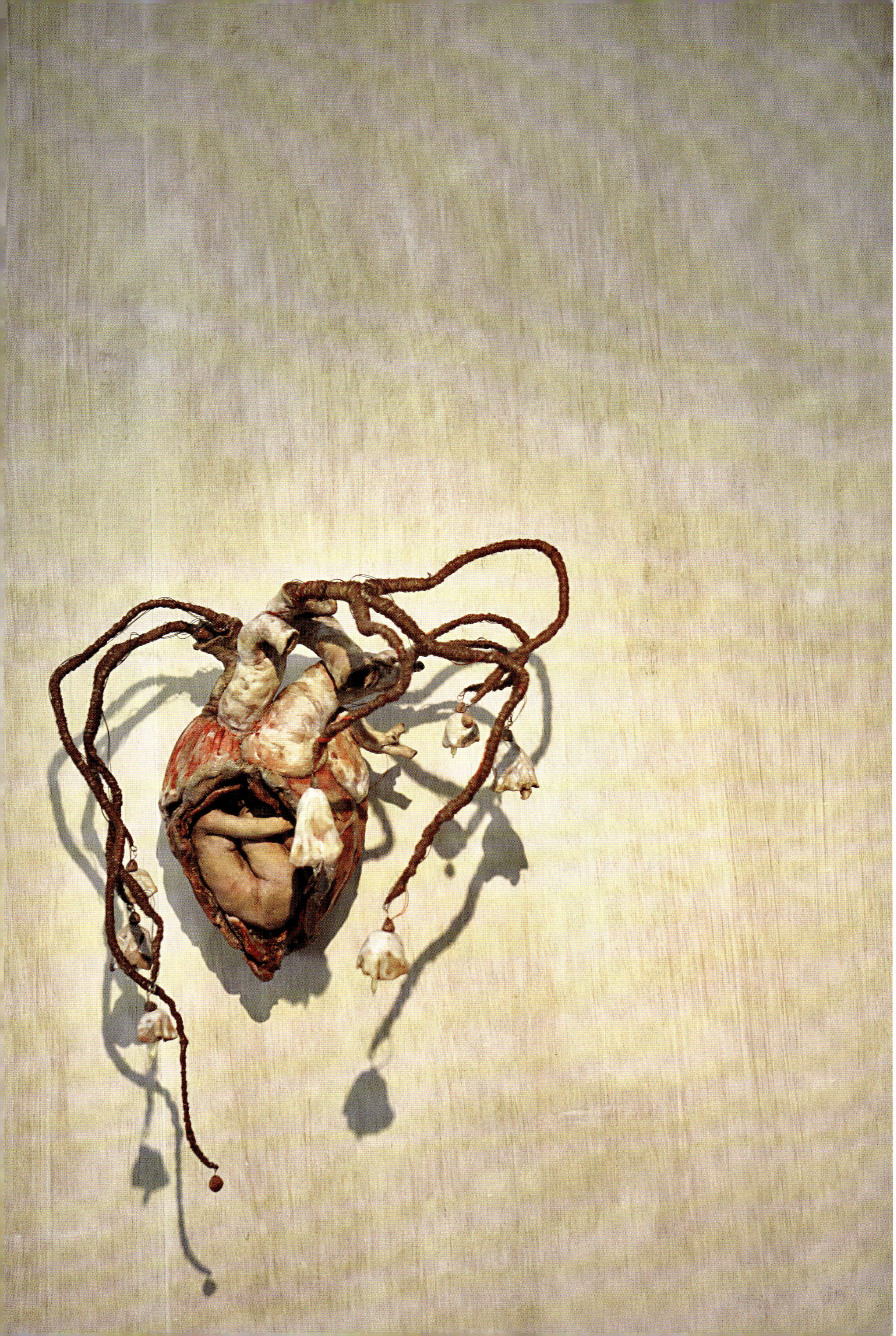

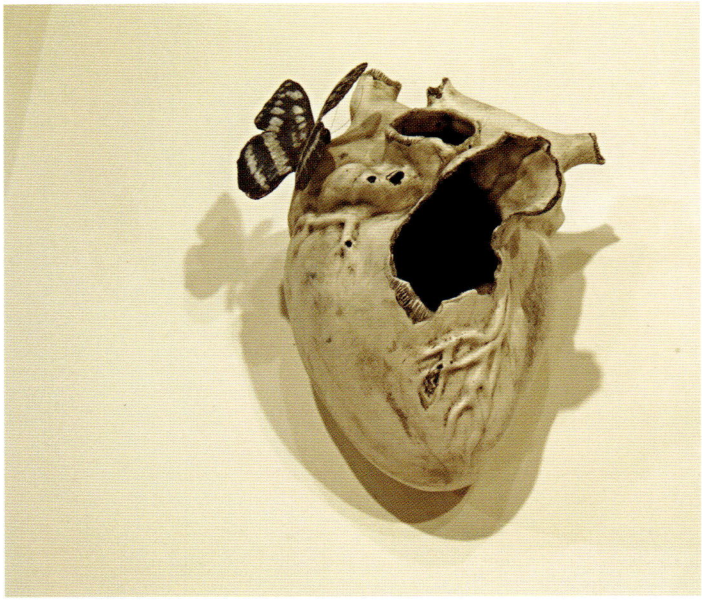

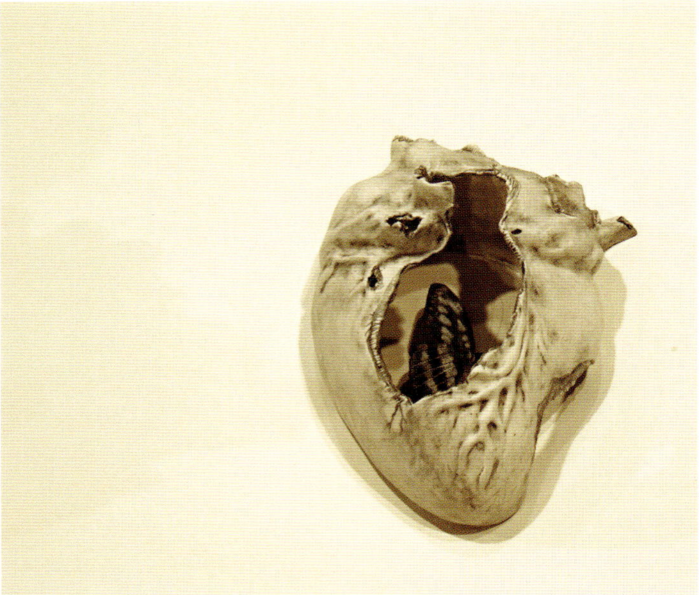

(Above, from left to right) The Touch of Tenderness #1 (Part 1 – Part 5)
Porcelain, 50x182x22 cm, 2007

(Right bottom) Life Goes
Earthenware, 14x16x26 cm, 2007

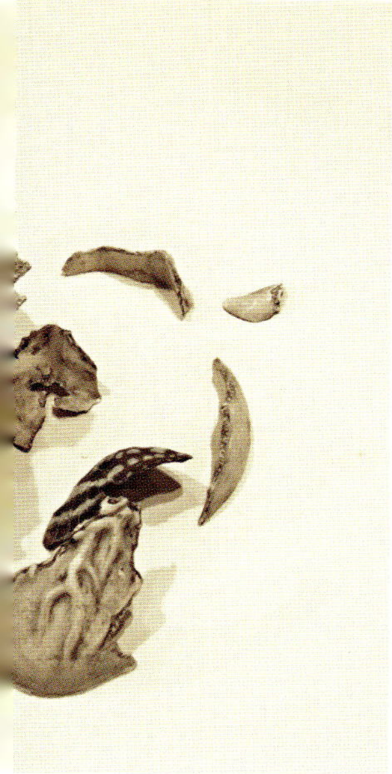
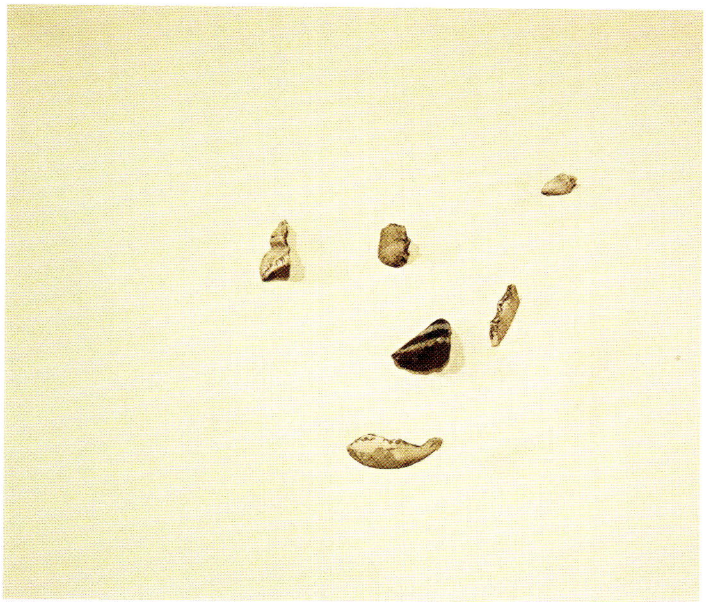
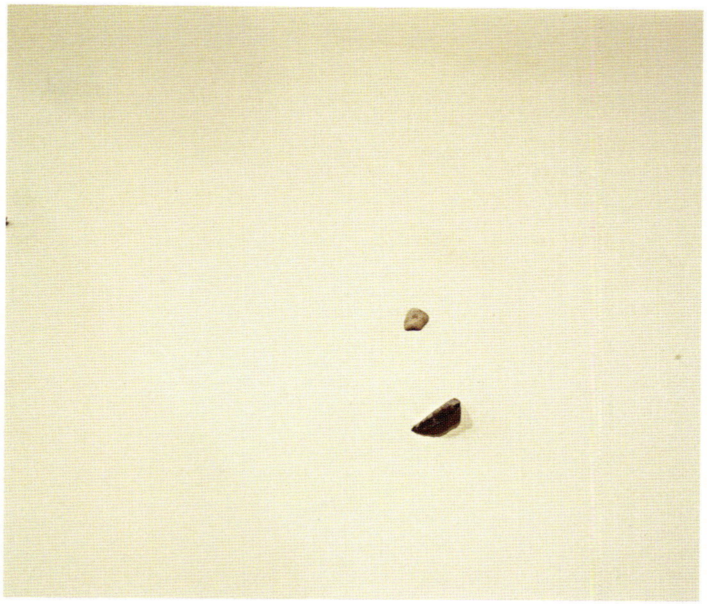
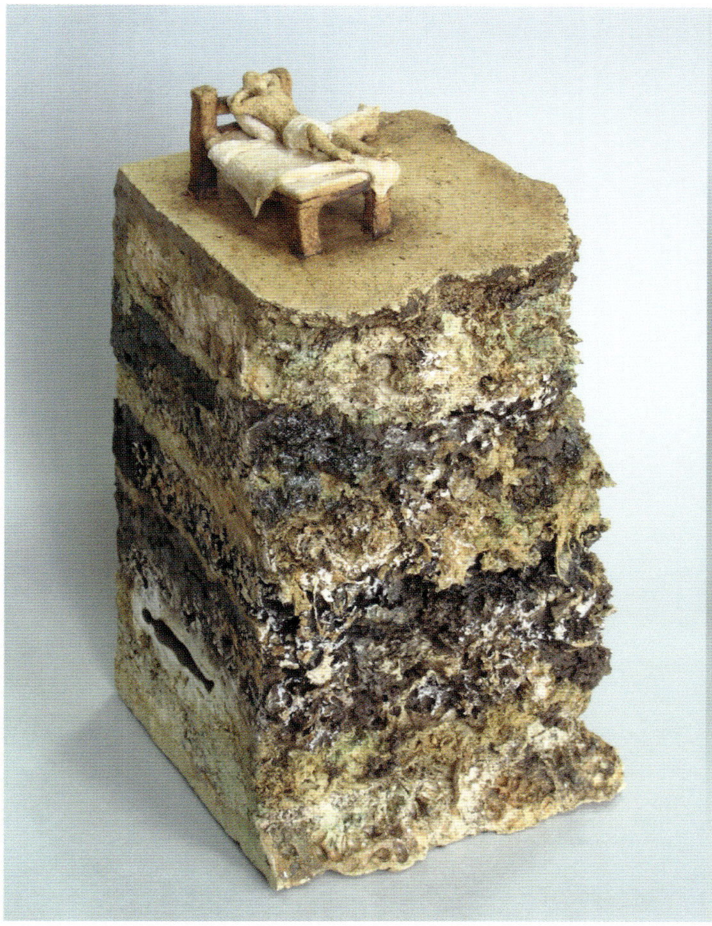
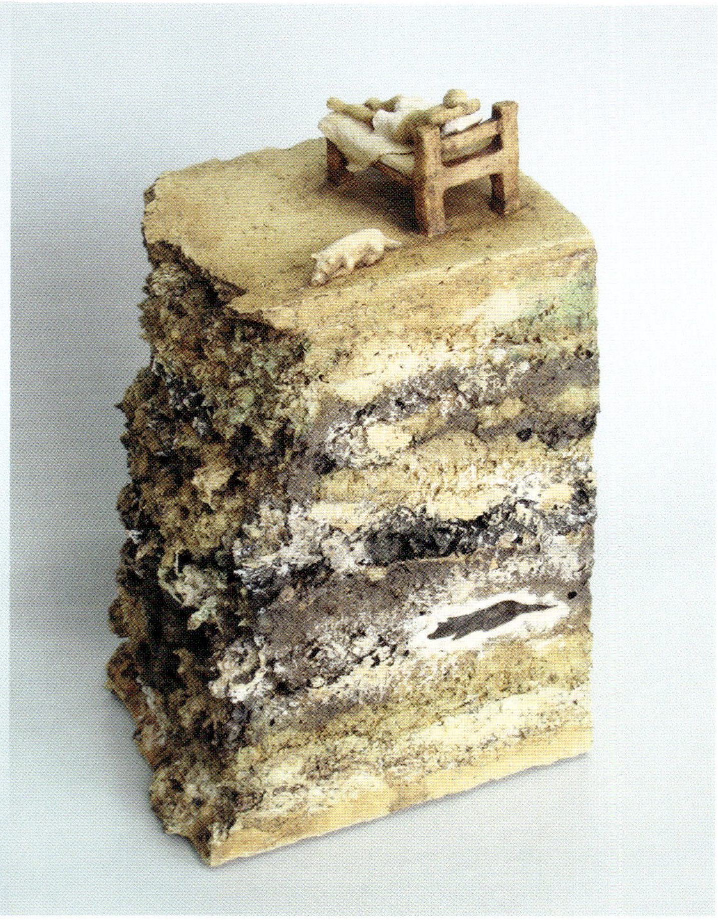

The Shared Studio

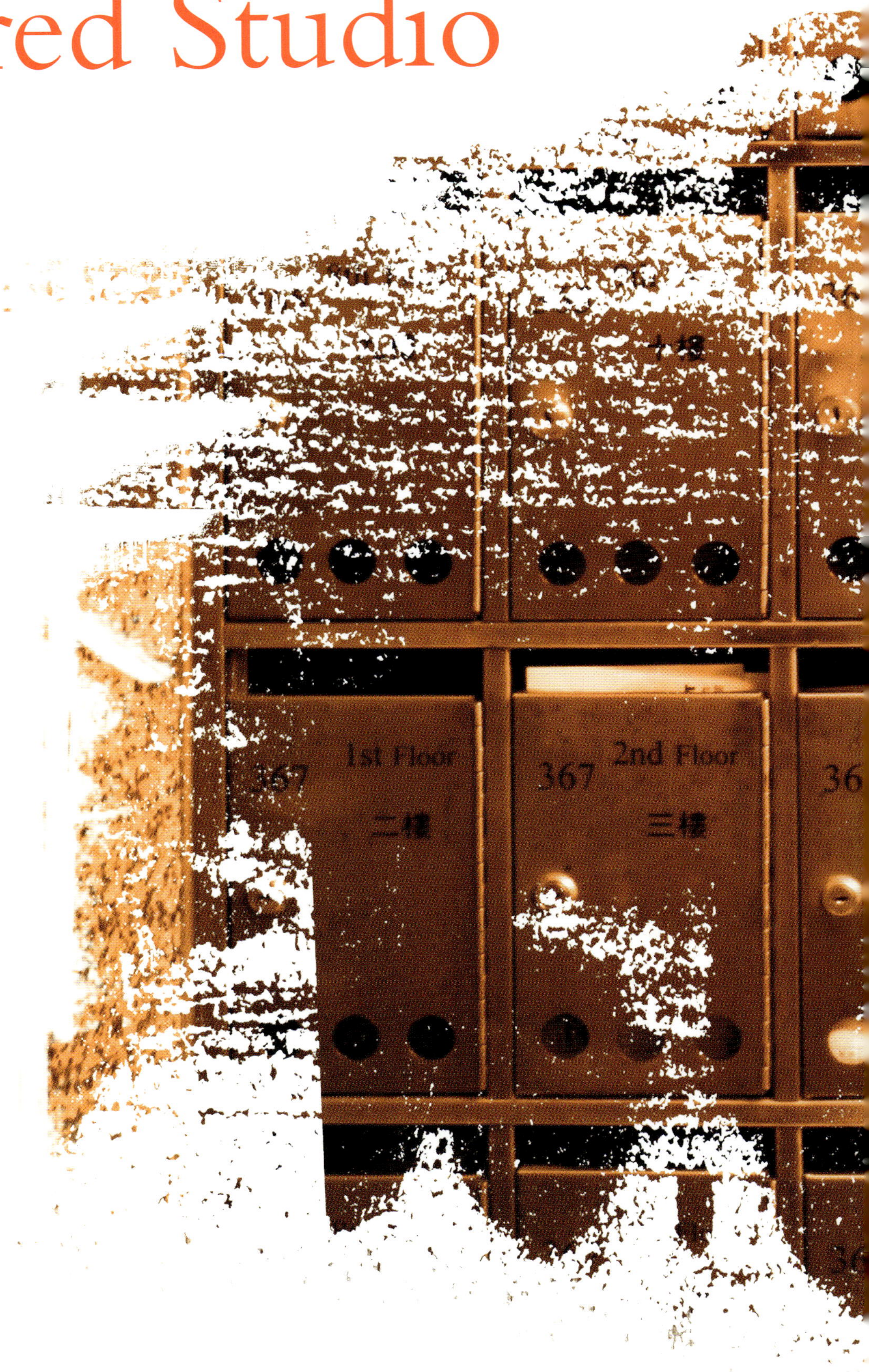

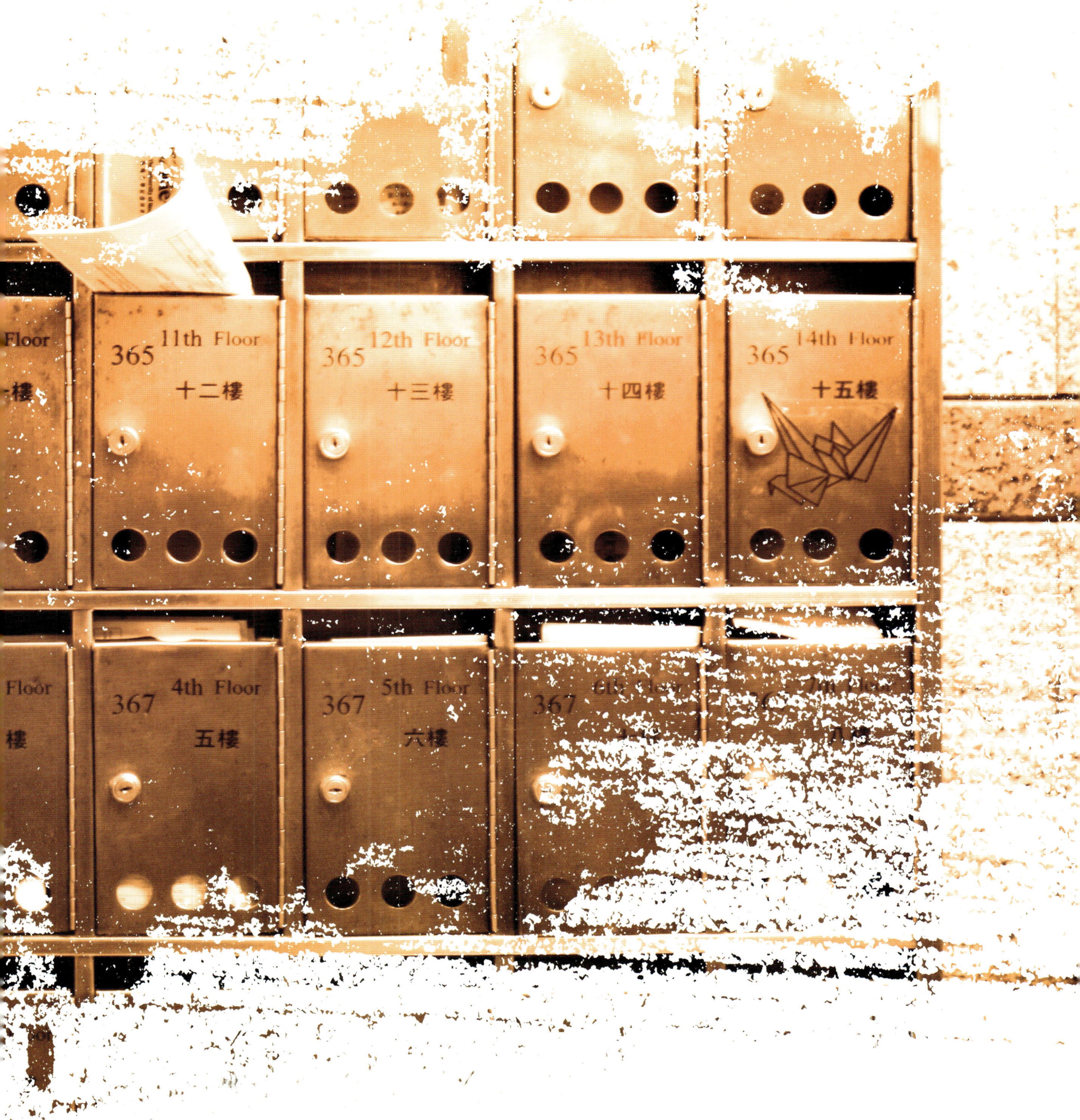
365 11th Floor
十二樓
365 12th Floor
十三樓
365 13th Floor
十四樓
365 14th Floor
十五樓
367 4th Floor
五樓
367 5th Floor
六樓
367

Choi Yan-chi and Hon Chi-fun

Lasting Devotion and Passion

By Alice Choi and Carl Cheng

Choi Yan-chi studied in the United States from 1973 to 1978, where she earned a Bachelor and Master's degree in fine arts from the School of the Art Institute of Chicago. She taught at the Hong Kong Polytechnic Swire School of Design from 1979 to 1986. In 1993 she was invited to the First Asia-Pacific Triennial in Australia and had her solo exhibition *Raumfarben (Room of Colour)* at Haus der Kulturen der Welt in Berlin, after which she lived in Toronto, Canada. She returned to Hong Kong in 1997, and in 1998 established 1a space, a non-profit making art space. In the same year, she resumed full-time teaching at Hong Kong Institute of Vocational Education, and in 2003 participated in the founding of the Academy of Visual Arts of the Hong Kong Baptist University, where she has been teaching ever since.

Hon Chi-fun attended private classes in childhood and later continued with formal schooling in Wah Yan College, Kowloon. He is a self-taught painter and started to paint in 1954, always joining his artist friends in painting and drawing outdoors. He had his first solo exhibition at the Chatham Galleries in 1963, and became a founding member of the Circle Art Group the following year. In 1969 he was awarded the John D Rockefeller III Fund Fellowship, and was the first Hong Kong grantee ever. He retired early in 1972 to become a full-time artist. He suffered from a stroke in 2000 but published *Space and Passion: The Art of Hon Chi-fun* in the same year. In 2005 his retrospective exhibition, *Secret Code: The Art of Hon Chi-fun* was organised at the Hong Kong Museum of Art.

Choi and Hon married in 1976, and their son Wang-kwong was born in 1979.

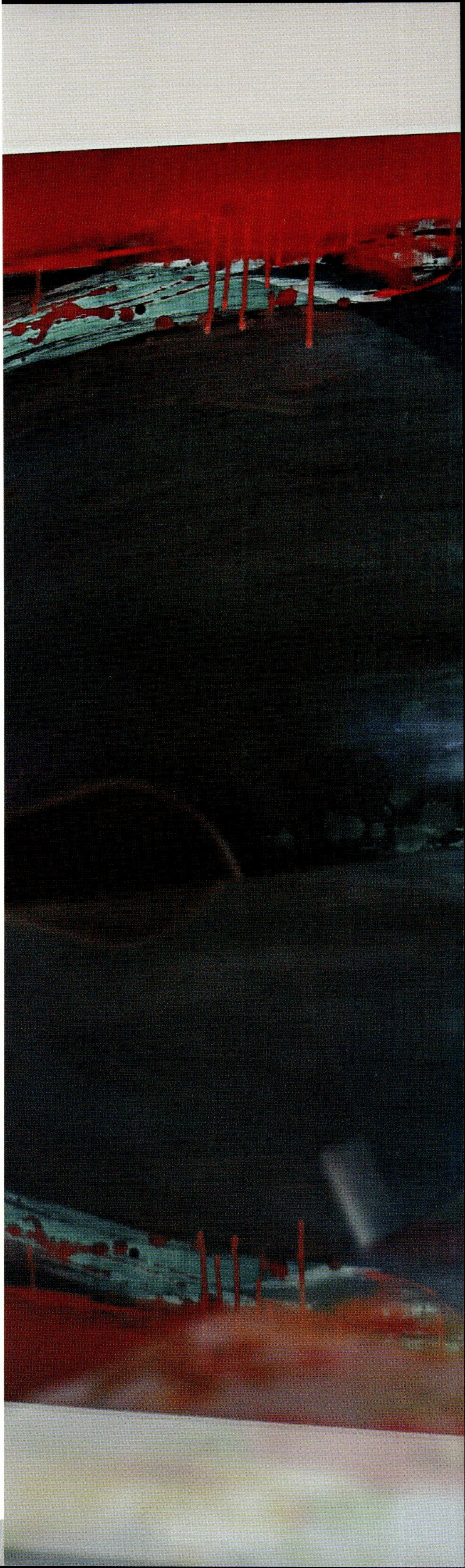

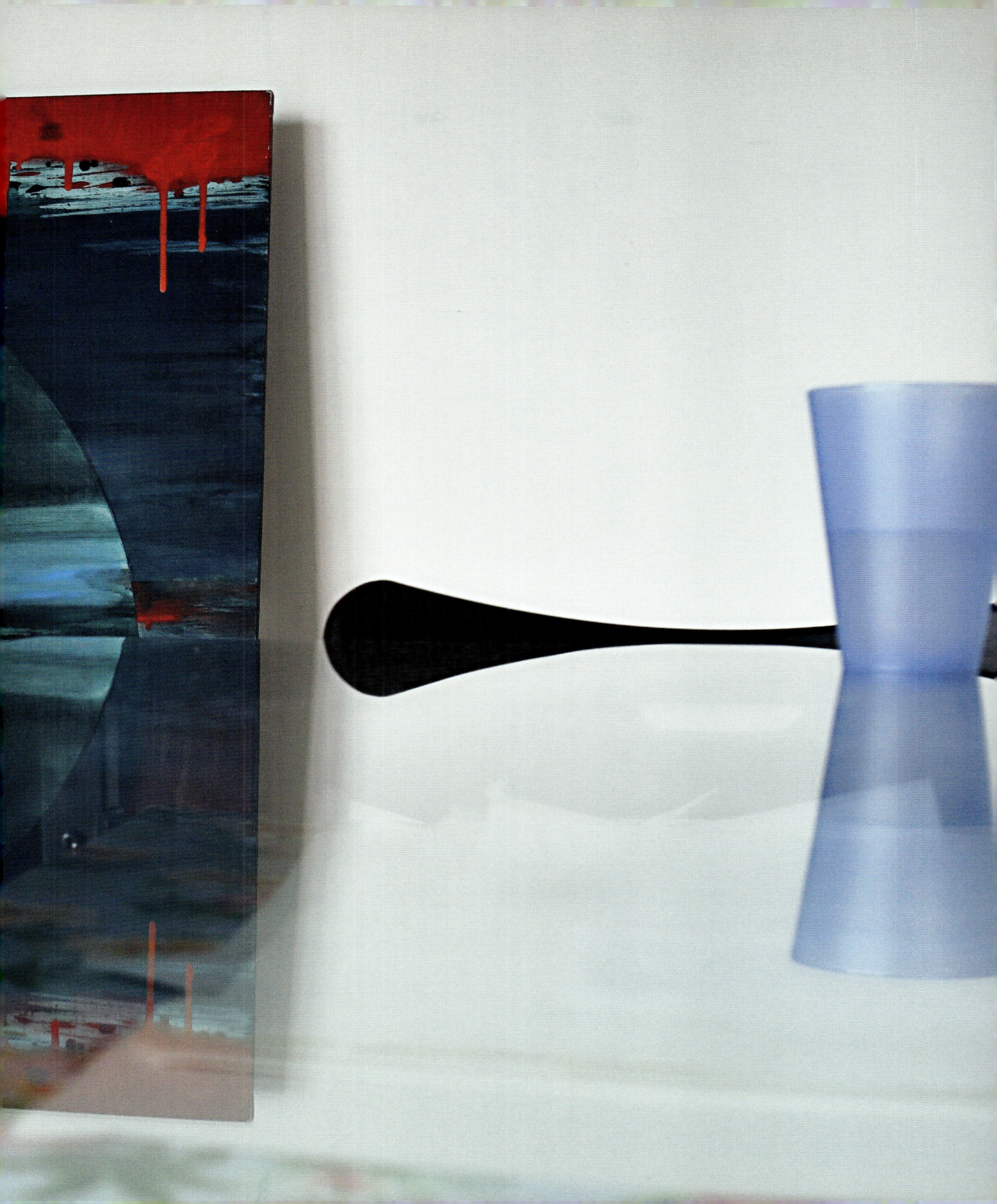

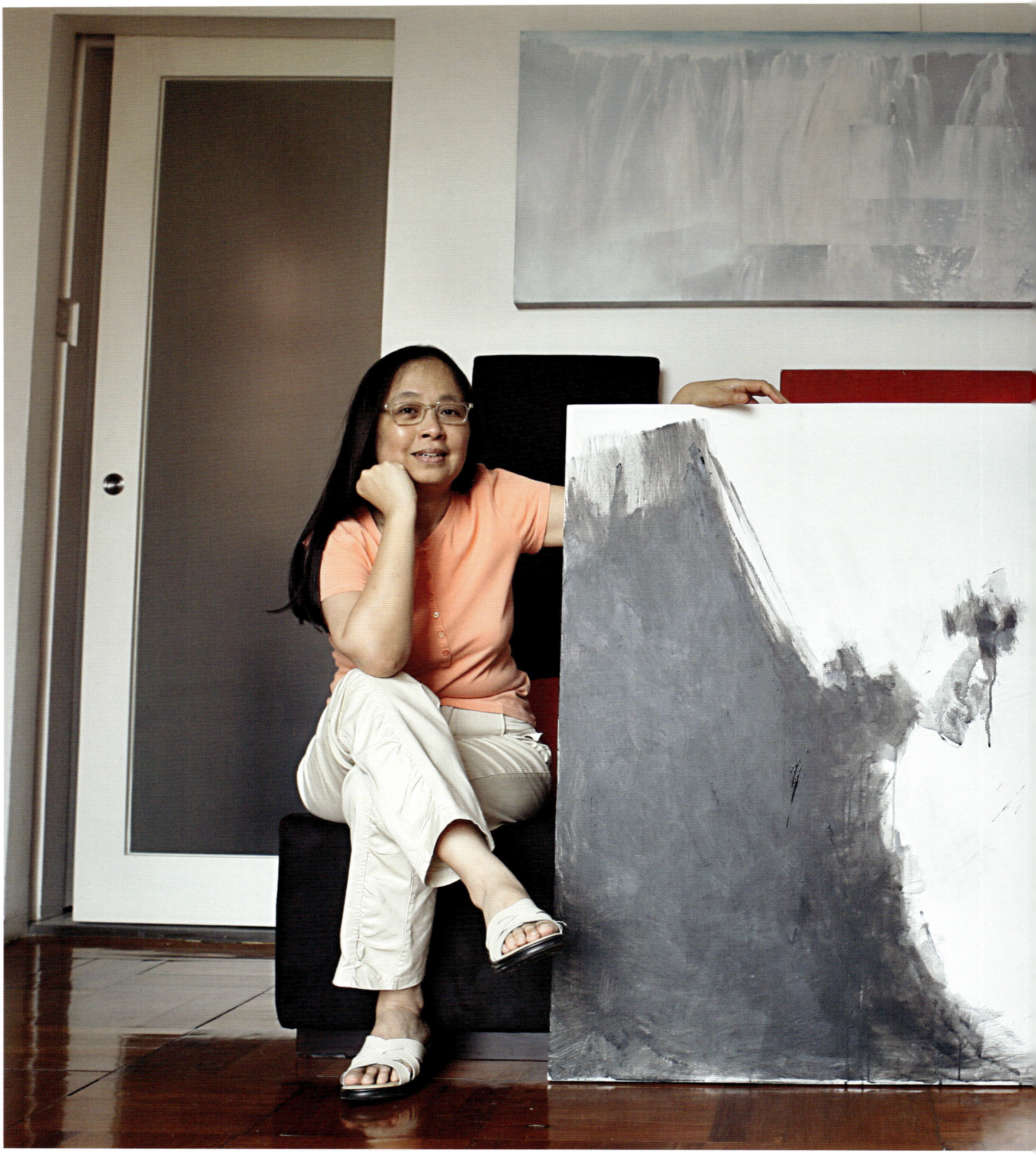

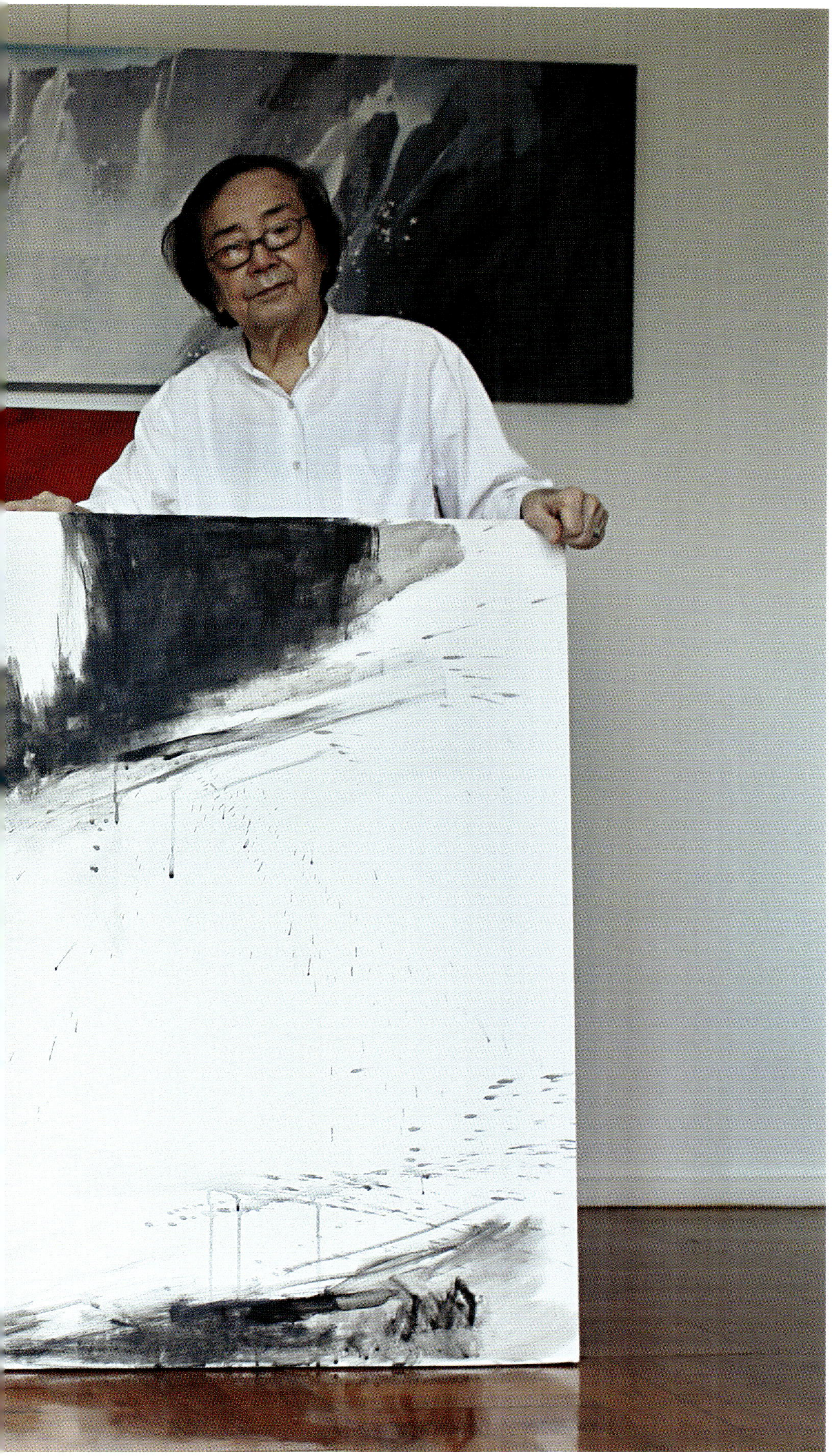

Hon Chi-fun's creativity is not limited by environmental constraints. His life experiences across two centuries have developed a certain adaptability. In the '50s and '60s, living space in Hong Kong was crowded. Hon did his large paintings in his narrow living room, drove around to do outdoor sketching, or travelled to different countries. Choi and Hon have had more than one studio, and they have shifted their focus as they progressed to different stages in life. The studio with the longest history is their old apartment on Penland Street in Kowloon City, adjacent to St Teresa's Hospital. They used to do their artworks there until Hon's retrospective exhibition *Secret Code: The Art of Hon Chi-fun*. From 1993 to 1997 when they were living in Toronto, Canada, they worked in the basement of their house. Hon recovered from his stroke in 2000, but climbing stairs had become a tough task for him and he has been working at his current apartment since then. The master bedroom is divided by a glass door, half is a place for rest and the other half is studio space. Hon mainly works in the living room, sometimes at the dining table and sometimes on the floor. The old apartment on Penland Street has been turned into a storage space for artworks.

Choi and Hon are different in many ways. They were born in different eras, and they received different kinds of education: the former received a formal university education while the latter was self-taught. Their media and styles differ, and their artistic paths were different. What happens when two persons of such diversity live under the same roof? "We both have very strong personalities," says Choi. "We insist on our own views towards art. In order to maintain our autonomy we have reached a consensus of not influencing each other in art, and we seldom discuss art."

"We have our own sphere of creativity and our own art circles yet we share common ground on some fundamental issues, like core values towards life, attitudes towards other people and views of social change."

Despite their different artistic paths, they have been companions to each other since the '70s. When Choi was studying art in Chicago, Hon travelled between Hong Kong and the United States, where he had opportunities to sit in lectures by artists like Harold Rosenberg and Allan Kaprow. But owing to his visa limitations

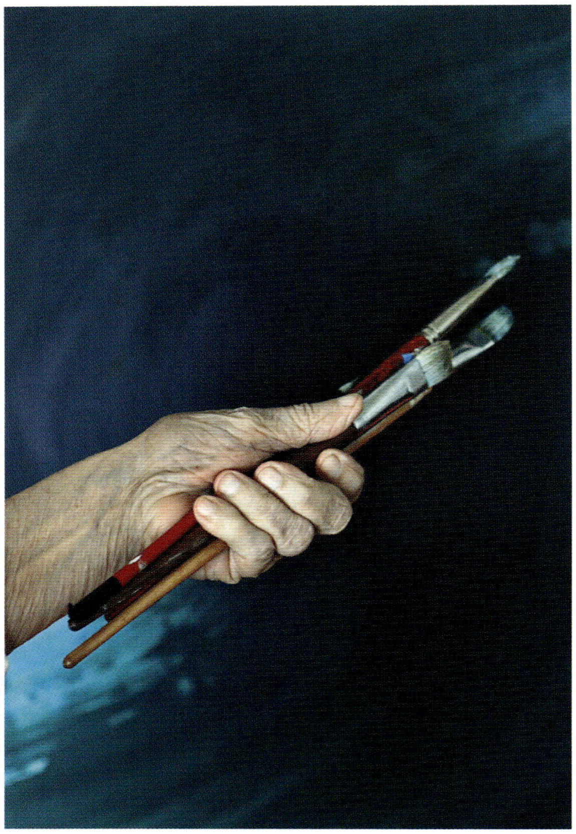

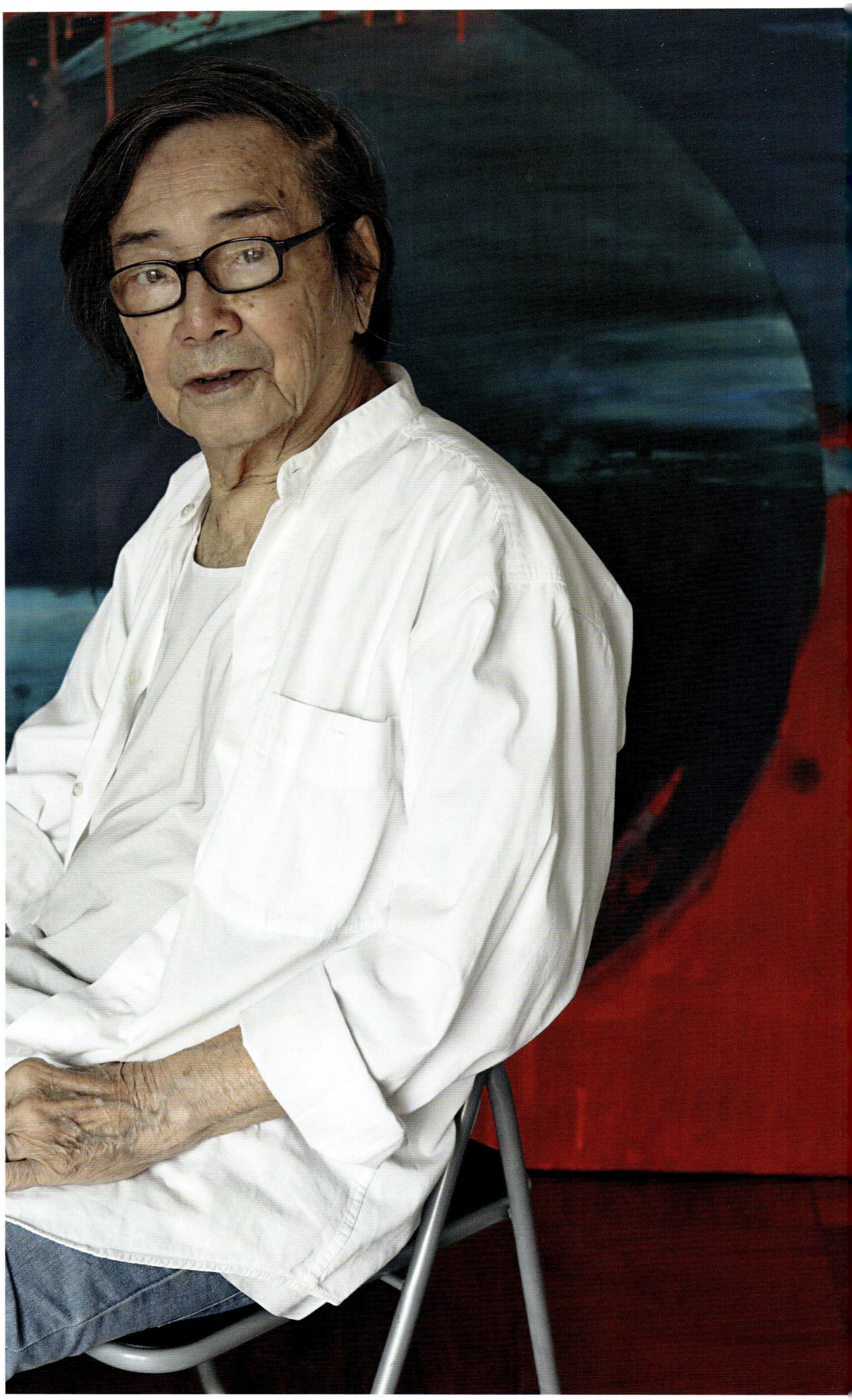

The artist's expression bespeaks insight into all matters of life

The watermarks on the old photographs carry his passion from the old days, which is still evident in his sparkling eyes as he tells his adventure with pride

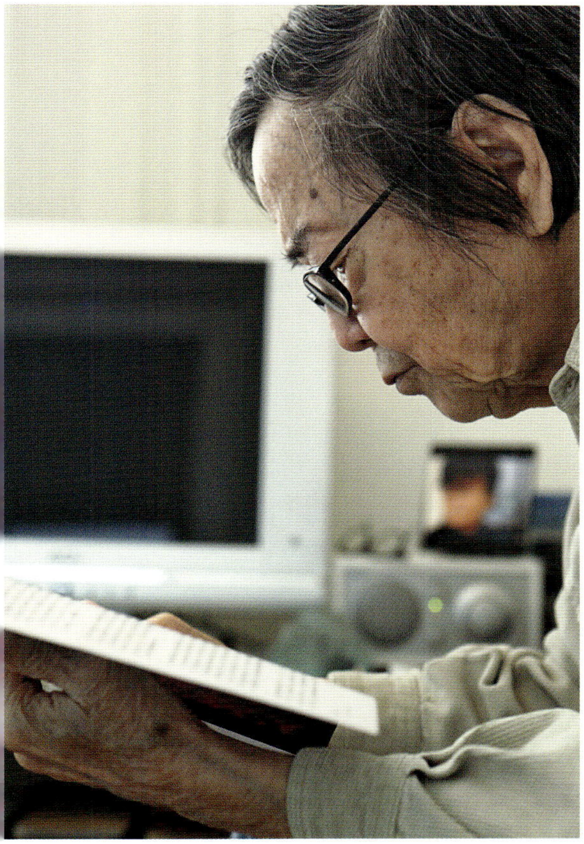

he could only stay in the United States for six months every year. In daily life, Hon assisted Choi in many ways, particularly with his craftsmanship in the installation of artworks. Now Choi has helped him. From attending to his daily needs, to helping with exhibitions and publications, Choi has given him unconditional support. Since *Space and Passion: The Art of Hon Chi-fun* in 2000, Choi has taken up the organisation and planning of Hon's exhibitions and publications.

Choi and Hon's devotion to art is evident in their works, though these differ in style and subject matter. They both have strong personalities and their underlying rebellious nature has not faded over time, it has just become more introverted. When Hon was young he loved speedy motorbike rides and adventure. *A Place that Was* and *The Wind Chaser* are vivid portrayals of those experiences. During the interview he told us stories of his journey to the Iguazu Falls on the border of Brazil and Argentina in 1970, while showing us pictures of his adventure. He fell into the water by accident when he was taking pictures of the waterfall. It started as an accident but he decided to enjoy the experience. The watermarks on the old photographs carry his passion from the old days, which is still evident in his sparkling eyes as he tells his adventures with pride. You can read his life experience and his power in his paintings, whether naturalistic landscapes or abstract paintings. His style was informed by brushstrokes from Chinese calligraphy and

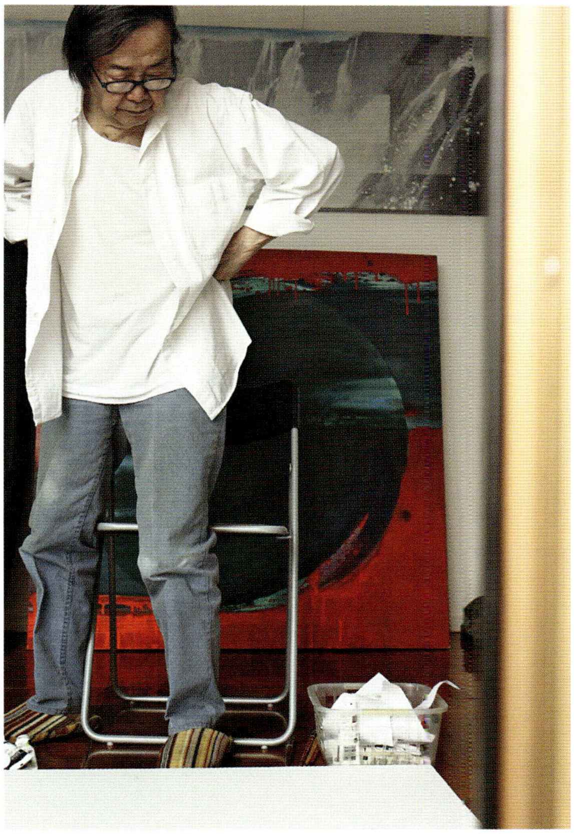

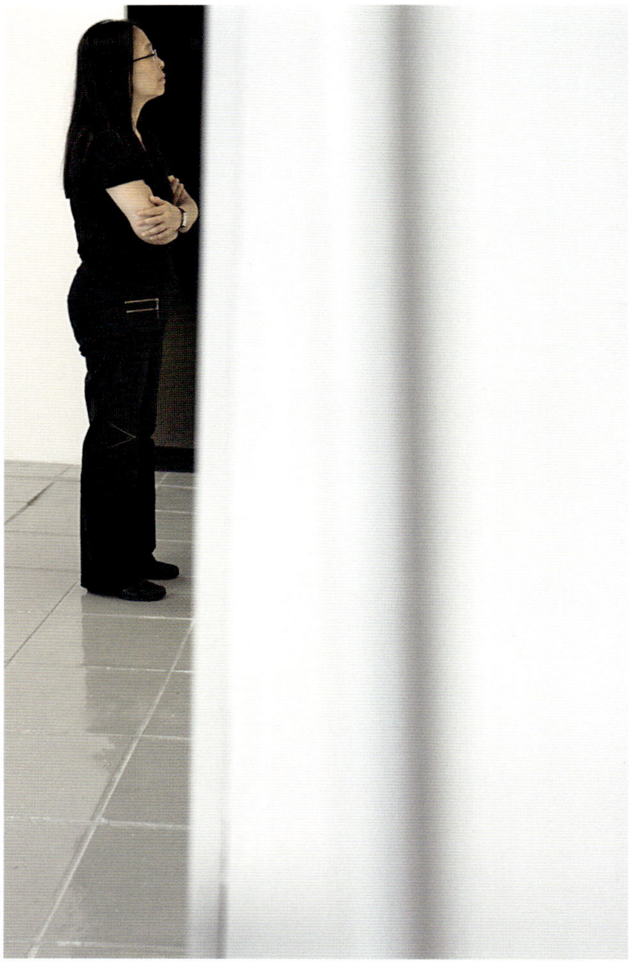

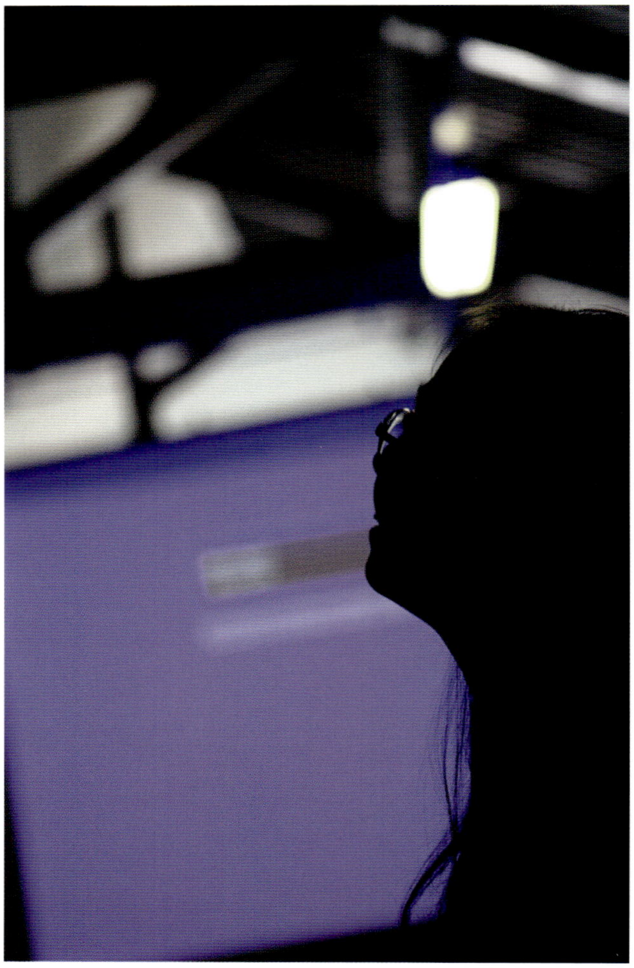

Buddhist texts. One can hardly tell that he has been a devoted Catholic since his adolescence at Wah Yan College.

Choi's rebellious nature is reflected not only in her life, but also in her art and teaching. She originally wanted to teach on a part-time basis at the Hong Kong Polytechnic Swire School of Design so as to spare more time for her art making. However only a full-time teaching post was available then, and so she tried to explore the art forms of her choosing through her teaching, benefitting both teacher and students. 'Environmental exploration' is her favourite subject. Without established course content or framework, she introduced unconventional materials such as light, air, time and space into her classes. Different themes were introduced in each semester, when teachers and students explored the creative process in different settings, for instance, in public spaces on campus, on streets and even on buses. That was a forward-looking approach in the '80s. "When I have an absolute belief, I will go for it," she says. "Young people are more sensitive and responsive to my strong character, which very often brings about new stimulation to the teaching and learning process."

In 1986 Choi felt that it was time for a change, and so she resigned and devoted her time to art. In the '90s she exhibited around the United States, Canada, Germany and Australia and in 1997 she returned to Hong Kong and resumed full-time teaching, first at the Hong Kong Institute of Vocational Education in 1998, and subsequently at the Hong Kong Baptist University, where she has worked since 2003. There, she had the opportunity to participate in the establishment of the university's Academy of Visual Arts.

She is determined to do meaningful work. Her versatile media, from performance, installation to photography, do not follow a particular sequence of development, but are only determined by which method is best and

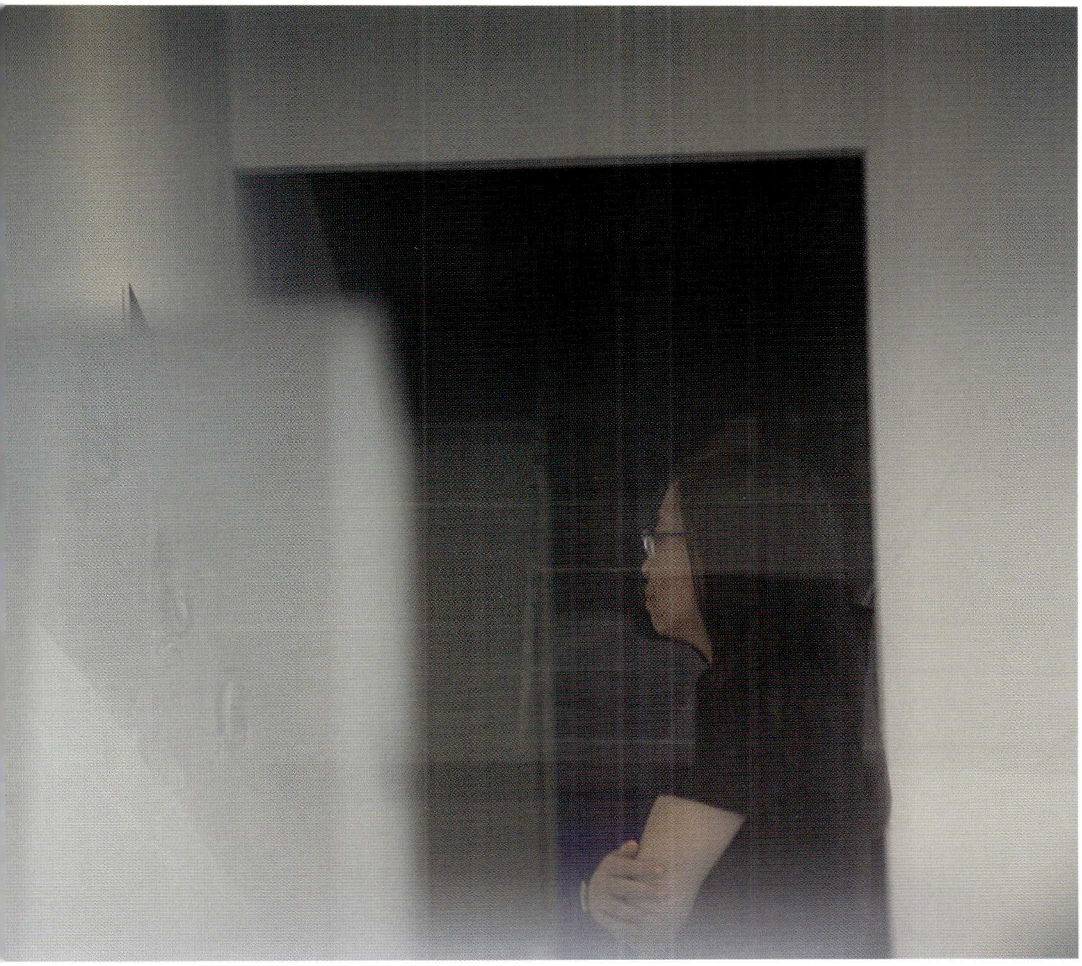

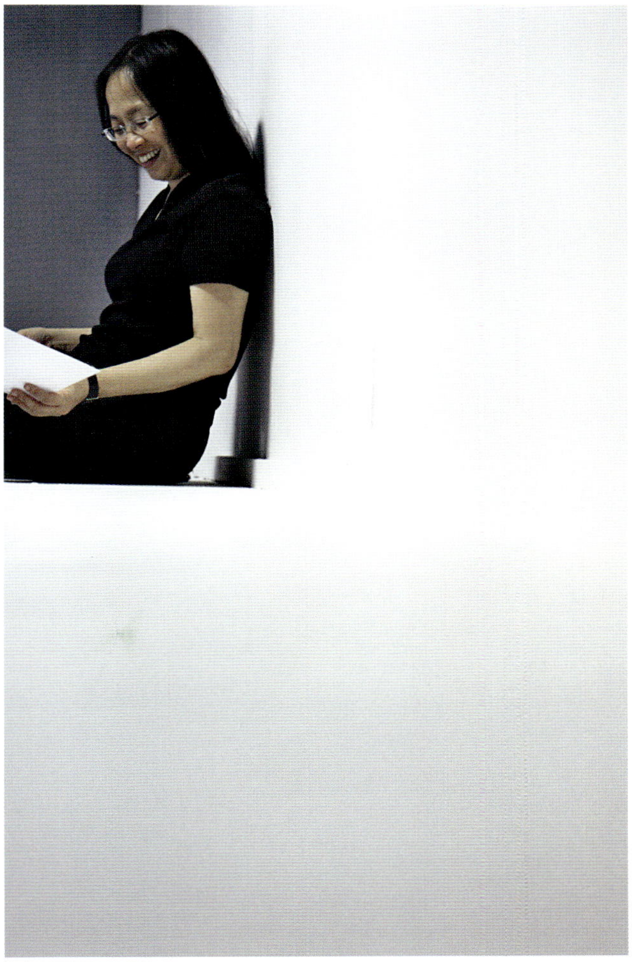

The richness and depth of her work take time to read and experience, as her rebellious nature and penetrative sentiments are expressed in an introvert, subtle and distant manner

most suitable for a particular subject matter. She emphasises concepts and thinking, but is not limited by the idea of concept, for instance sentiment is also a kind of thinking to her. Choi is among those early artists who practised installation art in Hong Kong. In 1985 *An Extension into Space*, her first installation show, was held at the Hong Kong Arts Centre. Such art forms were rare in Hong Kong in that era, and the Chinese term for 'installation art' was translated by her. The installation works then were not very mature, but Choi had successfully broken the boundary by transforming the idea of art from a stable to an unstable space. The richness and depth of her work take time to read and experience, as her rebellious nature and penetrative sentiments are expressed in an introvert, subtle and distant manner. Her works do not shock you instantly, but gradually fill you with their richness and complexity.

Choi and Hon have been observing the development of Hong Kong's modern and

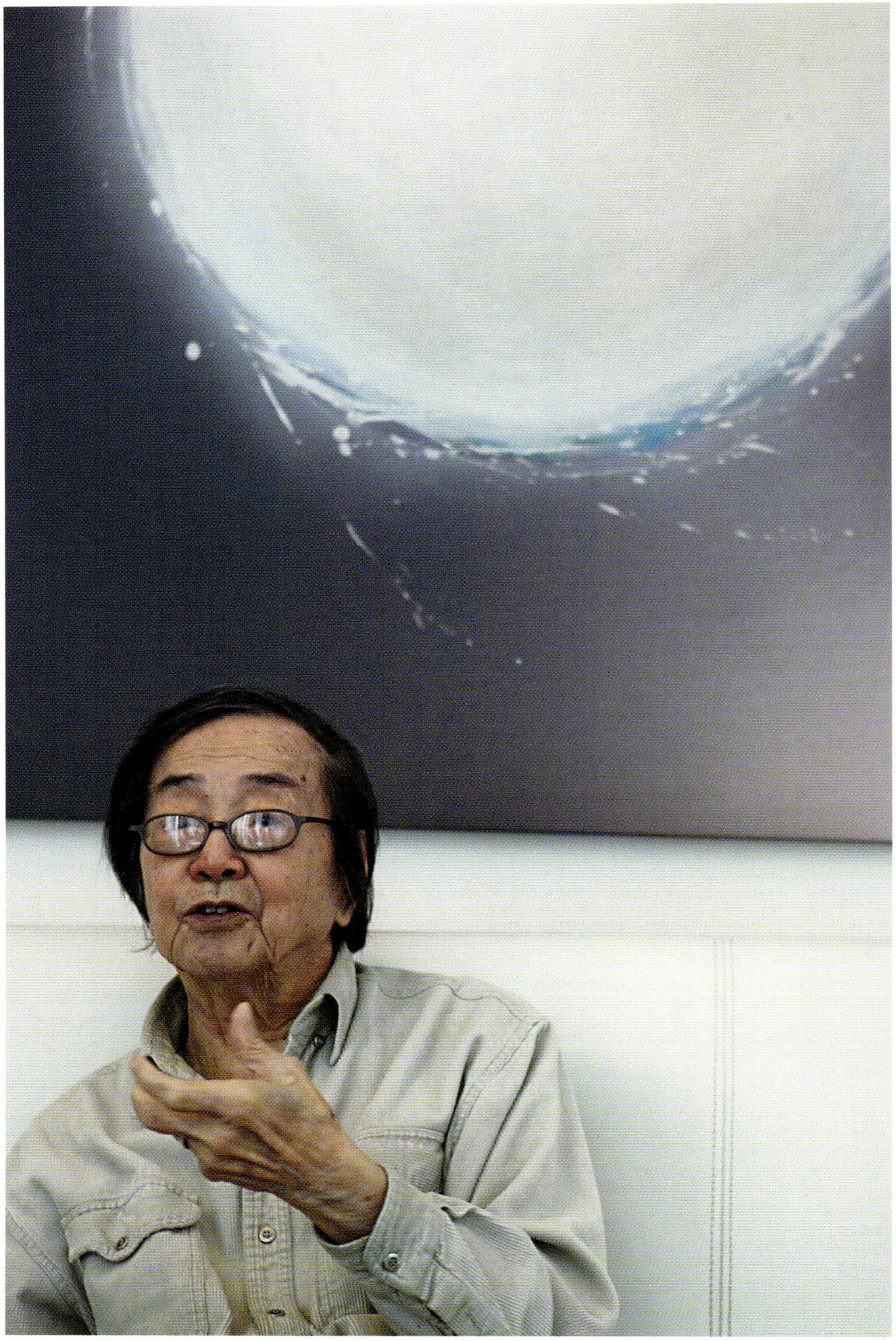

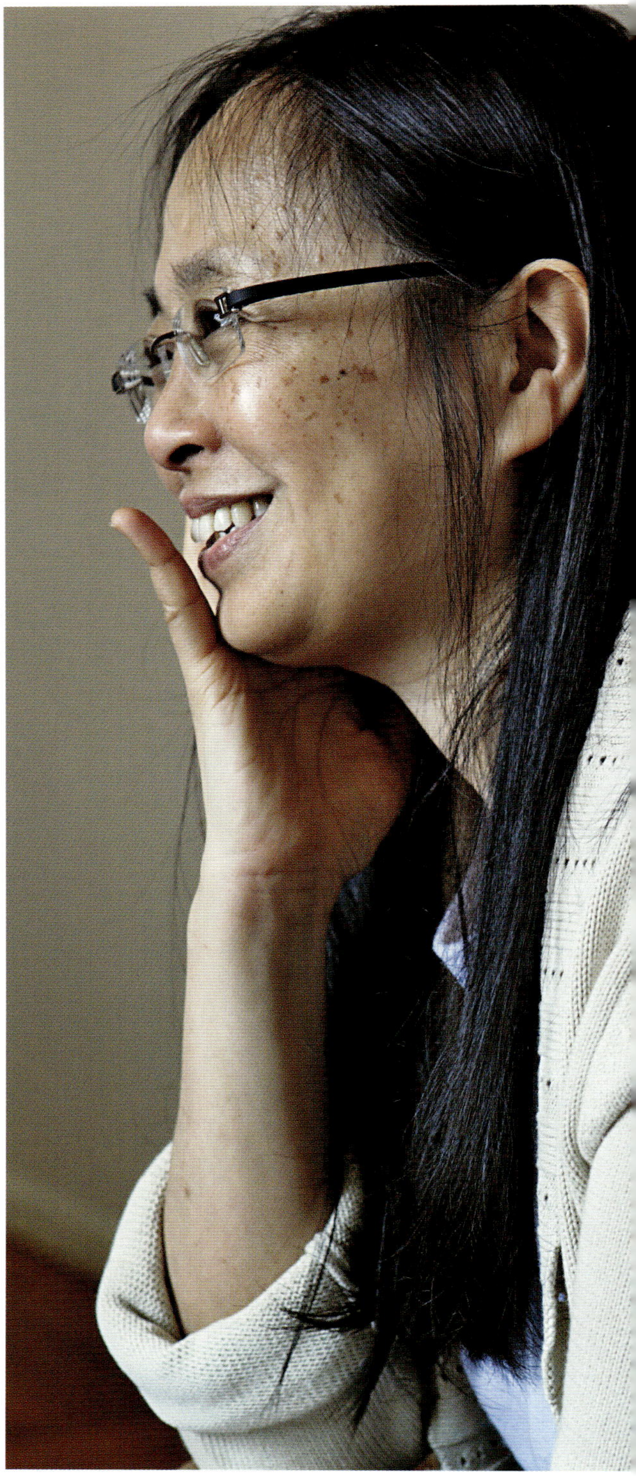

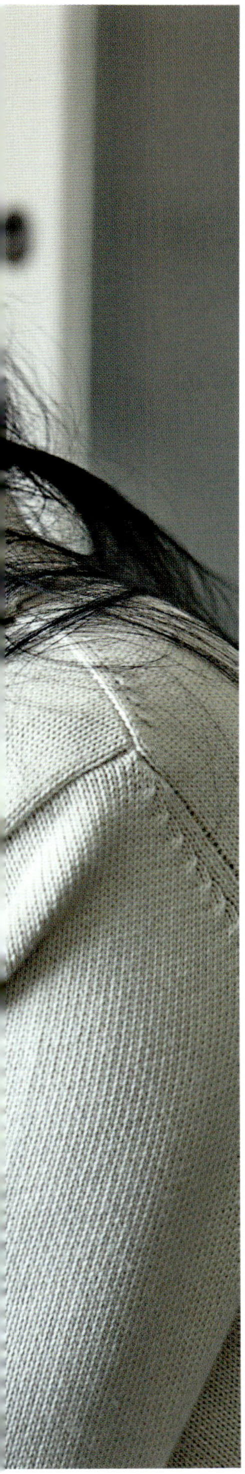

Together for over three decades, Choi and Hon are unique and independent in their own artistic pursuits, yet always with respect for each other

contemporary art scene, particularly Choi, who has a mixed feelings for its development locally. "The development of Hong Kong art has had both opportunities and crisis," she says. "One of the crises came from the drastic evolution of art in China, but more detrimental has been the comparatively insignificant status of Hong Kong art research in the academic arena."

"I treasure Hong Kong art. Hong Kong artists largely make art out of pure intention, and non-profit making art spaces deserve exploration as well. Nowadays, artists have more opportunities and together they have become an intellectual creative force with a conscious mind. If they are persistent in their pursuits, create from their hearts and build up a sound foundation, they will only need a platform to showcase themselves. This cultural aura of purity and sincerity is significant, as it has great potential for contribution to the art scene in Asia."

Together for over three decades, Choi and Hon are unique and independent in their own artistic pursuits, yet always with respect for each other. Sitting in their spotless living room, overlooking the Lion Rock skyline and sipping the Loong Jing tea prepared by Choi, we listened to their life stories, immersing ourselves in their world of life-long commitment, bitter sweet experiences and harmony beyond words.

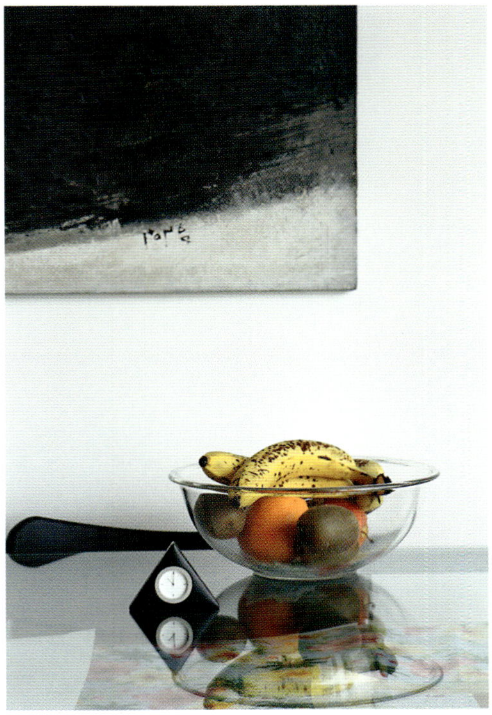

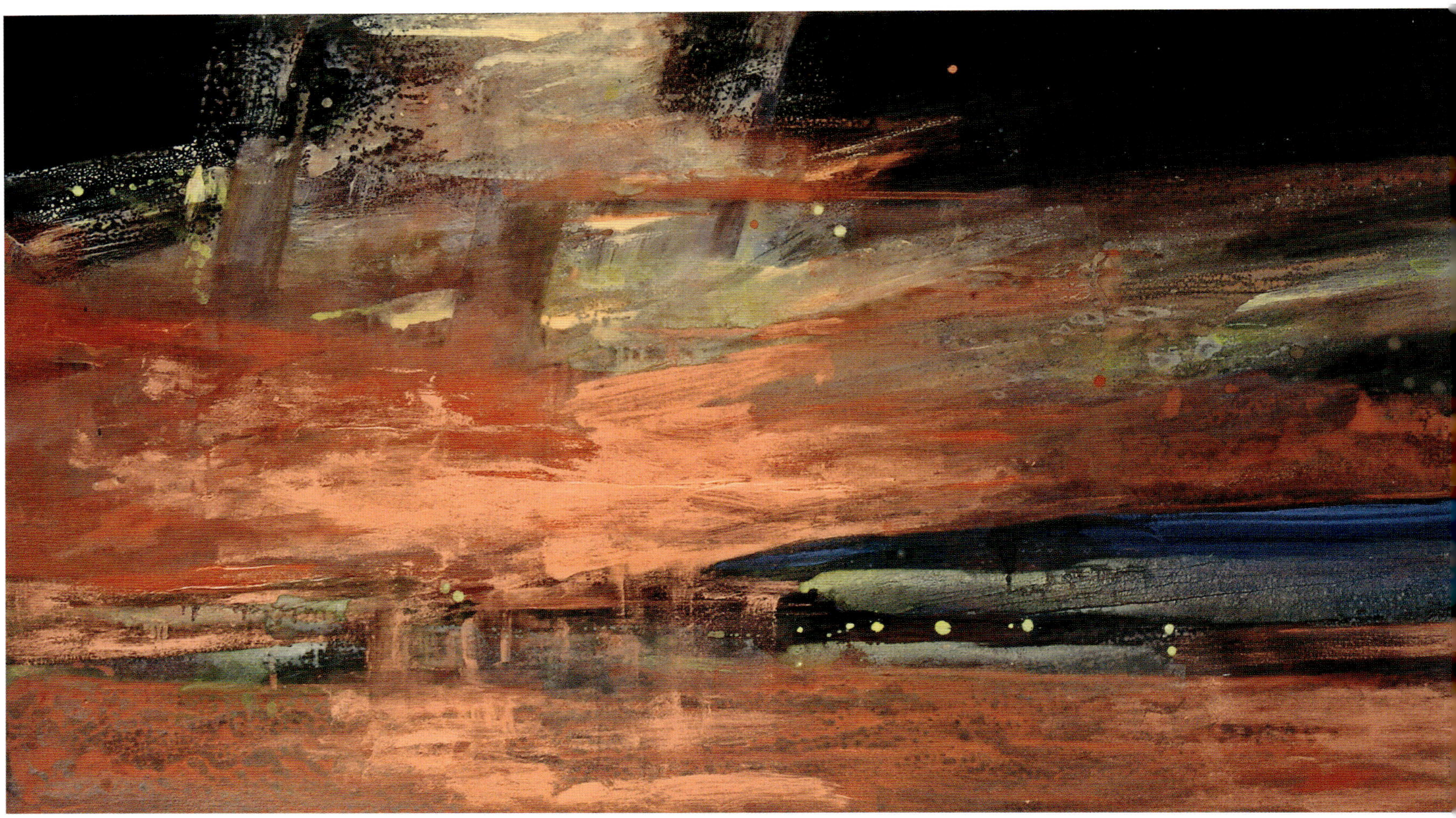

(Above) Hon Chi-fun/Those Lusty Years
Acrylic on canvas, 79x145 cm, 2003

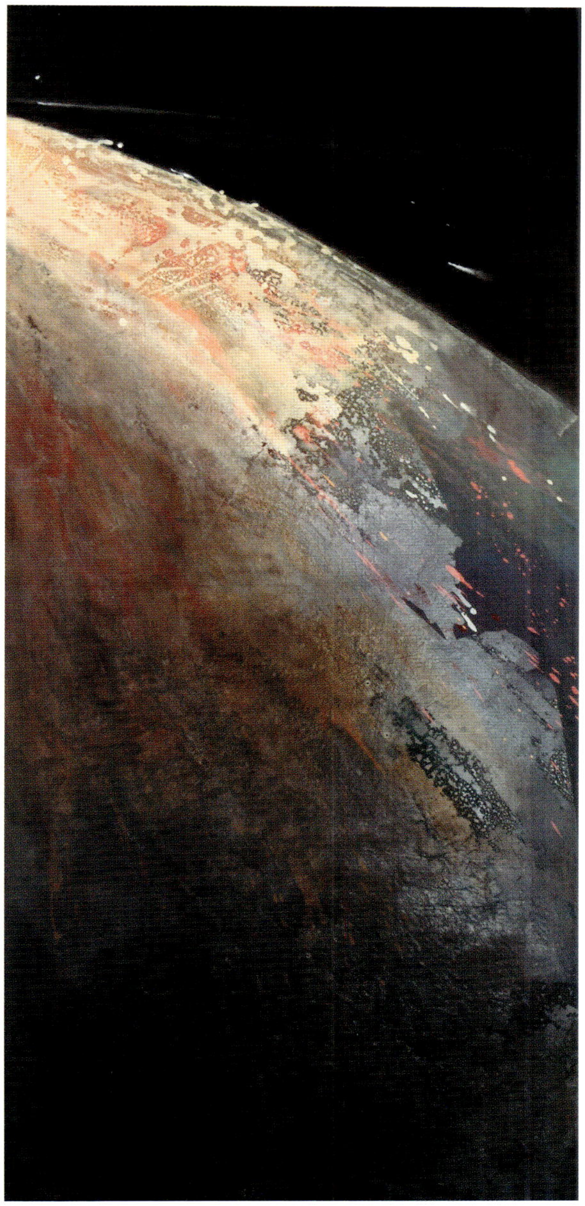

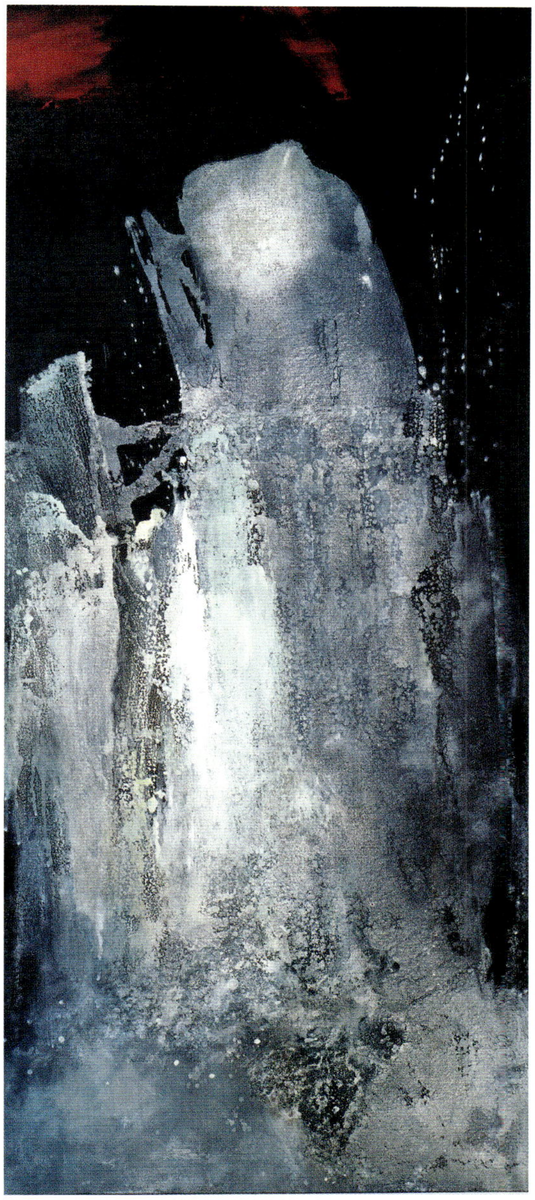

(Left) Hon Chi-fun/Moon Climber
Acrylic on canvas, 202x101 cm, 2004

(Right) Hon Chi-fun/Out of the Gorge
Acrylic on canvas, 202x101 cm, 2005

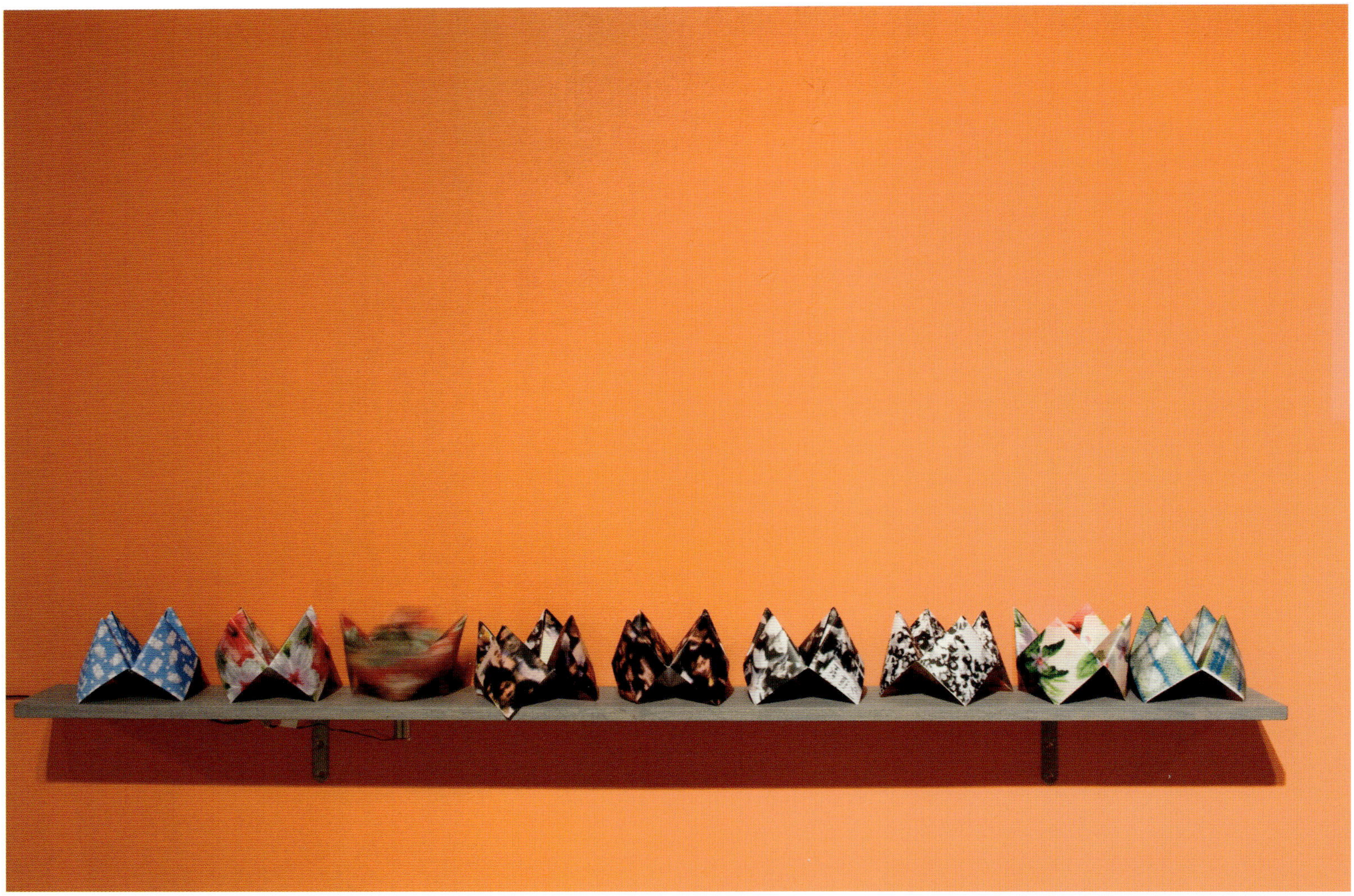

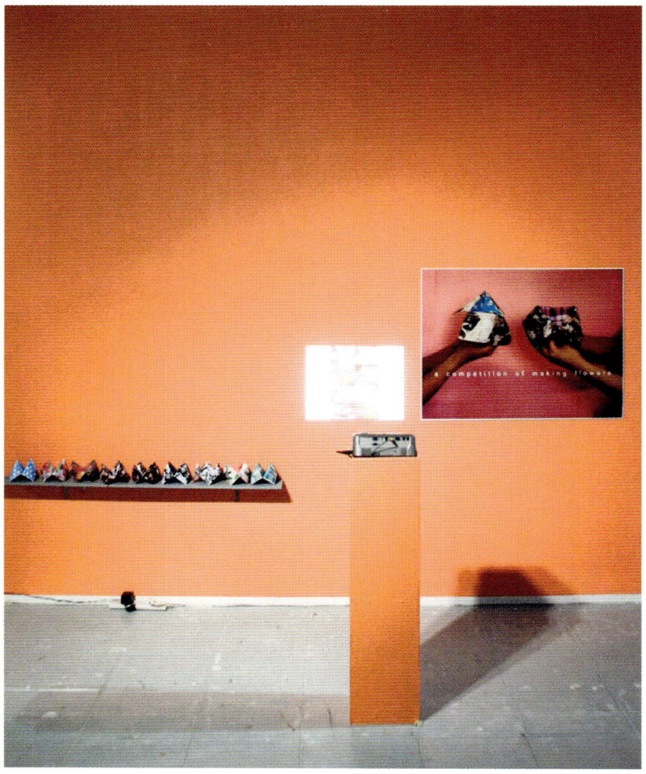

Choi Yan-chi/A Competition of Making Flowers
Installation, 250x280 cm, 2007

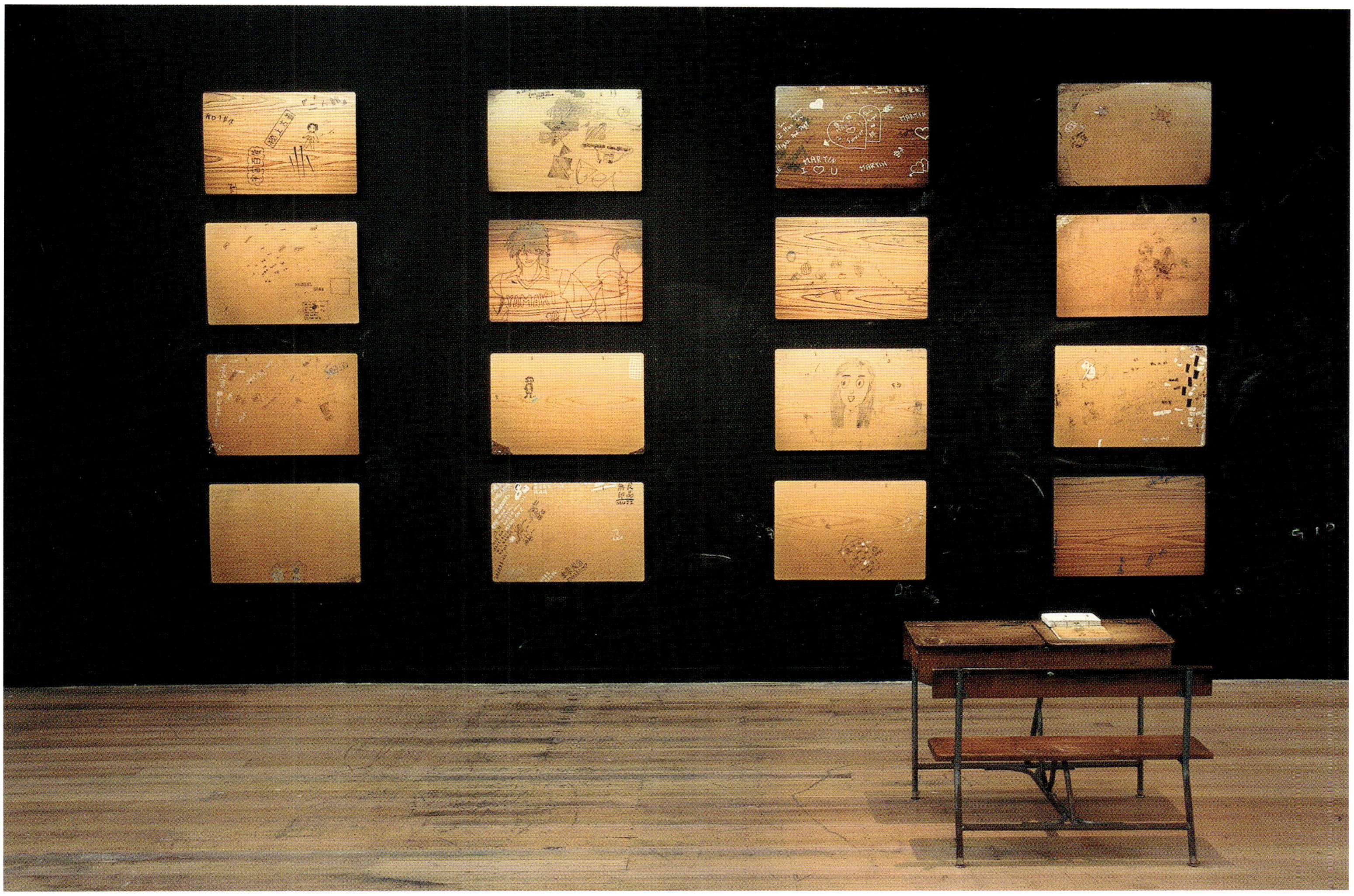

Choi Yan-chi/Past and Future III
Installation, 300x400x250 cm, 1998

Josephine Chow Suk-fan and Gaylord Chan

Happiness Forever

By Alice Choi and Carl Cheng

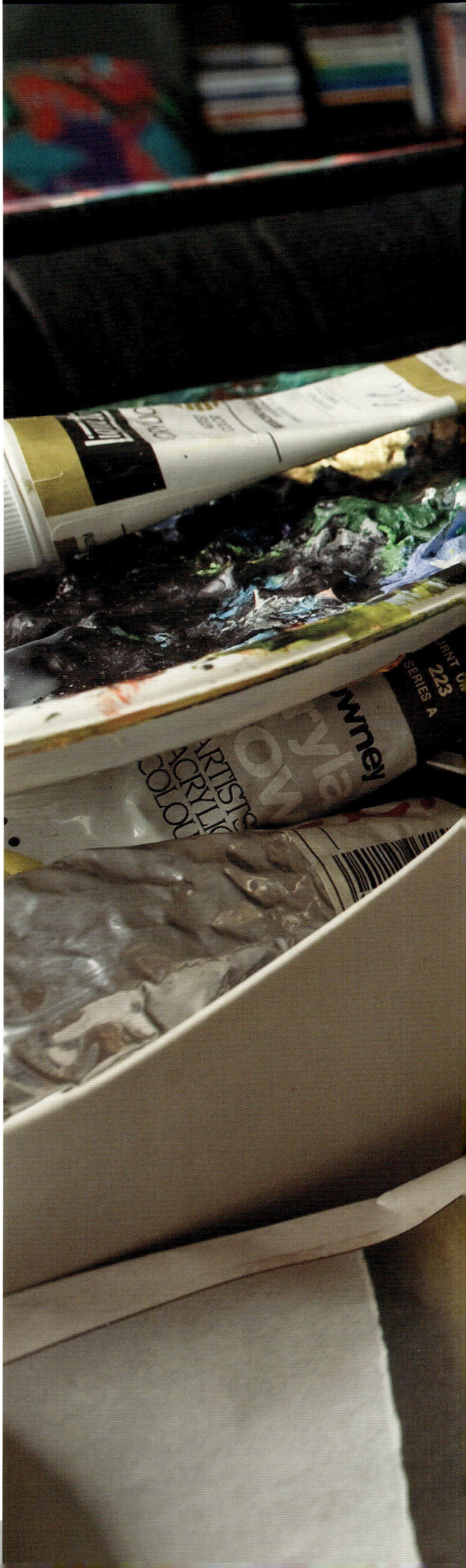

Josephine Chow Suk-fan graduated from the Chinese University of Hong Kong (CUHK) in 1989 with a Bachelor's degree in fine arts. She is devoted to art education, and has been engaged with children's' art education since 1985. She co-established the Cultural Corner with Gaylord Chan in 1989. Chow joined the Hong Kong Visual Arts Society (HKVAS) in 1991 and is active in art organisations and group exhibitions.

Gaylord Chan completed his diploma in art and design from the former Department of Extra-mural Studies of the CUHK in 1970. In 1974 he founded the HKVAS with his classmates and friends, and was its founding chairperson. He is dedicated to promoting art education and co-established the Cultural Corner with Chow. He has been an adviser to the Leisure and Cultural Services Department since 1993. His early works are mostly in acrylic, and recently he has been using Microsoft Paint software to create prints. Chan was awarded the Urban Council Fine Art Award in 1983, an MBE in 1986 and the Artist of the Year Award in Hong Kong in 1990.

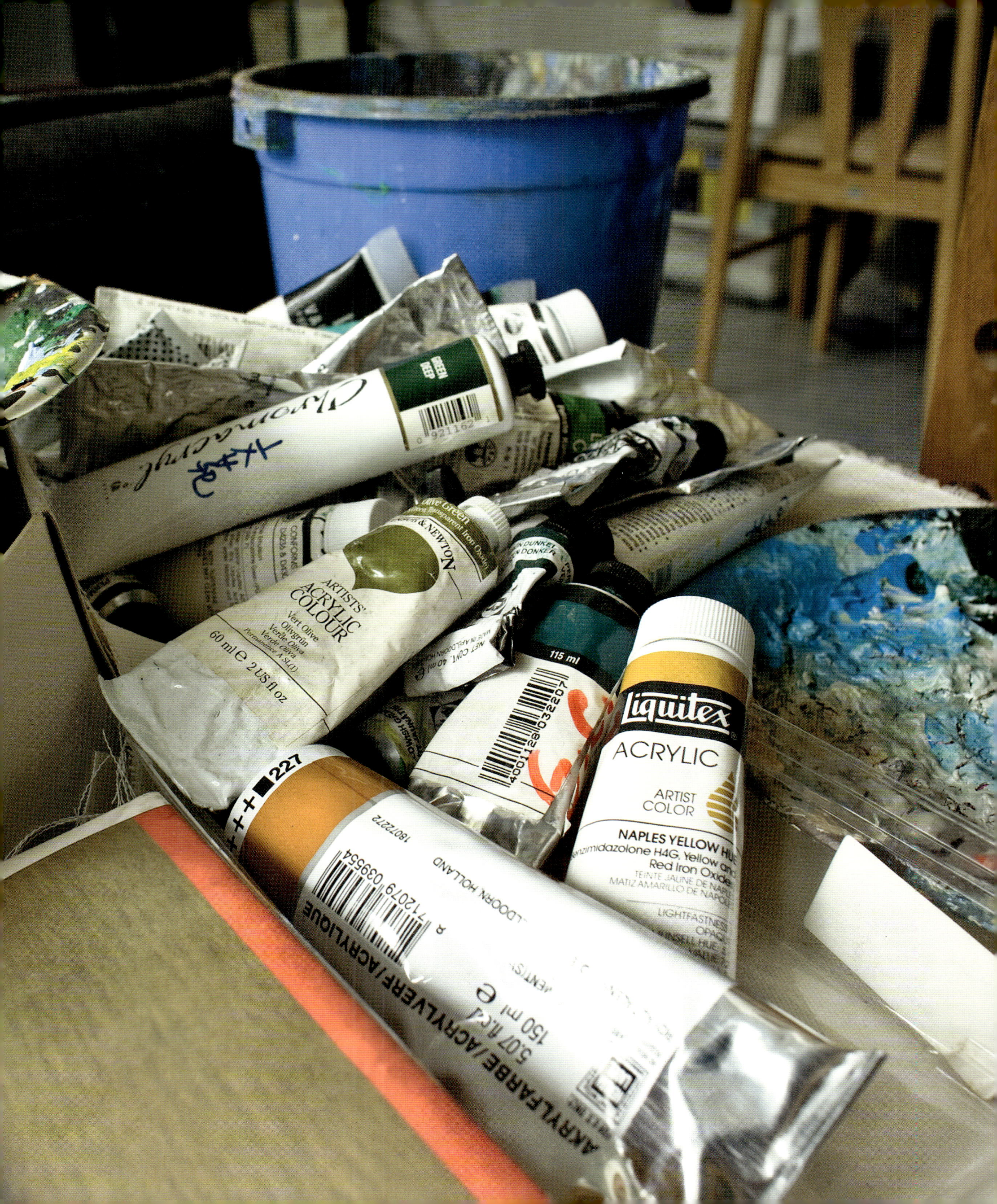
GREEN
DEEP
Olive Green
& NEWTON
ARTISTS'
ACRYLIC
COLOUR
Vert Olive
Olivgrün
Verde Oliva
60 ml e 2 US fl oz
115 ml
liquitex
ACRYLIC
ARTIST
COLOR
NAPLES YELLOW HUE
227
AKRYLFARBE / ACRYLVERF / ACRYLIQUE
150 ml e
5.07 fl.oz

Some say it is better to be happy together than alone. Most artists are content to be alone, and find that solitude is sometimes necessary for the art making process. At the same time, art is to communicate, and to make lives more beautiful. Josephine Chow Suk-fan and Gaylord Chan have chosen to share their art in education. In the same manner, they have been getting along with each other for years.

Chan was once an engineer. Out of his love for art, he enrolled to study for a diploma in art and design at the former Department of Extra-mural Studies of the CUHK. He recalls that they had four evening classes each week, and that the course was very demanding. In the end only two students were able to graduate. After graduation he was devoted to his art and organised group exhibitions, and was soon known to the art circle. Chan has a vibrant character – conversational, humourous, hospitable and informal. He is true to his feelings, and lives his life fully with a wide range of interests. He paints hard and plays hard. His unique personality has brought him many friends and students.

Every Saturday Chow and Chan's students and friends gather together at their studio,

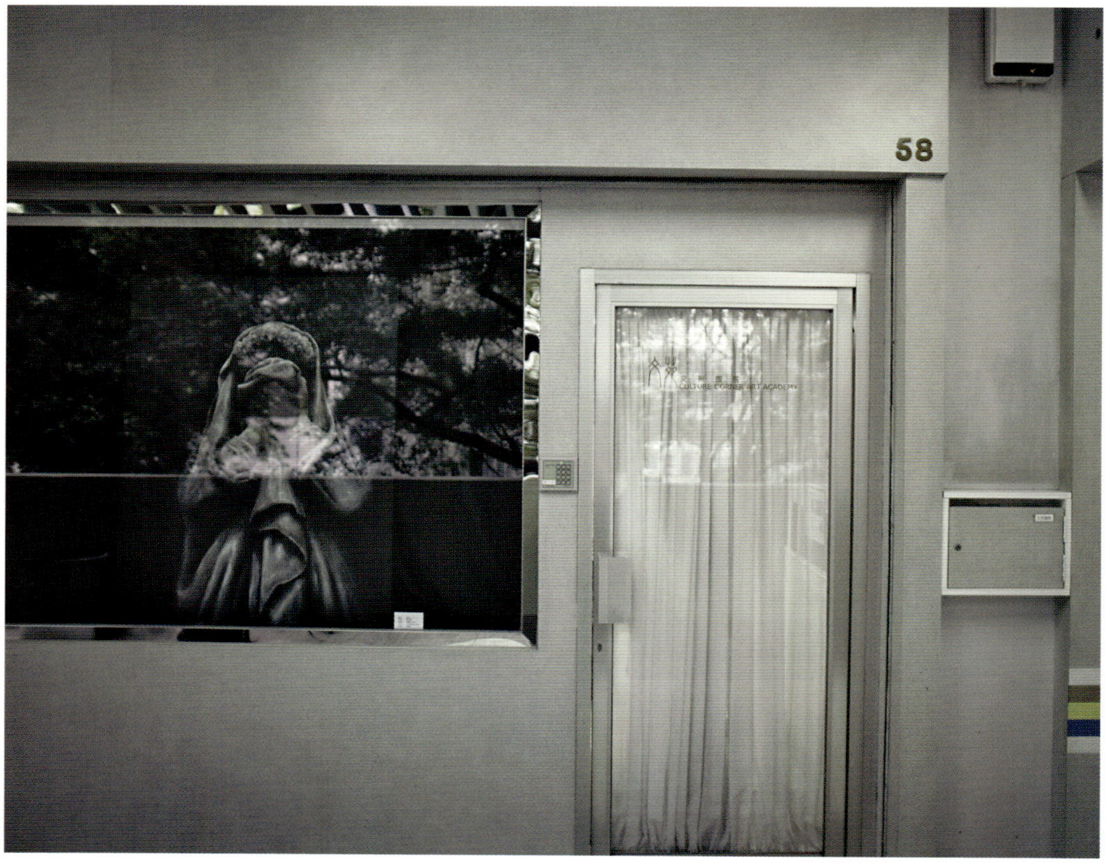

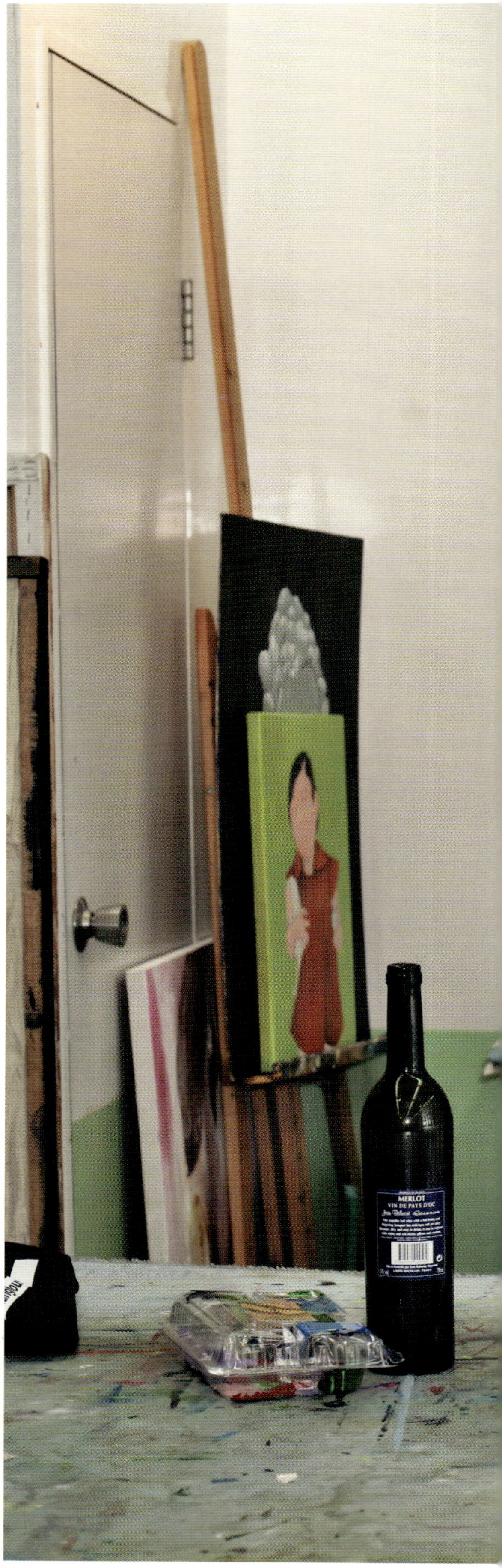

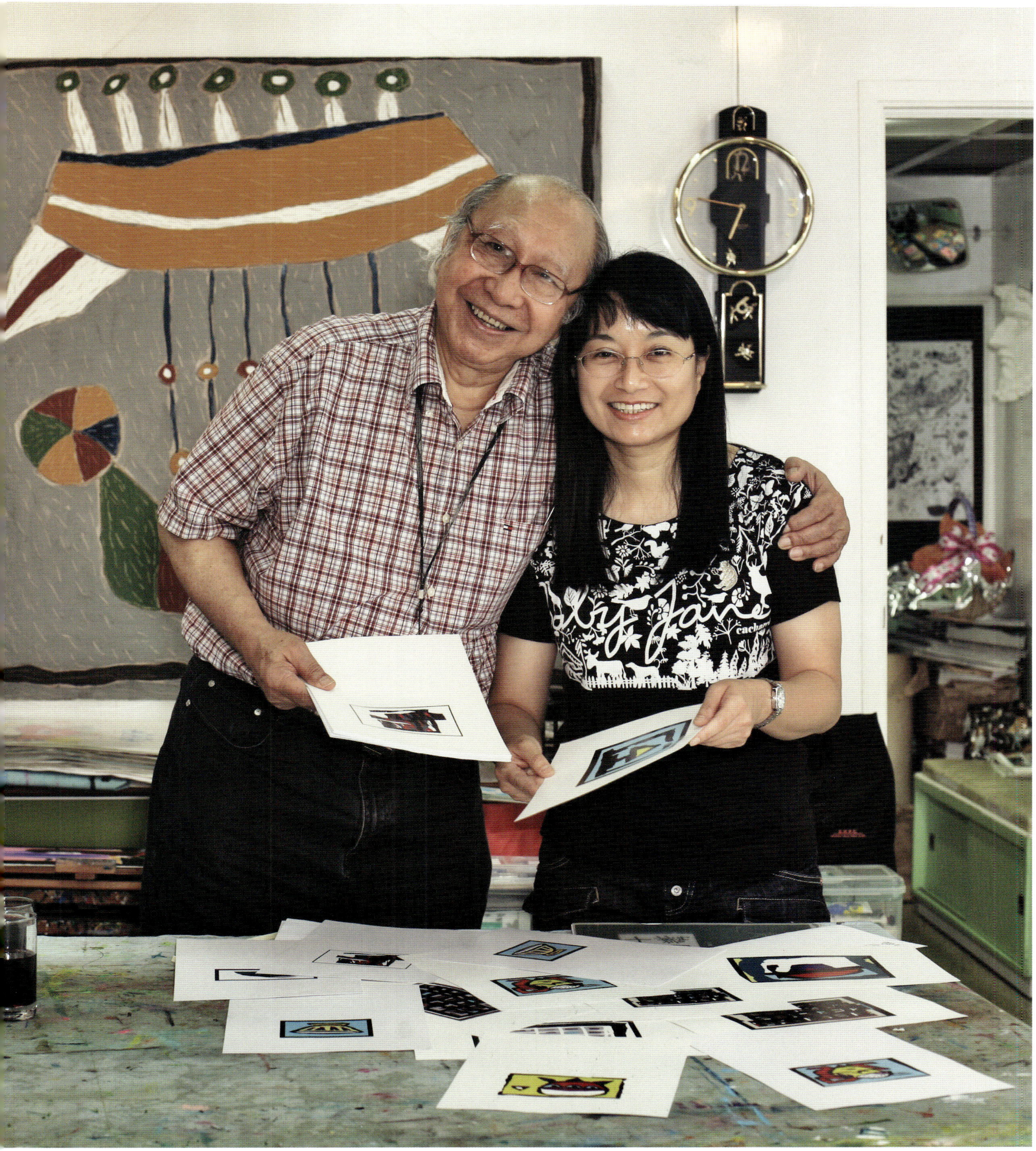

Spiritual communication and sharing in life bring success to their art

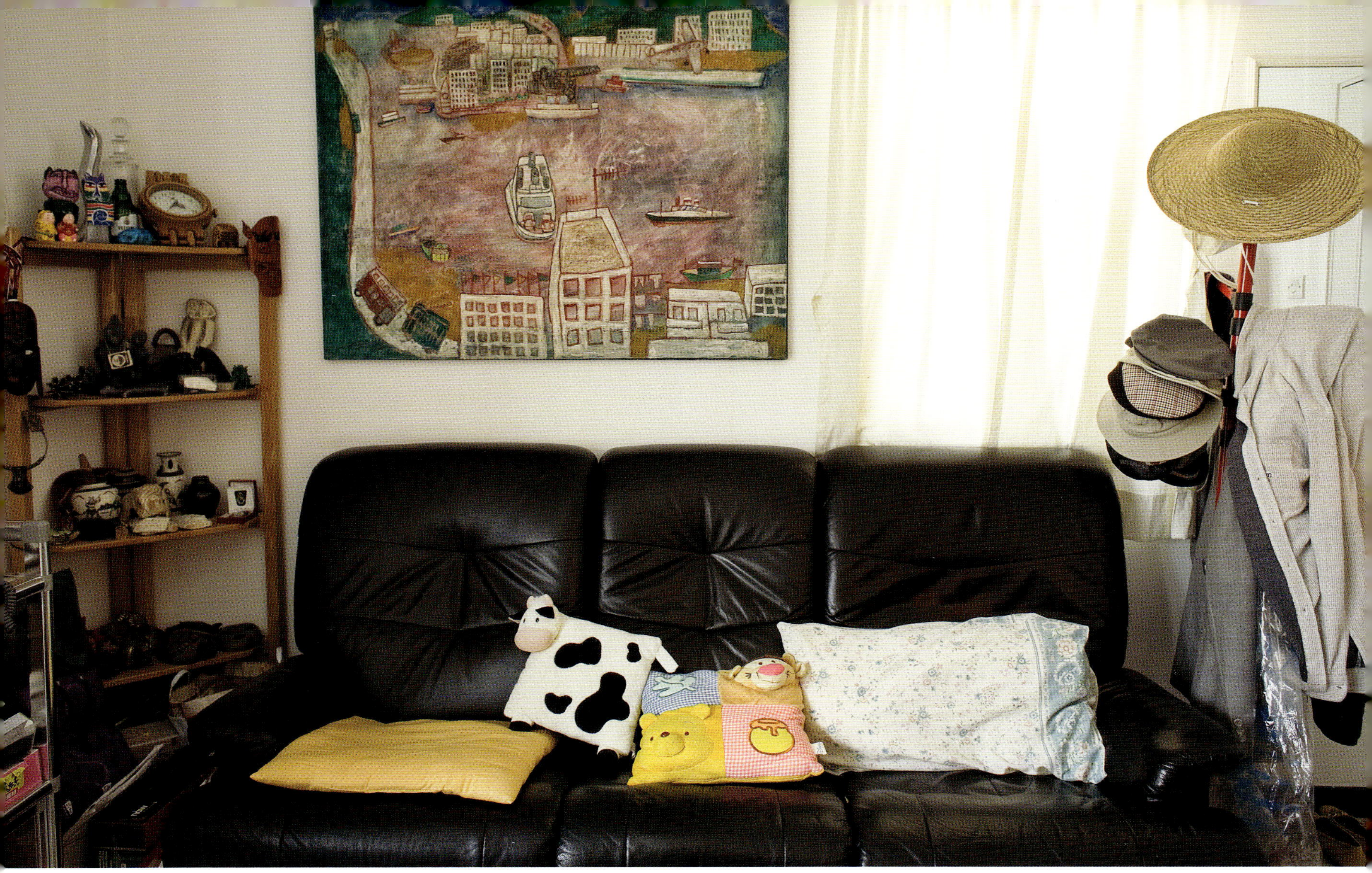

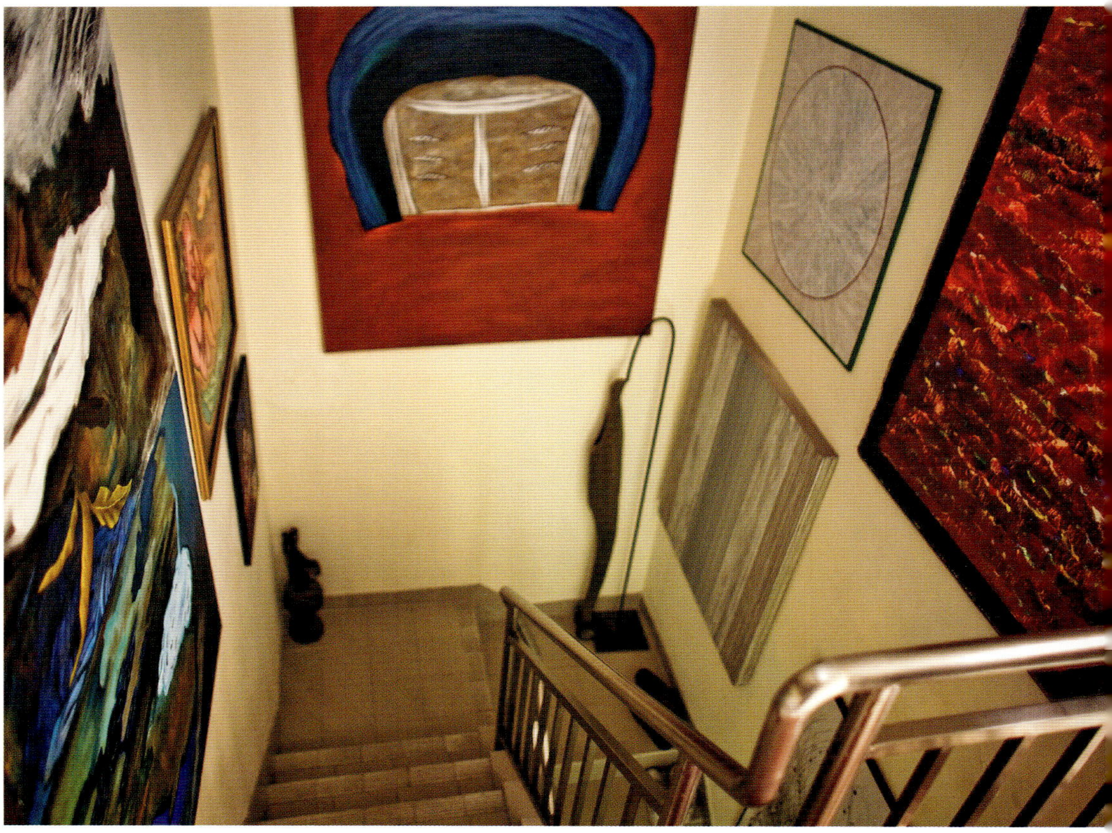

Cultural Corner, to drink and chat. They discuss a wide range of topics – casual and serious, happy and sad. Their studio is often full of excitement. They regularly critique art among their friends, commenting on each other's works and learning from each other in the process. As well as teaching and painting, they are very active on the contemporary art scene. Last year they formed a cultural tour of over 10 people to travel around Europe, and they visited the Documenta in Germany and the Venice Biennale in Italy.

Chow and Chan met in 1988 when Chow was still an undergraduate at the CUHK. Chan was very famous then, but Chow did not know of him until one day, she saw his painting *Heart of Shaman* and was deeply impressed. As a student representative of her class, Chow invited Chan to give lectures at CUHK, which was how their romance started. He had retired by then and with his pension he co-established the Cultural Corner with Chow after she graduated.

Chow and Chan are good companions. They have many things in common: art, education, friends, wine, but above all, communication

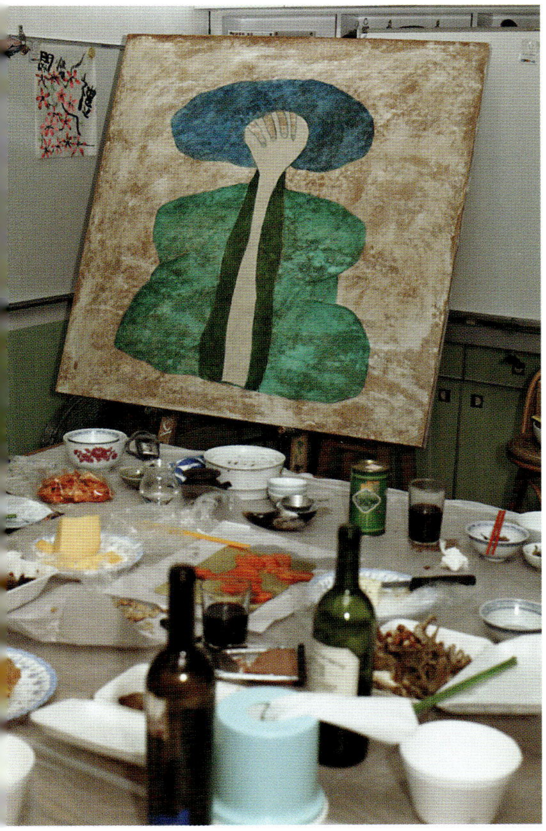

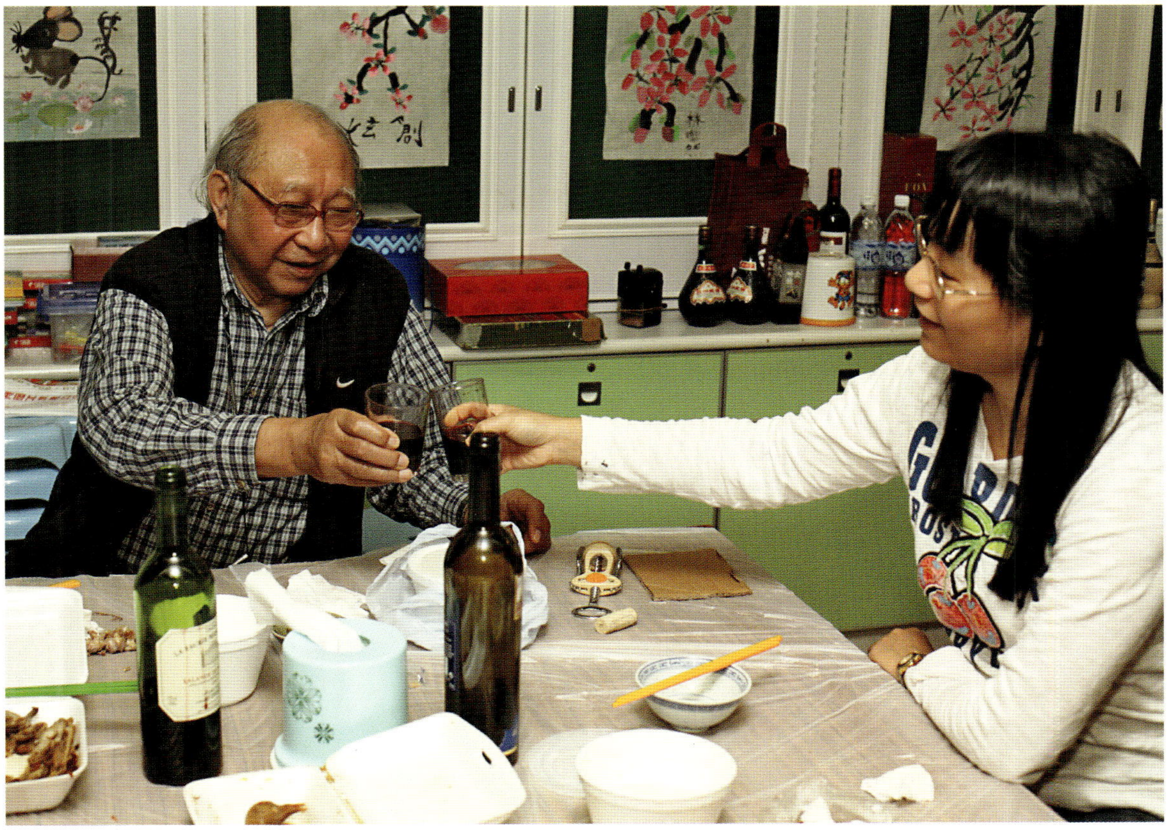

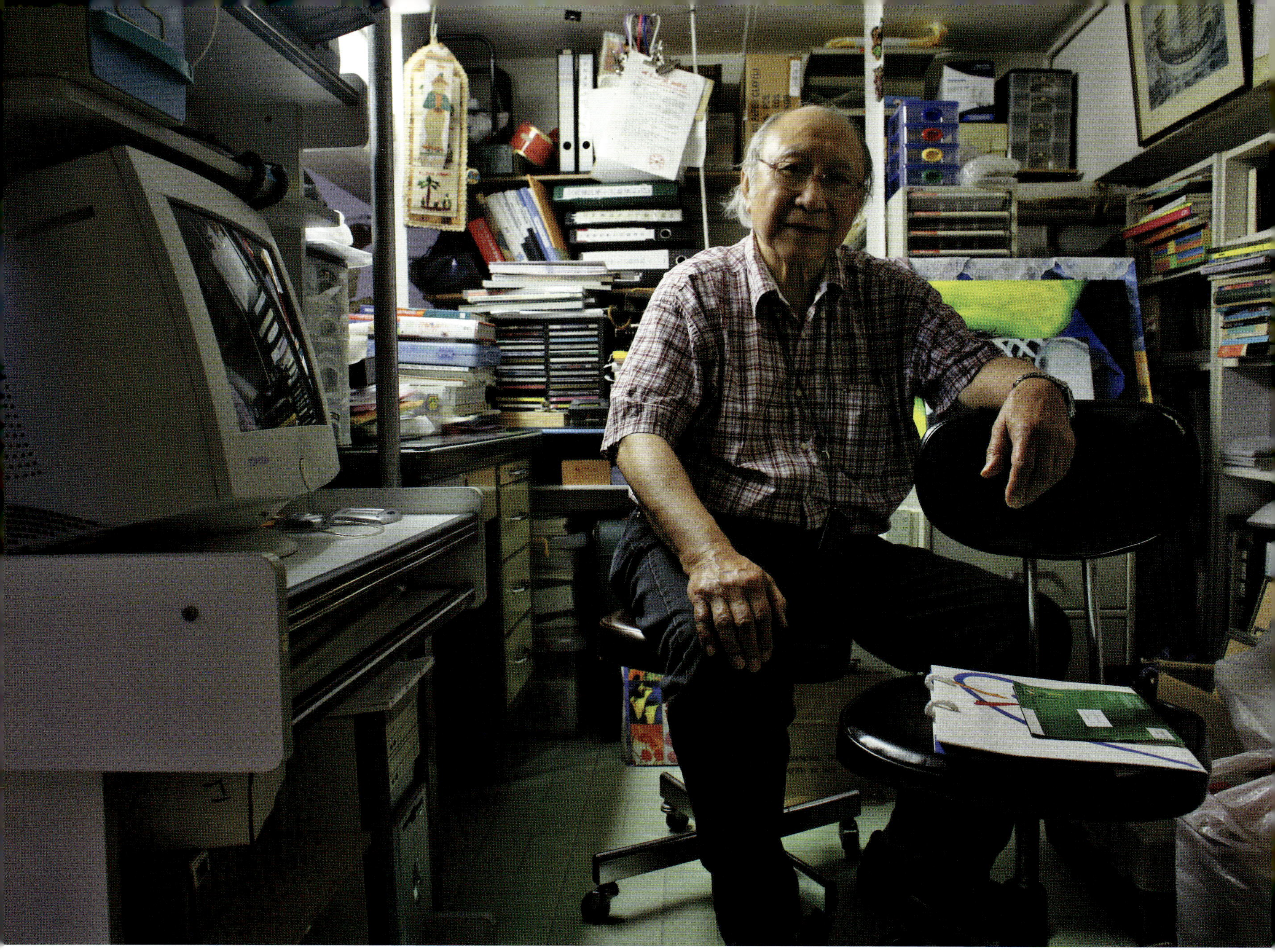

His images are impromptu, primitive, simple and humorous. He is curious about the world, and looks at things in a new light

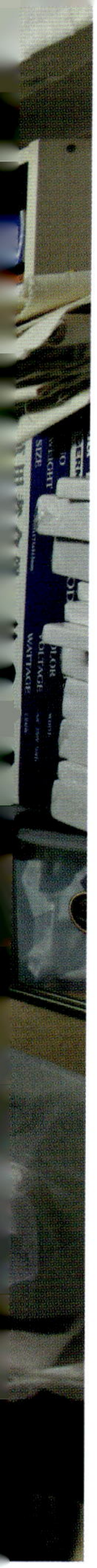

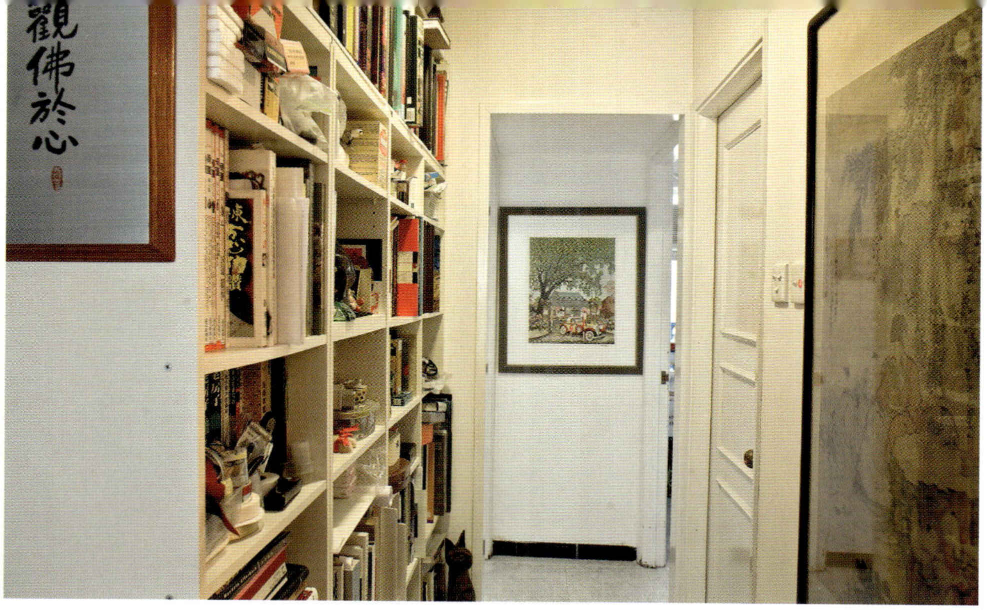

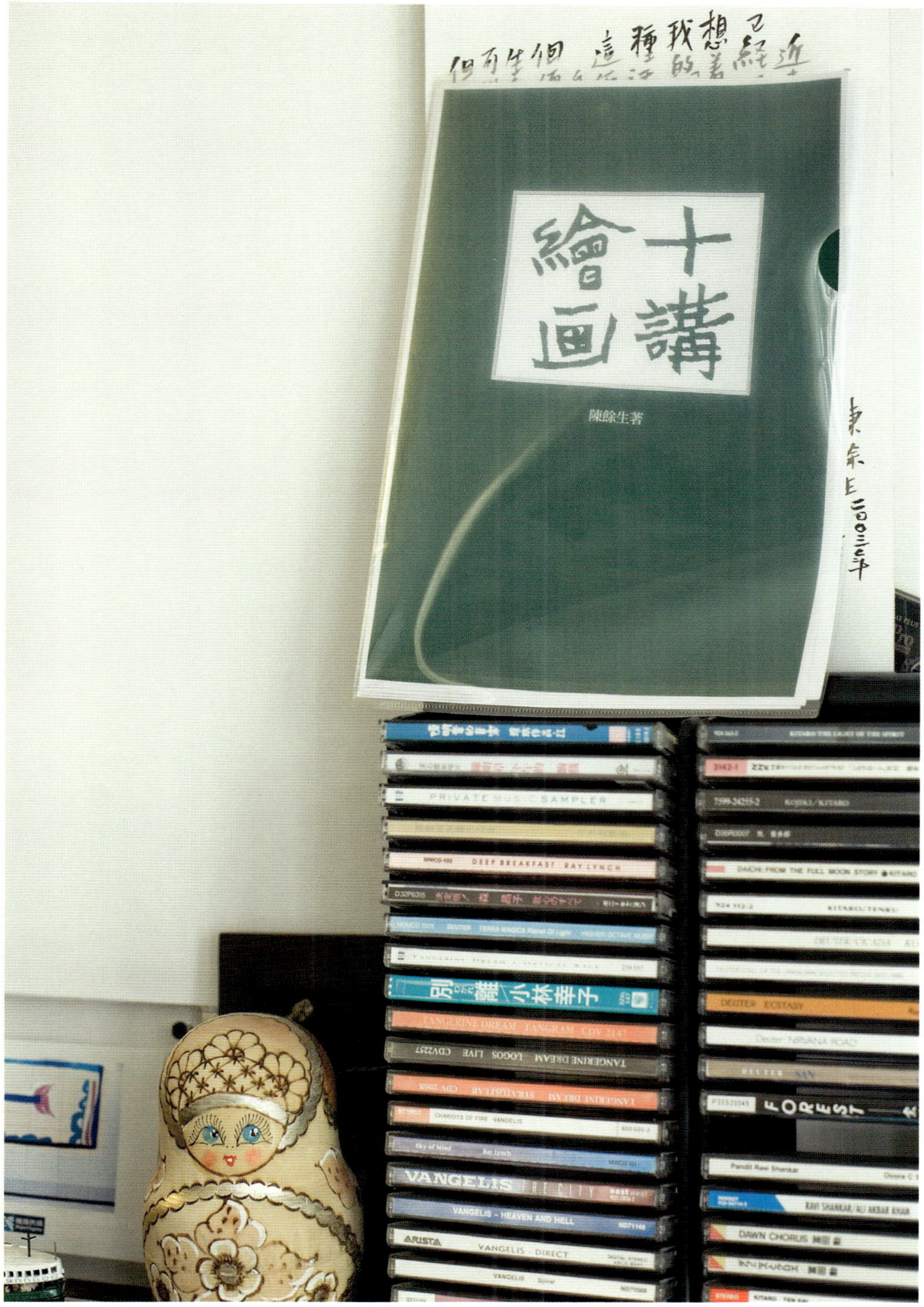

Notes from Gaylord Chan is a concise summary of his artistic method

Chow and Chan are good companions. They have many things in common: art, education, friends, wine, but above all, communication. They both have passion for art, and their world views are very similar. They understand and read each other's minds through their artwork. Chan appreciates the sentiment, imagination and mystery in Chow's works, which he lacks, and he can tell what she is thinking about. On the other hand, Chow admires Chan's attitude and diligence. They do not interfere with each other's direction, nor do they disturb each other while working.

When the Cultural Corner was initially established, Chan turned one room into his studio where he painted most of the time. Students were curious and wanted to have a look, yet did not dare to disturb Chan. His style discards technique and follows artlessness. His images are impromptu, primitive, simple and humorous. He is curious about the world, and looks at things in a new light.

You can tell how honest he is with his friends when you read their descriptions of Chan in his solo exhibition eight years ago, when he was 74:

> *"A person who does not admit his age," says Alan Zie Yongder.*

> *"...Loud, confident, attentive, satyric yet weak-headed..." comments Danny Lee Chin-fai.*

> *"...'Passionate', 'gallant', 'simple', 'indulgent', and even 'erotic' are all the 'true temperaments' you are pursuing in your works," opines Ho Tao.*

In recent years Chan has suffered from different illnesses and his health is no longer

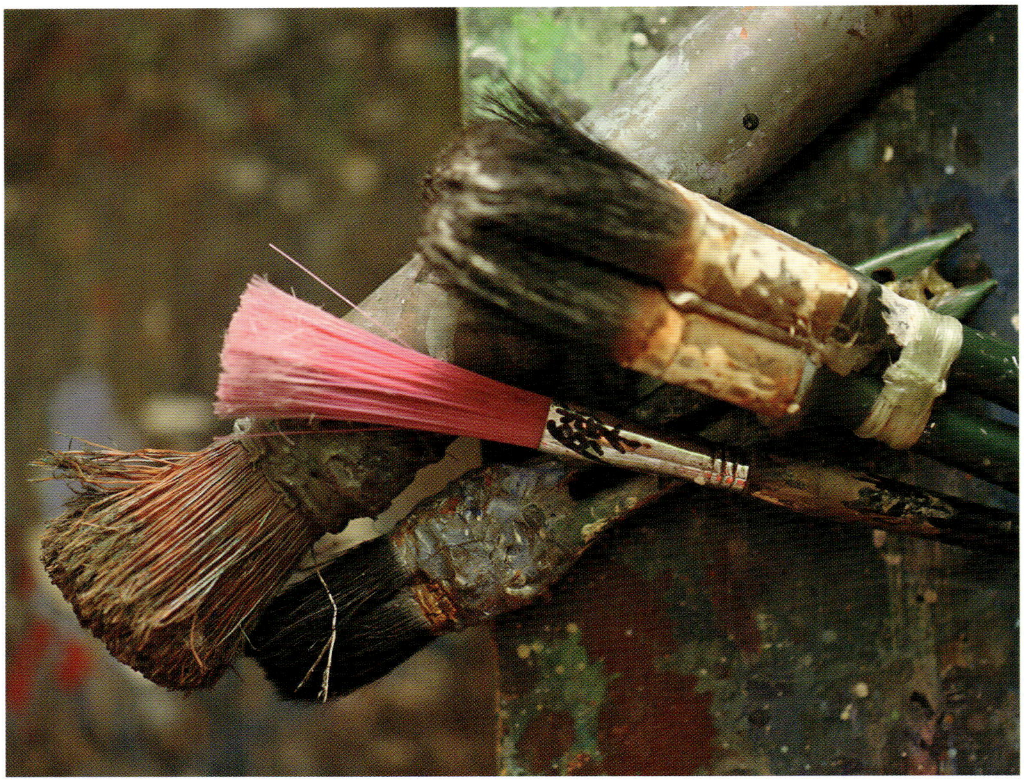

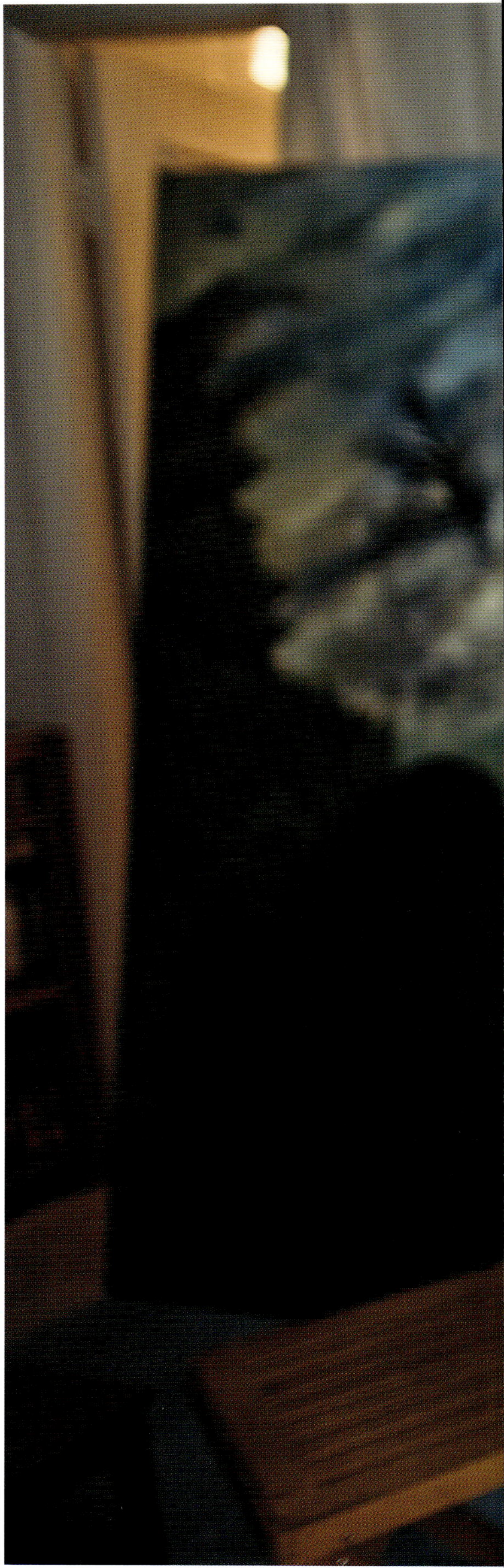

as good as it was. He then started to create with his computer. He uses the mouse as his brush and the screen as his palette, creating prints on paper with Microsoft Paint that have a similar mood to his paintings. An A4-size digital print often takes over 10 hours or more to finish, and then after numerous colour tests, only a few satisfactory prints can be selected. His art has risen to a new level.

Art originates from life. After over 40 years of art practice, Chan incorporates issues of life and death into his works. Recently he published a book, *Notes from Gaylord Chan*, in which he talks about his world views.

Chan loves Chow's quietness. Chow is a strong and outspoken lady who has her own views of art and life. She does not talk ceaselessly, nor is she submissive to her husband, as traditional Chinese wives are. For years, working and taking care of Chan have kept her busy, leaving her little time to paint. Eventually she decided to reduce her teaching load to spare more time for her to paint.

Acrylic is Chow's primary medium, but she occasionally does print and installation work as well. Her subject matters are the things around her, such as daily life, dreams, and nature. Her main concern is humanity, and her works are full of concern for it. Chow used to paint in the Cultural Corner, but cleaning up for classes made it hard to concentrate. Recently she turned one of her living rooms at home into her studio, where she paints without disturbance. She enjoys her mornings by painting and listening to her favourite classical music.

Chow thinks that having a studio of her own enables her to concentrate on her paintings. She does not make art for the sake of making art, nor did she set up a studio for the sake of setting up a studio. Art is not to follow suit. In the end, one is responsible for one's own art.

Chatting and drinking with Chow and Chan is a pleasant experience. They talk without taboos; they are true to their feelings. It is their open-mindedness that lets them create their own lives from art, and share that richness with other people.

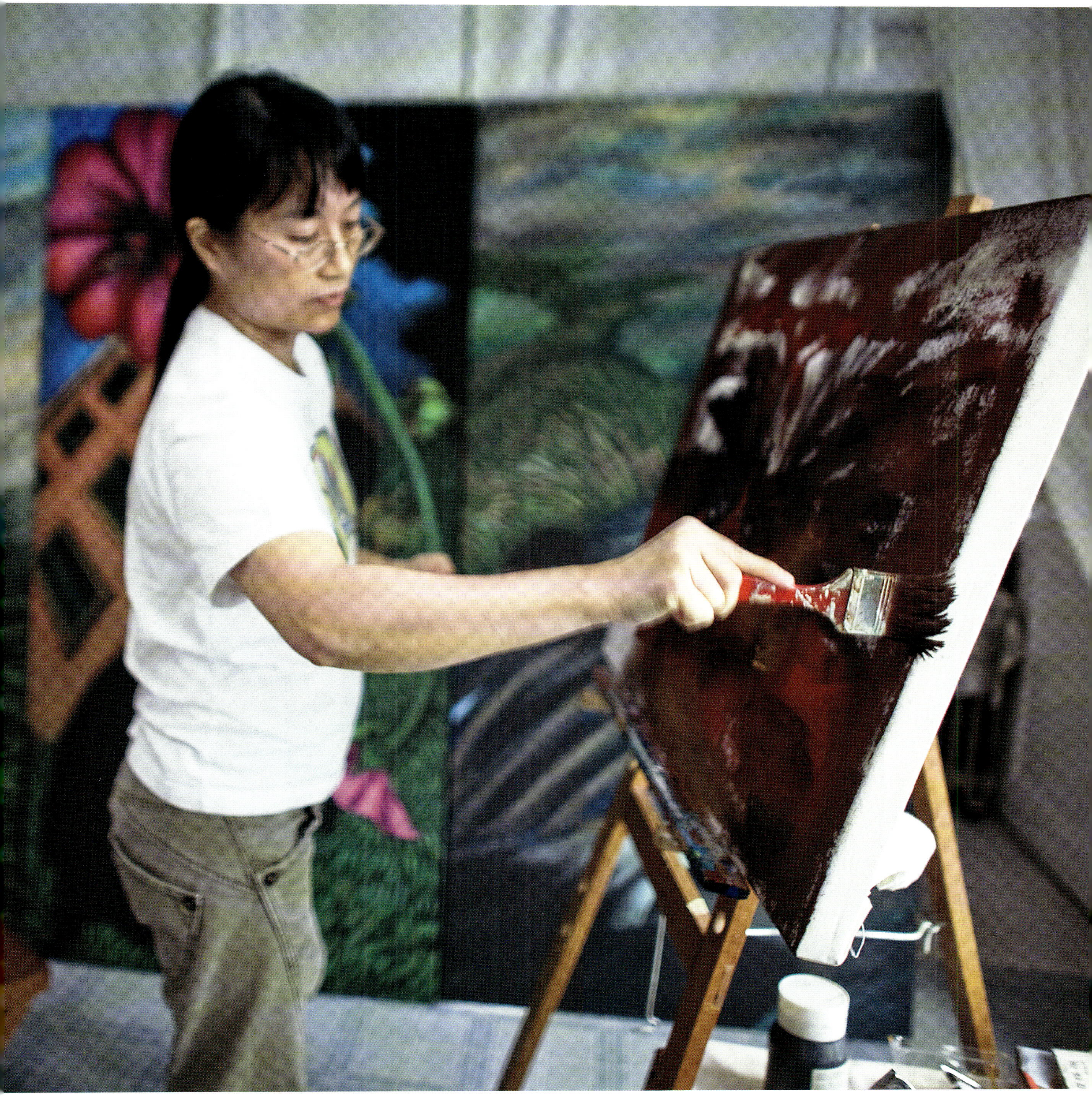

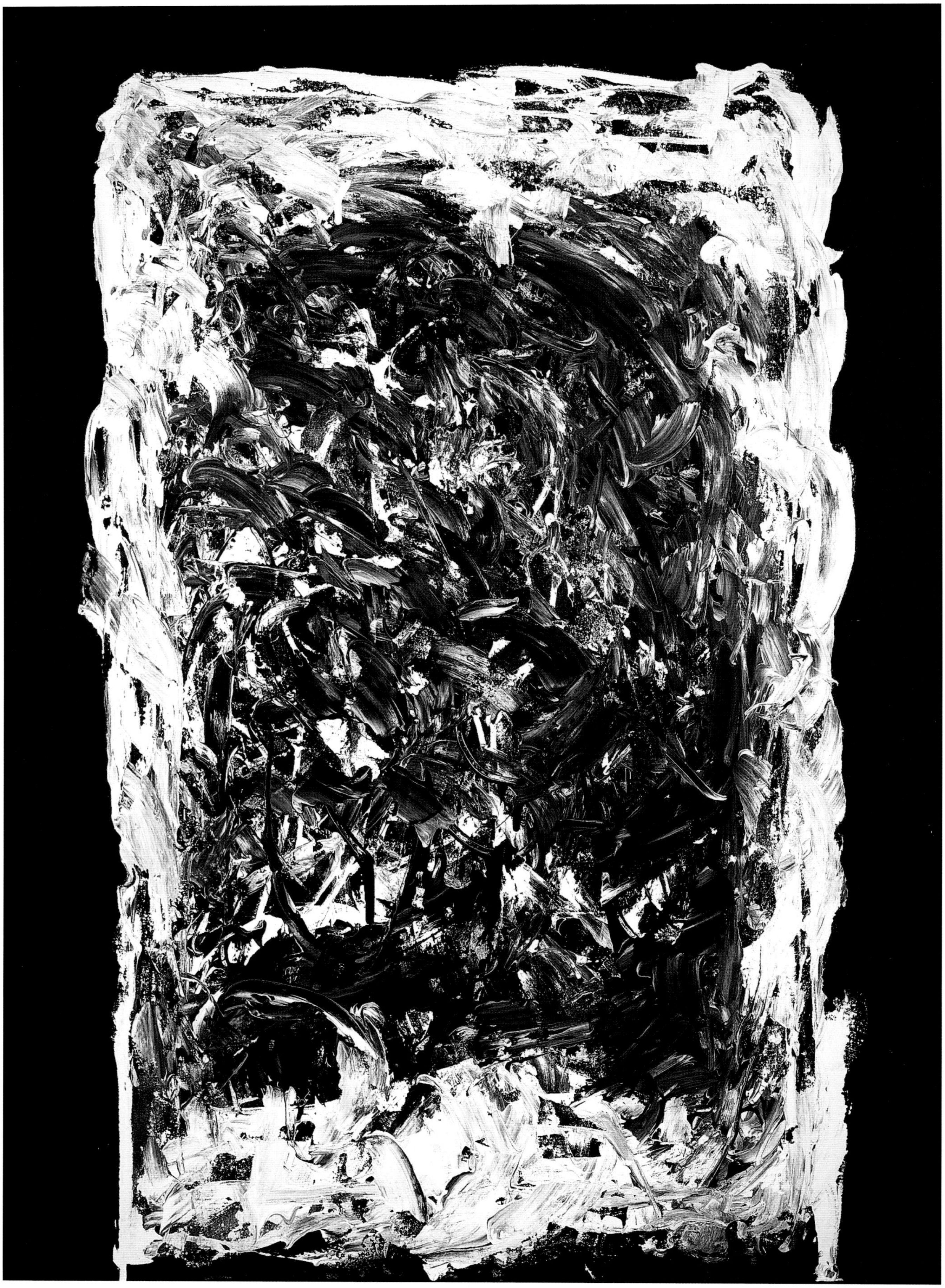

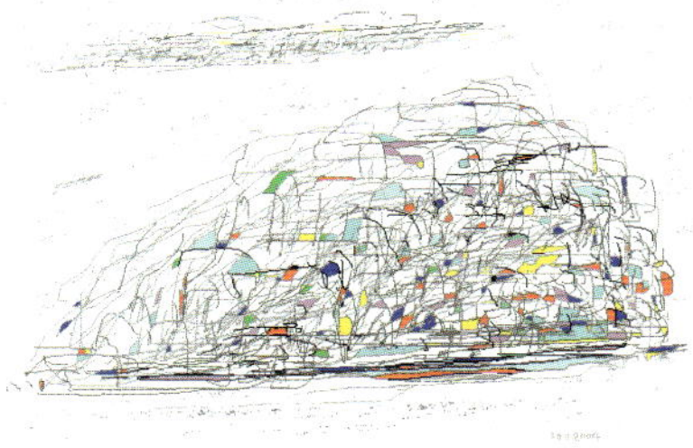

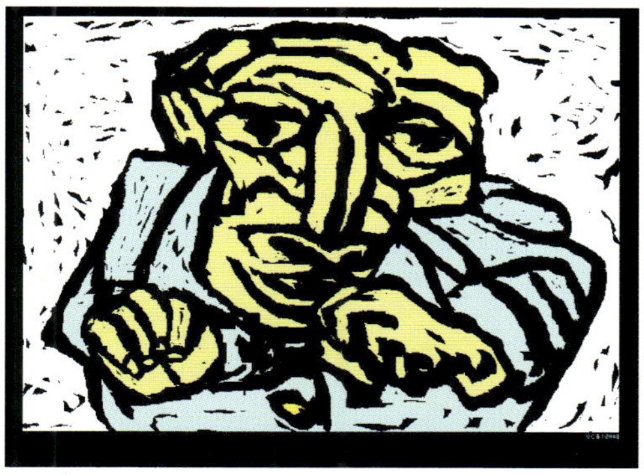

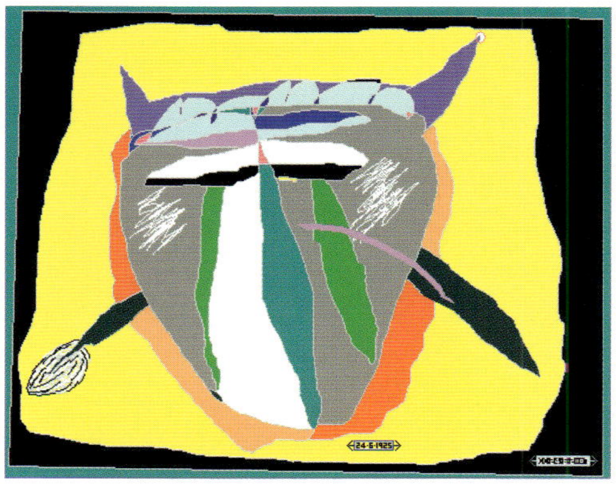

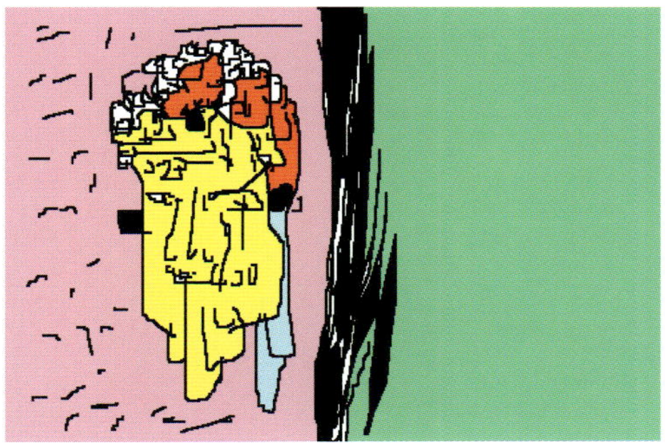

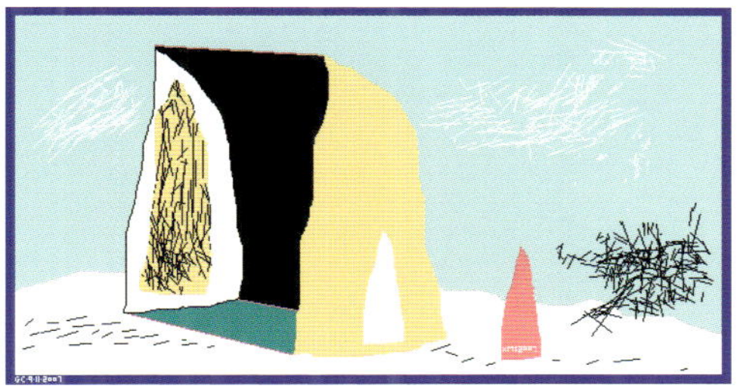

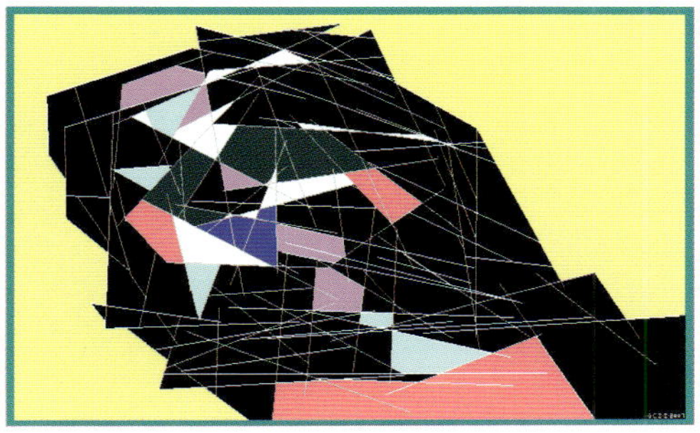

(Left page) Chan, Gaylord/Zero Point
Acrylic on canvas, 120x90 cm, 1999

(Right page, from left to right above)
Chan, Gaylord/Gems
Hybrid-Art, 210x297 cm, 2004

Chan, Gaylord/Oldfessor
Hybrid-Art, 210x297 cm, 2008

Chan, Gaylord/Old Mask
Hybrid-Art, 210x297 cm, 2007

(Right page, from left to right bottom)
Chan, Gaylord/Window X
Hybrid-Art, 210x297 cm, 2008

Chan, Gaylord/Xms
Hybrid-Art, 210x297 cm, 2007

Chan, Gaylord/Glass
Hybrid-Art, 210x297 cm, 2007

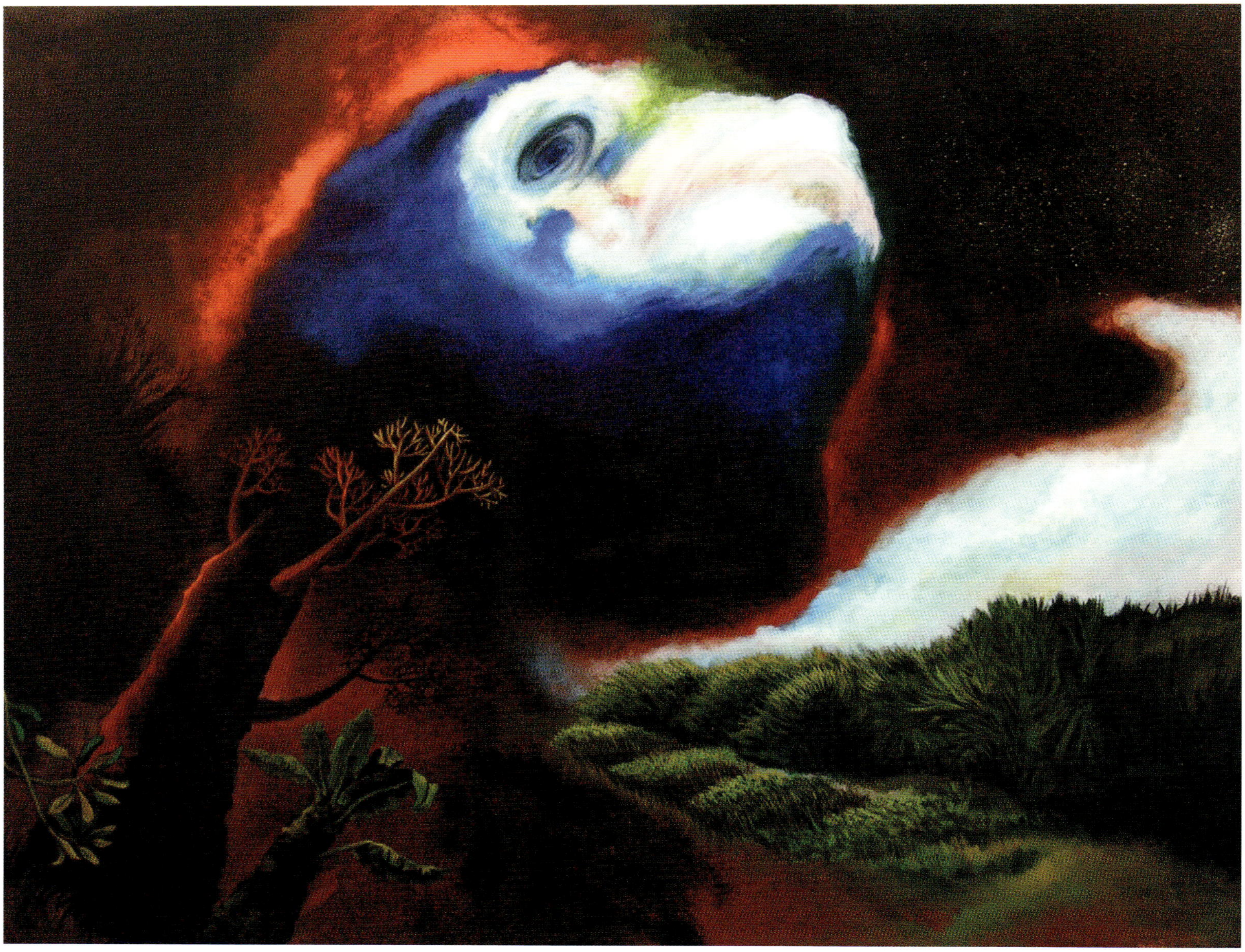

Chow Suk-fan, Josephine/Zone II
Acrylic on canvas, 92x122 cm, 2006

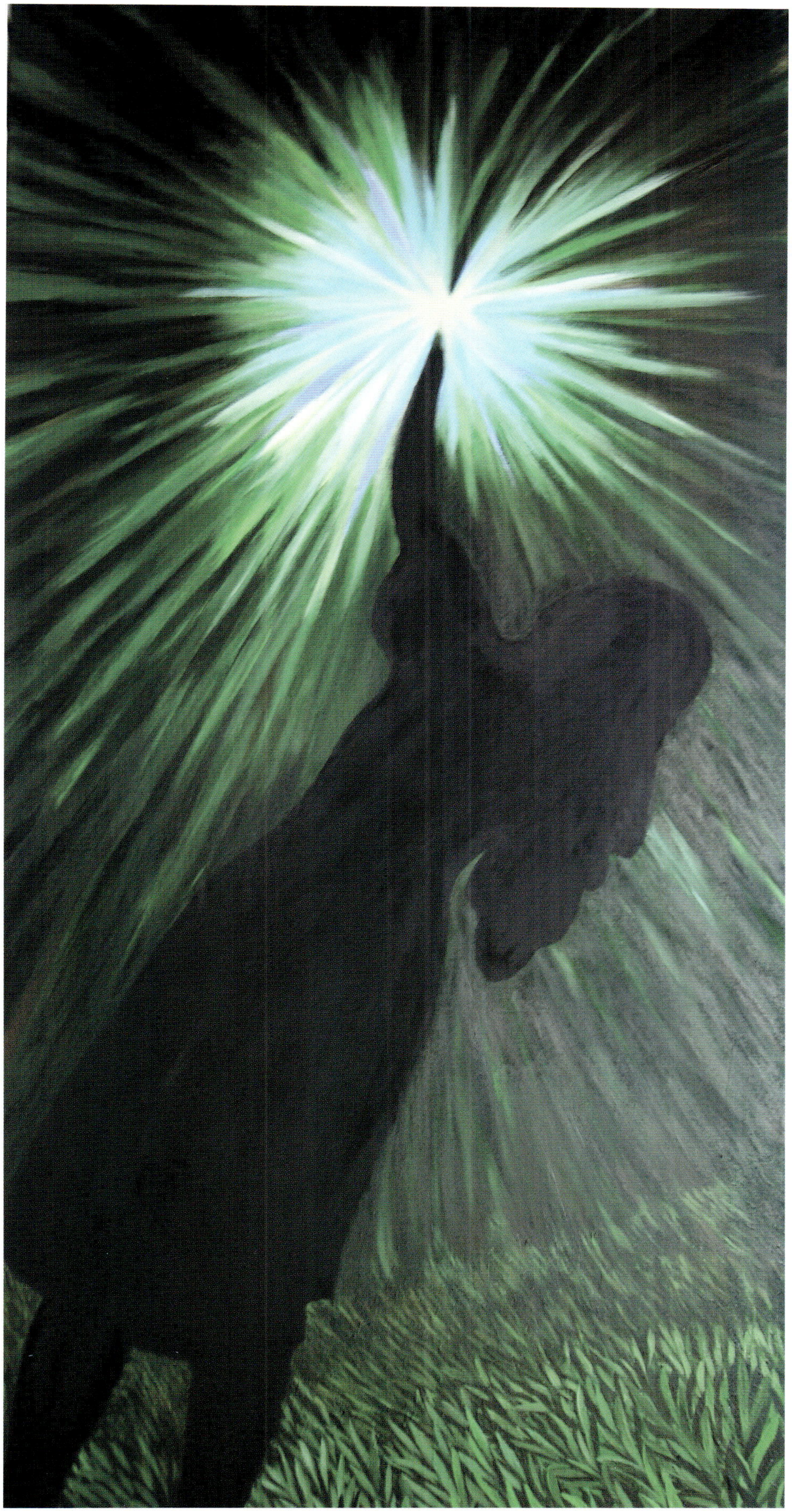

Chow Suk-fan, Josephine/Shadcw III
Acrylic on canvas, 183x92 cm, 2008

Celia Ko Tin-yan and Tony Ng Kwun-lun

Relativism

By Alice Choi

Celia Ko Tin-yan graduated from California State University in the United States with a Bachelor degree in fine arts, in drawing and painting. She has organised several solo exhibitions in Hong Kong and the US, and has participated in group exhibitions and community mural projects in Los Angeles and Long Beach. She is a visiting lecturer at the Hong Kong Polytechnic University, Hong Kong Art School, City University of Hong Kong, and is a part time tutor at the University of Hong Kong's School of Professional and Continuing Education (HKU SPACE). Ko was awarded the Vermont Studio Center Fellowship in 2000. Her works are collected by the Hong Kong Museum of Art and private collectors.

Tony Ng Kwun-lun got his diploma in Chinese ink painting from the former Department of Extramural Studies at the Chinese University of Hong Kong. He has vast experience in the framing, conservation and restoration of artworks. He teaches at the HKU SPACE, Hong Kong Chingying Institute of Visual Arts and CO1 School of Visual Arts, and has attracted public and commercial commissions. He has received numerous awards and his works are collected by the Hong Kong Heritage Museum, the Hong Kong Museum of Art and individuals.
Together they established 20C Studio in 2002, and their members' first group show, *20C Debut – Eclectic Visions*, was held in June 2008.

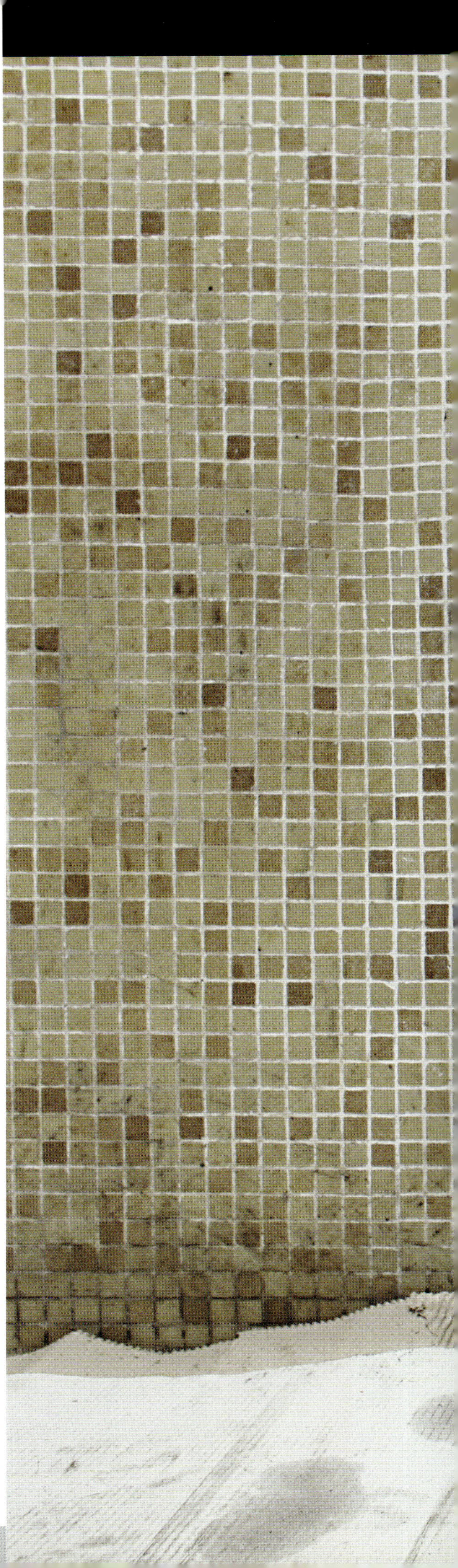

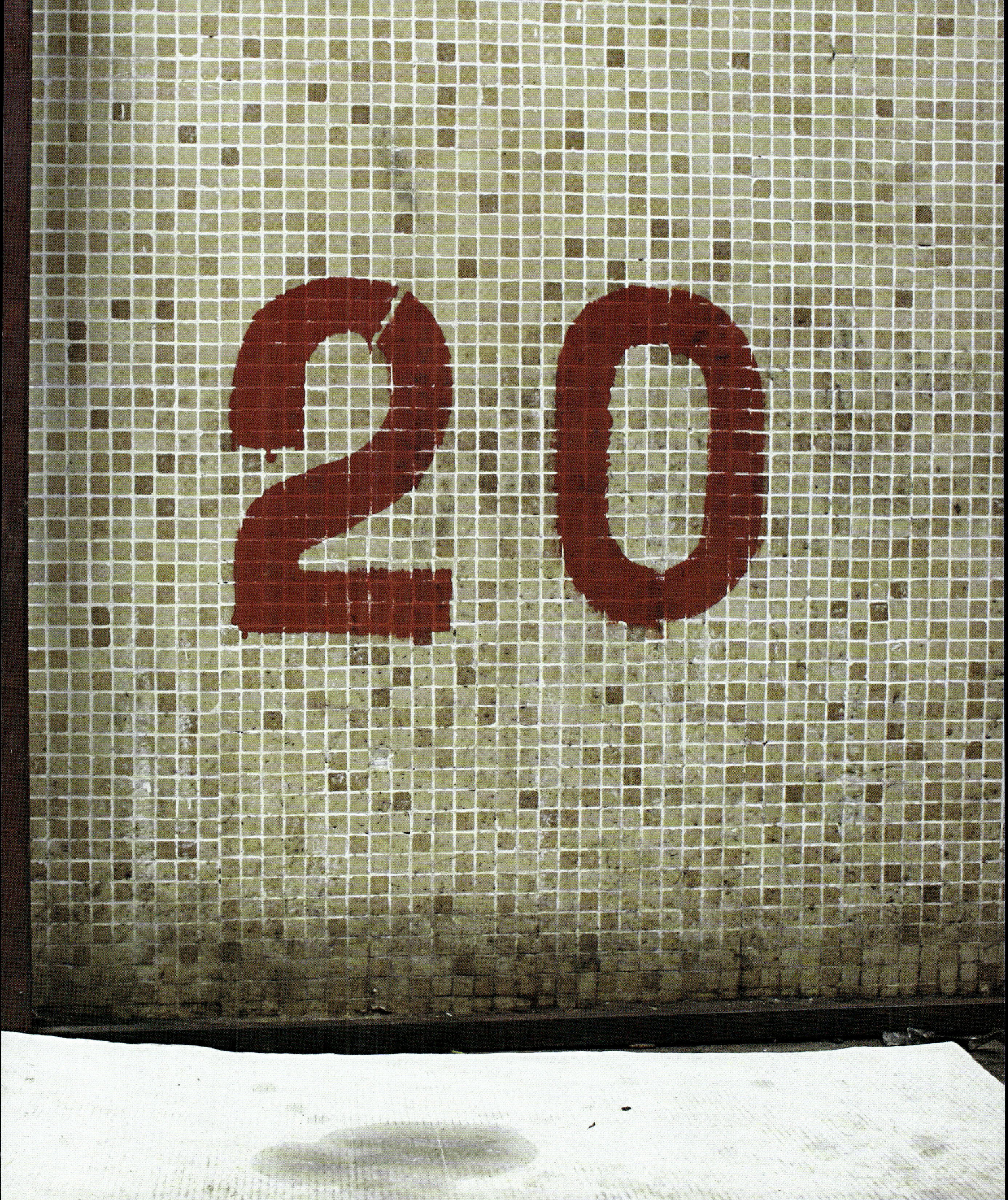
20

Celia Ko Tin-yan and Tony Ng Kwun-lun's studio is located on the top floor of an industrial building in Sai Wan, the western part of Hong Kong Island. It has a frontal sea view and a rear mountain view. Established in August 2002, it was originally intended as a place for art making. However as more and more students indicated an interest in art, in 2003 Ko and Ng decided to open up the space for their students to use every Thursday evening.

For six years Ko and Ng have been witness to the development of the neighbourhood. A luxurious apartment building was built next door and the old stone houses along the hillside behind them were demolished by the government, leaving traces of the old floor tiles, seen like crackers from a distance (and reminiscent of a cityscape in Piet Mondrian's *Broadway Boogie-Woogie* from 1943, only without the hustle and bustle). The value of the industrial building which they are using has also risen drastically over the past few years. Since the studio is not their property, if they are asked to leave one day, they will have to do so, albeit reluctantly.

In the past the artists have worked at their homes, but this had its limitations. Ko recalls the day that they decided to have a casual look around with agents; they had not made the concrete decision to rent a studio, but when they first saw the space they fell in love with it. Ng is very content with it now and feels

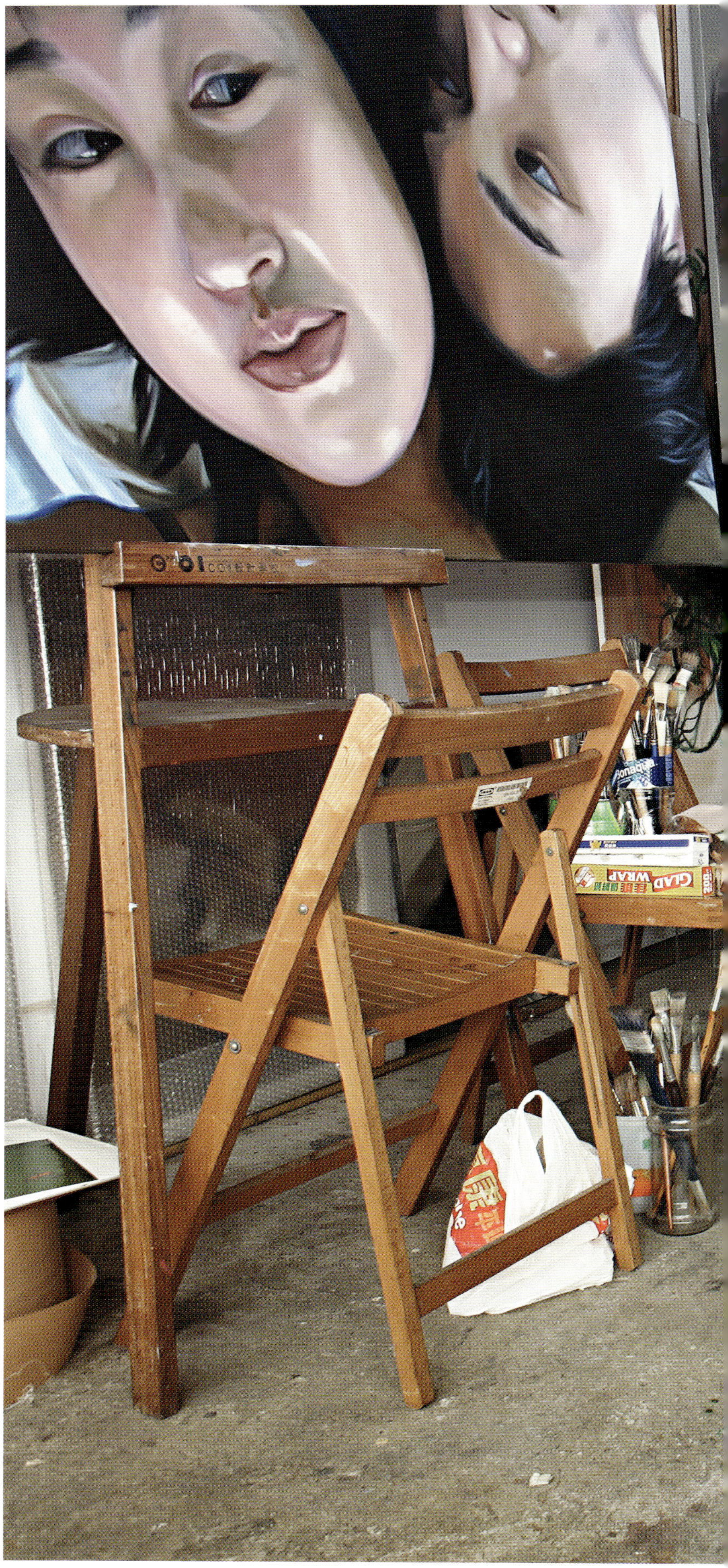

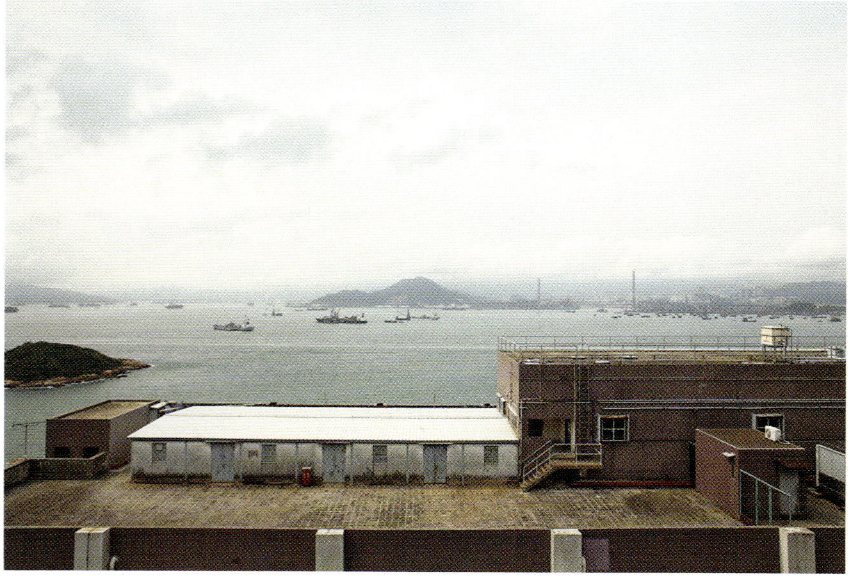

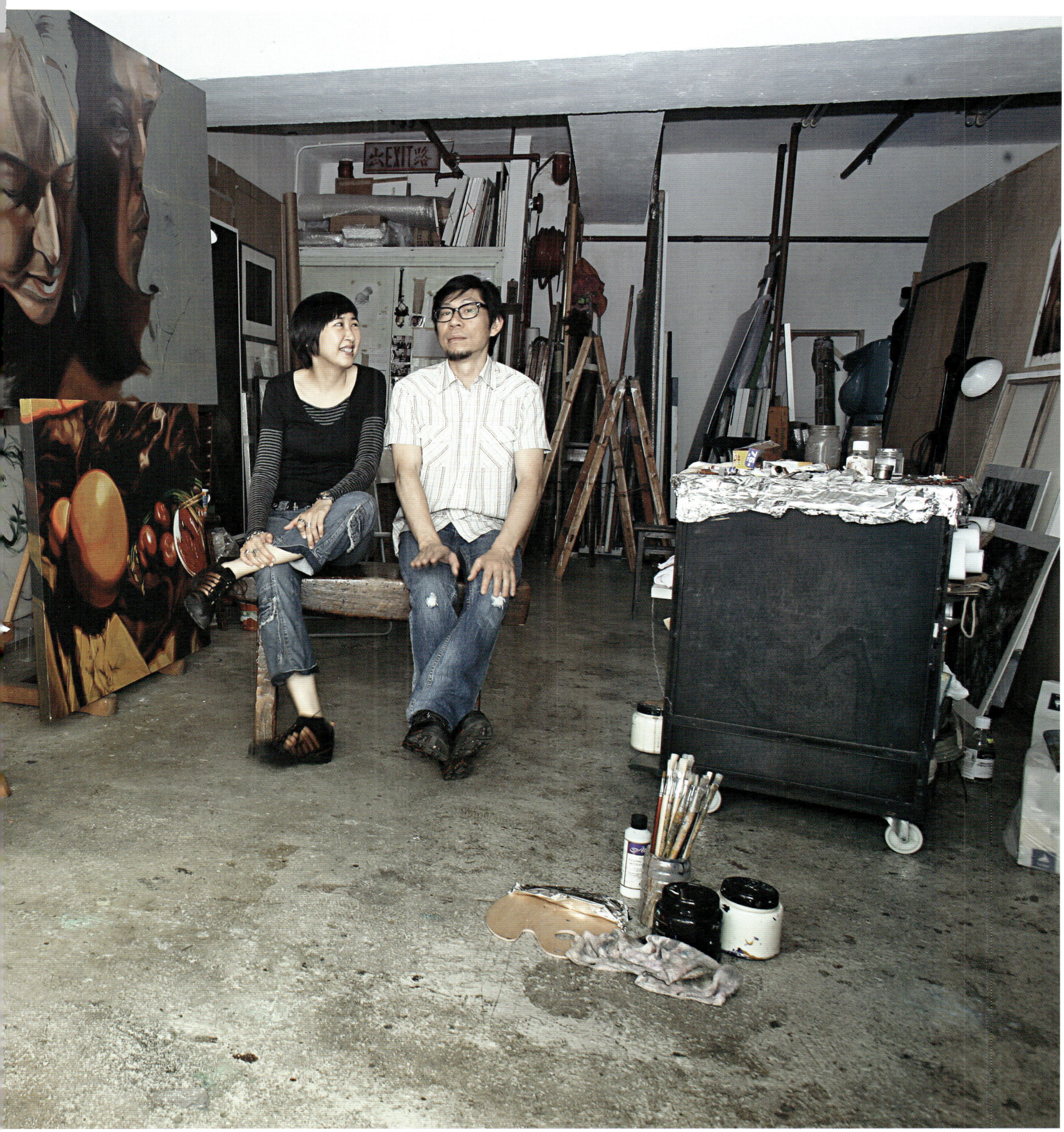
EXIT

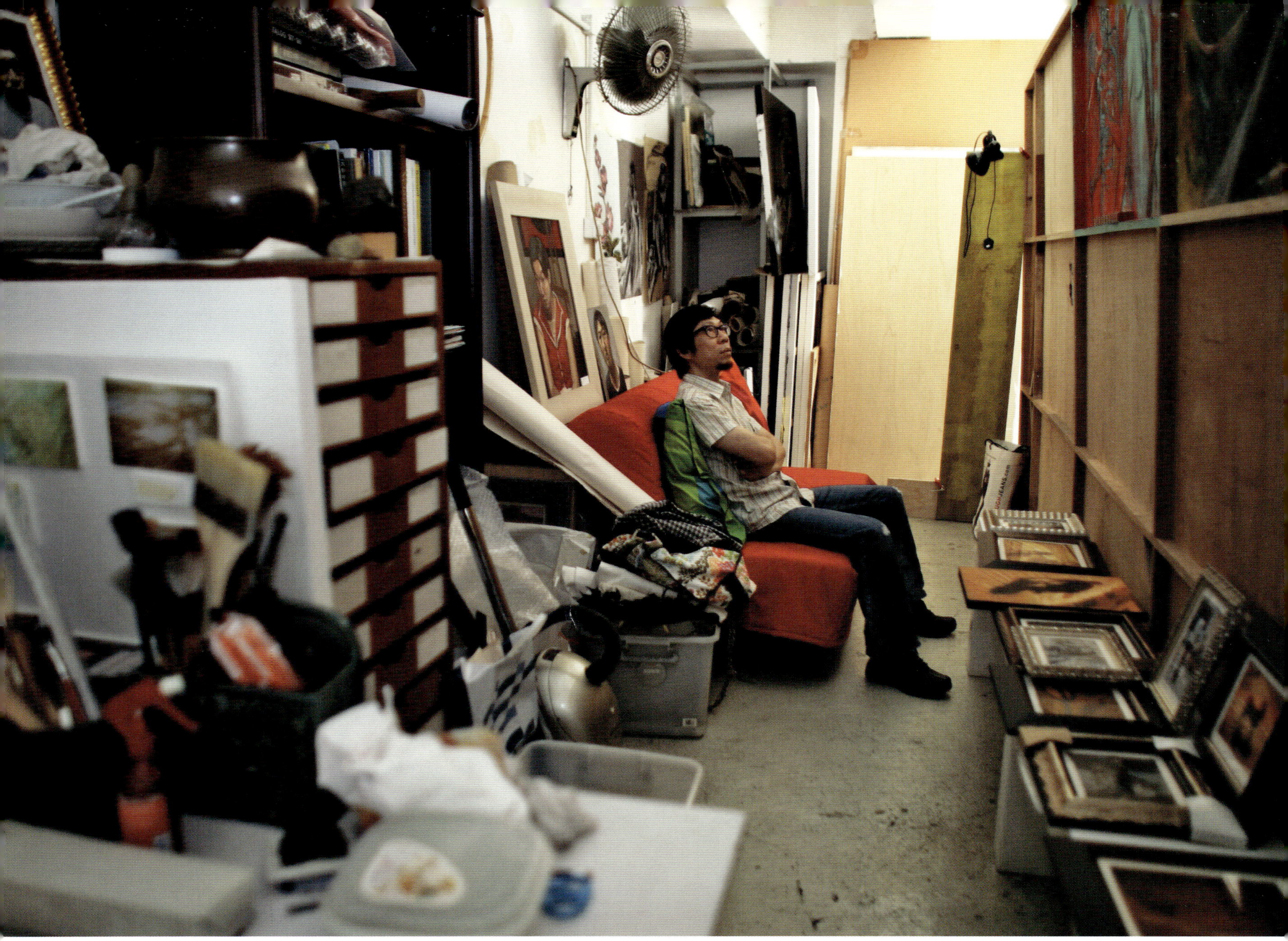

On the dark surfaces mountains and rocks are rich in texture and vitality, as if they are being oppressed, breathing heavily. His works have a strong contemporary character, yet also the scintillating, intrinsic quality of the literati at home there. "It takes time for me to adjust to an environment," he explains. "Now I have got used to this studio, which has become a stable creative space for me. In the past when I worked at a framing workshop or at home it was flexible, but tough and uncomfortable."

Despite sharing the same studio, Ko and Ng are independent in their art. In fact they have their own schedules and seldom work there at the same time. Whenever they have spare time they try to work there, but owing to the lack of space, they accommodate each other's needs too. For instance, if one of them has to do a large work, the other will make an adjustment, and the studio layout therefore keeps changing.

It only takes a second to contrast Ko and Ng's personalities. Ng is more reserved and cautious, while Ko is outspoken, enthusiastic and active. It is their similarities and differences that make the space unique and interesting. Artworks often reflect an artist's character. It is not difficult to tell which work belongs to whom.

Upon entering, Ng's well-known ink stone paintings immediately come into my sight: layers of form and a dark colour scheme, with a heavy and reserved character. Yet his style has nothing to do with traditional Chinese landscape painting, and the techniques were invented by Ng himself, creating a unique persona of his own. On the dark surfaces mountains and rocks are rich in texture and vitality, as if they are being oppressed, breathing heavily. Ng's works have a strong contemporary character, yet also the scintillating, intrinsic quality of the literati. No wonder some people describe his works as depicting 'spiritual landscapes'.

An artist's creativity often has many facets. To more comprehensively understand Ng, his three-dimensional works should not be missed. For the past decade he has created many sculptures and installations. He applies the same level of thinking to his two-dimensional and three-dimensional works, and both kinds are consistent with his style, though the former is richer in its diversity of materials. For his sculpture *Clouds* he made use of more than 30 pieces of transparent acrylic board to convey the phenomenon of three-dimensional space. In another sculpture, *Heroic* (on display at the Police Headquarters), pieces of steel are used, creating multiple reflections on the red-painted back of the sculpture. These change in accordance with the movement of passers-by, creating a subtle symbolic effect.

In spite of his busy teaching, Ng has also taken up art consultancy, and he takes commission on.

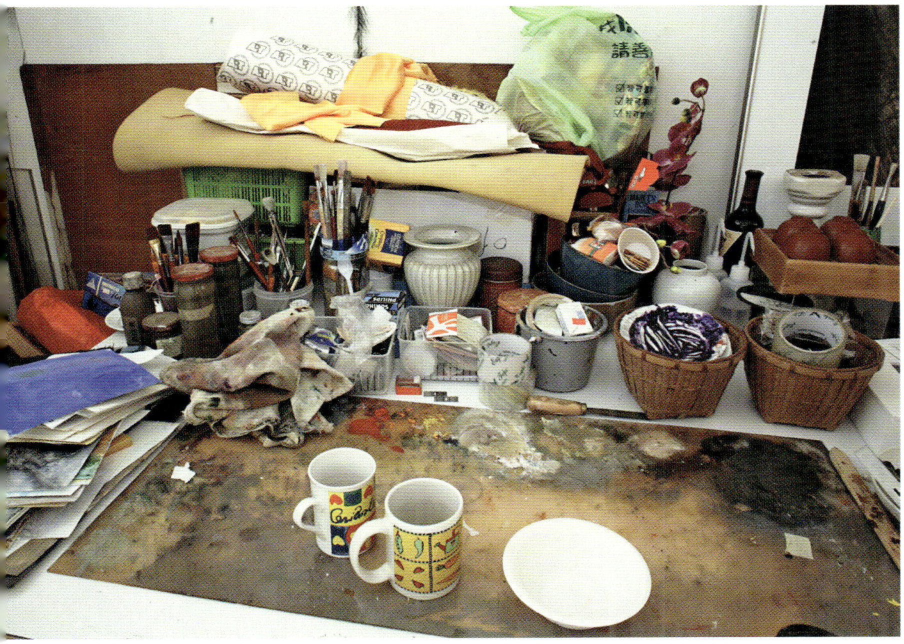

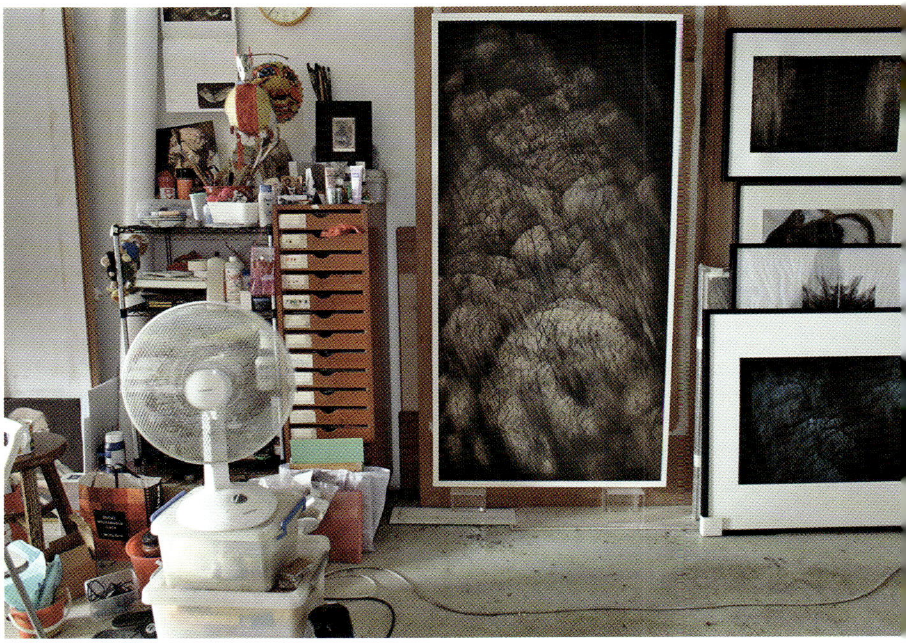

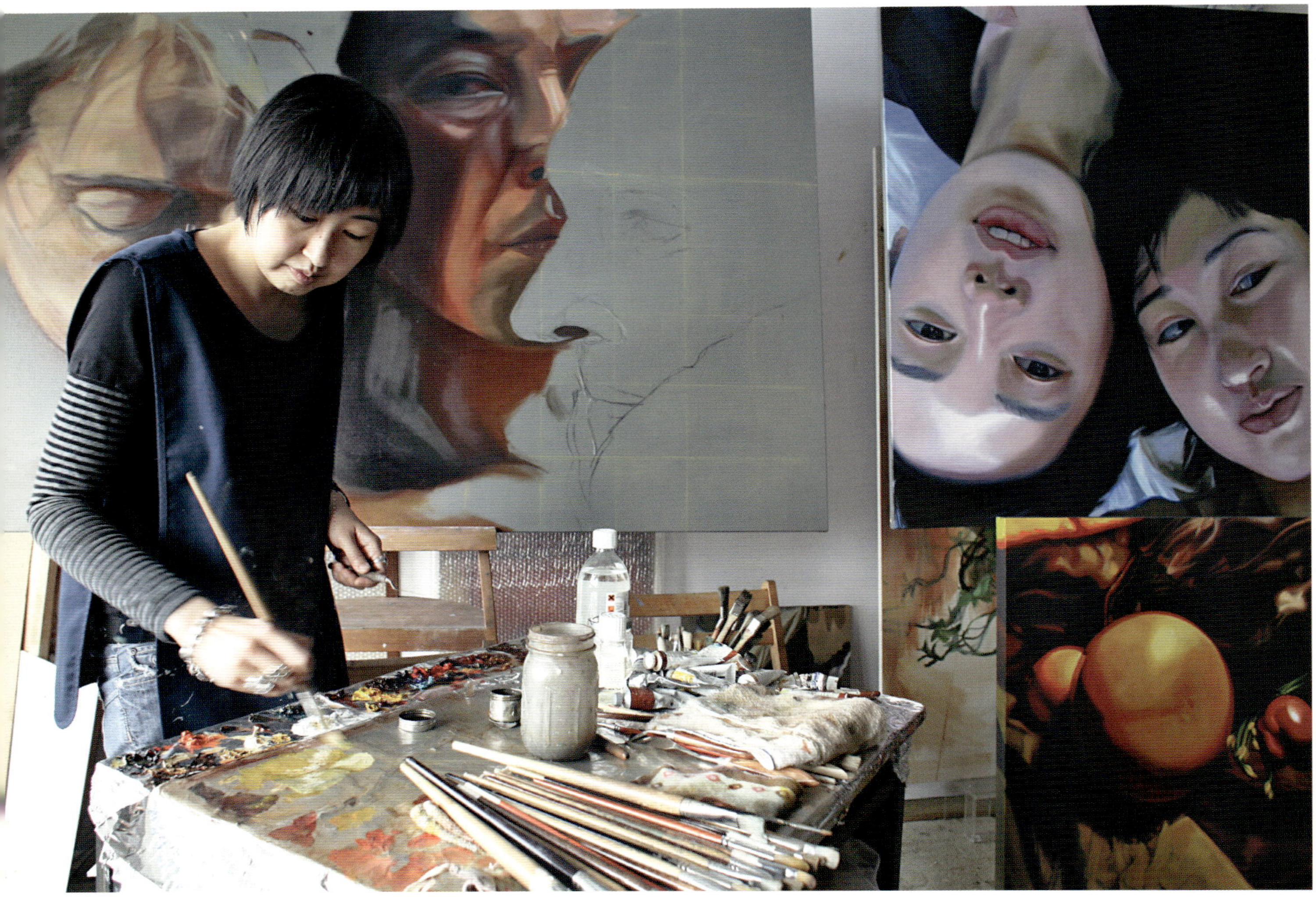

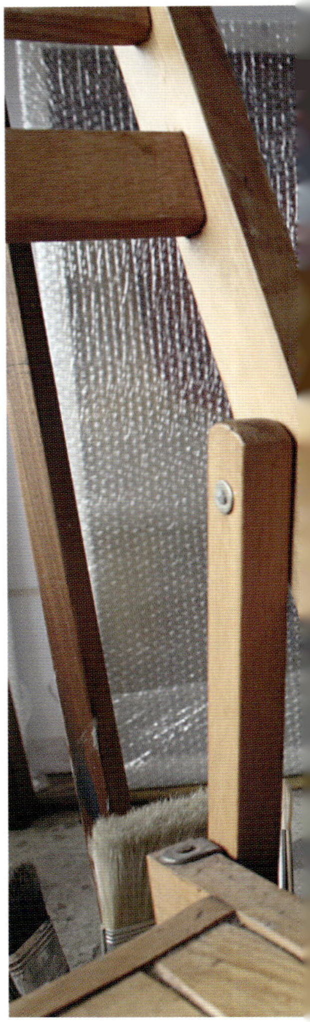

His works are widely seen in government departments, at the Hong Kong International Airport, the Hong Kong Wetland Park, the Urban Council Centenary Garden, and in large hotels in Hong Kong and China. Ng has always tried to strike a balance between his creativity and users' needs, considering viewers' points of view together with the uniqueness of the site. "Artists' concepts are important," he explains. "However we also need to consider the feelings of users, particularly in public art, because the sites are public and some are even working spaces; the people using the space may need to face the same environment frequently or even every day. I want my work to be human-oriented and multi-functional. Therefore people, time and place are equally important in my consideration."

Ko currently concentrates on oil painting. In the studio we mainly see huge paintings of human figures. Both the subject matter and mood of the paintings are meticulously

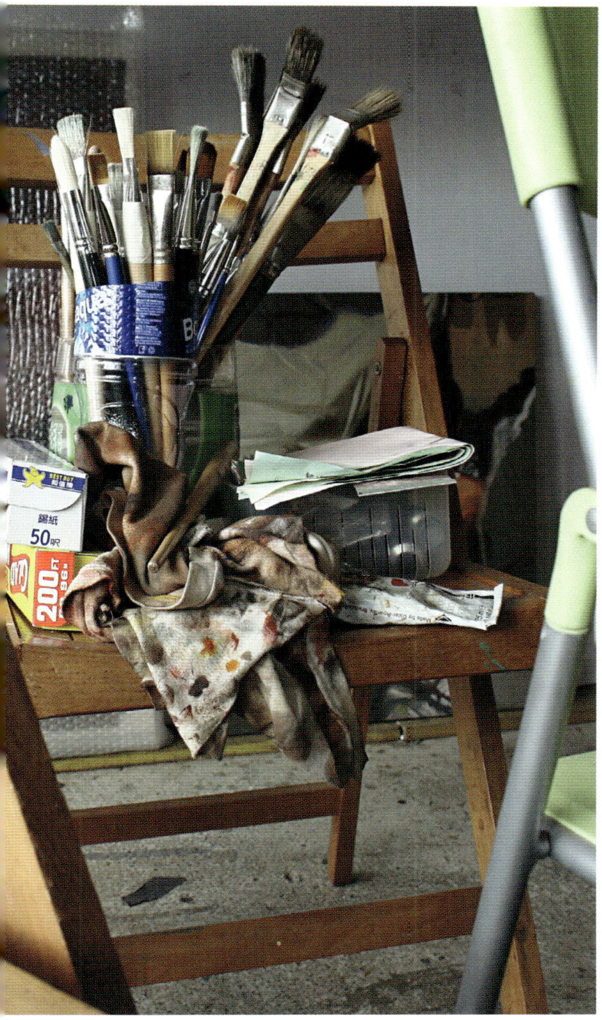

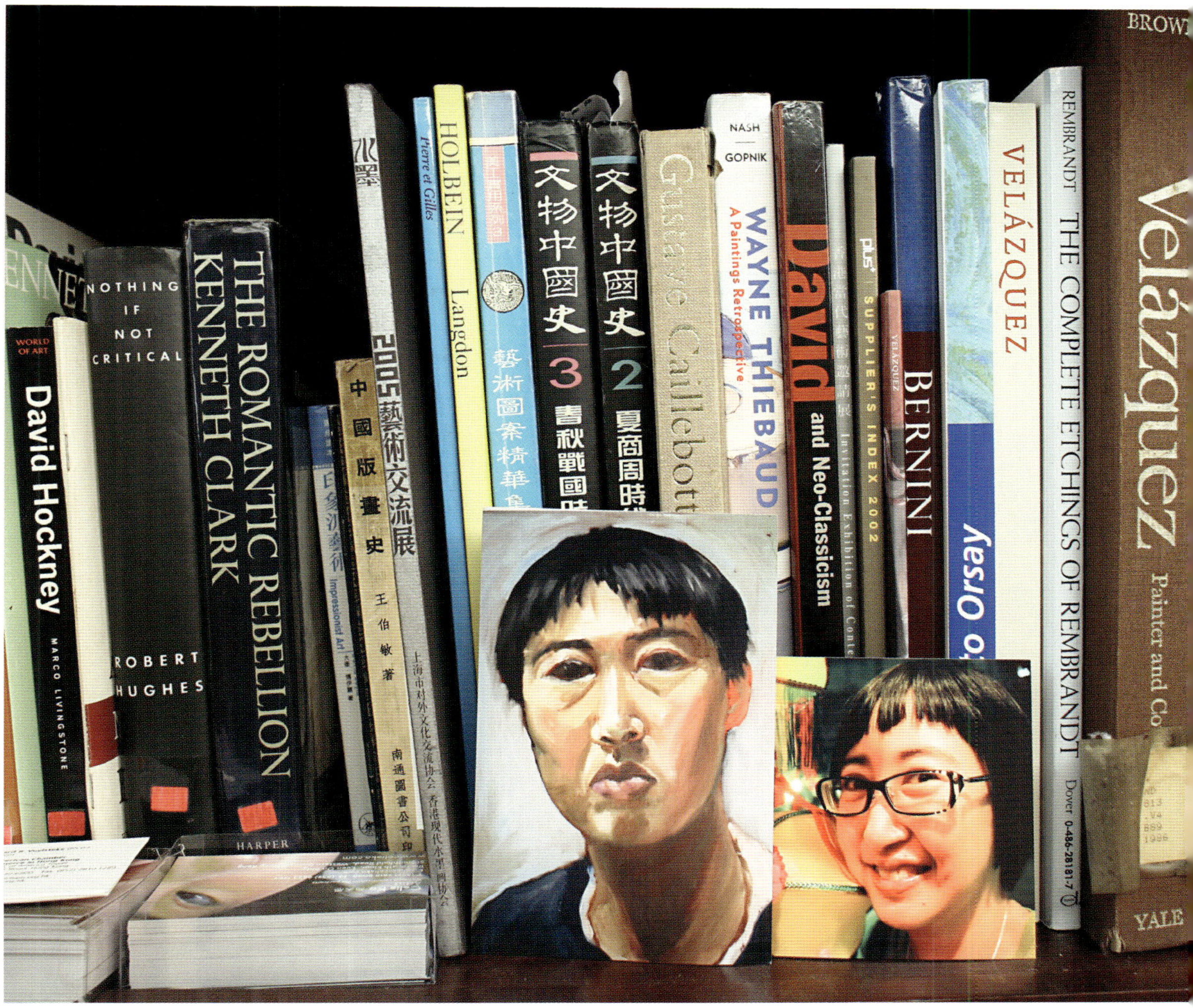

arranged. Her style and subject matters are unique. She often uses her acquaintances and students as models, staging them in different scenes. For instance, Ng has appeared more than once in her works. She is fascinated with people as a subject matter. The depiction of people represents a deeper side of herself. After all, representational and abstract art are both sides of the self. Ko is fond of the purity of painting, and she opines that what is represented in the paintings should be accessible to viewers. "Like music, visual art should be able to visualise and communicate beyond words," she says.

When Ko was studying painting in the US she explored different media, such as installations, video, photography and mural painting. She had been fascinated with Chinese history and literature from a very young age, so when she was in a non-Chinese context she was drawn into thinking about her cultural identity even more. That was when the *Wearables* series came about. Developed in the early '90s, this series ranged from earrings, belts, decorative collars and jewellery. Each piece is handmade, using materials steeped in culture and personal history, such as childhood pictures, imageries, text and jewels.

When she returned to Hong Kong, Ko brought the Southern Californian mural tradition and its techniques with her. From the 1990s until now she has been involved in countless lectures and mural projects for those such as the Hong Kong Museum of Art, the former education department and the housing department, plus art organisations and schools. The techniques that she has taught are still being widely used.

Although Ko and Ng both use traditional materials to create art, their subject matters and methods are contemporary and unique. They both believe that art has no boundaries; the media chosen should depend on the purpose and focus of the piece. "Pluralism

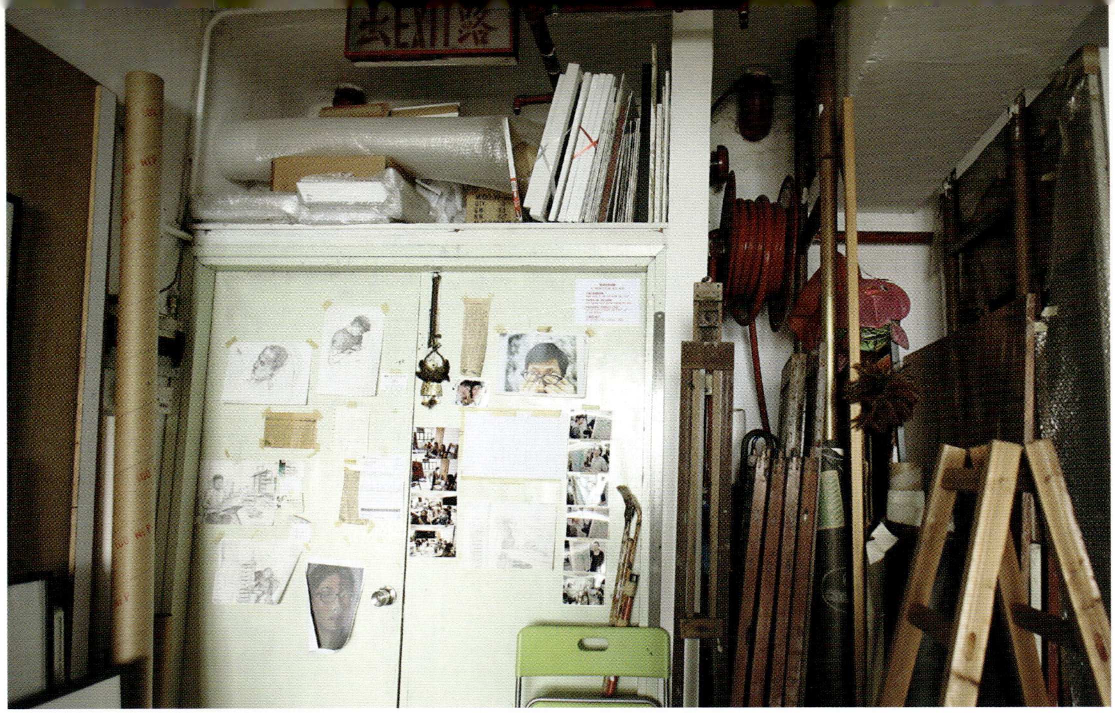
EXIT

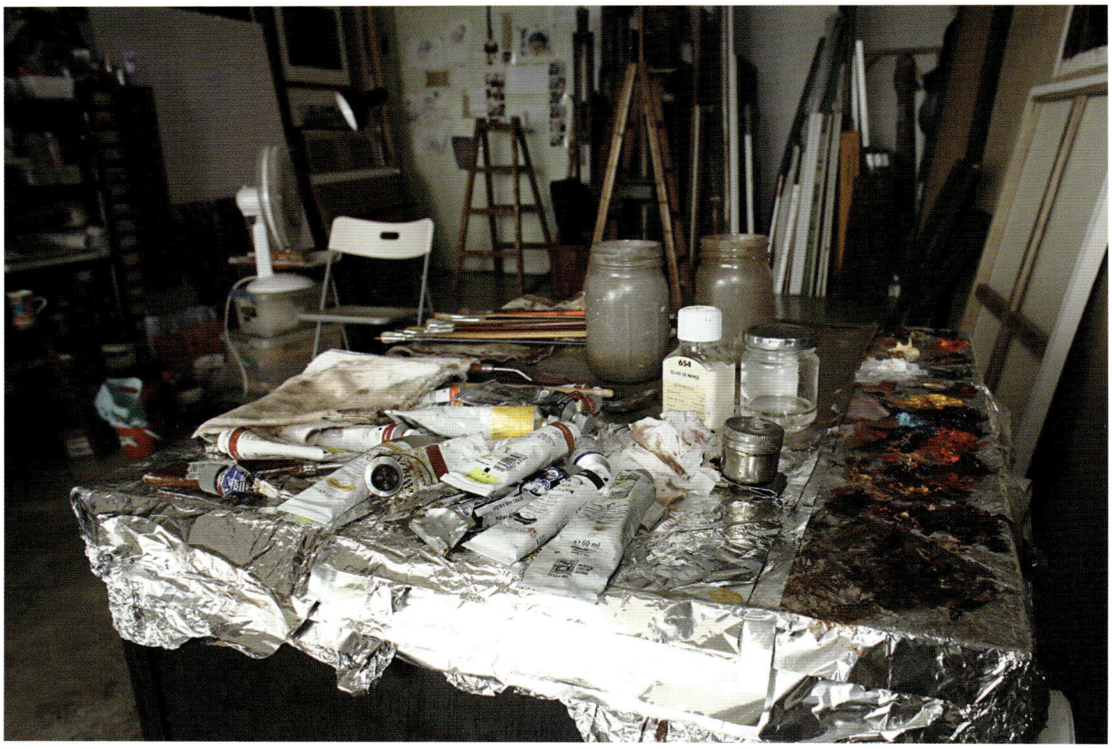

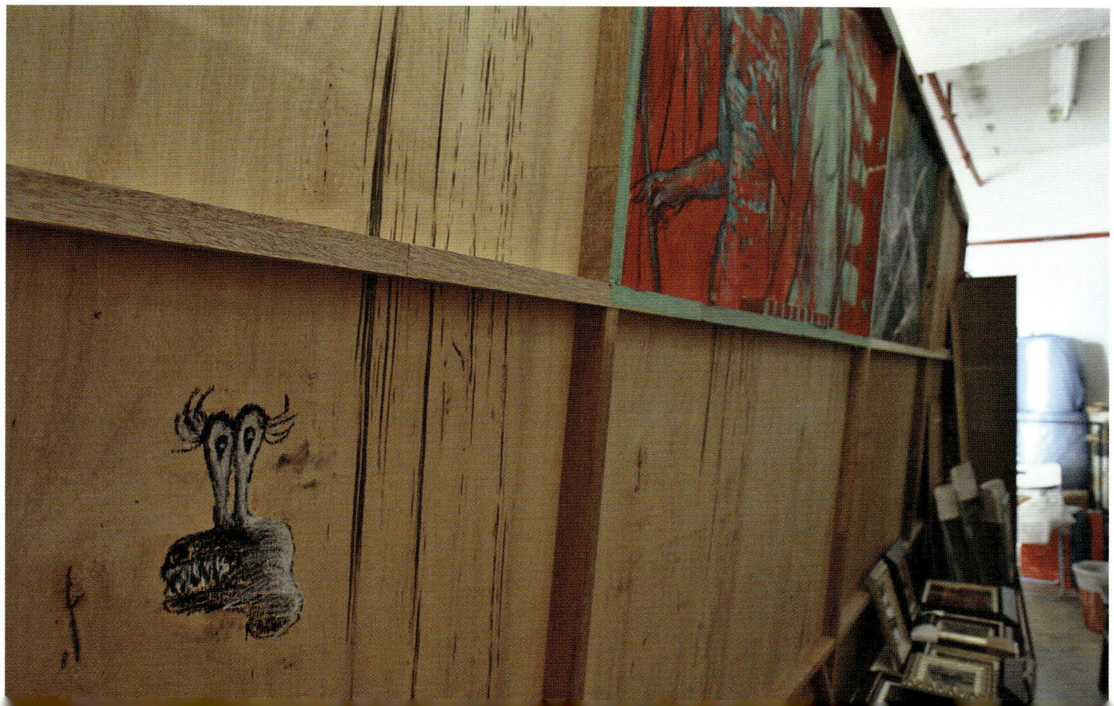

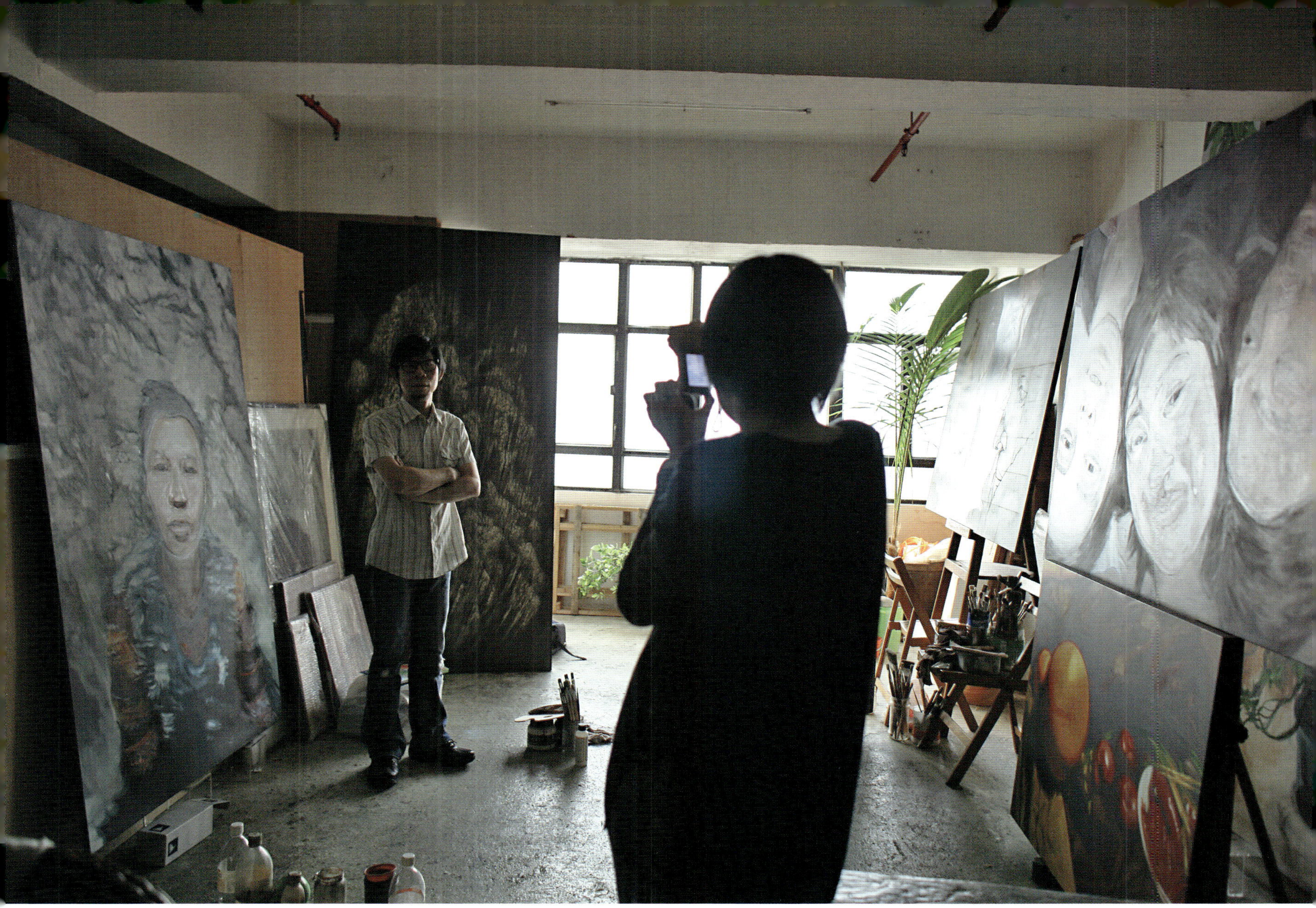

Opposite in appearance yet harmonious in nature is their way of getting along with each other

has been discussed for 40 years," Ko says. "Comments like 'painting is old-fashioned' or 'installations are avant-garde' are really outdated."

Talking to Ko and Ng is an interesting experience. Very often the same question will receive a totally different response, yet when you listen carefully, they actually have the same views presented in different ways. For instance, Ng thinks that being an artist is a lifestyle choice reliant on inner drive while Ko thinks that choosing the artist's path has nothing to do with choices, but is a matter of instinct, and that no matter what happens in life, one will eventually return to the same path.

Ko and Ng have both done different jobs before to earn a living, and found that they lost focus once they stopped making art. The process of art making may not always be enjoyable, and there are difficult times when one strives for perfection. All these require persistence and inner drive. Ko shares a trick: "At a point when you find that your job is a burden, this is an indicator that it is not your cup of tea." Art chose her, she says; it was a gift from above, which is incidentally the meaning of her Chinese name, Tin-yan.

Men are from Mars, women are from Venus. Two individuals can appear to be incompatible on the surface yet be harmonious in nature Ko and Ng share beliefs and strive for excellence in their art. It is their choice. It is their fate.

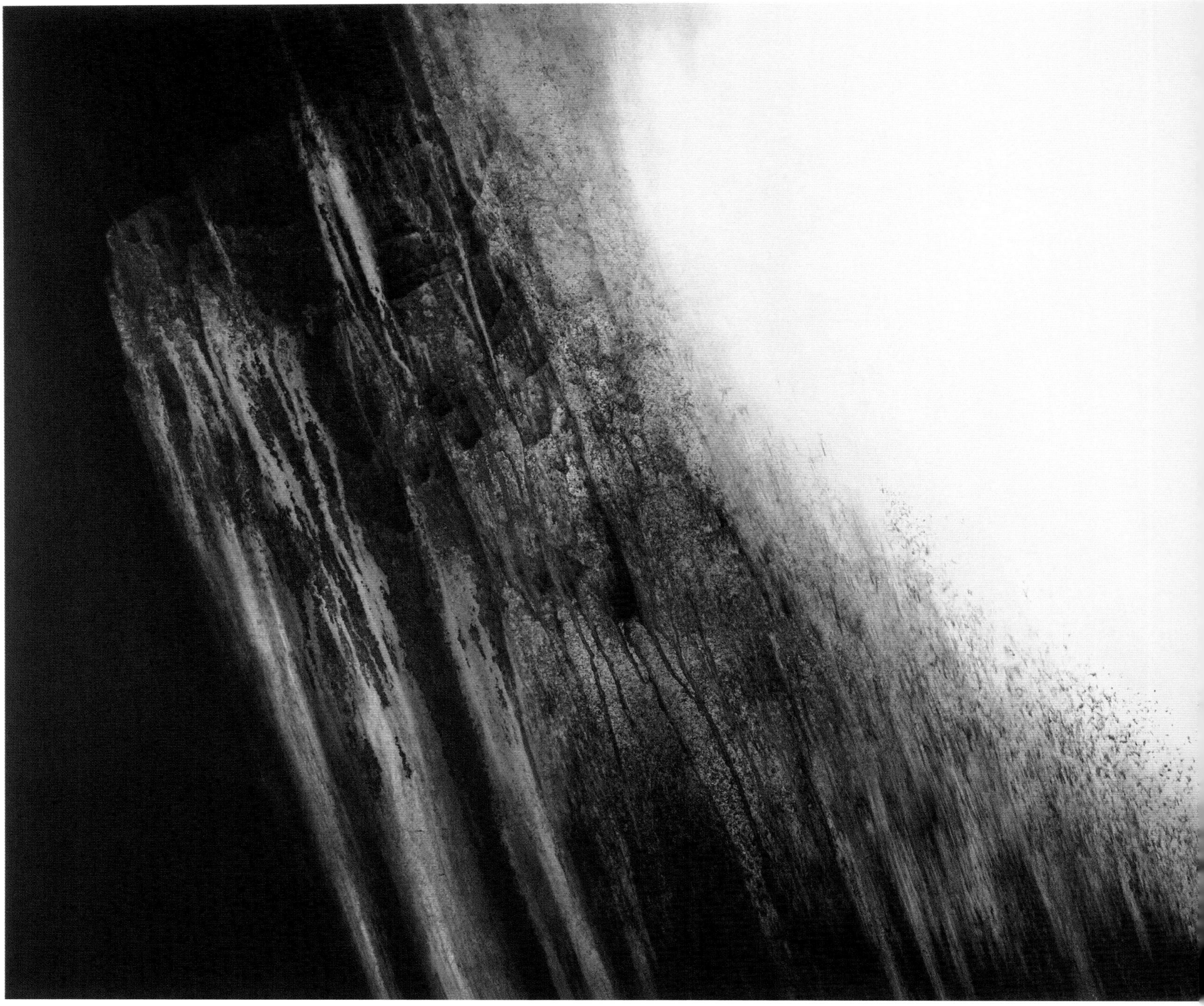

(Left) Ng Kwun-lun, Tony/Orbit
Ink & colour on paper, 88x162 cm, 1993

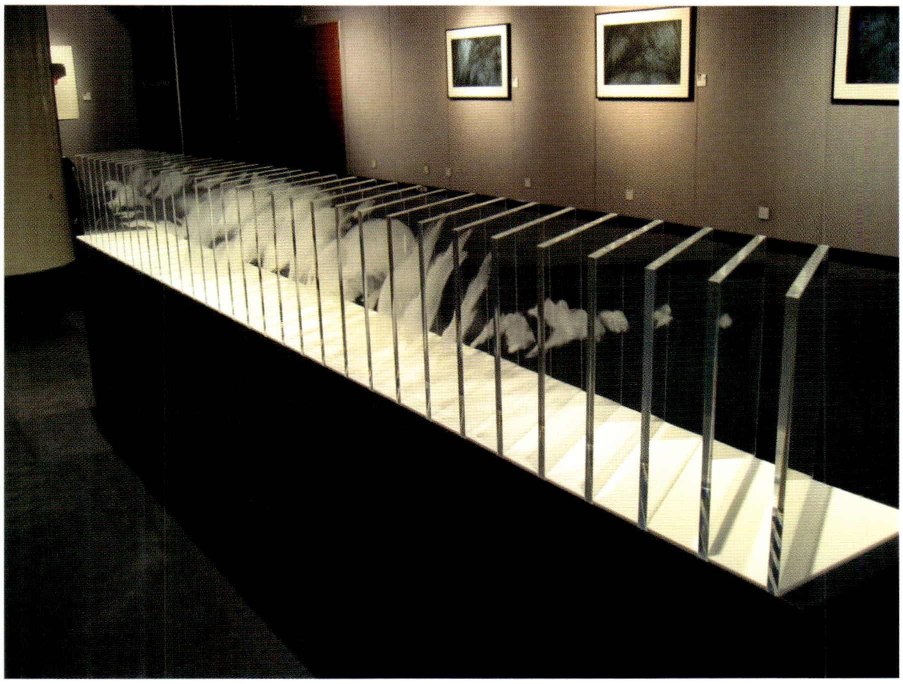

(Right) Ng Kwun-lun, Tony/Clouds
Acrylic sheet, 30x30x300 cm, 2004

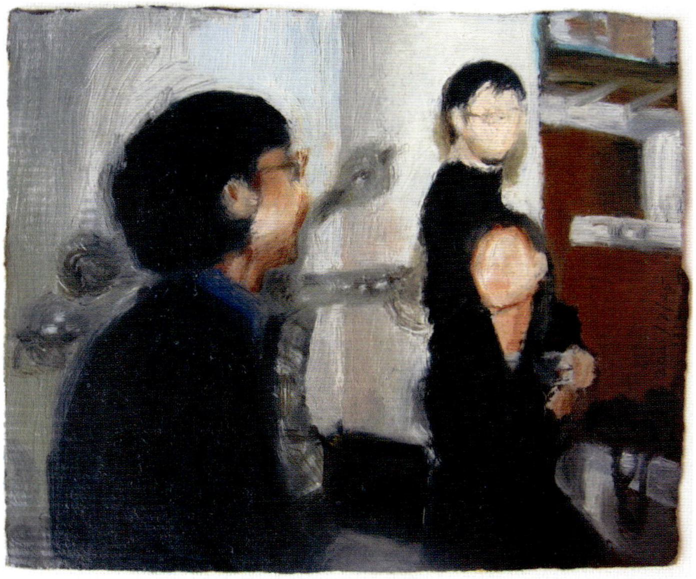

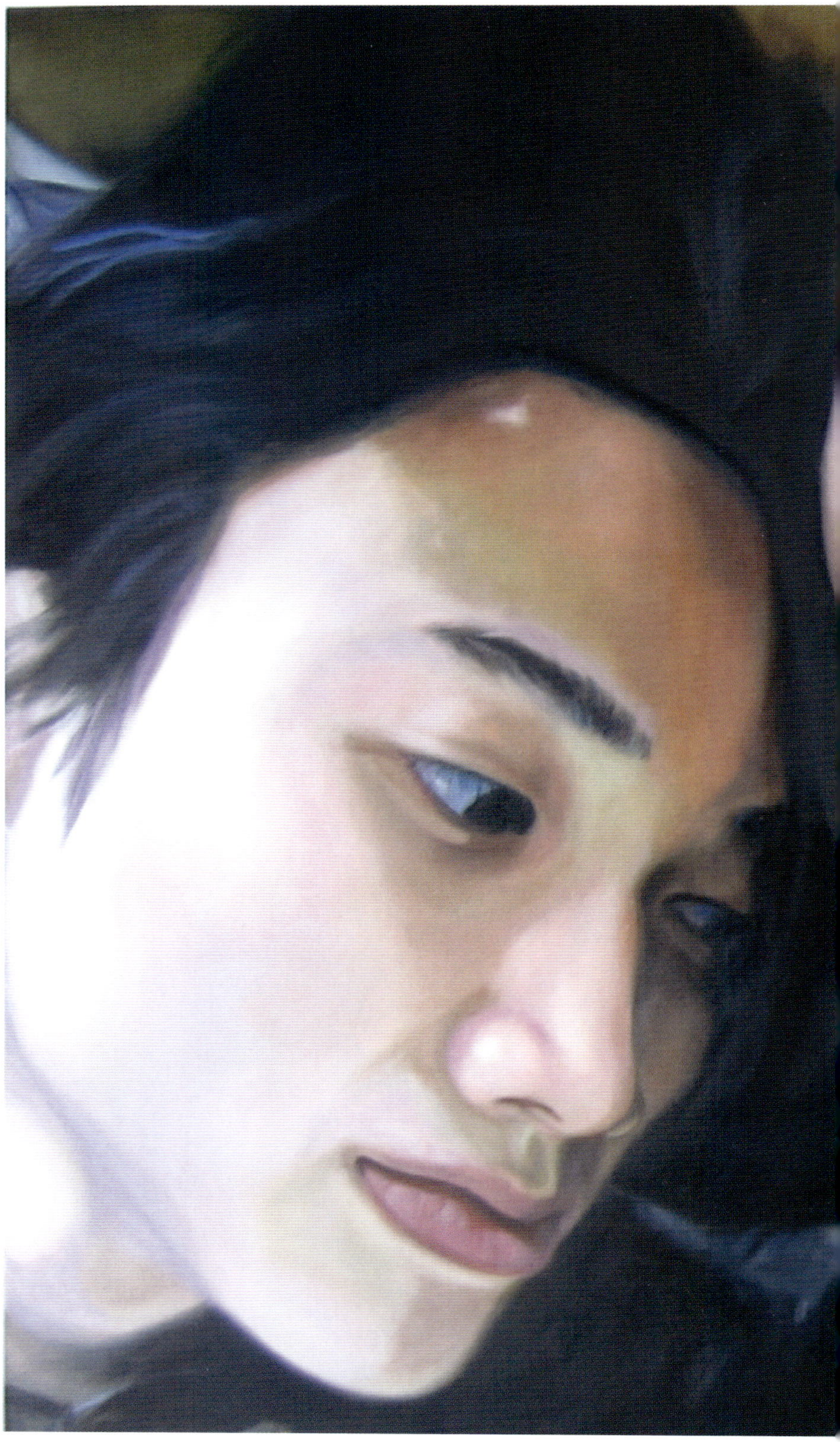

(Left) Ko Tin-yan, Celia/Tea time II
Oil on paper, 15x19 cm, 2000

(Right) Ko Tin-yan, Celia/Boy Girl Boy
Oil on linen, 122x118 cm, 2006

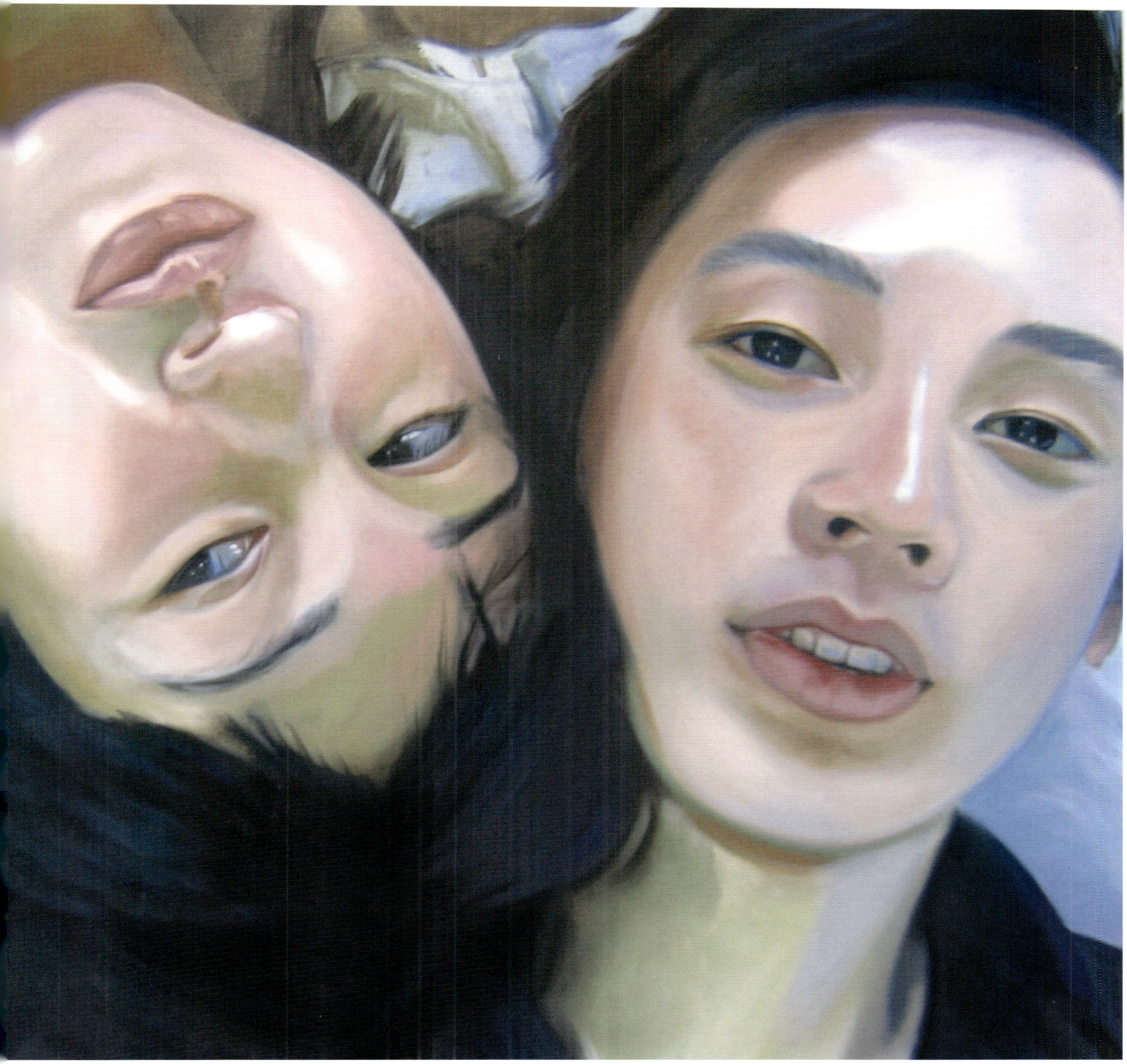

Cheung Chung-chu, Fung Ho-yin and Yung Sau-mui

A Long Relationship with Graphic Art

By Teresa Chan

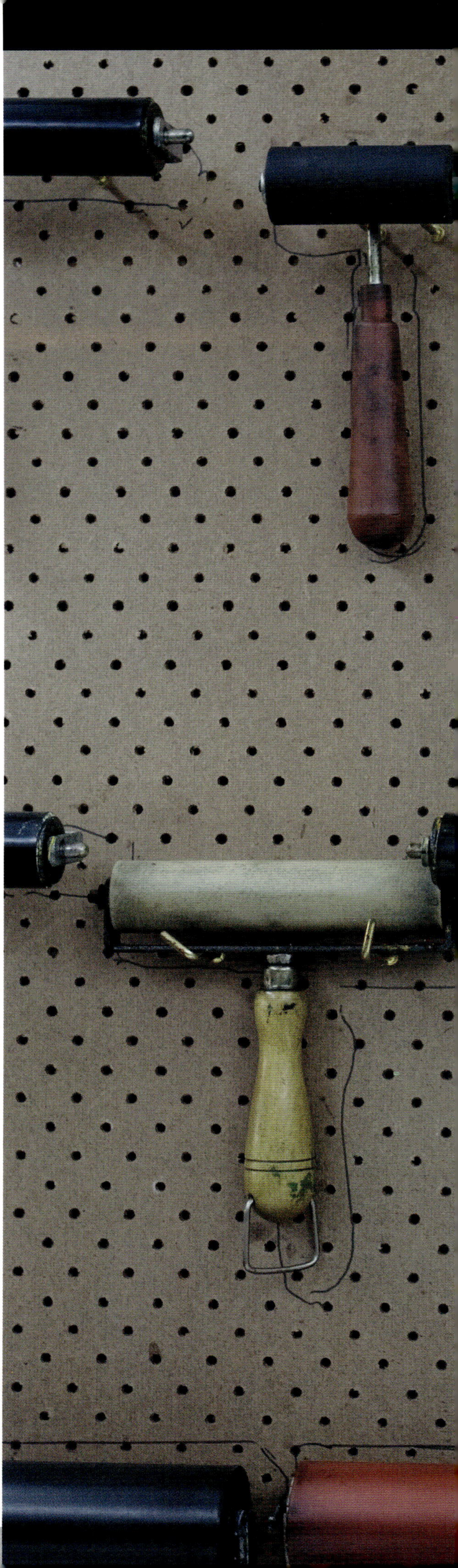

Cheung Chung-chu, Fung Ho-yin and Yung Sau-mui are founders of the Hong Kong Open Printshop. Cheung is an experienced printmaker and a versatile artist who practices Chinese ink painting, calligraphy and ceramics. His works have been shown at the Hong Kong Art Biennial. Fung was trained in photography and design, and is now an assistant professor at Hong Kong Polytechnic University's School of Design. His recent works have focused on the application of alternative photographic processes. Yung has studied printmaking at the Hong Kong Polytechnic University, the University of Alabama and the Tamarind Institute at the University of New Mexico. She is now the programme manager of the Hong Kong Open Printshop and an instructor of printmaking in a number of educational institutions.

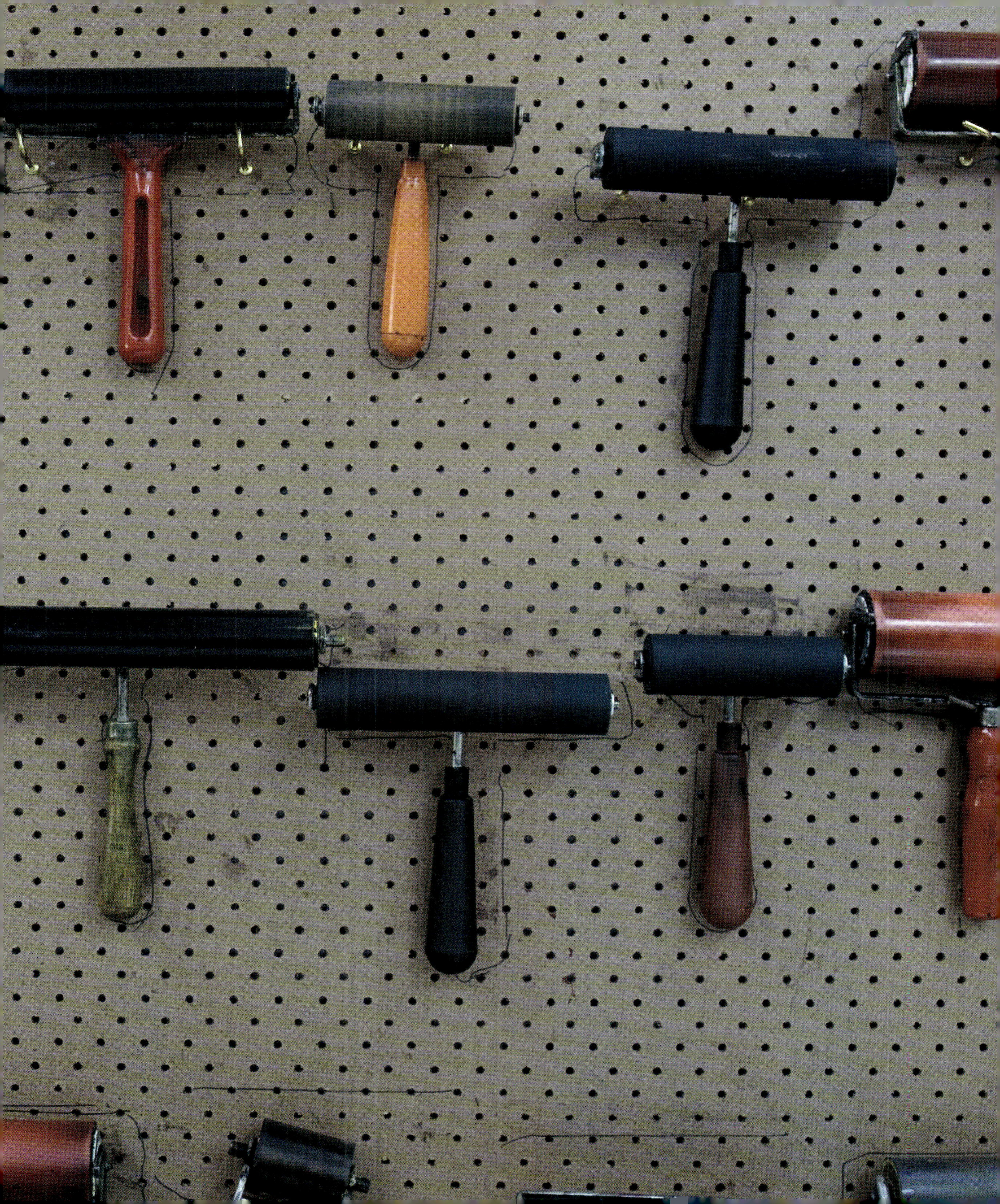

As a feature writer for the *Oasis* series, I have had the chance to visit the studios of a number of artists in the past year. Sometimes, before an interview, I let my imagination run free and make a guess about how the studio I am visiting will look. Will it share any similarity with the artist and the artworks, or show no apparent connection with its owner? This visit to the Hong Kong Open Printshop (HKOP) at Kowloon Bay however, leaves little to the imagination. This is because I had classes there when I was a student artist and I can still remember the space. Instead I may need to take a good last look at the place. Yung Sau-mui, one of the founders, told me on the phone that they will soon bid farewell to the Kowloon Bay studio they have used for years, and move to the Jockey Club Creative Arts Centre at Shek Kip Mei.

Entering the HKOP studio I can see that the printing presses are still in their old places. In the air is a faint smell unique to paper. Sitting around the long working table are Cheung Chung-chu, Fung Ho-yin and Yung Sau-mui, the three artists who founded the studio, and renowned figures in the art community. Though the interview should be centred around the studio, I decide to also ask the artists about printmaking. Is the number of people using this traditional medium on the decline due to the advances in technology? How do the three of them see this language of art that they have chosen?

When hearing the word 'printmaking', many people think of the illustrations they have seen in books — prints with fine lines made from engraved wood. In fact a more exact definition is the 'making of graphic images', which includes a wide range of techniques and materials. Cheung, Fung and Yung are experts at different techniques in printmaking. Cheung is experienced in copper engraving, but the technique he chooses for each work depends on the image he is making. He loves copper engraving because it allows him to manage fine details and make subtle changes,

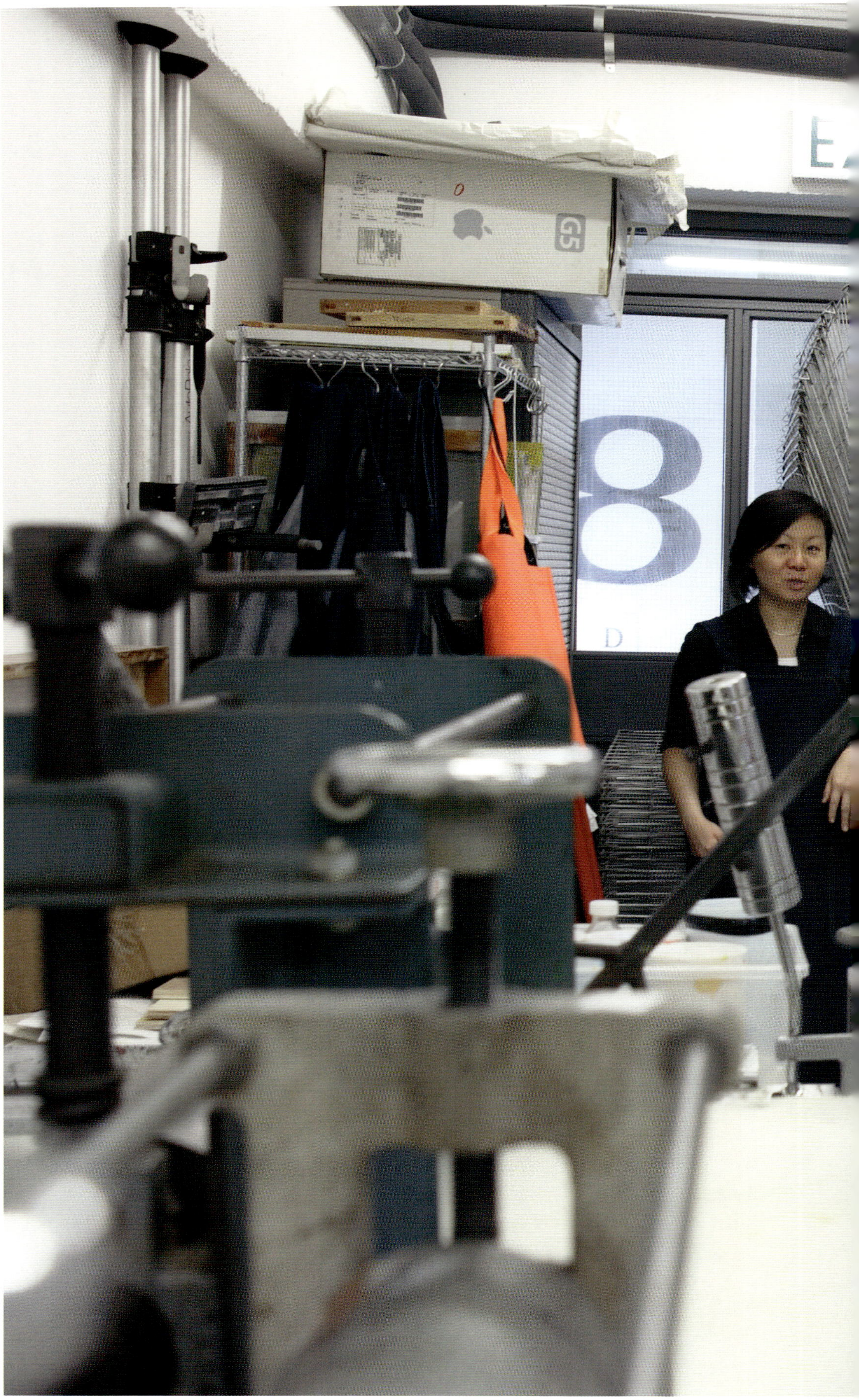

From left: Yung Sau-mui, Fung Ho-yin, Cheung Chung-chu

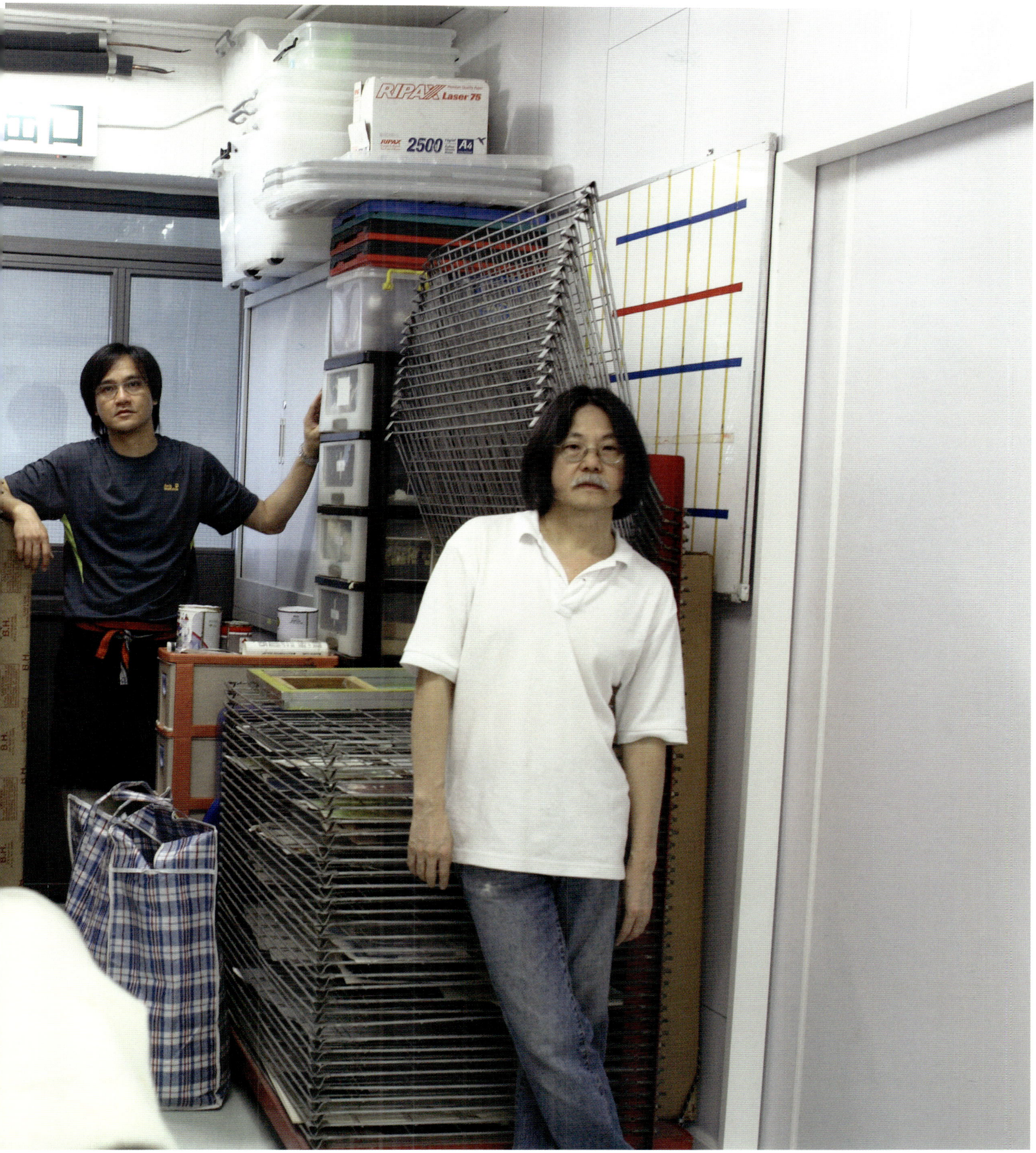
RIPAX Laser 75
RIPAX 2500 A4

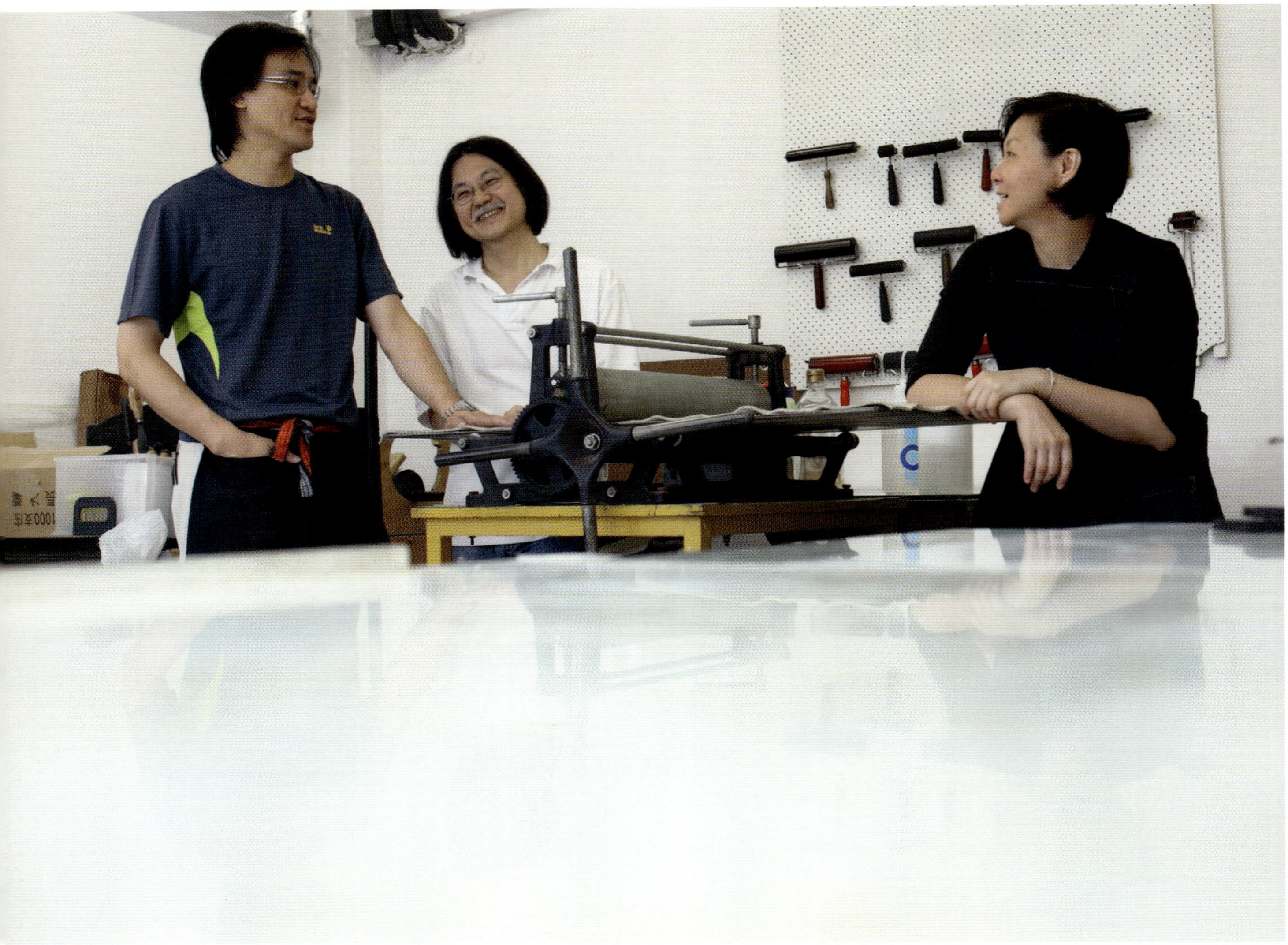

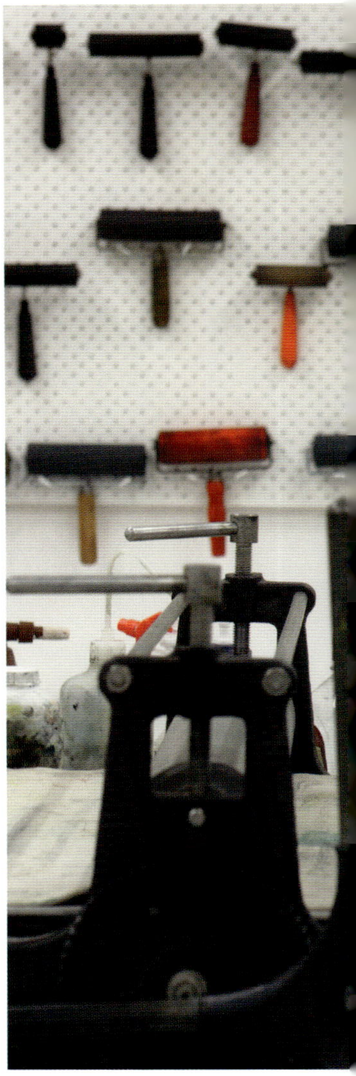

Sharing a studio space, sharing the experience of art making

inducing variations in the images and telling stories with them. Cheung is well-versed in a number of other media. Calligraphy has influenced him the most.

Fung teaches design at the Hong Kong Polytechnic University. Since he has solid training in photography and design, many of his prints feature photographs as a starting point and alternative printing processes as the medium, like cyanotype printing and gum bichromate printing, which give the photographs new layers and looks. Yung has received professional printmaking training in the United States and has employed planography and silk screen printing in recent years. She considers printmaking a collaboration of the brain and the hand, and enjoys giving the printing process her undivided attention.

While many people associate printmaking with complicated steps and skilled hands, the three artists believe that each art medium has its own techniques, and that patience and practice are important for good works no matter which medium one employs. They point out that printmaking has a close relationship with printing. A process as simple as frottage can be used to make a print, and stamping on paper is itself a way of making a graphic image. Viewed from this angle, printmaking is not so distant.

In founding the HKOP, Cheung, Fung and Yung did not just aim to create a studio space, but to promote the art of printmaking by breaking down the myths around the medium. Before the establishment of the HKOP in 2000 there were not many open venues suitable for printmaking, apart from the facilities at

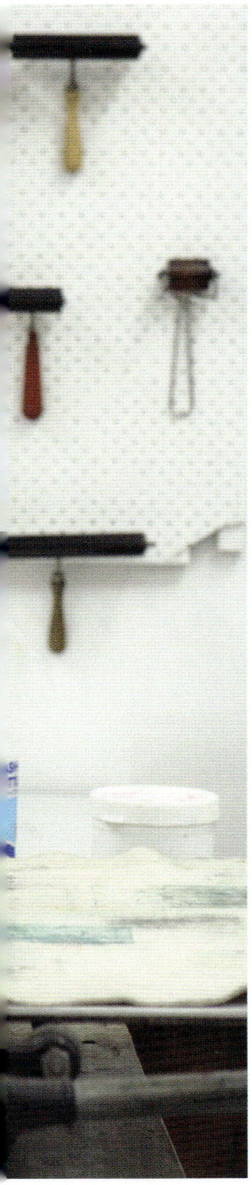

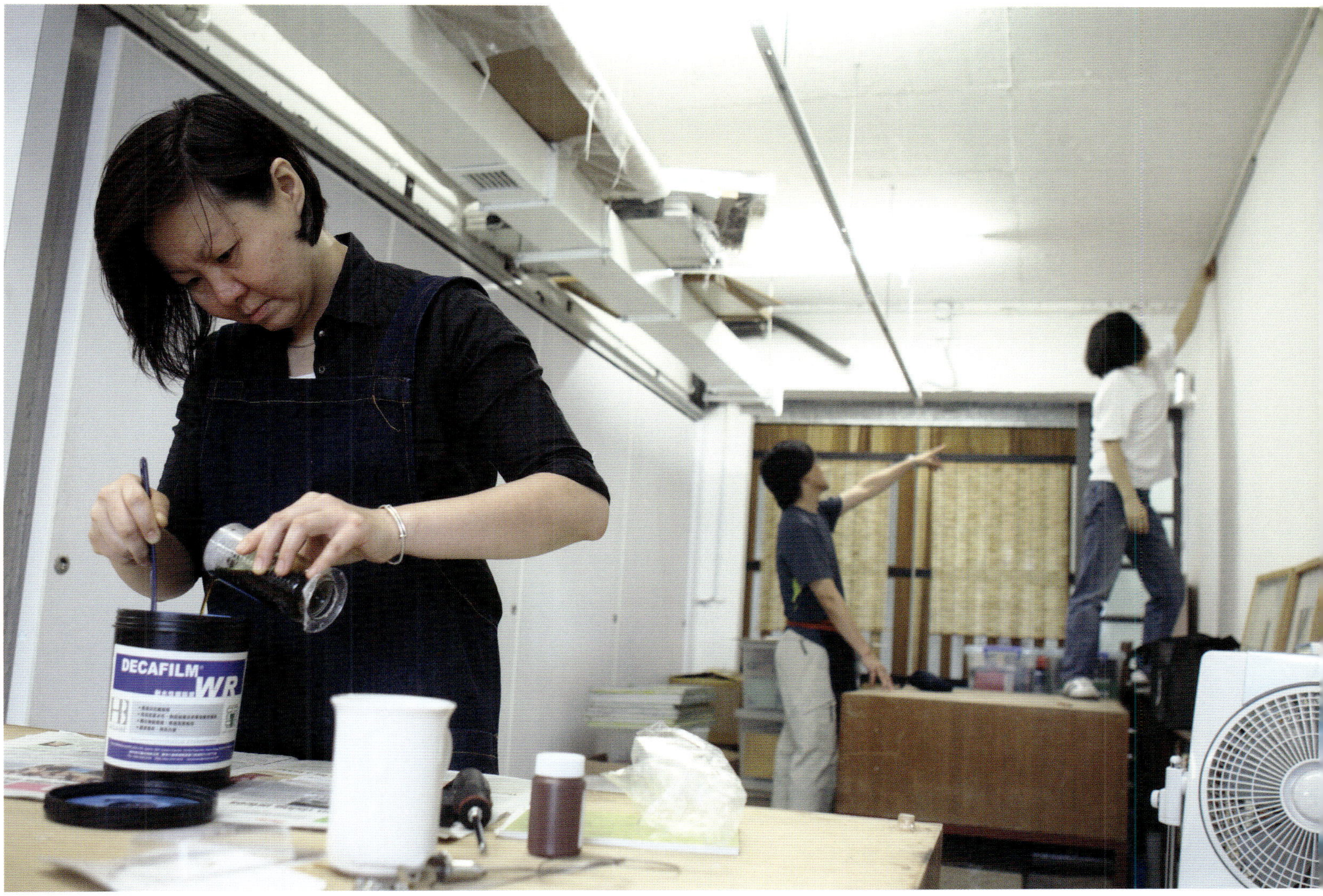

the Hong Kong Visual Arts Centre, which are available for rent. Cheung recalls that people who learned printmaking techniques in a course might not have been able to continue making art with the medium due to the difficulty of finding space and equipment.

Many overseas printmaking studios are commissioned to make prints, which means that they are really 'working studios', but when setting up the HKOP, Cheung and the others wanted their space to help promote printmaking, not just provide a physical place to work. Over the last seven years they have organised various printmaking courses, allowing people of different ages to learn the techniques. They have also lent the studio to other artists and launched artist-in-residence programmes.

Yung says that they were not that optimistic at the beginning, since setting up a studio requires both 'hardware' and 'software'. However an opportunity emerged at the turn of the millennium, a time where old and new technologies were crossing paths. Digitalisation and networking were the general trends, and some schools were giving up their old equipment to set up computer rooms. Among the equipment being disposed of were printmaking tools. According to Yung, the printing presses still functioning at the HKOP were items given up by schools years ago. At one point these abandoned presses signified the disappearance of printmaking from school syllabi, but they unexpectedly gave the medium new life by making the HKOP possible.

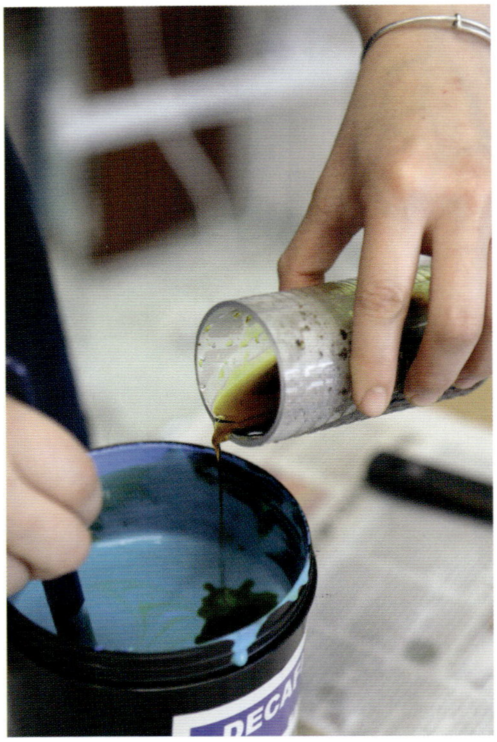
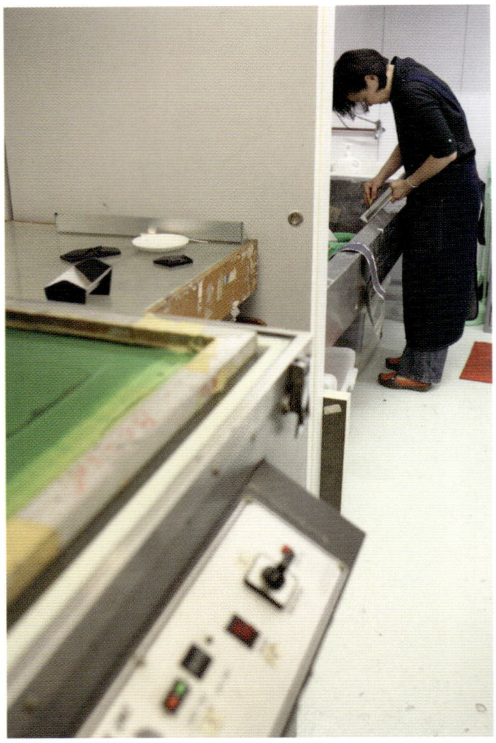
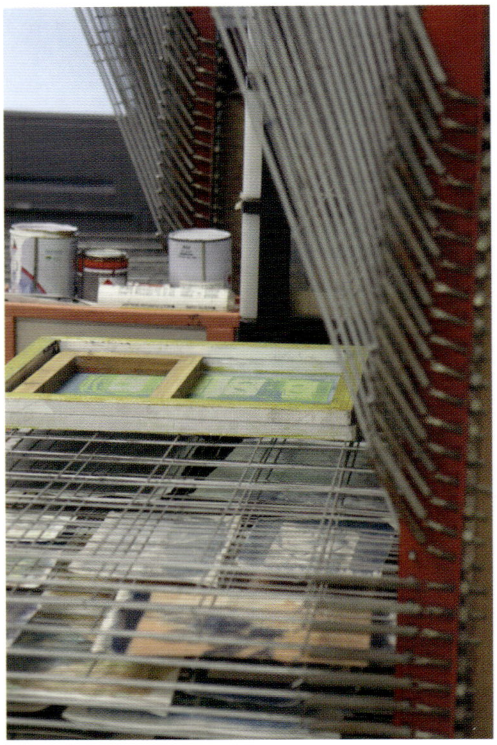
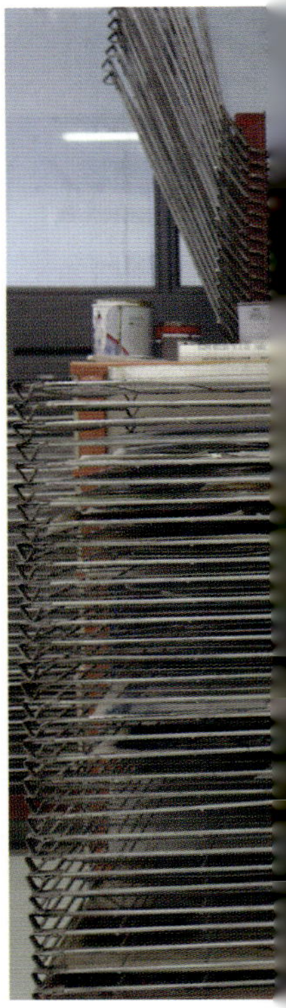
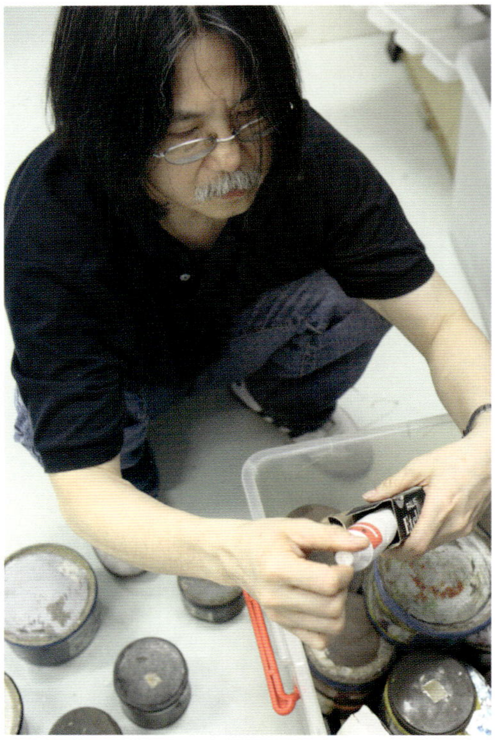
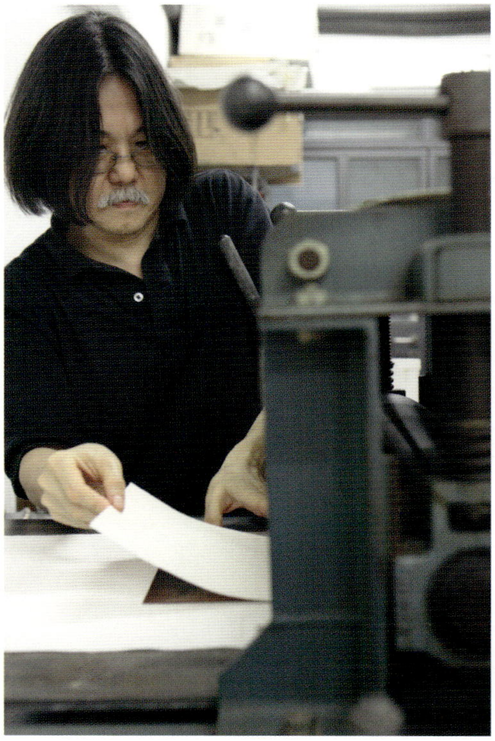

Stamping on paper is itself a way of making a graphic image. Viewed from this angle, printmaking is not so distant

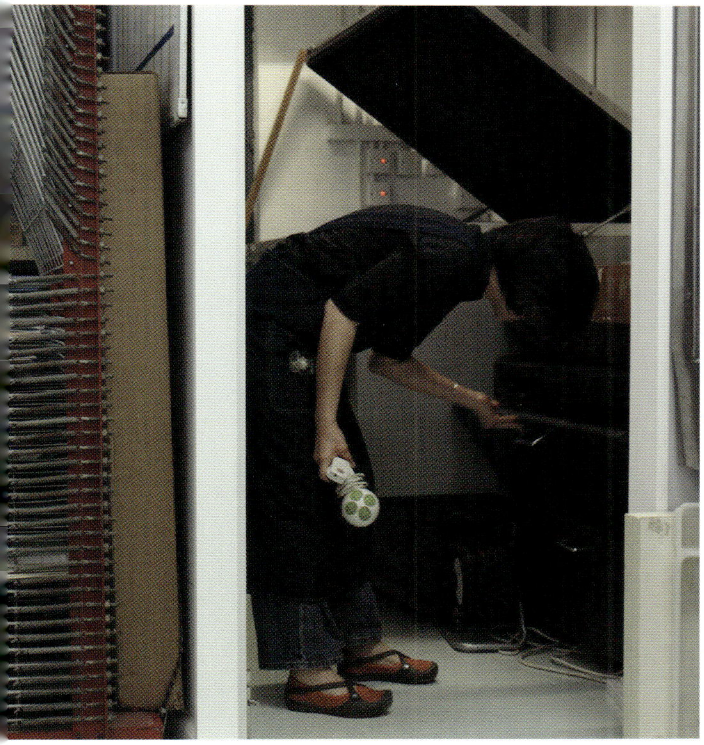

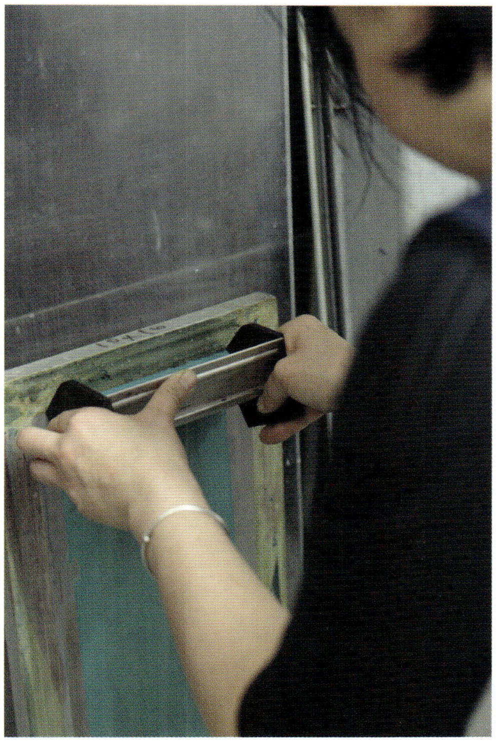

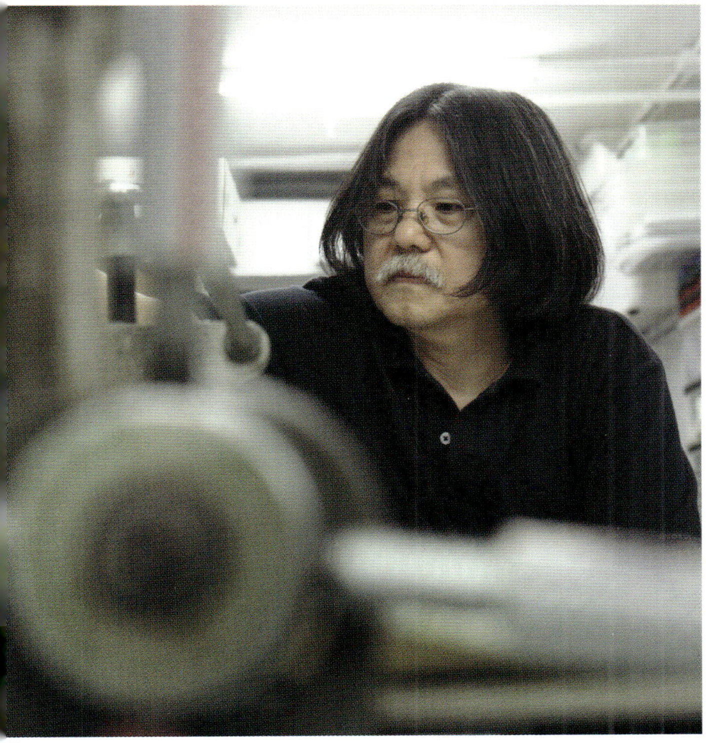

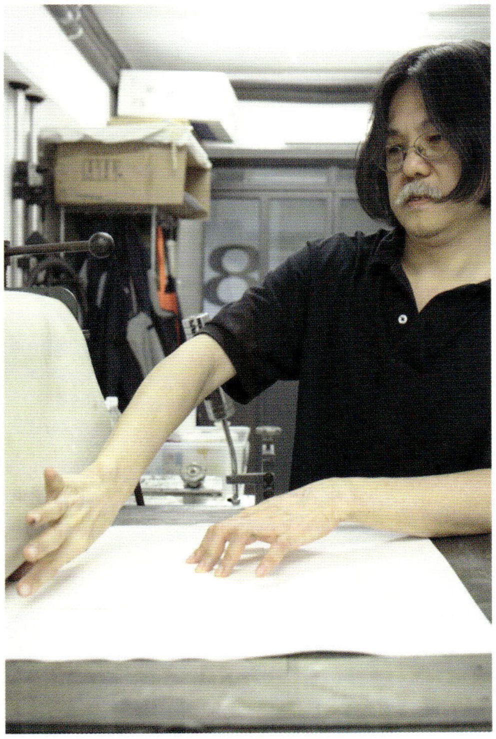

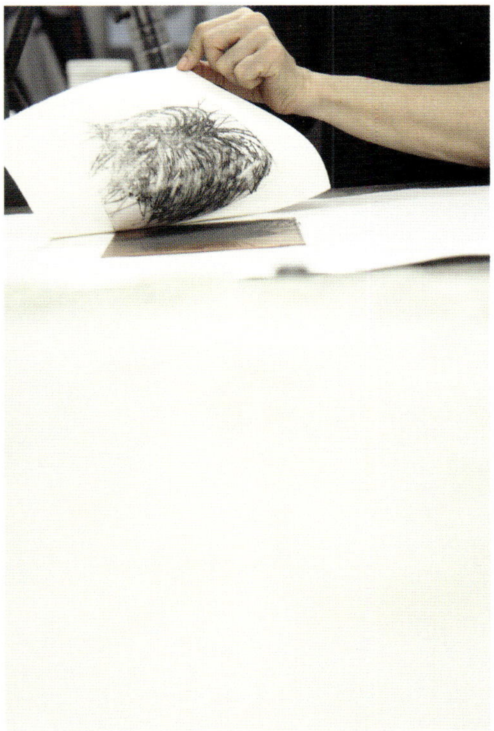

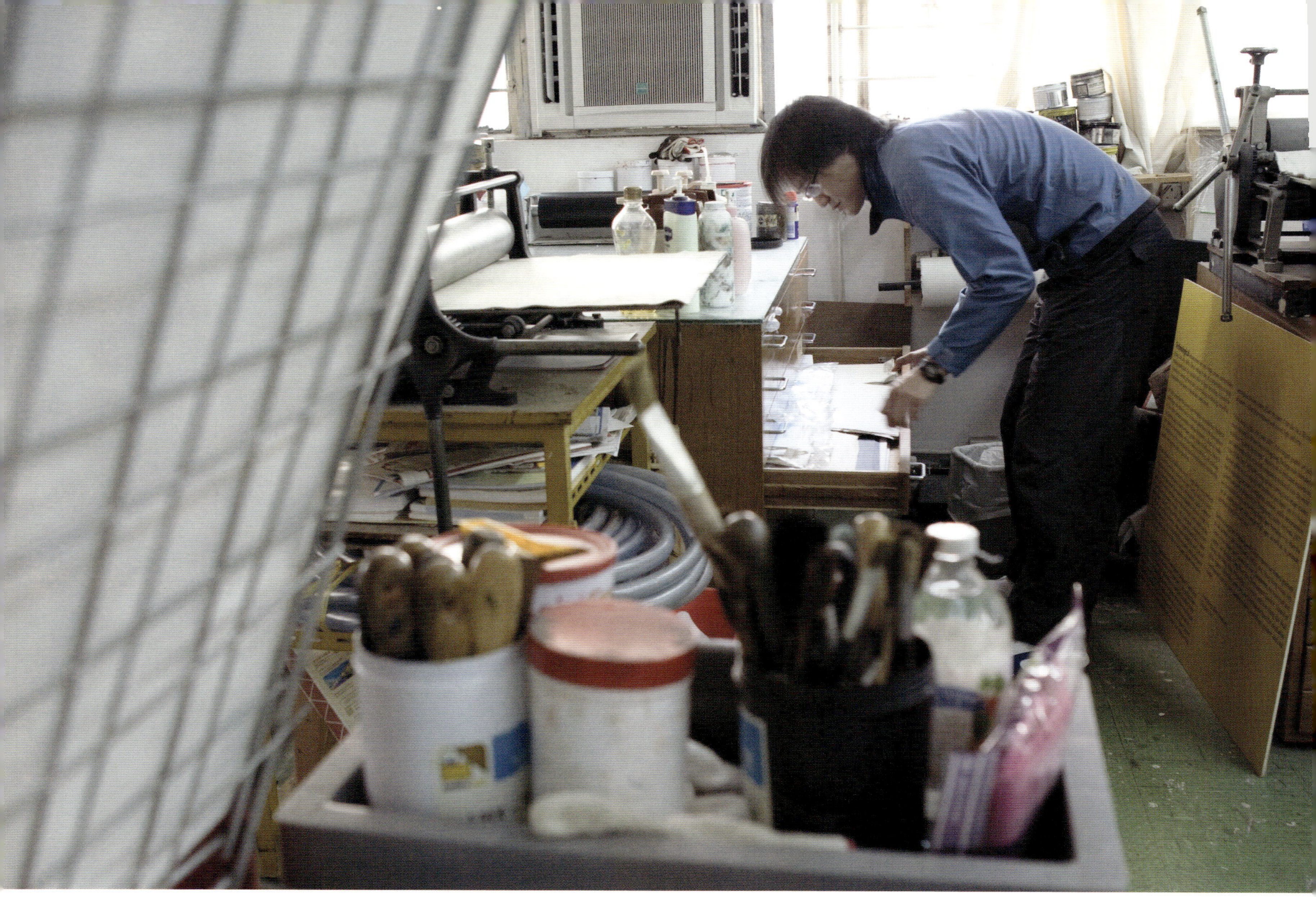

Art may look fragile compared to the rapid development of the world, its life is stronger and may be longer than we expect

Time flies and we are almost at the end of the first decade of the new century. While many predicted that traditional techniques would be replaced in the computer generation, to the contrary, it seems that more people are seeking to express themselves through hand-made works. The courses and workshops held by the HKOP have allowed many to re-discover the joy of working with their hands. Fung's belief is that as mass production dominates the market, people are starting to call for the uniqueness of hand-made things.

Browsing through the newsletter of the HKOP gives an idea of the effort they have put into promoting printmaking. Apart from regular courses, they have organised community-based workshops and activities for people of different ages, in different professions and from different places. A good example is the visual arts programme held for the elderly since 2004. At the Hong Kong Graphic Art

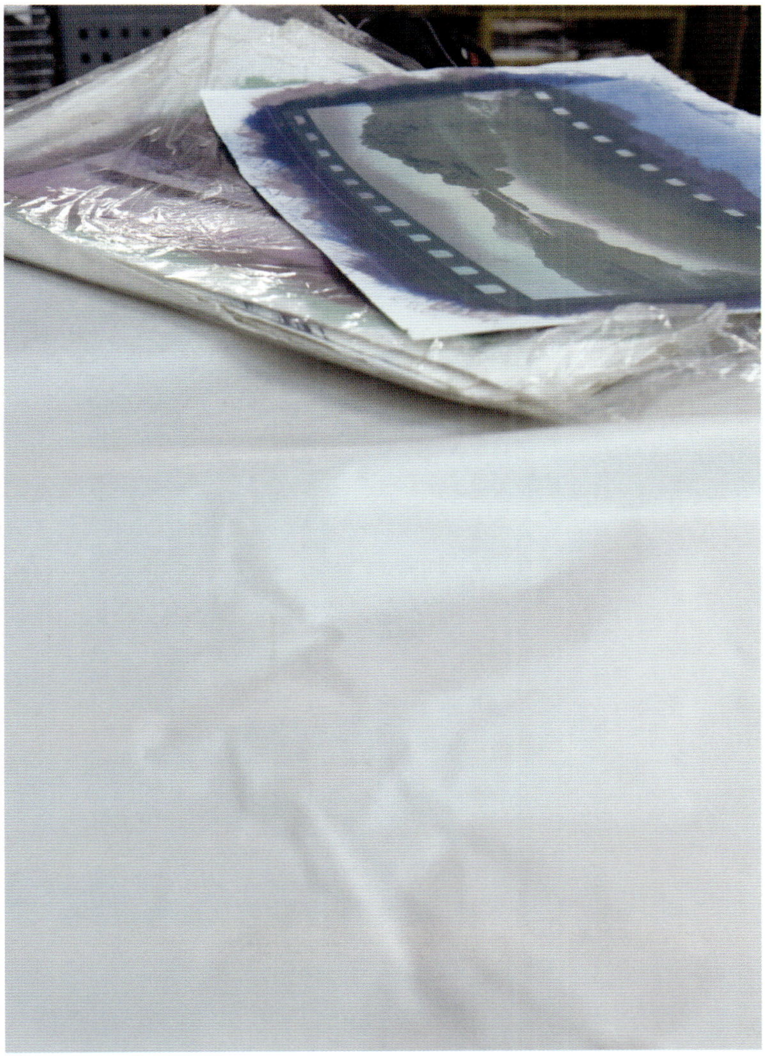

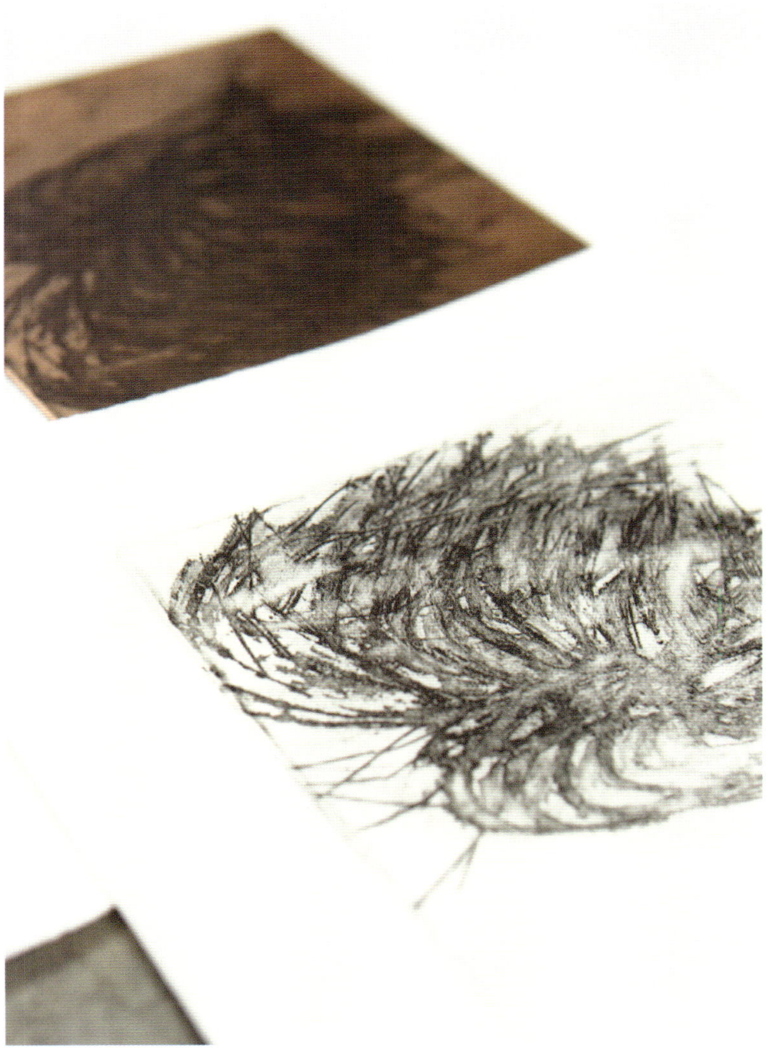

Fiesta 2007, a collaboration with the Leisure and Cultural Services Department produced two exhibitions. *Cross Boundaries — An International Print Exchange Exhibition* showed works of printmakers around the world and *Hot Off the Press* provided new printmakers in Hong Kong with a platform on which to stage their works.

Whether art is something difficult for the public to grasp or whether closer links should be forged, is a topic that has attracted much debate. For Fung, the 'strategy' of the HKOP is to attract more people and arouse interest in the medium, so that more people know that it is something they can handle. After mastering the basic skills, they can learn more advanced ones and develop more mature works. Besides, if few of us know about printmaking then this form of art will be short of an audience as well as artists. With promotion as their objective, the HKOP constantly adds new elements to their courses and activities, such as combining printmaking with animation and creating three-dimensional prints.

Will technology replace traditional forms of art? After listening to the three printmakers who continuously try to strike a balance between making and promoting art, I think the answer is no. Fung says that in a modern world, with its myriad choices, the space and time required for making art are often considered something people cannot afford. That said, the team has never given up hope. Looking at the few printing presses that have walked into a new century and are ready, once more, for a new home, and recalling the stories of their rebirth here, I start to believe that while art may look fragile compared to the rapid development of the world, its life is stronger and may be longer than we expect.

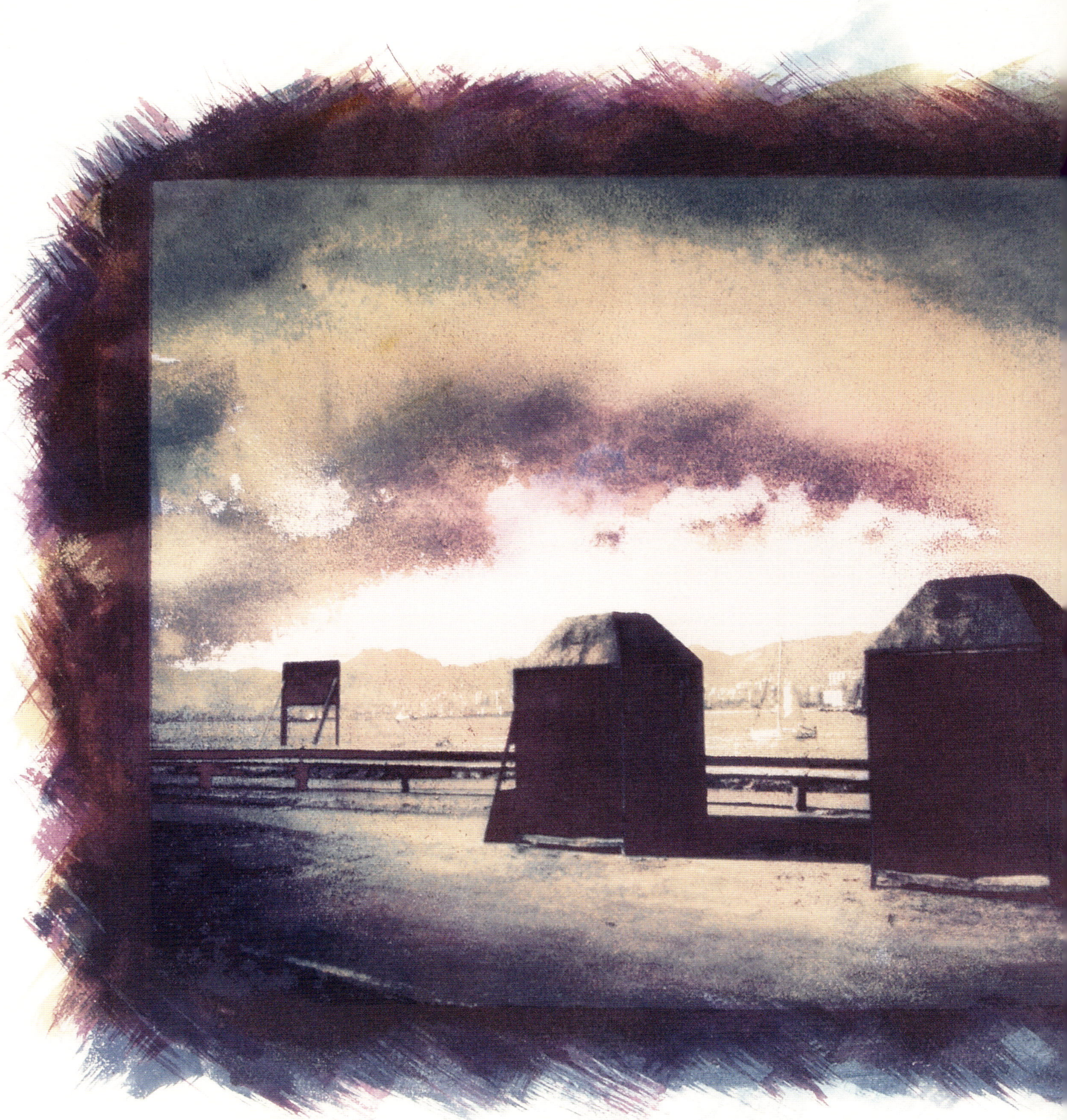

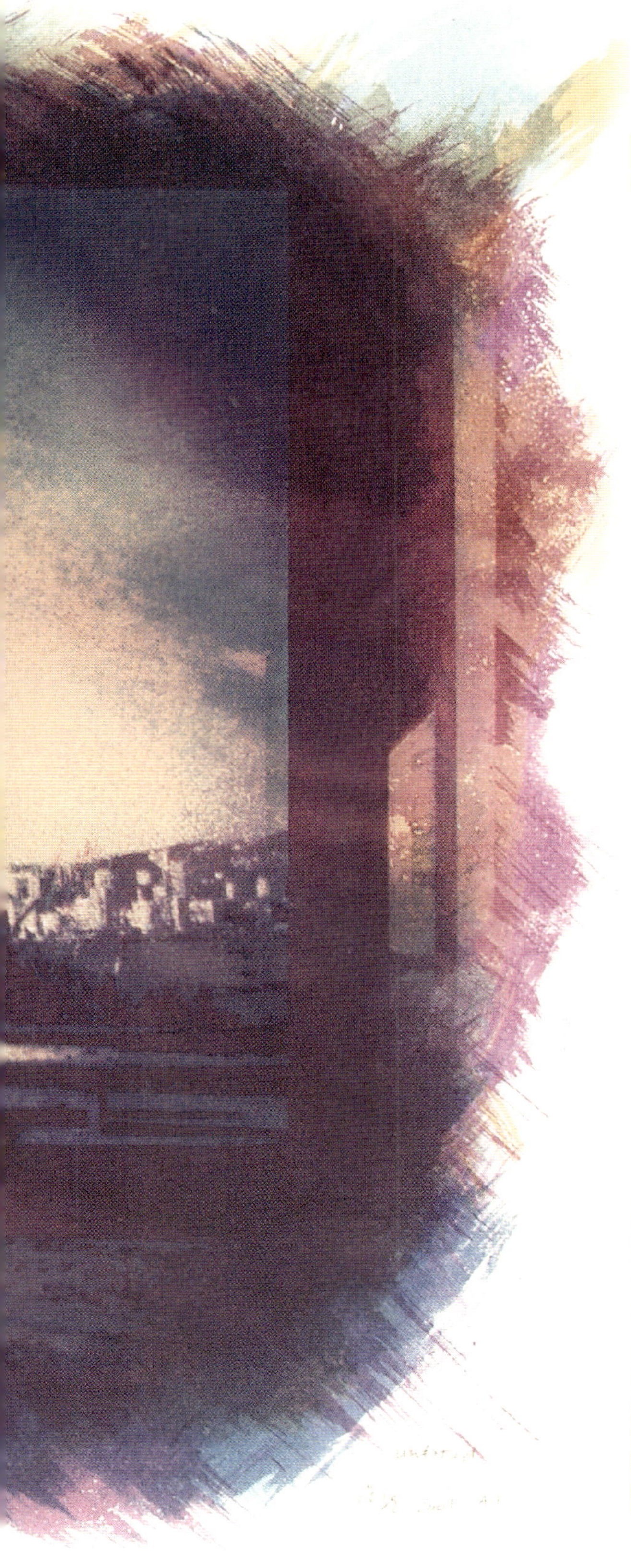

(Left) Fung Ho-yin/Untitled
Gum bichromate print, 56x76 cm, 2000

(Bottom) Fung Ho-yin/Untitled
Gum bichromate print, 56x76 cm, 1999

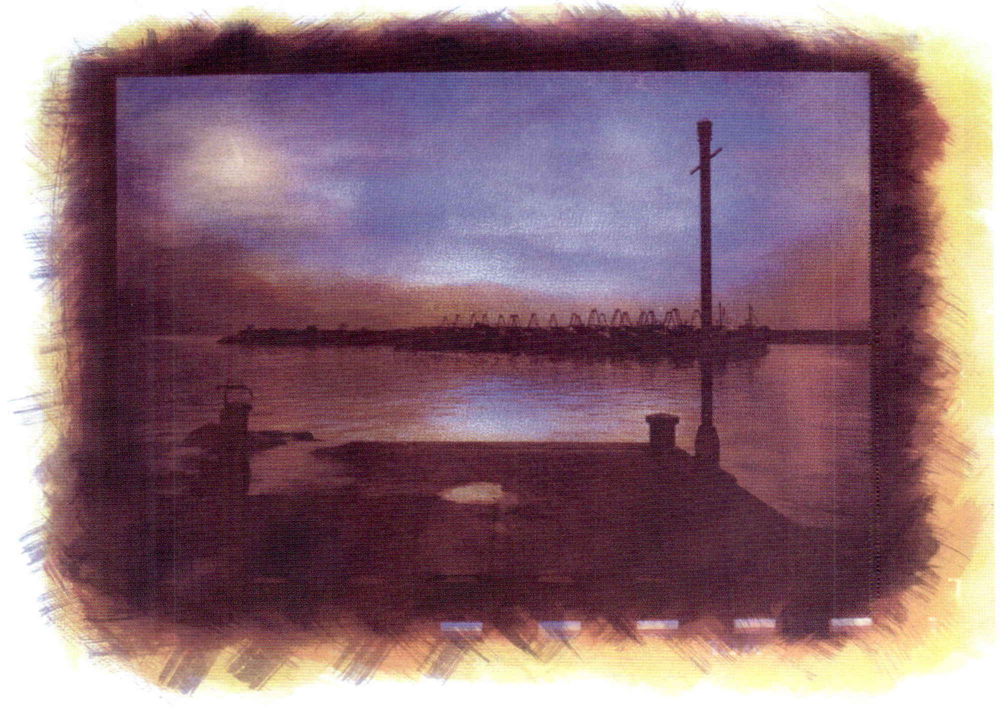

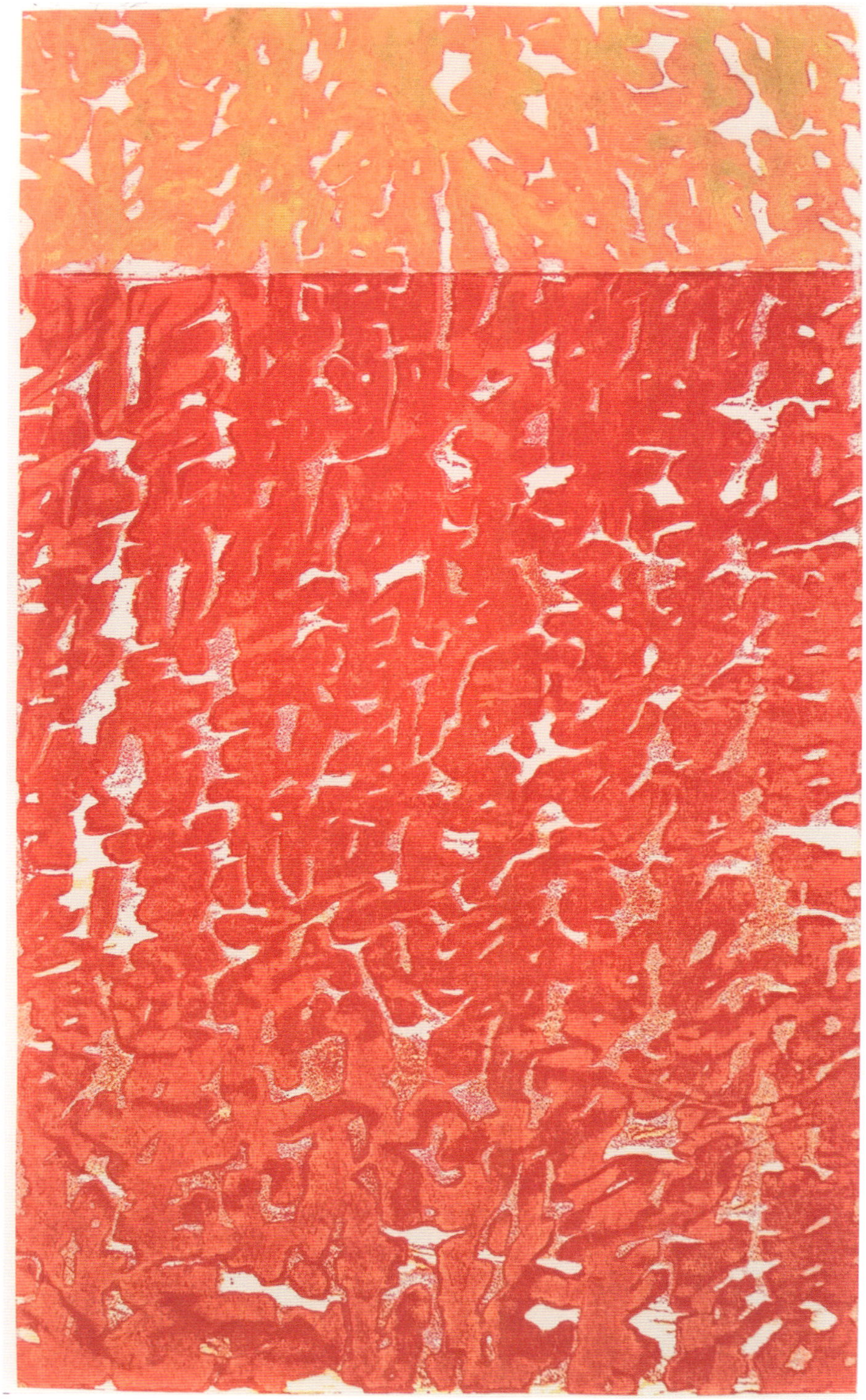

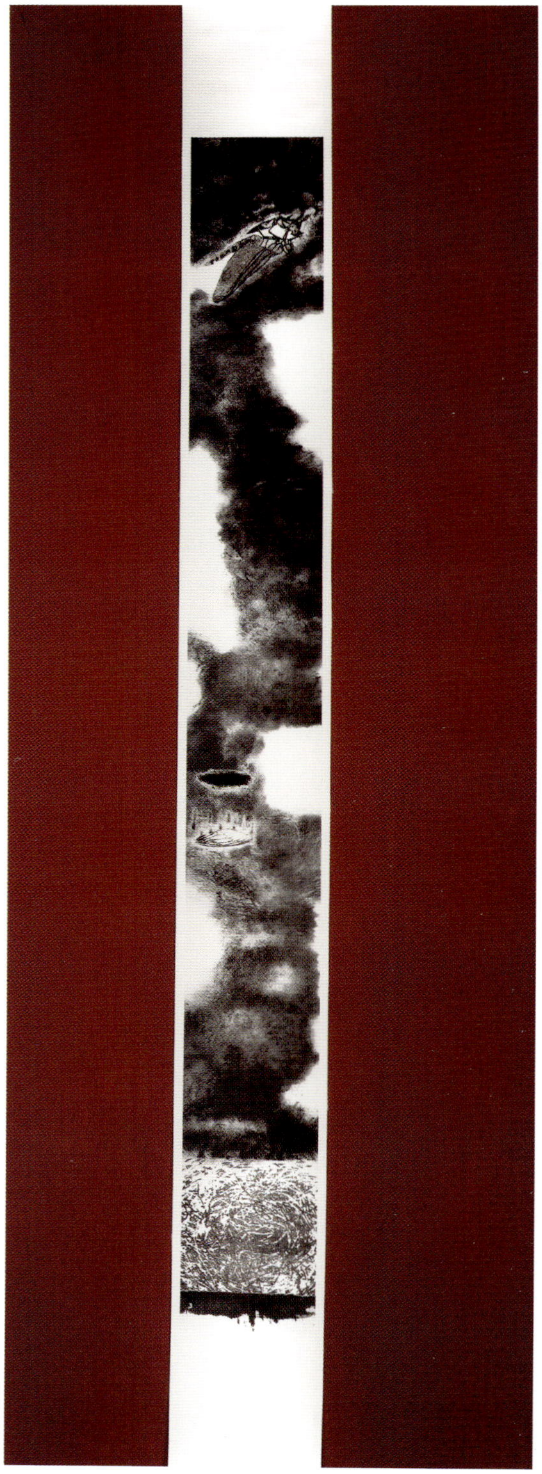

(Left) Cheung Chung-chu/The Book of Songs
Woodblock print, 76x57 cm, 2007

(Right) Cheung Chung-chu/Sketch
Intaglio frottage, 110x20 cm, 2006

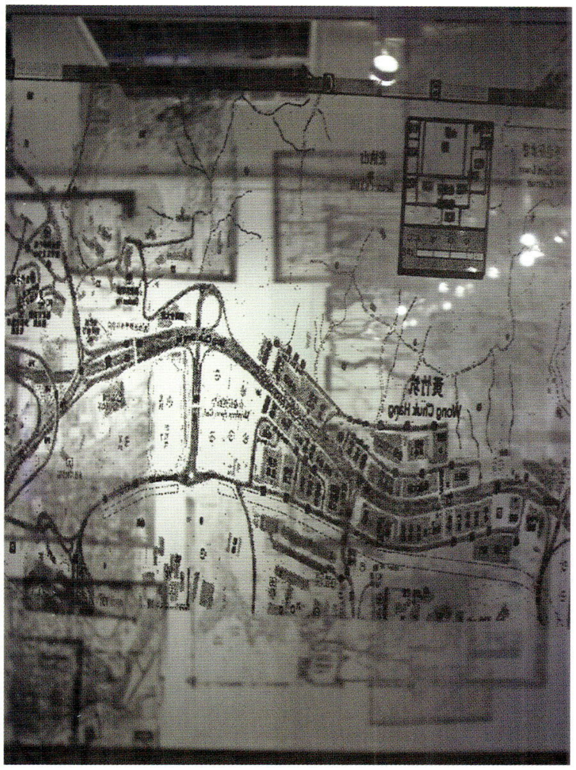

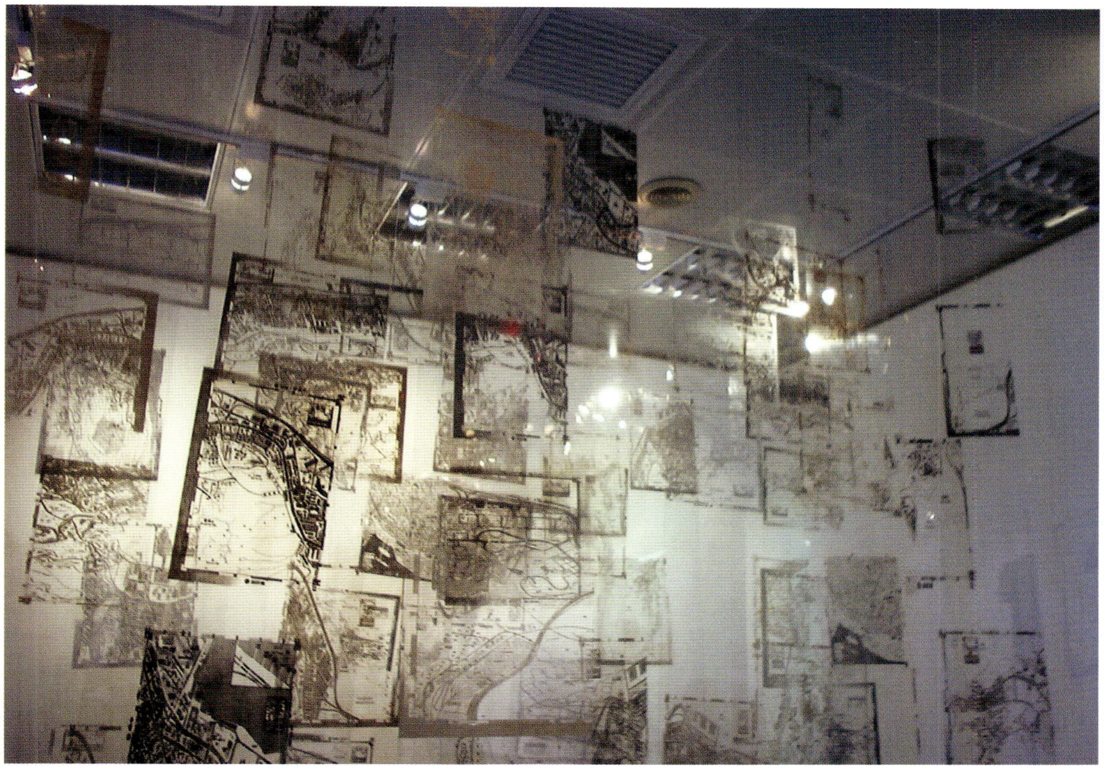

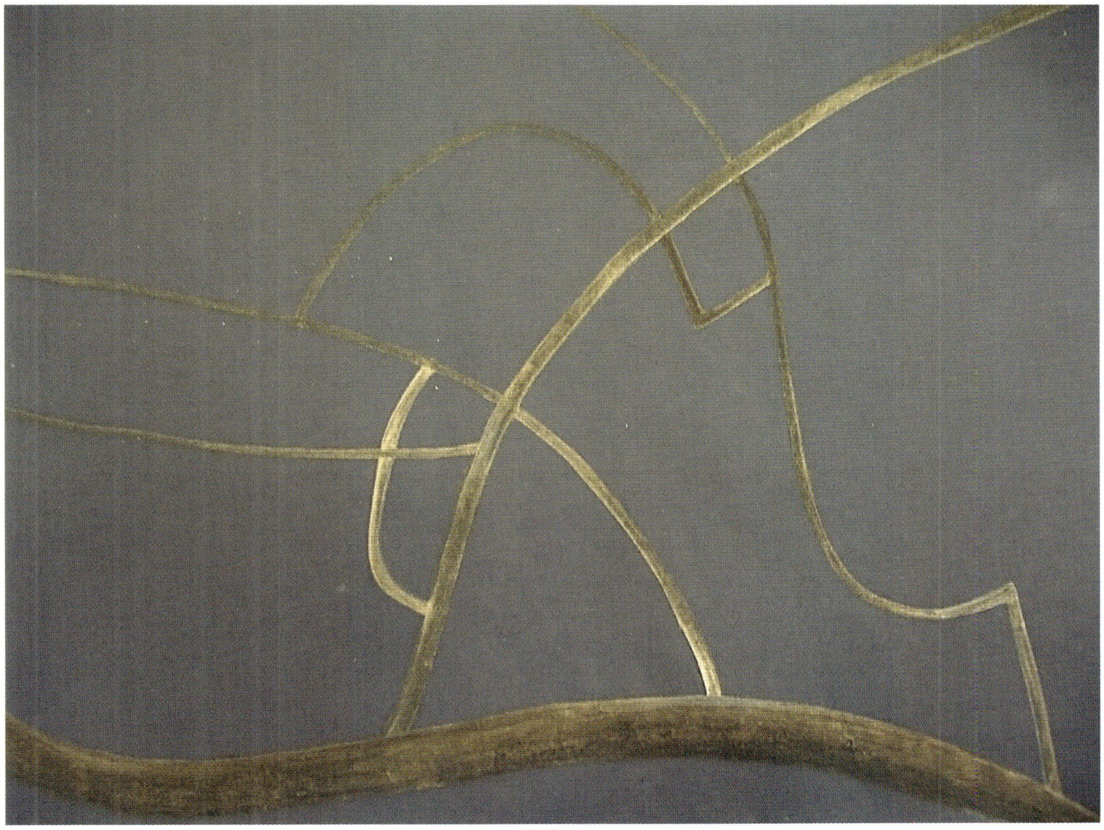

(Left above) Yung Sau-mui/Mapping 2004.1 (detail)

(Right above) Yung Sau-mui/Mapping 2004.1
Pronoto plate lithography,
30x240 cm ,60x240 cm (each), set of 24, 2004

(Right) Yung Sau-mui/Mapping 2006
Mixed-media on hand-made paper, 40x60 cm, 2006

Lee Chi-hoi and Kong Khong-chang

A Taste of Fruit

By Ronny Leung

Lee Chi-hoi (known widely as Chihoi) studied food and nutrition science at the Chinese University of Hong Kong. After graduation in 1999, he started a career in comics. His publications include *The Writer and Her Story* (1999), *Still Life* (1999), *Train* (2007) and *Hijacking — Comic Hong Kong Literature* (2007; co-authored by Kong). His works have been published in *Ming Pao*, *Shing Pao* and *East Touch*, among other publications. In 2007 he held a solo exhibition at the Hong Kong Arts Centre entitled Hochaaa! Chihoi's Comic, 10-Year Retrospective!

Kong Khong-chang (known as Kongkee) graduated from the Department of Fine Arts at the Chinese University of Hong Kong in 2000. In 2005 he received a Master's degree from the School of Creative Media, City University of Hong Kong. His online series *Rice-gas* has received massive support. He is a regular contributor to *Ming Pao*, *East Touch*, *Ming Teen's* and *Shing Pao* and has authored a series of comics titled *Imperfect Shoes*. In 2007 he collaborated with 29s and published *What If We Talk About Love?* In 2005 his video, *Name of Wu Mei*, was selected by the Hong Kong Art Biennial exhibition and received a special mention from the ifva Short Film Festival.

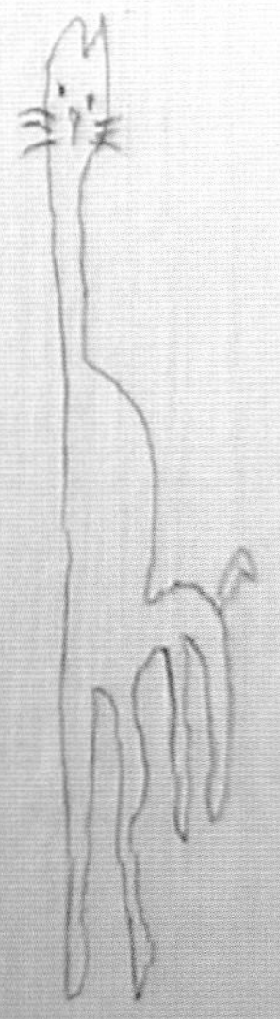

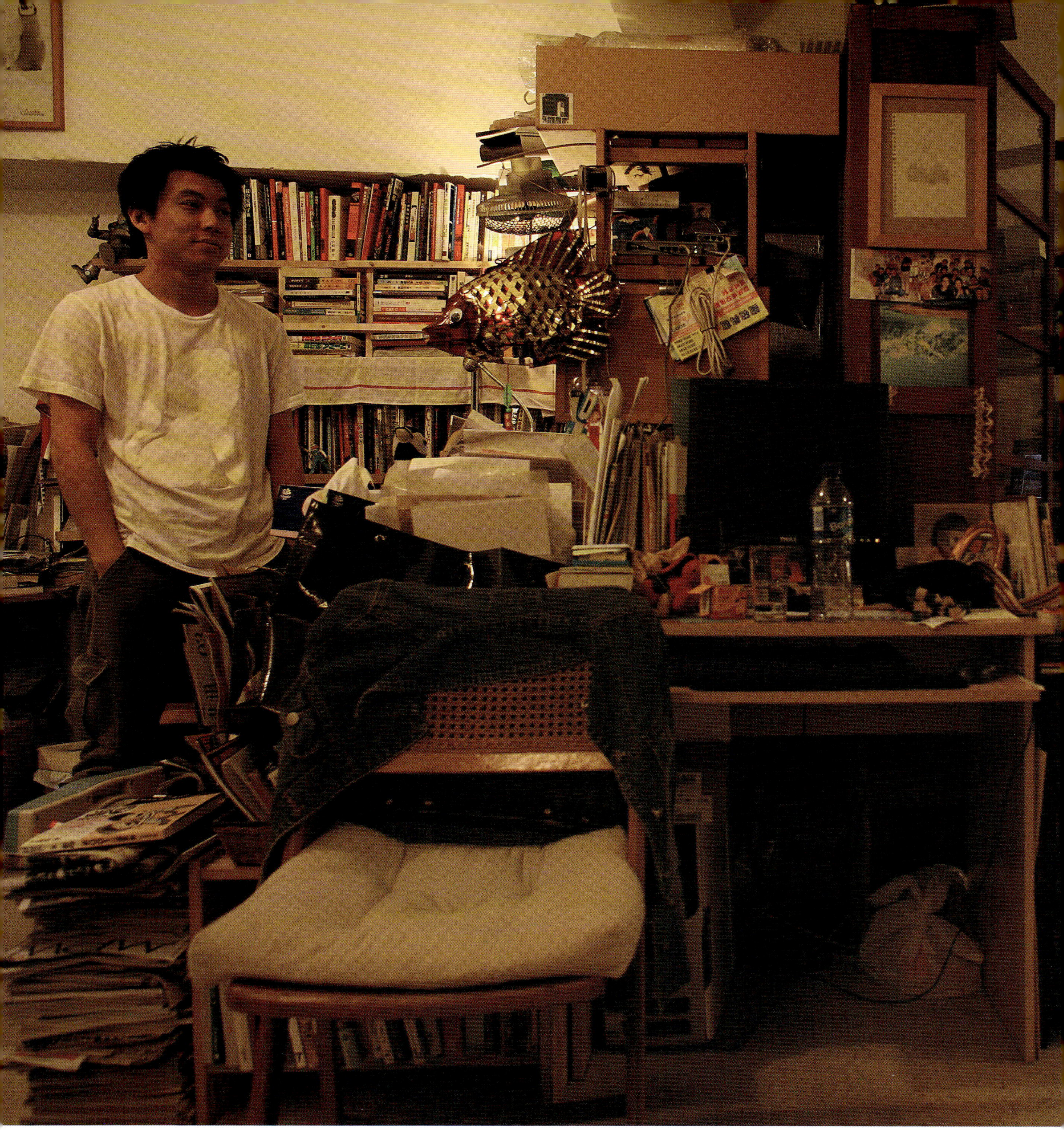

Kong Khong-chang (left) and Lee Chi-hoi (right)

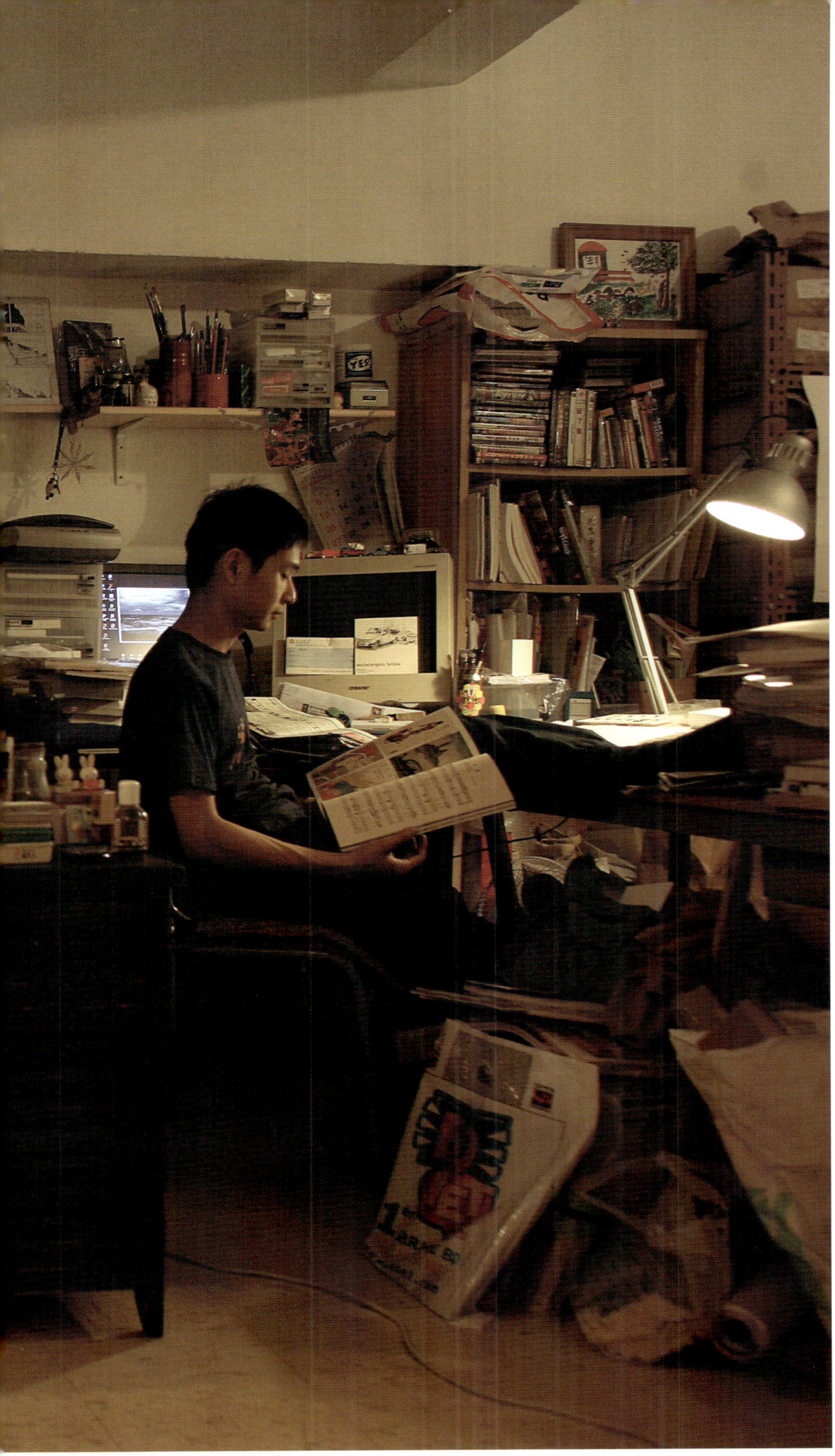

When I was young, there was a drama series called *Rainbow Around My Shoulder* on TV, a programme about a young man striving for a career in comics. Over the past 20 years the publication industry has gone through its ups and downs and local comics, at most, are just middle-of-the-road. However Chihoi and Kongkee are determined to venture into the road not taken.

Many know that Chihoi was not formally trained in the fine arts. After giving up his specialty and devoting himself to a new field, the difficulties and his frustrations were overcome by his passion for comics. When he was an undergraduate he frequently filed his works with newspapers and magazines; some were published by *Magpaper*, *Express* and *Young Express*. Failing to secure a subsidy from the Hong Kong Arts Development Council he hand-made his first comics album, *The Writer and Her Story*. The 80 odd photocopied copies were consigned to the East Bank Bookshop and Eureka Bookshop and sales were good. Confidence and opportunity always go hand-in-hand.

Kongkee graduated from the Department of Fine Arts at CUHK. In his undergraduate years he contributed works to Japanese comics magazine *Comic Teens*. When the magazine shut down, he stopped creating that kind of work. His hiatus ended with his collaboration with 29s, a publisher founded by a creative team. The collaboration turned out to be *Imperfect Shoes*, a series of comics in a new style. His output has been ceaseless since graduation. *Creating Rice-gas*, however, was coincidental. The series, silly but fun, was intended to wake up his 'rice-gassed' (a Cantonese expression for the sleepiness induced by a heavy meal) friends. It was circulated widely on the Internet and received enormous support.

In 2003 Kongkee founded 29s with seven other culture lovers. A year later, they rented a workshop in Foo Tak Building in Wanchai. Foo Tak Building is a legend in the art field. The whole block is managed by Dawei Charitable Foundation Limited and the apartments are rented to artists and groups at a rate much lower than market price. The low rent has attracted lots of aspiring artists and culture practitioners, and it has turned Foo Tak Building into a cultural hub. After learning about the bargain from artist May Fung, Kongkee and the other 29s become occupants.

Cosy and warm, the studio feels like home. Some of 29s' members work on words and edit the cultural magazine *Fleus des Lettres*. Kongkee and Chihoi are involved in the magazine's artistic direction. Such a job does not require a lot of space; all the artists need are a drawing table, a light box and a computer. They can actually work at home. But Kongkee and Chihoi, both living in Tai Po, prefer to travel all the way to Wanchai.

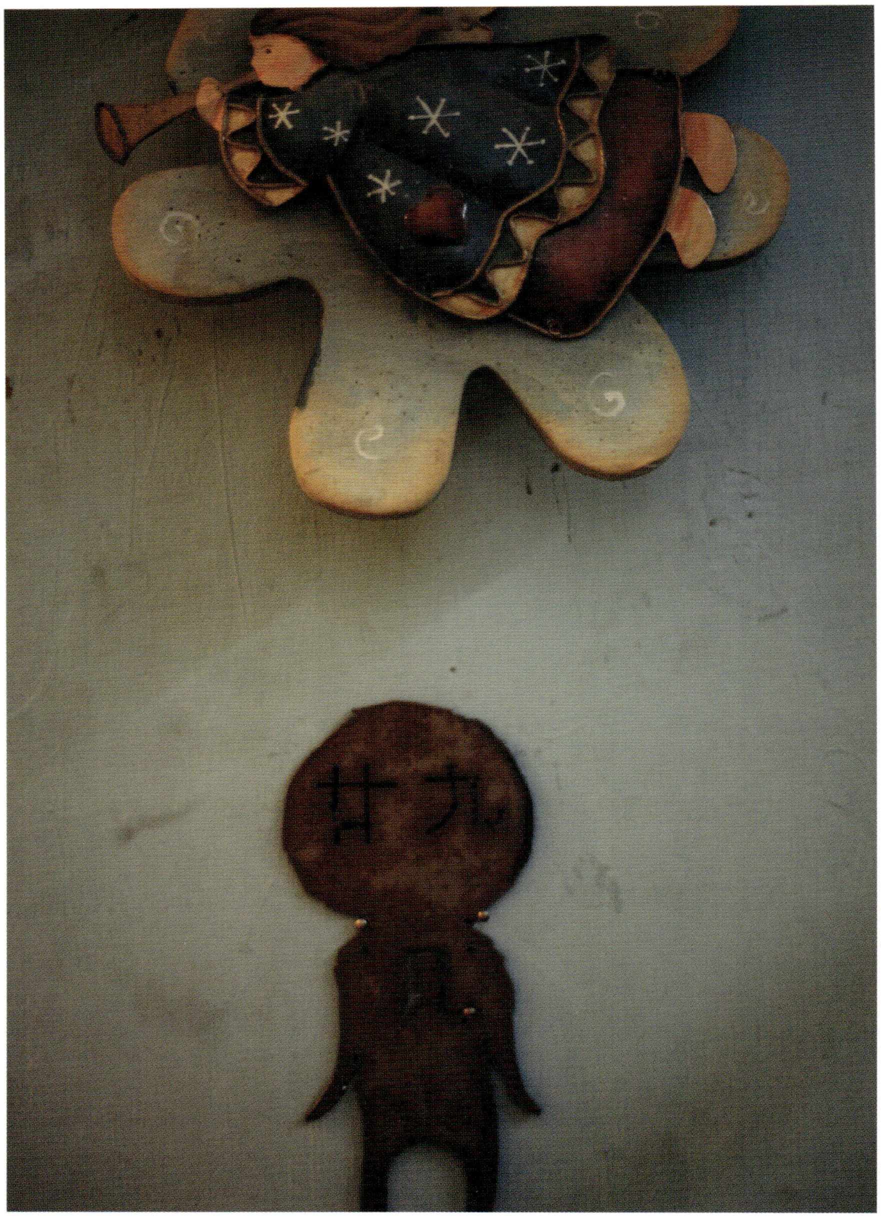

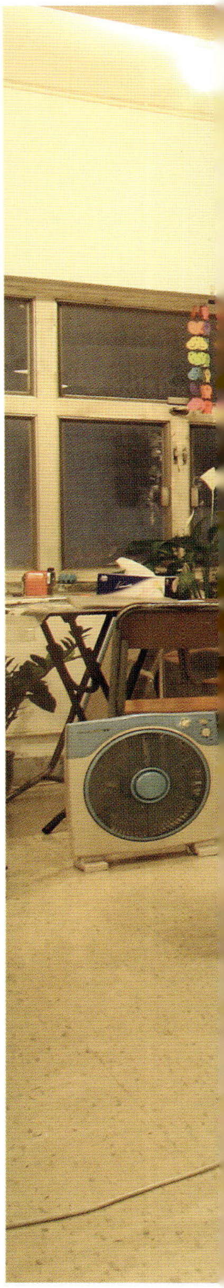

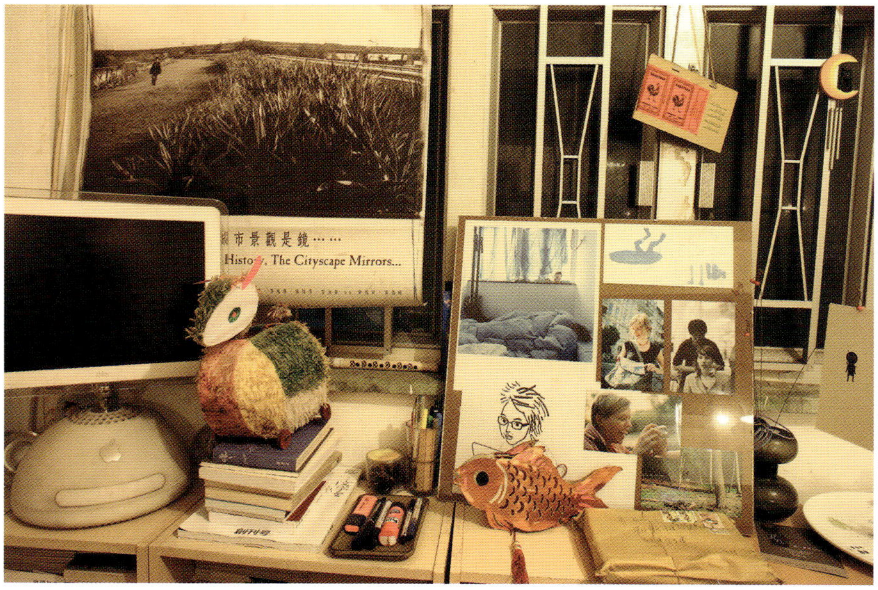

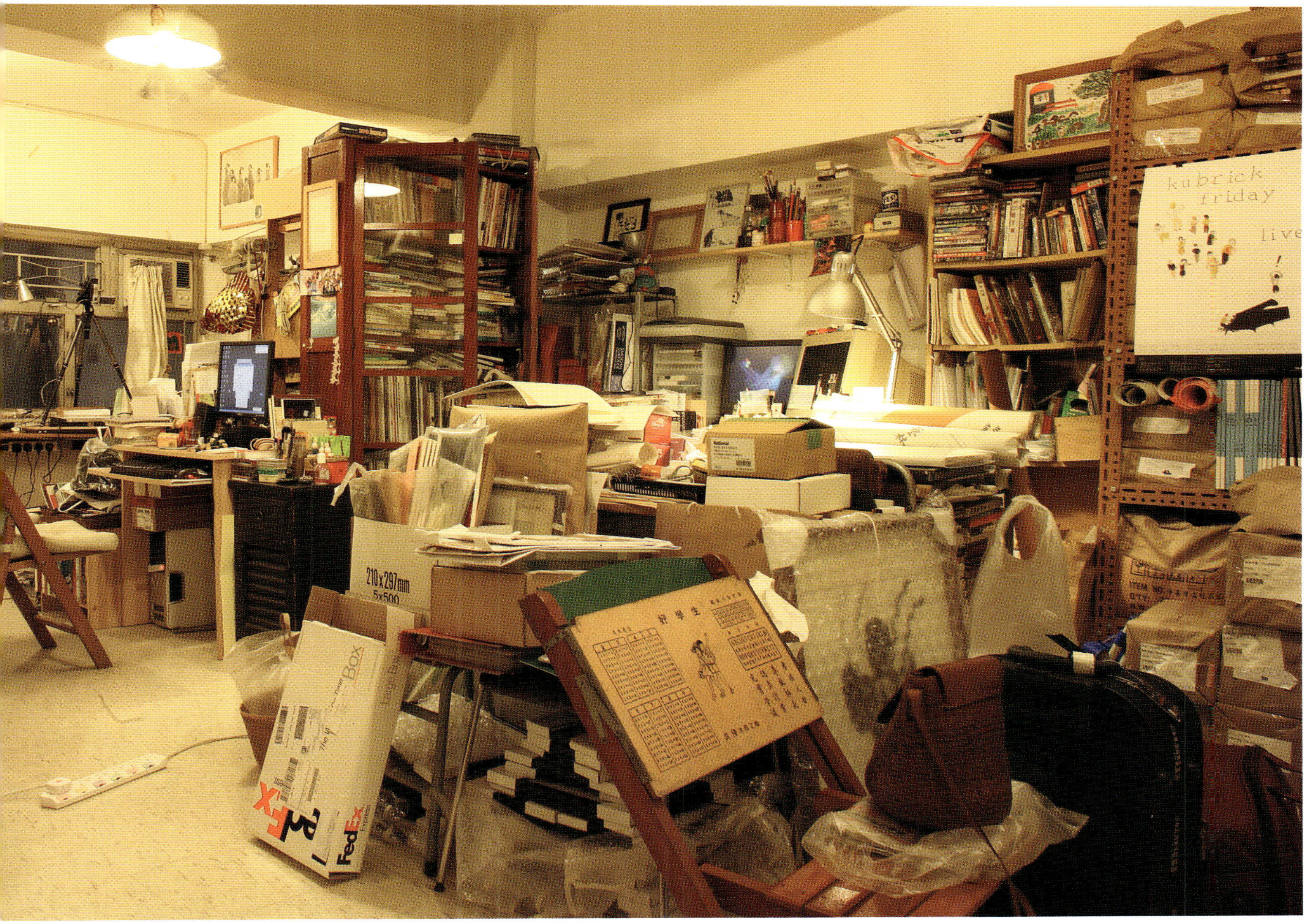

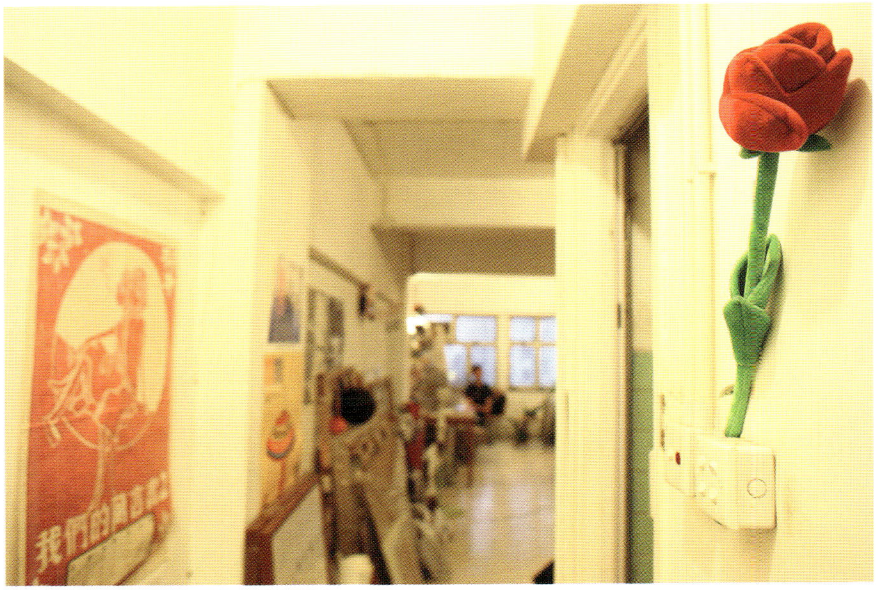

A homelike studio is a good meeting point for young people who love literature

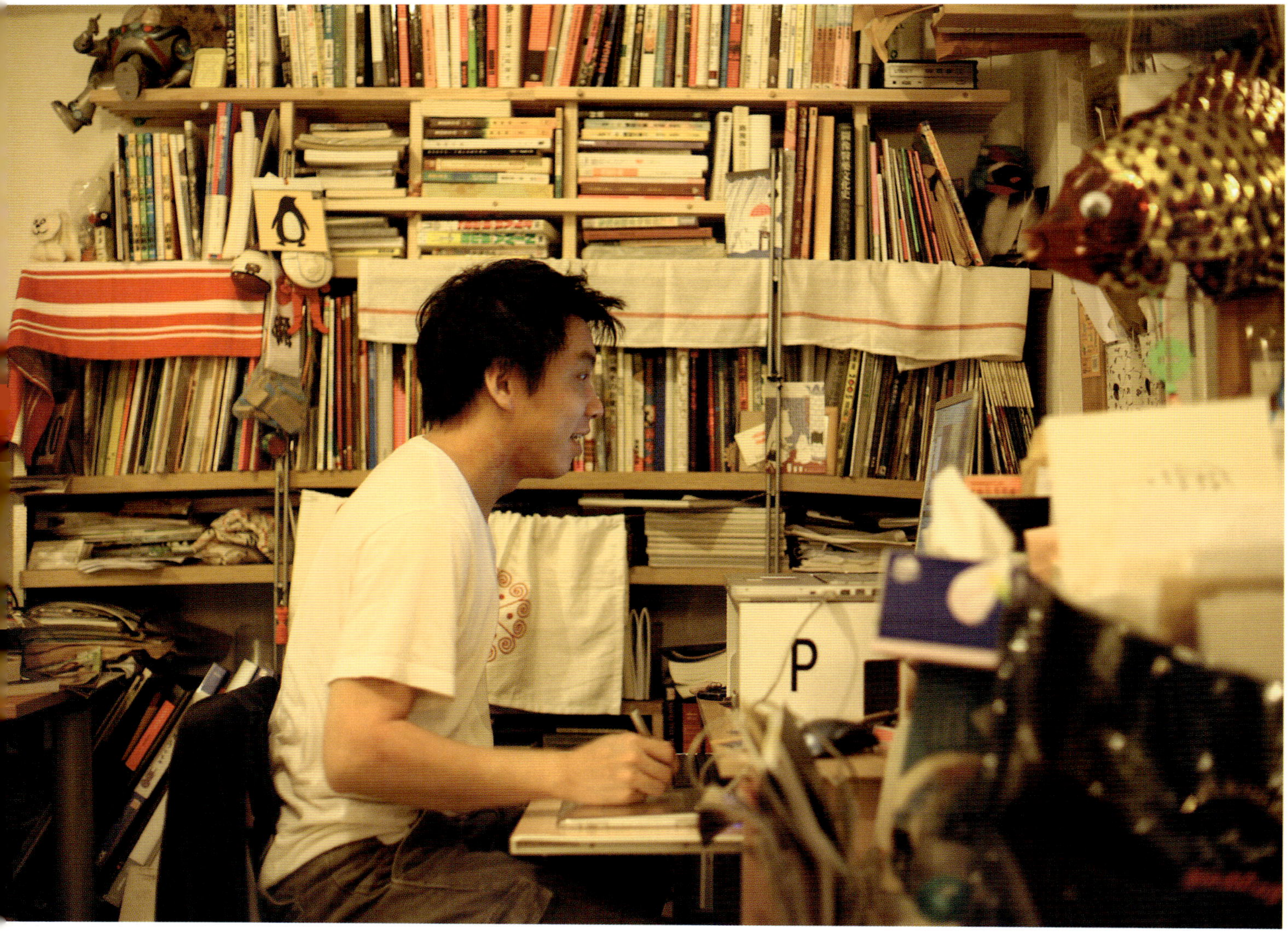

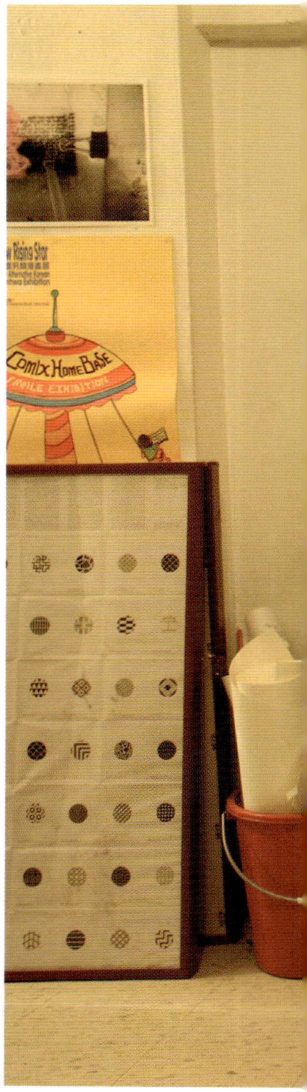

This makes it easier for them to work with the team as well as hang out with friends and exchange information. As Chihoi says, "there is technical support here! There is help when the computer breaks down."

The popular image of a cartoonist is a workaholic with designer stubble. This is somewhat of an exaggeration, but Chihoi comes close. At the end of 2007, Chihoi had been working flat-out for both the publication of *Train* and for *Hochaaa!*, his comic retrospective at the Hong Kong Arts Centre. For two months he was buried in work. He got sick towards the end. The Chinese doctor's diagnosis was 'liver gloom' — excessive tiredness. It was a hard but great time for Chihoi. He reached his full potential. The works done in the hectic days are his best.

Because of his health condition Chihoi rarely works overnight. He says that meeting deadlines is tough but that faulty outputs are even more annoying. On the other hand, delight comes with the independent lives of his characters. When they voice what has never crossed his mind, and open a new world to him, he is always overjoyed.

Over the years his career in comics has had a tremendous impact on Chihoi's character. When he was a student he was a loner. He had difficulty communicating with his teachers and schoolmates, who thought it was weird when he gave away his own comics. Having befriended the partners of 29s, who shared the same interests, Chihoi opened up. Calm on the outside but impetuous on the inside, he thinks that "creative work helps improve [his] character." During the interview he repeatedly suggested that he enjoys making friends. I also believe that this is what he has harvested from his devotion to comics.

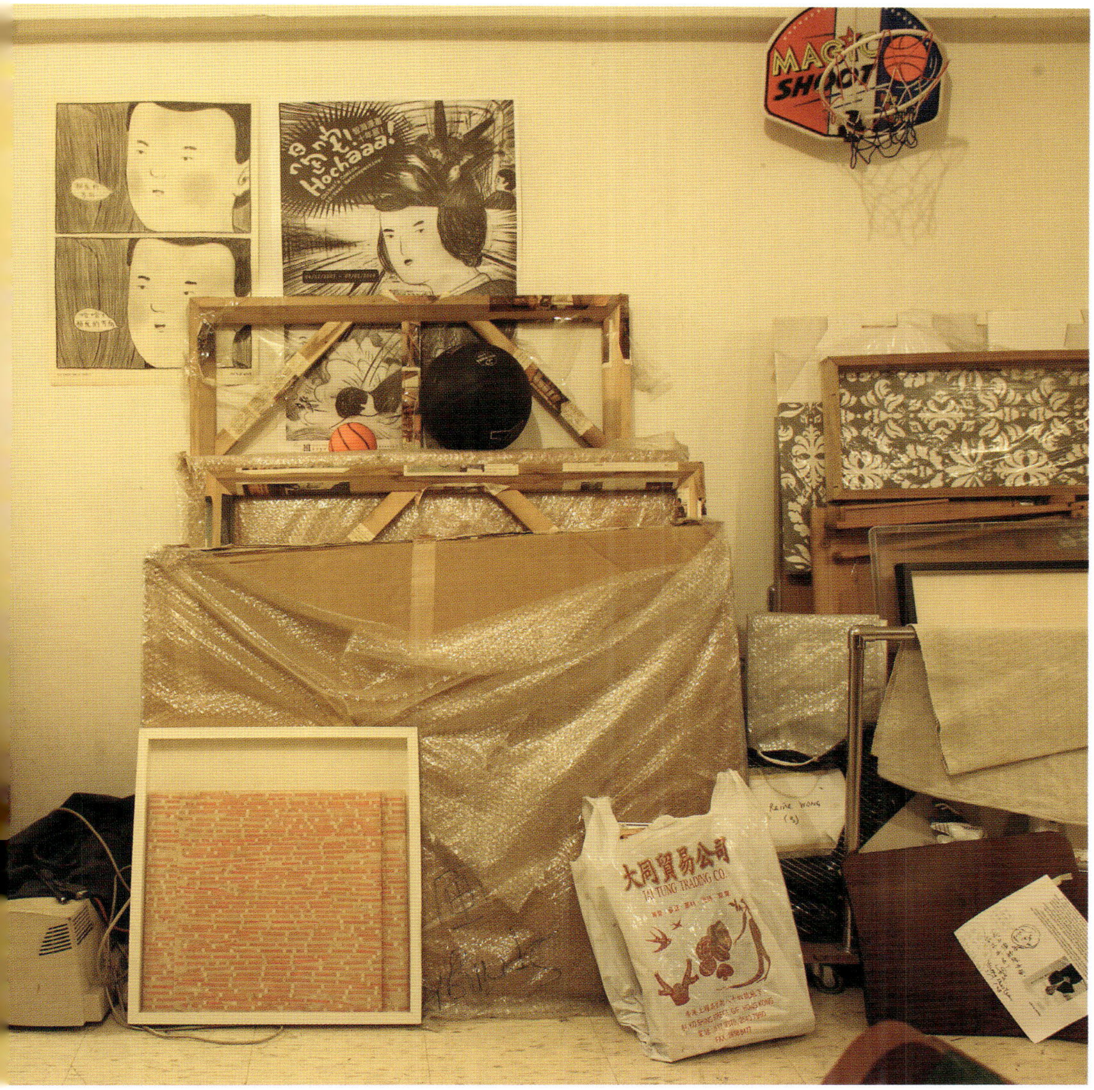

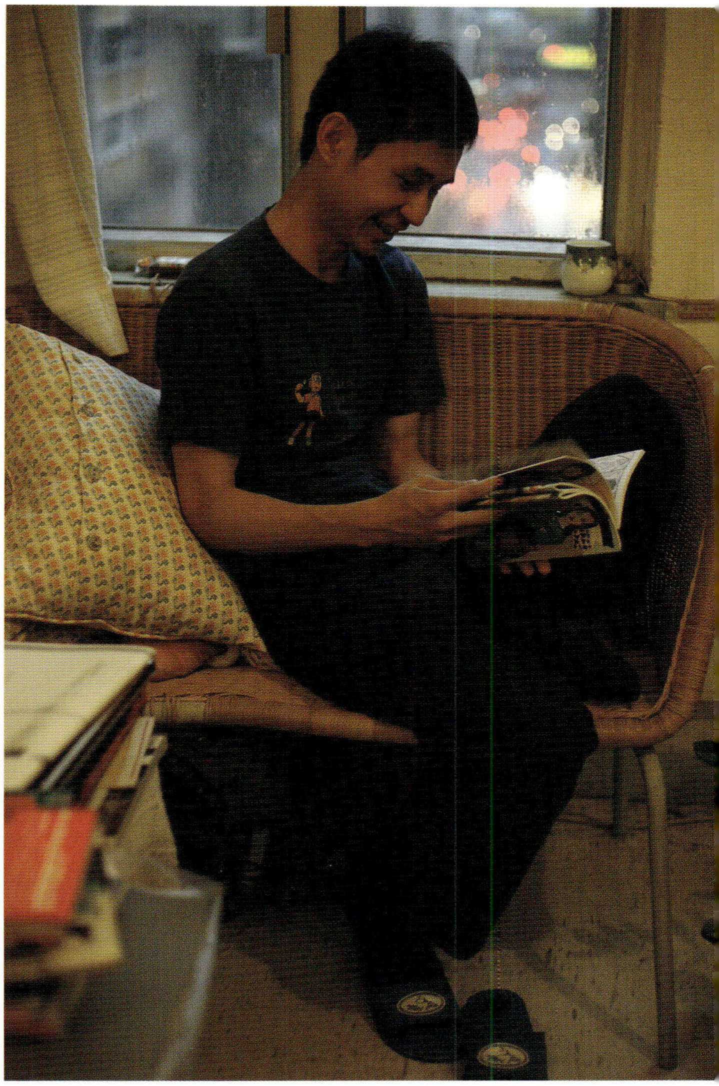

Kongkee meanwhile, describes himself as capricious and this comes through in his work. His interests are ever-changing and his work has a kaleidoscopic view.

Many project their own stories or characters onto their work, but this is not what Chihoi wants. He just wants to tell stories with comics, and it does not matter whether the story is one of his own. Kongkee sees creating comics as a way to communicate feelings, but there is no defined aim. The choice of subject is mercurial. For example, *Hijacking* reacts to Hong Kong literature and promotes it.

Chihoi and Kongkee both think that there are too few new faces on the local comics scene. Even if publishers are willing to invest, there is nobody to invest in. Kongkee cites an example: "If a university graduate goes for catering, in a few years' time he could become a manager.

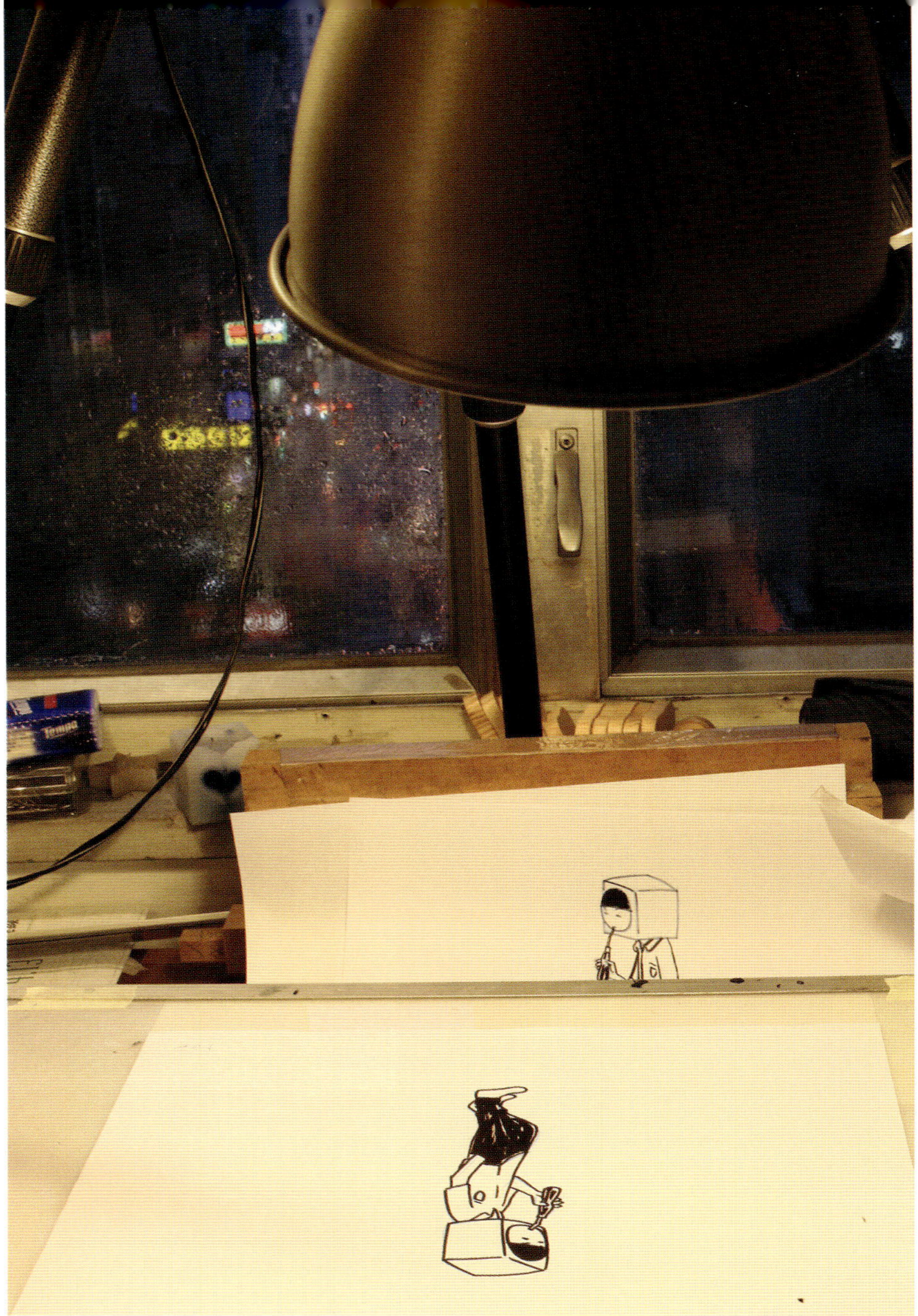

But working in comics is different. It is not easy to get promoted." The unrewarding job, together with financial and family pressure, has put many young people off.

Nevertheless, both of them are full of hope. Chihoi reckons that local comics are starting to be accepted and that there has been a rise in their variety. Sales have not been too much of an issue for Chihoi, who bases his work on whatever he wants. If sales are not good, he can publish less. Kongkee however, dismisses the myth that cartoonists can feed only on their passion. Some publications see that young people need exposure, so they take advantage of them and exploit them financially. This only drives people away from the industry. Excitedly, Chihoi mentions Author D, a young author whose photocopied compilation was able to hit newspaper stands. Chihoi stresses that Hong Kong needs more daring new forces like Author D. He hopes that his work can inspire interest in comics and attract more newcomers to the scene.

Many people have hobbies but few are committed to them. Kongkee and Chihoi have turned their hobby into a career. Looking at them, one is envious. But they deserve the fruits of their endeavours.

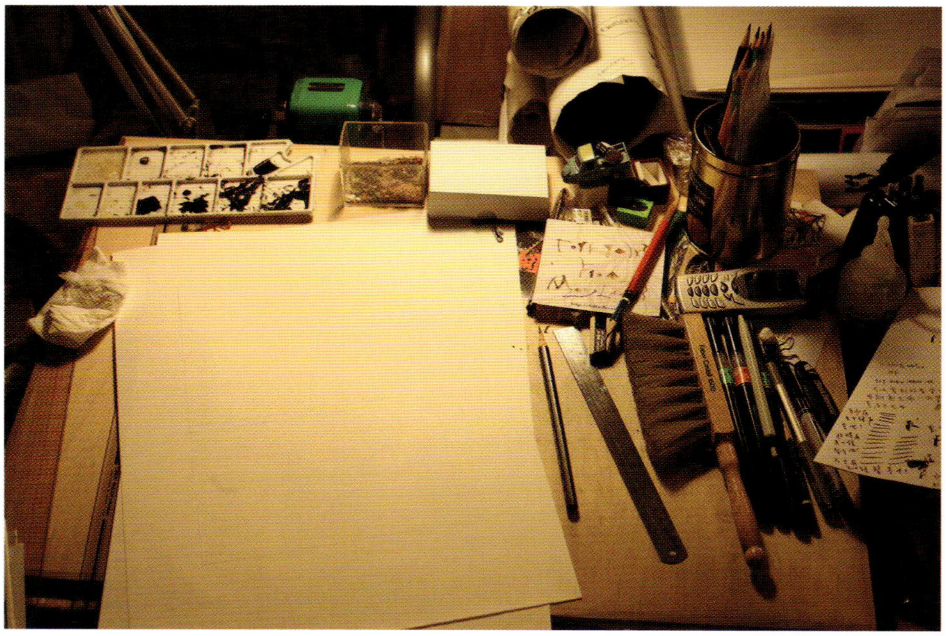

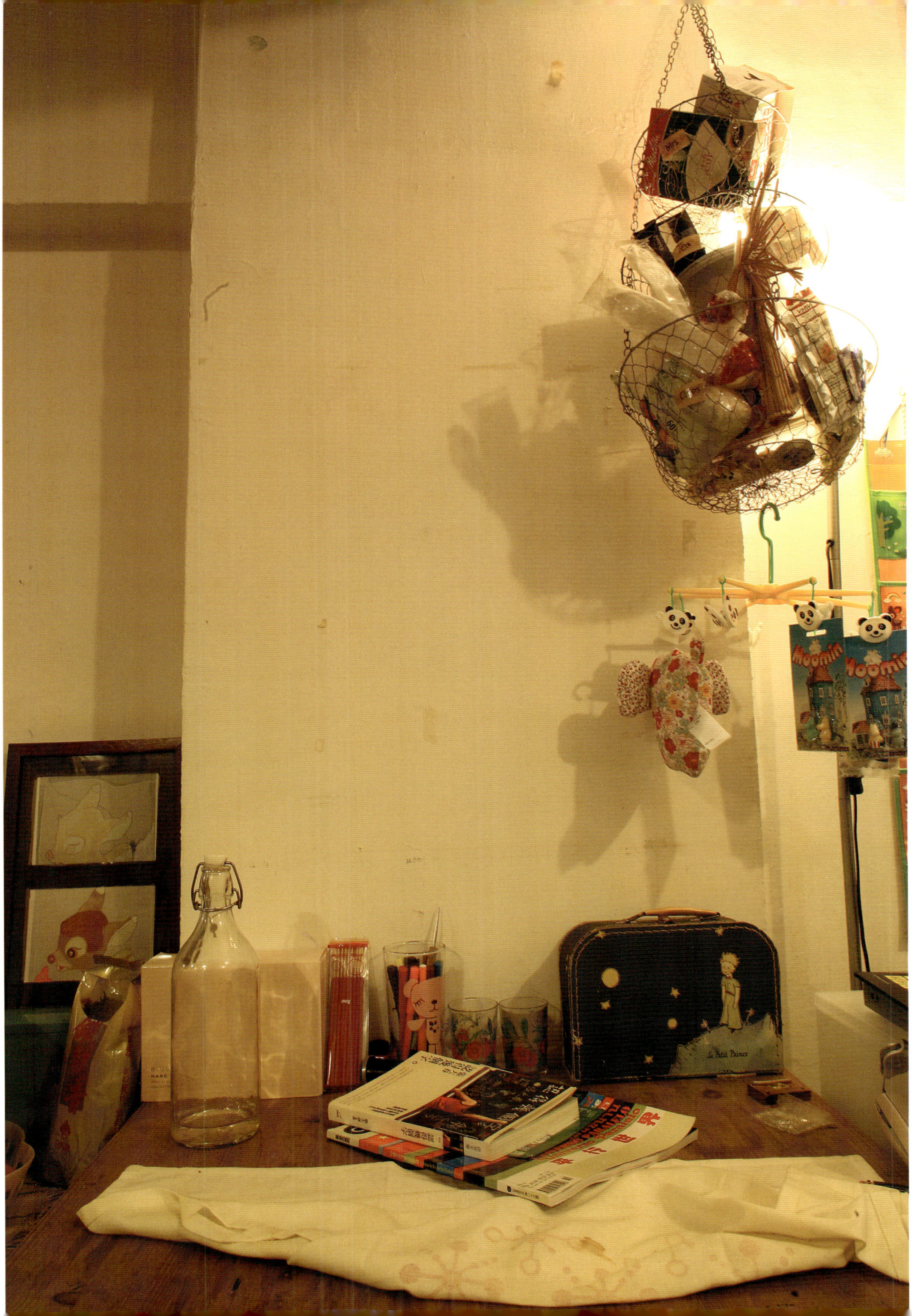
Moomin
Moomin
Le Petit Prince

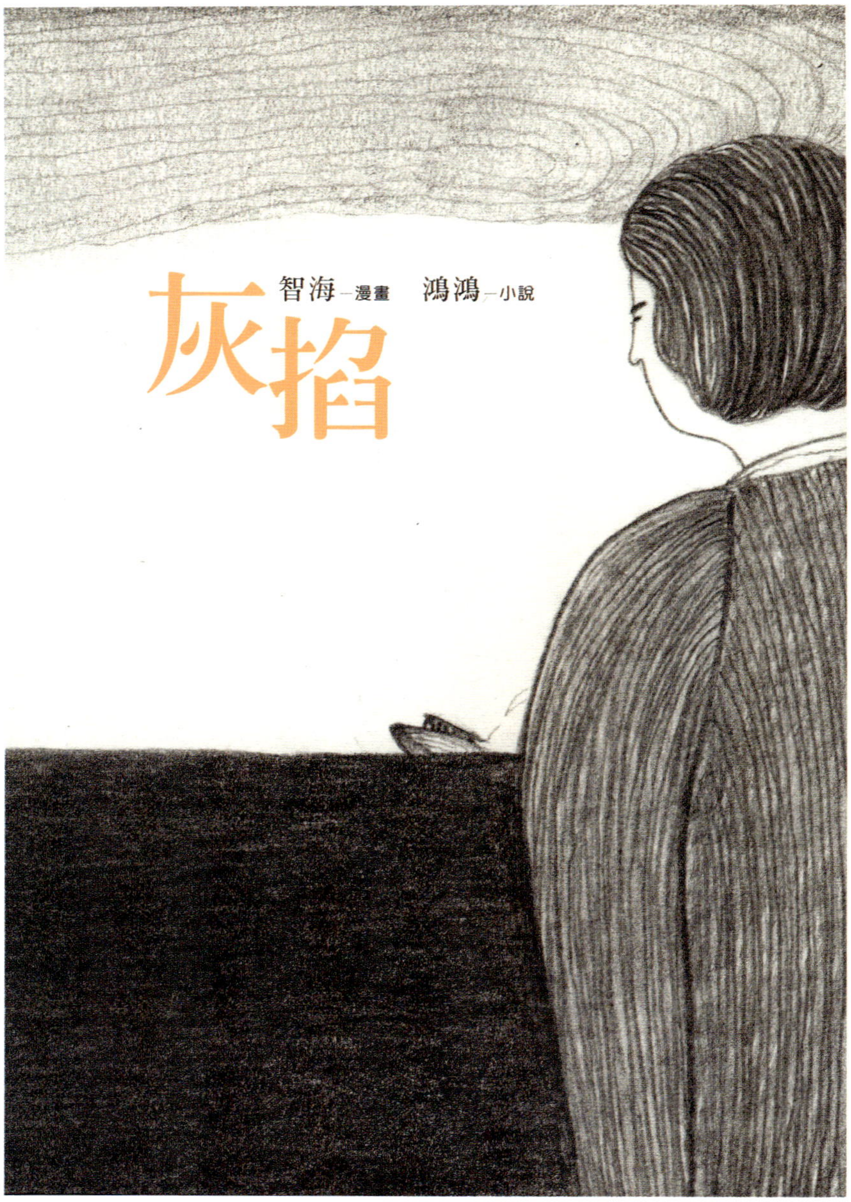

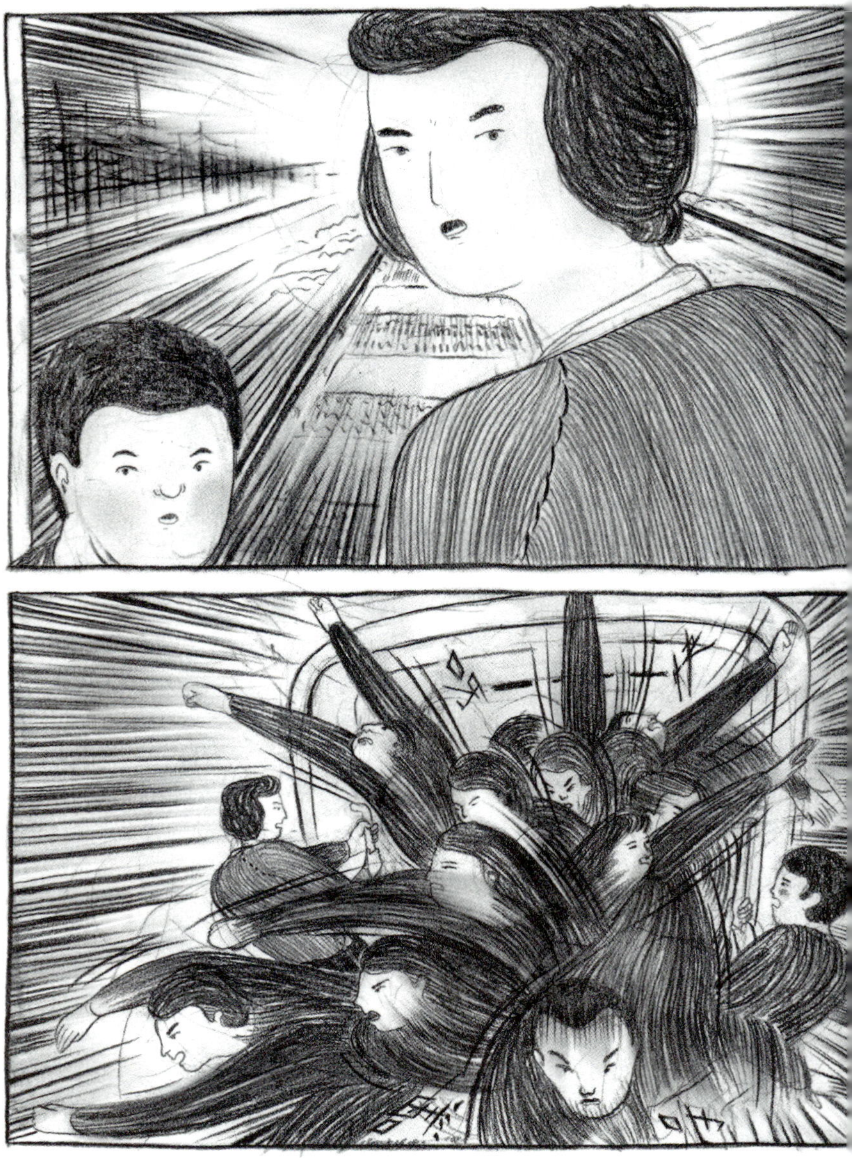

(Above, from left to right) Chihoi/The Train
Pencil on paper, A4, total 64 pages, 2007

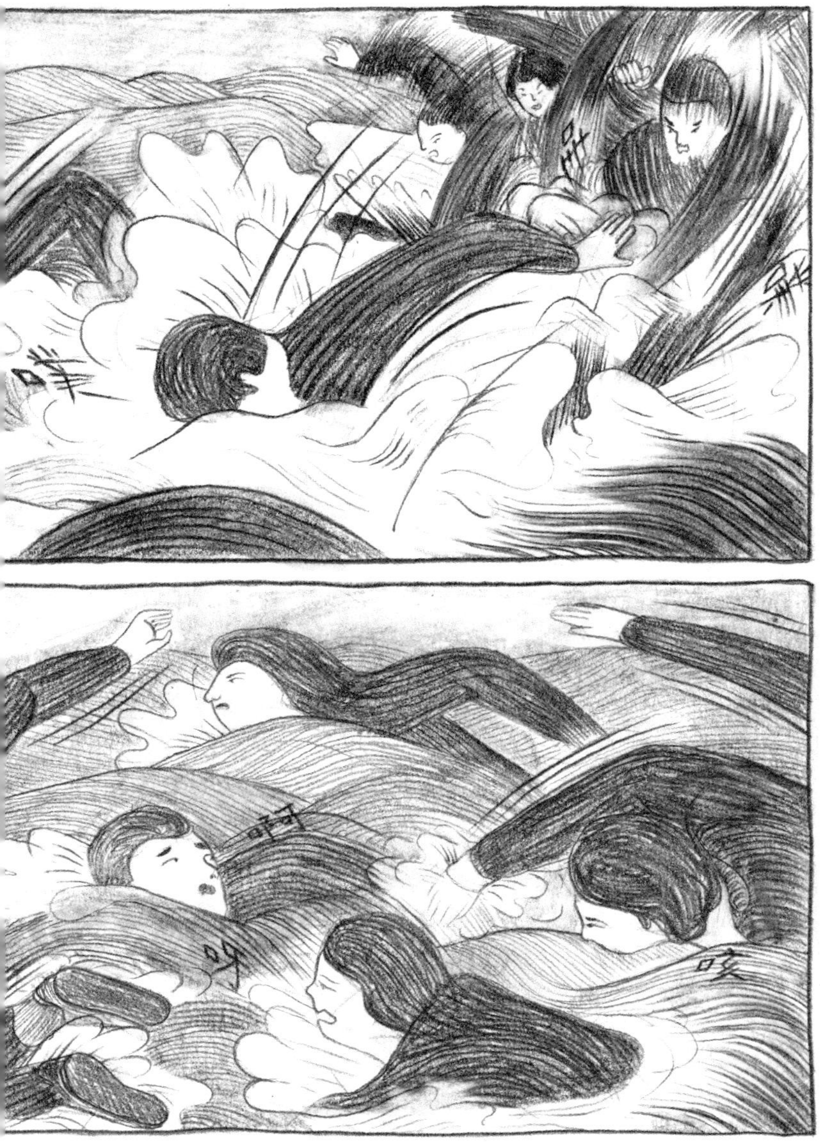

(Bottom) Chihoi/Rain in Spring, collected in Hijacking – Comic Hong Kong Literature,
Ink on paper, A4, total eight pages, 2006

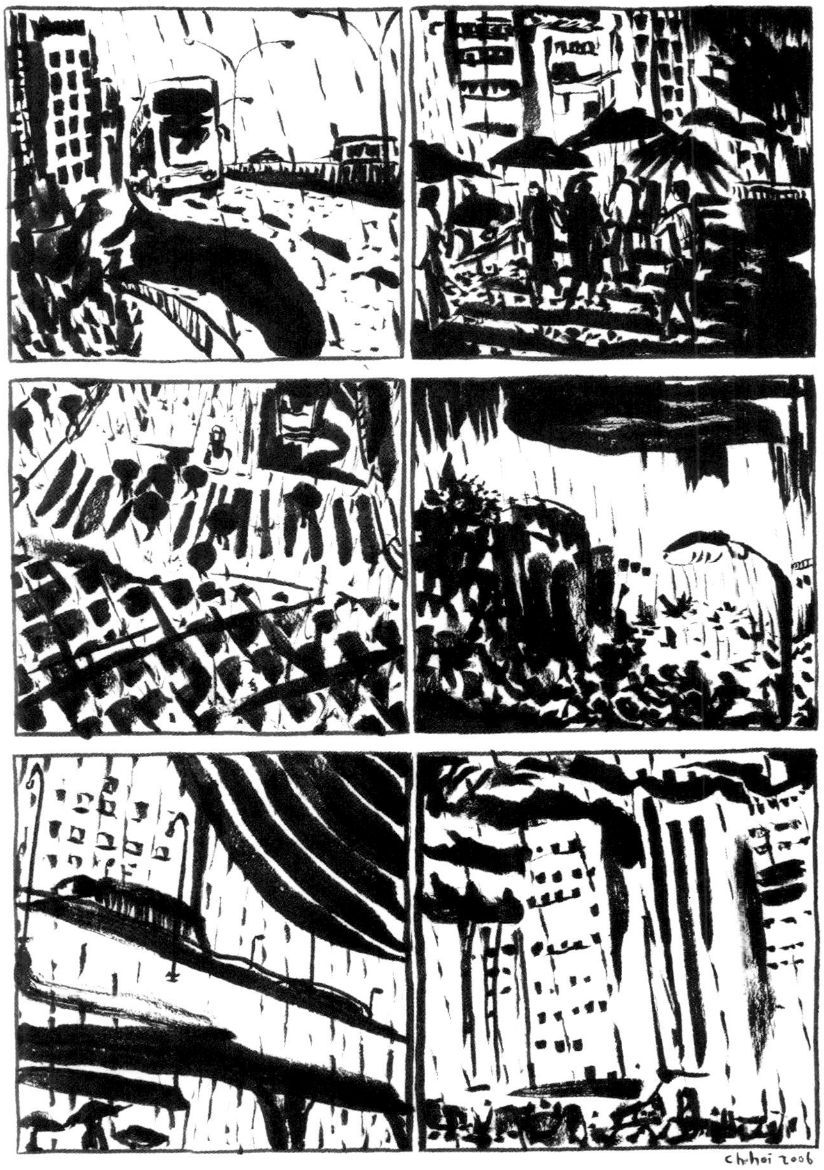

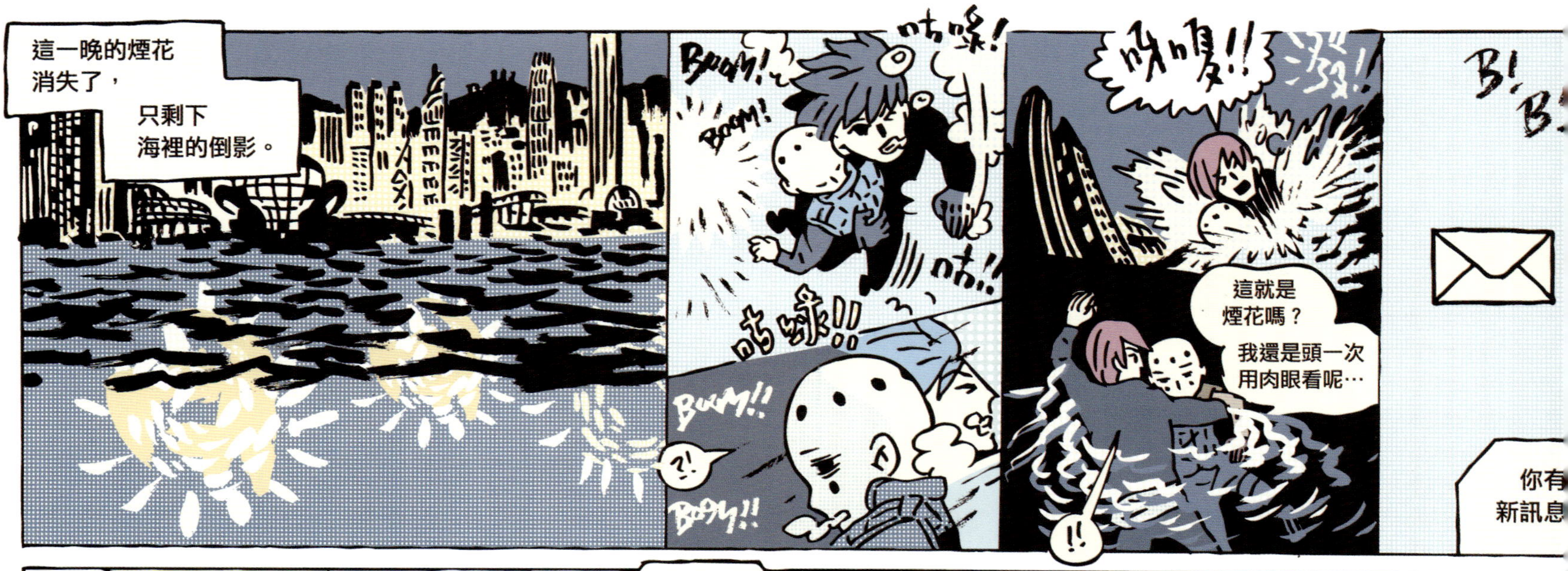

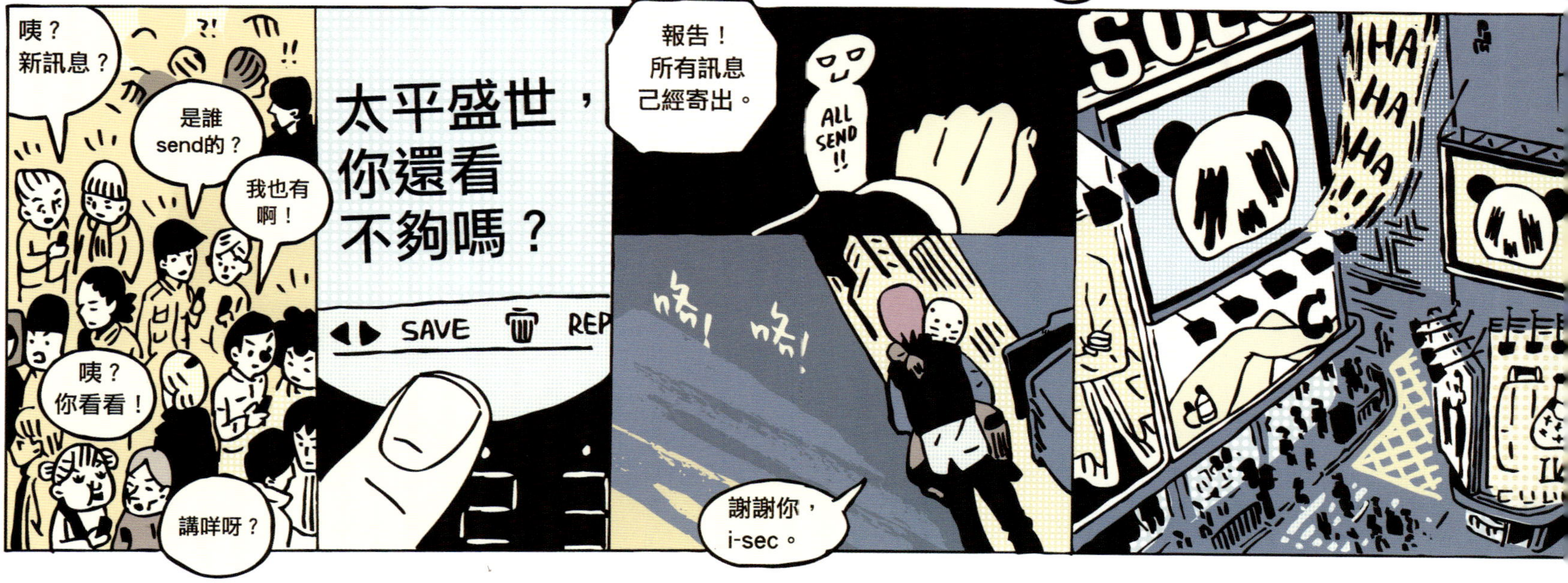

(Left above) Kongkee/2020 H.K. Crisis: Pandaman series every Sunday, Mingpao Comic, 2006-07

(Right above) Chihoi & Kongkee/Hijacking – Comic Hong Kong Literature Publication, 2007

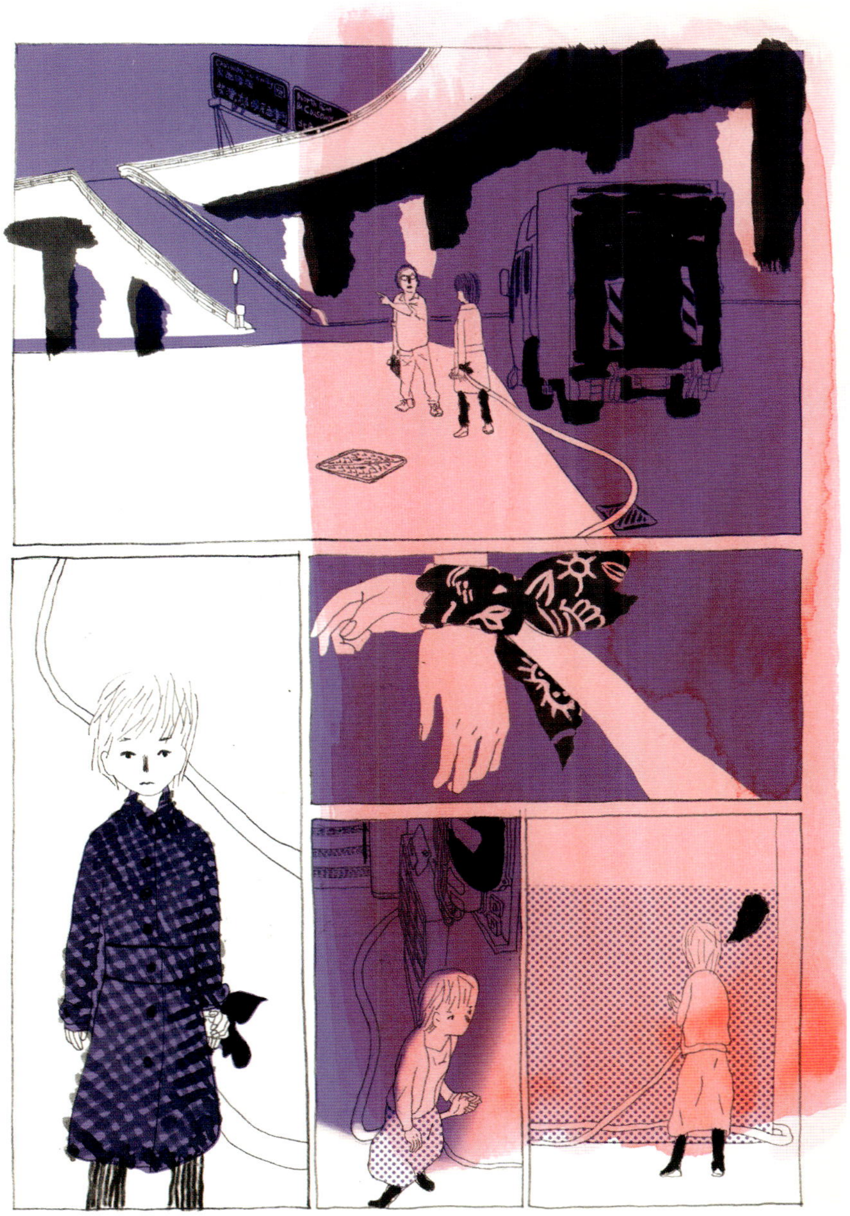

(Bottom) Kongkee/Guoduo Zhixun (Excessive Information)
Art Train Design Competition (organised by the Mass Transit Railway Corporation, Radio Television Hong Kong, and Hong Kong Arts Development Council)

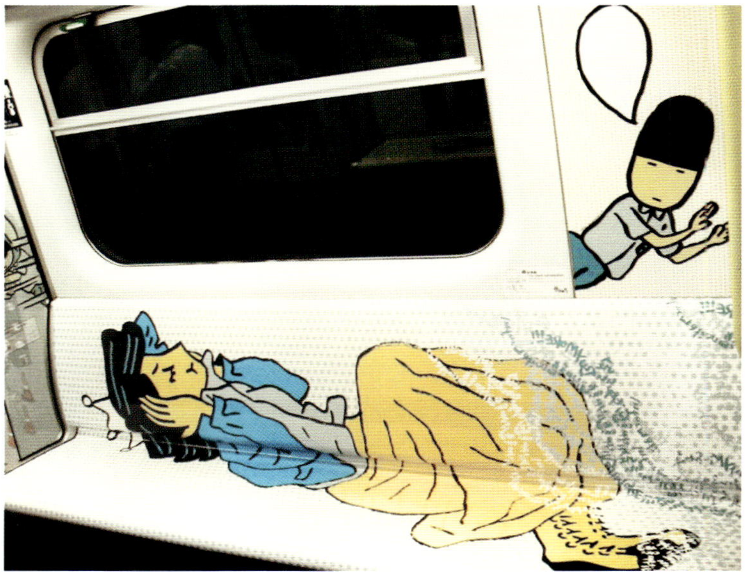

Ten O Four

Reach the Sky. Embrace the World

By Livia B Garcia

Ten O Four comprises Hanison Lau Hok-shing, Stanthony Shek Chun-yin, Winnie Chan Hiu-ting, Jasmine Ho Sze-man, Stephanie Sin Long-yee, and Cyrus Fung Kwok-hai. They are all graduates of the Bachelor of Arts (Fine Art) course co-presented by the Royal Melbourne Institute of Technology (RMIT) University and the Hong Kong Art School. Lau completed his Master's in fine art in 2008; Chan finished her BA in 2005, she is now an undergraduate at the Chinese University of Hong Kong, majoring in cultural studies with a focus on gender studies; Shek, Ho, Sin and Fung completed their degrees in 2007 and work mainly on paintings and installations.

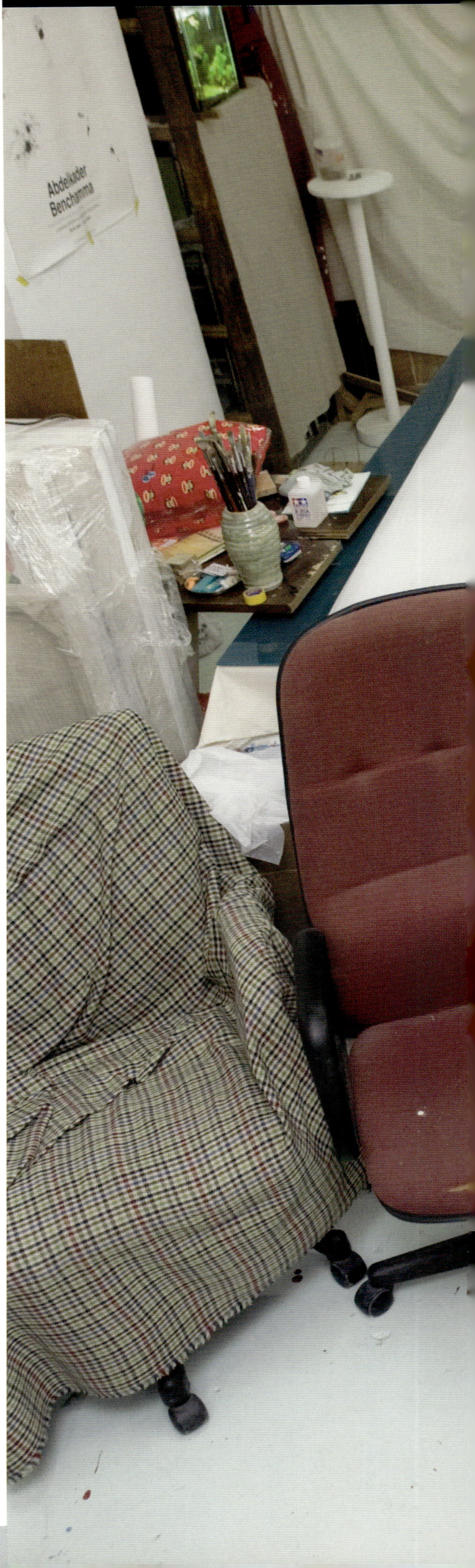

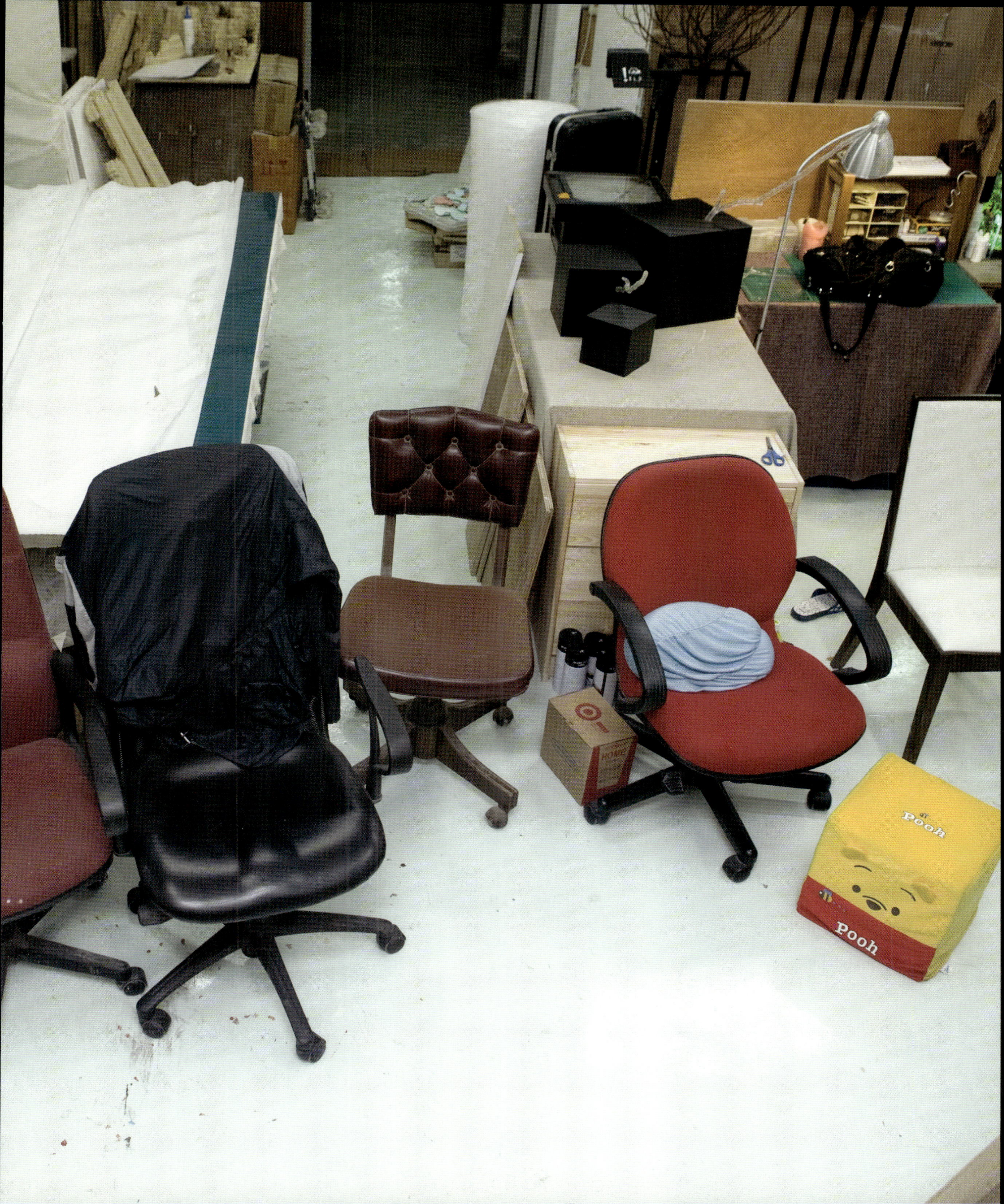
HOME
Pooh
Pooh

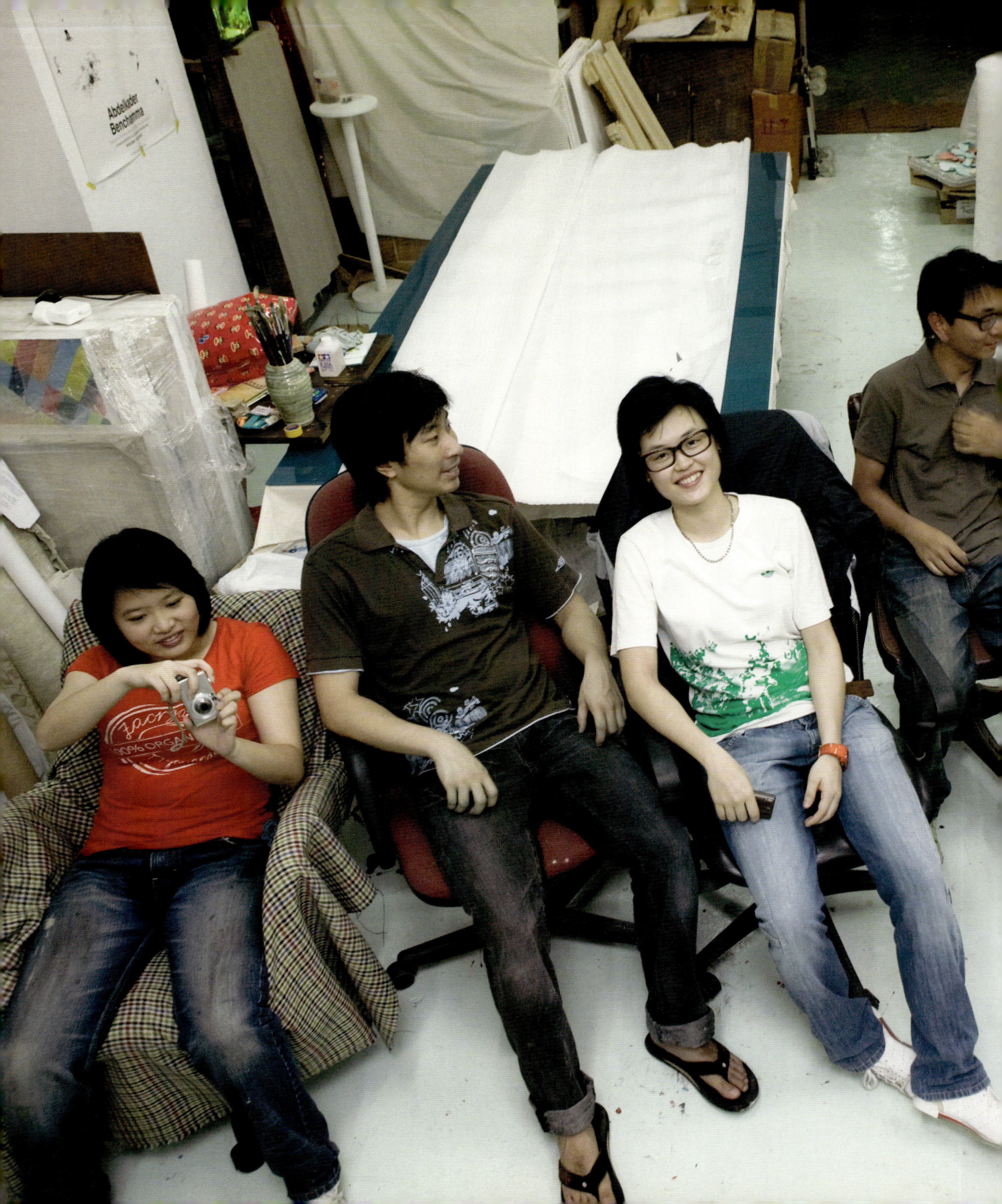
Abdelkader
Benchamma

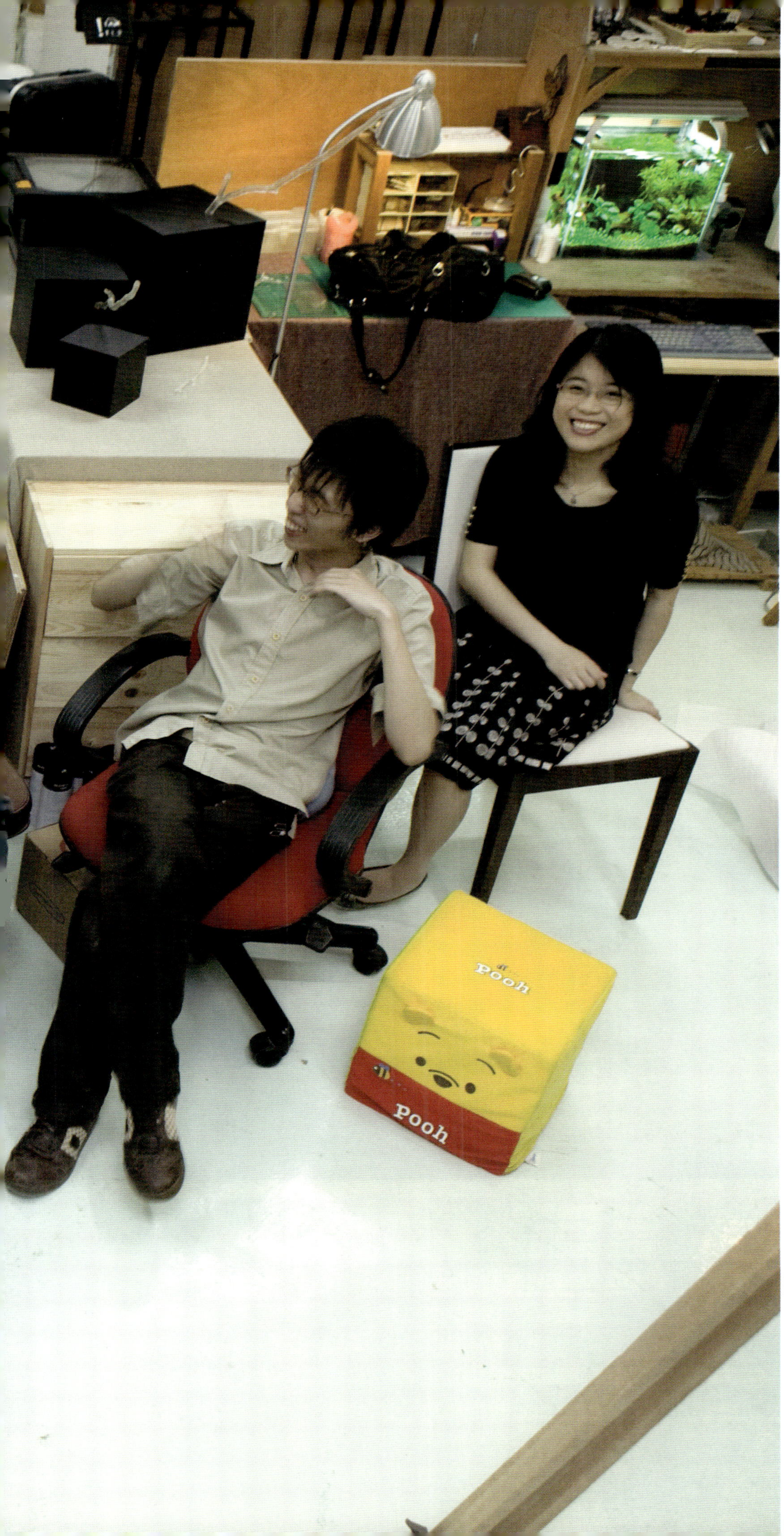

From left: Stephanie Sin Long-yee,
Cyrus Fung Kwok-hai,
Jasmine Ho Sze-man,
Hanison Lau Hok-shing,
Stanthony Shek Chun-yin,
and Winnie Chan Hiu-ting

As soon as we step into the 1,200 sq-ft space, the photographer beside me cannot help but say, "This place is playful!" This team of artists moved into their current studio in Fotan in December 2007.

Occupying the spaces on the two sides of the main entrance are Cyrus Fung and Hanison Lau. Fung finished his BA in 2007. He left Hong Kong to study in the United Kingdom when in form two, and then studied product design in Kingston University and at the University of Hertfordshire, obtaining a BA with honours. Besides being an artist, he is a swimming coach. Fung repeatedly uses two kinds of materials in his art works: yellow plaster and rolls of plastic bubble wrap that are normally used for packaging. He pours the yellow plaster on the bubble wrap in its liquid form and when the material has solidified, the bubble wrap gets peeled off. Fine traces of the bubbles remain on the yellow plaster surface, which resembles the texture of beehives. To add layers to the work, the final installation of the plaster units embraces the concept of architectural planes. Yellow plaster itself is rather fragile and bubble wrap is meant to provide protection. When the two materials come together they generate a delicate relationship.

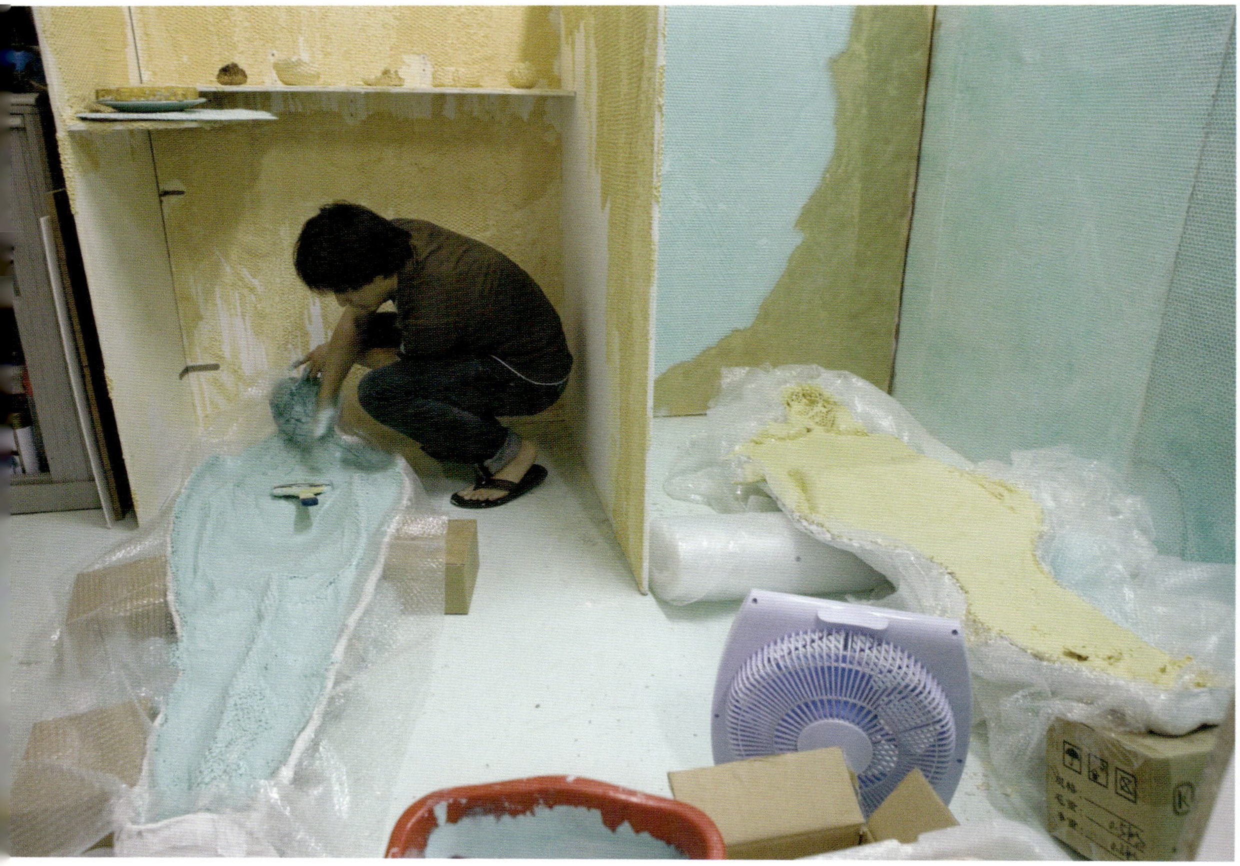

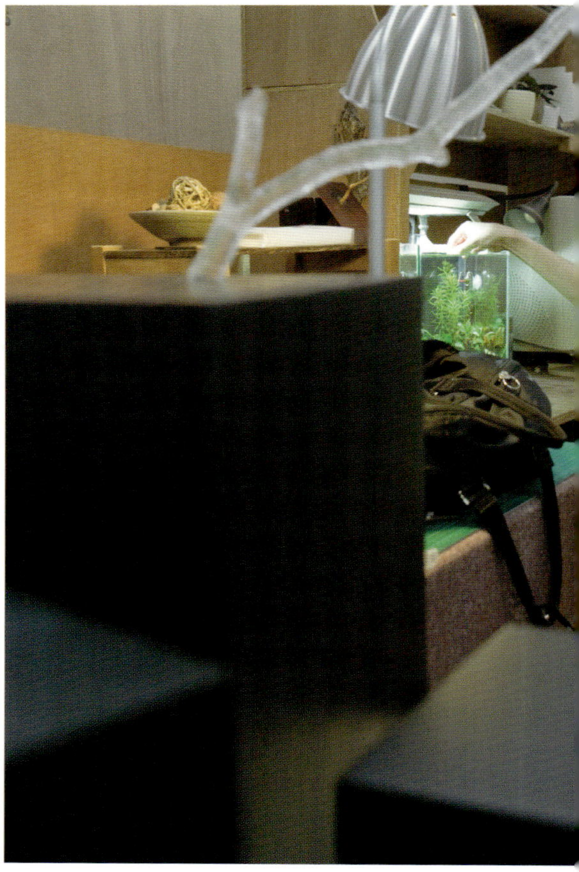

About his past studios, Fung says, "The size of a studio is not of any concern to me. A studio should not become a burden either. I see art as a life-long career. Now that we have a studio, it is up to me to develop my works freely and see how far I can go on the path."

Hanison Lau's corner is stacked with little hills that resemble those used in landscape garden designs. They are made by gluing together layers of saw-cut timber sheets. The space is also equipped with a wire cutter. Lau attained a higher diploma in graphic design in Australia, followed by a BA(FA) in 2005. He worked as a teaching assistant at the Hong Kong Art School between 2005 and 2007, and in 2008 he obtained his Master's in fine art. Lau's installation works are informed by classical Chinese literature.

"My focus is to explore the culture of the Ming dynasty and try to infuse this into the contemporary world," Lau says. "Many people have neglected the characteristics and interesting elements of classical things." Lau has also learned to play the classical Chinese musical instrument, the 'guqin' in his free time. Since Hong Kong is ceeply influenced by Western culture, I wonder if the mainland would be a more suitable environment for making his works, which are very oriental. "That may not be true," he responds. "The fact that I am using classical Chinese literature as reference material while I am in Hong Kong shows that I truly like this topic. I wish to refer to Chinese culture, but adopt a Western way to present the concepts, so as to form a new viewpoint."

I asked if his family members have encouraged him to study art. "They think that it is fine to study whatever subject I want," Lau says. "Things that still exist in this society still have their own value, otherwise they would have been rejected long ago "

Like Lau, Stanthony Shek often makes use of timber to create his art works. He studied for a certificate in the arts and a diploma in fine arts in 2002 and 2005 respectively, at the Hong Kong Art School, and in 2007 finished his Bachelor in fine arts. The space that he occupies is tidily arranged; there is a small tank of fish by his working table.

Shek's works often make people consider nature and the power of life. "Sometimes I don't quite know what my focus is during my explorations. It is often after the works are completed that I evaluate them as a third person," he says. "Reviewing the works that I have been developing, I find that they are closely intertwined with humans and their environment. Living in the city involves a kind of pressure. Man and nature should co-exist, but nowadays most people have neglected the importance of nature. Urban people should ask themselves when the last time was that they raised their heads to watch the sky or reached out to touch trees."

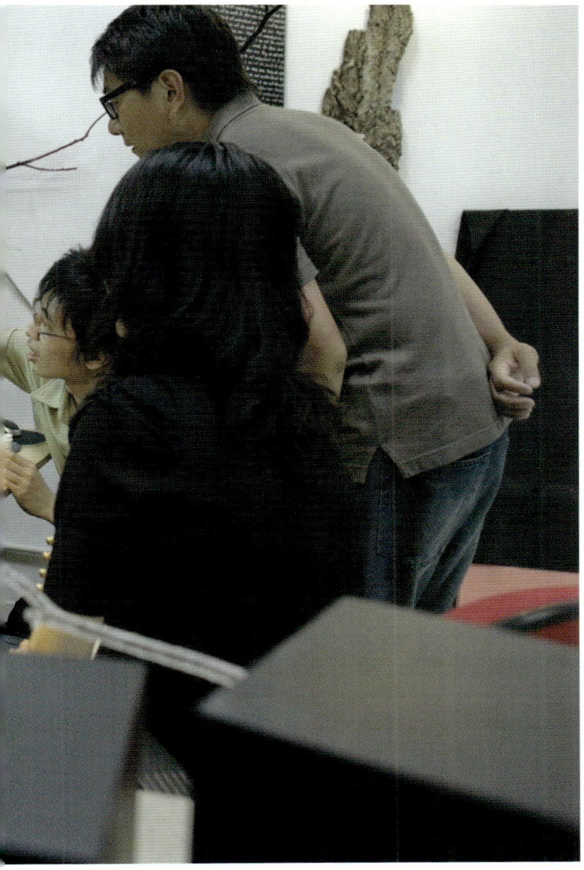

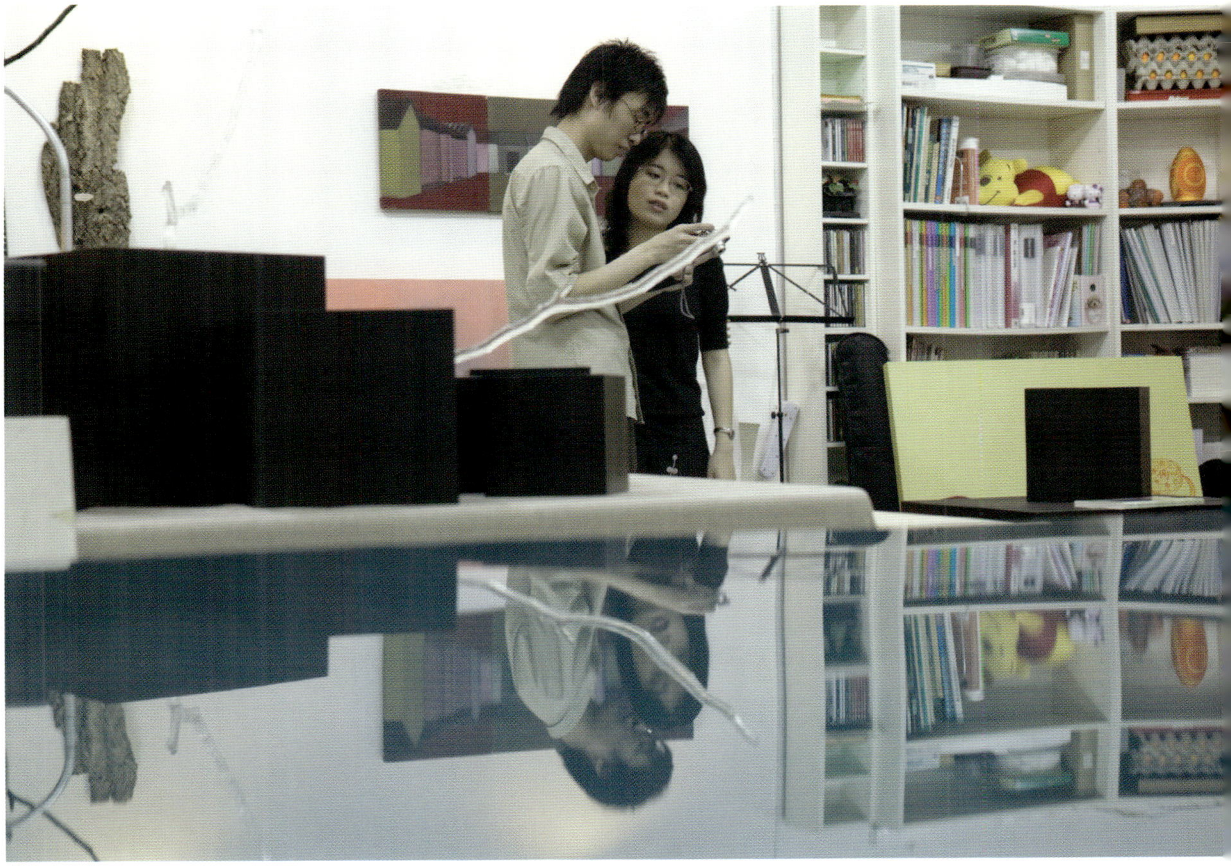

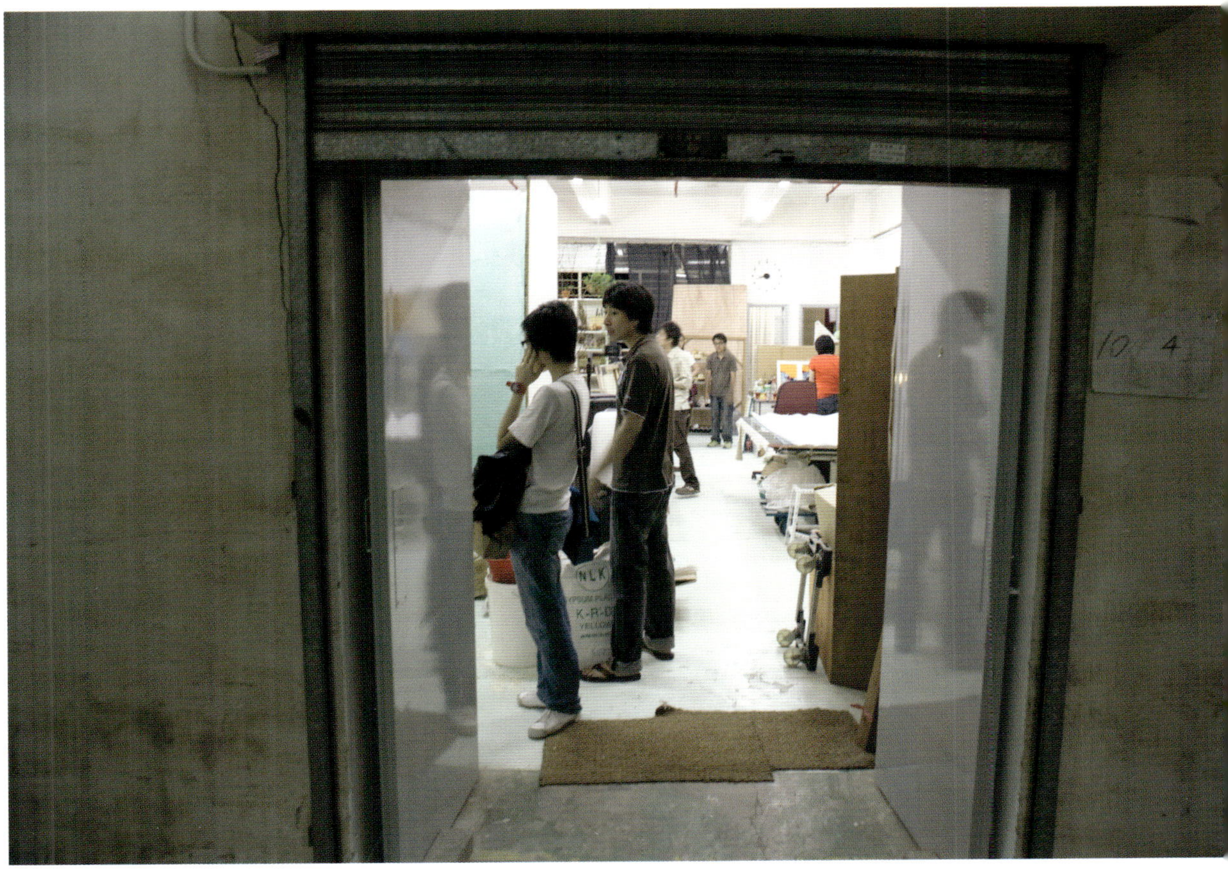
10 4

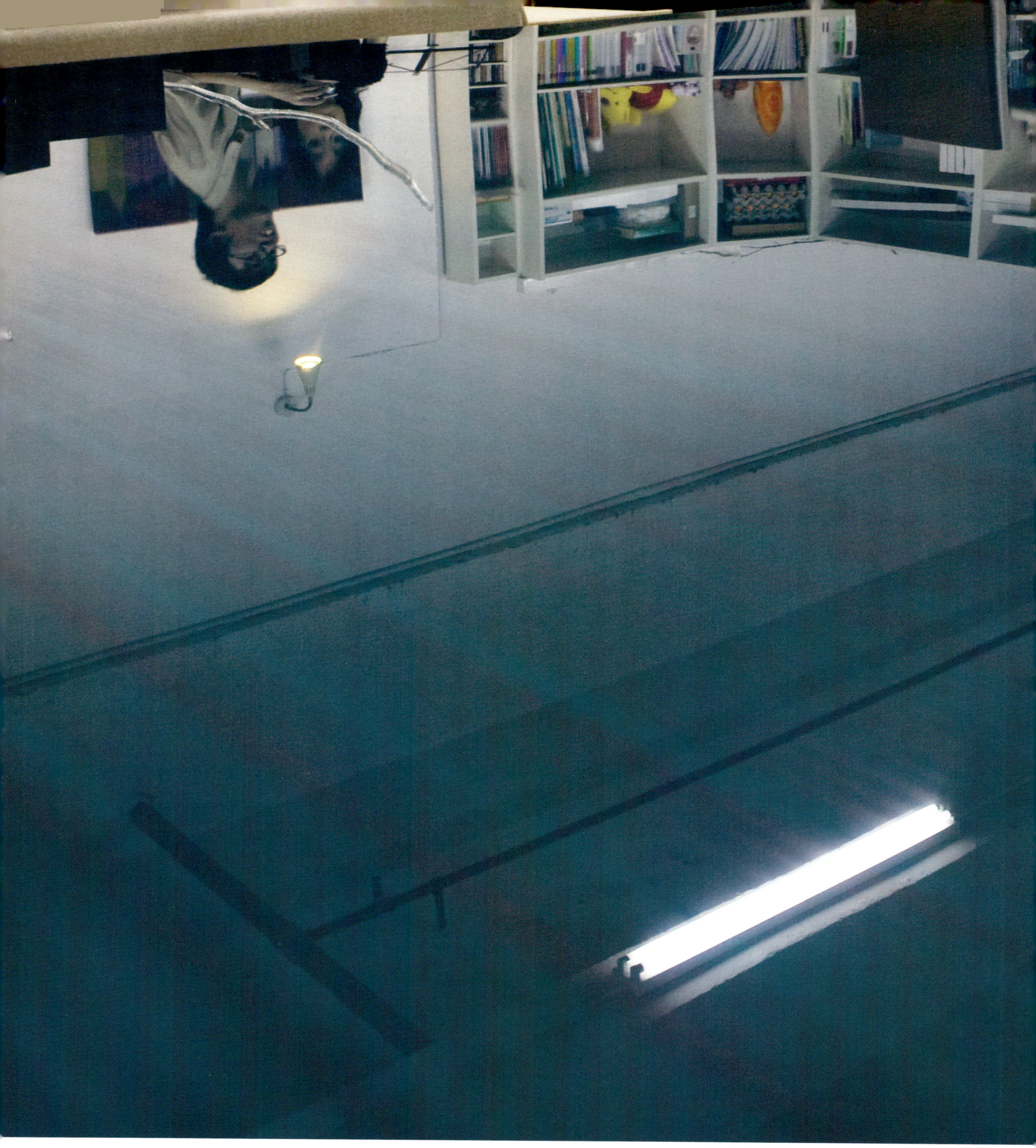

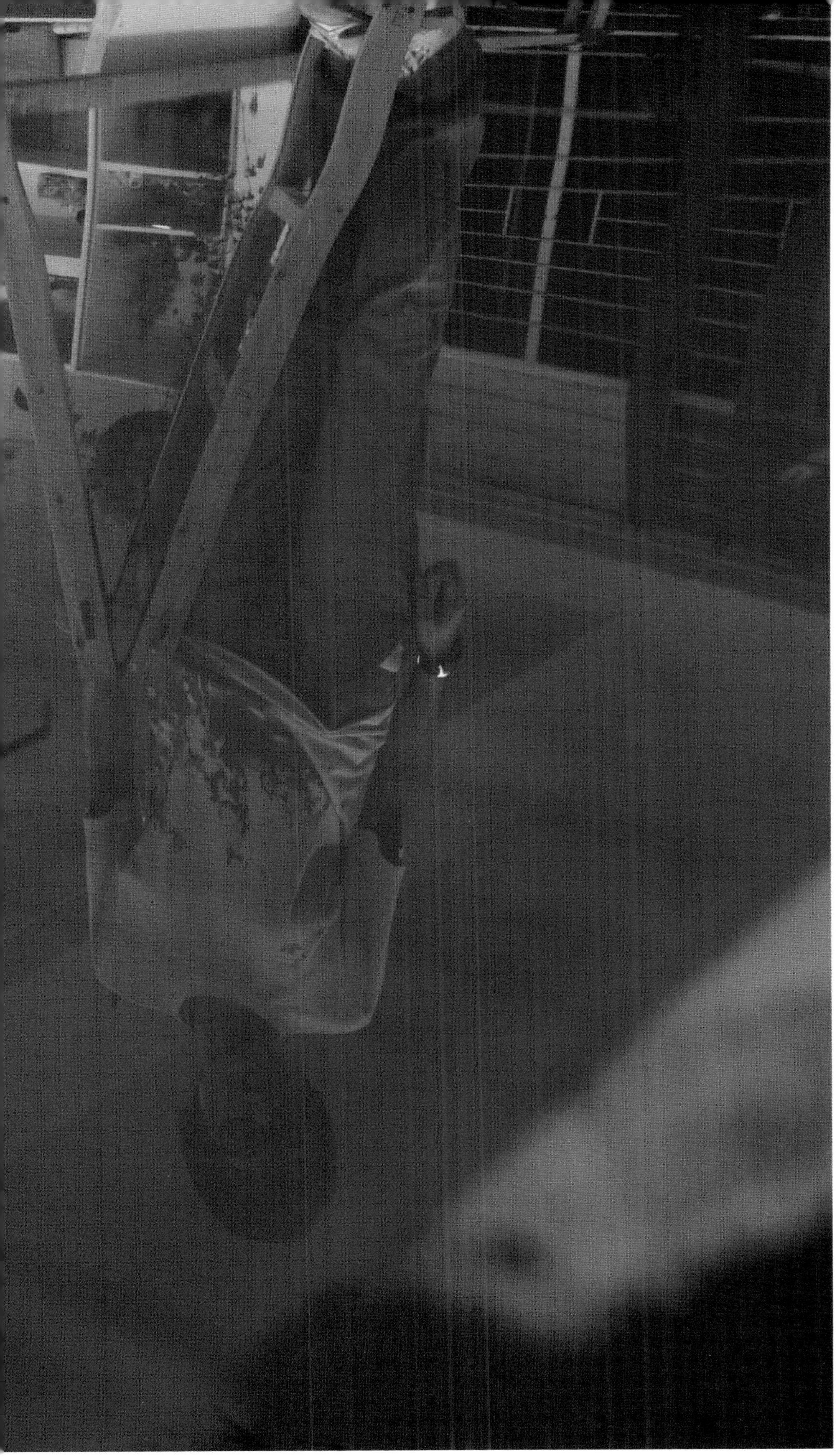

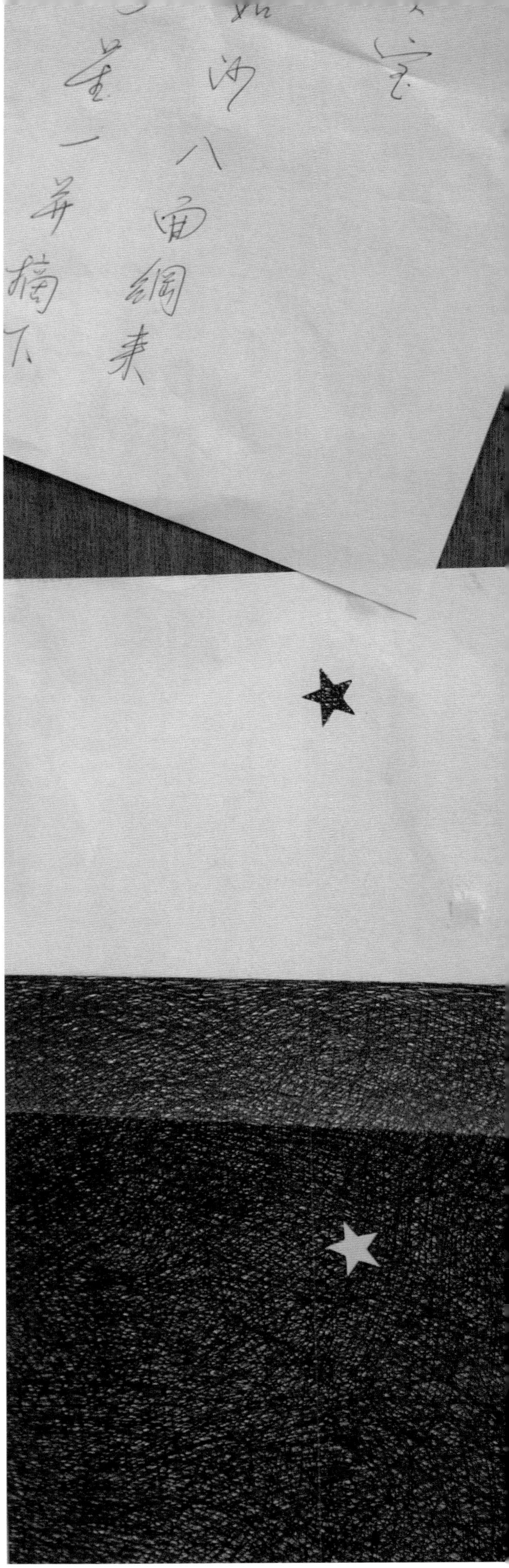

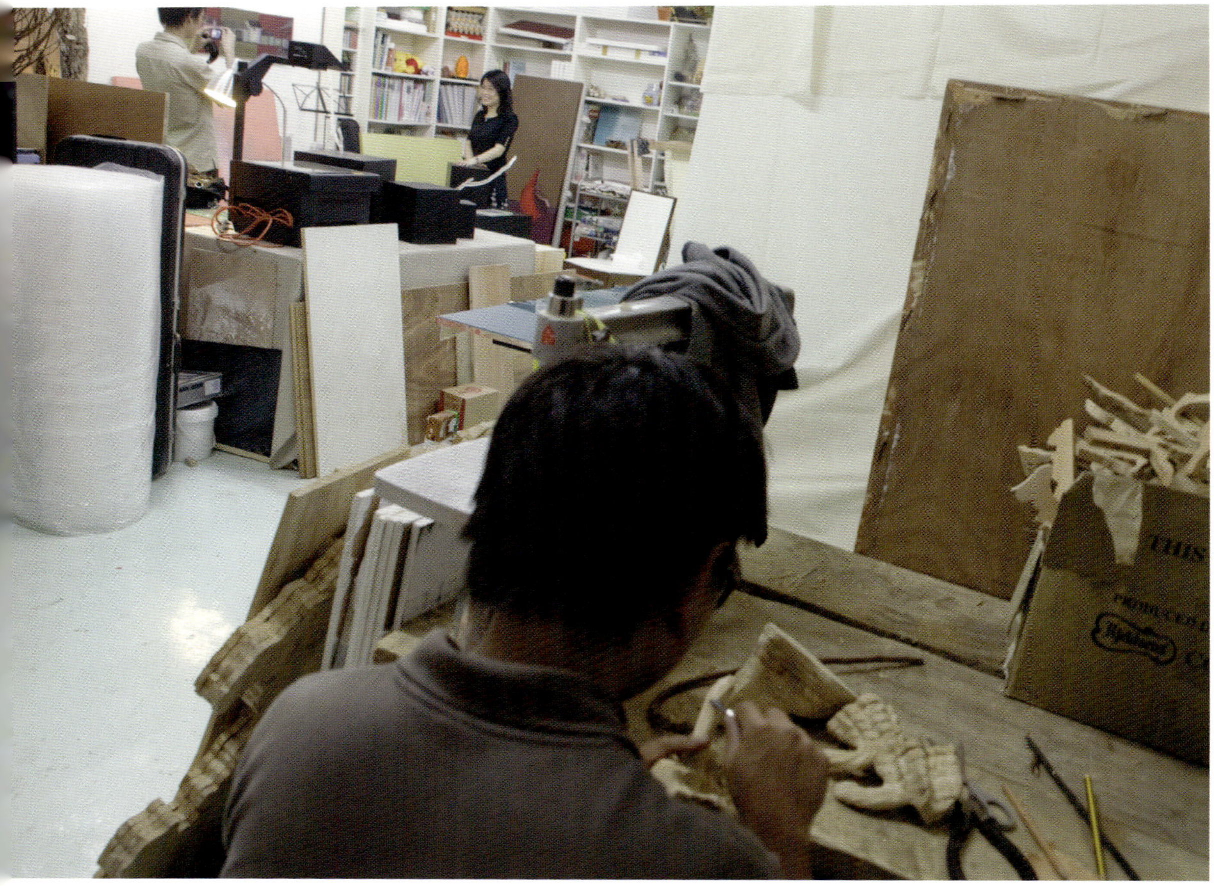

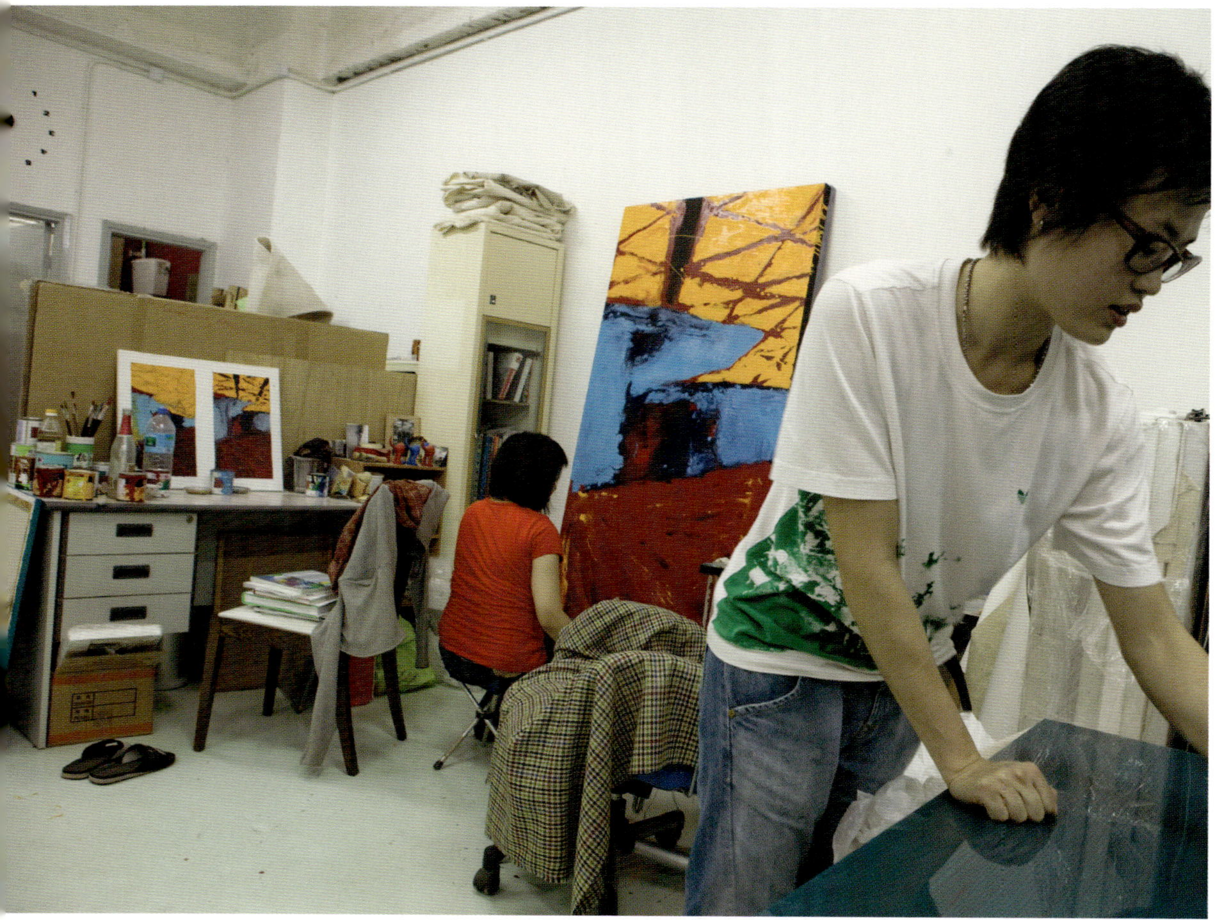

"It is also about reading human mentality and desires," he adds. "For example, many people wish for longevity. I try to ask questions and through the process of art making I find answers." Shek mentions that his father often makes furniture, and this had an effect on why he chose art. Both require skills of the hands – tools that Shek also uses to play the piano beautifully.

Winnie Chan finished her BA degree in 2005, and is studying at the Chinese University of Hong Kong. "When I was studying art history at the Hong Kong Art School I had the chance to learn about the works of some feminist artists," she remembers. "There was a saying which stirred up my emotions: 'Men made art; women did crazy little things'. This made me start to re-think the position I took as a female art student." Chan consciously explores the topic of gender through her works, mostly oil paintings. Weaving into them are her own experiences of growing up in a family which originates from Chiu Chow, a region known for gendered socialisation.

As a student assistant Chan has had more of a chance to explore gender-related activities and this has helped with her art making as well. "In 2007 I took part in the collection of heritage items for Women of Hong Kong – a Century of Contribution and Development," she says. "I accompanied workers from the Hong Kong Institute of Asia-Pacific Studies Gender Research Centre to collect an infant-carrying strap from the home of this old lady Mrs Choi. Mrs Choi had embroidered on the strap words of greetings like 'Innocent and Playful Baby', which are full of strong feelings. So why can't handicrafts made by women be considered art?" she asks, before raising other issues, such as whether women must get married, and why male fashion is always regarded as unisex.

As someone who has studied fashion in the United Kingdom, Jasmine Ho has her own theories about the trend of going 'unisex'. "Spirituality is not divided into any sex at all," she notes concisely. Ho completed her BA degree in 2007 and is most concerned with painting. When the medium of painting has come to a point where there seems to be little room for breakthrough, she re-explores material choices and tries to push the medium forward. She often makes use of transparent

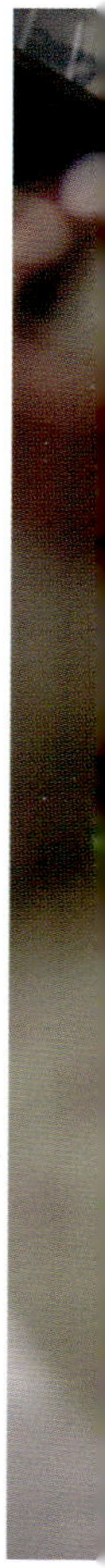

Six people sharing one studio means everyone must make the best use of what limited space is available

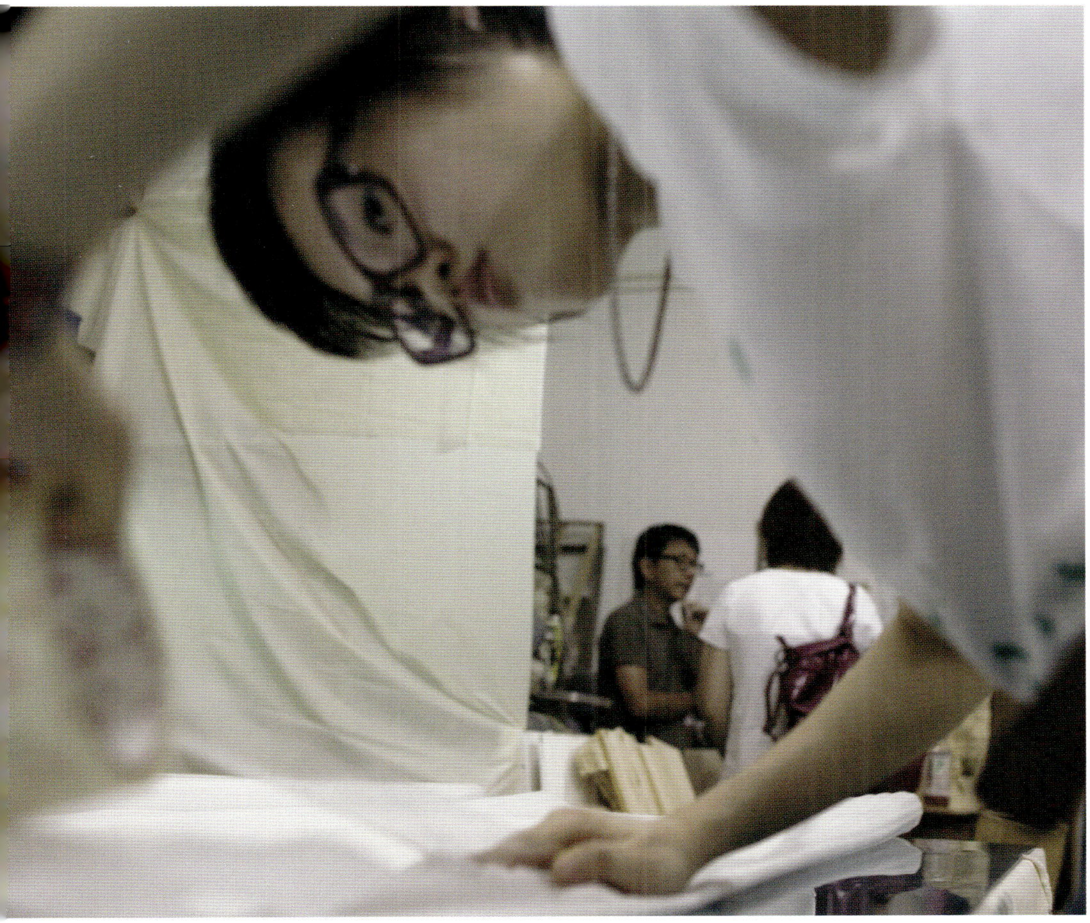

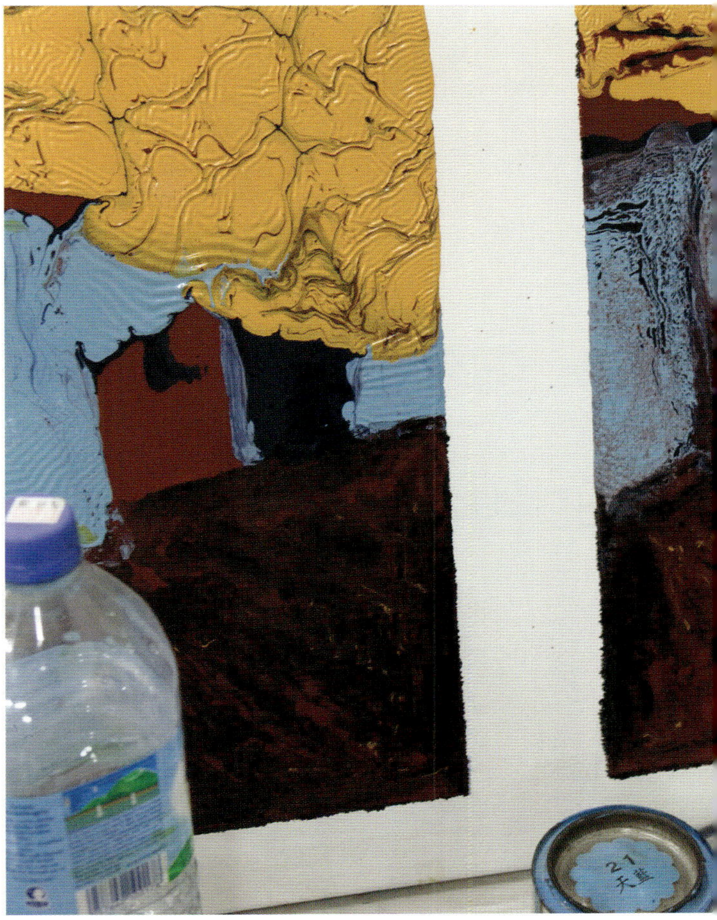

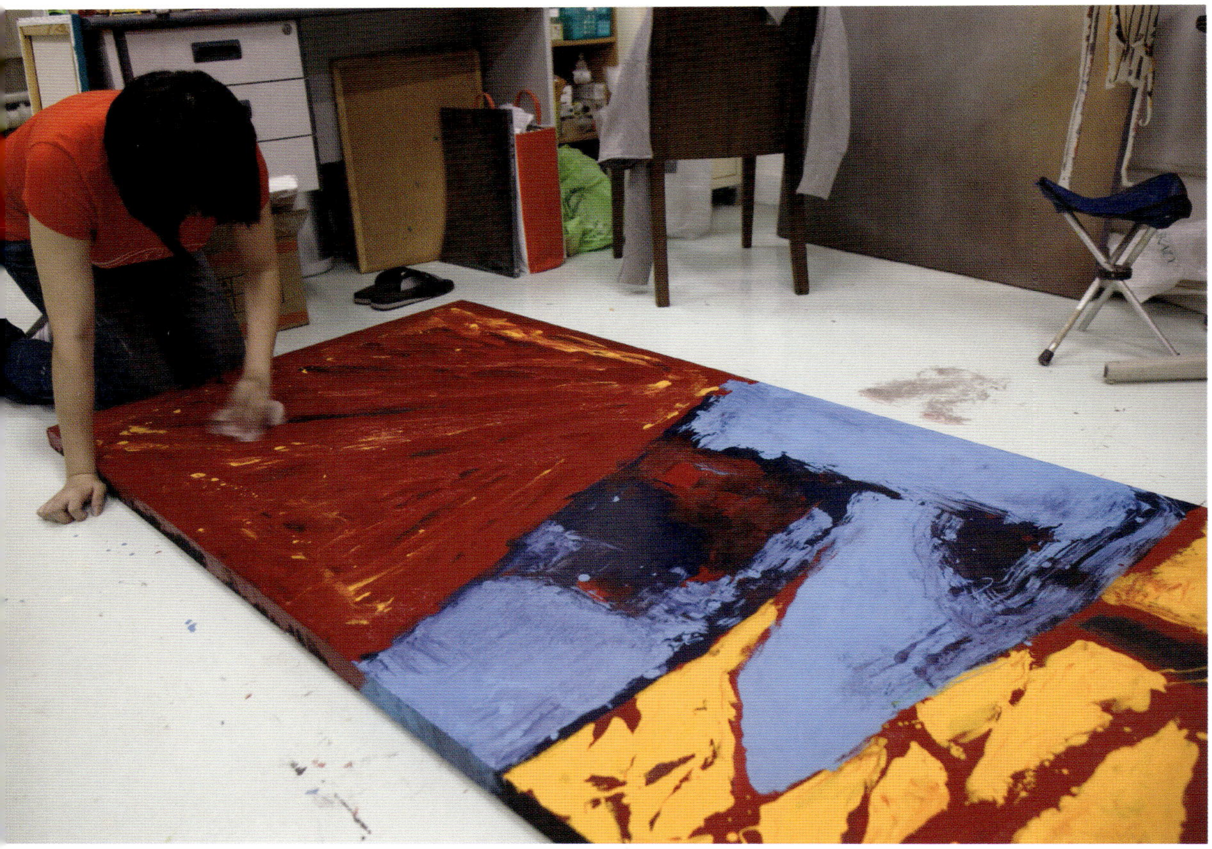

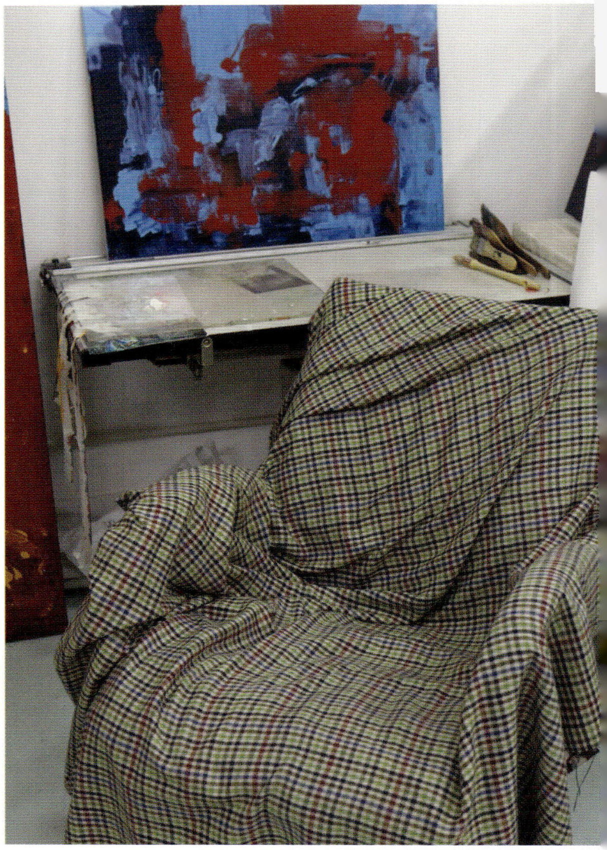

acrylic sheets and engraves them with thin fine lines, before covering and filling the lines with acrylic paint. When viewed from the other side of the plastic sheet, one sees layers of paint coming through. Since the grooves are of different depths, the colours that come through look three-dimensional. The works seem to be a fusion between painting and sculpture. Ho says, "I try to find the truth and I think colours are truest of all things. That's why my works always evolve around this topic. I wish to concentrate on one thing at a time. I also prefer to use materials to bring out the characteristics of paint, such as its pigments and the idea of layering." As to the composition, Ho insists on starting with something figurative and then slowly moving on to the more abstract.

Another young artist who works in this studio is Stephanie Sin. Like Fung and Ho, Sin received her education in the United Kingdom. After she finished secondary school she went to Lincoln University for an arts foundation course. Early on she had the chance to learn about photography, architecture, graphic design, fashion design and other aspects of art and design. By the latter half of the course Sin had decided to major in fine art.

Sin always works within the realm of abstract painting. Her references are to flashbacks and snapshots of everyday life, like the view one gets the second the doors of a lift open. "In three years of having classes at the Arts Centre, I had to use the lifts there every day," she says. "The images that I saw when the lift doors opened became repetitive and they formed some kind of sub-conscious images in my mind. My works are to capture these images." Sin's parents both taught painting, and she has been watching them work from the wings ever since she was little. Sin's mother was also a fashion designer, and her grandfather was in the jewellery business. Perhaps her sensitivity to art was implanted then, again, the kind of sub-consciousness that Sin mentioned before.

When we chat about the little things that happen in art studios, Lau remembers sharing a shed on the roof of a building in Kwun Tong. "The rent then was only 200 dollars per month but there was no water available!" he says. Shek had another story. "I rented a place in Sheung Wan some time ago. There was no toilet inside the flat and so we just had to use the public ones on each floor." Regarding the artists' current digs, he says, "I know who has been working when I see the wood shavings on the floor. Even though I may not see anyone in the studio, I can still feel the air of people here."

As Ho then points out: "The world of art is universal. Seeing art is a kind of sharing." Having the opportunity to share with these young people has indeed given me a comprehensive art lesson.

"The world of art is universal. Seeing art is a kind of sharing"

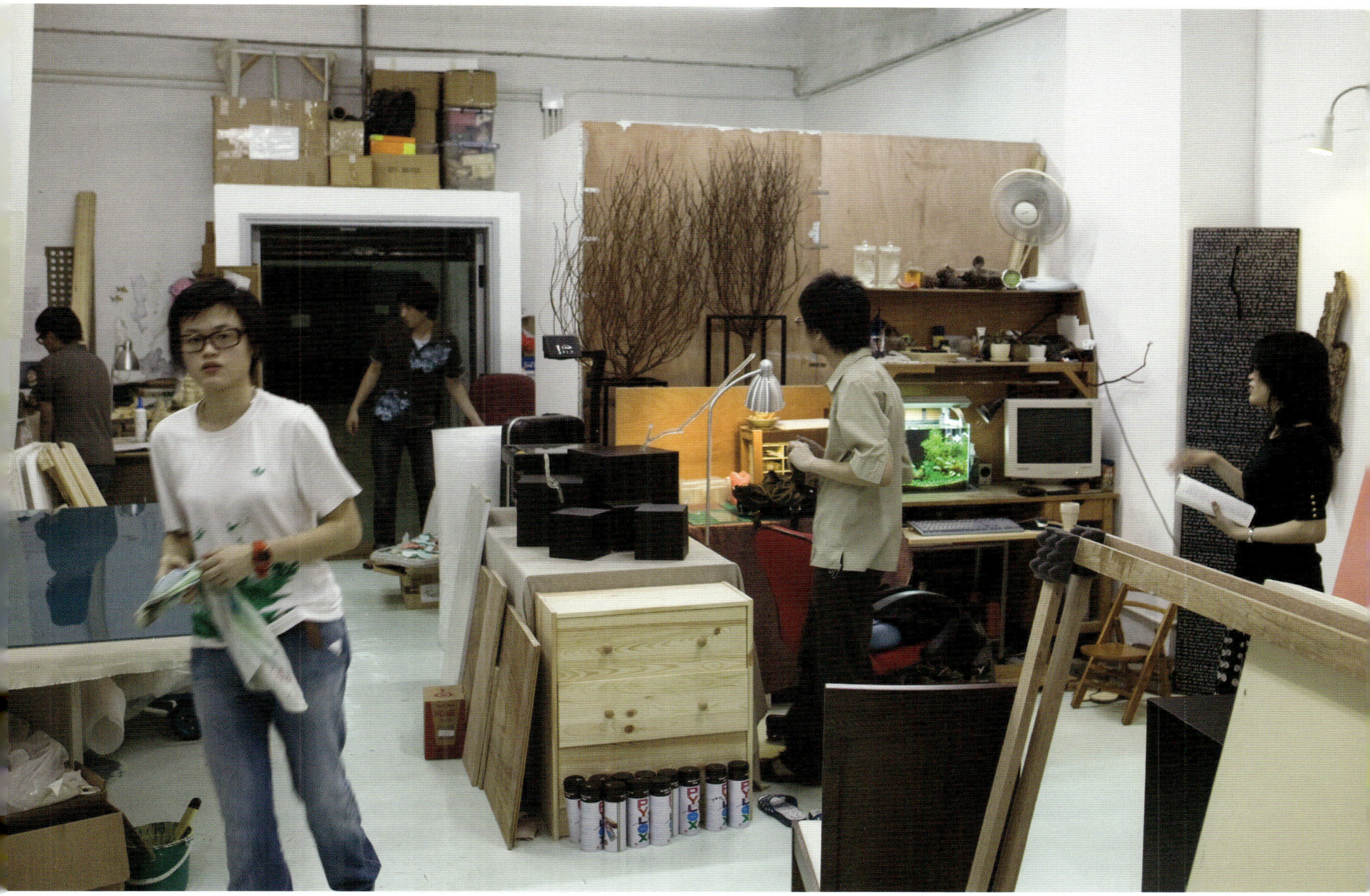

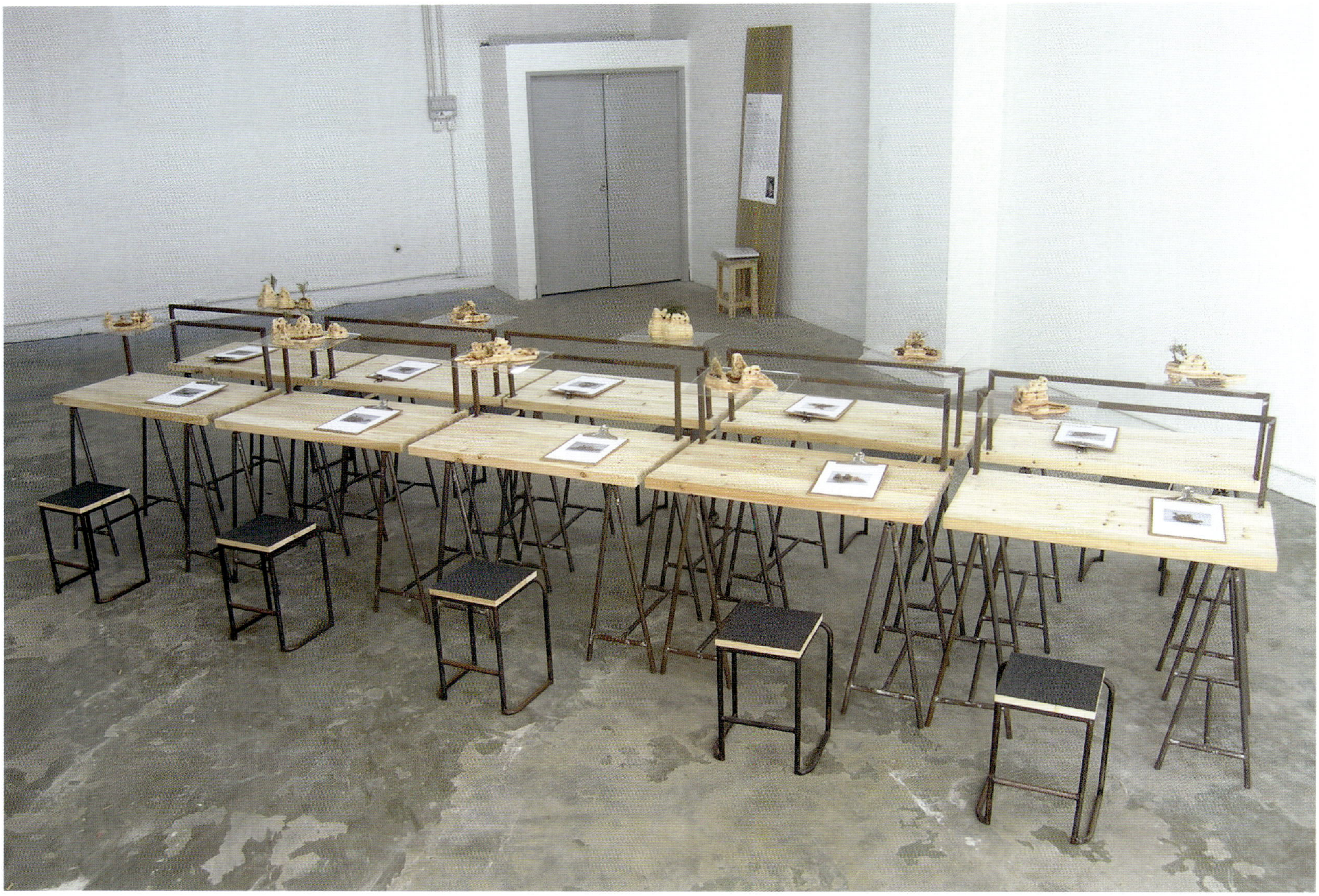

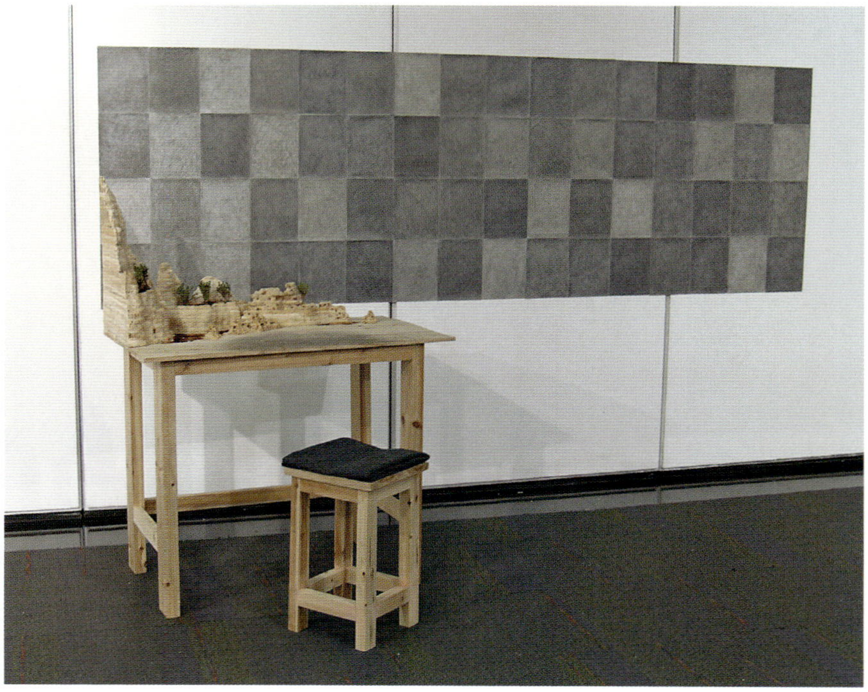

(Above) Lau Hok Shing, Hanison/Tabletop Garden
Sculpture, dimensions variable, 2007-08

(Bottom) Lau Hok Shing, Hanison/Land
Sculpture, dimensions variable, 2007-08

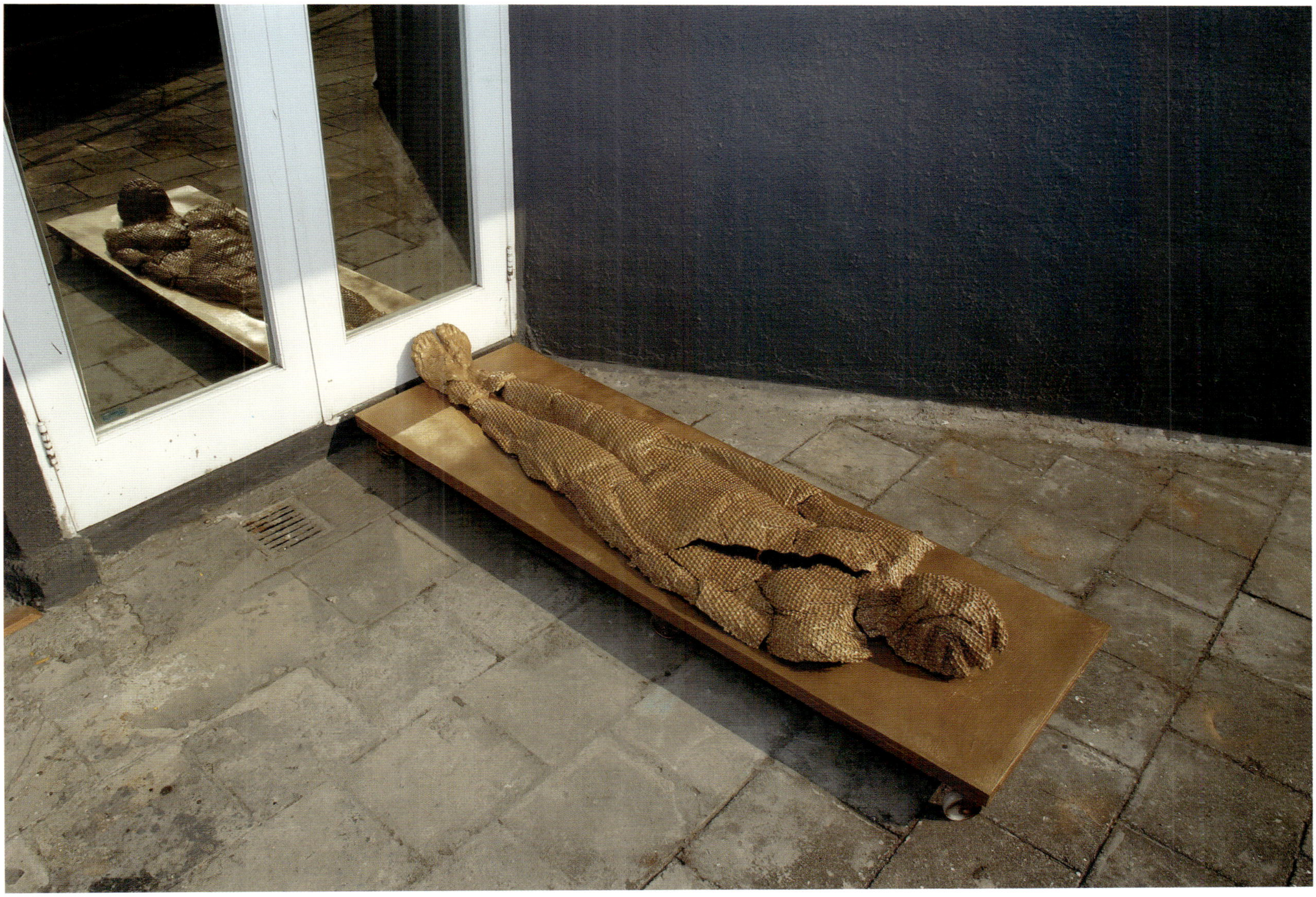

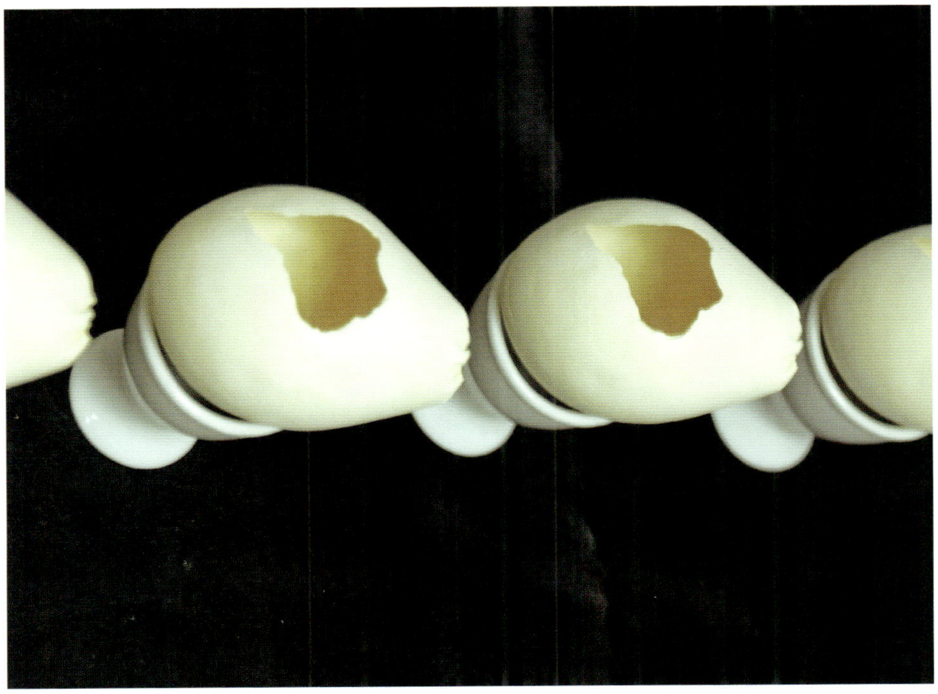

(Above) Fung Kwok-hai, Cyrus/In the memory of human and nature
Mixed-media, dimensions variable, 2008

(Bottom) Fung Kwok-hai, Cyrus/Breakfast Set A – Egg & Sausage
Mixed-media, dimensions variable, 2007-08

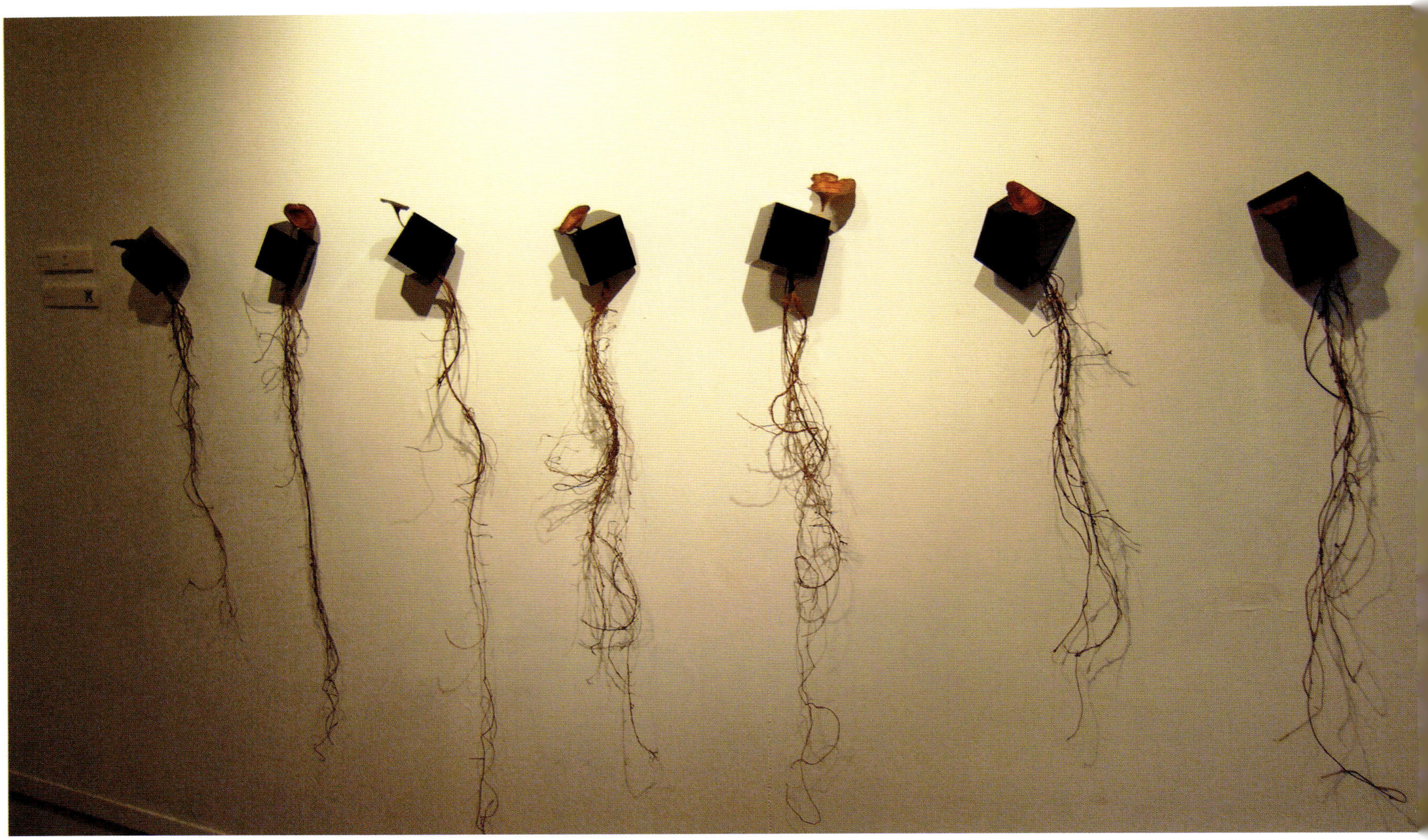

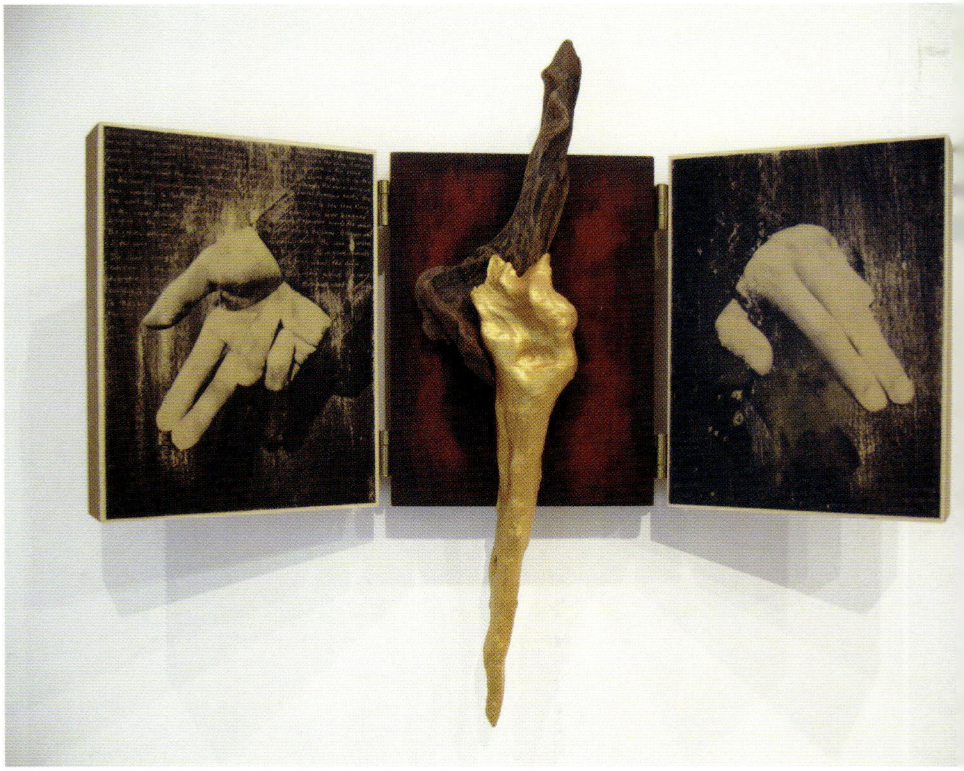

(Above) Shek Chun- yin, Stanthony/Essence
Mixed-media, 7x7x7 cm (each), 2007

(Bottom) Shek Chun-yin, Stanthony/Tête-Bêche
Mixed-media, dimensions variable, 2007

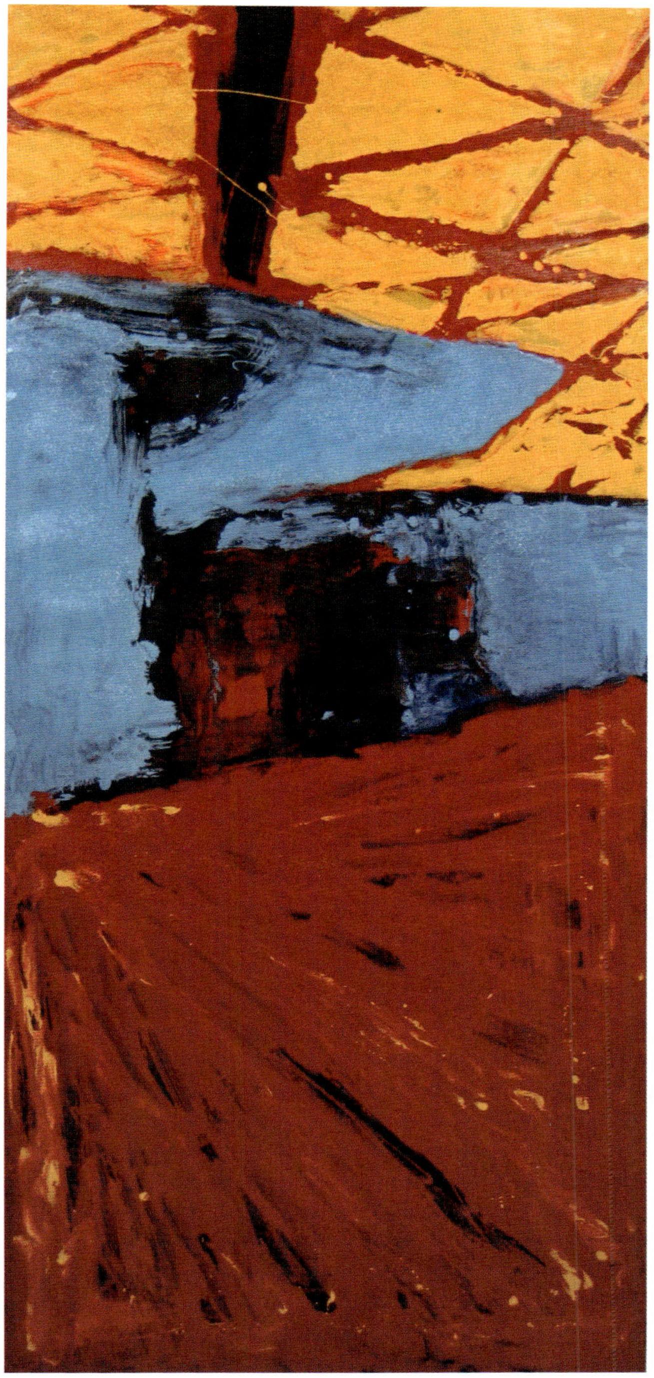

(Left) Sin Long-yee, Stephanie/15th Floor, HKAC
Oil on canvas, 210x100 cm, 2007

(Right) Sin Long-yee, Stephanie/The Extinct Moment
Enamel on canvas, 210x100 cm, 2008

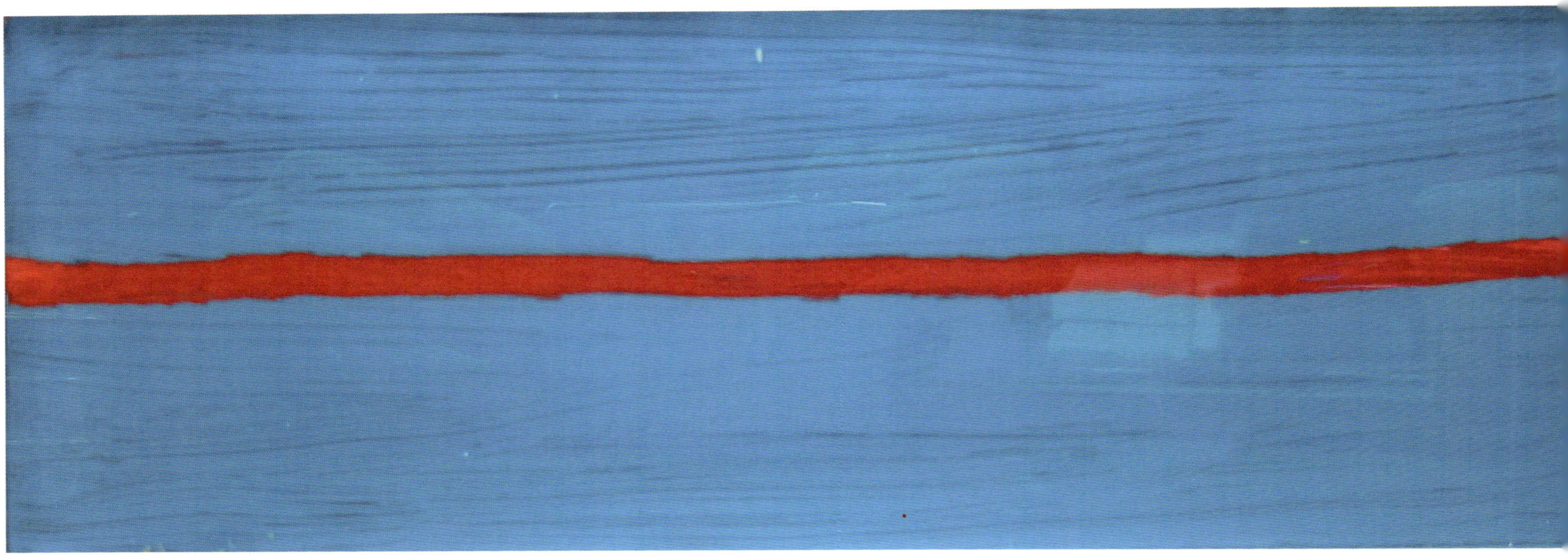

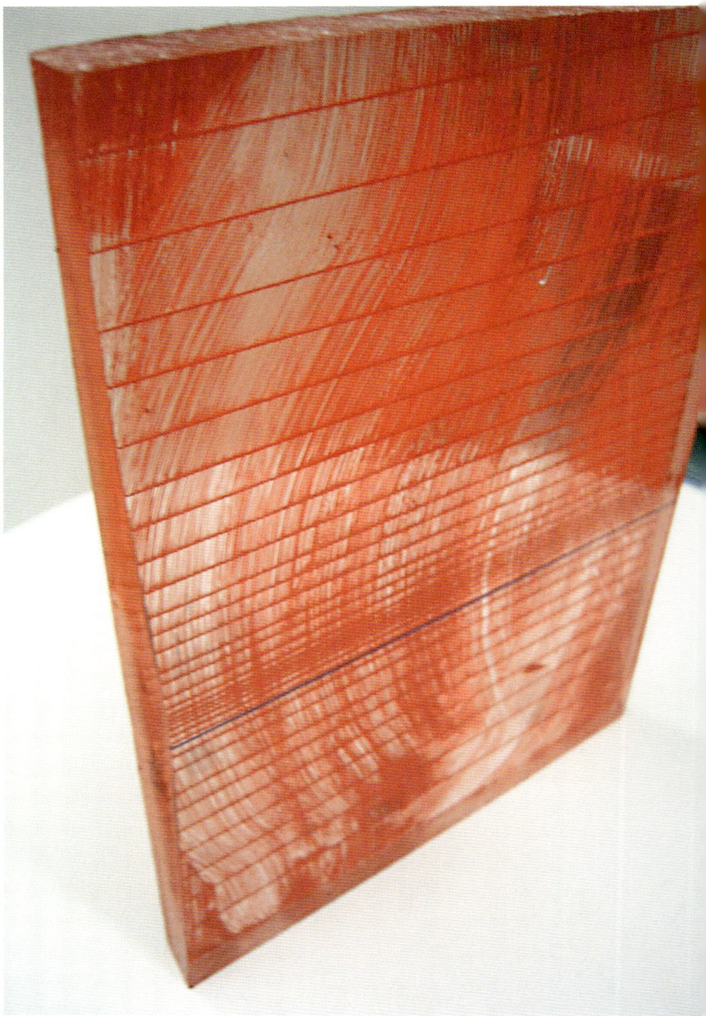

(Above) Ho Sze-Man, Jasmine/Colour #01
Acrylic on acrylic board, 21x6.8 cm, 2007-08

(Bottom) Ho Sze-Man, Jasmine/Colour #03
Acrylic on acrylic board, 17.8x11 cm, 2007-08

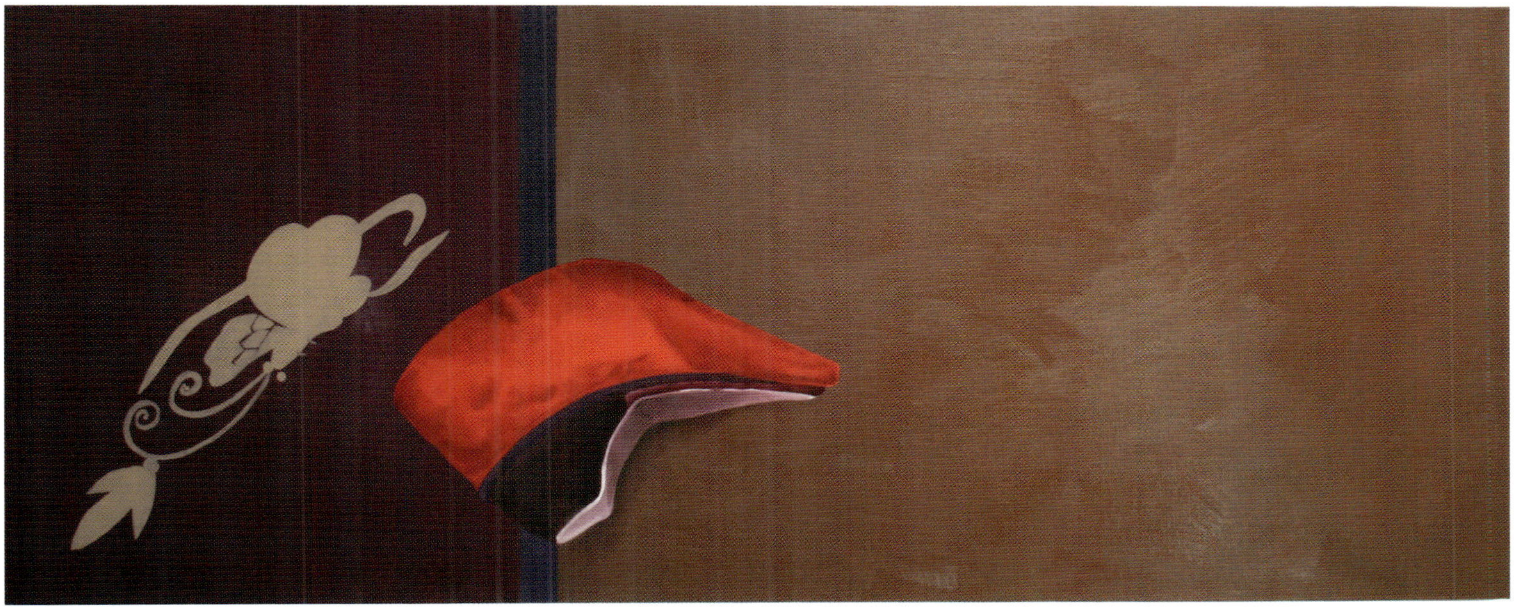

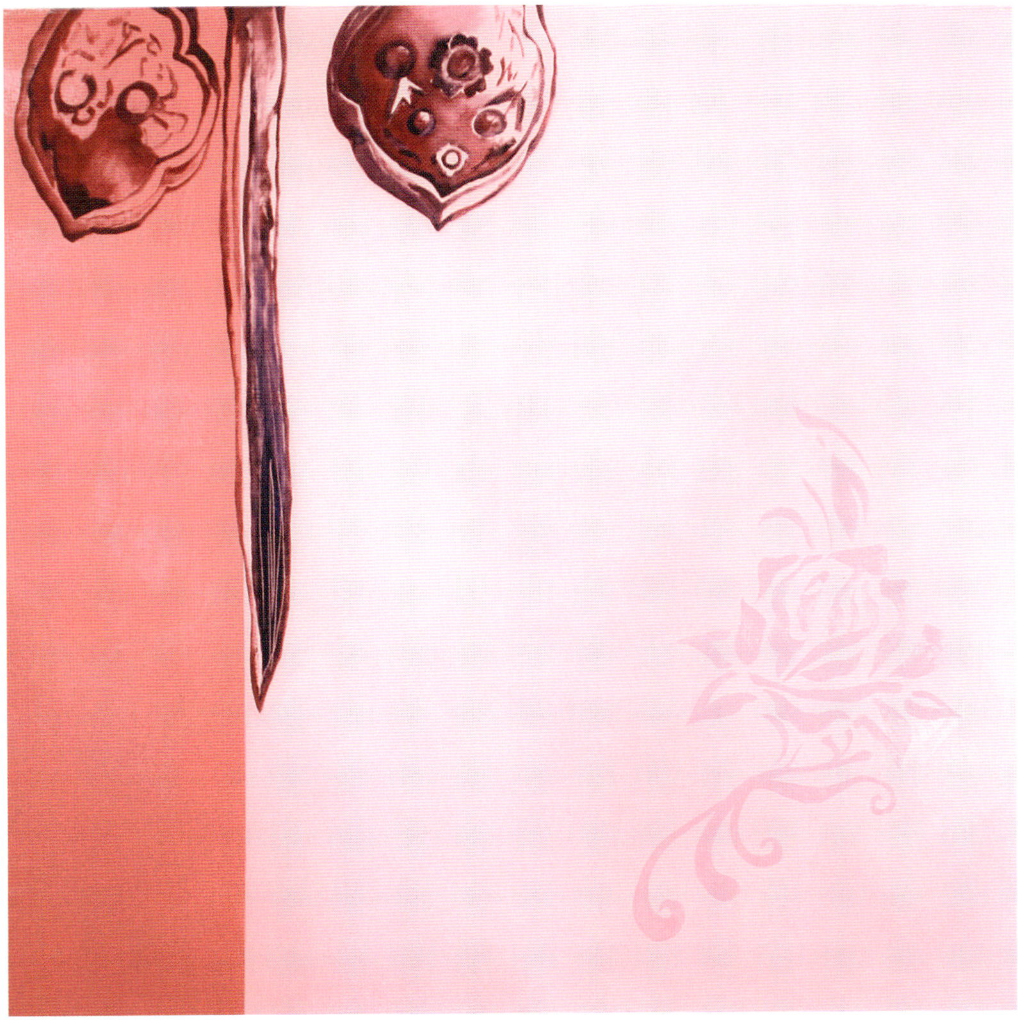

(Above) Chan Hiu-ting, Winnie/Ideal of Beauty
Oil on canvas, 90x90 cm, 2005

(Bottom) Chan Hiu-ting, Winnie/Ideal of Beauty
Oil on canvas, 90x90 cm, 2005

The Freestyle Studio

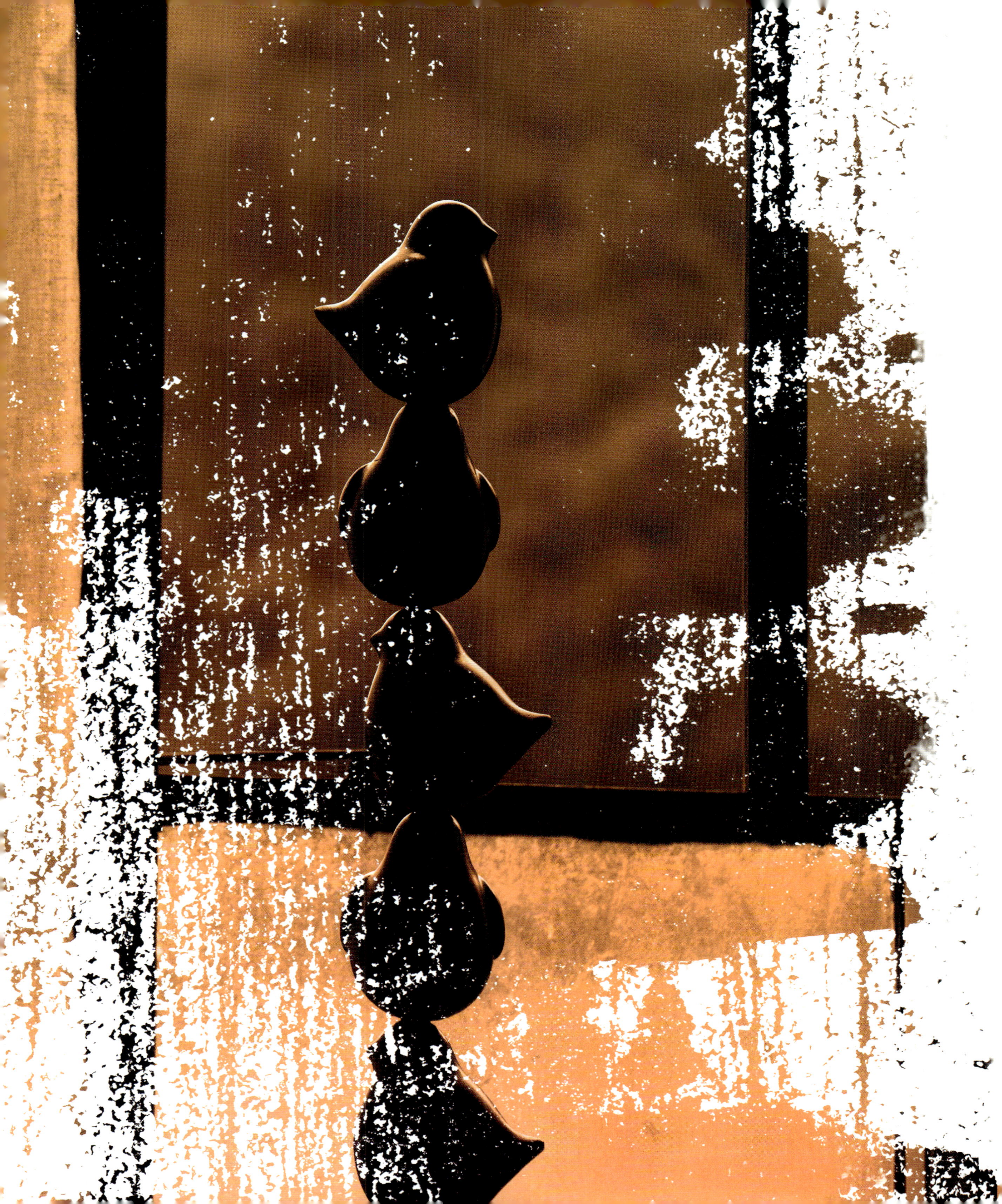

Van Lau

Literati Sculpture

By Stephanie Cheung

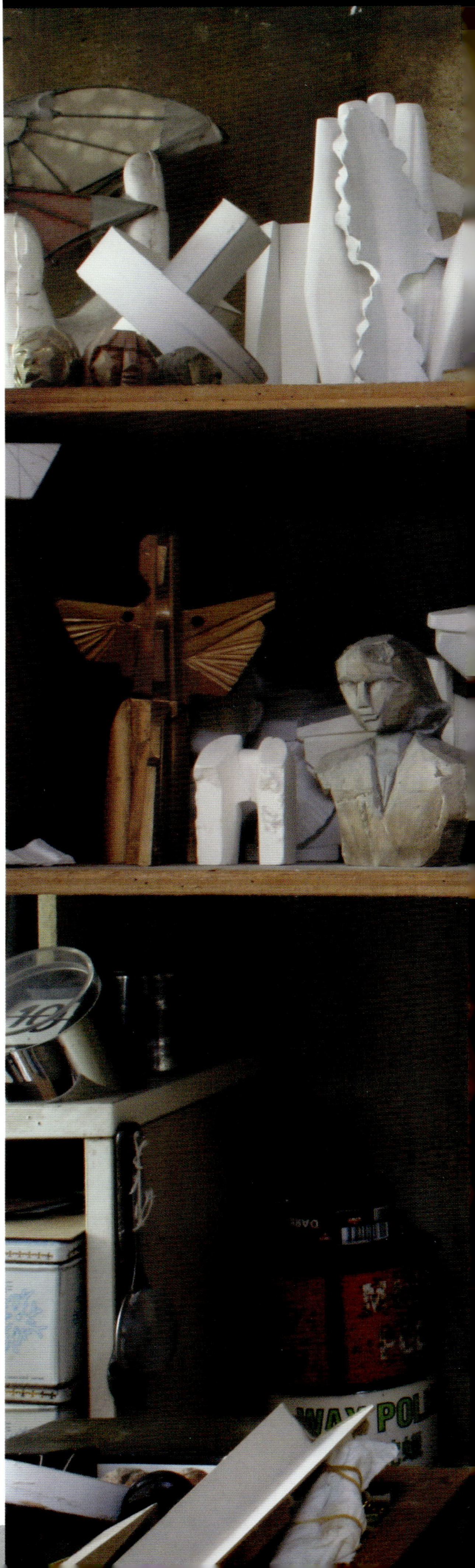

Van Lau was born in China in 1933. He moved to Vietnam in 1934 and has been residing in Hong Kong since 1960. Van's work expresses a 'Hong Kong style', synthesising Chinese and Western aesthetics. He has founded a number of art-related publications and organisations, such as the Hong Kong Sculptors Association and the Hong Kong Institute for Fine Arts. An active advocate of Chinese art and culture, he was chairperson of the Hong Kong Institute for Promotion of Chinese Culture (1985-97) and has served on the People's Political Consultative Committee of the People's Republic of China (1993, 1997) and the Culture and Heritage Commission of Hong Kong (2000).

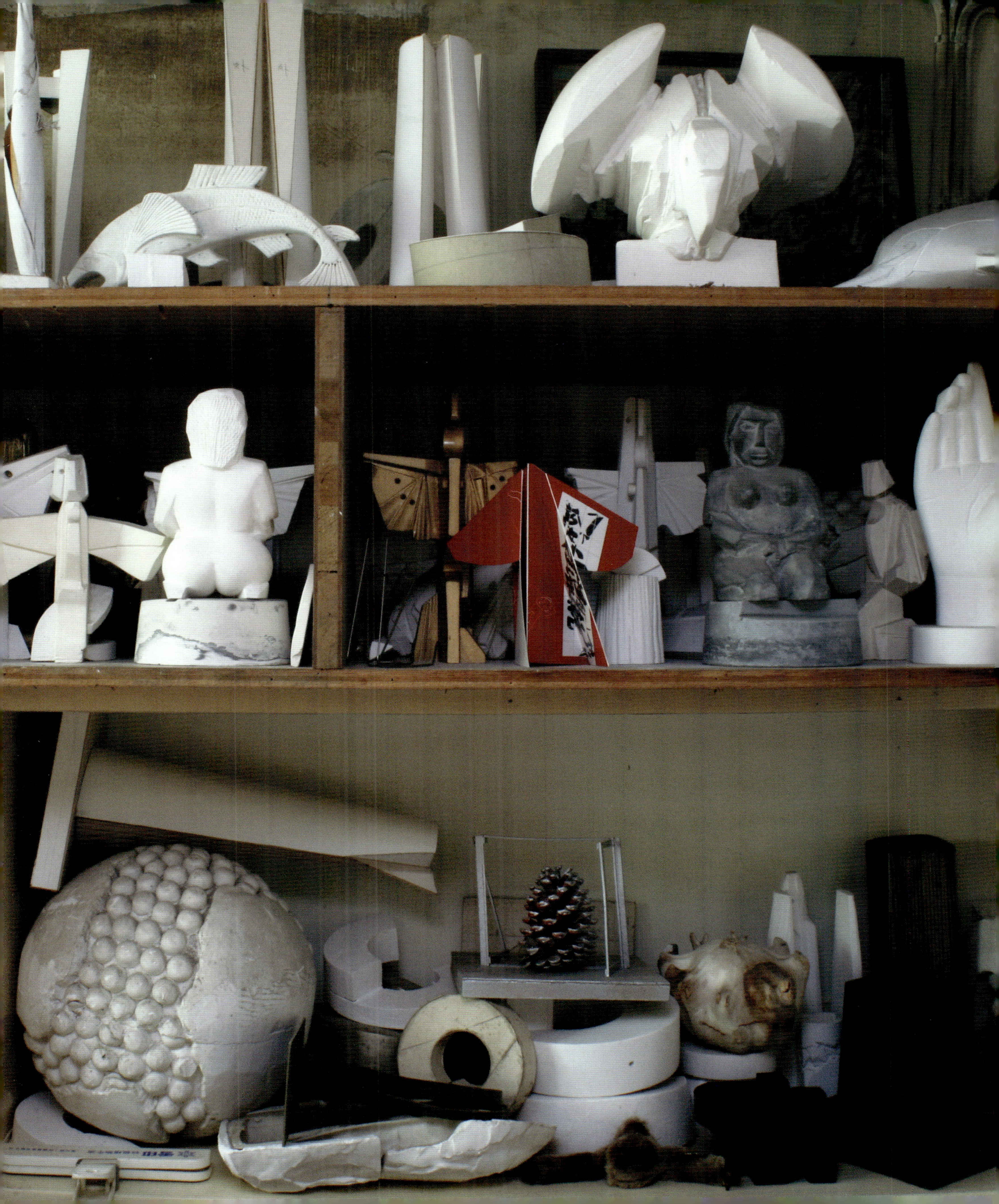

Van Lau works at home in Shatin. "This is where I work, live and meet friends," the artist says. Traces of work, daily life and hospitality infuse the space. A pair of sculptures welcomes visitors at the door. Shelves of art periodicals flank the staircase. His study is right next to the living room. Enlivened by his sculptures and bamboo paintings, it is where he spends time with friends. On the day of the interview, a few books on Picasso and a sketch occupy the coffee table.

Van is a sculptor. He calls his work 'literati sculpture.' In Chinese art, the term literati is used as an adjective to describe paintings by scholars (and sometimes bureaucrats) who are well versed in traditions, and are expected to contribute to the nation. This spirit continues in Van's work.

Van's childhood was spent in Vietnam. In 1953, according to his father's will, he went to study architecture at the Cheng Kung University in southern Taiwan. There he met

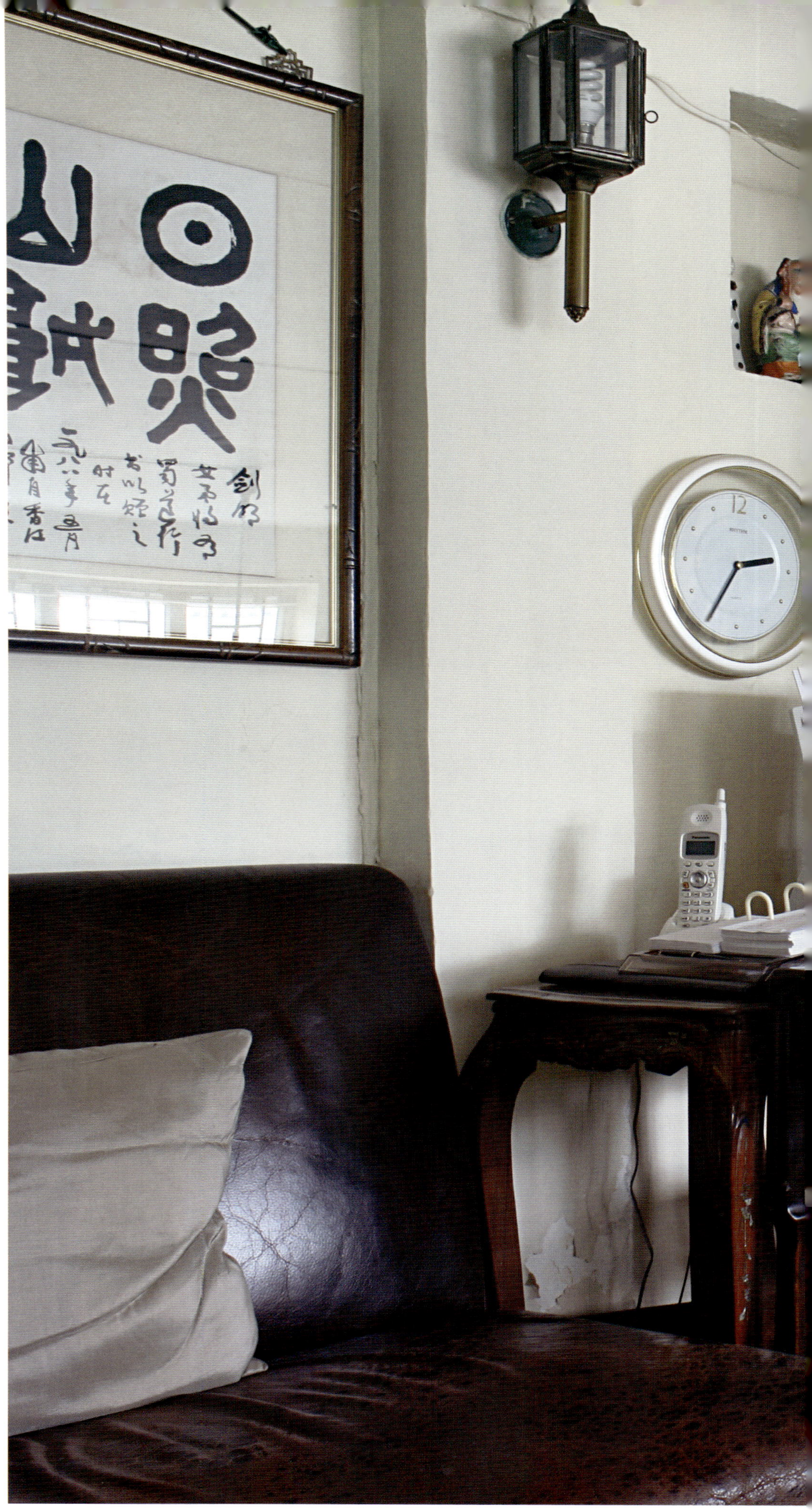

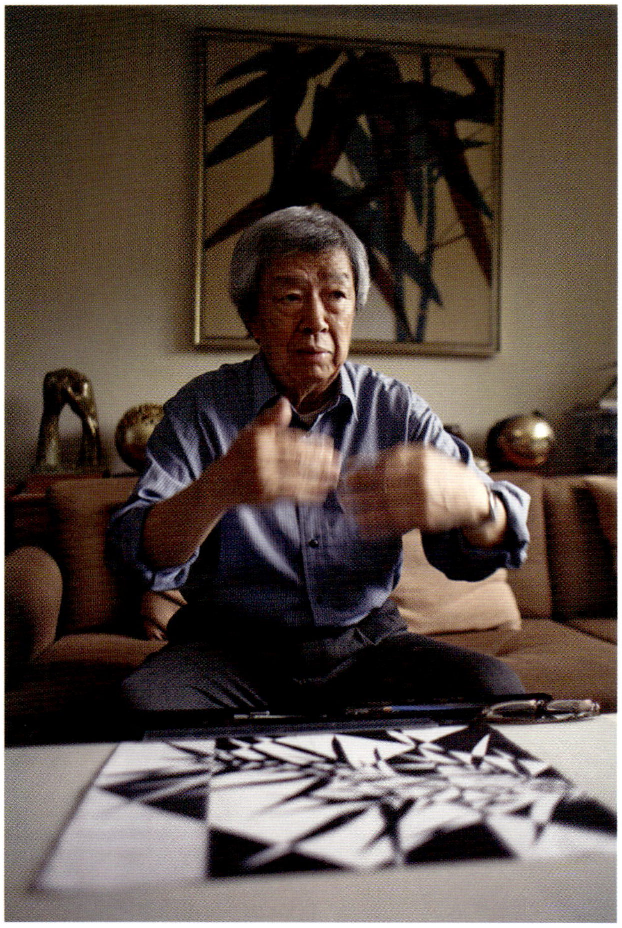

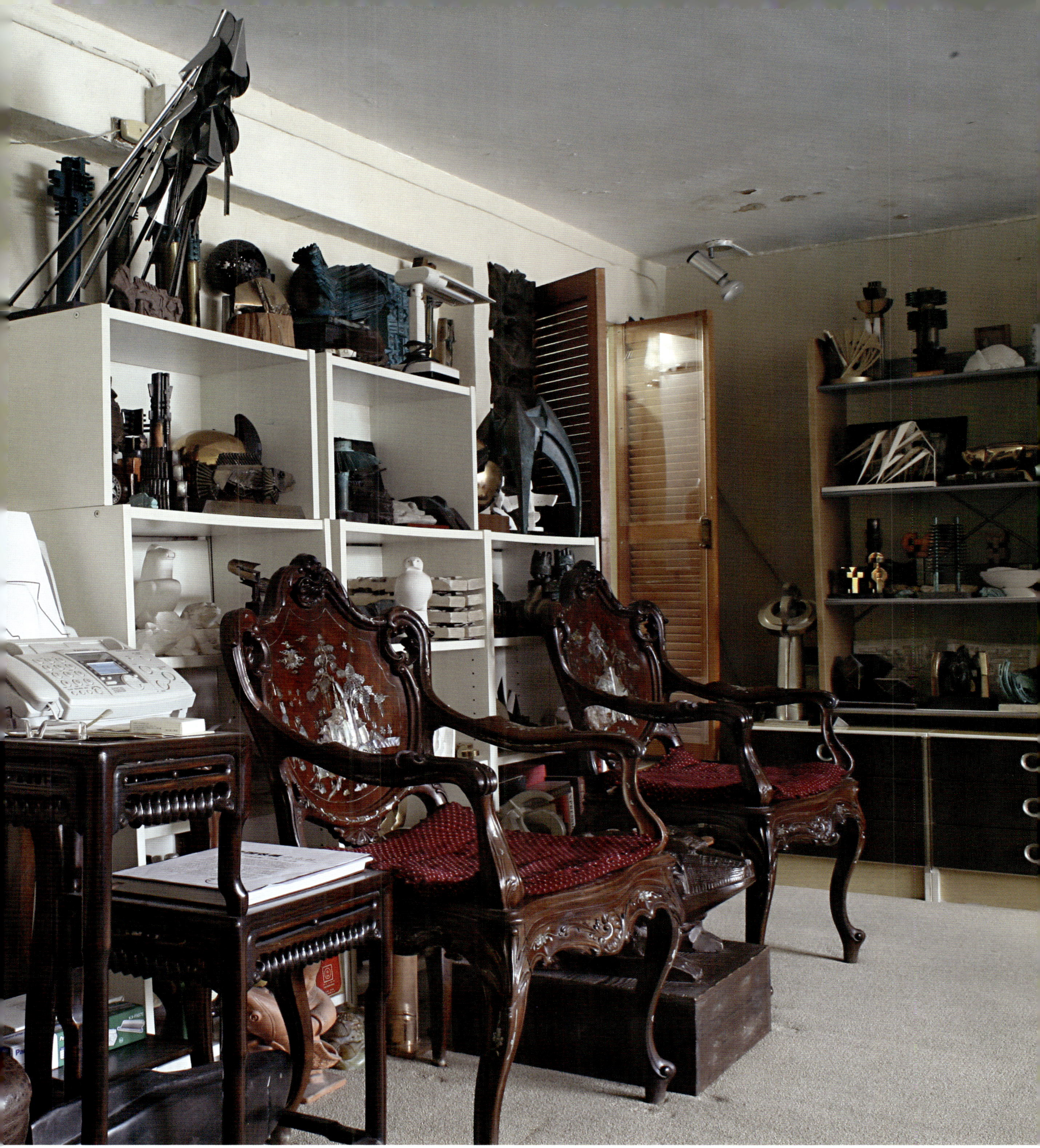

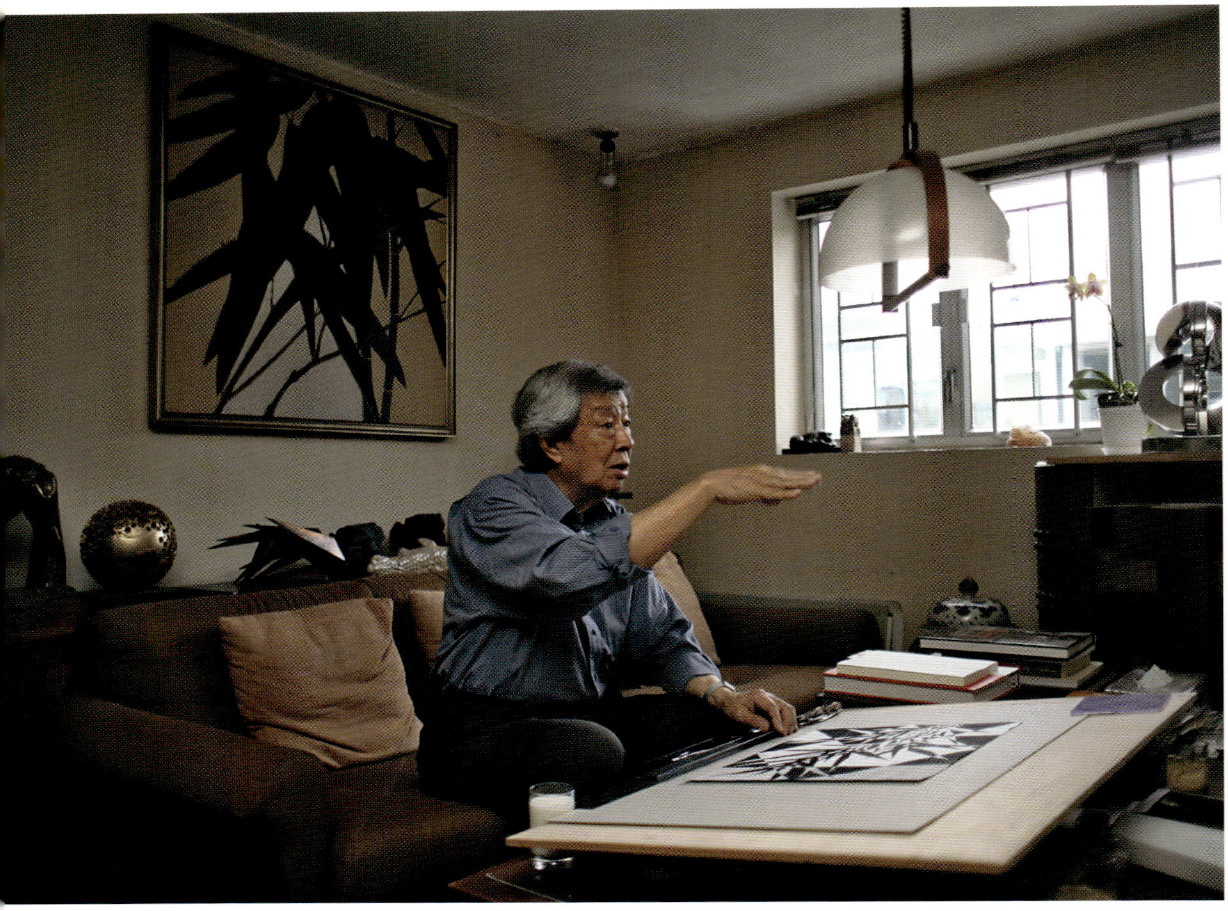

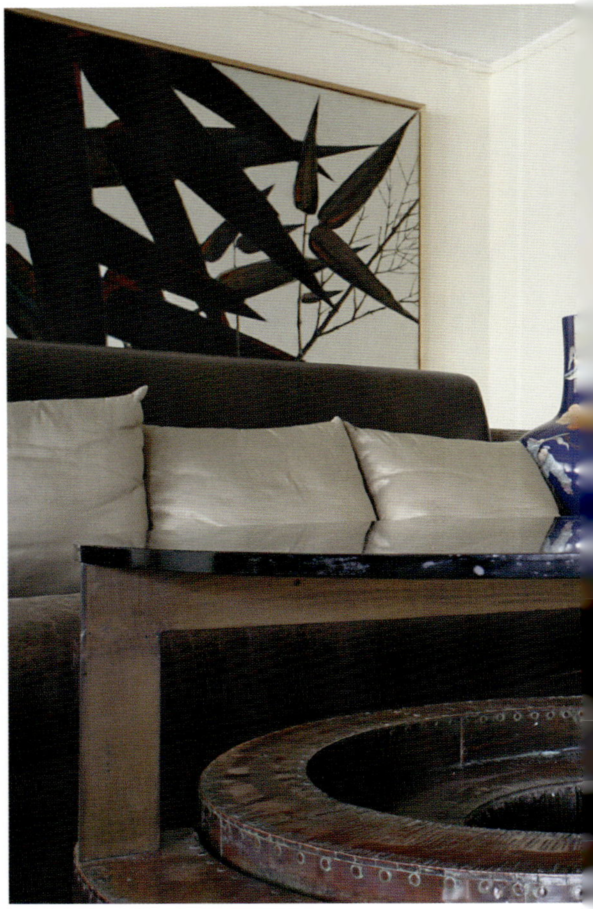

"This is where I work, live and meet friends"

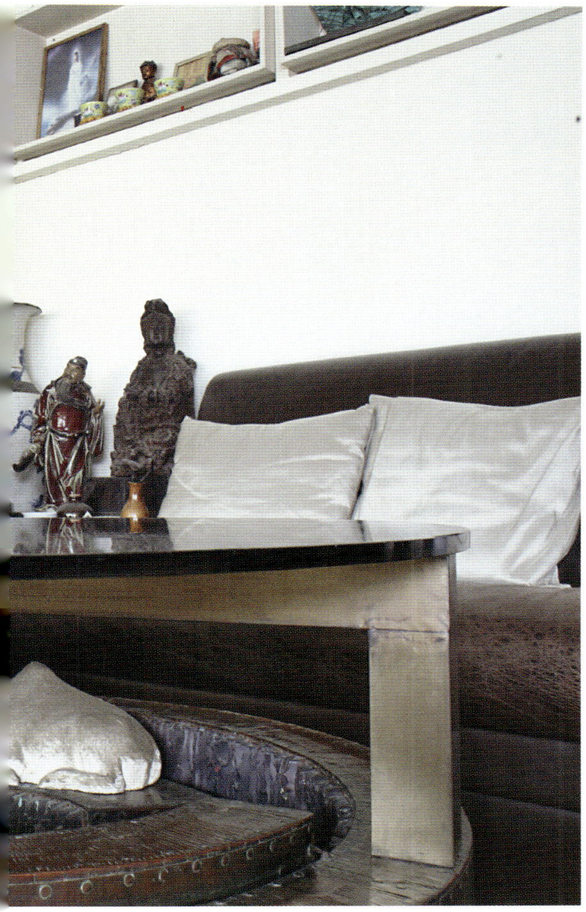

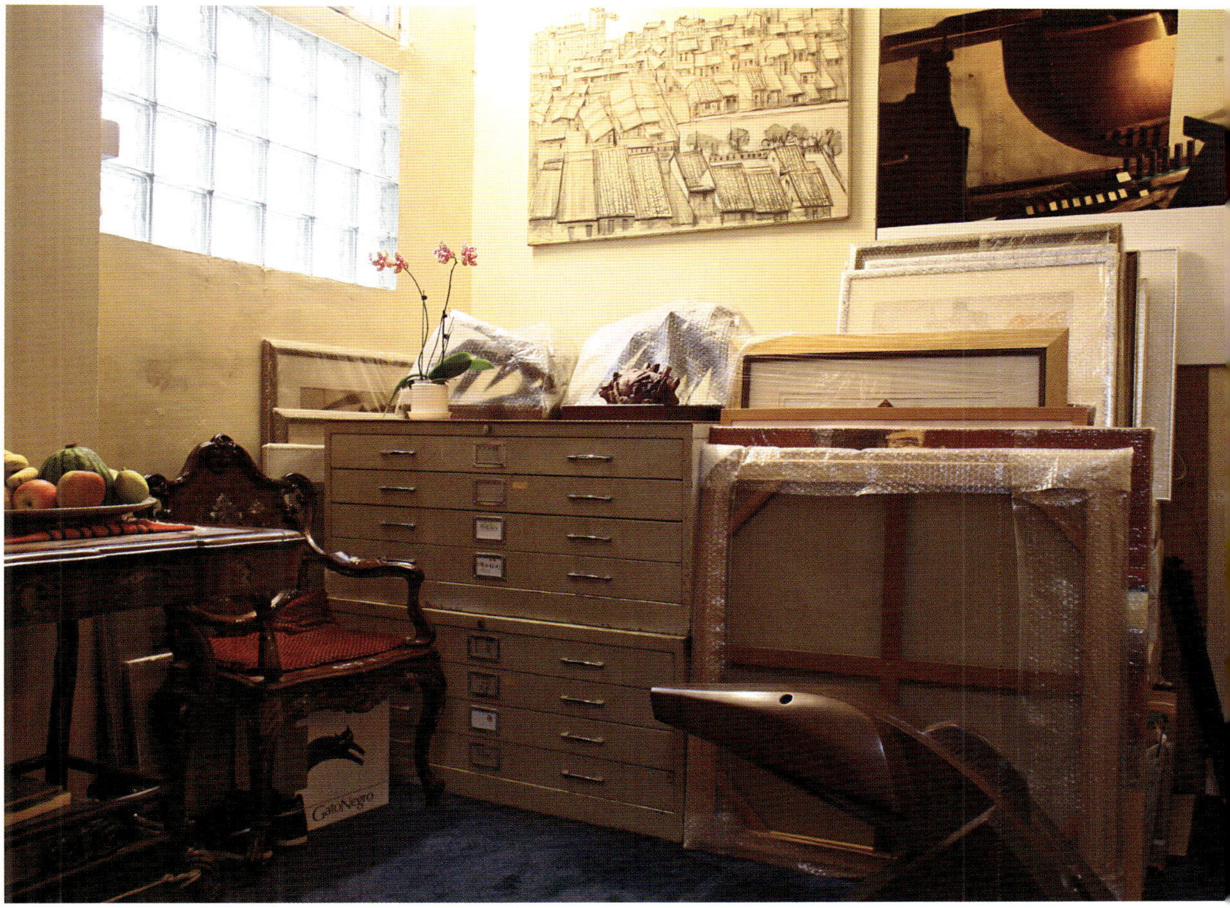

his first mentor, Kuo Po-chuan. The painter spotted the young man's artistic talents. "Quit architecture and go for fine arts," he advised. Van followed his advice. He then moved to Taipei and found a place at the Fine Arts Department at the National Taiwan Normal University, where he met his second mentor, Yu Junzhi. He told Van to learn more about aesthetics and logic, so Van started obediently sitting in on philosophy classes. At that time he did not have a clue what it was all about. Years later he has seen how it has helped his work and is grateful for Yu's farsighted advice.

Upon graduation Van moved to Hong Kong and became a full-time artist. When he began his career, he was represented by a gallery in Central and also did portraiture for tourists in Tsimshatsui. In 1965 Van received a visiting grant to the United States from the Institute of International Education. This sojourn had a tremendous impact on his later work. In the 1960s the New York art scene was thriving. Driven by the war and market factors, many avant-garde artists had fled Europe for the United States and New York was the gathering point of the émigrés, who stimulated groundbreaking developments. During his stay, Van lived in the same block as Giacometti, the Swiss master of post-war sculpture. In such an environment Van had access to a feast of contemporary art.

Finding himself among other European and American artists, Van thought about his own identity. "In the United States I tried to live in the American way... but I couldn't do it," he admits. There is no way that he could assimilate into another culture, being Chinese to the core.

With this in mind, Van went on a root-searching journey to China in the early 1970s, years before the opening of the mainland. When he was a university student Taiwan had given him a certain idea of China, but seeing the country with his own eyes gave him a different feeling. In order to foster better understanding in others, he started organising cultural exchange programmes between the mainland, Taiwan and Hong Kong. As he learned more about China he became aware of the complexities involved.

Having spent time in three differing Chinese environments, Van feels that he gained an insider's understanding of their conflicts. However he believes that their conflicts can be resolved. The three places share the same language, history and culture: a shared root and therefore platform for all Chinese. "This platform is very important. On this platform, we can reach up and set off," he says.

Van's oeuvre has been built on this platform. His 'literati sculpture' feature many Chinese elements. A notable one is the bamboo motif. In the history of Chinese painting, bamboo has been a favourite subject among scholars. The plant's botanical character is that it can withstand harsh conditions, is upright and is hollow inside (which is taken to stand for humility and honesty — essential qualities of a virtuous person). Interpreting the spirit of bamboo, Van uses the language of Constructivism, addressing two cultures at the same time: abstraction makes the plant look timeless; fragmentation of the leaves responds to modern art's spatial explorations. The artist believes that by expressing Chinese contents in Western idioms, Chinese culture can be brought to the world.

Van considers Hong Kong his home. Long before 'red-white-blue' and cha chan ting (Hong Kong-style coffee houses) became fetishes in Hong Kong's collective memory, Van was an advocate of creating a local style. He is critical of Hong Kong's 'importism': "our automobiles, our TV sets... are all imported," he says. "Even if there are more West Kowloon Cultural District projects, more large 'stalls', we still lack the goods. Our art and culture lack local character." His creative approach to this problem is the synthesis of East and West.

Besides making art, Van is also active in art education. When he looks at young people's work he is delighted by their daring, but saddened by their lack of direction. His own experiences in the United States inspired him. He remembers his American colleagues taking turns to use the studio facilities, and sleeping in them to seize every moment. Impressed by their passion, he wanted to encourage students to be as committed when he taught at the Chinese University of Hong Kong (CUHK). His home being close to the campus, he would open his doors to students who stayed up late. Sometimes he made them congee.

But regrettably at that point, the university did not share his vision. After his tenure at CUHK Van went to the University of Hong Kong, but still could not realise his goals because the department's specialty was art history.

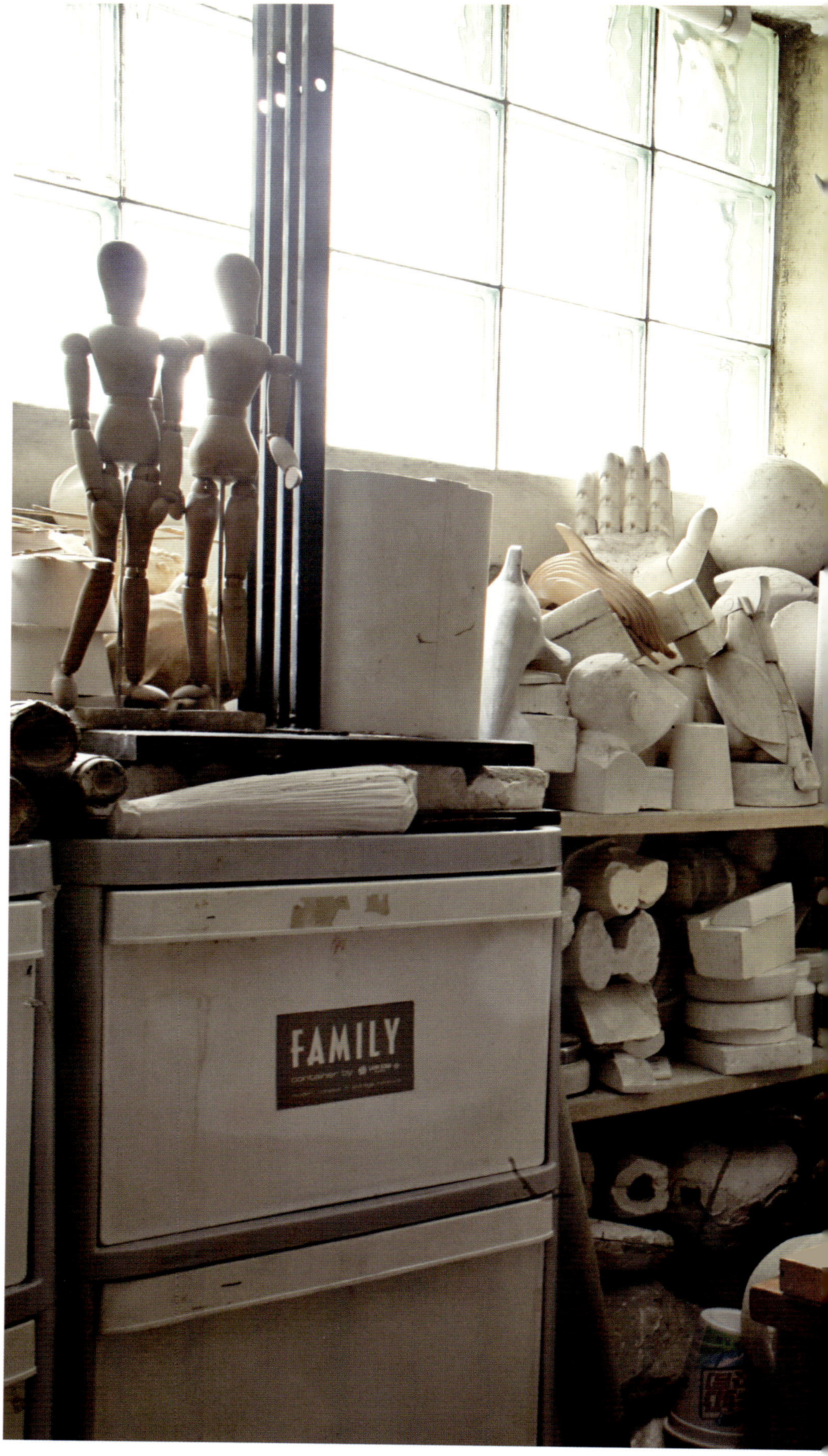

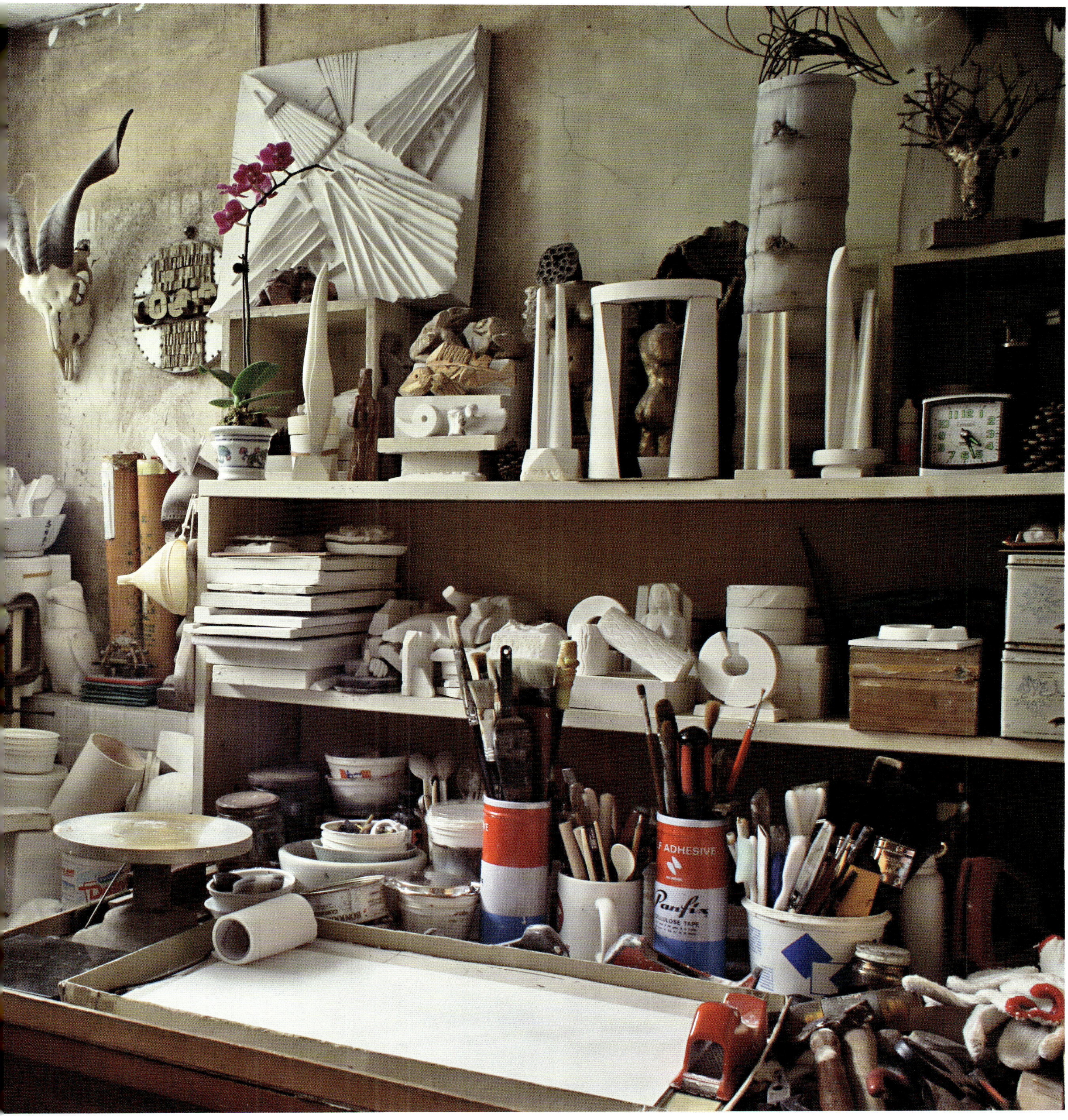

Van Lan's studio is filled with finished and unfinished maquettes

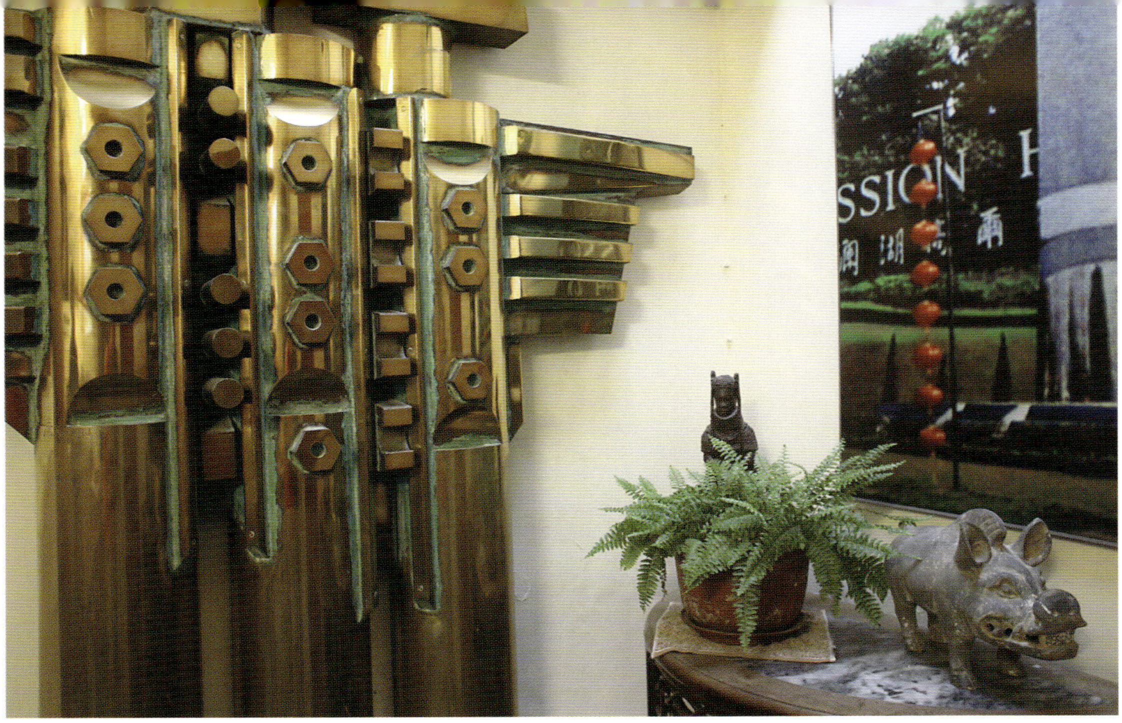

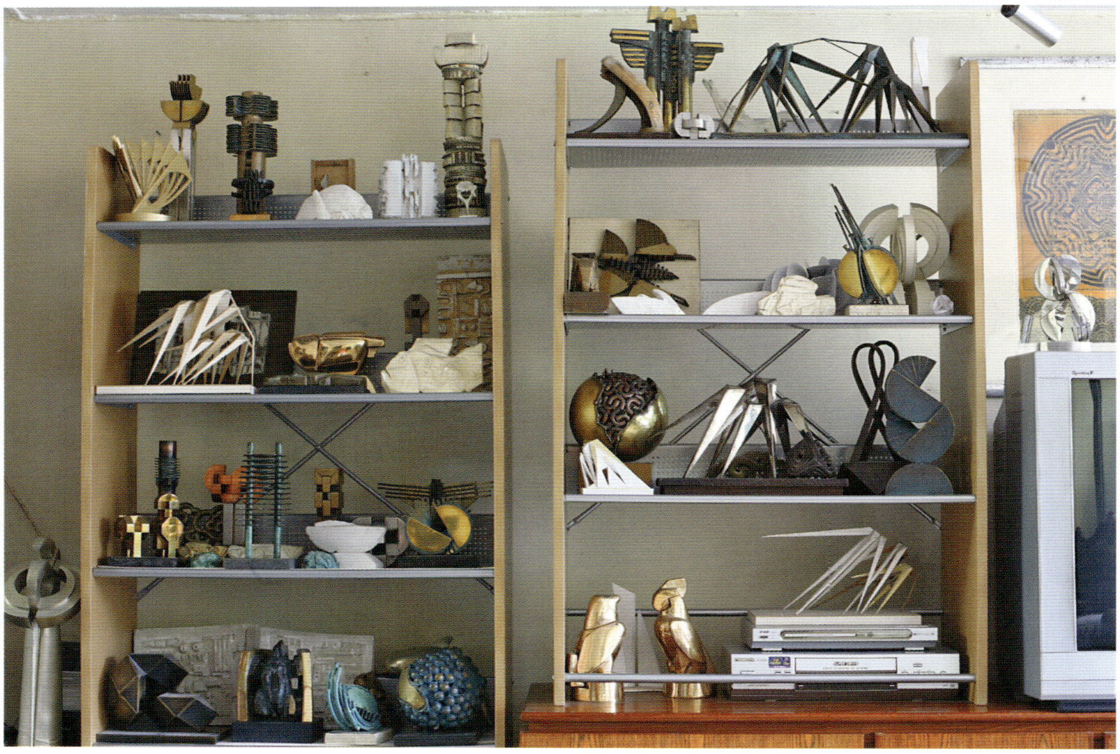

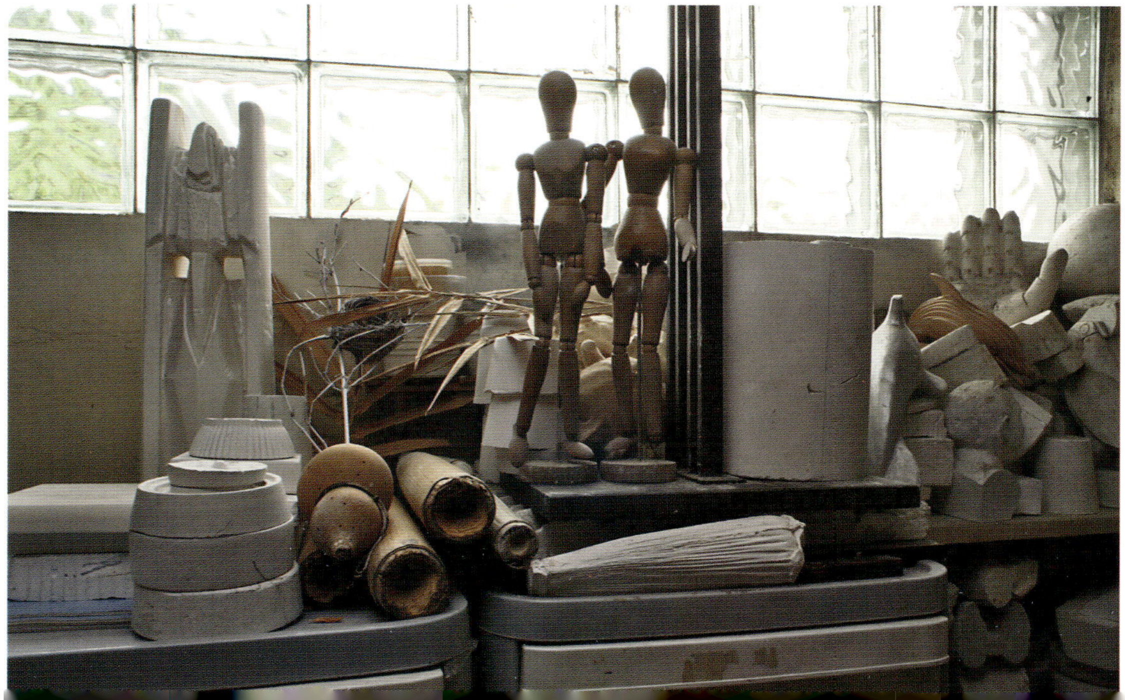

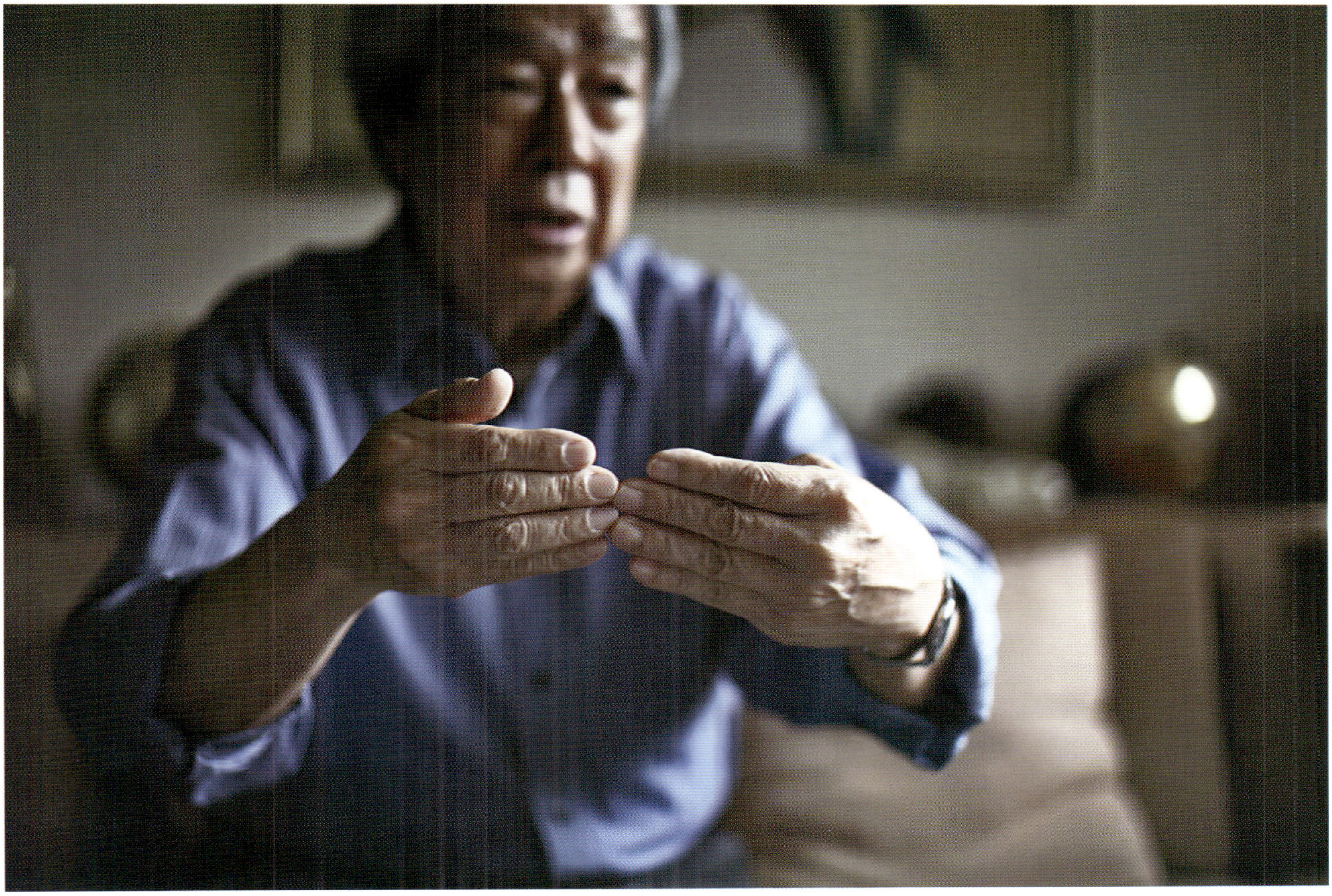

He knew that fundamental and long-lasting changes are only brought about by those in power, so he took part in committees and commissions, including those for the design of the SAR's emblem and the monument of reunification, the Basic Law Consultative Committee and the Culture and Heritage Commission.

Unable to realise his ideals in Hong Kong, Van turned to the mainland in the 1990s. He applied for a subsidy from the United Nations Development Programme, a body supporting the flow of technology from developed to developing countries. In his case, he in Hong Kong proposed to import the technology of sculpture to China, which was then still considered a developing nation. Setting up a project in China can be daunting, but Van made use of his earlier experiences and succeeded in introducing his 'technology' and vision to China. His move was timely. "China was opening and needed talents," he recalls. "Expats were being hired from Russia but they did not understand China's situation. Only Chinese people, with insight into the country's problems, could act as a bridge."

Van is proud of his success in China. His contribution to art education has been recognised by many leading institutes: a metal workshop is named after him at the Central Academy of Fine Arts; the Guangzhou Academy of Fine Arts and Fudan University's Shanghai Institute of Visual Art have honoured him with the role of Visiting Professor. His studio assistant, who has been helping him for years, has just received his doctorate, and has translated and edited an artist's manual called *Living Materials: A Sculptor's Handbook*. In the publication he credits Van by including his work in the illustrations.

Van currently spends part of the year on the mainland and the remaining time in Hong Kong, where he works as a full-time artist from his home-studio, surrounded by bamboo. This is different from literati painters of the past, who insisted that they were amateurs. In his monograph, writer Gu Zhaoshen suggests that he belongs to the literati because he continues their spirit. During our interview Van, however, repeatedly suggests that "his art, teaching and life are all together."

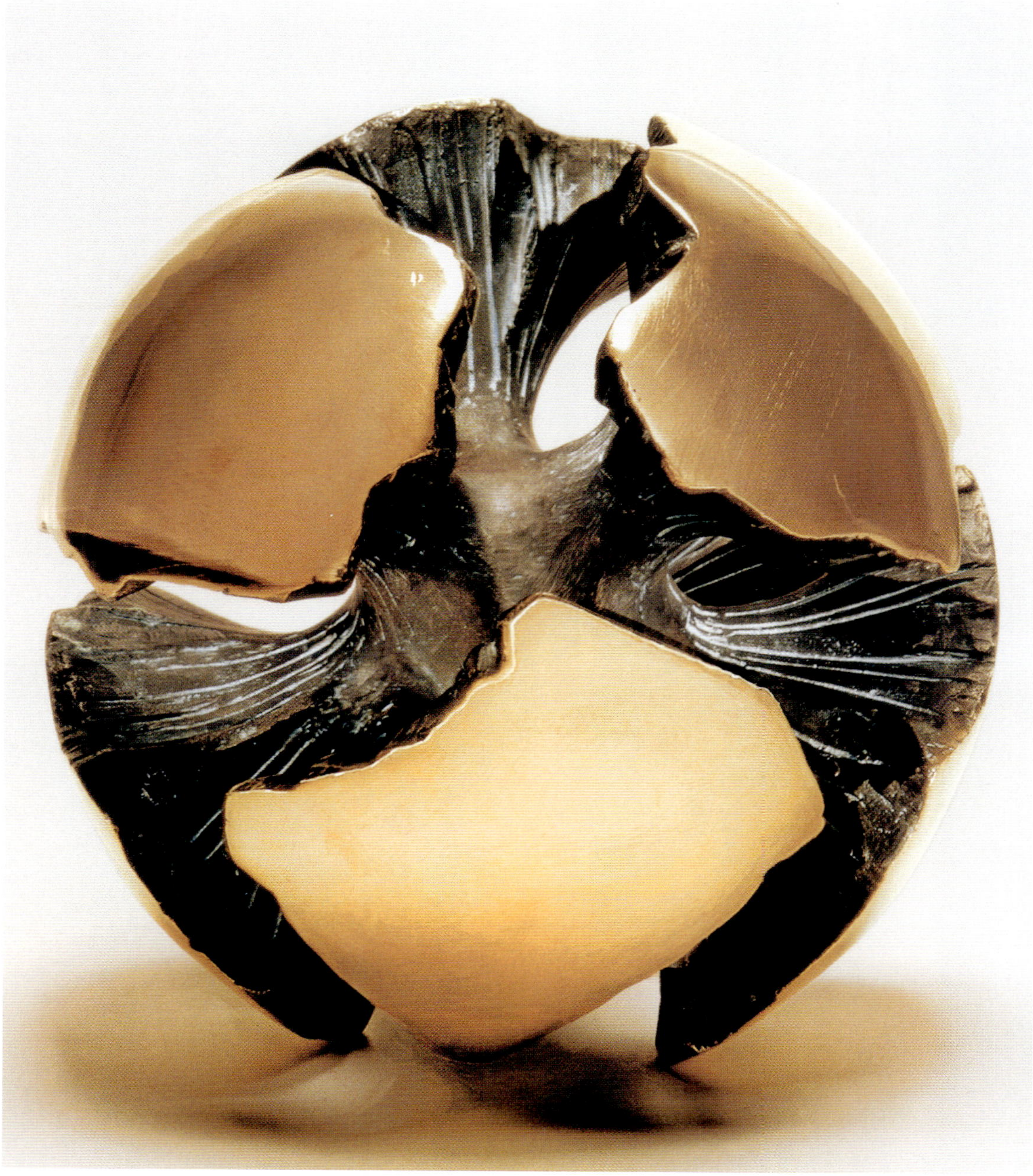

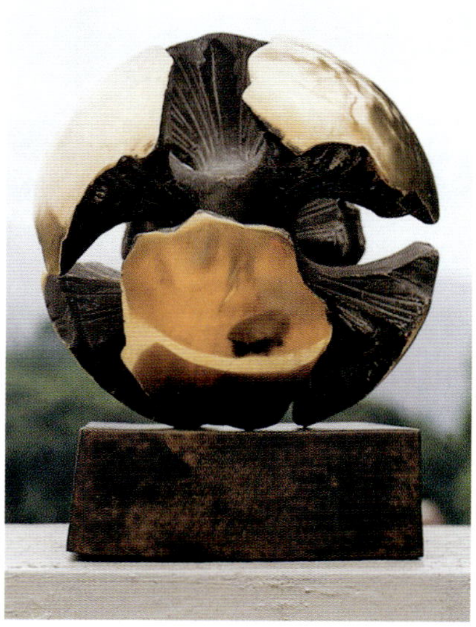

Release
Bronze, 100x100x100 cm, 1992

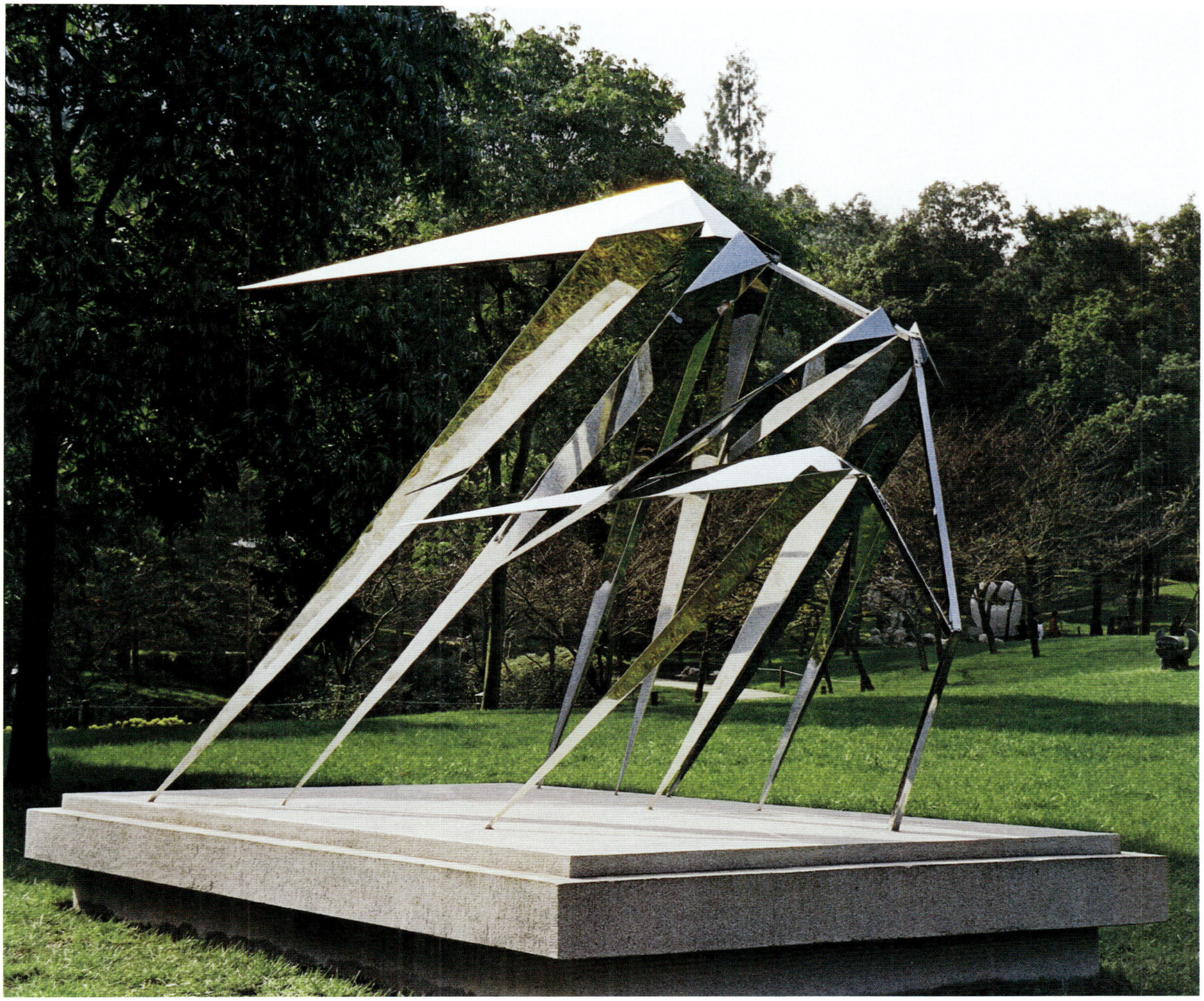

Geese Form in the West Lake
Stainless Steel, 600 cm (H), 2000

Wan Qingli

This Place is My Home

By Carl Cheng

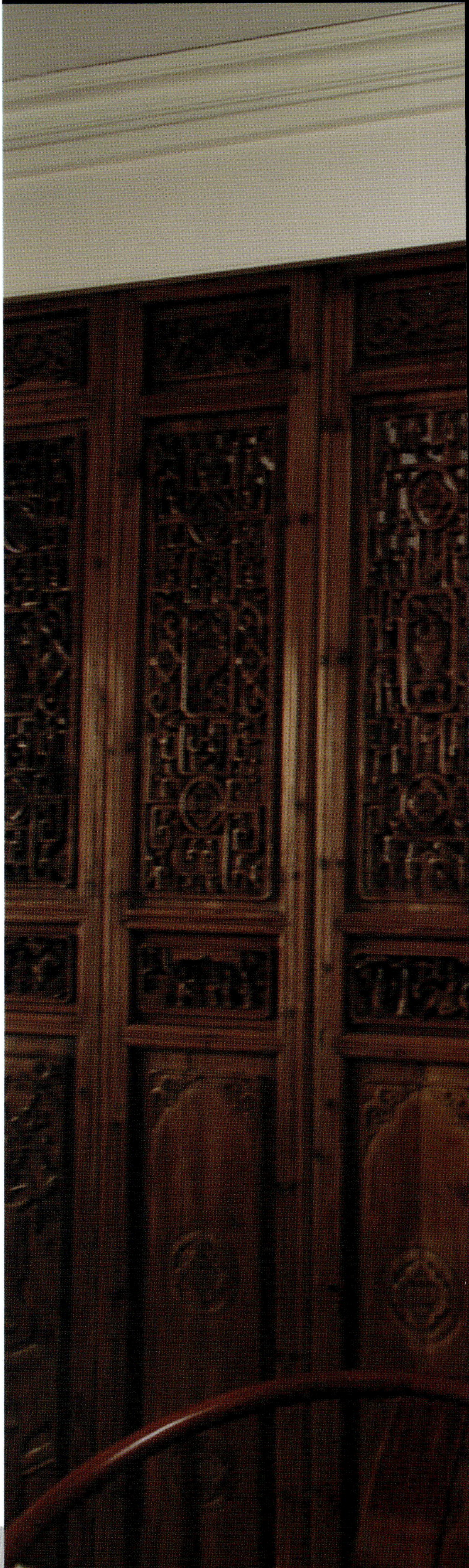

Professor Wan Qingli graduated from the Central Academy of Fine Arts in Beijing with a Bachelor degree in art history and a Master's in Chinese painting. He left for the United States in 1984 for further studies and was awarded a Master's in art history and a PhD by the University of Kansas. He came to Hong Kong in 1989 to teach in the University of Hong Kong (HKU), and became the founding Director and Chair Professor of the Academy of Visual Arts of the Hong Kong Baptist University (HKBU) in 2006. He is also an honourary professor of the HKU Faculty of Arts. Wan is a renowned art historian and a leading authority on modern Chinese art history, and has published 19 books and over 130 journal articles. He is an outstanding artist and his works are collected by museums around the world, including the National Art Museum of China, the Palace Museum and the Hong Kong Museum of Art.

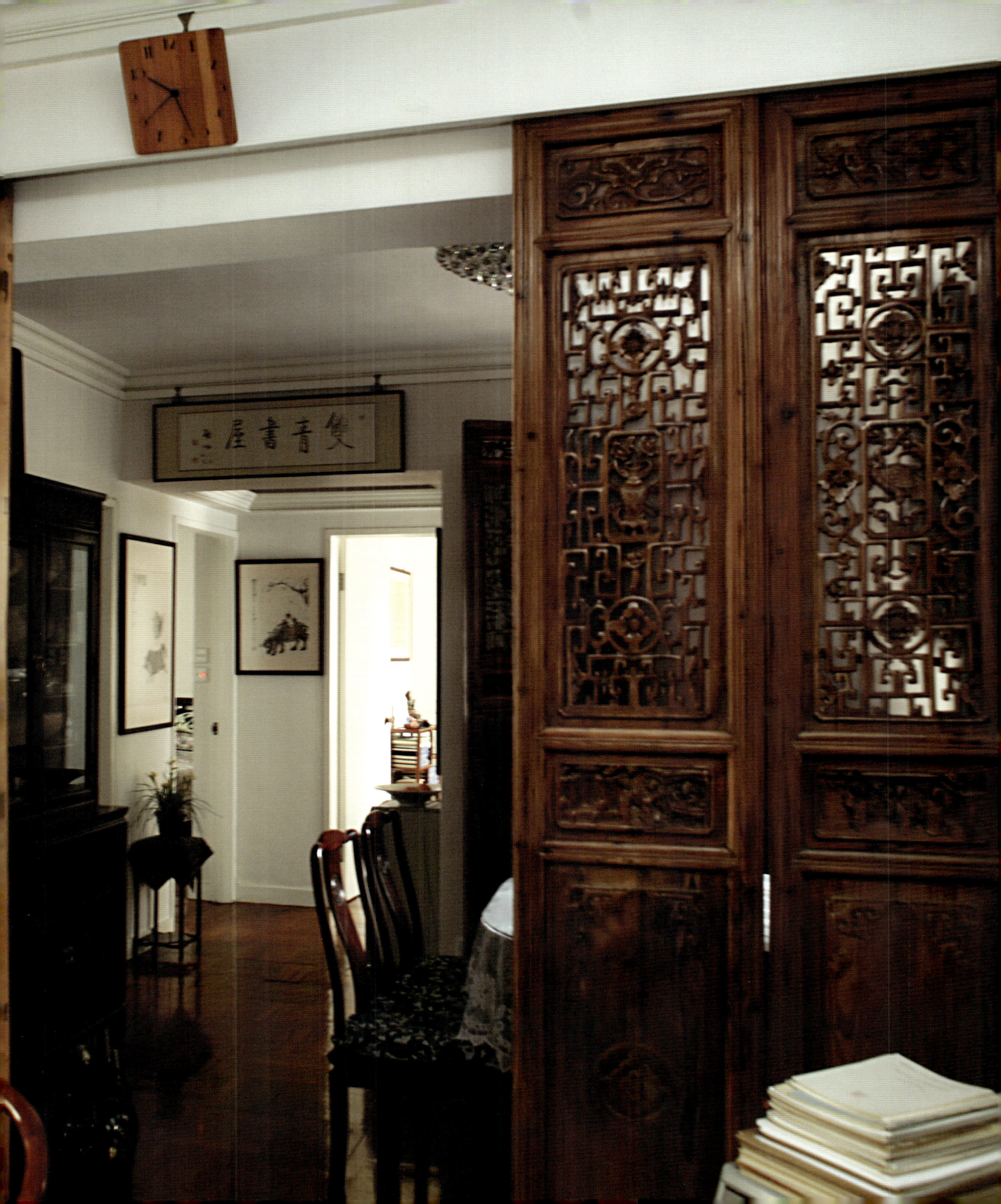
雙青書屋

Artists should have a forward-looking perspective as well as a solid background in the theories and history of art, so that their works can respond to contemporary society and lead the cultural development of their time and place. Professor Wan Qingli has based his studies and practice of art on his own life experience and learning, and so contributes to the nurturing of talent.

Wan first came to Hong Kong and taught at HKU in 1989. Born and brought up in Beijing, Hong Kong was stranger to him than the US. Walking on congested streets where people talk in Cantonese, Wan felt isolated by the hustle and bustle of this new place. But as time has gone by, Wan has not only settled down well in the city, but has also allowed the characteristics of Hong Kong culture to become a source of inspiration for his art making.

For those who are engaged with art history research and art making, it is impossible to limit themselves to one place in this globalised world. Wan was born in Beijing, educated in the US and teaches in Hong Kong. The three decades he has spent in Hong Kong has given him a wide perspective and an open mind. According to Wan, life was full of difficulties when he first arrived as he knew no Cantonese and nothing about the related culture. But as he adapted to the life here, he has gradually come to appreciate the characteristics of the local culture. Although there are still things he does not fully understand, he now considers himself a 'Hongkonger'. He is able to enjoy the local movies, which many people find difficult to respond to. He even treasures items from the culture that are despised by some Hong Kong people, like the gags of cinema star Stephen Chow, Cantonese pop songs and political satires in the comics by Zunzi[1]. Wan believes that although the pop culture is simple and easy to understand, it has its own beauty and can also be treated seriously. The culture created by the public is rich and valuable, and can become elements in art.

Away from his homeland, Wan can view the life of Hong Kong people from the angle of an outsider. He finds Hong Kong people's enthusiasm for making money understandable, as everyone likes to earn more. But Hong Kong people often put more emphasis on this than others elsewhere. What is more difficult for him to comprehend is the Hong Kong people's love of gossip columns related to show business. However, in the eyes of Wan, the 'nosy' locals are very professional at work. For example, when the city was plagued by SARS, Hong Kong people joined hands to stand against the disease, showing a high level of professional performance. He recalls

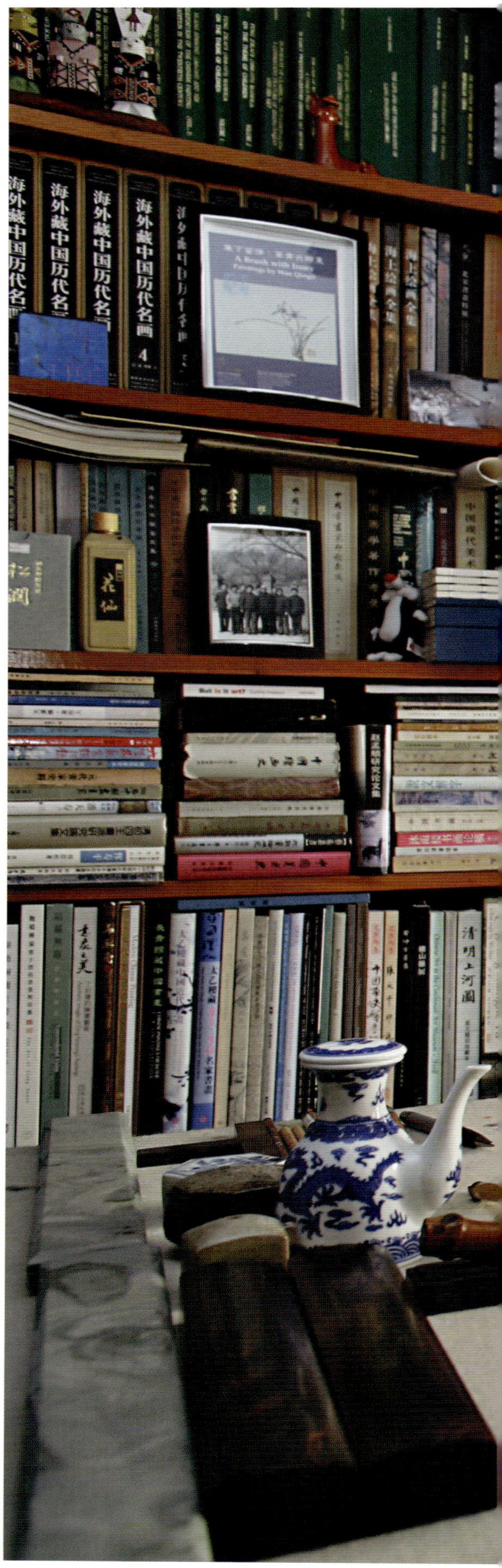

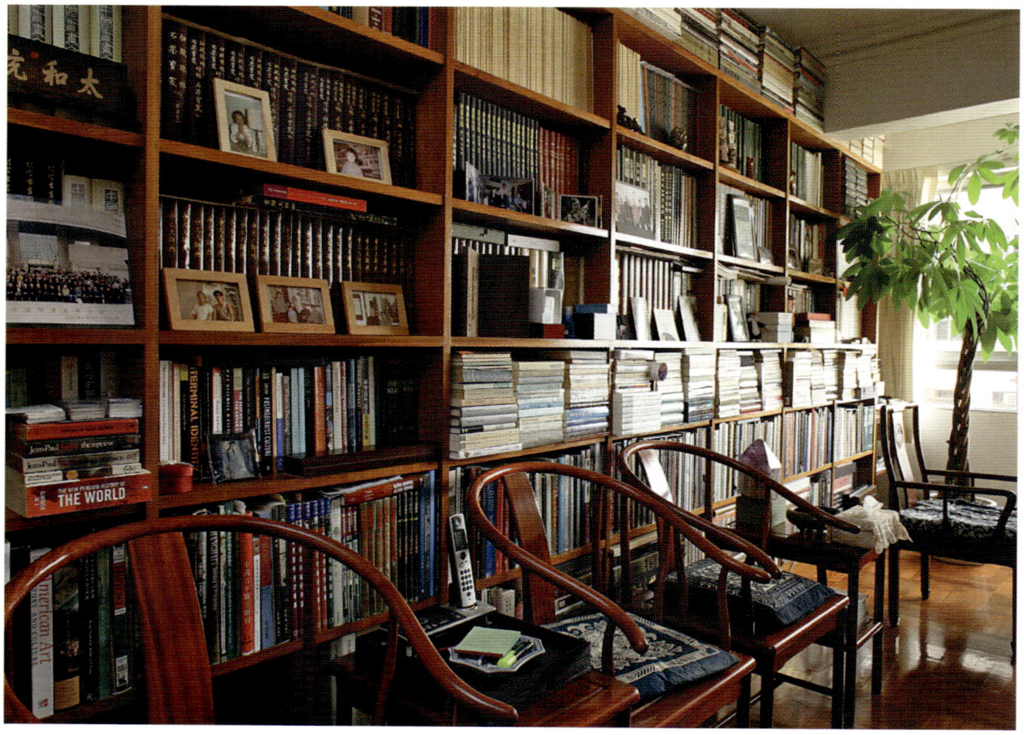

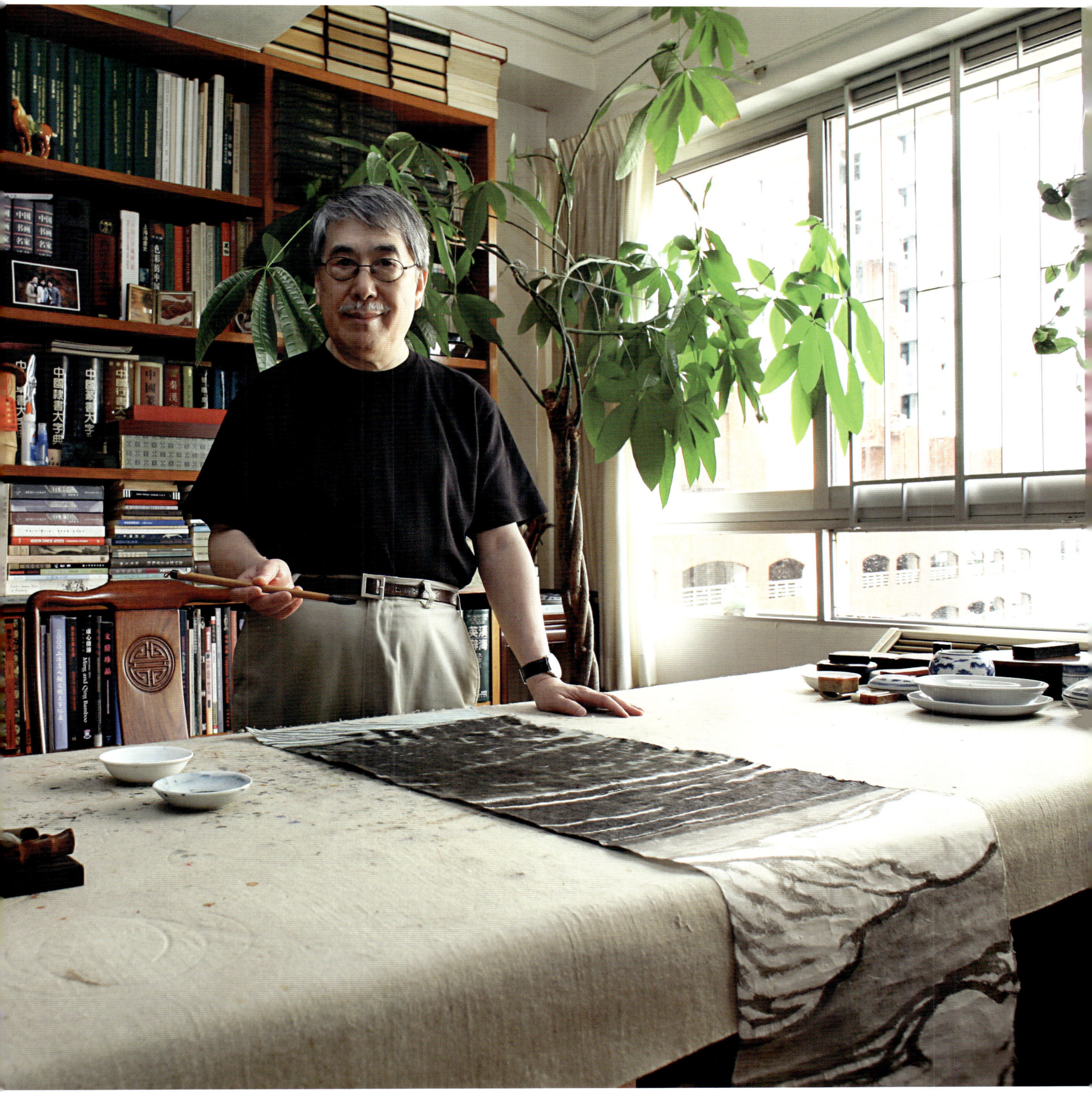
Ming and Qing Bamboo

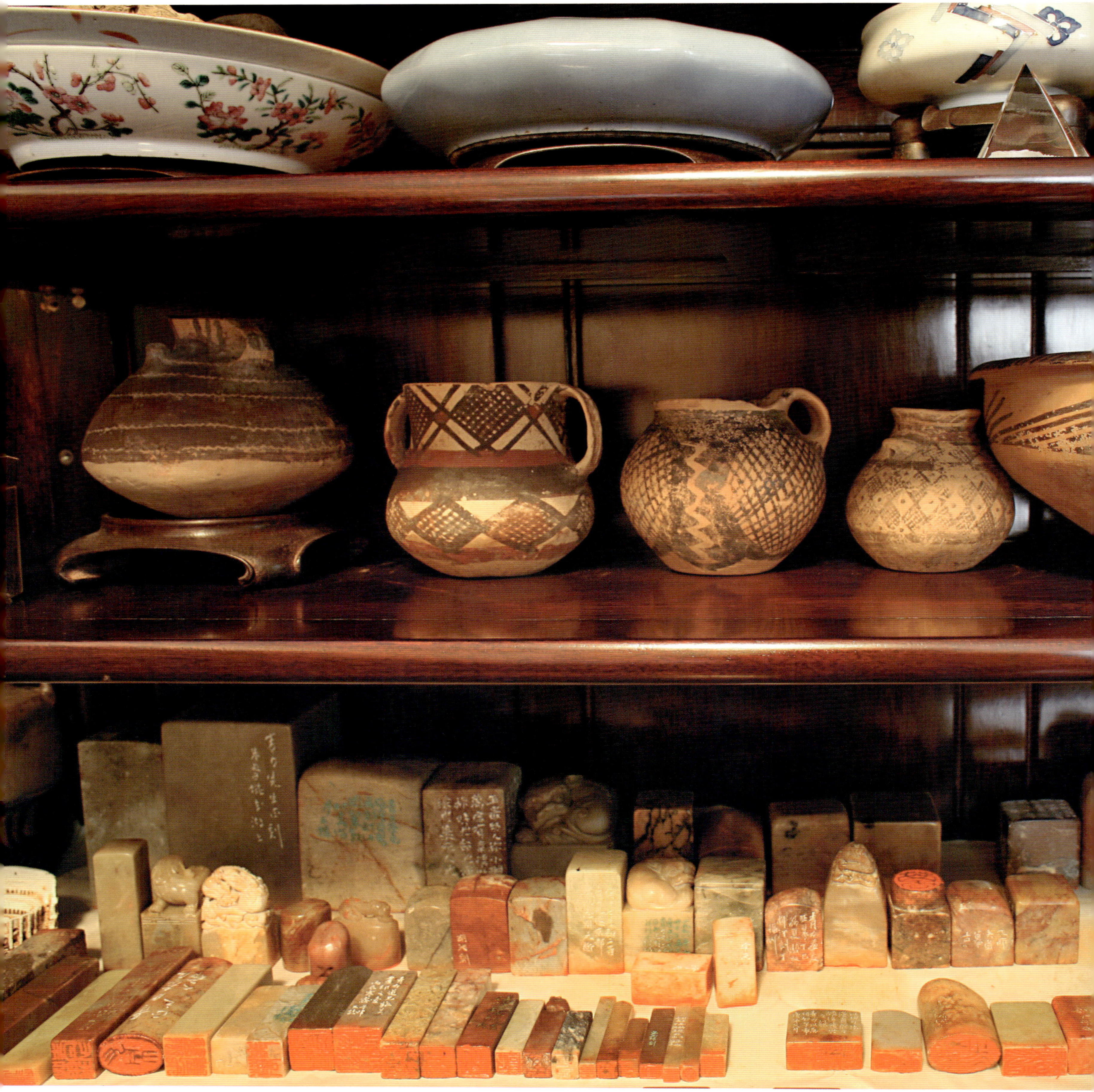

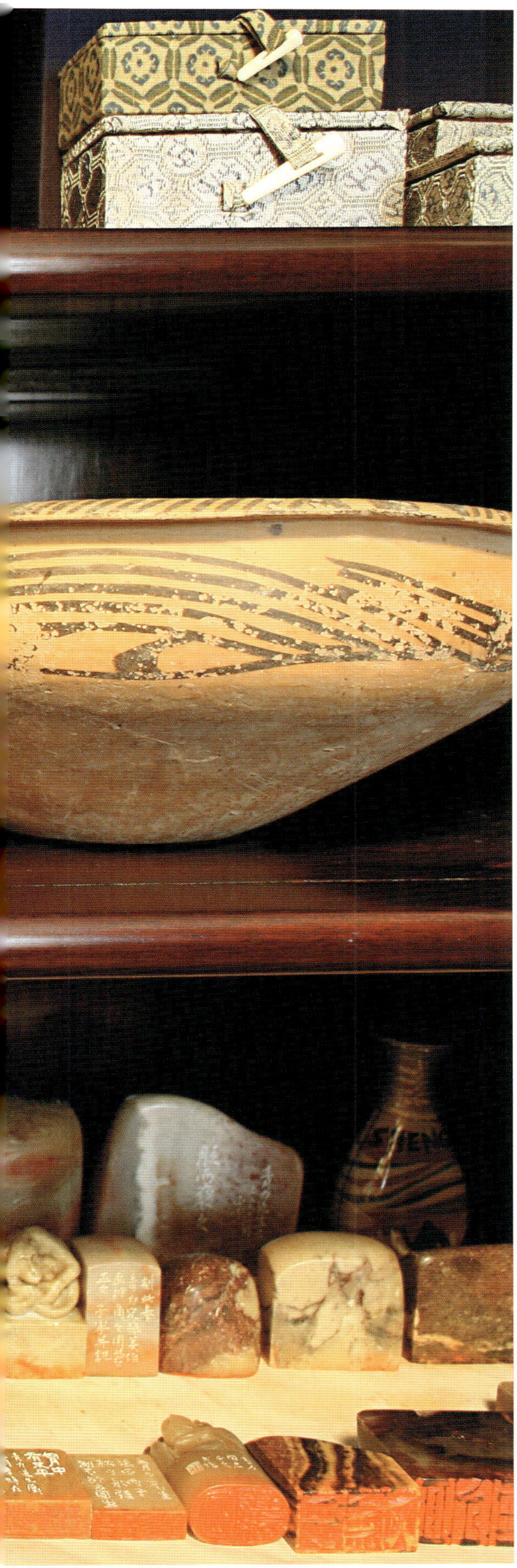

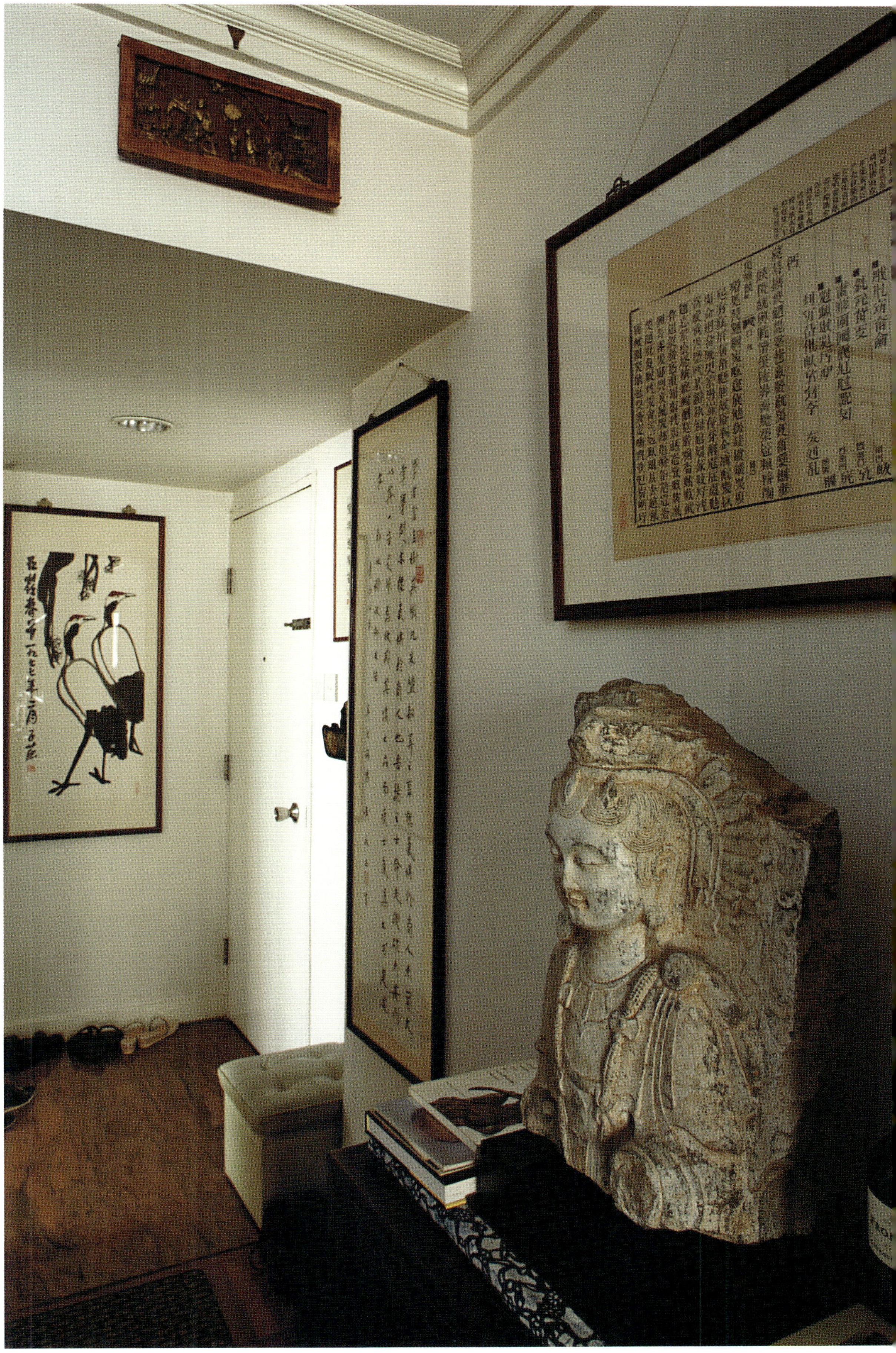

that in the most difficult moment of the SARS period when everyone was low-spirited, a salt water crocodile appeared in the Shan Pui River in northwestern New Territories and the whole city got very excited with the news. The Government had tried every means to capture the croc — which was dubbed Pui Pui — but she was eventually caught by local experts. Wan says that he often thinks about Pui Pui, as she brought warmth to Hong Kong in a time of difficulty, but most Hong Kong people are too busy to remember the crocodile after the excitement. Every time Wan imagines Pui Pui spending her days alone in the Wetland Park, he wants to find her a partner.

Wan is a serious academic but he never sticks to one approach in his studies and research. Spending years abroad and visiting so many places, Wan has been much impressed by the freedom in Hong Kong. He mentions Tsang Tsou-choi[2] who claimed to be the Emperor of Kowloon. Obviously, Tsang suffered from psychiatric problems, but as he lived in Hong Kong he had the freedom to continue with his calligraphy graffiti on the streets. He would not be allowed to form such valuable 'street culture' in any mainland city.

With the heavy administrative work related to the academy and teaching, Wang often buries himself in computer work, telephone calls and meetings. He can only focus on art making in his free time. He says that he needs to be highly focused before starting to paint, and his emotional status is much more important than the physical environment. Therefore he has not purposely set up a studio space but makes paintings and calligraphy works on the table in his living room. As full attention is crucial, he does not talk during the process and may work continuously for a few hours. It is not uncommon for him to only pick one satisfactory work after finishing a number of them. When he reviews his works after one or two weeks and find them unsatisfactory, he will paint them again. Wan's works are the result of repeated polishing and refinement.

Living in Hong Kong for more than 20 years, Wan has gradually turned from an outsider to one of the community. He has incorporated many Hong Kong elements into his works. Pui Pui, the crocodile he misses, pollution problems, gossip news and political ecology are all localised themes. Sometimes only Hong Kong people can feel and respond to the

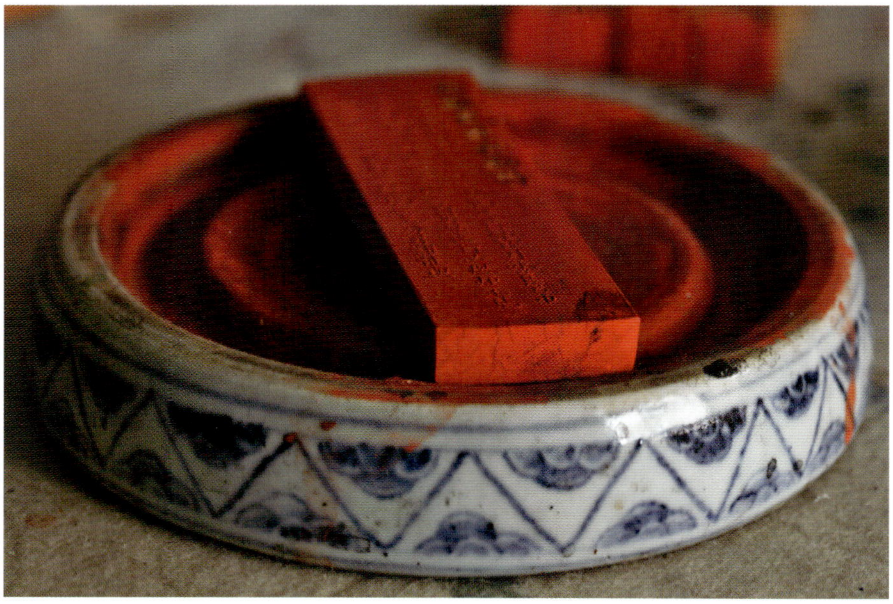

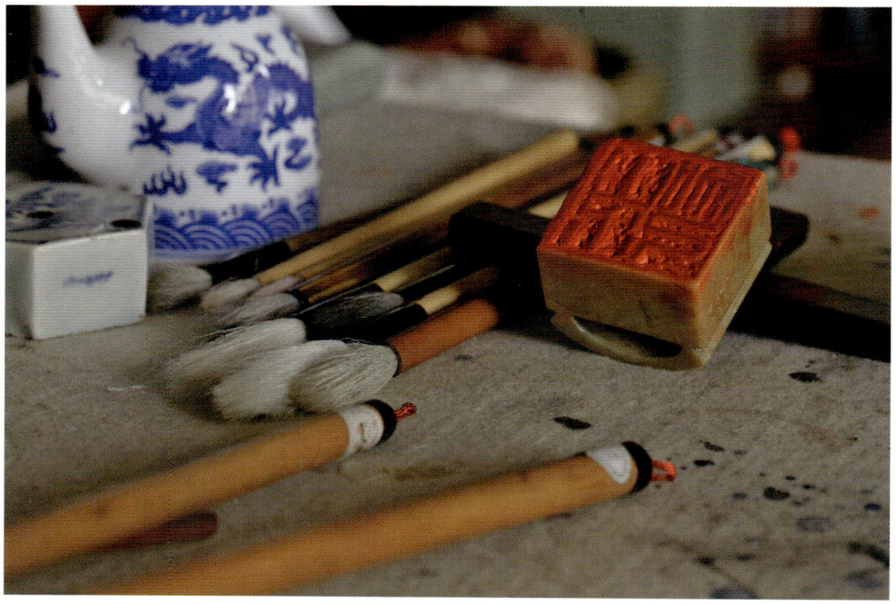

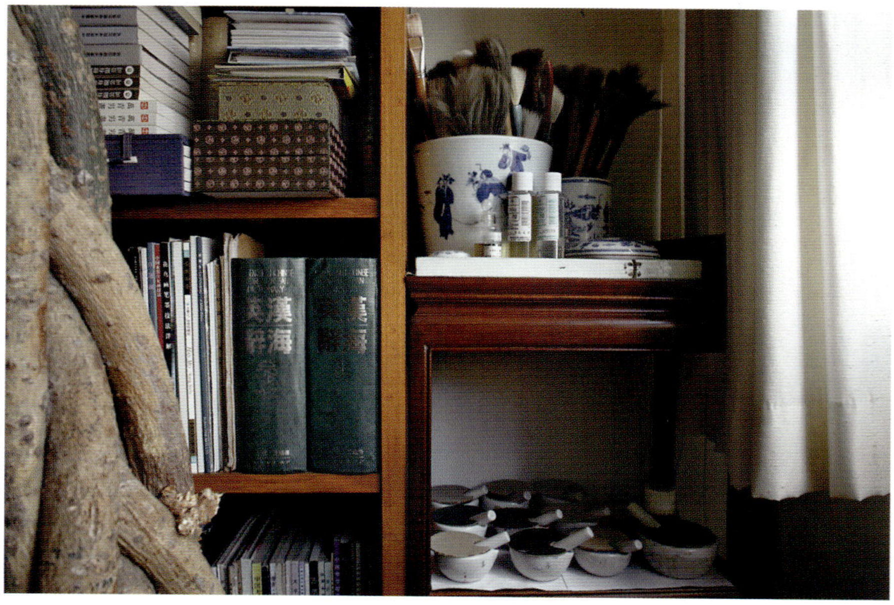

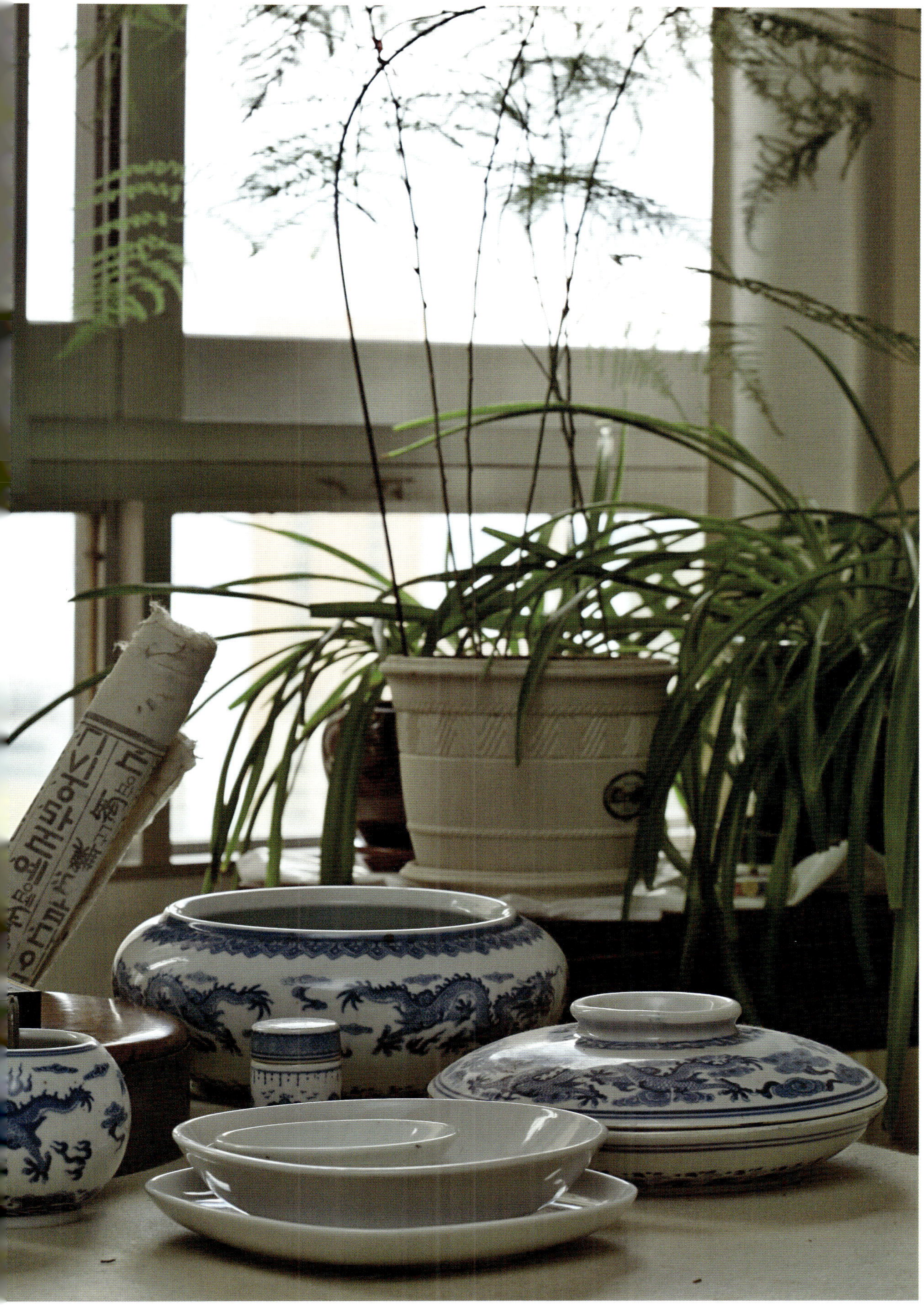

He needs to be highly focused before starting to paint, and his emotional status is much more important than the physical environment. Therefore he has not purposely set up a studio space

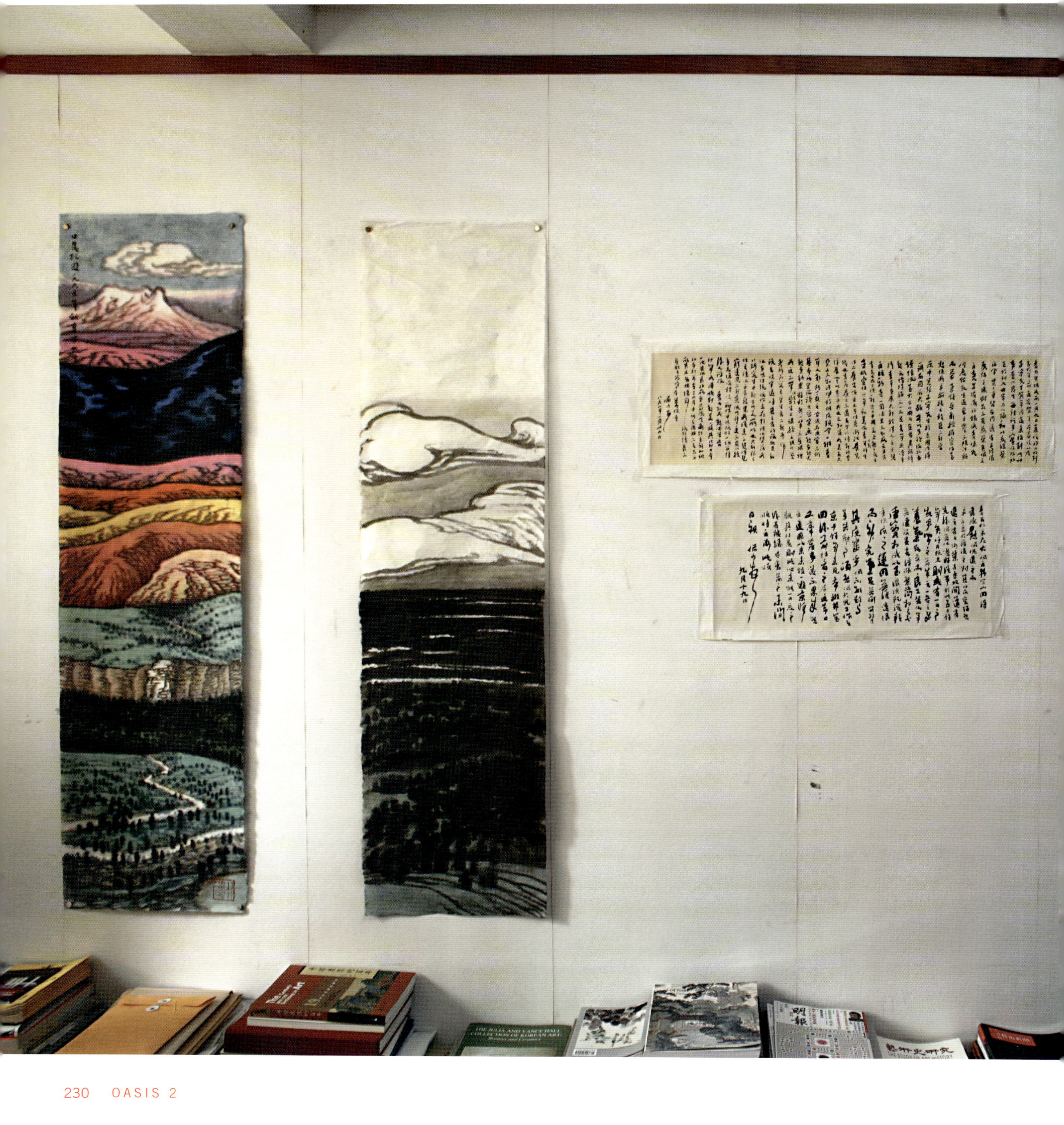
明報
藝術史研究

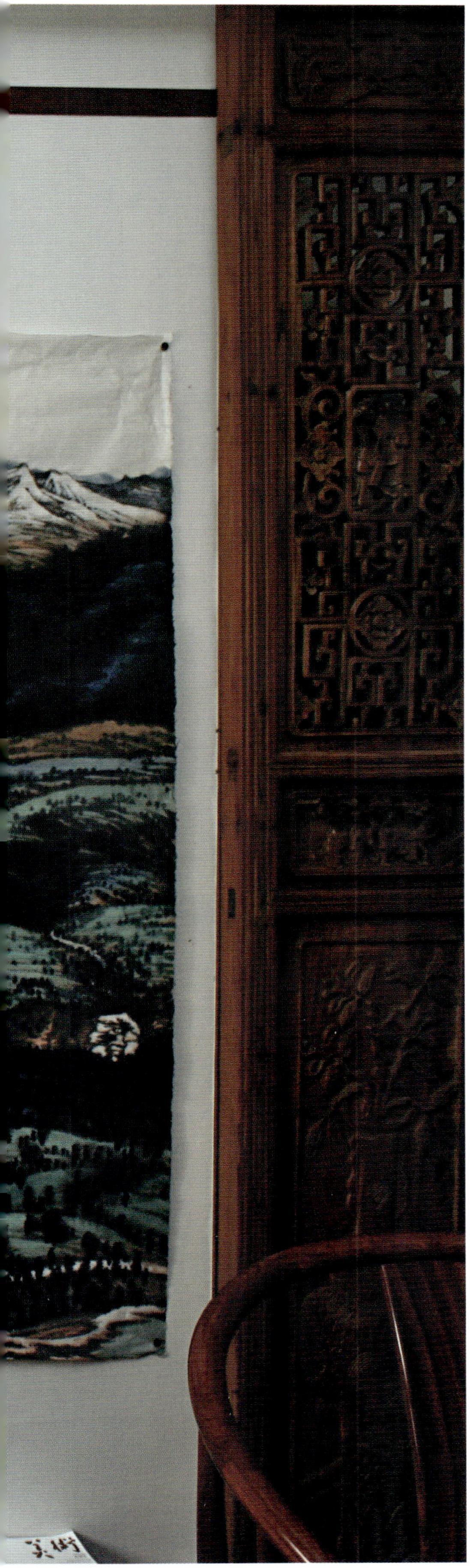

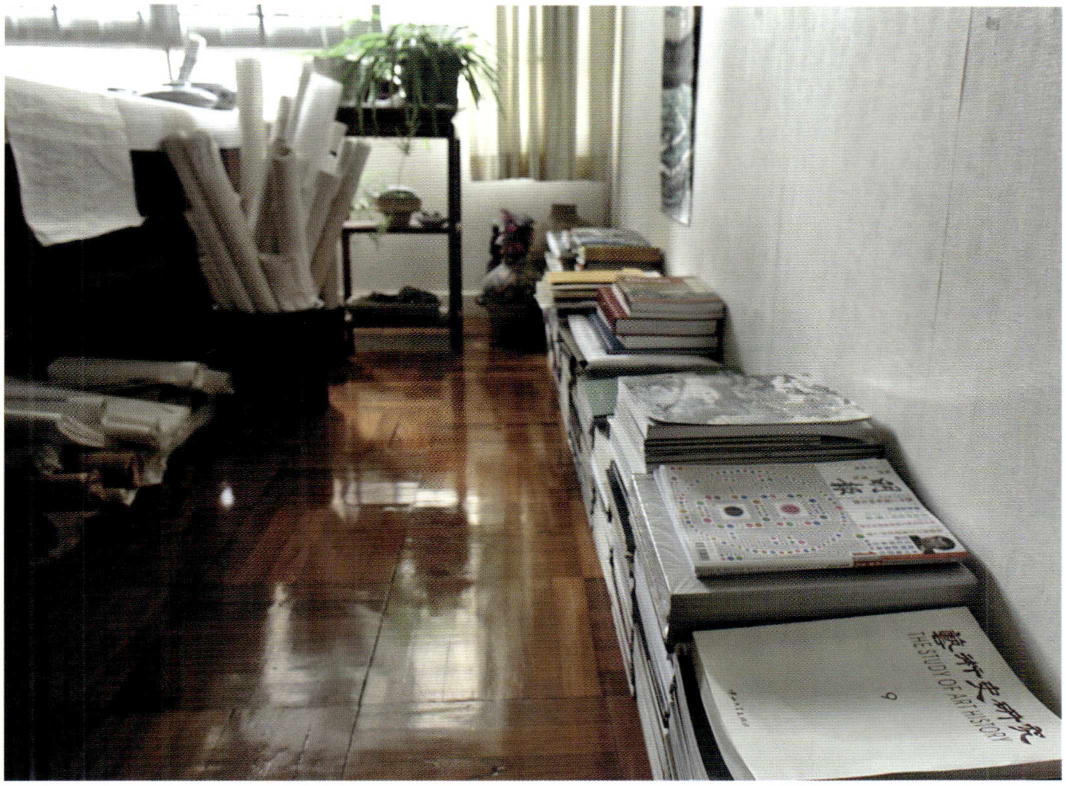

satire. Wan's friends from Beijing are amazed at the local subjects found in his recent works. It seems to them that Wan is becoming a 100 percent Hongkonger. Wan has added his own observation of daily lives into the structure of traditional Chinese painting, his perspective on the community and social issues. The special humour in his works has made them a contemporary form of literati painting[3]. In his art history research Wan extensively studies the creativity of Chinese brushstrokes and ink painting. He puts his belief into his art and uses brushes and ink to express his feelings and thoughts, echoing the myriad faces of the modern world.

Wan believes that artworks should be linked to the place in which they are made and the people there. The cultural context and living environment have their own impact on artists. He sometimes finds topics in academic research too specific and disconnected with the public. What interest him the most are issues of the current time, place and people. That is why he uses a traditional medium and style but subject matters that are always contemporary and worldly. This strong contrast has become a special feature of the works he has made in Hong Kong.

With most of his career dedicated to academic research, Wan has not been satisfied with just living in the academic circle. He cares a lot about art and cultural development in Hong Kong, which is why he has taken up the leading role at the Academy of Visual Arts of the HKBU. He hopes that the academy can train more graduates with versatile abilities in visual art, who will then serve as a driving force for the creative development of the city. Wan says that local cultural development should go faster and the establishment of the West Kowloon Cultural District is a project too important to be further postponed. Hong Kong also needs more professionals in art administration to work in line with future developments.

According to Wan, there are many good artists in Hong Kong and the local culture is also unique, but there is a lack of communication between artists and the community. This is where education can play a role. Wan has identified such a need, and introduced a Master's programme in visual art, which is tailor-made for the long-term development of local art and culture. Wan sees the programme as a good opportunity to train art administration professionals who can contribute to the art development of our city.

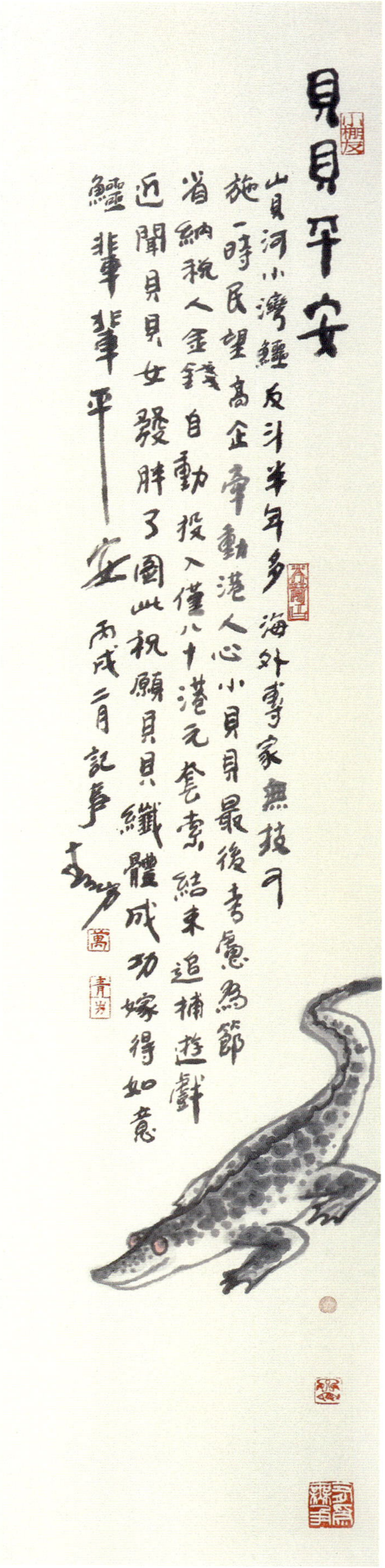

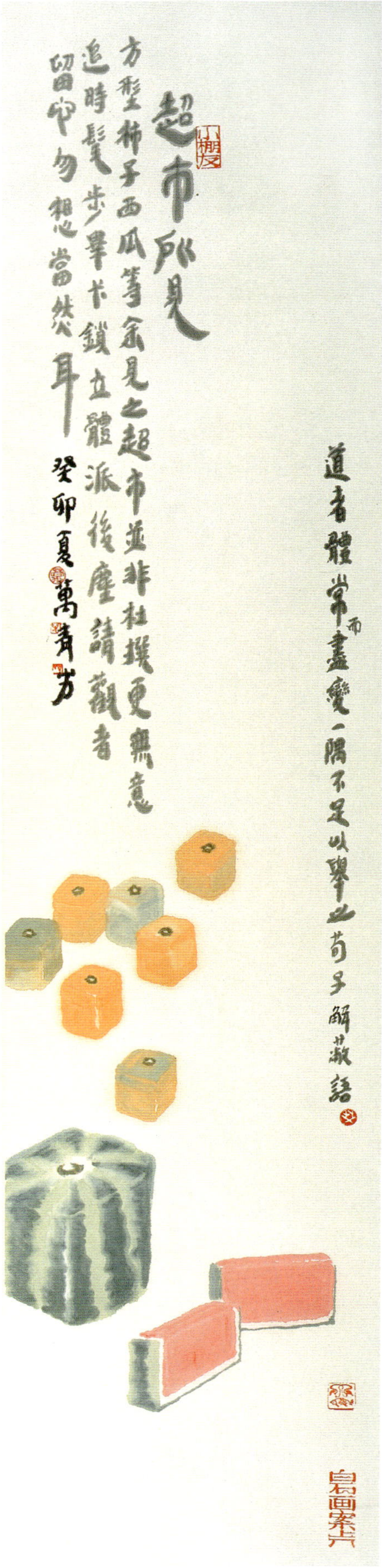

(Left) Pui Pui Safe and Sound
Ink and colour on paper, 138x36 cm, 2006

(Right) Seen in a Supermarket
Ink and colour on paper, 138x36 cm, 2003

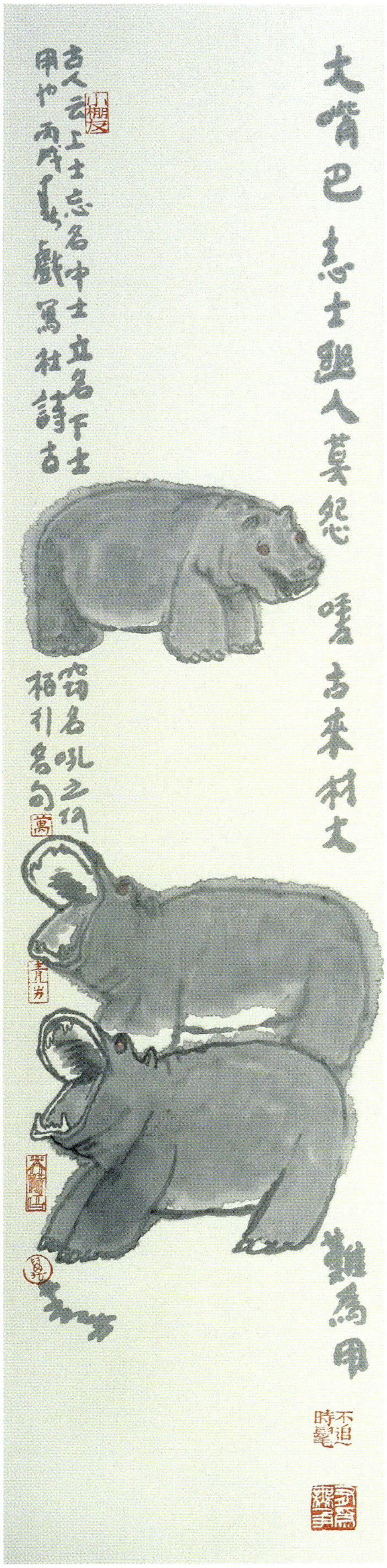

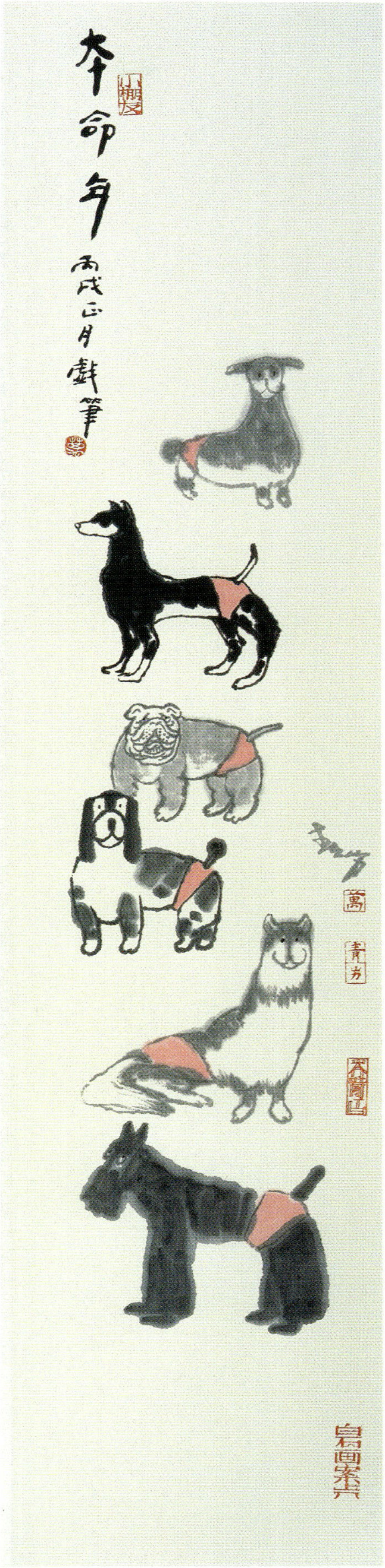

(Left) Large Mouth
Ink and colour on paper, 138x36 cm, 2006

(Right) My Zodiac Year
Ink and colour on paper, 138x36 cm, 2006

John Li Tung-keung

Following One's Heart

By Ronny Leung

John Li Tung-keung graduated from the Department of Fine Arts at the Chinese University of Hong Kong (CUHK) in 1962. After graduation he taught at the department for nine years before accepting a scholarship for further studies in Iowa, in the US. There he completed a Master's degree in printmaking and another in drawing, before going to New York and then the UK to study lithography. When he returned to Hong Kong he again taught at the CUHK. His work has been exhibited in Hong Kong, US, UK and Shanghai. In 2000 Li received an Artistic Development Fellowship from the Hong Kong Arts Development Council. His works have been published in a number of volumes, including *The Drawings of John Li* (1975), *Works of John Li* (2000) and *Colour East and West: Ink Painting of John Li* (2004).

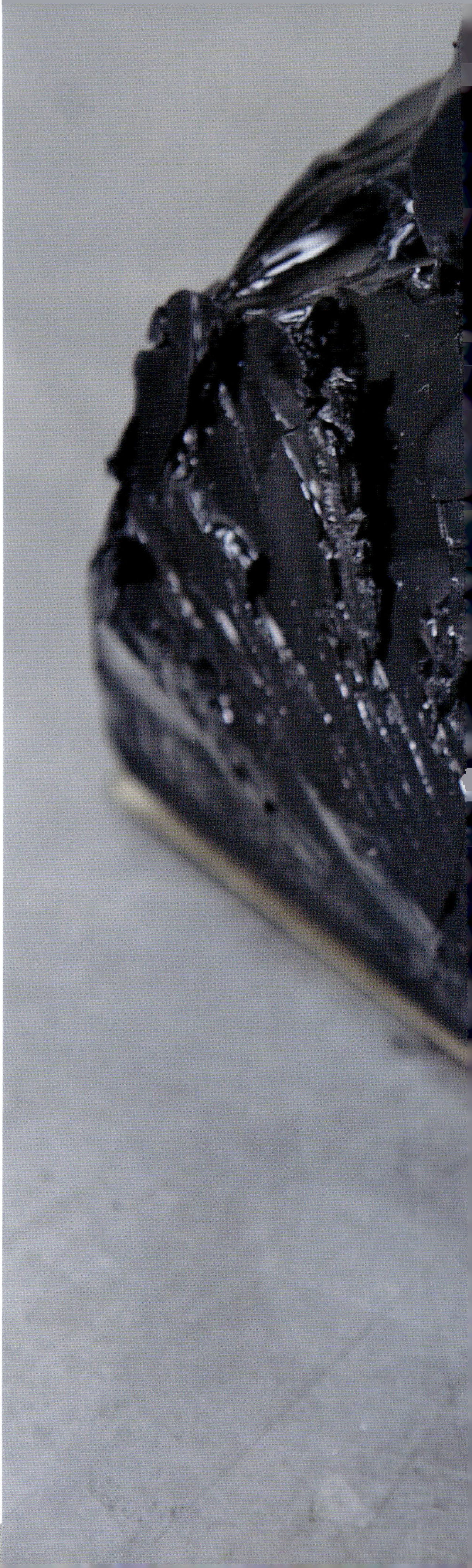

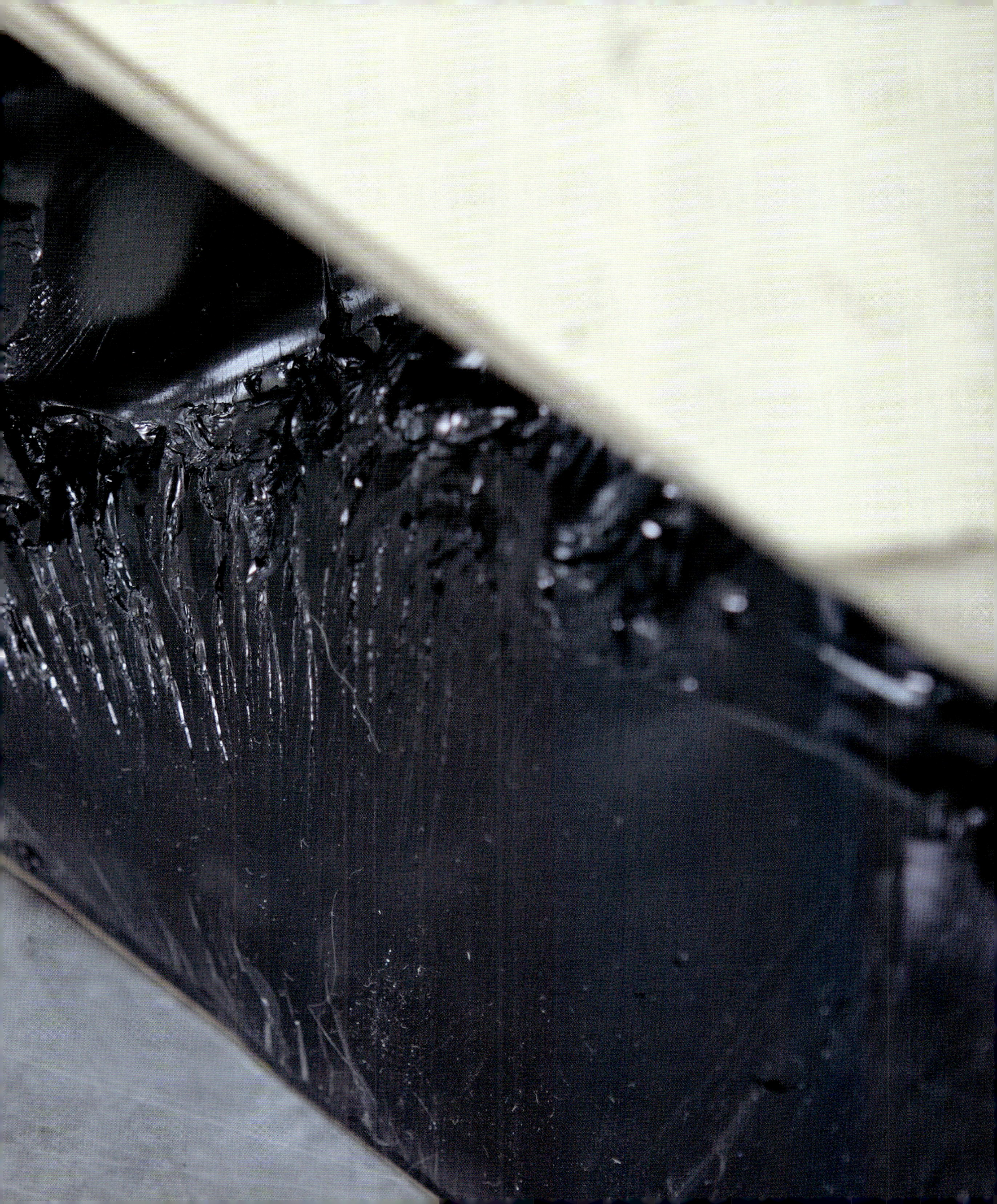

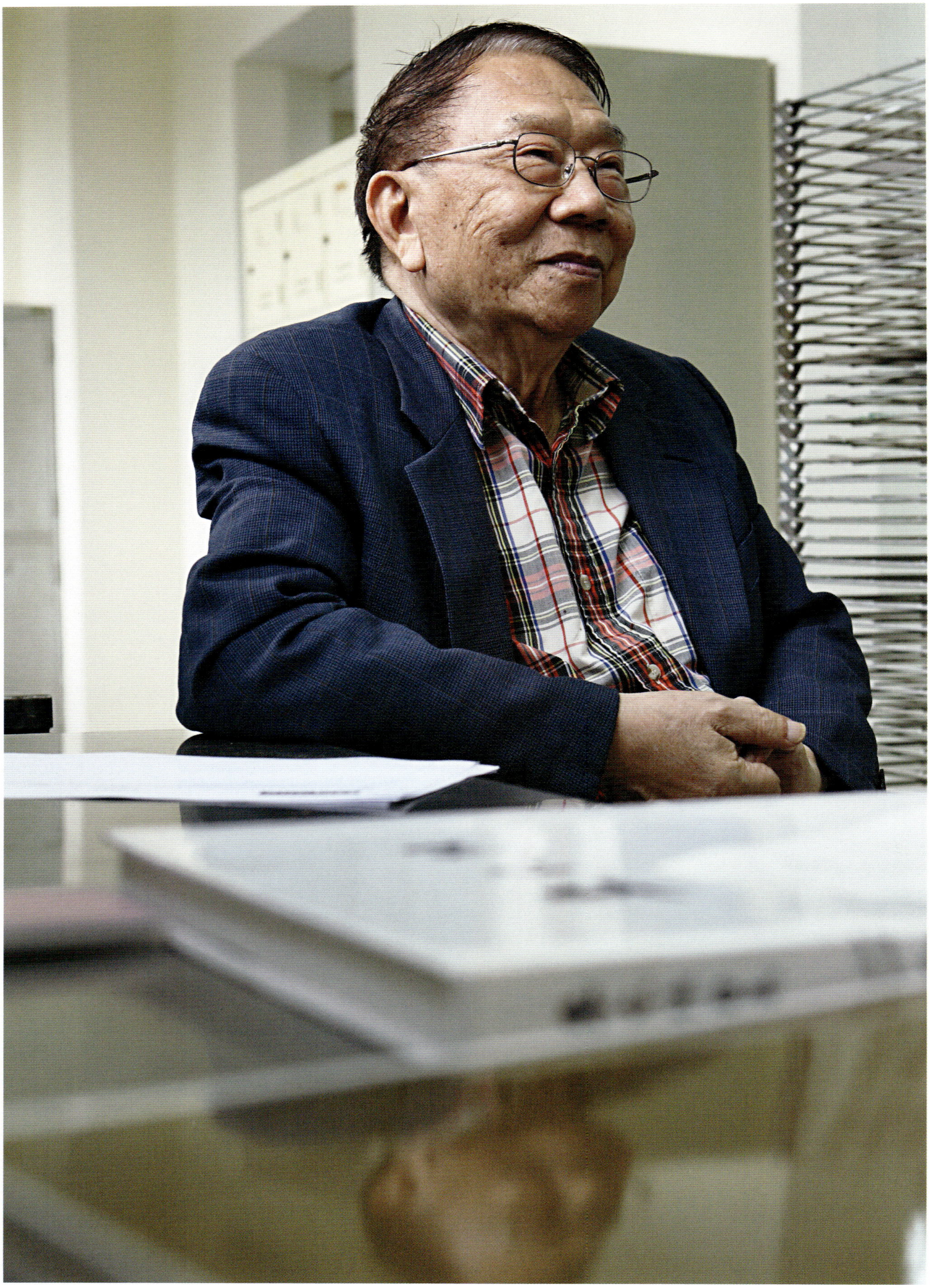

The artist expresses snapshots of his life in a calm and unhurried manner

Born in 1931, John Li Tung-keung certainly does not look his age. He moves about nimbly. During the interview he is like a little schoolboy, his smile innocent.

Li's work looks fresh; in the words of Ding Yanyong, "His art, seriously made, showers one with delight".[1] Li is considered a master of portraiture, good at capturing characters and expressions. When I was a student in his drawing class he always used to say, "If you can draw people, you can draw anything". The statement was picked up from a former teacher of his and it has inspired his life-long interest in portraiture. He has depicted obstinate girls, playful children, ladies and fools. All these are real characters. They are from among his students, friends and family members. The relationships give Li a good grasp of his subjects' personalities, which subsequently stand out in his work. He cherishes the time spent with friends and when he works he chooses to be relaxed, rather than pursuing formal precision or exhibition opportunities. To him, art is about self expression.

Li thinks that drawing is the foundation of all art, believing that since printing and calligraphic characters are drawings, so writing is too. Li's drawings feel like Chinese calligraphy; they convey perspective, structure and texture. A veteran of both drawing and calligraphy, he does not combine the east and the west by depicting forms. The essences of the two fuse in his lines.

The smoothness in Li's line work is reminiscent of Matisse or Picasso. Li does not mind these comparisons: the artists are similar in their love of lines, but they have developed different styles. Just as Li's use of his brush and the way he forms characters are influenced by his teacher Tsang Ke-tuan, the styles of the two men are nonetheless very different.

Every artist has his or her own views about aesthetics. To Li, art needs 'capability', 'brilliance', 'spirit' and 'freedom'. 'Capability' refers to technical competence while a tasteful and delightful work, to him, is 'brilliant'. 'Spirit' describes a work's character. 'Freedom' transcends vanity and gives room to self expression. Li believes that art is the union of one's knowledge, experience, world view and spirituality.

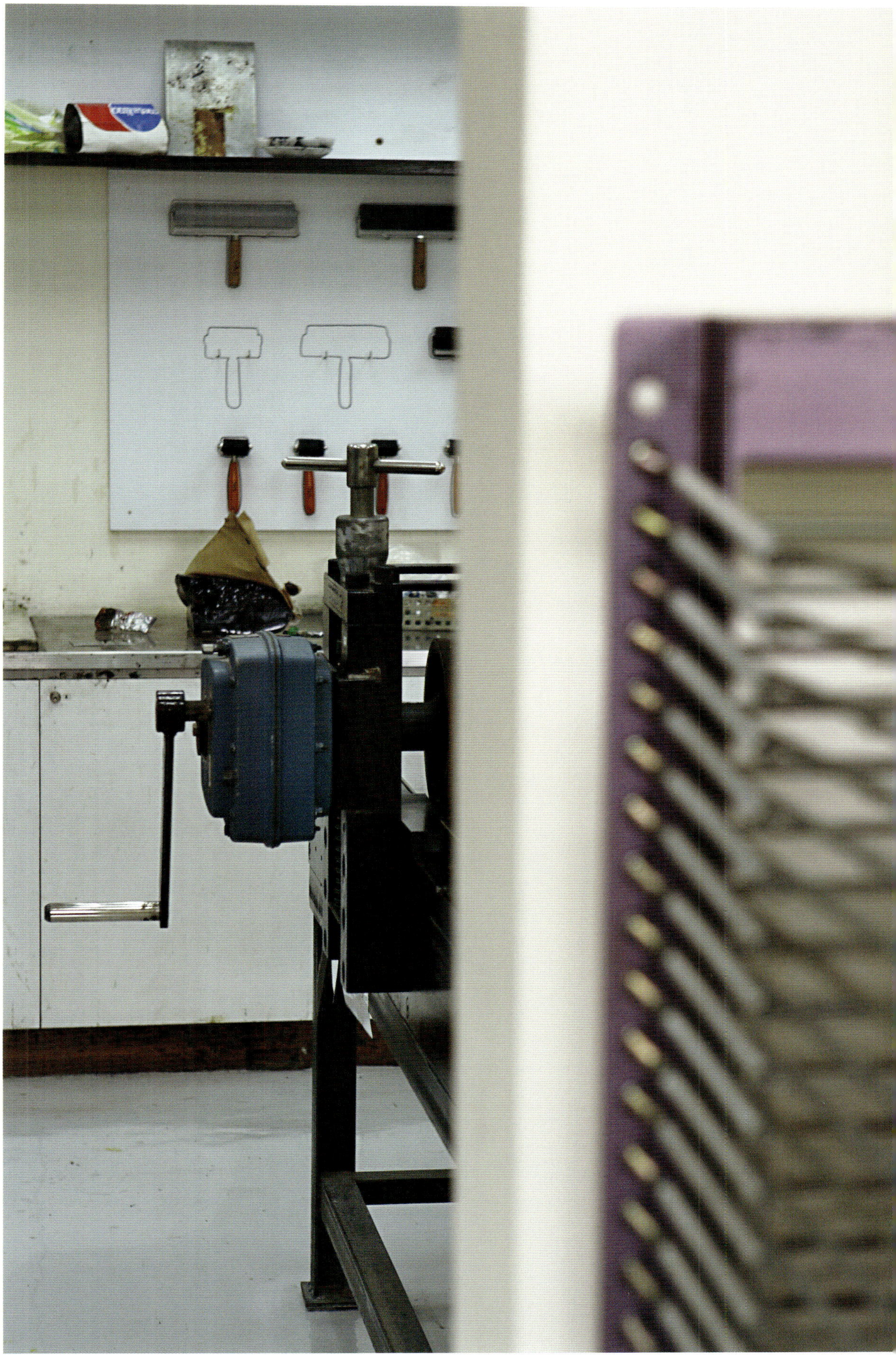

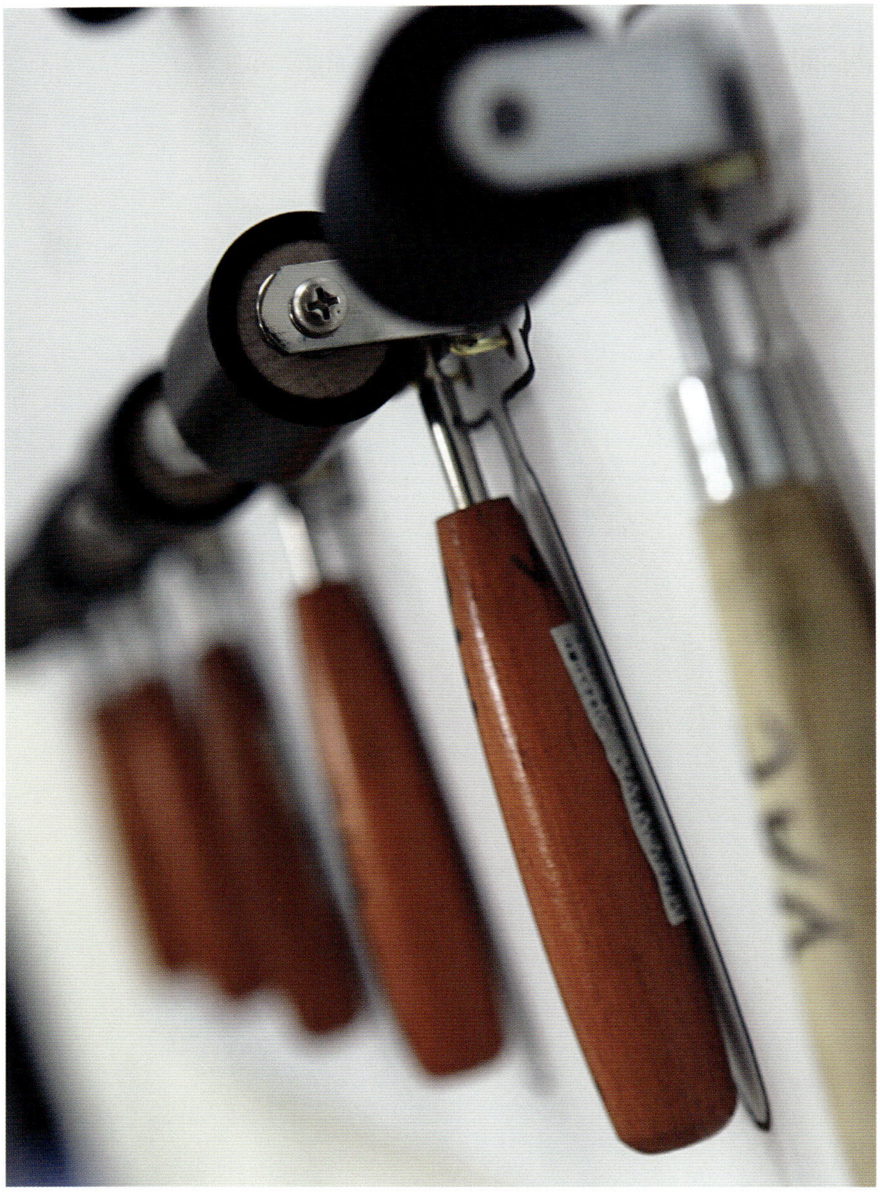

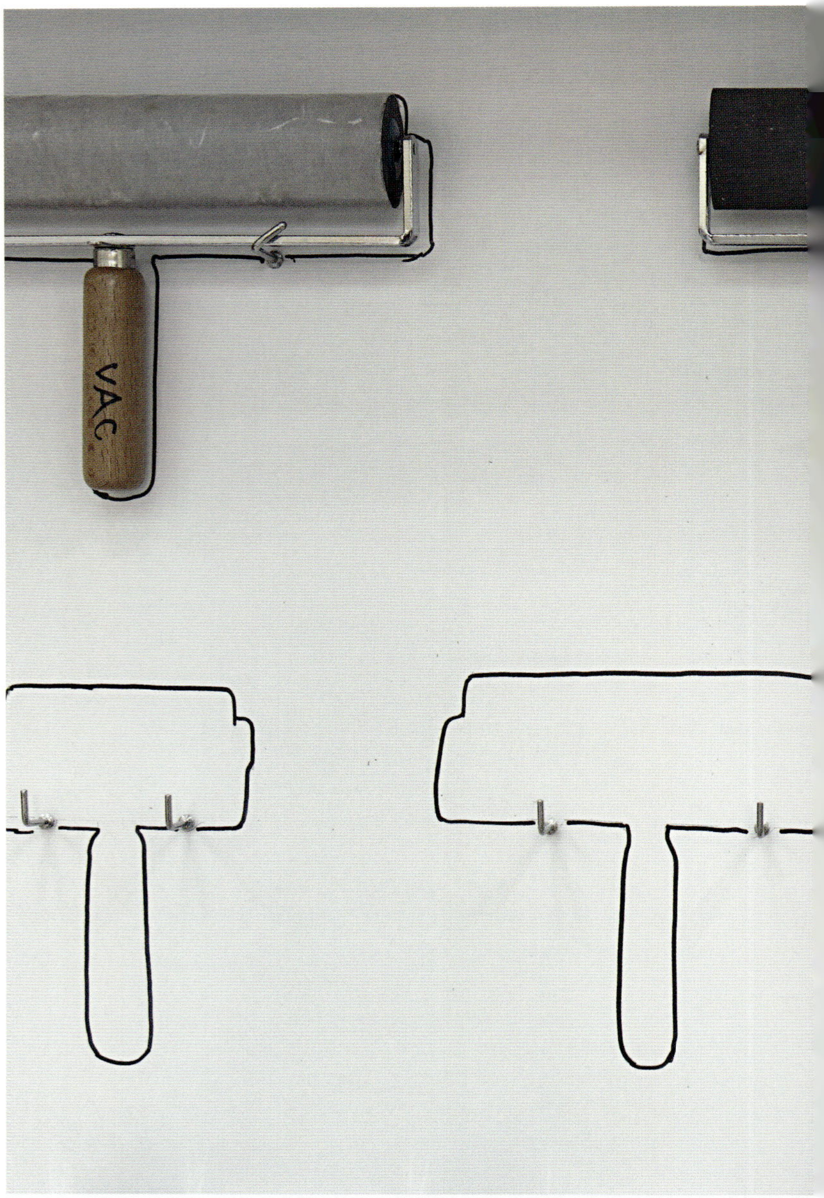

Art is the union of one's knowledge, experience, world view and spirituality

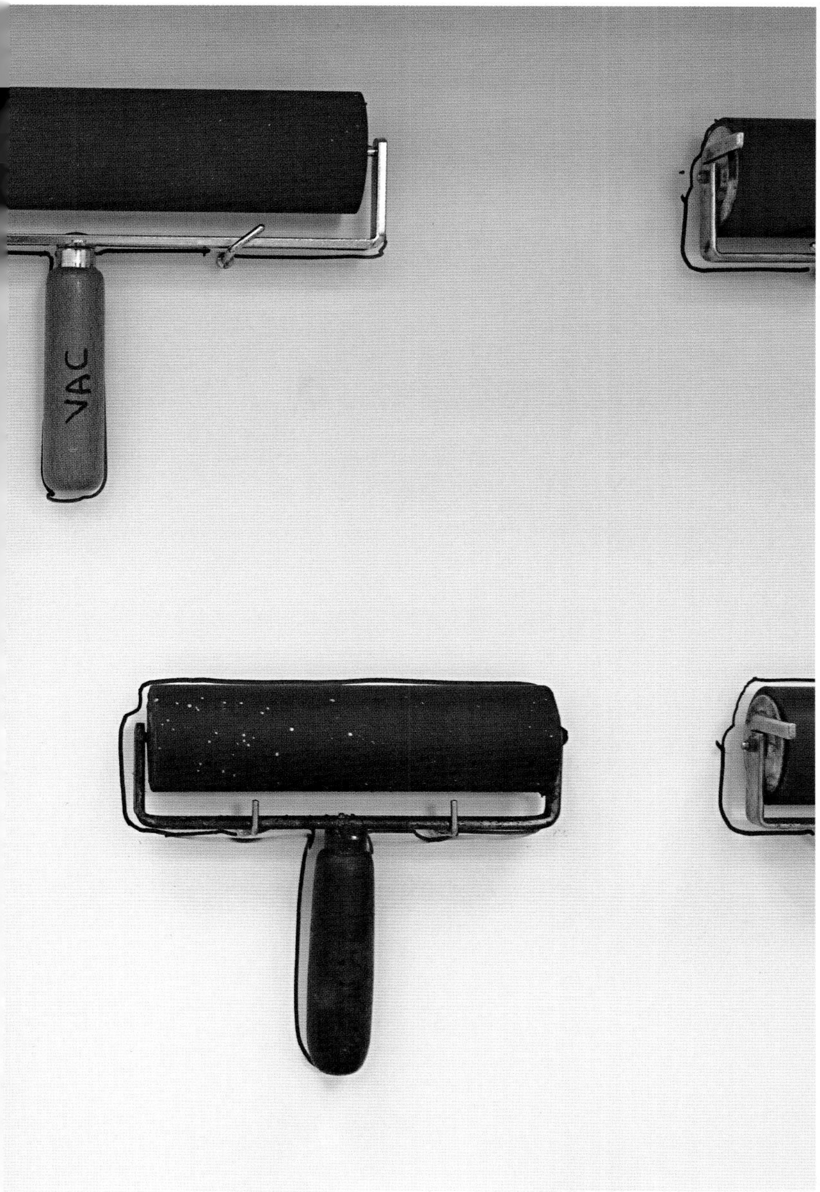

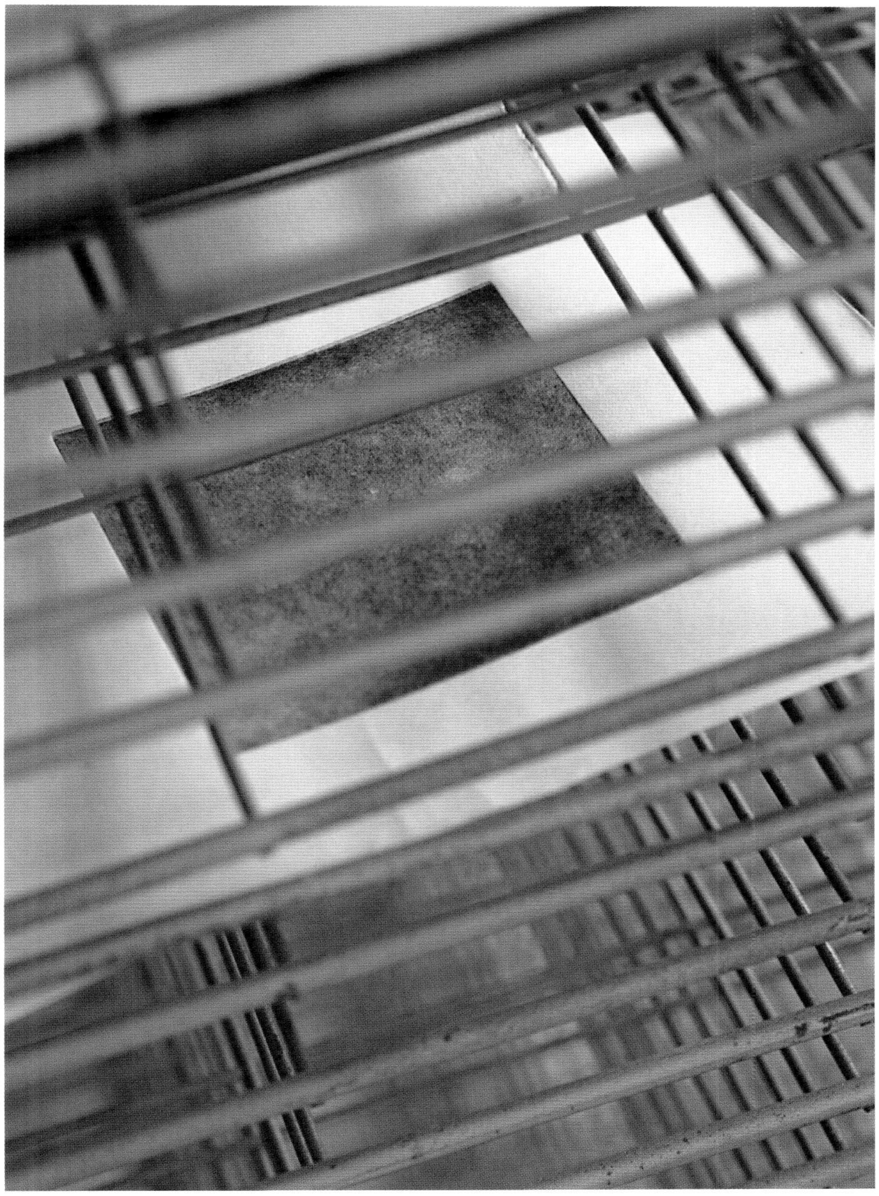

Li has a studio in Vancouver where he can work on a large scale. In Hong Kong he always works at home, his ink paintings done on the floor. When he needs equipment for printmaking he goes to the university. Whenever he has time, he paints — not for anything in particular, but as a habit. Li has never taken a break from art making. His latest work is a calligraphic series that portrays the 14 stations in the story of the *Passion of Christ*, each with an illustrated poem. Now that he is old, he says, it is time to follow his heart and work on whatever he likes. His only worry is that there will not be enough time to work on everything he wants to.

All alumni of the CUHK remember Li for his drawing instructions. He would tell students to draw figures with circles, triangles and squares. The repetitive circles have bored many, but Li sees them as a form of training. The shapes can link form and background with an array of identical shapes. This is similar to painting and television images in China, which are also shaped by dots of varied shades. He says that most students focus only on form and miss the background, and that although students now are more receptive, most of them think that drawing is unimportant and rarely take the training seriously. Even so, Li likes teaching, and wanted to teach since

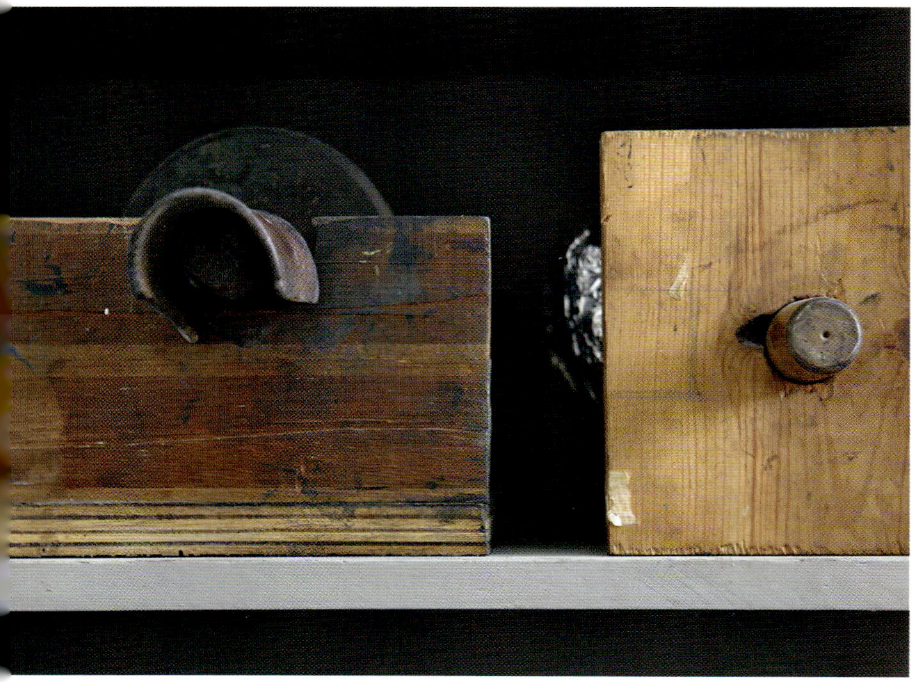

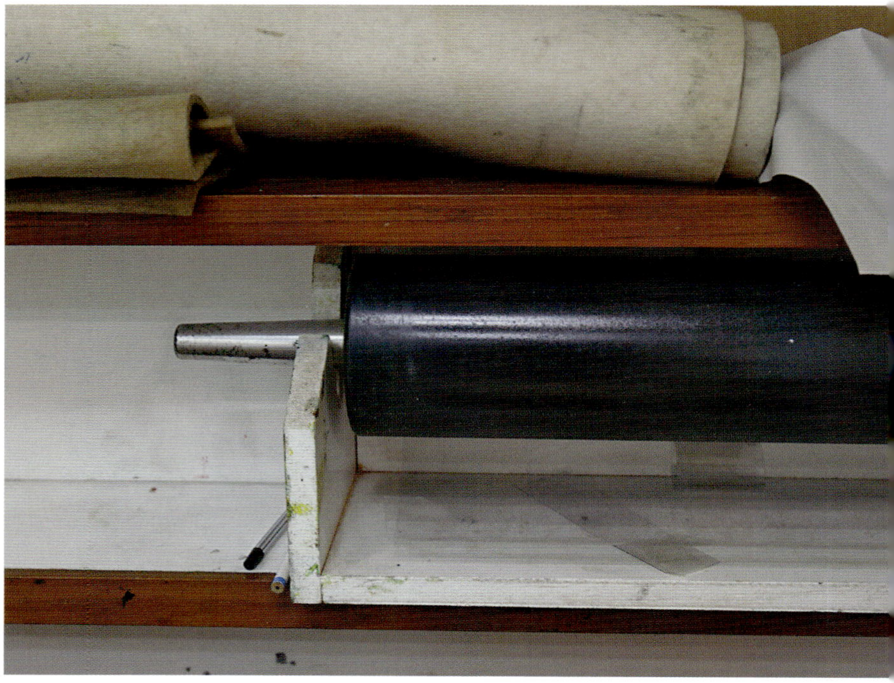

he was young. He believes that art is a lifelong pursuit and he always considered art education his mission. Though he retired many years ago he is still an active guest lecturer at the CUHK and at the Hong Kong Baptist University, and it enriches his retirement. Once in a while he teaches printmaking at the Hong Kong Visual Arts Centre.

Li is a virtuous scholar; he is humble and courteous. When he talks he smiles sincerely. I ask him how one can gain artistic merit. He replies: "People should look for truth, goodness and beauty. Religiously, look for the divine. They should be nice to others and fulfill their roles." Li is a Catholic and has a philosophy based on treating others well.

I ask him whether he has ever done anything wrong, or mischievous. "Nothing that I can think of at the moment," he says with a smile, "I have always lived like this. Nothing special has ever happened yet I feel blessed." To many this may not seem exciting, but what is wrong with living an uneventful life? When one sees Li's satisfied smile, one gains an understanding of bliss.

1. The Drawings of John Li (1975), published by the Department of Fine Arts Publications New Asia College, The Chinese University of Hong Kong

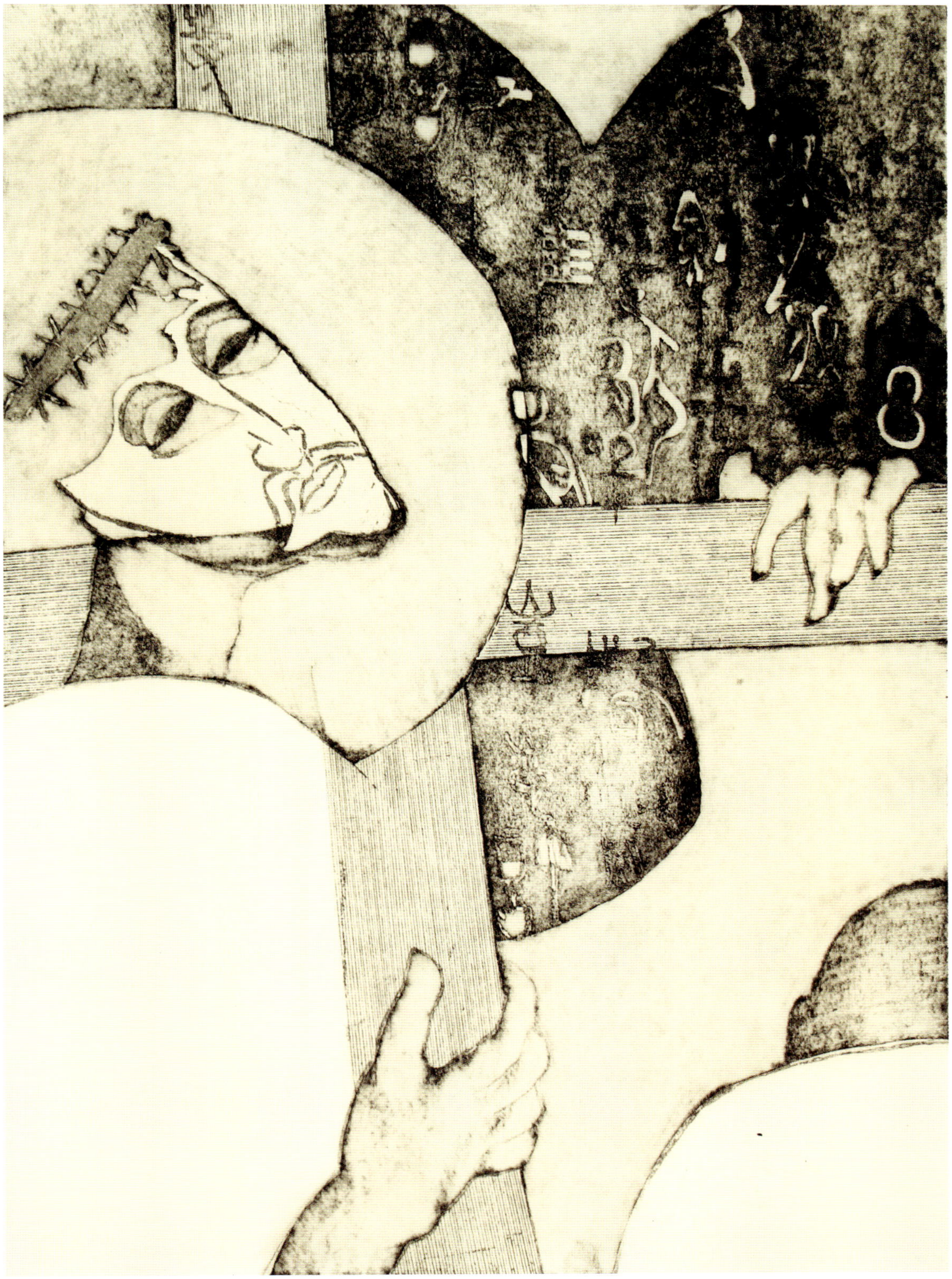

2nd Station
Etching, 80x60 cm, 1997

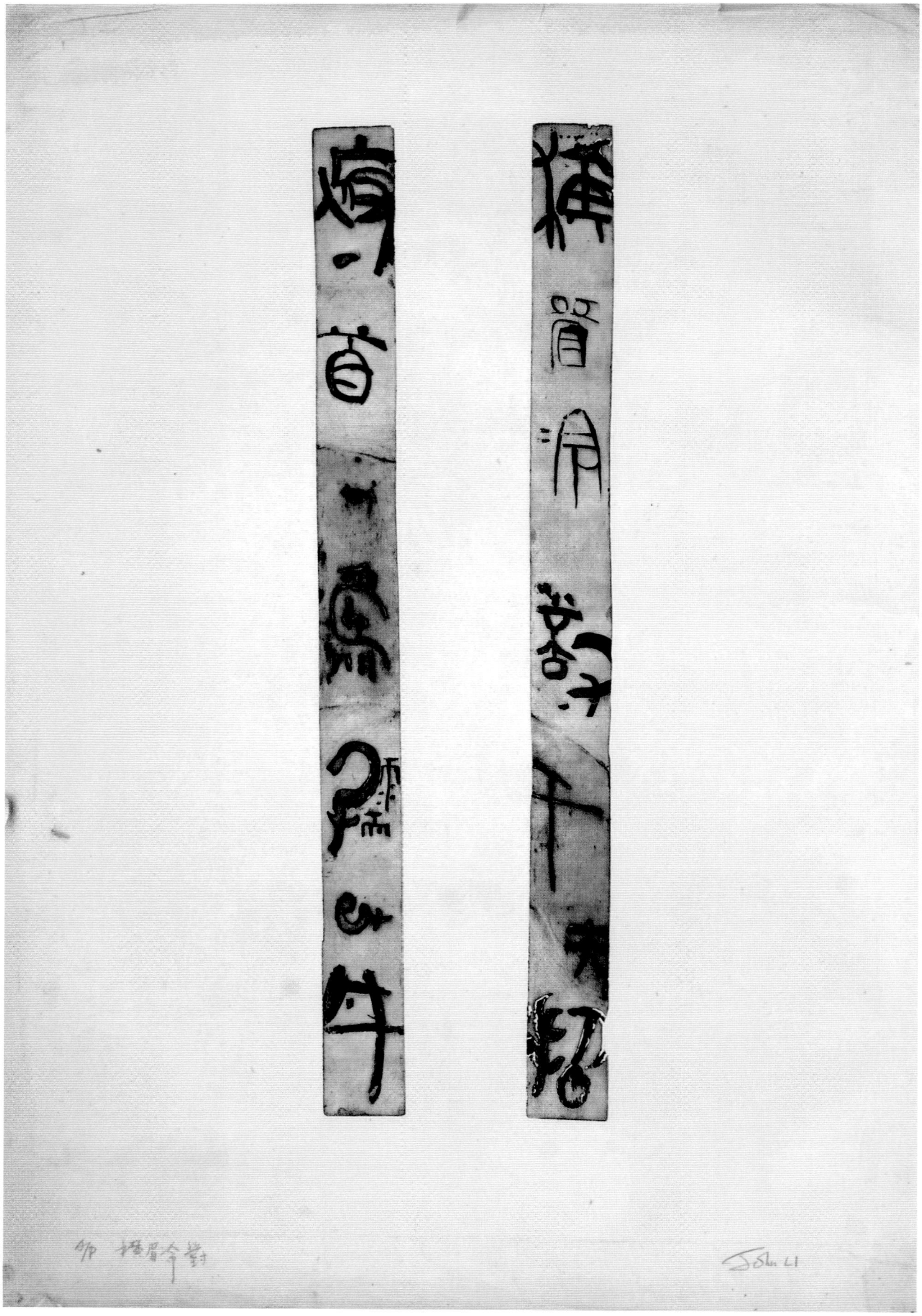

Calligraphy
Etching, 76x54 cm, 1978

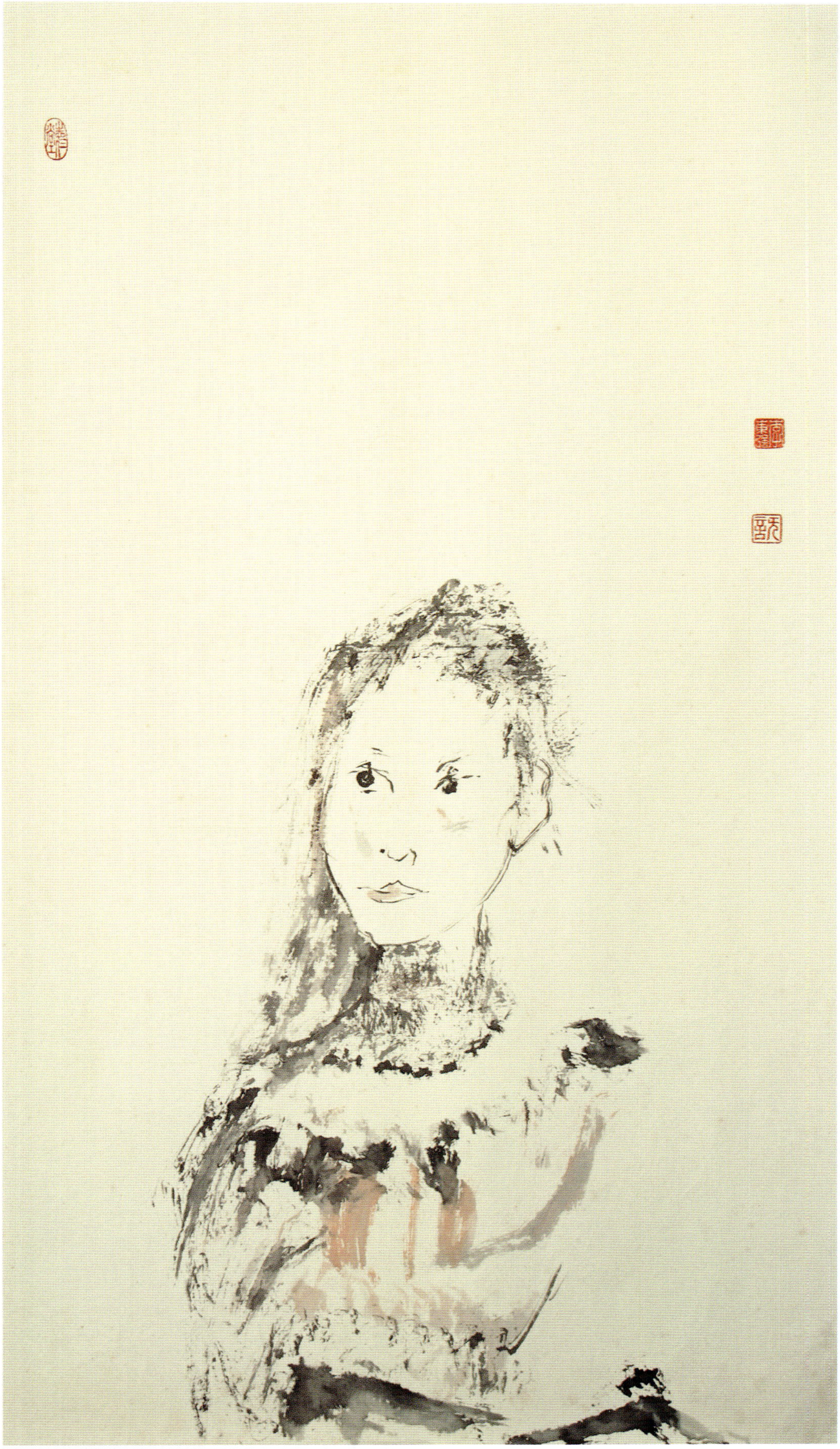

Phoenix
Ink colour on paper, 86x56 cm, 2002

Liew Come-tong

A View from the Study

By Stephanie Cheung

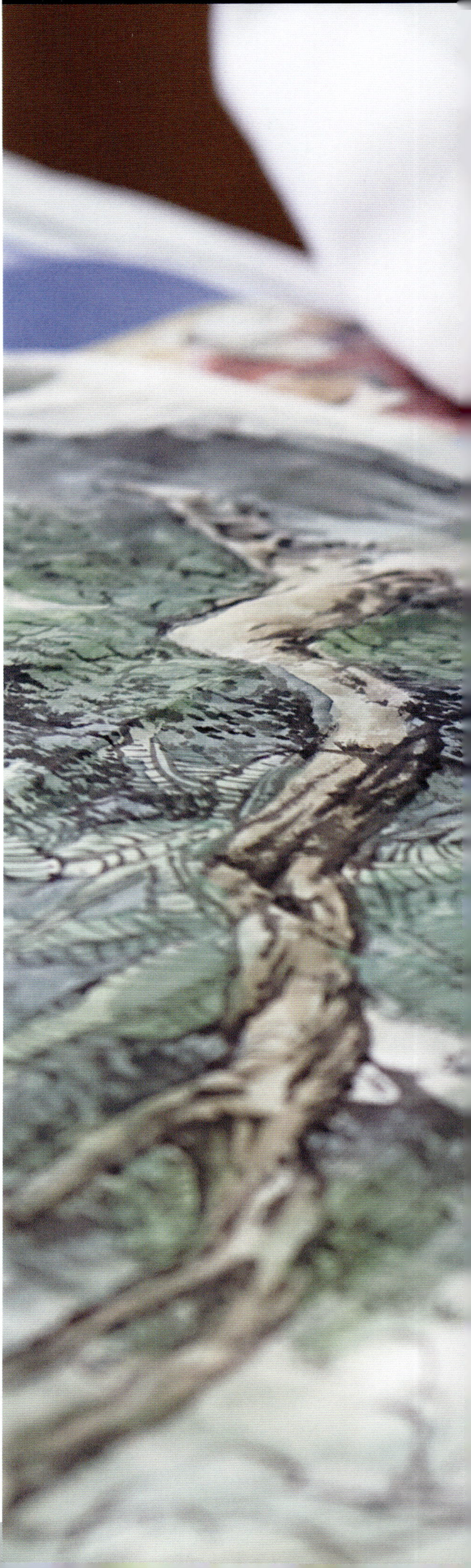

Liew Come-tong was born in Malaysia in 1949 and has been living in Hong Kong since 1972. He works in a variety of media and styles. His art has been shown in 10 solo exhibitions and more than 100 joint exhibitions, locally and overseas, and they are collected by museums, public organisations and individuals. He has published a number of monographs and is listed in *The Collectors' Dictionary of Contemporary Artists of Chinese Painting (Vol. 2), The Encyclopedia of Achievements by Chinese Artists in the World* and World VIP Centre. He also contributes art-related writings to various publications. He has taught at a number of tertiary institutions, including the School of Continuing and Professional Studies at the Chinese University of Hong Kong, where he has been teaching for over 30 years. He is currently guest lecturer for the Department of Creative Arts and Physical Education of the Hong Kong Institute of Education.

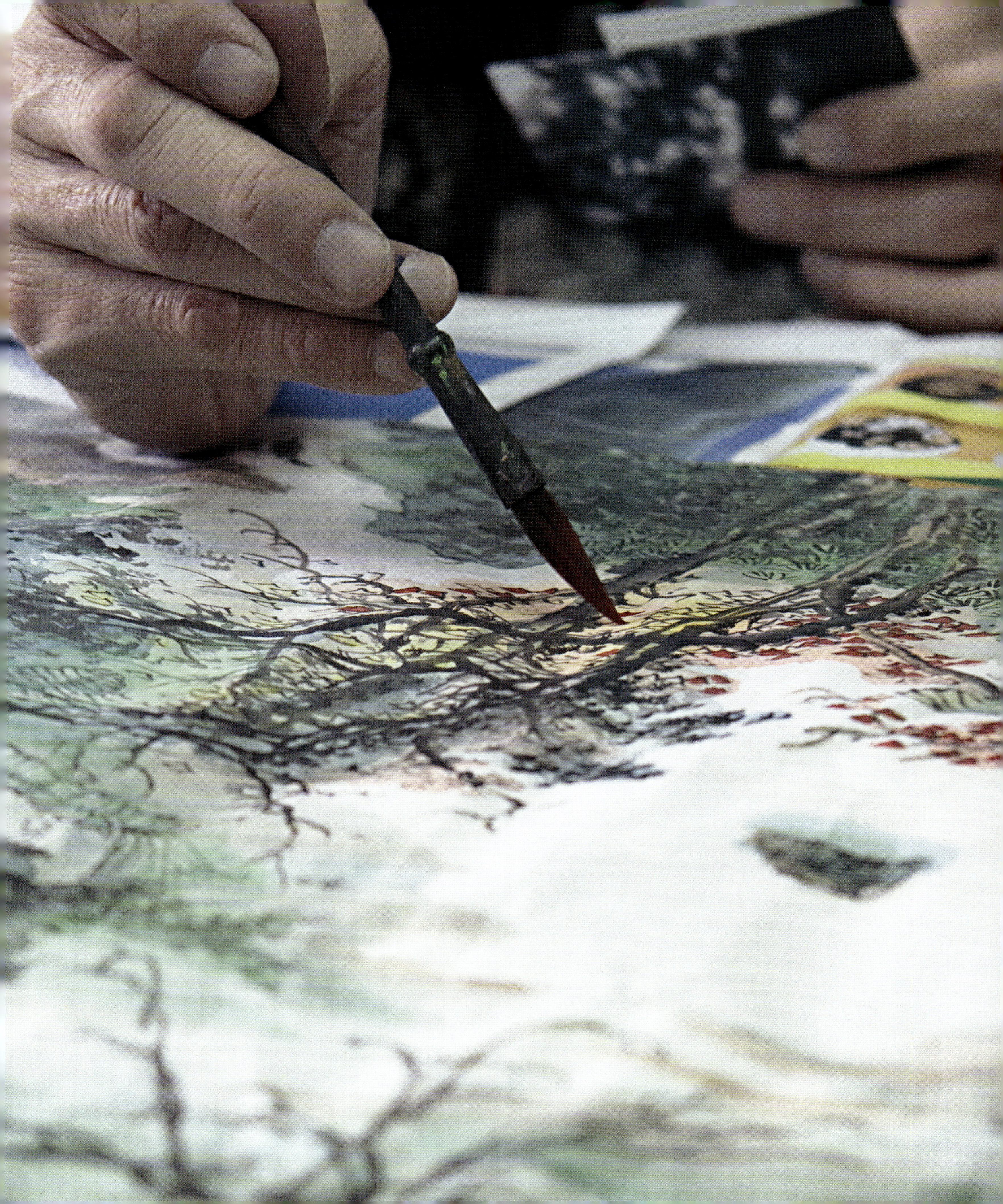

Liew Come-tong works in his study. He paints in the middle of his room. Behind him, there is a library of books covering every area, from art, literature and philosophy to history, geography and flora and fauna. The shelves are also filled with souvenirs and photographs. The pictures show Liew's mother, back in Malaysia, his travels with his wife and a group with professor Ambrose King, former president of the Chinese University of Hong Kong, professor Tay Lian-soo from its Department of Chinese and Literature and Dr Chang Chak-yan from the Department of Government and Public Administration.

On the other side of the room there is a view of the factories in Fo Tan. Liew's studio is above that horizon and overlooks the greyish buildings at a distance.

On the day of the interview the artist's desk is occupied by two works-in-progress. One of them is a forest in ink and colour. The other is a snowy mountain; its iciness conveyed with corrugated paper and sprayed paint.

These are not mundane views from outside — Liew paints his own mental landscapes.

Liew was born a third-generation Chinese migrant in Malaysia in 1949. Influenced by the diaspora and his family's strong Chinese values, Liew always wanted to understand Chinese culture from the inside out. In 1967 he made his way to Taiwan, a Chinese environment, for immersion. There he received his tertiary education in fine arts at the National Normal University.

"My teachers were renowned artists and connoisseurs of the Palace Museum," he says. "They showed me the cream of Chinese culture." In due course Liew learned the exquisite rendering of ink and colour, but more importantly, he took on the spirit of the Chinese literati.

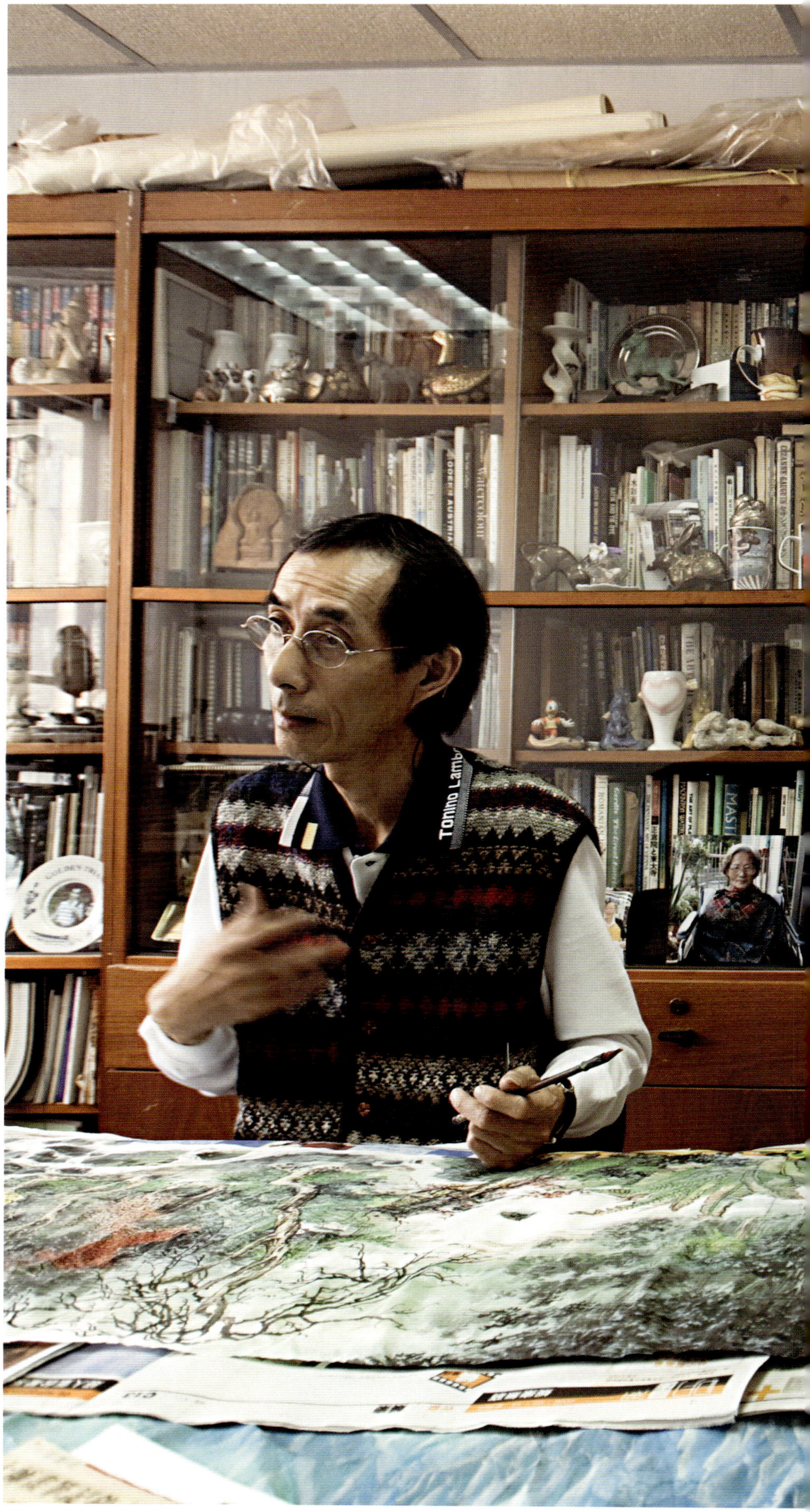

The artist paints ceaselessly in his studio

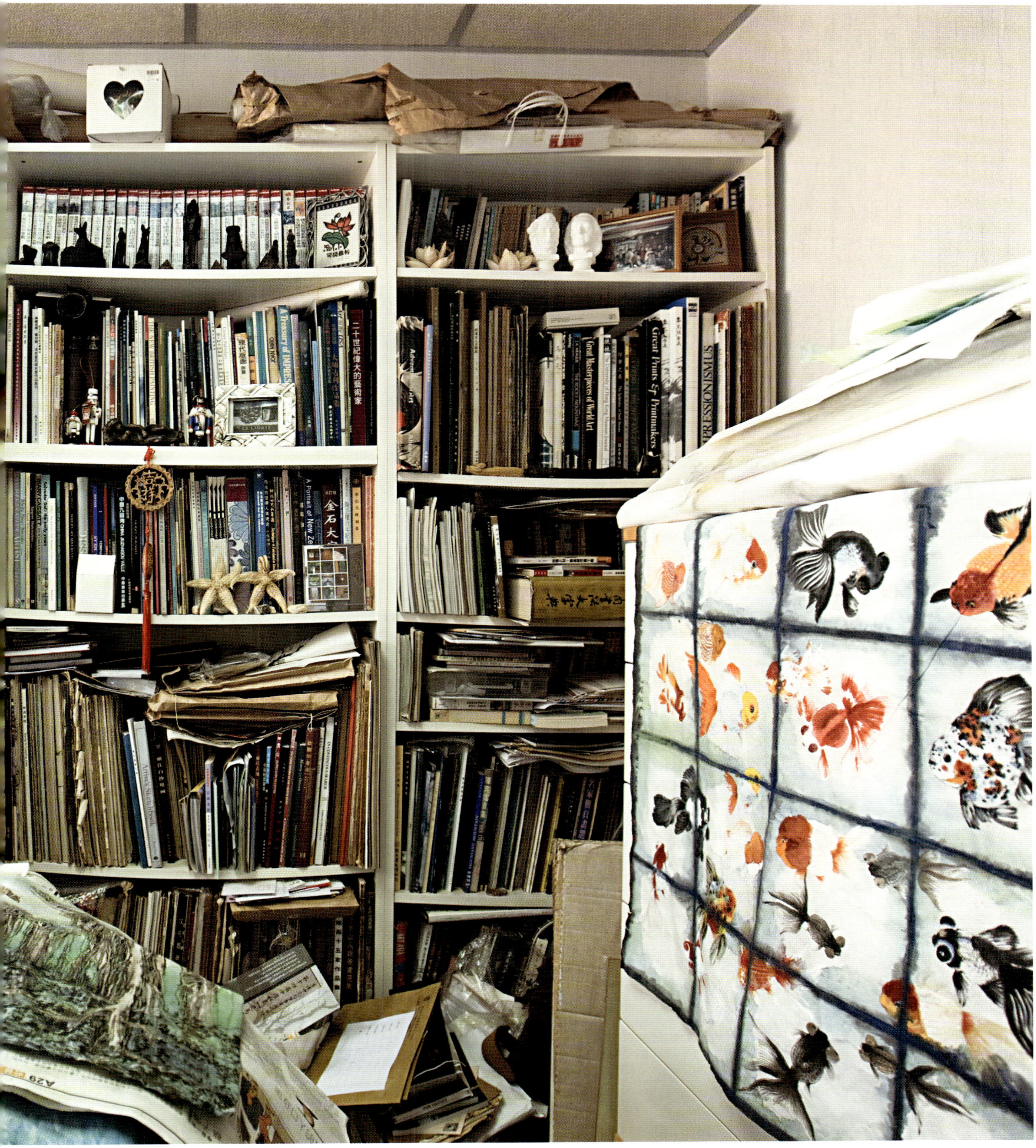

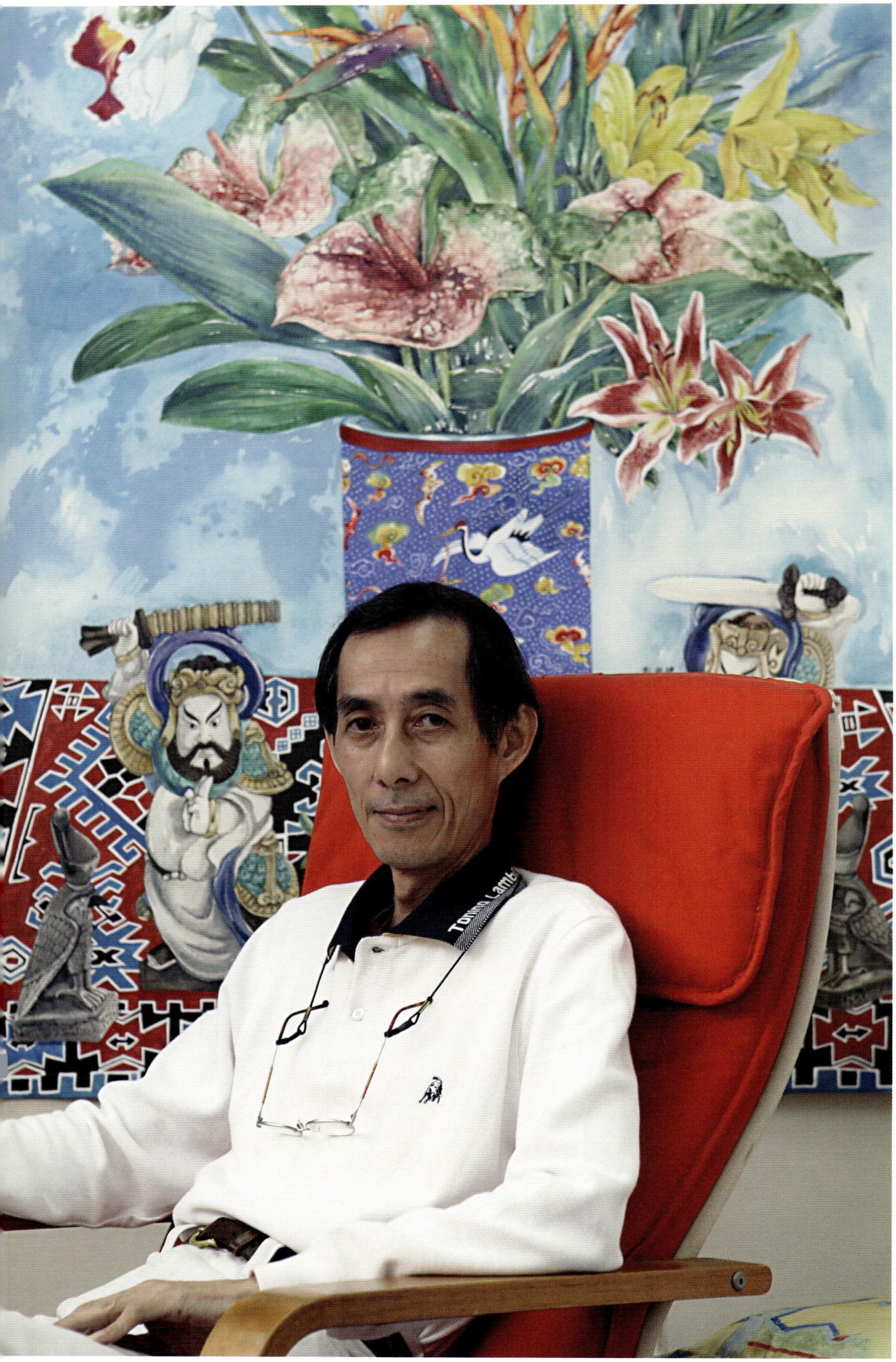

"Substance is essential," says Liew, and by 'substance' he means erudition. In a monograph of his ink paintings done in the 1980s there is a 3,000-word epilogue that details his study of the art, in which he notes that "a survey of classical paintings and artists' notes such as *Xuanhe huapu* (Xuanhe painting list), *Kugua heshang huayulu* (the sayings of Monk Bitter Melon), *Tangwang youcheng shanhsuijue* (the Right Minister of Tang on landscape), *Jing Hao Shanshuifu* (Jinghao on landscape), etc, presents the profundity, meticulousness and wisdom in the work of painters across time." [1]

To Liew the pursuit of knowledge is part of art making, and the foundation of artistic excellence. He backs his work with a library of books. He befriends scholars. He embarks on travel as a series of epistemological quests. For example in 2006 he made a trip to Anhui in China, the hometown of the celebrated Longmei inkstones. The artist, who insists that "calligraphy is more than putting brush to paper," delves into the story. "Longmei stone is also called She stone," he says. "It has earned its name ever since the Southern Tang dynasty (937-975). The material is from Mount Longmei, whose minerals… "

This breadth of knowledge broadens one's horizons. Liew sees a vast vista with Chinese vision. The artist relates his point of view to landscape painting. "The West conquers nature," he explains. "This is an act of self-centredness. The Chinese believe in the union of man and nature. Between heaven and earth, human beings have just a tiny share. We strive for harmony. We respect nature. Chinese landscape paintings are all about appreciation and respect." He points to the painted forest on his desk. "I enjoy every view of this tree. I also find beauty in another."

Besides Chinese ink painting, Liew also utilises Western-style painting, collage and three-dimensional works. He experiments with style. His ink paintings display a mastery of traditional techniques — as in the aforementioned landscape — as well as innovative methods such as the corrugated paper and spray used in the snowy mountain scene. When he works with Western media he employs realism — as in a series of cityscapes painted in the 1980s; see later discussion — and abstraction — such as the *Gates* series discussed later — at will.

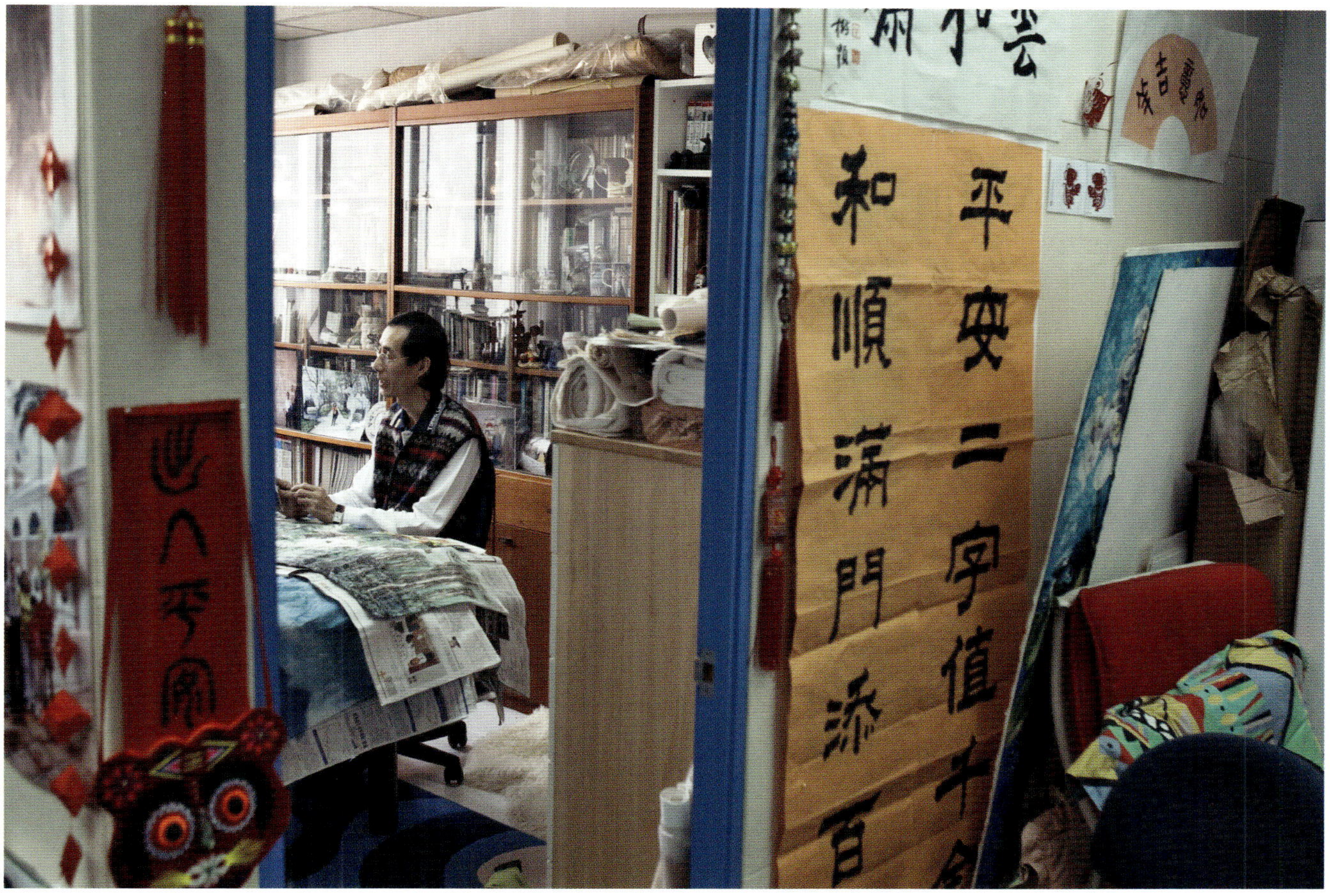
平安二字值千
和順滿門添百

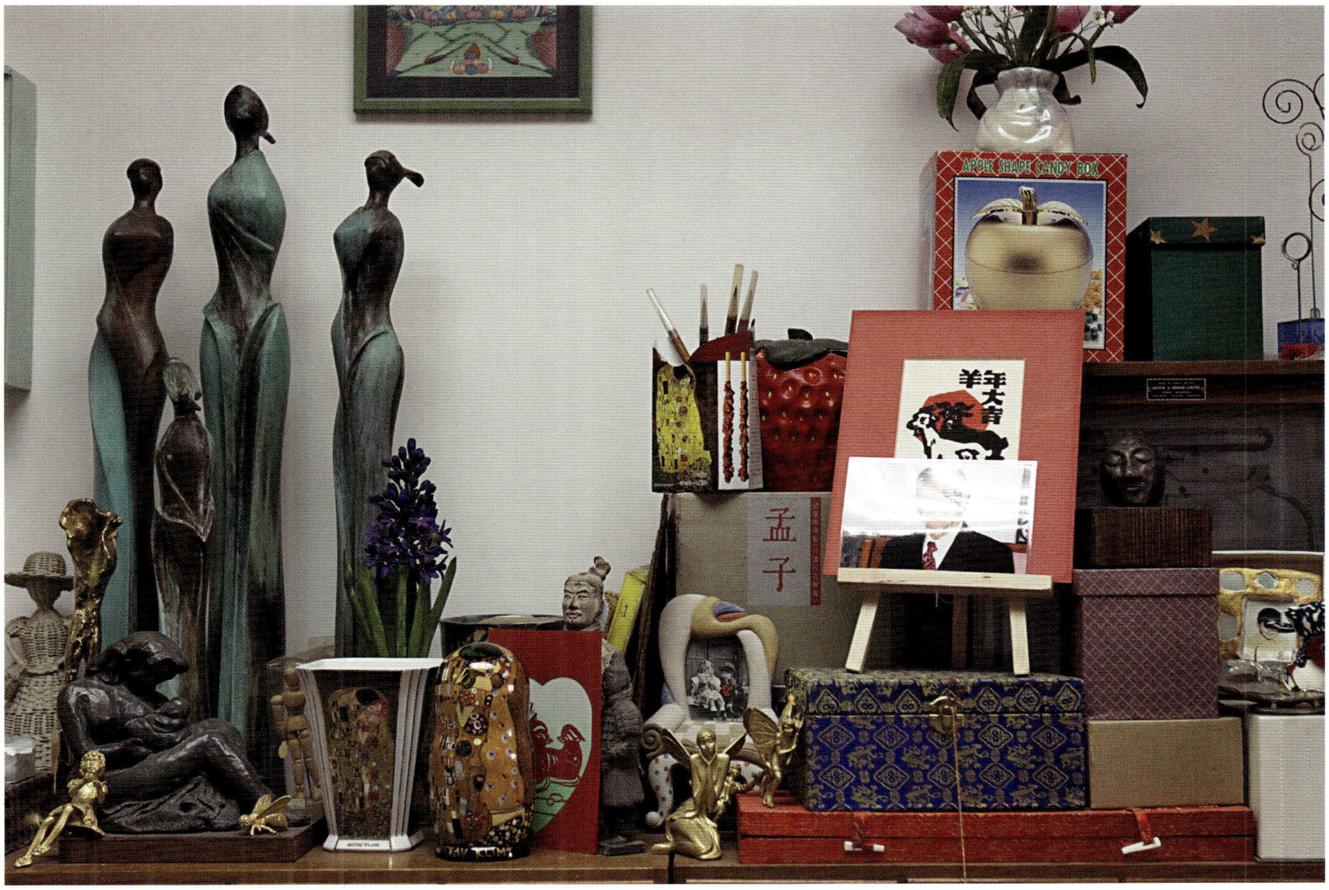
APPLE SHAPE CANDY BOX
羊年大吉
孟子

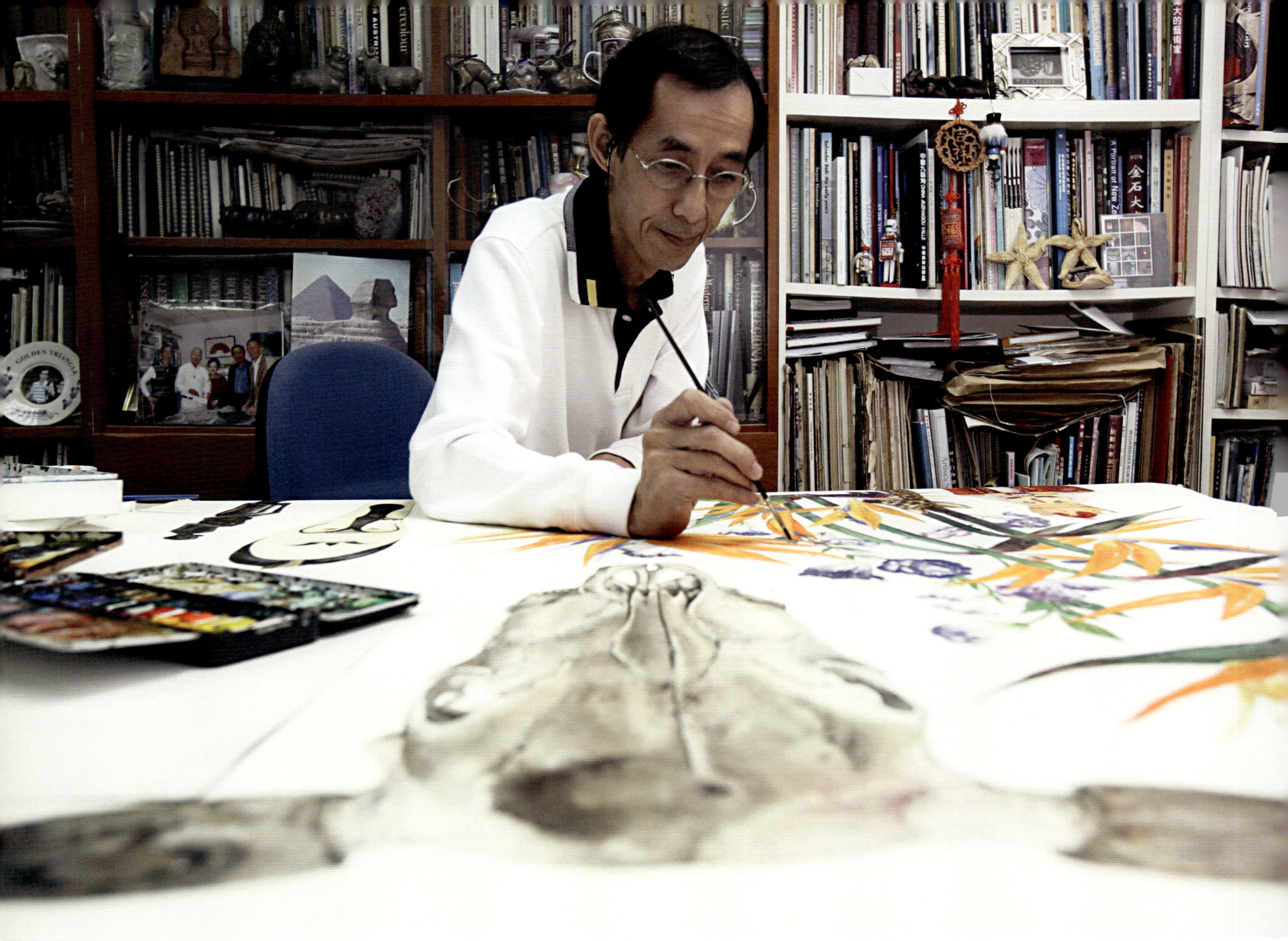

Liew's stylistic versatility is a result of his training and exposure. As a student he benefited greatly from the comprehensive curriculum at the National Taiwan Normal University. Upon graduation his move to Hong Kong (where he teaches) placed him in a much freer environment, in which he could start his cultural pilgrimage around the world. Thanks to his love of books he has a store of art knowledge that reaches across time and space. In the 1980s he contributed to a handful of Hong Kong and Taiwanese publications, covering subjects that ranged from *The Five Buffaloes*, a classic Chinese work by Tang painter Han Huang, to Pop Art such as Richard Hamilton's *Just What is It that Makes Today's Homes So Different, So Appealing?* [2] Liew embraces all these with open-mindedness. "There is no point in limiting oneself to one style — this is bigotry," he opines.

The night before this interview, Liew was working on an article for *Hong Kong Literature Monthly*. It was a request from the editorial staff on the question of where inspiration comes from.[3] The artist's opinion is that "when a sensitive person is absorbed in something, inspiration comes naturally". His own case is summarised in the introduction to a monograph of watercolours and drawings that were produced in the two decades leading up to the volume's publication in 1997. Called *The Gates*, the series reflects

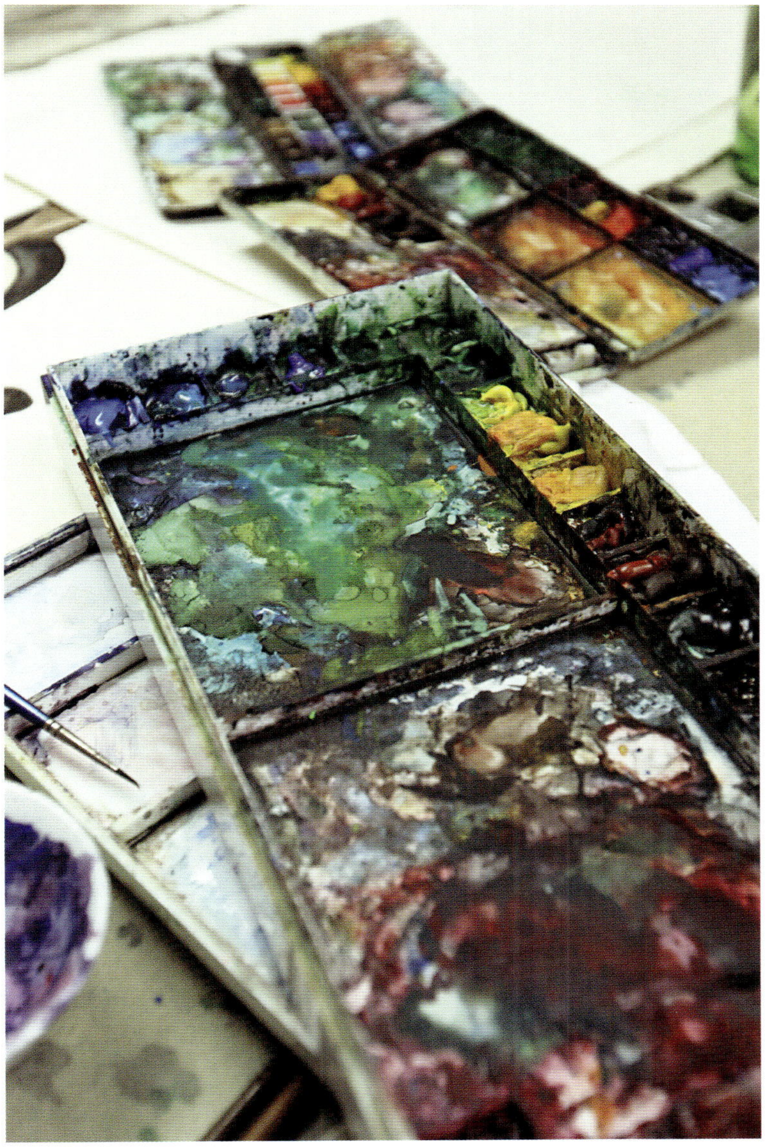

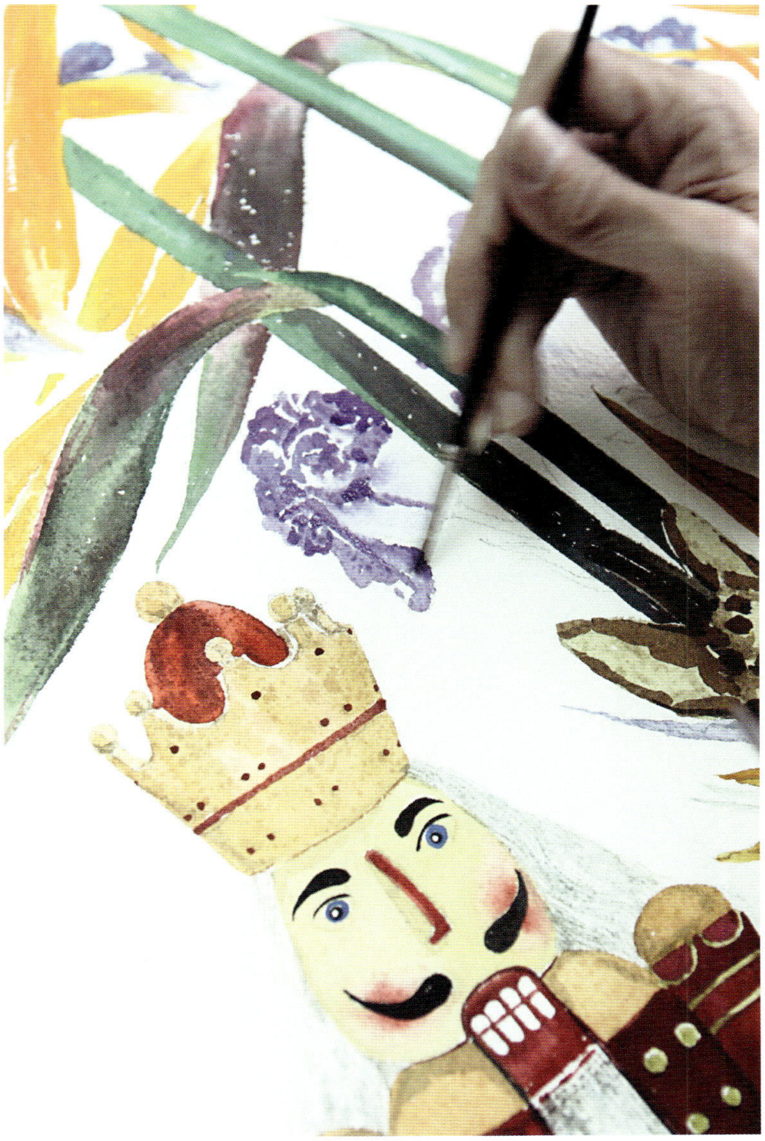

the claustrophobia in the psyche of Hong Kong people in the 1970s, in which temples become symbols of spirituality, where people seek refuge. "In the 1980s, new buildings sprouted everywhere in Hong Kong. Glass walls replaced historical buildings," Liew says. "On the reflective surfaces, the overlapping of reality and illusion highlights the city's rapid transformation". [4] On 30 June 1997, the eve of Hong Kong's return to China, he marked the date with a collage of newspapers headlines, a calendar page, the day's tickets and a pasted inscription by professor Jao Tsung-i, guru of Chinese studies. The text reads: "a historical moment".

Art is an artist's meditation on the environment.

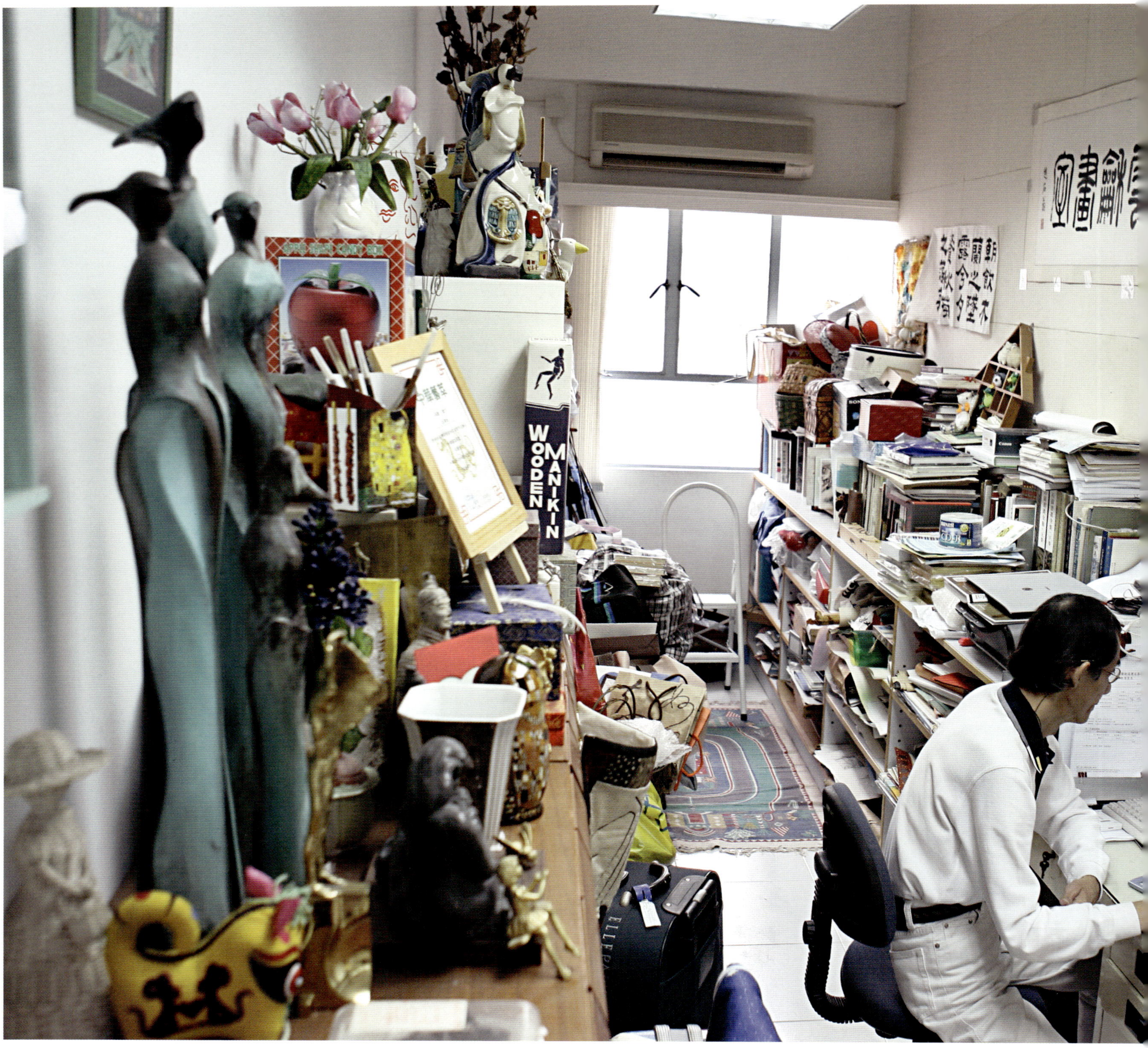
WOODEN
MANIKIN

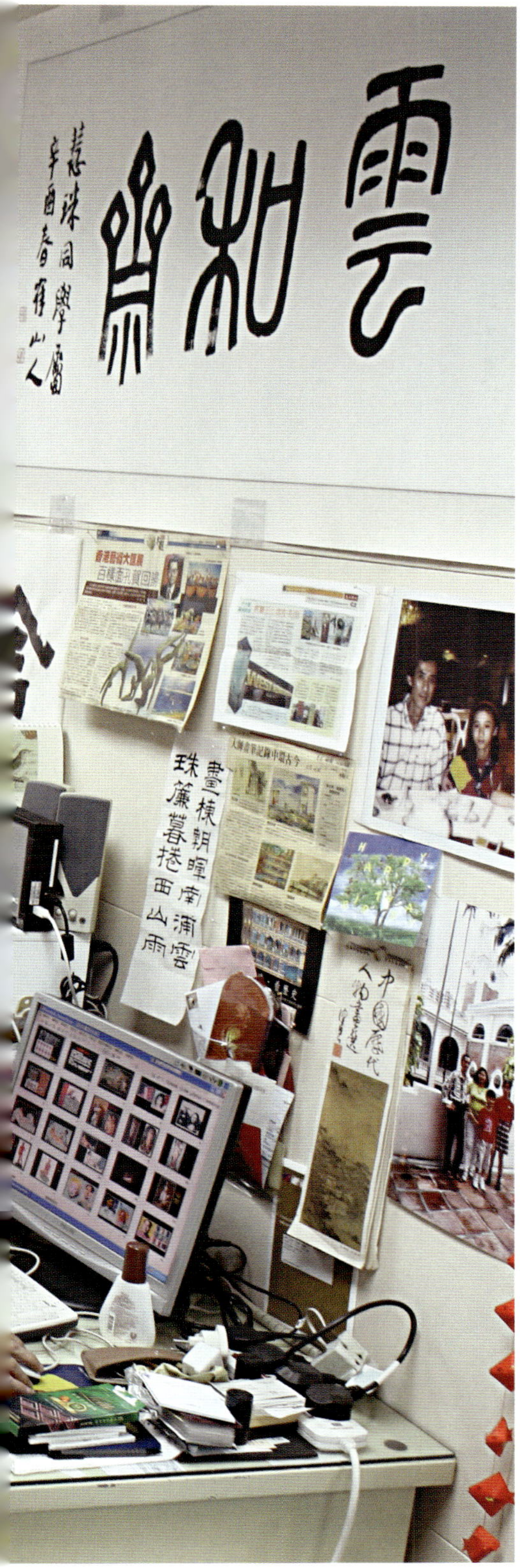

Liew thinks that the contemplative artist should have a clear mind, unbothered by earthly trivia, so Chinese painters prepare for painting: they tidy their tables, clean their windows and make the ink; all are rituals of serenity.

Except for a post as guest lecturer at the School of Continuing and Professional Studies of the Chinese University of Hong Kong, and at the Hong Kong Institute of Education, Liew currently spends his time reading and painting. In 1990 his recovery from cancer prompted a new outlook. "When I took paintings for mounting, the person at the shop said, 'Your paintings were all very dull. Why have they turned colourful?'" he remembers. Illness reminded him of the frailty of life, so now he looks for the eternal. "Do you know Leonardo da Vinci? Do you know Vincent van Gogh?" he asks. "We don't know them in person but we all know their work." In an article about Paul Gauguin's *Where Do We Come From? Who Are We? Where Are We Going?*, written in 1993, he makes it clear. "Life is short. A person's spirit lives on in his creation. Artists live on in their work," he writes.[5]

During the interview Liew takes a figurine from his bookshelf. It is an old work of his: a little seated figure, glazed in ochre. "This is well done. I like the shape," he says. He looks at his work with a satisfied smile.

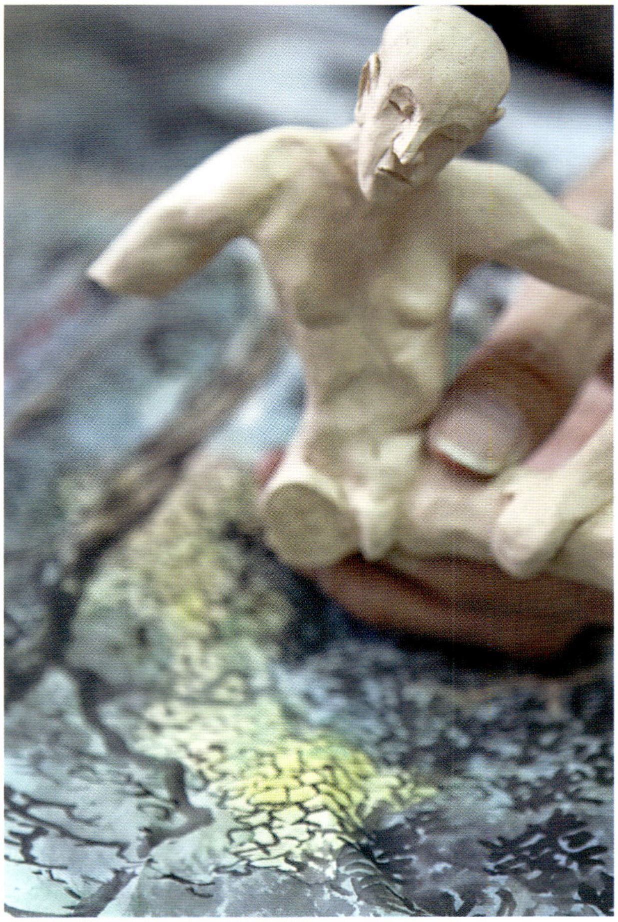

1. Ink Painting by Liew Come-tong, Liew Come-tong, Artistic Gallery, Hong Kong, 1991.

2. Liew has published articles in Hong Kong newspapers such as Oriental Daily, Overseas Chinese Daily News, Wenweipo, Mingpao and Mingpao Monthly; and in Taiwanese publications that include Artist Magazine and The World of Collectors. The articles cover his thoughts on Chinese and western art, his reviews of local exhibitions and his ideas about art education. A selection of 173 articles is collected in Art Criticism East and West (Hong Kong, 1997).

3. 'Yishi linggan helai', Liew Come-tong, in Hong Kong Literature Monthly, No, 3, Vol. 3, April 2008, pp. 49-52, 97-98 and back cover.

4. Watercolour Paintings and Drawings by Liew Come-tong, Liew Come-tong, Hong Kong, 1997.

5. Art Criticism East and West, Liew Come-tong, Hong Kong, 1997, p. 83.

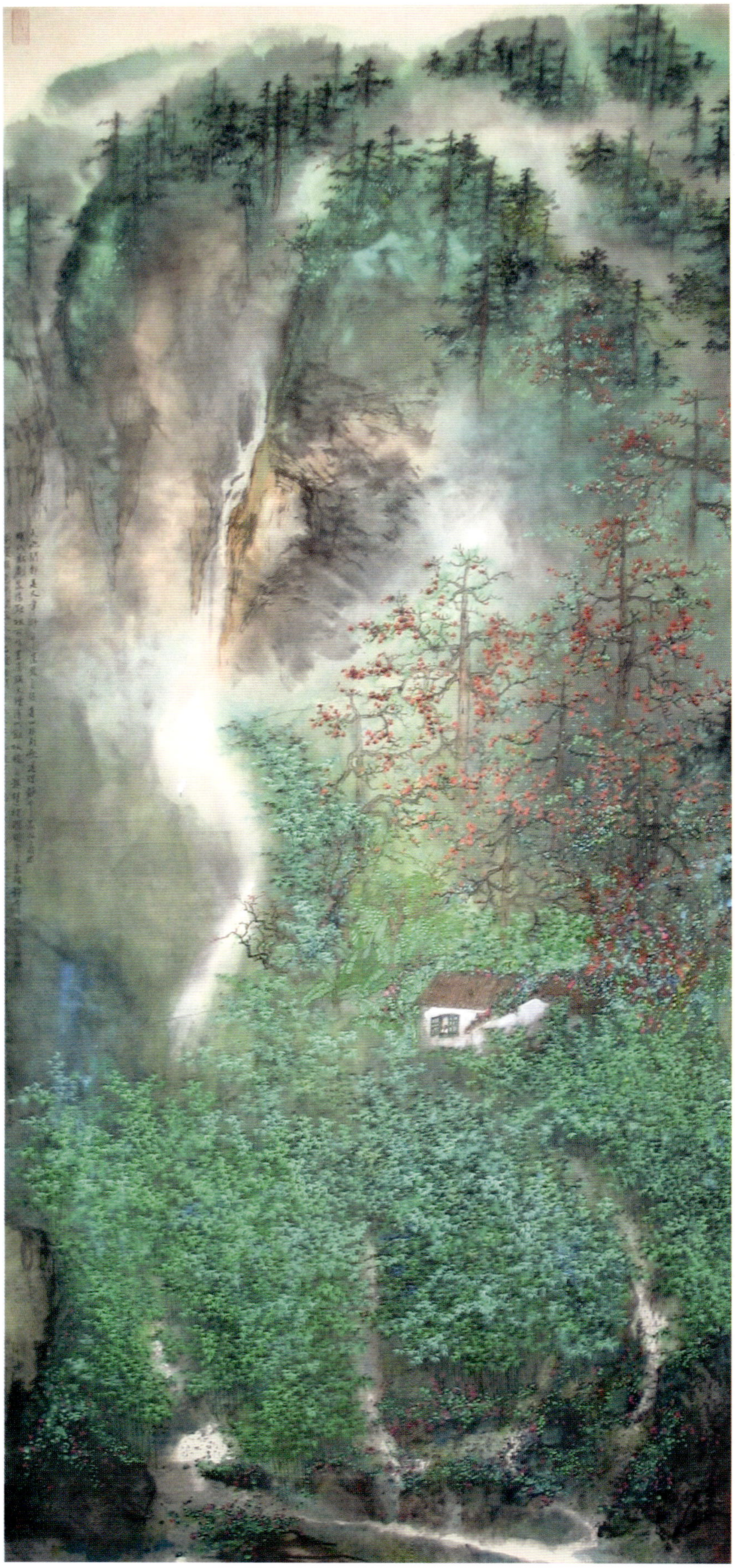

Retirement Lodge
Ink painting, 191x90.5 cm, 2001

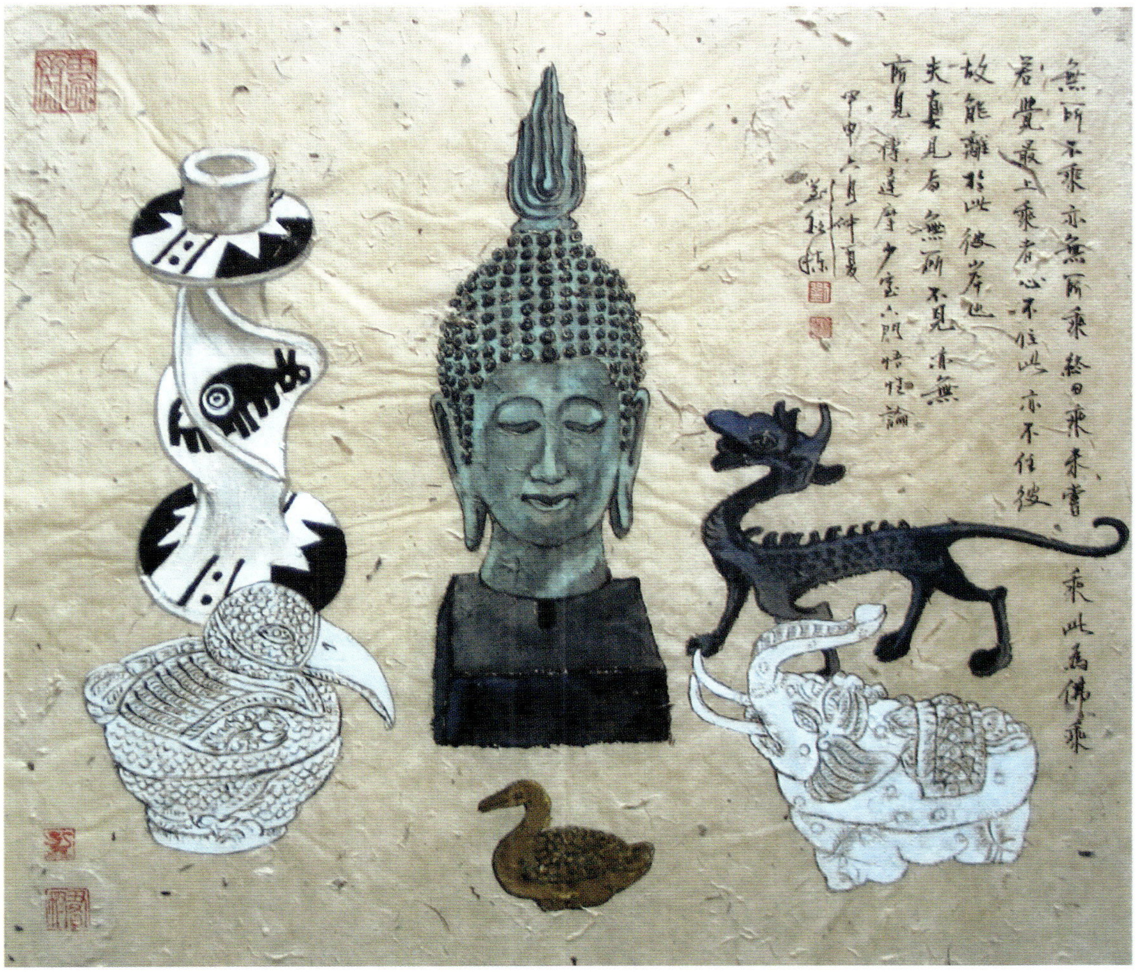

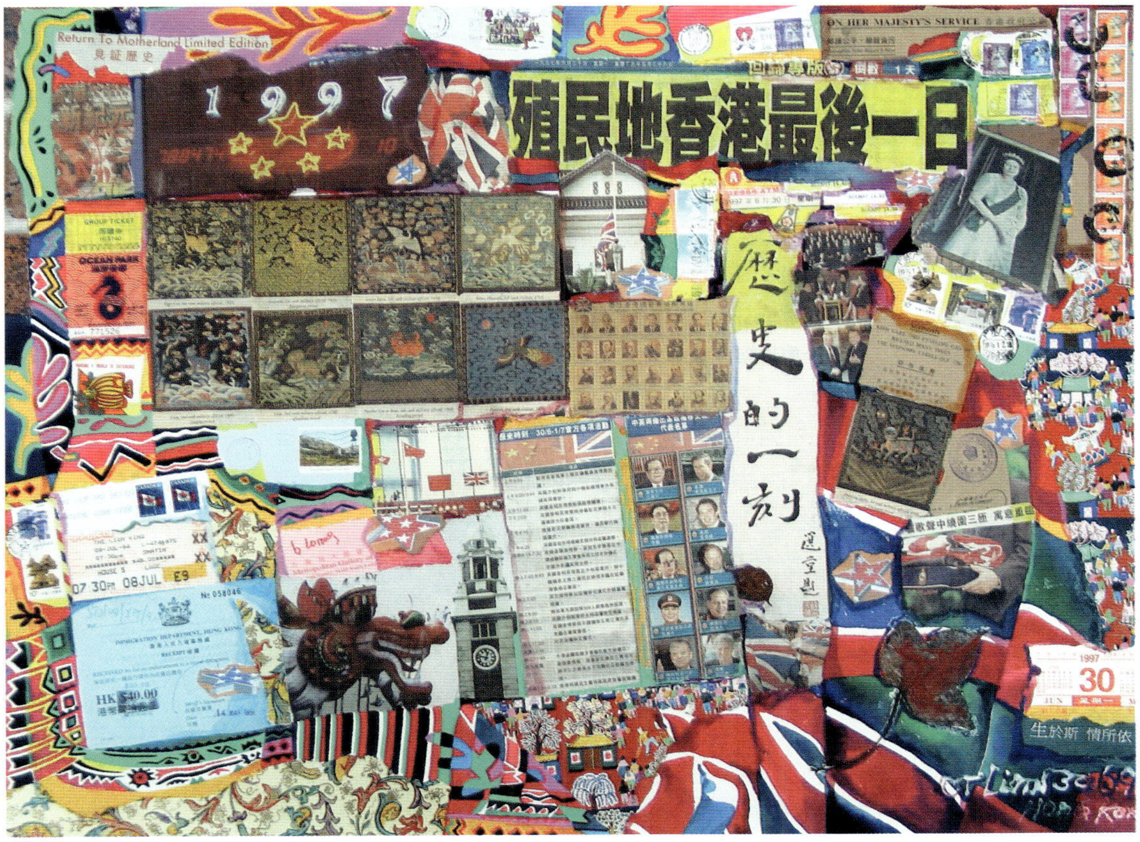

(Above) Still life
Ink painting, 55x70 cm, 2004

(Bottom) The 30th Day of June, 1997 (I)
Collage, mixed-media, 56x76 cm, 1997

Leung Mee-ping

The Value of a Pause

By Livia B Garcia

Leung Mee-ping was born in Hong Kong. She graduated from the L'Ecole Nationale Superieure des Beaux Arts in Paris in 1991 and received her Master's in fine art from the California Institute of the Arts, USA in 2000. Media that Leung adopts include mixed media, video, multi-media installations and site-specific projects. She is a lecturer at Acdemy of Visual Arts of the Hong Kong Baptist University. Exhibitions that she has taken part include the Hair Dialogue Installation Art Exhibition at the Hong Kong Museum of Art in 2006 and Reversing Horizons at the Shanghai Museum of Modern Art in 2007.

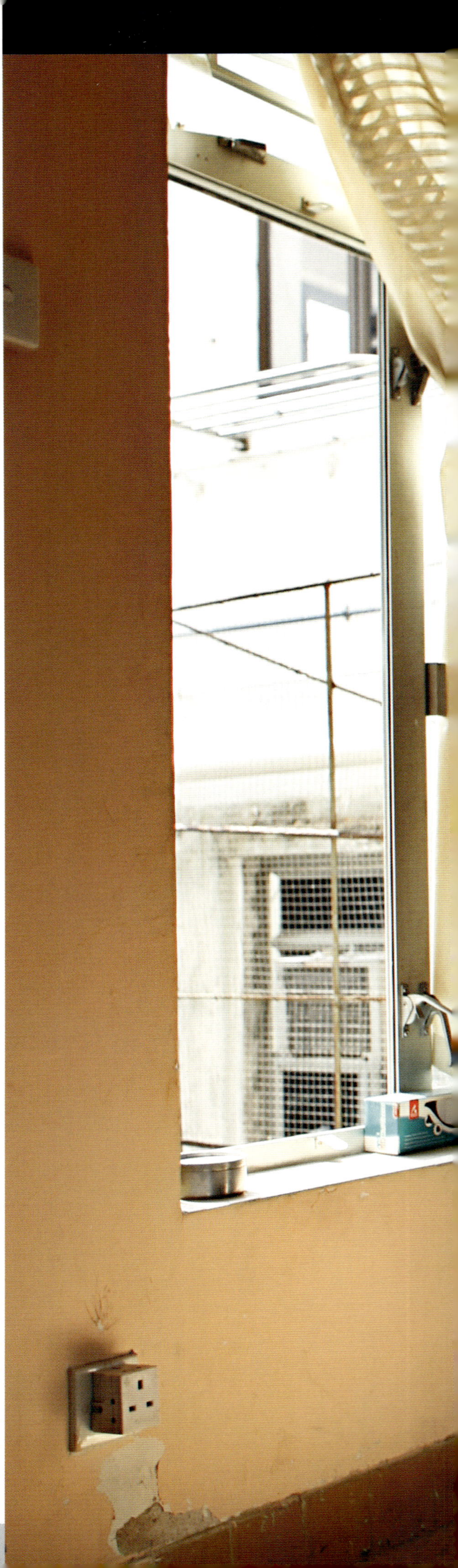

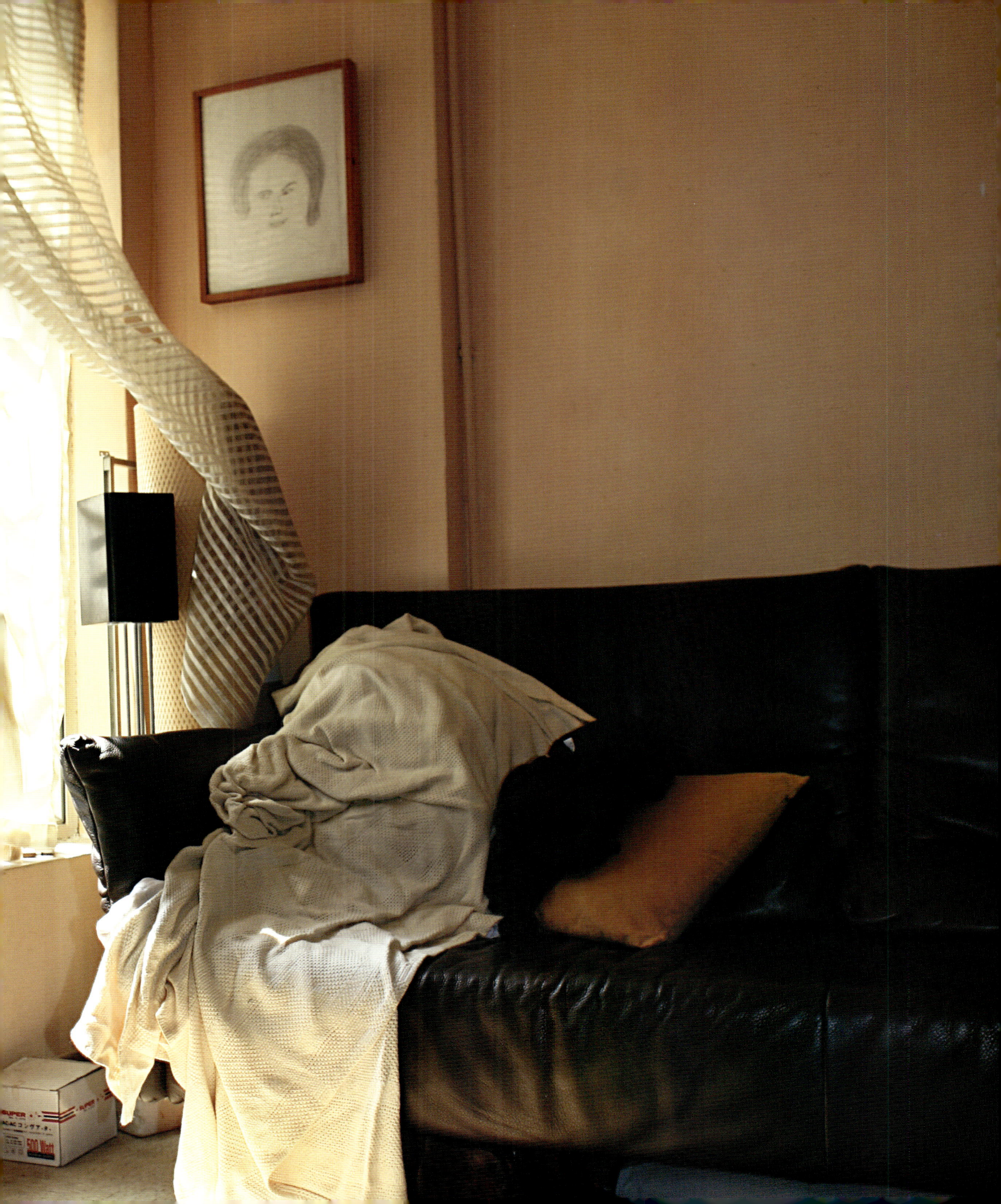

"My views on studios are very contradictory. I hope that my studio is not piled up with too many things. I want it to be empty with a big chair or table right in the centre. I don't care too much whether I can see hills or water from there, but it would be ideal if I could see vehicles on the streets. Actually the kind of studio that I have in mind is not a working space or a place to live in; it might as well be described as a pre-studio for the brewing of works and for people to pause in. It is a place that no one can invade."

In reality, the studio space of Leung Mee-ping is actually where she lives. "All along this place has been neither here nor there. It didn't start off as a studio. I have never rented any place in Hong Kong as a studio and I don't want to find a place where I have to travel to deliberately, as this would only make me feel troubled. Actually my working style has always been very free. Nowadays I go and work at my mother's place from time to time, but an ideal

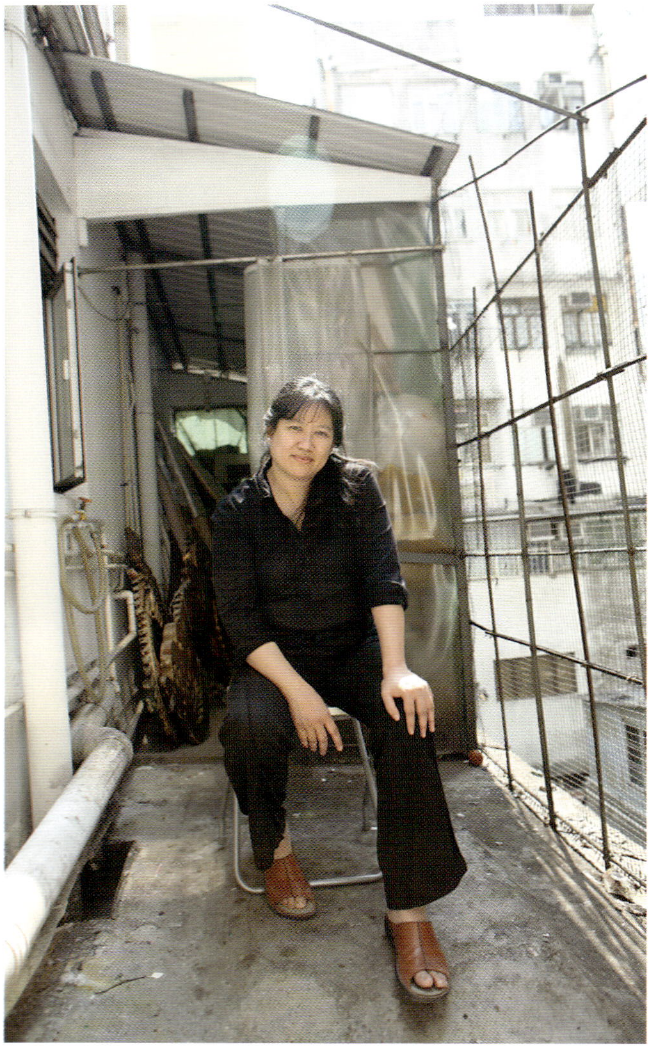

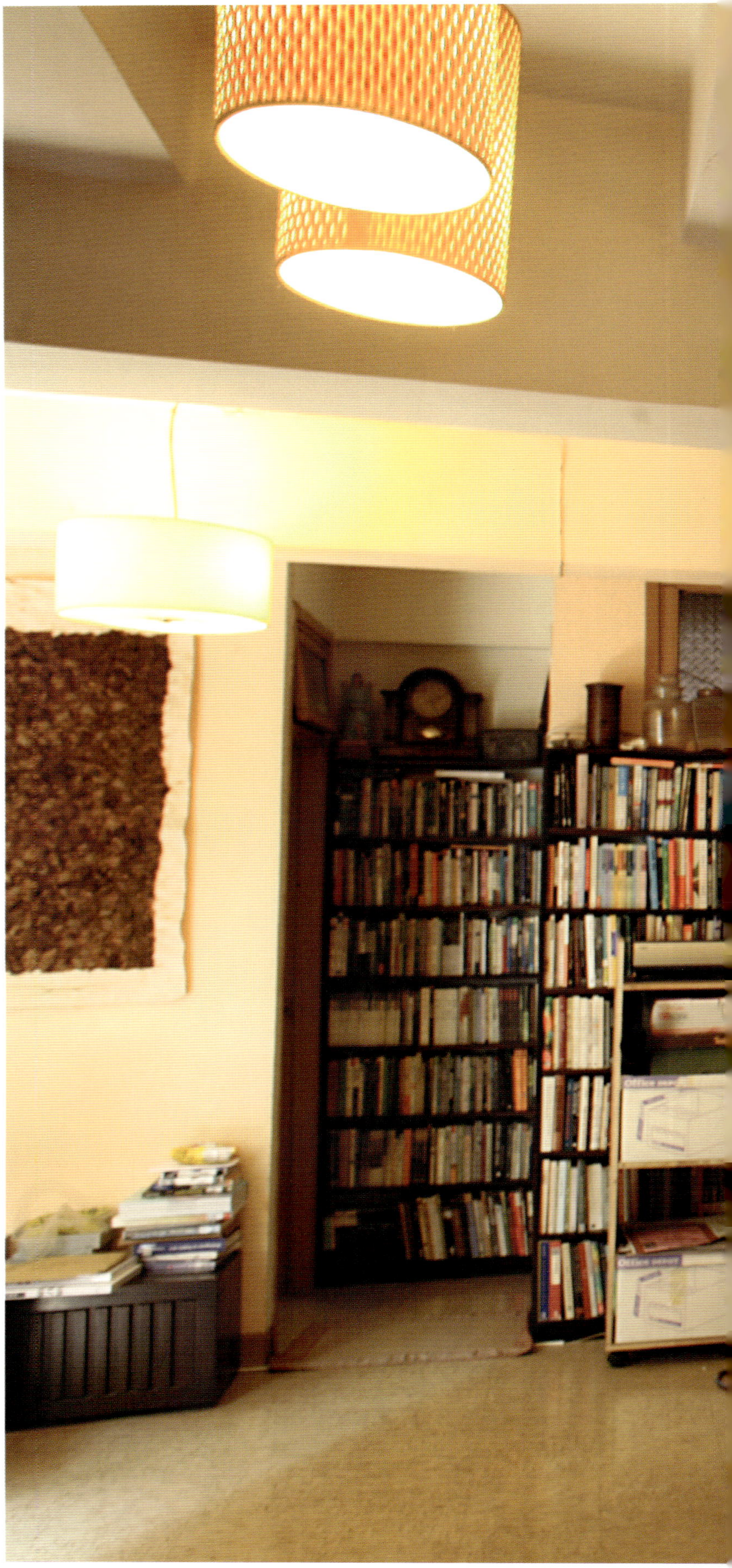

Reading enriches one's life experience which breeds creativity

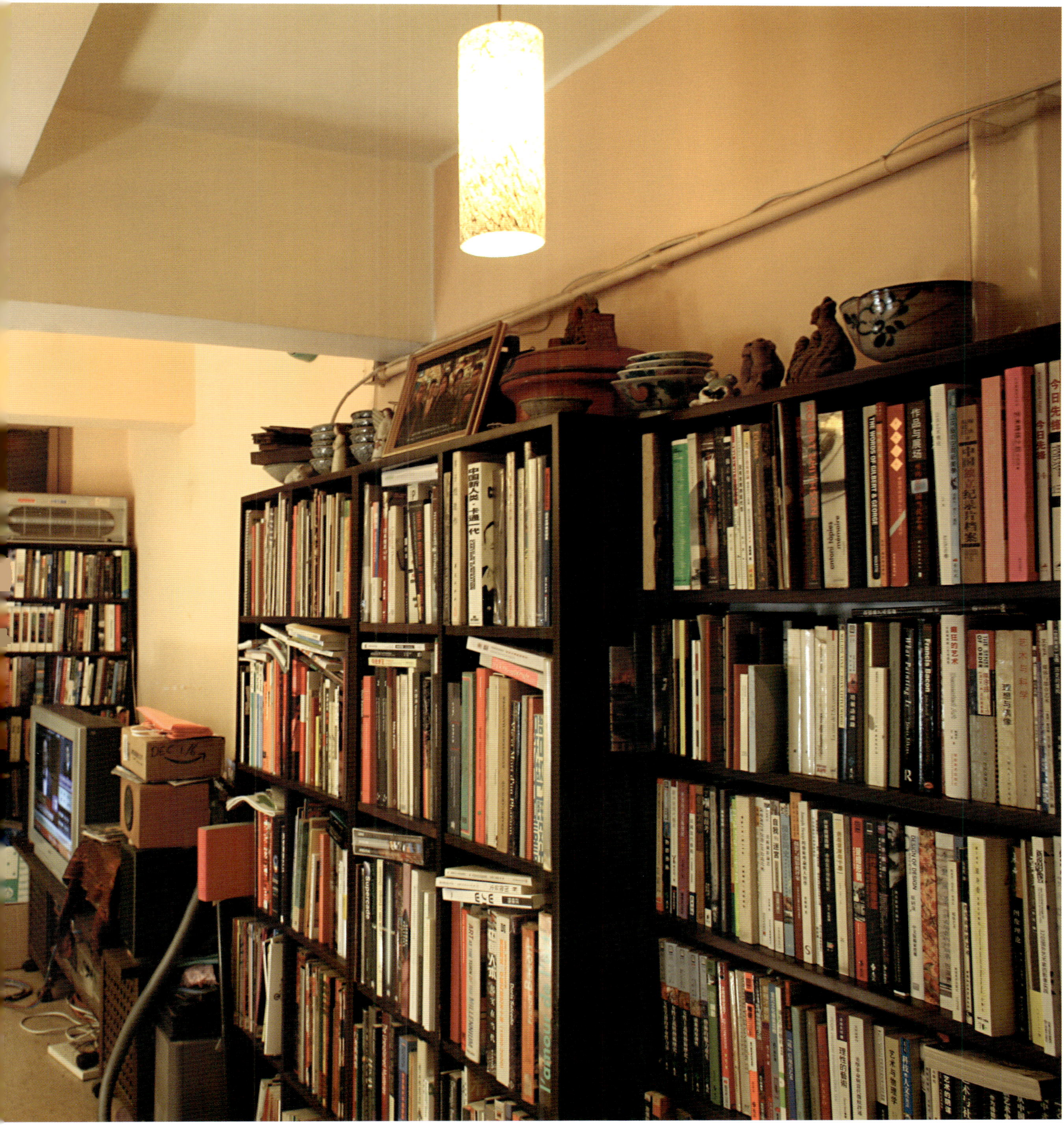

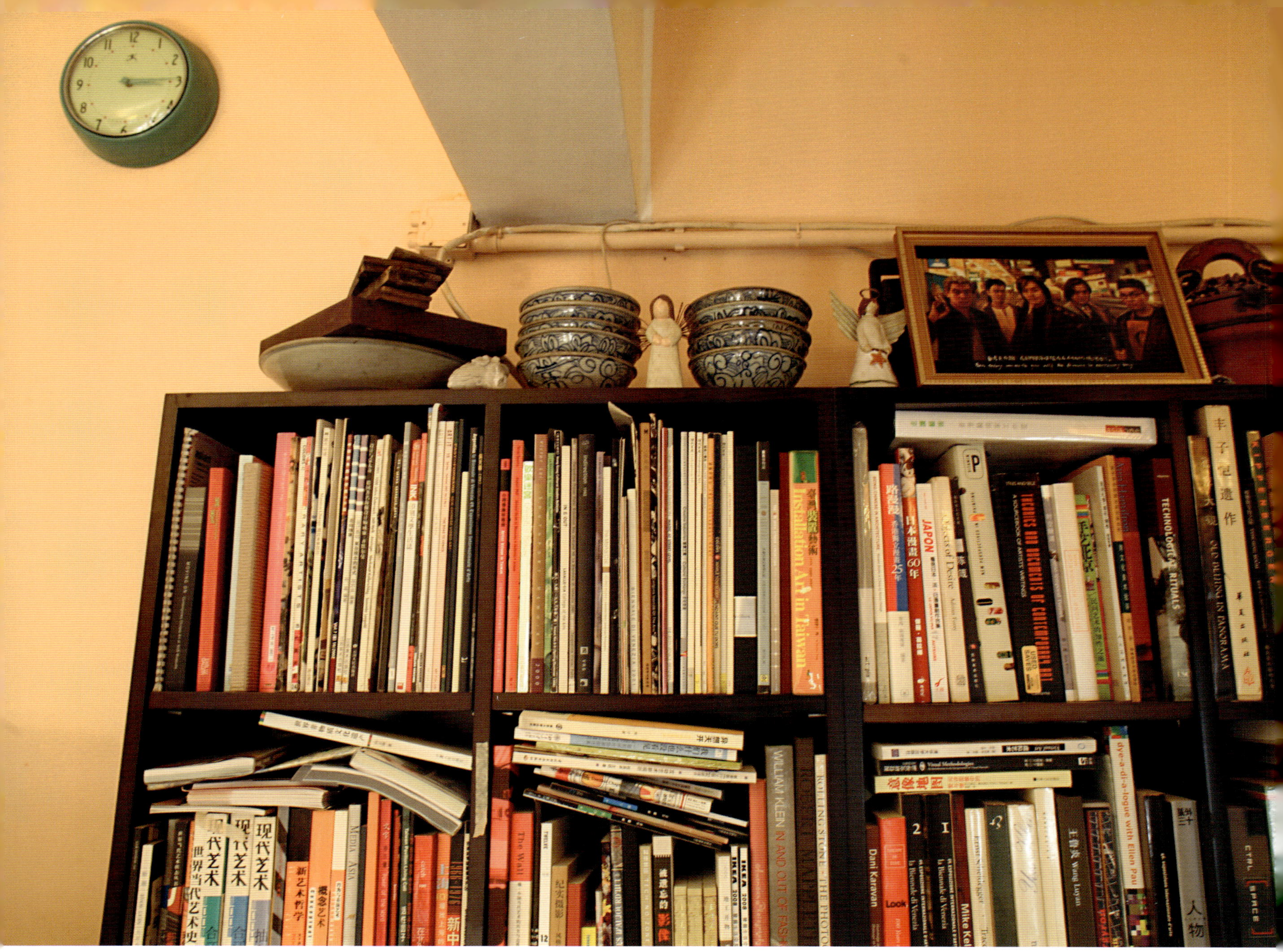

臺灣裝置藝術
Installation Art in Taiwan
JAPON
日本漫畫60年
Dani Karavan
WILLIAM KLEIN
现代艺术

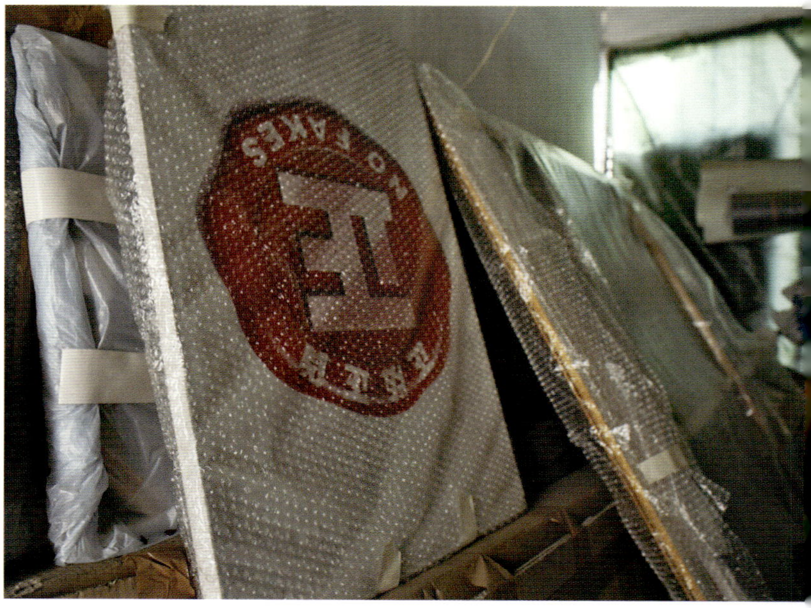

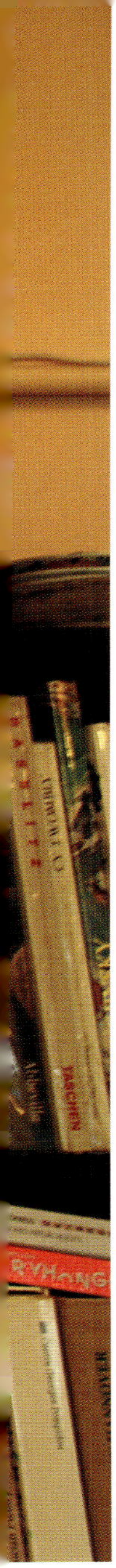

studio would be best not as part of home, but next door to home."

Leung told me that the unit right next door to hers has been left unoccupied. It is owned by an old lady and normally it would be used to store things. Leung has always hoped that she could buy it, and she once wrote to the old lady asking her to take a look at her artwork. They would chat when they ran into each other, and the old lady would ask, "Where are you storing all your things now? I often see you running up and down." But there seemed never to be any sign of her selling the place. Leung thinks this is a pity, as the old lady does not really care about it at all. She owns a few other shops on the ground floor. Moreover, her children have no intention of selling the properties either. Leung says, "I wish I could just drill a hole in the wall and simply climb in from there!"

Leung's home or 'studio' is located in an old building in Mongkok. There are two rooms in the unit and each room is around 150 sq-ft which is rather spacious compared to flats in new buildings. One of the rooms is used as a bedroom and office while the other one is used for film cutting and storage. Leung points out that she does not like places to be too lively. However she likes to mingle in crowds. She would wander in the streets when she got tired of working on her art pieces. "The sense of deep thoughts strengthen when you become part of a busy street," she says. "When I am back in the studio and lock the door, I get silence immediately. Of course with shops within a reasonable distance it is always easy to buy any material I need." There is an outdoor terrace of more than 100 sq-ft, half of it covered and the other half open. This is where she can store her work. From inside the flat, one has to climb through a window to get to this landing. "My works are kept here and there. For example I have collected pairs of big dragons and phoenix from closed-down Chinese restaurants, and they are now kept in a vacant office space in Fotan that belongs to my friend," she says. "Another example is a boat that I made, which is covered with mirrors. Someone who specialises in the business of decorating shopping malls liked it and decided to keep it."

"Luckily, most of my works are rather conceptual. As such, most of the time the planning part becomes crucial. It is then followed by installation at the exhibition site. Some works are exhibited around the world, so I don't need to store too much material at home."

Leung started teaching at the Hong Kong Baptist University in September 2007. The courses that she teaches include 'Visual Culture and Arts' and 'Concepts in Contemporary Arts'. She also teaches drawing, the foundation concepts of design and career preparation workshops. Courses that are coming up soon are 'Creative Thinking and Application' and 'Hong Kong Industries of Handcraft: Tradition and Transformation'. Leung says, "About revitalising Hong Kong industries of handcraft — we are planning to use diagrams to break down elements of some traditional handcrafts, such as the construction of reinforced steel in concrete; structural joining methods in buildings that do not require the use of bolts and nuts; the making of lanterns and so on. All these will be included in a book, ultimately. I hope that these handicrafts can be preserved and that at the same time, students can incorporate these handcraft tradition into their art making."

"I hope that I can make suggestions at a time when schools are not yet too burdened, so that they can employ suitable teachers early," she continues. "This would bring different voices into the school. I also hope to revolutionise the admission interview. Since secondary schools always follow the entry standards and requirements of universities, they will never respond if there are no changes made to the tertiary institutions. Take, for example, the subject of drawing, which has been removed from the admission examination for the Hong Kong Baptist University this year. I think that students can learn drawing after they have entered university. What's more important is how they use their own imagination to express their perception of art, and that they not simply just bring along a rigid portfolio."

There is a story about one candidate that left a strong impression on Leung. "This candidate had brought a lot of drawings on plaster figures to the interview," she recalls. "Amongst

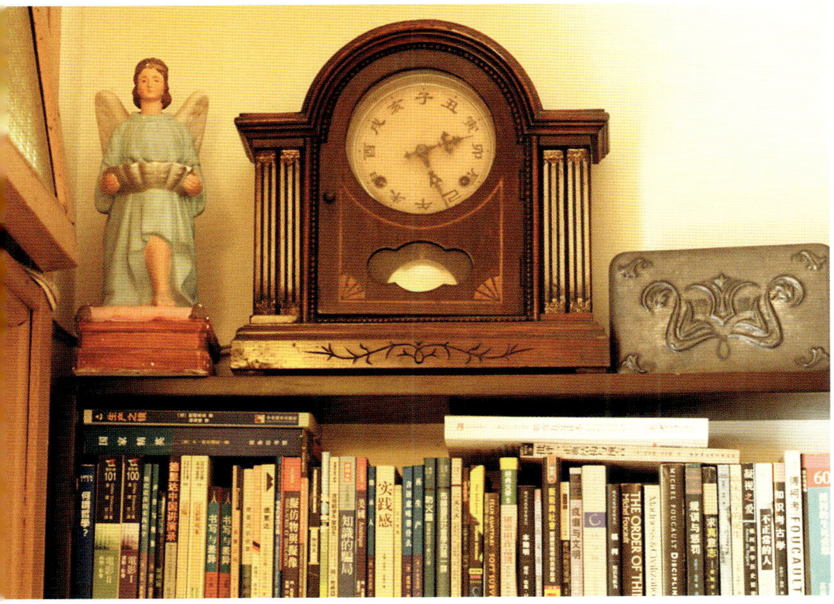

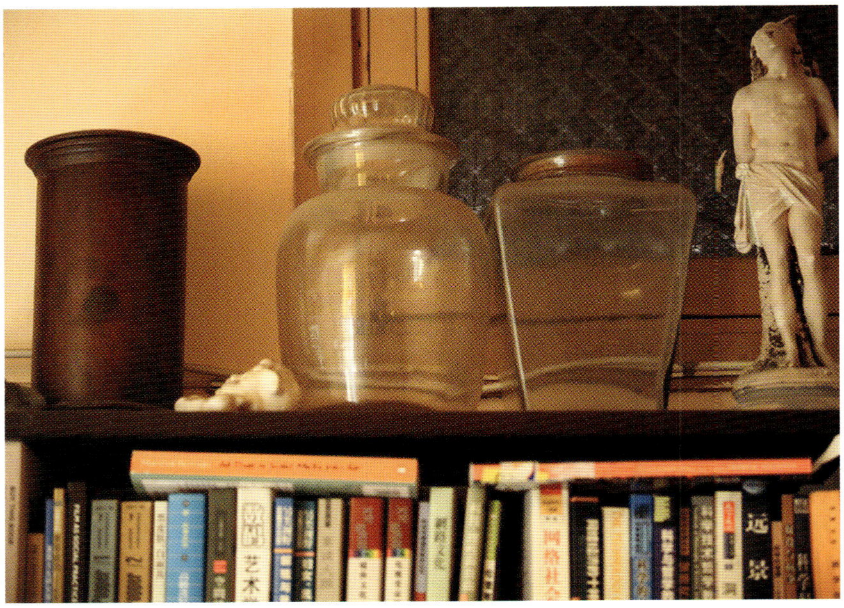

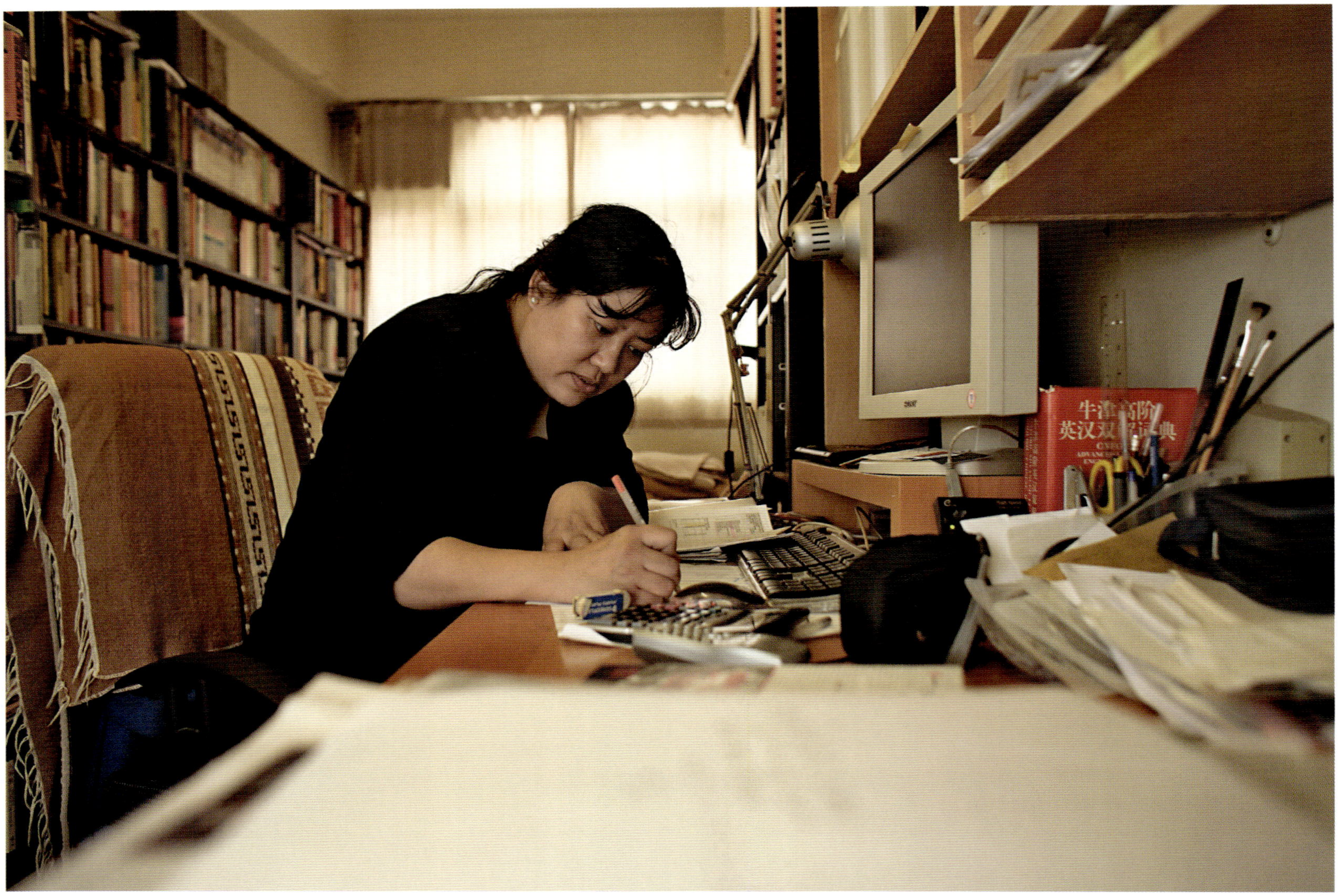

the drawings there was a photo of himself with his face painted white. I asked this candidate why he had to paint his face. He replied that he was so used to drawing plaster figures that when he did his own self-portrait he needed to first turn himself to plaster. I think that this candidate in fact possesses very clever problem solving skills, yet at the same time this incident triggered very strong emotions in me."

Leung reckons that the core that needs to change in art development is not the education system, but the value of free time held by society as a whole. "Some people think that it is unbearable to have too much free time," she says. "They are busy every minute and every second. Can we just slow down for a moment? To me, my best work was often made when I was mucking around and not when I was rushing or thinking too hard. I am not saying that whenever people take a break they should do art. It is fine if they decide to do nothing at all. If the concept of precious time cannot be changed, then improvements made in the hardware cannot do much to help. Cities rich in culture like Paris, New York and Berlin all get formed by leisure."

From time to time Leung leaves Hong Kong and goes to live in some foreign country for a period of time, to unwind and pause from her busy life for a moment. Not long ago she stayed at a town that is an hour's drive away from Paris. From the mayor she obtained the keys for a church which was built in the 13th century. "There were rivers around the place," she says. "Covers of manholes were all marked with Year '18xx'. I would dig up these covers and see if there was water flowing underneath. There was no power inside the church so I would lay some long electric wires for the vacuum cleaner and clean the place with candles lit. I would also clean the feet of the statue of Jesus. Later on, I filmed this act of myself collecting dust continuously and washing things. That kind of emptiness and labour-intensity cleared my mind."

"I would stroll along to a graveyard and watch the smoke that rises from the nearby nuclear plant," she says. "I would tidy up piles of bones that I saw lying on the ground. I would chat with retired people. I would also carry a ladder with me to go to places and rest it on tree trunk so that I could climb up. It was about discovering during the process of doing, and this gave me a very rejuvenated feeling. At times I would jot down in notebooks what I thought and saw. These records often become

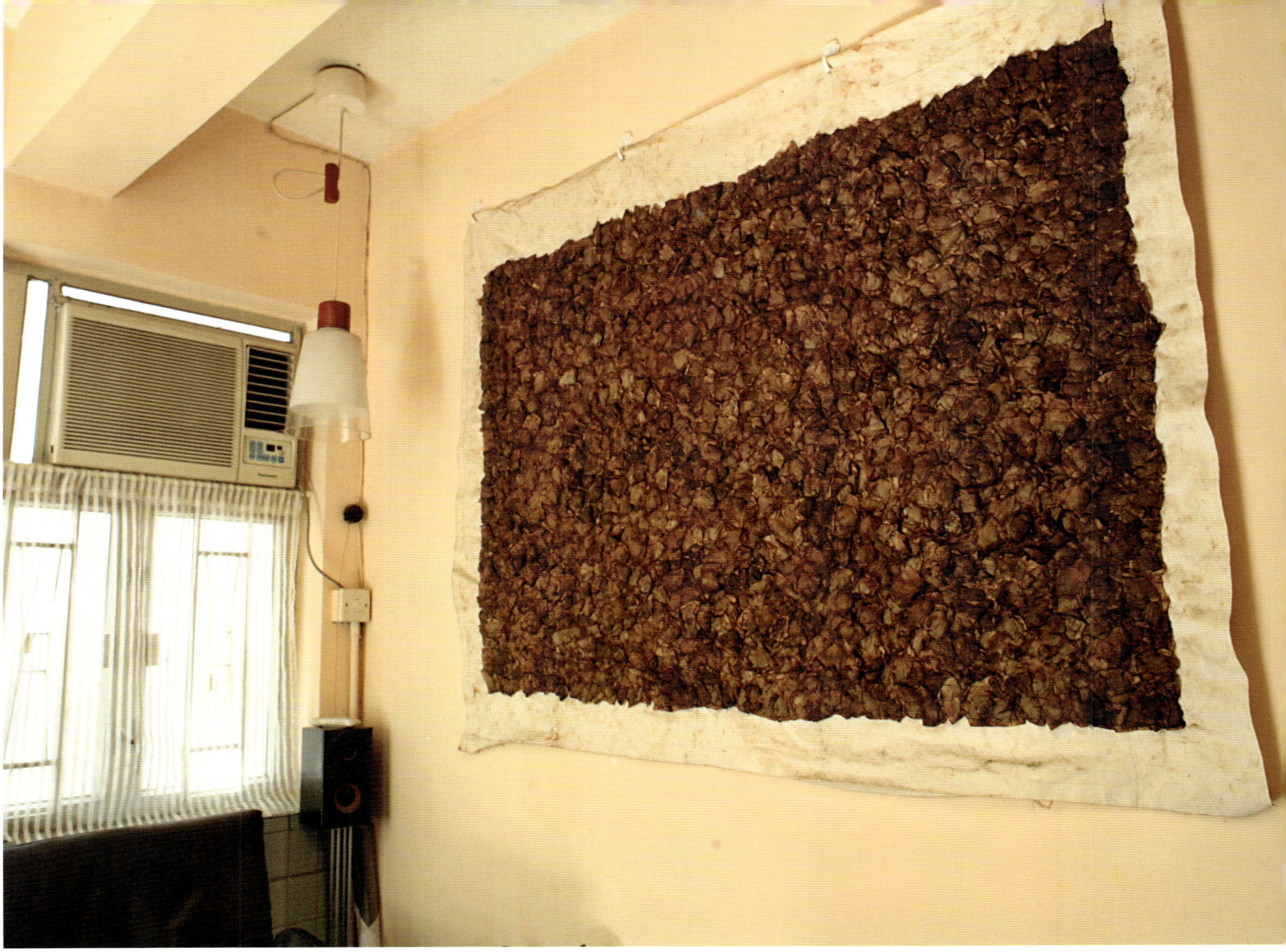

the starting point of my art pieces some time down the track. This is the lifestyle I want to have at this moment in life to be able to enjoy this kind of space whenever I can." For summer 2008 Leung has planned a trip to Italy. She is going to stay in a castle and continue to search for the 'pause space' in life.

"Some people think that it is unbearable to have too much free time. They are busy every minute and every second. Can we just slow down for a moment?"

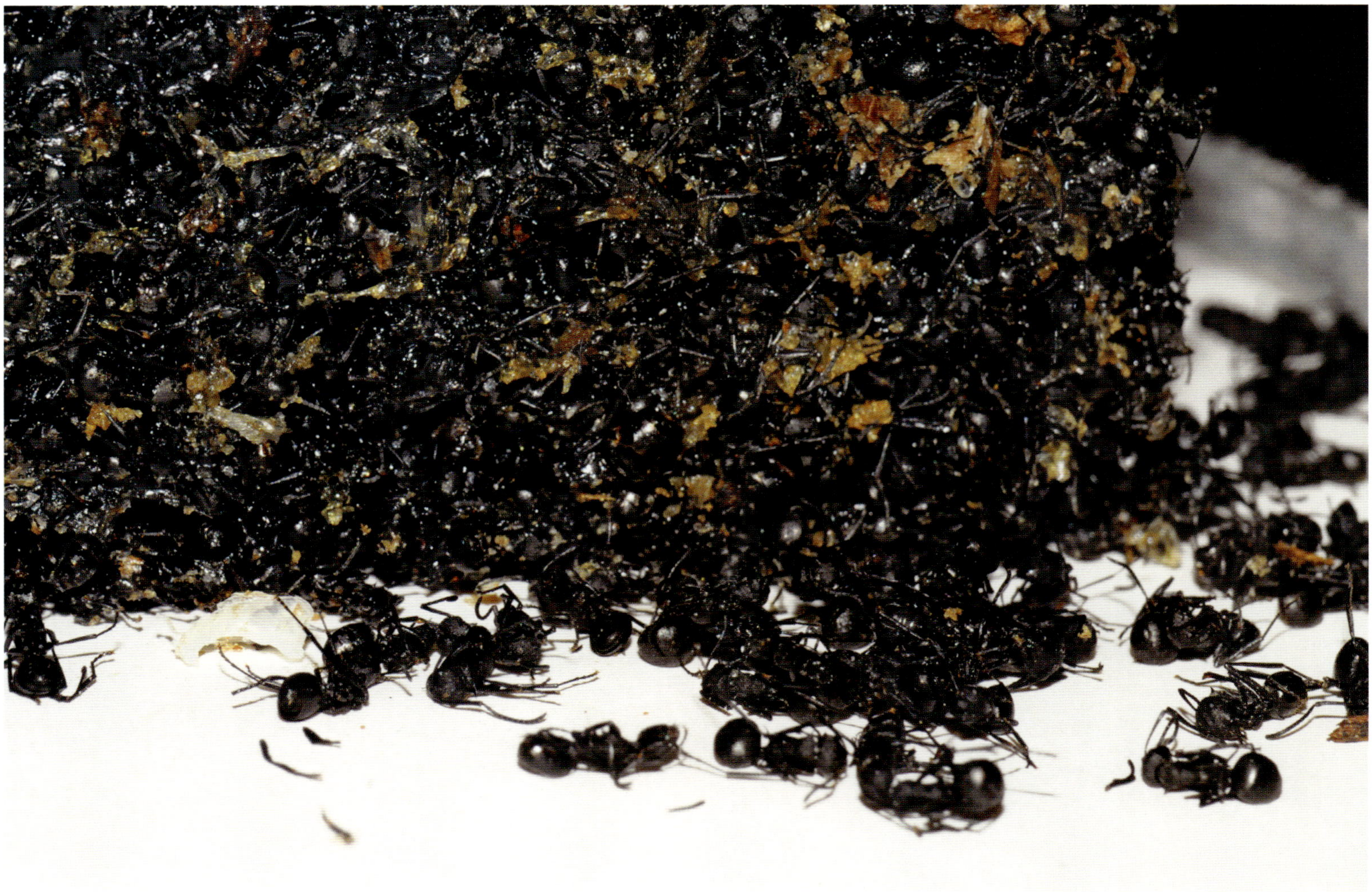

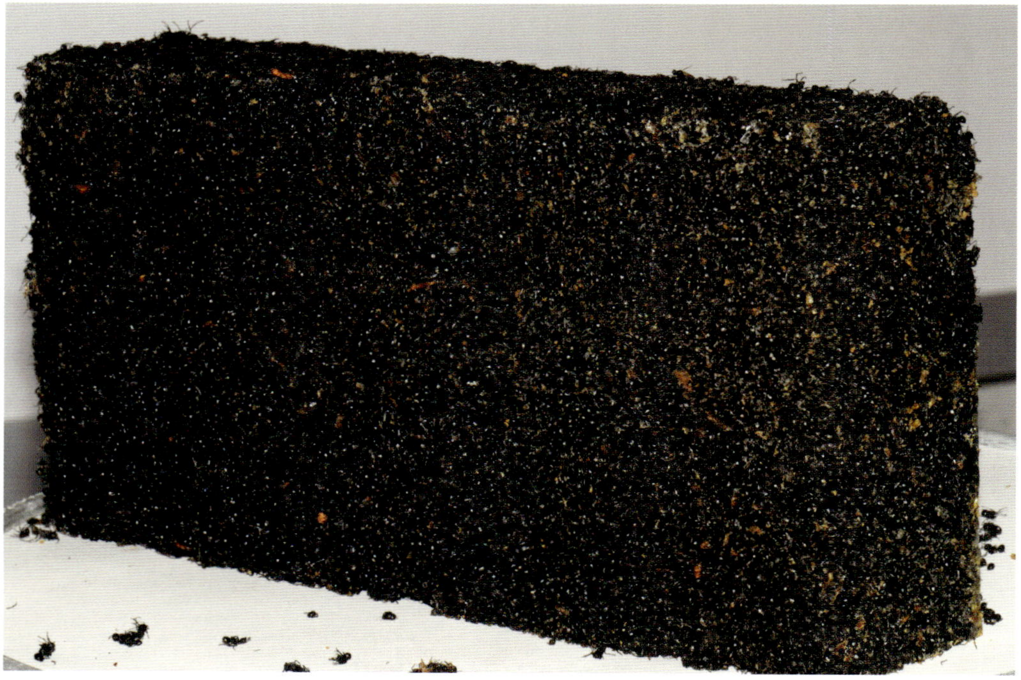

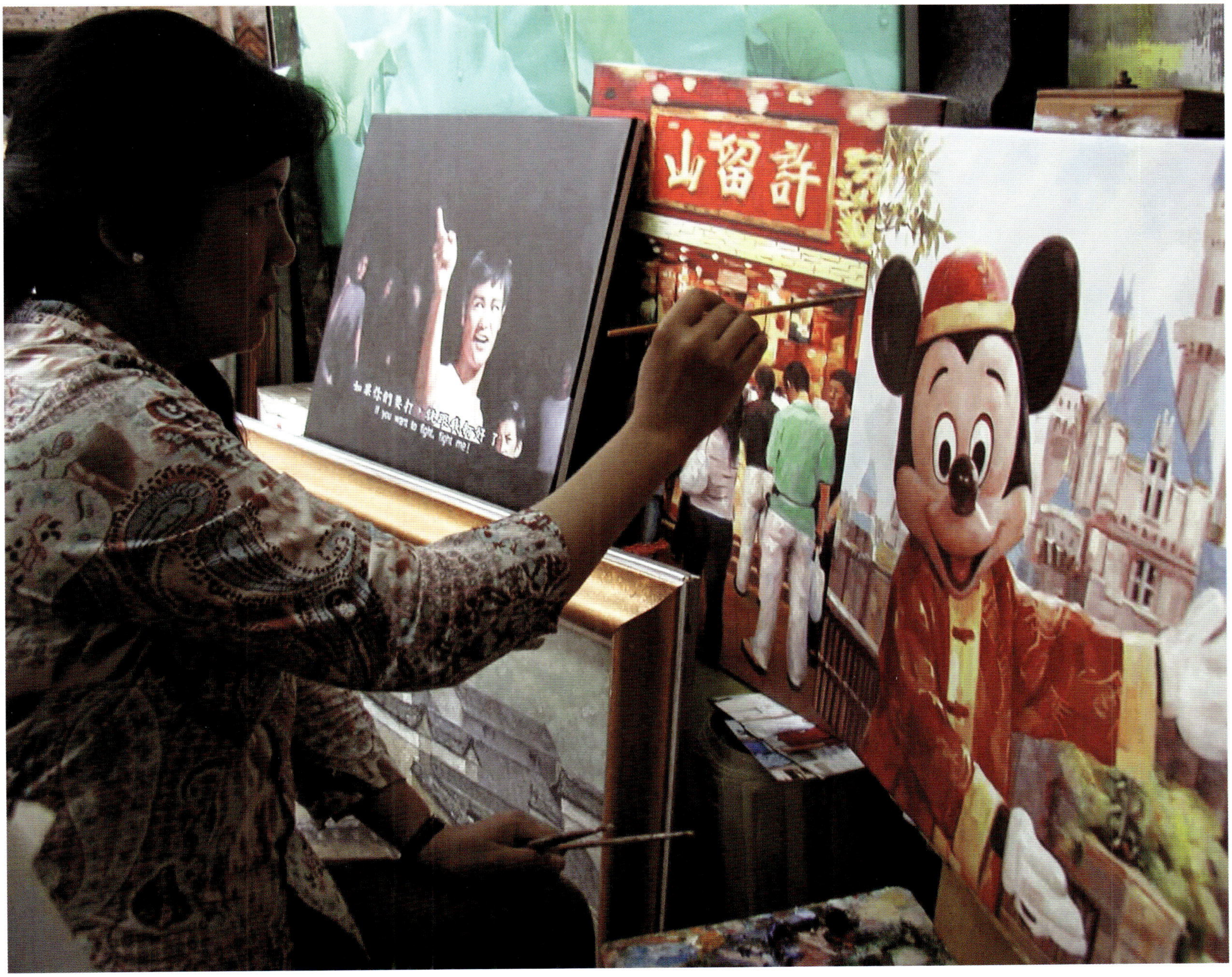

(Left above) Underneath the Feet, is Ground (detail)

(Left bottom) Underneath the Feet, is Ground
Mixed-media, 132x127x10 cm, 2008

(Right) Made in Hong Kong
Installation/performance, dimensions variable, 2007-08

So Yan-kei

Extraordinary Works by an Ordinary Person

By Livia B Garcia

So Yan-kei graduated from the Hong Kong Polytechnic University School of Design in 1993. She was awarded the Asian Cultural Council Fellowship to study for a Master's in fine art between 2001 and 2003. In 1999 she became the first artist representing Hong Kong to take part in the artist-in-residence scheme held by the PS1 Contemporary Art Center in New York. So has received a number of art prizes and scholarships both locally and overseas, including the Rising Artist Award from the Hong Kong Arts Development Council in 2003, the Freeman Foundation Asian Artist Fellowship in 1999 and the Ten Outstanding Young Persons Selection of Hong Kong in 2006.

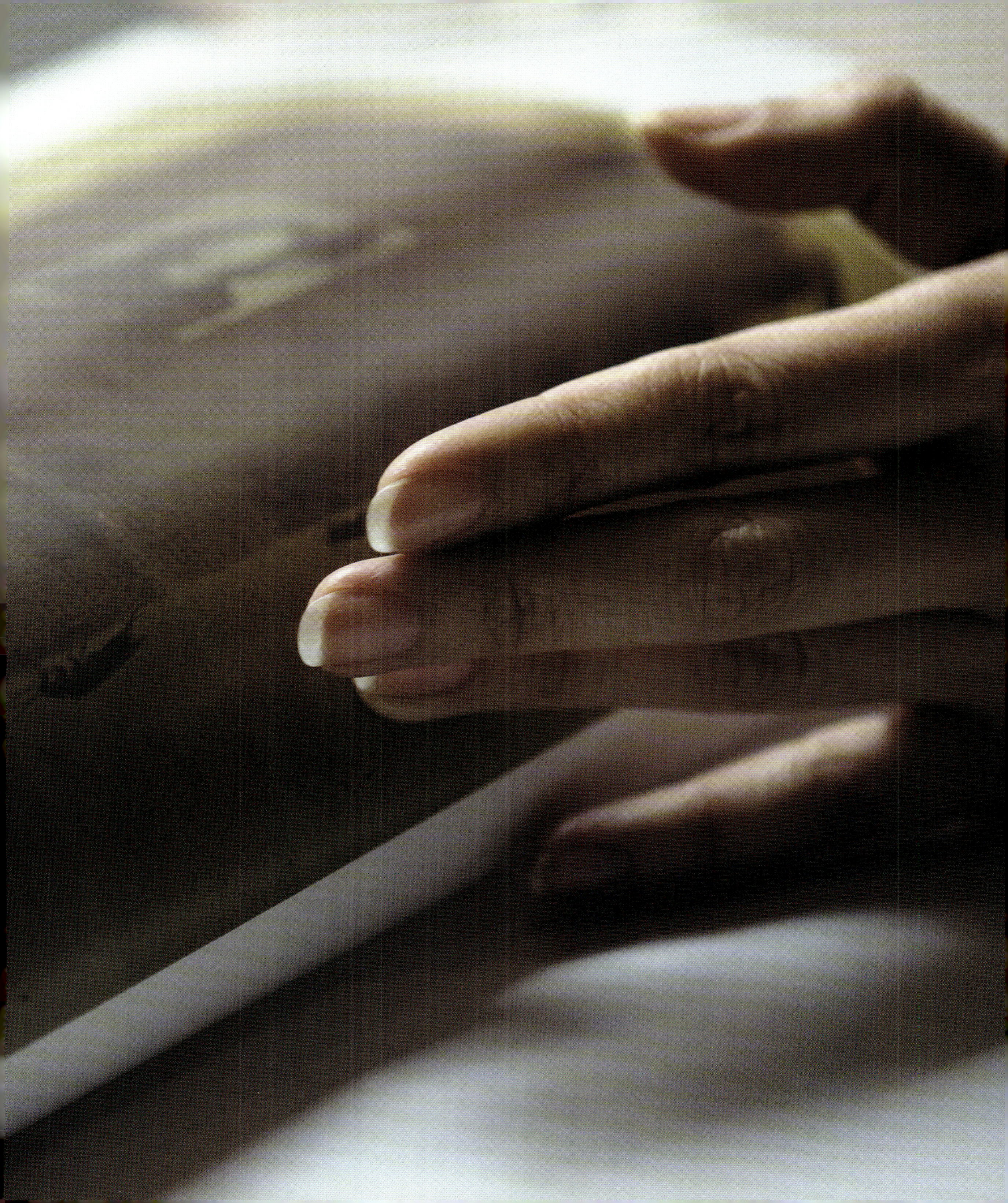

During our interview So Yan-kei emphasised quite a few times that she does not want her face to appear in the book. People always have subjective thoughts about which 'kinds' of people make certain kinds of work, she told me. Then let me not use words to describe what kind of person she is, but instead to concentrate on her artworks and the history of her art creation. For the rest, I will leave it to the readers to imagine.

When I browsed through So's curriculum vitae I realised that she has resided in quite a number of places: she lived in New York for two years, Vermont for three months, Los Angeles for three years and Holland for a year. She has also participated in some artist-in-residence schemes in Japan, Germany, France and Italy. So claims that her will to travel is so frequent that she does not need to clean out her suitcases at times. "It's natural, I simply feel that there is a need for me to do art," she says. This concise sentence has completely explained the reason for her art making.

So graduated from the School of Design of the Hong Kong Polytechnic in 1993. She worked as a designer for half a year soon after her graduation. After that, she worked full-time or part-time as an art director for advertising companies. Between 2001 and 2003 she took up the Asian Cultural Council Fellowship, studying for her Master's in fine art in Los Angeles. She was actually offered a scholarship to study in the United Kingdom at the same time, but after speaking to professors from both places over the phone So chose the States, as she believed that her thinking might be closer to that of the people of that country.

I ask if she thought about becoming an artist when she was a child, and she said yes. Apparently there was a time at school when So did not utter a word, and this lasted for over a year, so there were suggestions made that she should study at other schools instead. I find it hard to imagine that someone who was chosen as one of the 'Ten Outstanding Young Persons' today would have had this kind of experience in her upbringing. Out of curiosity I ask her if she can remember why she would not speak. "I was bored," she says. Then there was a time when she spent hours in libraries reading books that interested her. "I admired Picasso back then, so I read lots of books about him in the library," she recalls. "I also put photos of his works inside my wallet. Of course as I grew up I become fond of other artists' works as well. Actually my family has had a lot of influence on me; my father has given me lots of freedom all along." Perhaps it is this freedom that has given the artist the support and space to create.

So has a younger brother, an accountant who "wears glasses with a thin metal frame". Both of them are sensitive to numbers, and they both like mathematics. From her artworks one can easily notice her sensitivity to science and physics. In 1997 she created a piece of work which was made up of ice blocks and photographs. The work was installed inside a refrigerated truck which then toured around Hong Kong. It was named *Bitter Gourd No. 5*. When I view So's work, besides appreciating its appeal in its setting, I am tempted to think about the process of making it; for example how could the artist insert life-size photographs into ice blocks? What are the implications of a mobile exhibition, in a truck? "A lot of research had to be done beforehand, then I would think about how to realise the ideas," So says. "The ice blocks needed to be free of air. I had hired a few guys from Harbin to help cut up the ice blocks before the photographs could be put inside. Then I need to use some ice powder to fill up the openings."

"As for the mobile exhibition, I was wondering how I could create a sculpture about 'city'. The way the truck travelled around the city and the ways people could weave through buildings already formed part of the work. I wanted people to firstly feel the coldness, before they went on to appreciate other elements of the work."

As someone who liked painting from an early age, So says that the concepts behind her early installation works came from painting.

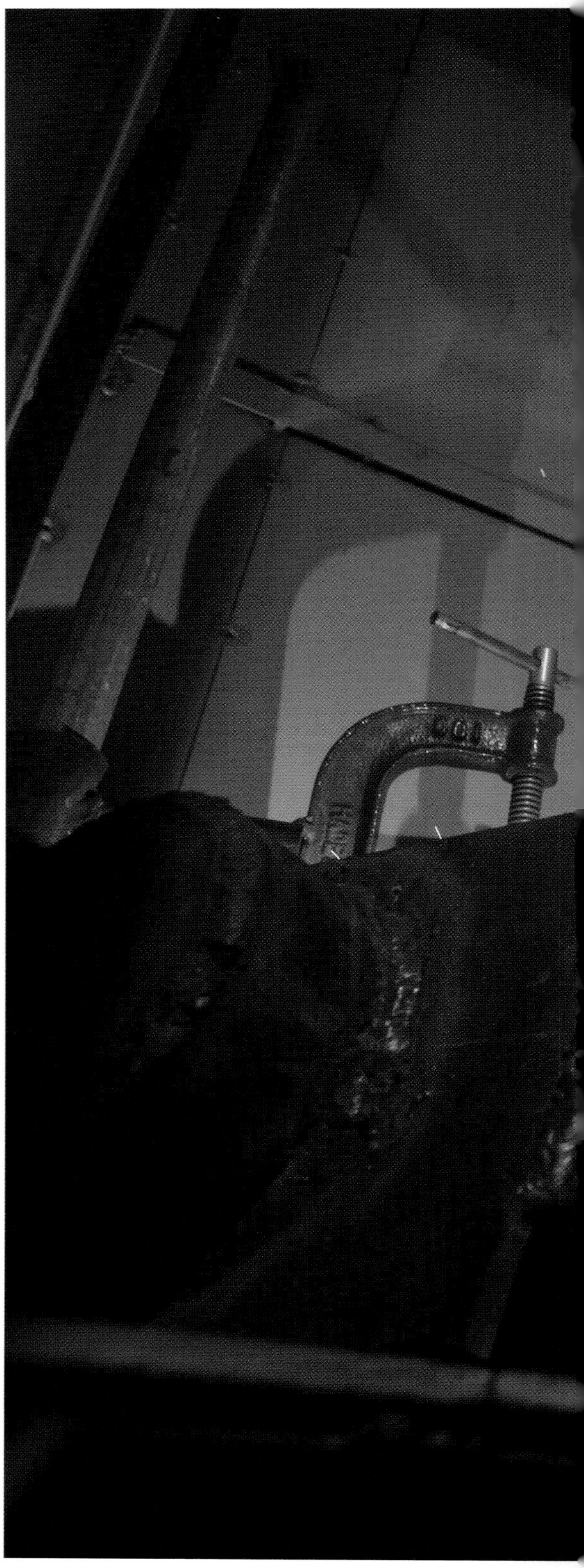

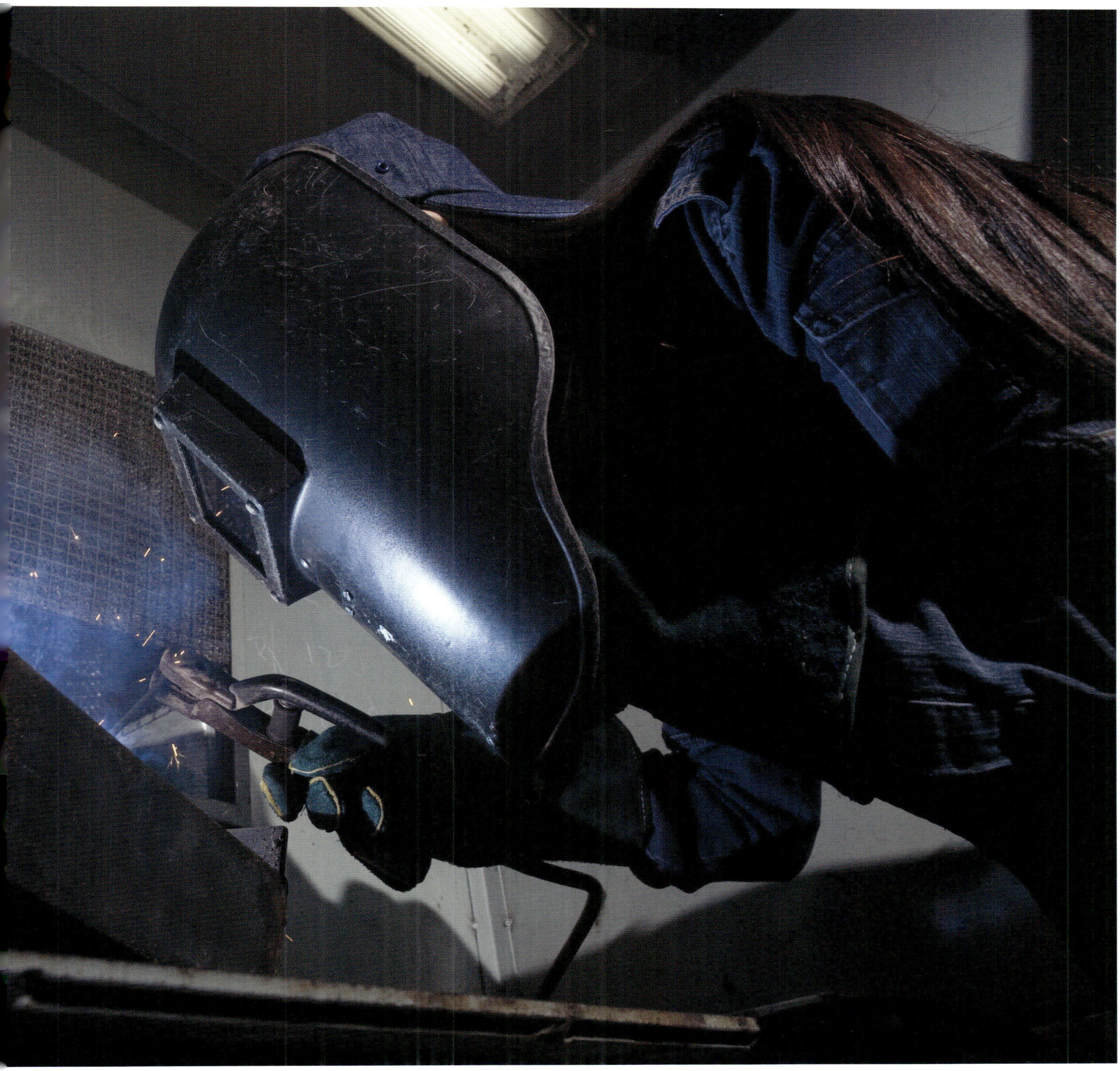

Welding and making art in different rented workshops requires extraordinary resolution

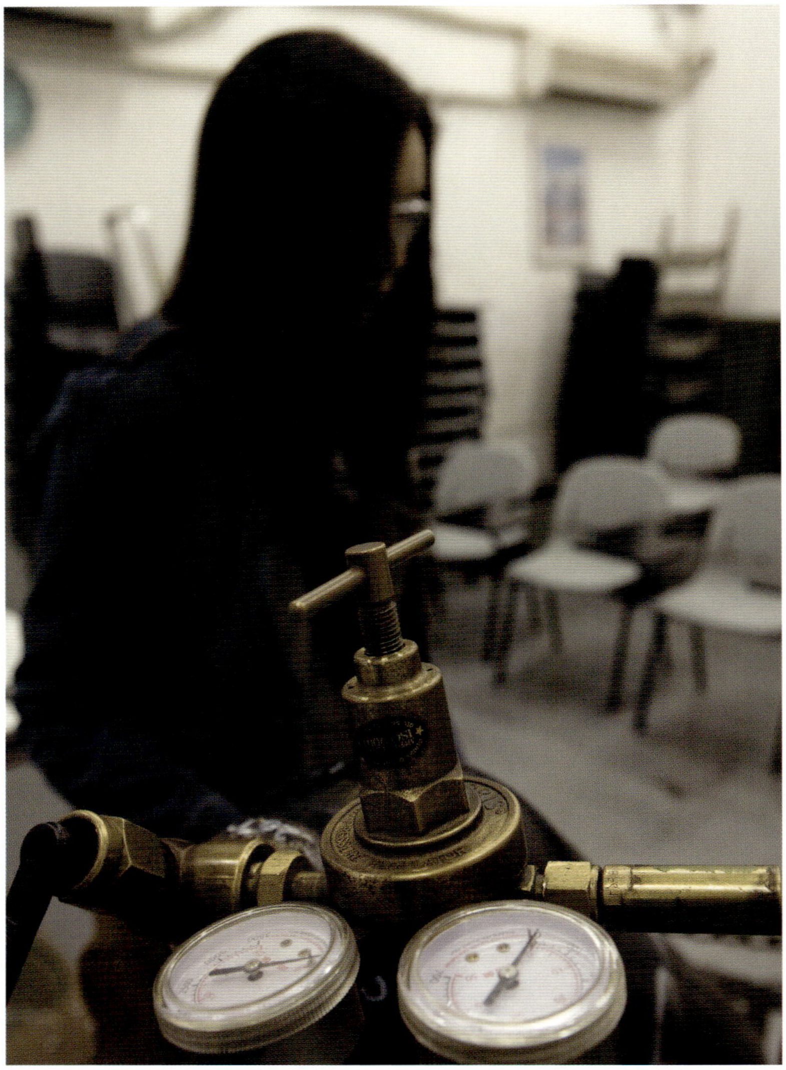

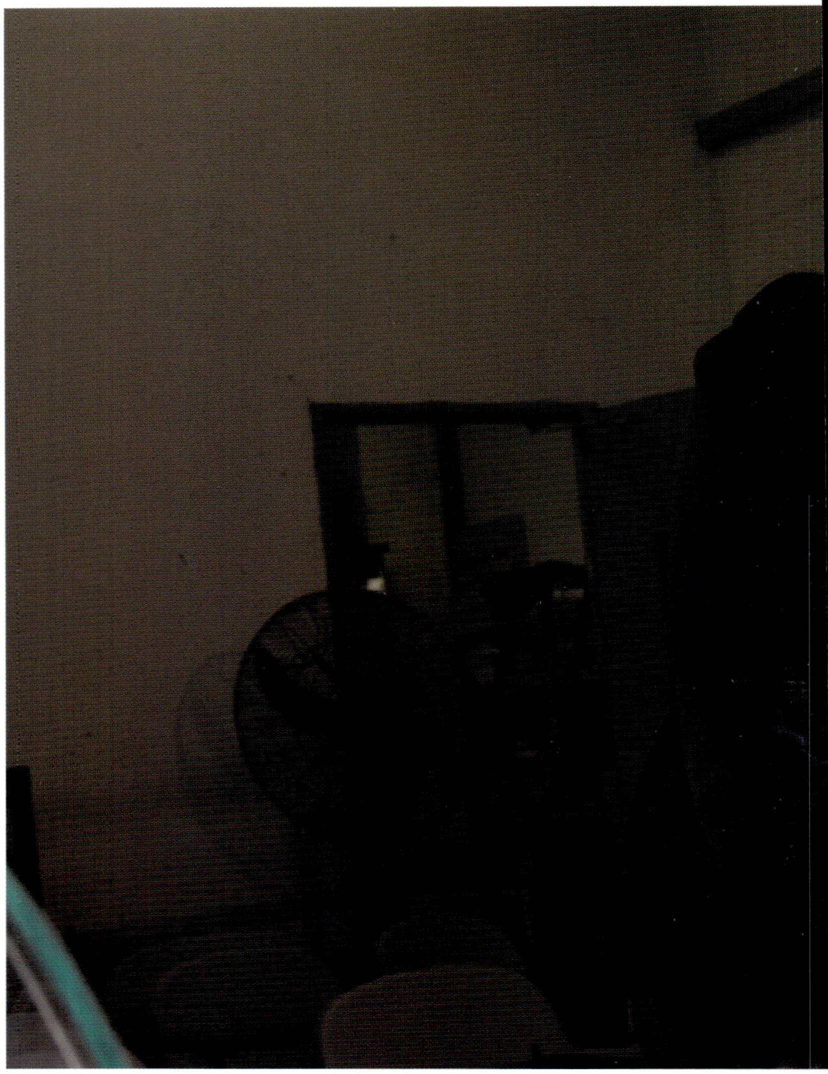

Rembrandt Harmenszoon van Rijn and Francis Bacon were some of the artists whose works gave her inspiration. She would think about how she could transform paintings into three-dimensional installations. Her installation piece, *Hair Dryer for Francis Bacon*, is one example: pieces of rusted blades on the walls of a small glass room that built up heavy pressure. This echoed well with the feelings of fear and mental instability evoked by Bacon's paintings.

Memo (1999) is a lighter work. She used only memo pads and pens. Besides the artist herself, viewers participated in the creation of the work — they decided what to write on the memos and where to stick them on the walls of the exhibition space. "When I was studying for my Master's degree in the USA Charles Ray was one of the teachers," she says. "He taught me how to see the whole personal development in art with a bird's eye view; for example one should pay attention to the influences and relationships between each art work. I think that *Memo* affected the other piece, *Red*, which I made in 2003. The former is about written messages and the latter — messages burning." For *Red*, So had hung a piece of red cloth in the middle of a highway in Los Angeles, and within seconds the cloth was burnt to ashes. She adds, "When I was living in New York I had the chance to come into contact with some well established artists like Mary Kelly and Paul McCarthy. Working with them made me realise that success really does not come about by luck alone."

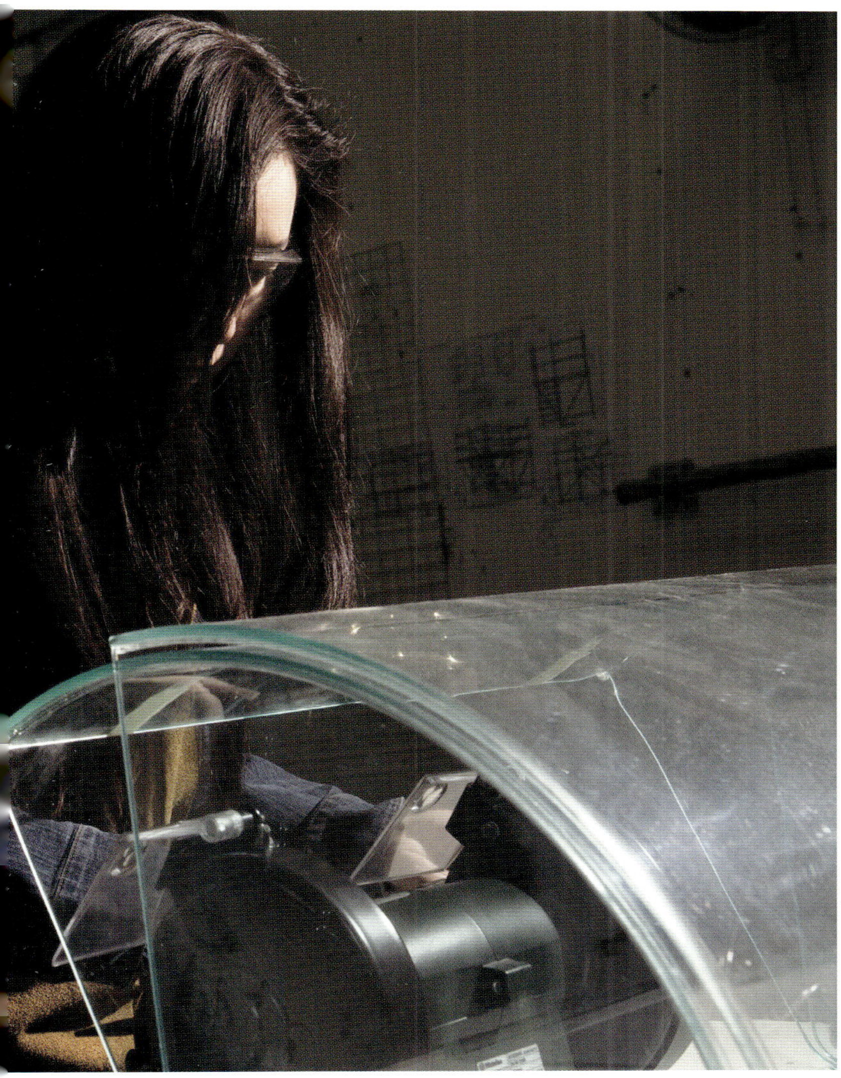

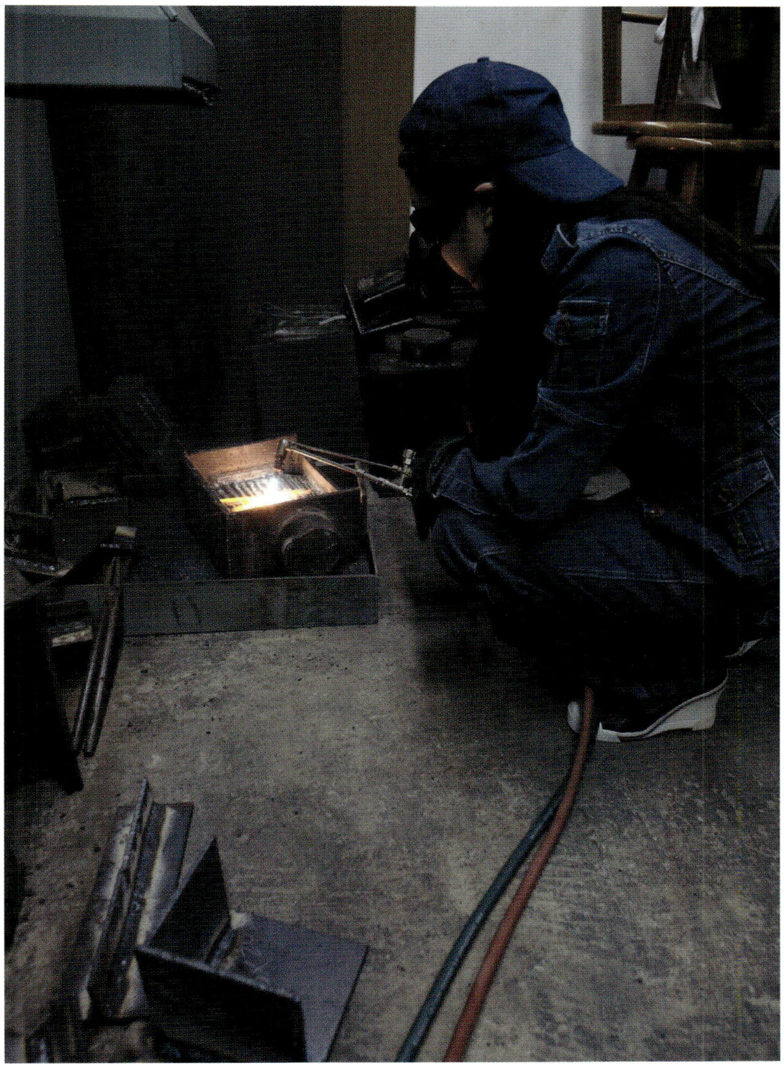

So's art works are known for their scale. They cannot be accomplished within a studio space. Due to the need to travel frequently she does not have a studio in Hong Kong right now. However she has rented workshops in the past in which to do her welding. "I go to different places to do welding, and where depends on whether they are electric or gas welds," she explains. "I had tried doing some of the creation processes at home, for example drilling holes in materials, but it took a long time to drill just a small hole. Moreover, sometimes the smell of materials would affect other family members in the house. I reflected on whether I should avoid making big scale works, but in the end I continued." So has had studio space in Shek Kip Mei and Yau Tong before. As to whether she may set up a stable studio in the future or not, So says yes, but she will leave that for destiny to arrange.

While storing ordinary materials at home may not be a problem, the kinds of things that artists choose to use always come as a surprise. Imagine having a few dozen cockroaches inside the house! In Bad Art Show held at the Fringe Club in 1997, cockroaches were amongst the materials So used. She describes, with great detail, the experience of catching them and the characteristics of those she examined during the preparation process. "I went to the back of a Chinese restaurant in Sai Wan Ho to catch cockroaches every day," she remembers. "Dusk is the best time. Cockroaches have strong powers of survival but their own bodies are very weak, so I could not wear gloves when catching them."

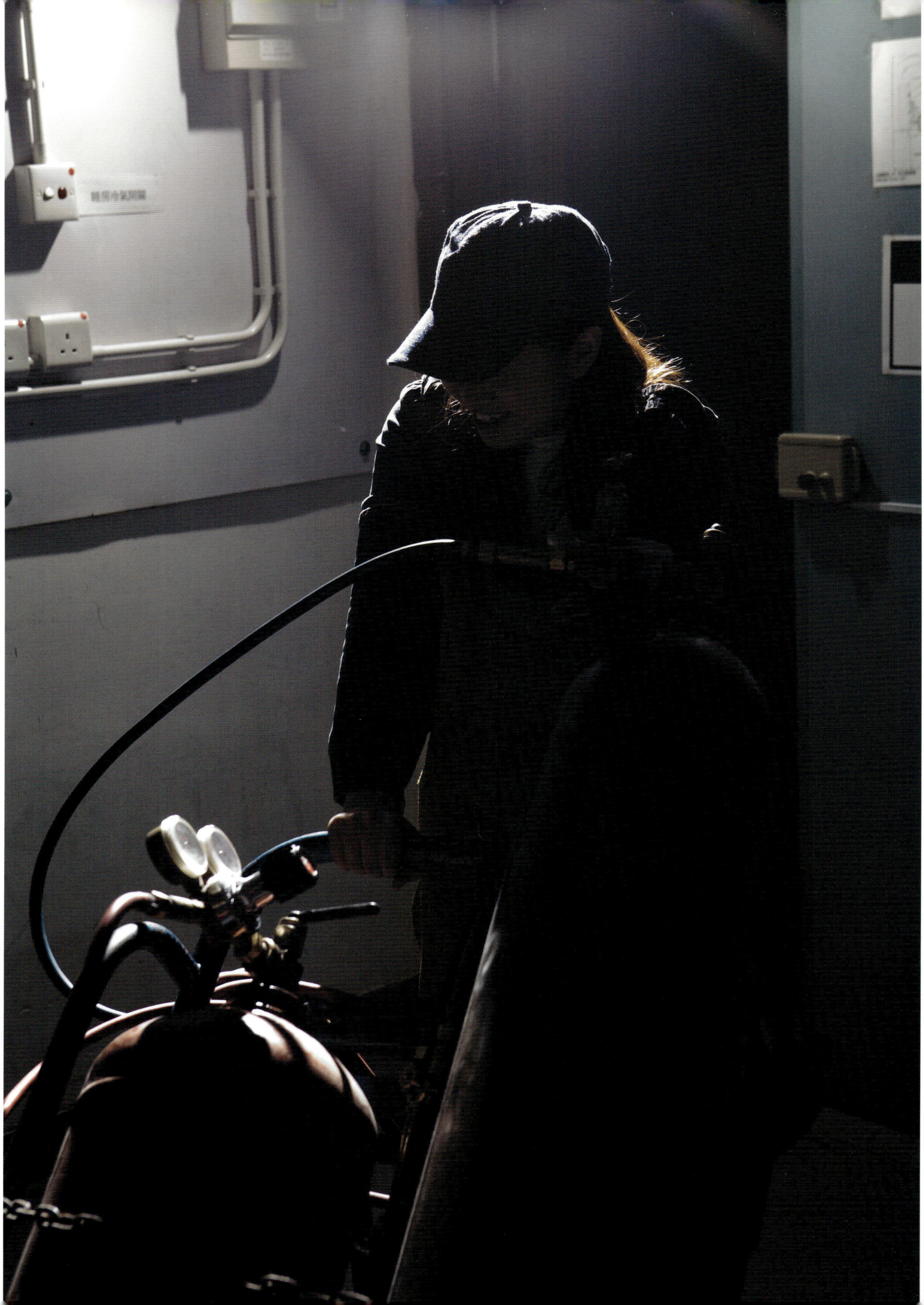

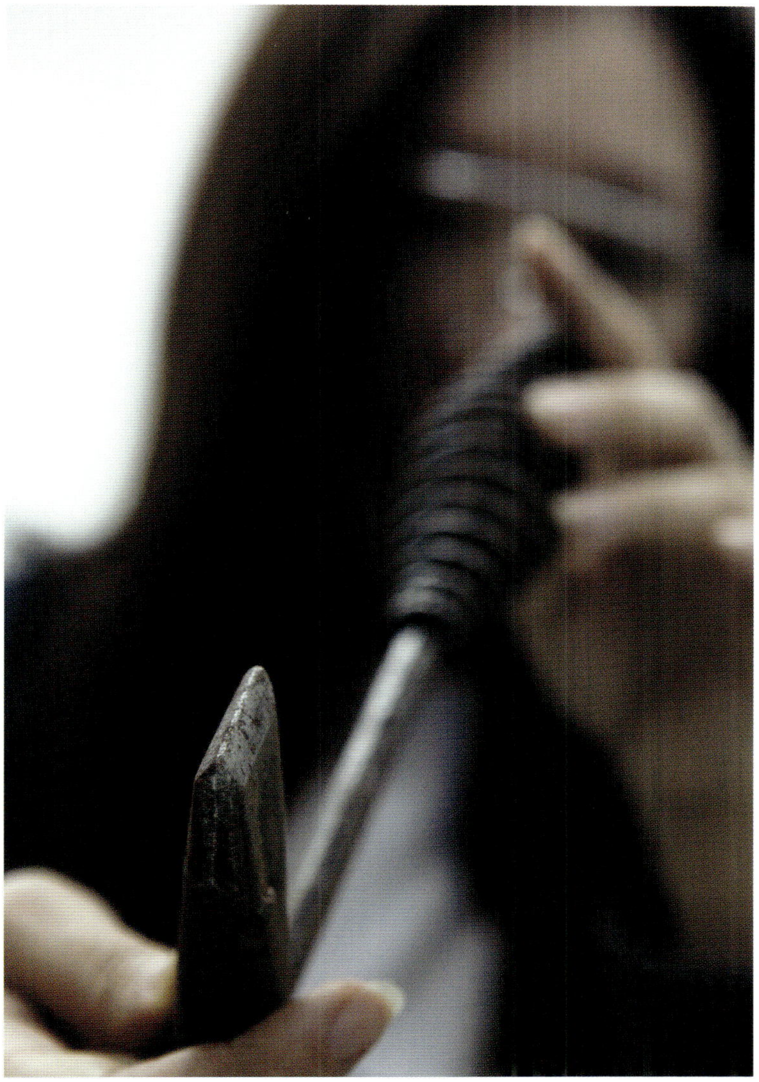

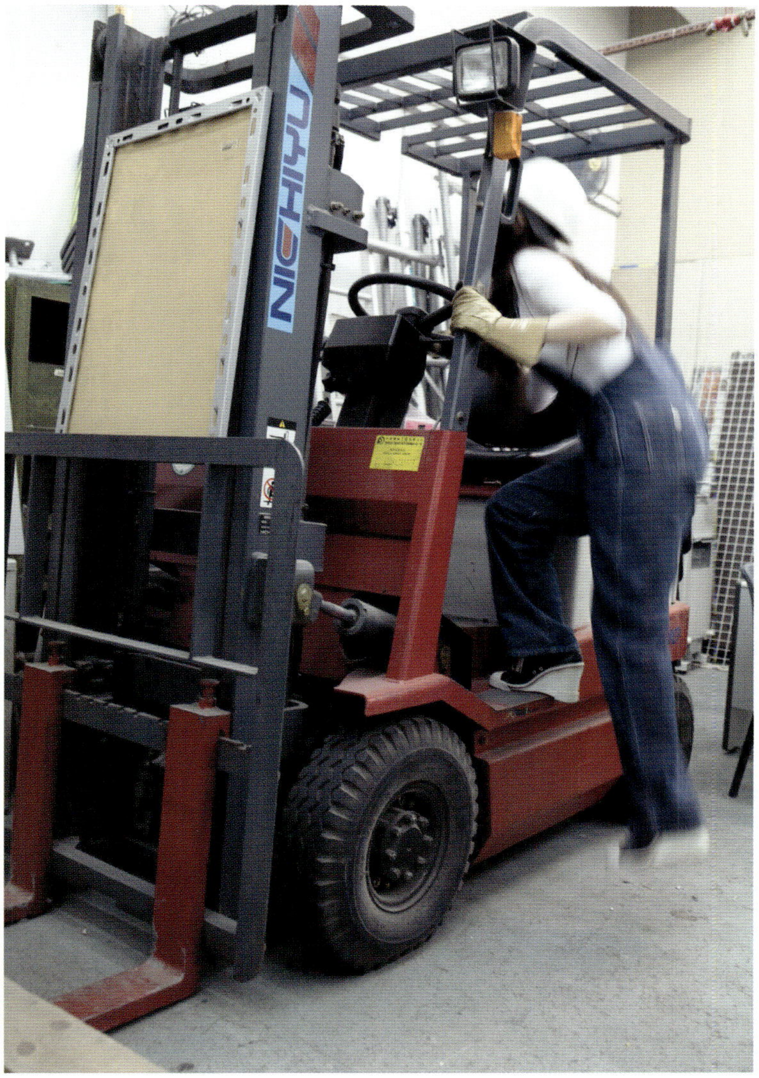

"What's more, they actually like to be clean and they like having their own space. They are keen to unite, but attack the weaker ones. The one thing they like most is eating the heads of their partners."

The latest piece of work to be fine-tuned by this artist is her *Self-Immolation* Exercise Machine. It is like the kind of photo booth that one sees inside train stations. The only thing is, with So's version, people who take pictures will end up receiving a handful of ash instead of photographs. "This is about cycles," she explains. "Human life seems to be compressed into several minutes." The artist does not need to think hard to come up with these strange concepts, they just appear in her mind naturally. "The first thought is subconscious, then the details that need to be attended to next," she recounts. "For example, the distances between each element in the work. I have to face lots of difficulties in the process, but I really want to get things completed properly. One shouldn't start by questioning whether he or she has the ability to finish the work, or whether there are enough resources or not. All these problems can get resolved step by step."

"Time goes by very quickly and I always imagine that life will end tomorrow. Therefore, I do everything that I want to do today. This is not limited to art-making, it applies to other matters such as showing care for my family and so on."

So continues: "I am only an ordinary person who has somehow become an artist. Actually living is already art, if you can pay attention to things around you." Perhaps she is right — she may just be an ordinary person who has somehow done something that is not quite ordinary.

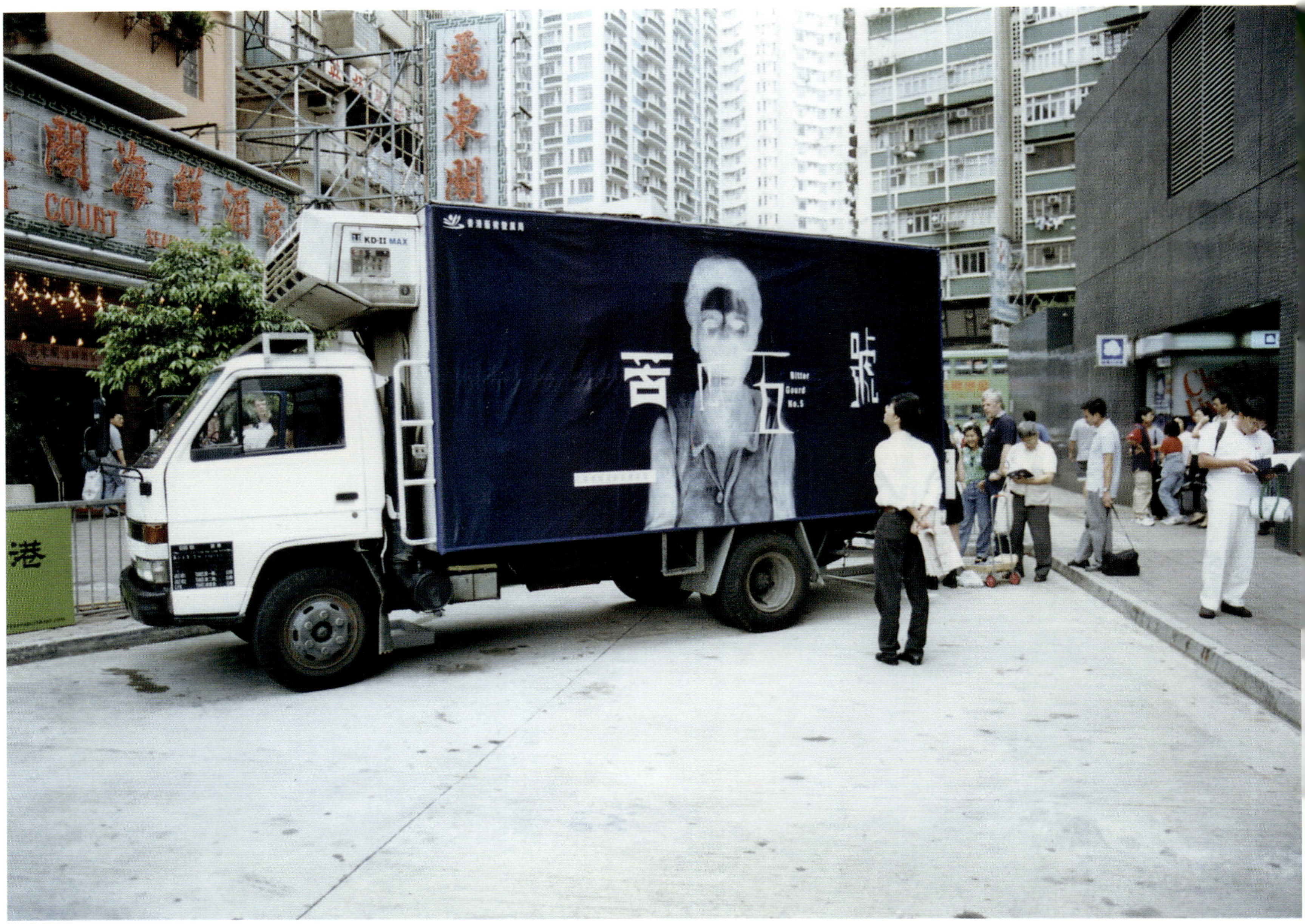

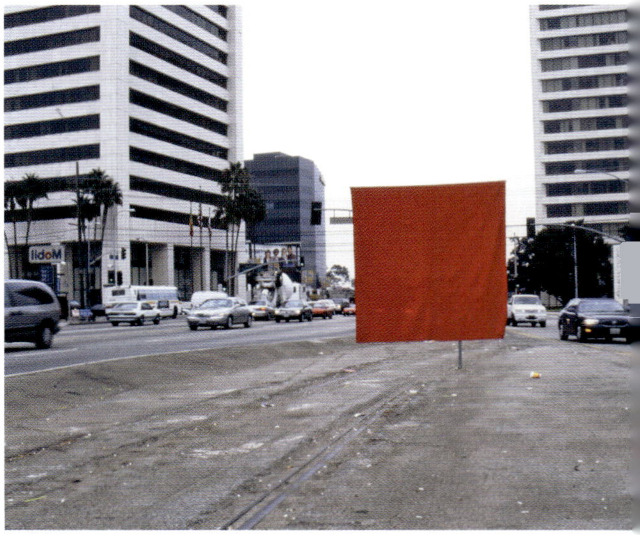

(Left and right, above) Bitter Gourd No. 5
Mixed-media, 570x275x275 cm, 1997-98

(Bottom) Red
Mixed-media, 112x112 cm, 2003-04

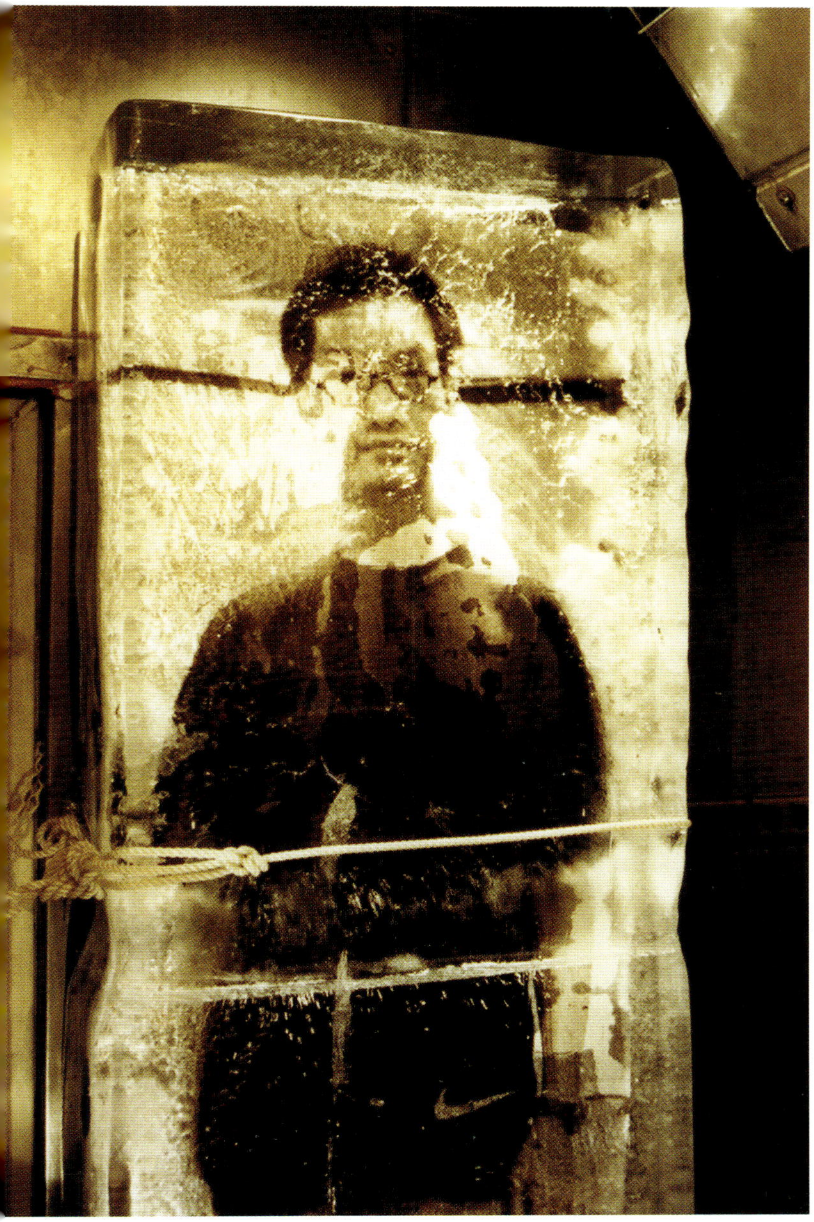

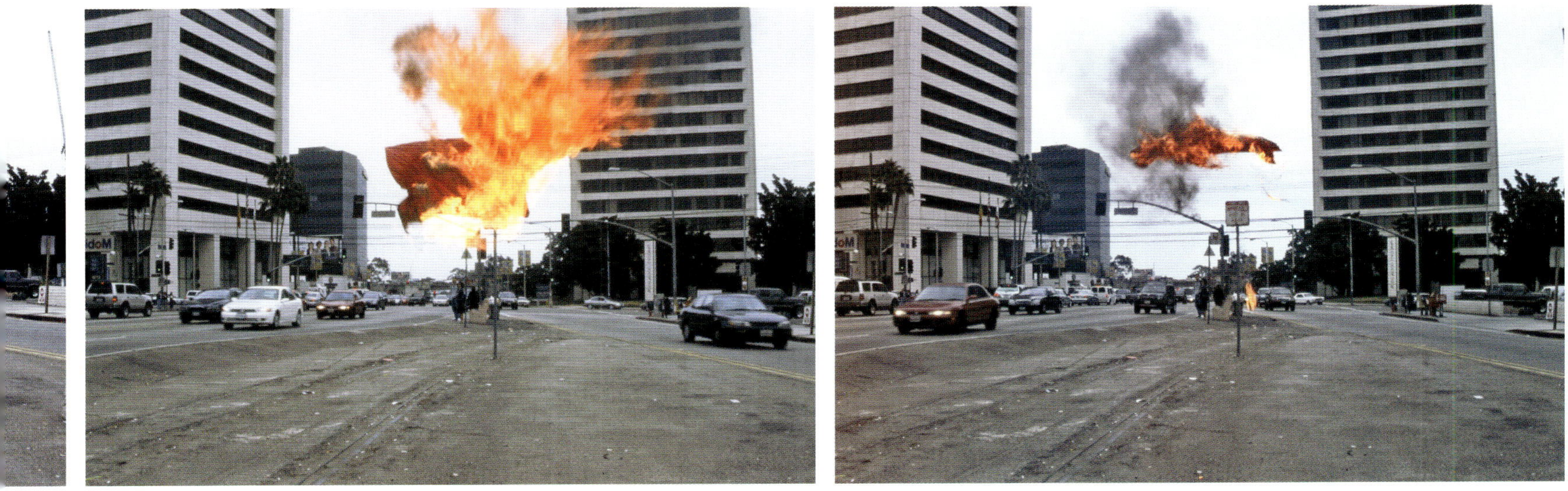

Luke Ching Chin-wai

Stephen Chow and the Scientist

By Ronny Leung

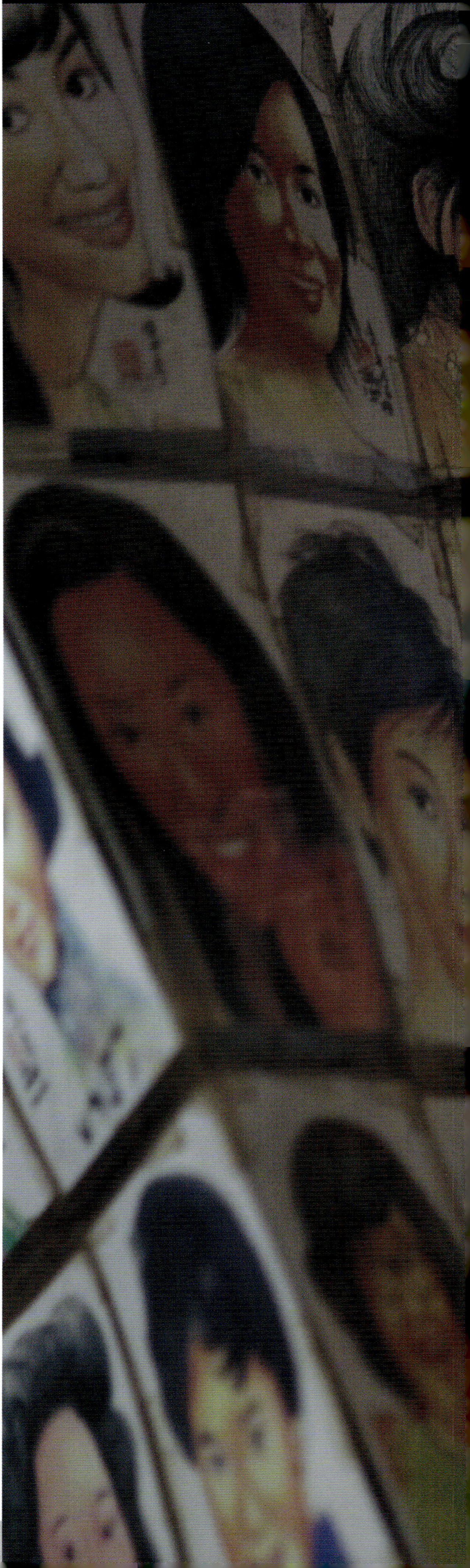

Luke Ching Chin-wai received a Master's degree from the Department of Fine Arts at the Chinese University of Hong Kong in 1998. His oeuvre includes *Folk Art Series: Cockroach*, *Easy to Learn Cantonese Chapters 1-6*, *Public Sculpture: Dog Footprint*, *Wet Print: Rainbow and Room as Pinhole Camera*. He recently completed residencies at the Vermont Studio Center in the United States and at the Fukuoka Asian Art Museum in Japan.

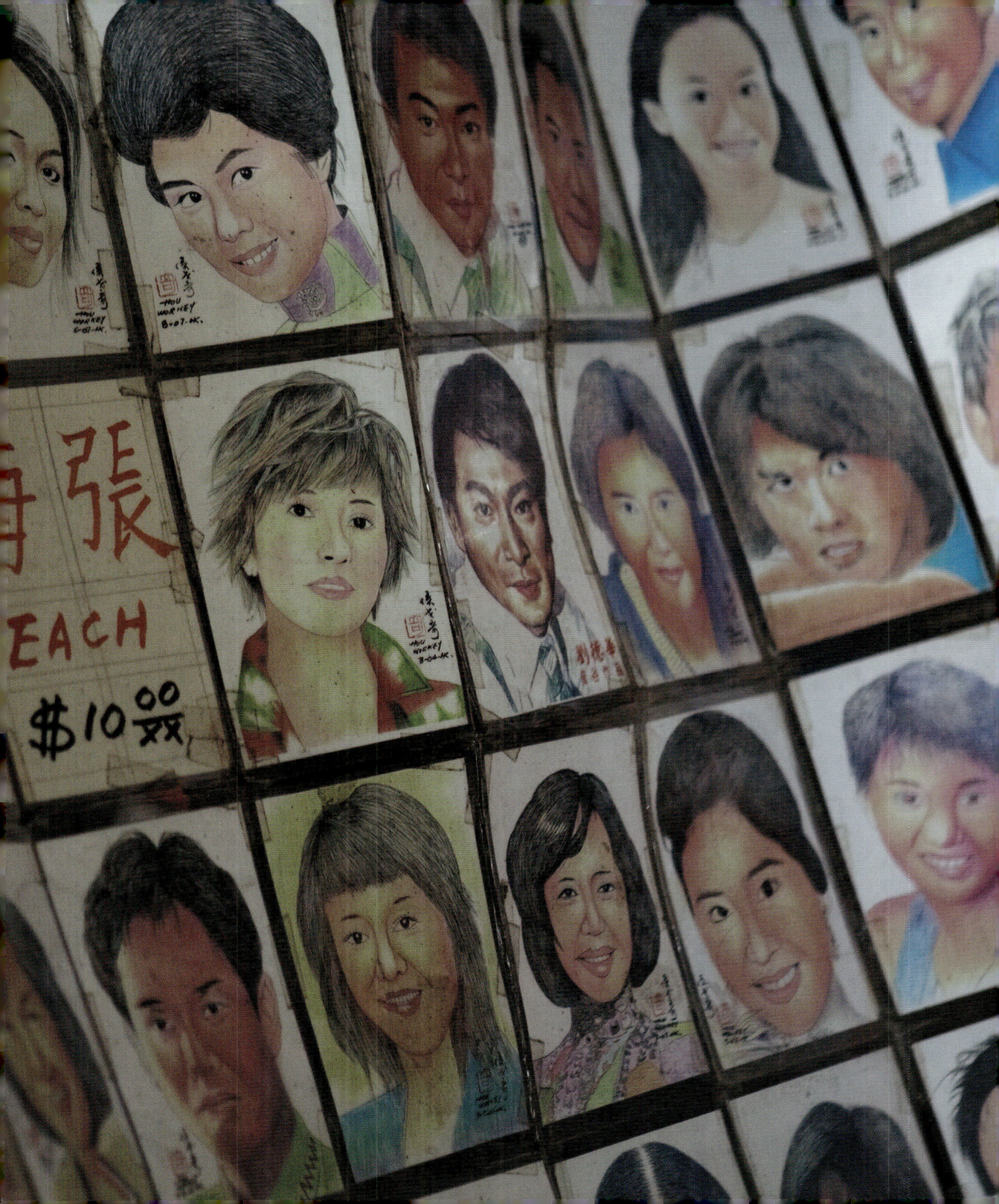
張
EACH
$10.00

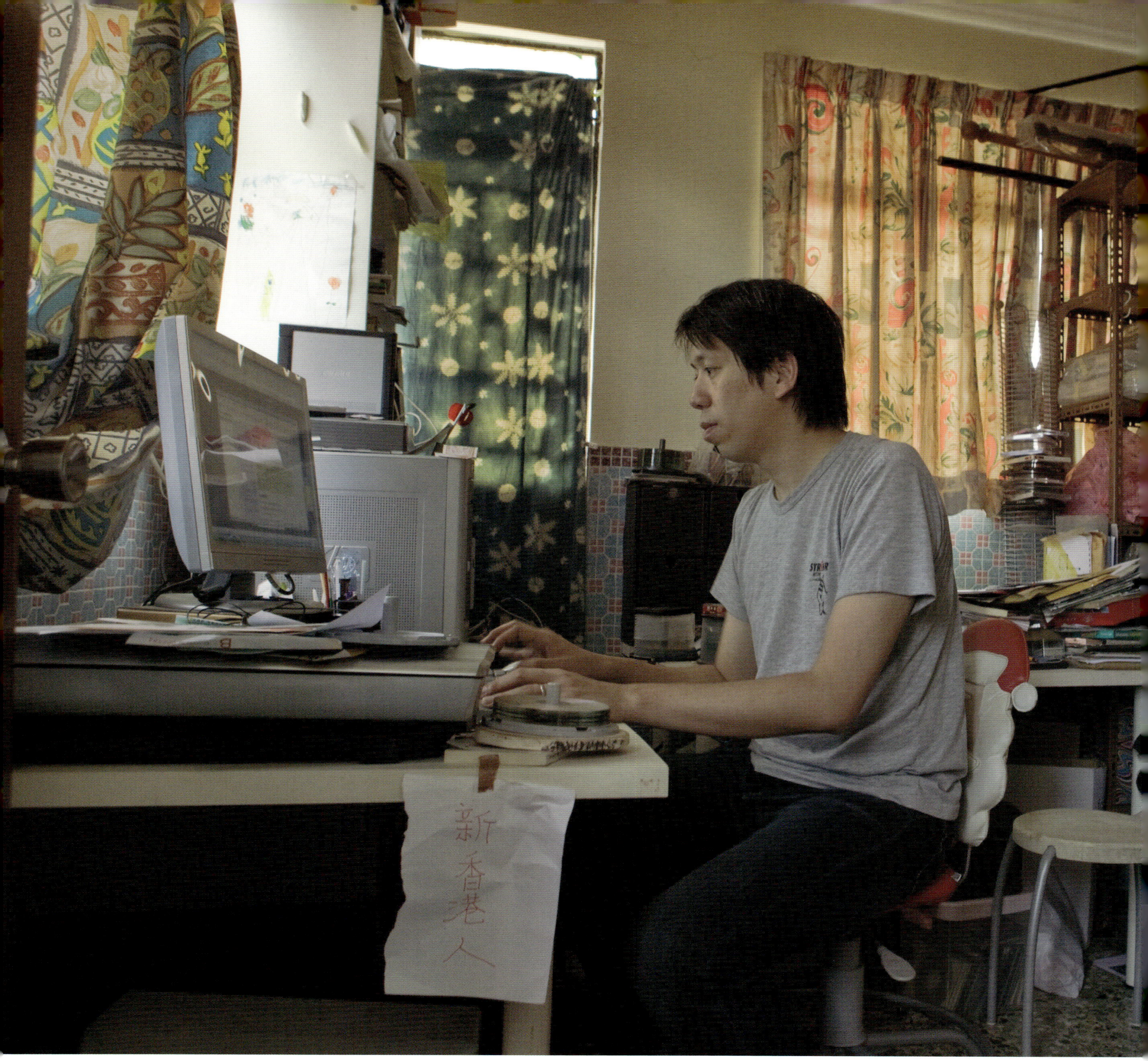
新香港人

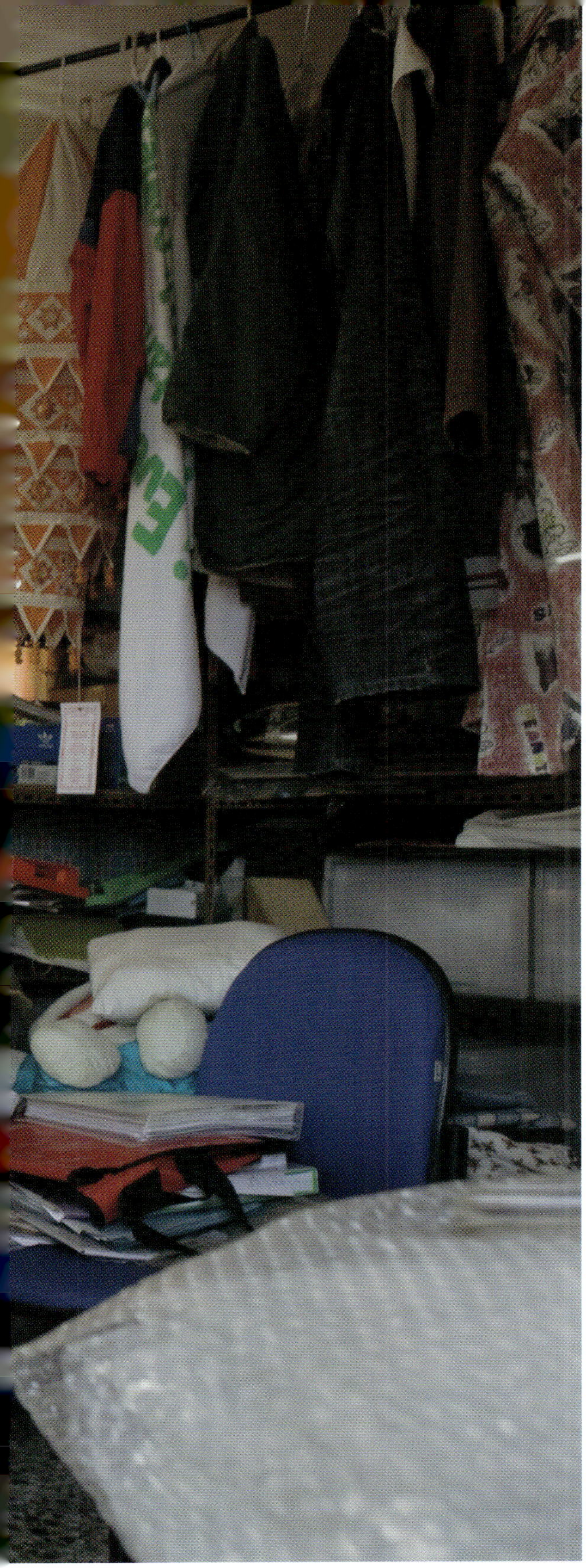

Picnicking in Times Square, flying balloons in City Plaza, painting rainbows on footbridges and saying "ngo5 oi3 nei5" (Cantonese for 'I love you') to foreigners of all ethnicities. Are these examples of art? Yes, indeed. They are the art projects of Luke Ching Chin-wai.

Ching has written: "I live in this city and at the same time I observe the city as if I am an outsider. I react to the city spontaneously. I deconstruct the city. And then, I observe it again." By 'deconstruct', Ching is saying that he likes to give new meanings to the commonplace. Such a creative strategy is typical of his personality. He says that he does not like formality. When he got married, it was in a T-shirt instead of a tuxedo. Ching likes things simple and direct.

When he was a kid, Ching loved art classes. He remembers his first work of art, done when he was in Primary Two. It was a vase, a work of papier collé using bits of paper from a magazine, with a wriggling carp on the inside. His freshman year in the Department of Fine

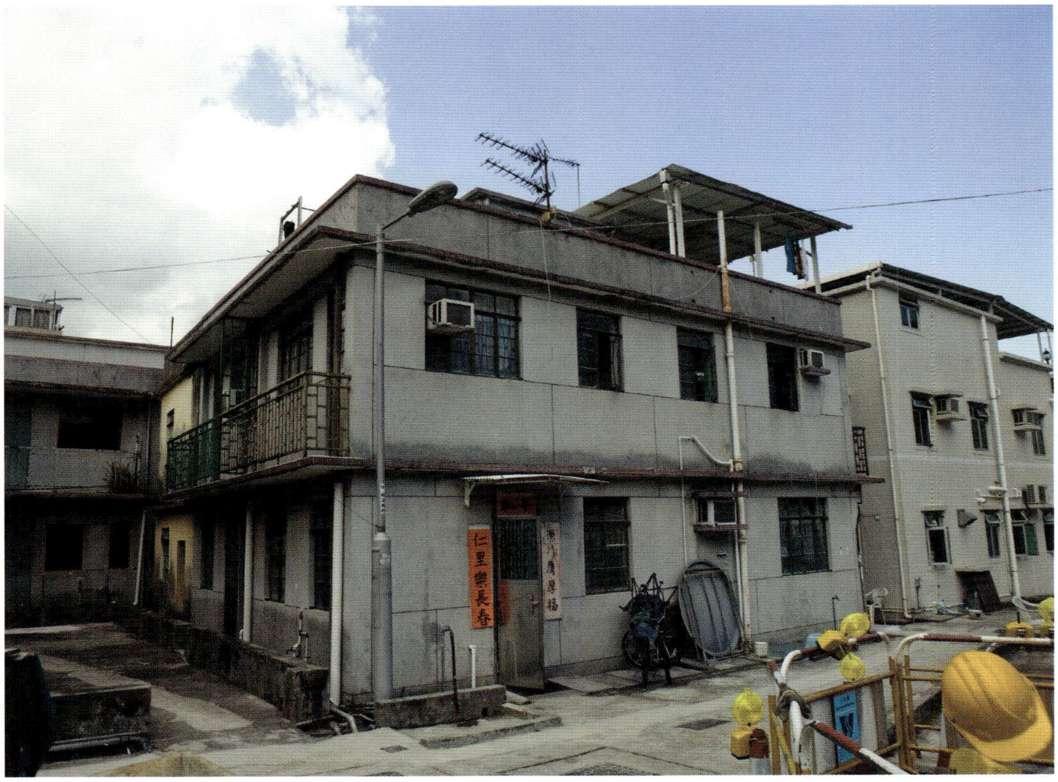

Ching believes that art is not confined to artistic media. When forced to put himself in a category, he picks 'conceptual art'

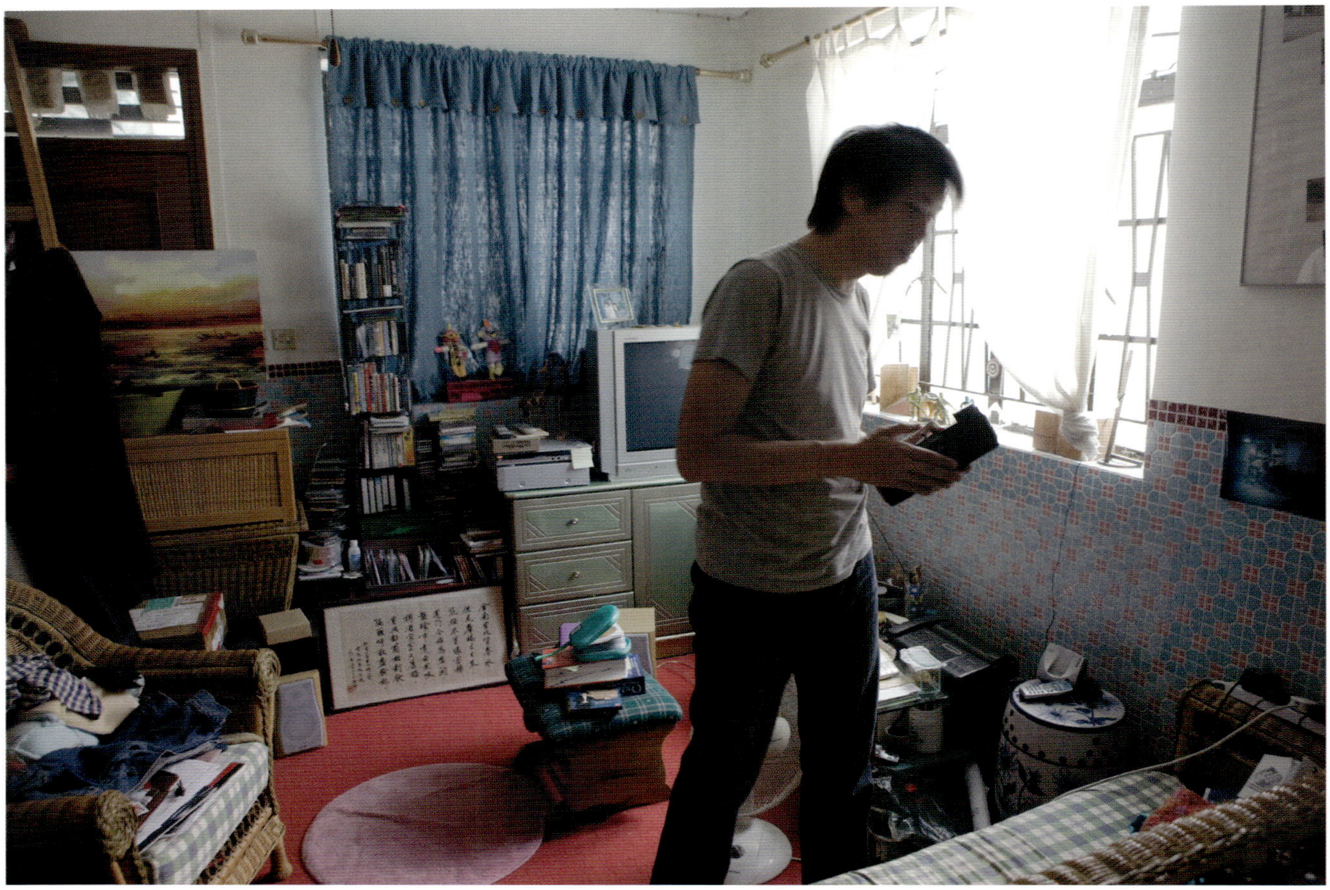

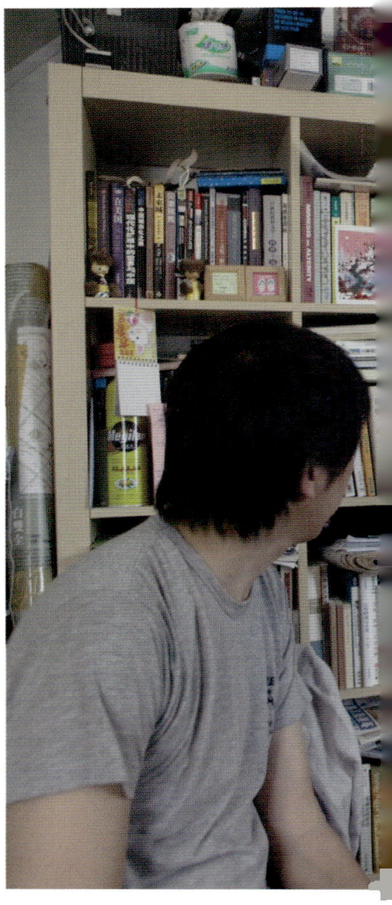

Arts at the Chinese University of Hong Kong was spent in exploration. He painted for a while, tried out different media and developed a 'signature style' using double-sided tape. His work was isolated from society then — very different from his socially-oriented projects today.

Ching believes that art is not confined to artistic media. When forced to put himself in a category, he picks 'conceptual art'. This direction started during an artist-in-residence programme at the PS1 Contemporary Art Center in New York in 2000. His project then was to teach Cantonese. More than 400 participants of different ethnicities have learnt how to say 'ngo5 oi3 nei5' from Ching and he recorded their hesitant movements and blank faces for the work, *Easy to Learn Cantonese Chapter I: 'I Love You'*. It is the artist's attempt to start conversations with strangers. As well as learning to say 'ngo5 oi3 nei5', the participants also shared the stories of their lives with Ching. This liberated the artist from his double-sided tape. From that time on, people become a key element in his art.

The artist has turned to conceptual art for two reasons. The first has to do with pragmatism. He says that for one to keep on creating, one's work has to fit into one's life. He works at home, which has him avoiding anything too big or smelly. His work needs to fit into his living environment and busy life. In this way he works and lives happily.

Secondly, he wants to discover new possibilities in simple ways. Minimal modifications to things that have always existed can bring about new ideas, triggering

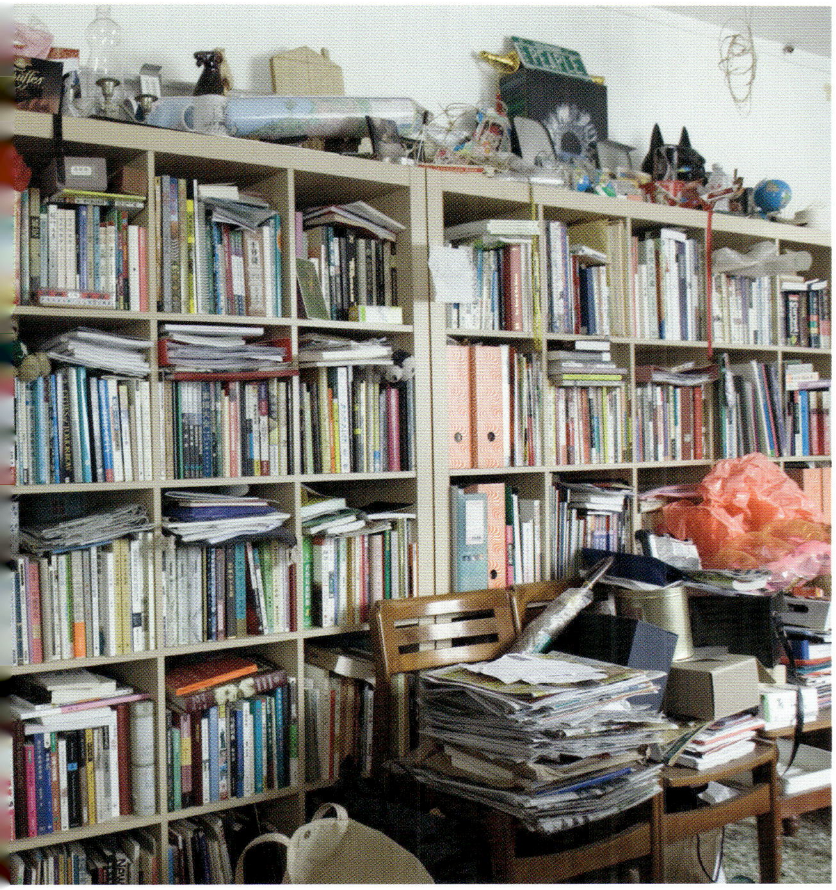

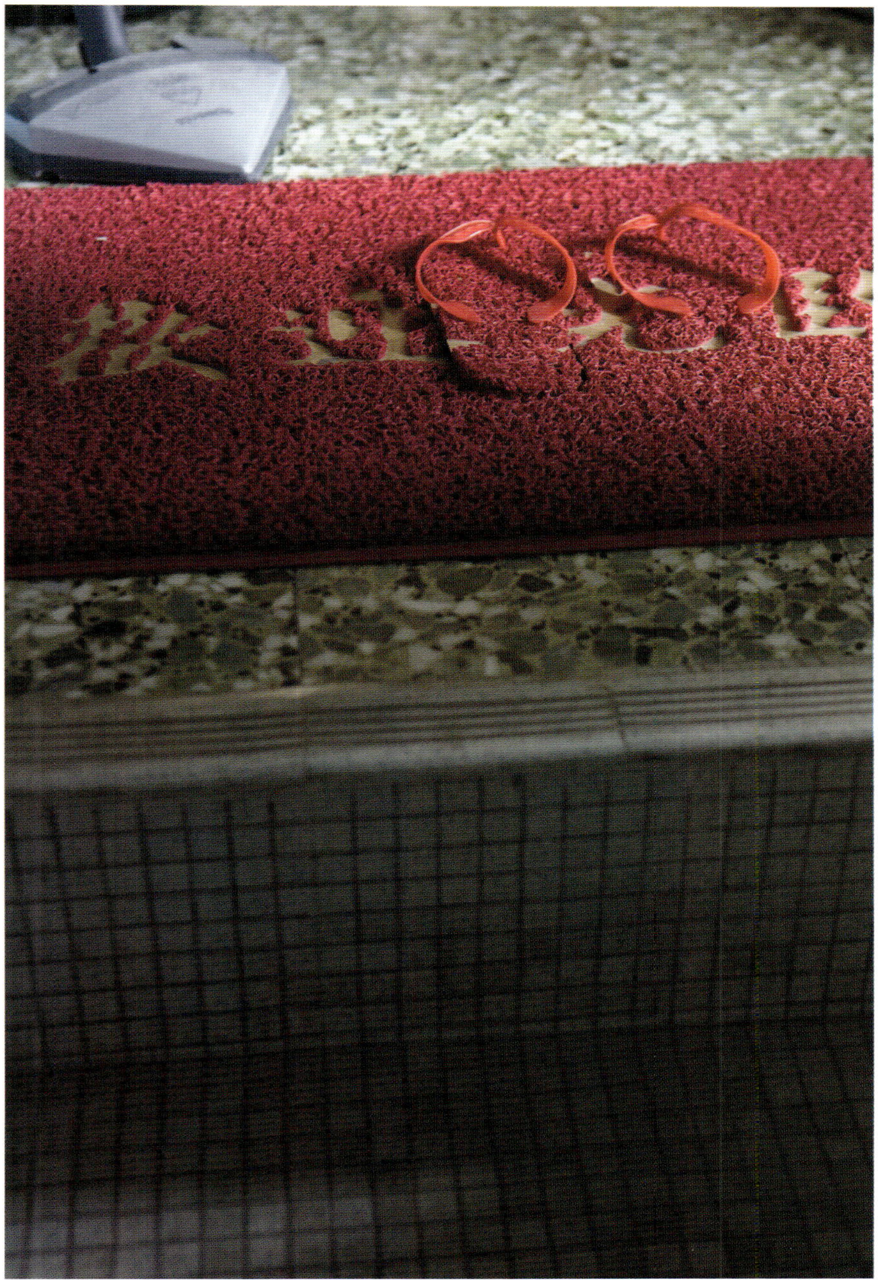

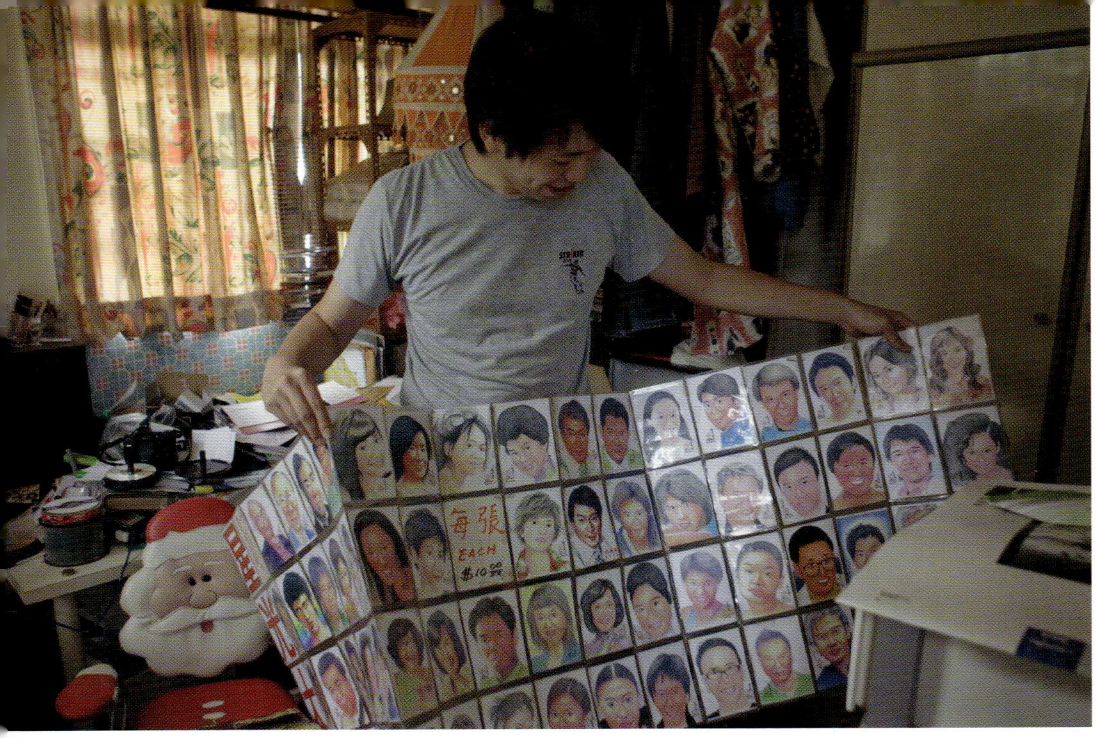

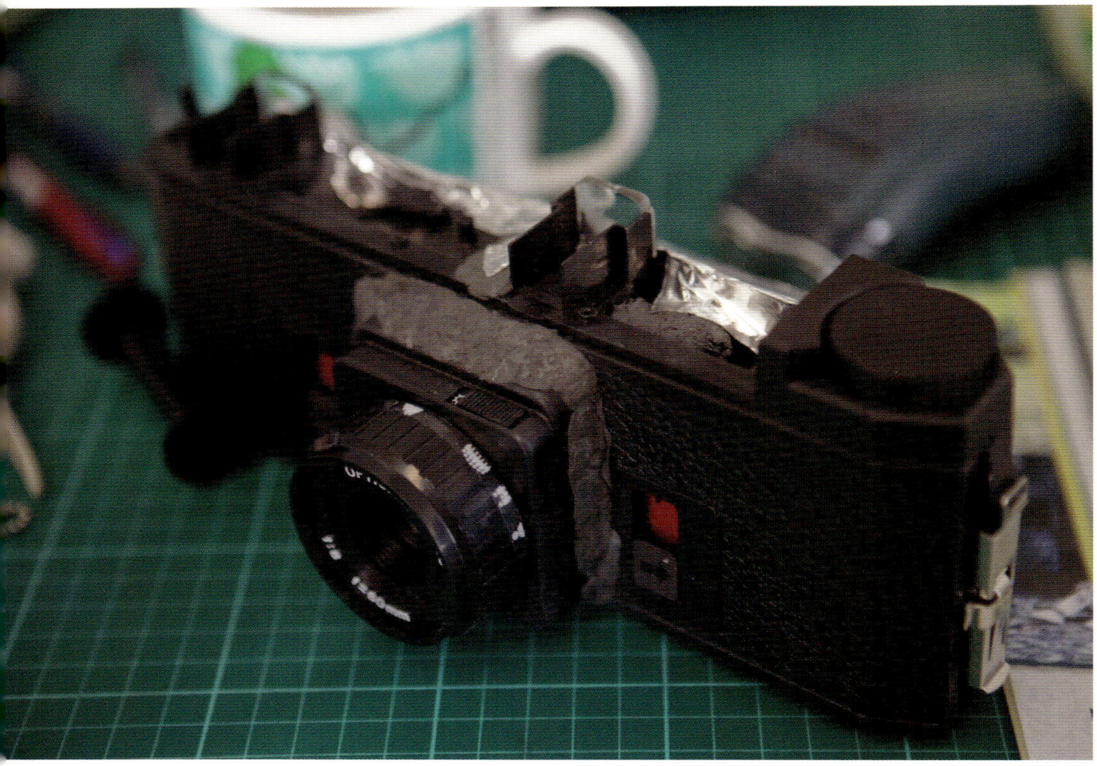

a dialogue between art and life. For example, in the series *Two in One* he had discovered that one day, the picture used for the top story in *Wenweipo* (also known as *Wenhuibao*) was the same as that used by *Apple Daily*. He then wove the two pages together. As a result the text is all mixed up but the picture is still the same. So which story is true? Do the headlines tell us anything about the event? Ching wants to stimulate thinking by modifying the mundane.

Ching is like Stephen Chow; both of them shock their audiences with nonsense. For example, he speaks of flying to Taiwan specifically to have a lawful smoke in a cha chan ting (Hong Kong-style coffee house) and to London to lawfully eat a banana in the 'tube' or subway. These are like anecdotes in a Stephen Chow movie! Yet though his actions may seem nuts, his viewers, becoming aware of his ridicule of the Hong Kong laws, may share his sentiment. Maybe then they might decide to try eating bananas onboard. Recently Ching has taken to picnicking with a few local artists in the open area of Time Square. This is a form of rebuke for a management that annexes public space for commercial purposes. The act has resounded in a series of online discussions, so does its impact, or capacity for stimulating public discussion and rethinking, make this work legitimate public art?

Ching says that his work has been significantly influenced by professor Kurt Chan Yuk-keung of the Department of Fine Arts and Hong Kong artist Ho Siu-kee. He was very much inspired by the mixed media classes of professor Chan who, by transforming simple things in clever ways, endowed objects with new forms and meanings. Ching says that for him, realism is powerful. To show what is real, close observation is as vital as the skills learnt during academic training. In the 1990s Ho came up with a visionary study of the body. It overwhelmed Ching and made him want to incorporate the 'people' element into his own work.

Because Ching works with concepts, any place can become his temporary studio. His pinhole cameras series is set in dark rooms with windows that are used as shutters, turning them into larger-than-life cameras. Light gets in through the 'shutter' and a photograph is taken on photosensitive paper pinned on the

Luke Ching Chin-wai is truly living in art — his tools and artworks are all over the place at home

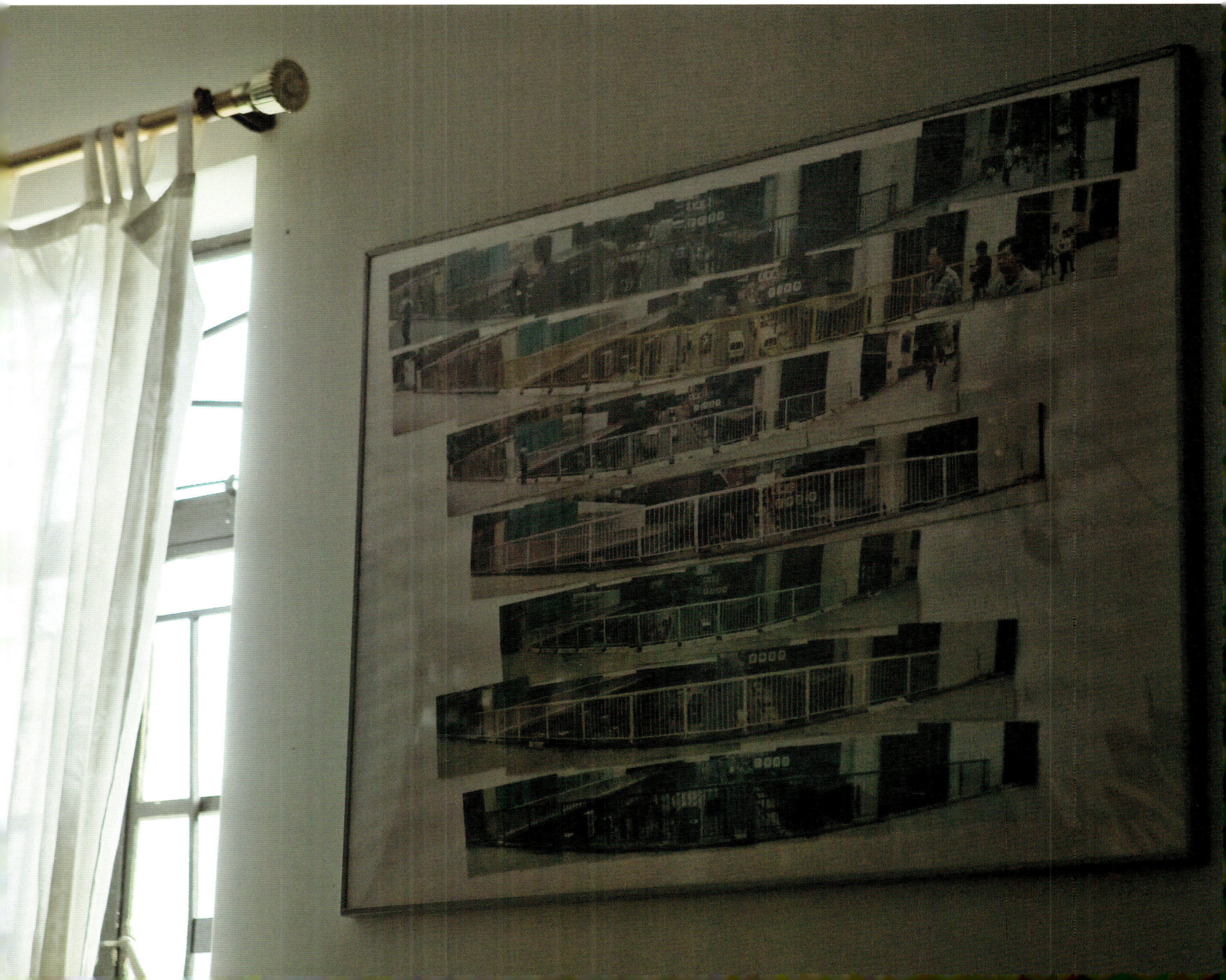

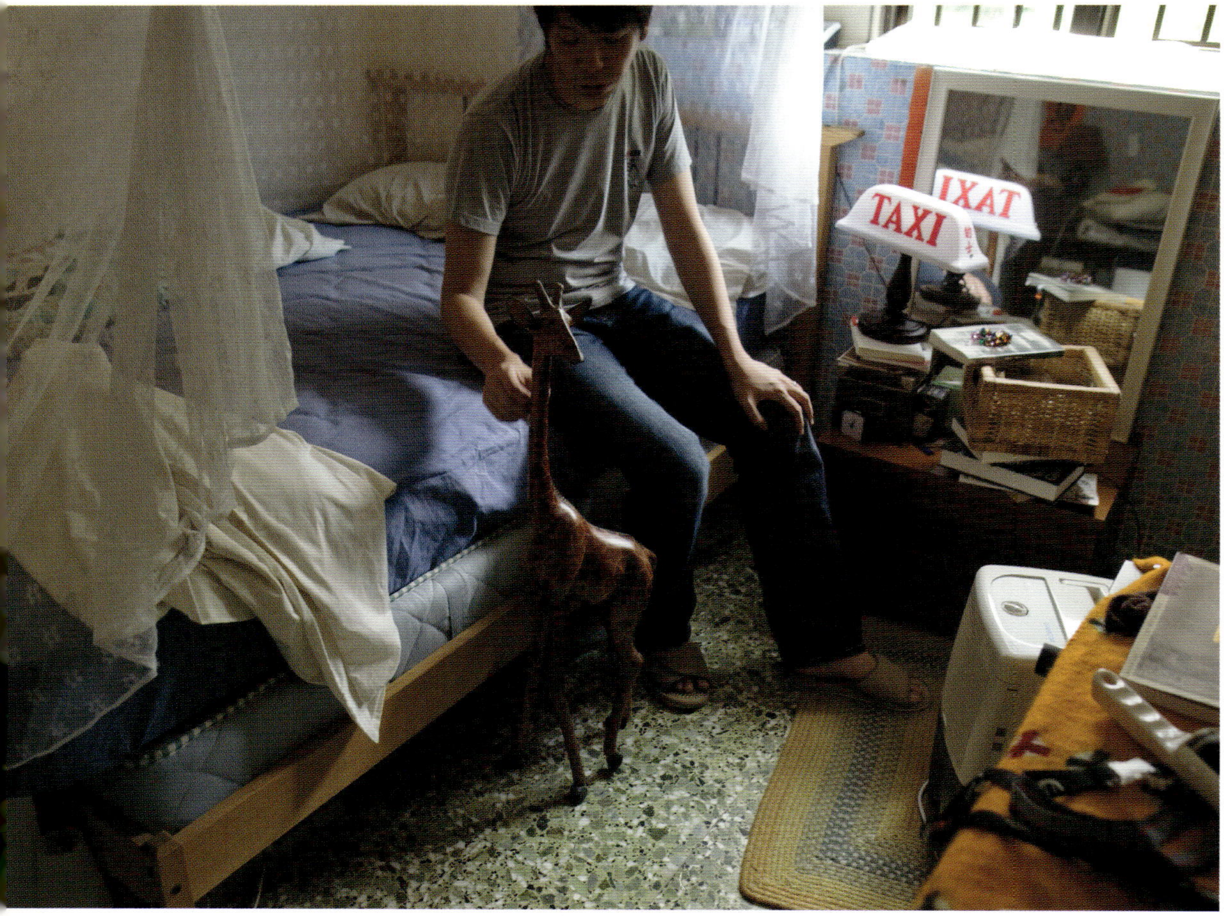
TAXI

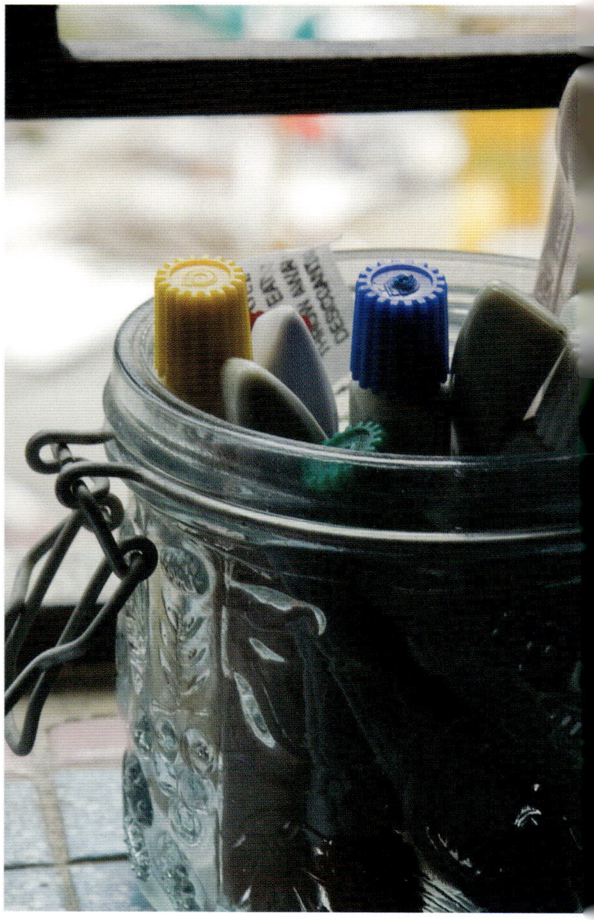

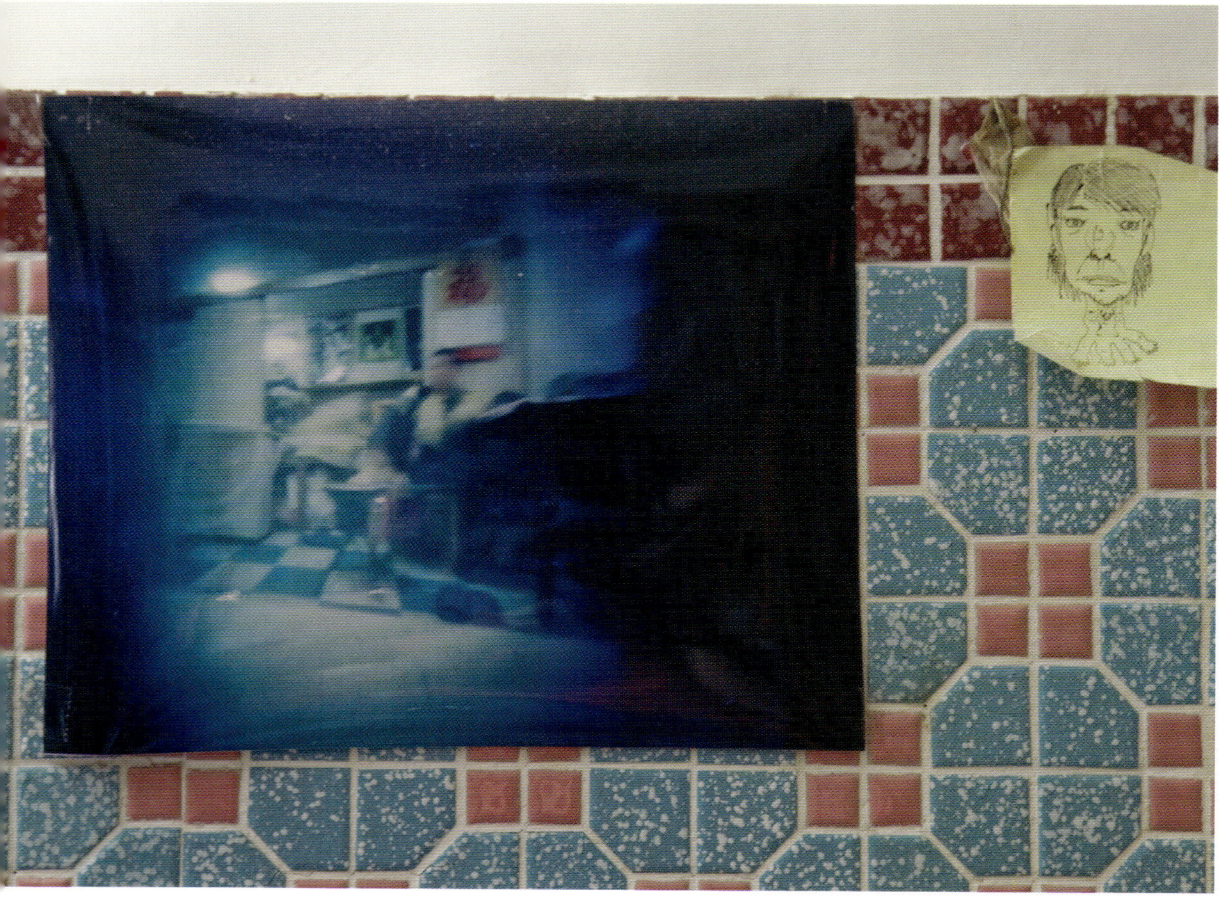

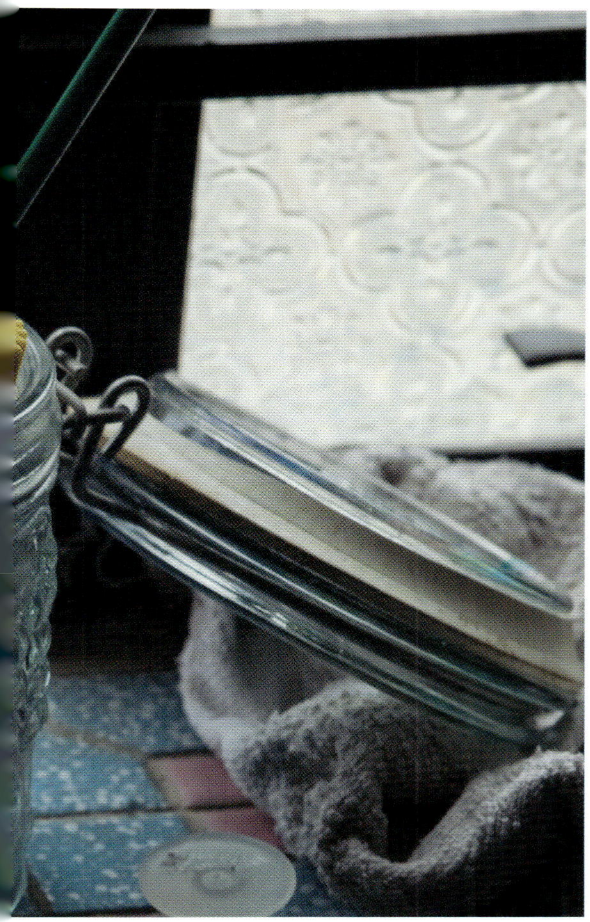

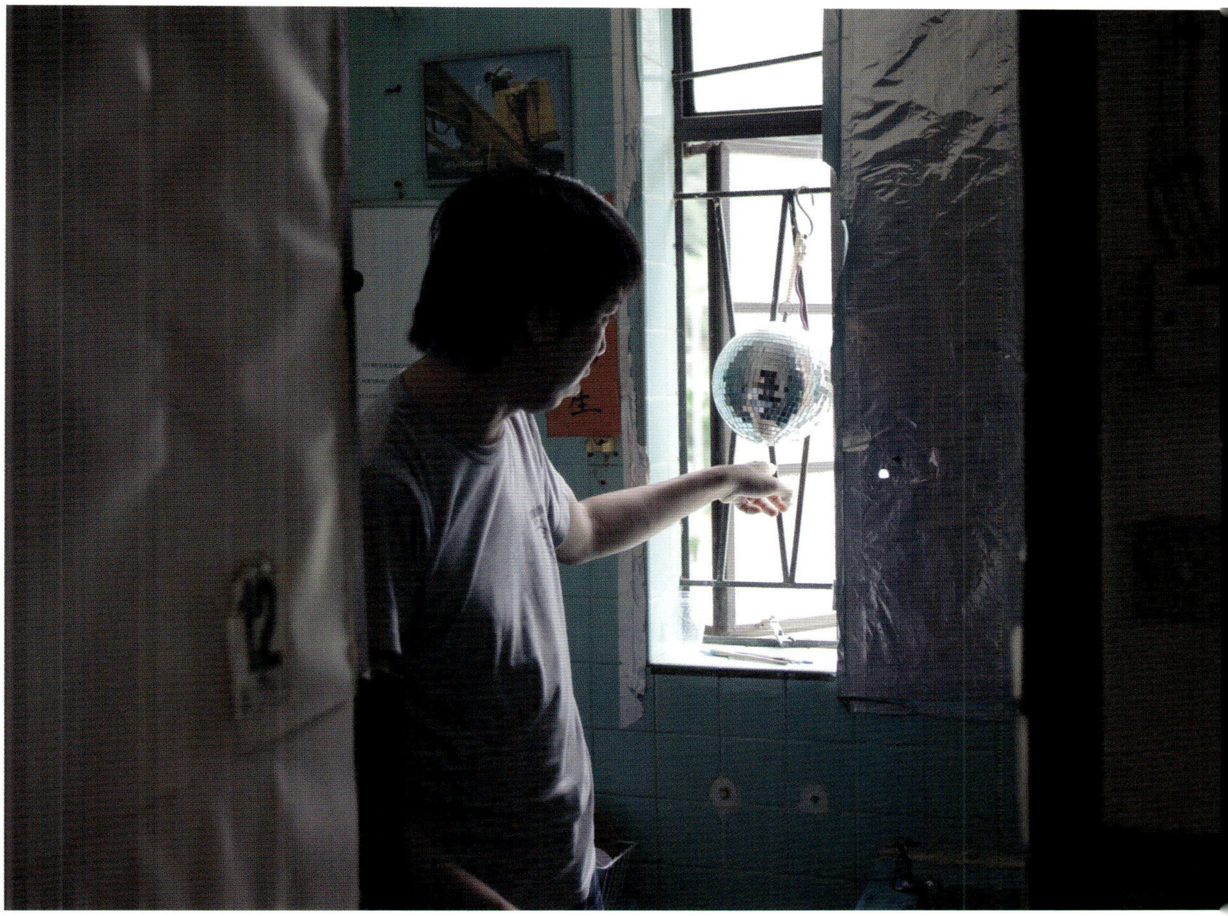

other side of the room. The rooms, borrowed from friends, become his temporary studios.

The word 'studio' does not mean too much to Ching. His art merges with his life to the extent that it is hard to tell them apart. In another series, titled *Shang Yue* (Moon Watching), he flies helium balloons in a number of shopping malls. He sees the balloons as the moon, and a picture in his blog shows him shopping for groceries with one. However do not mistake this is as a symbol. The truth, he says, is that he was simply shopping with his wife while he flew that particular 'moon'. He seizes every opportunity to make art.

Ching's ideal working space is one that does not have to be tidied. "My place is always messy," he admits. "My wife gave up tidying it long ago!" It seems that a tidiness-free space is what most artists want.

Compared to art made in the 1980s and 1990s, artists' work today is more pluralistic. As the audience has grown in size, so has its acceptance of the new and the novel. Ching likes the current situation, and thinks that Hong Kong is a strange, inspirational place, full of farce and distortion.

Ching's art is like a series of experiments. He starts with an idea or a hypothesis then tests it in different ways to come to a conclusion. Sometimes there are mistakes and surprises along the way, yet these add to the work's meaning. Ching is like Stephen Chow and a scientist. Does he give you new ideas about art?

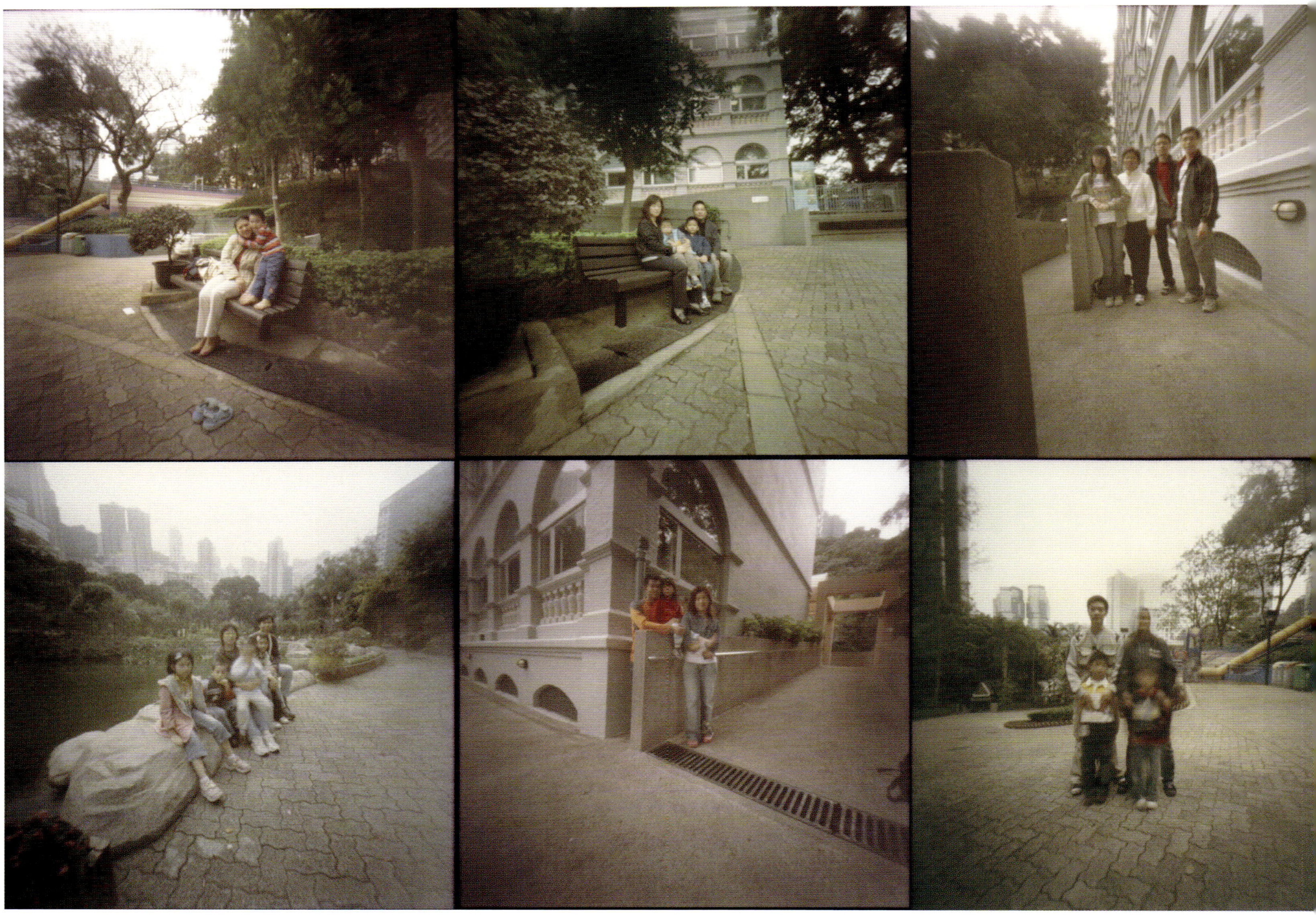

Family Pinhole Photo Project
Happening, 2007-08

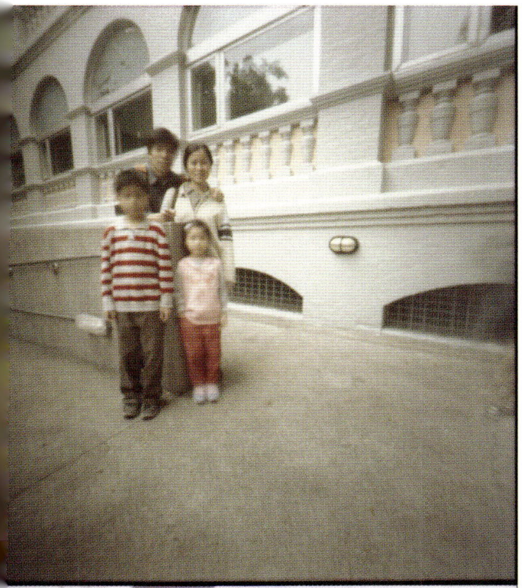

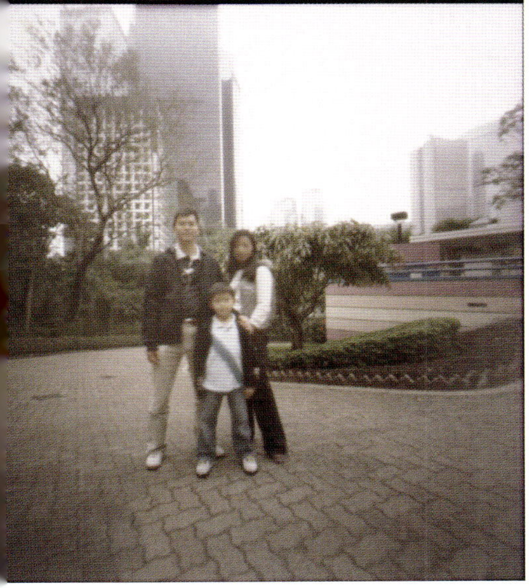

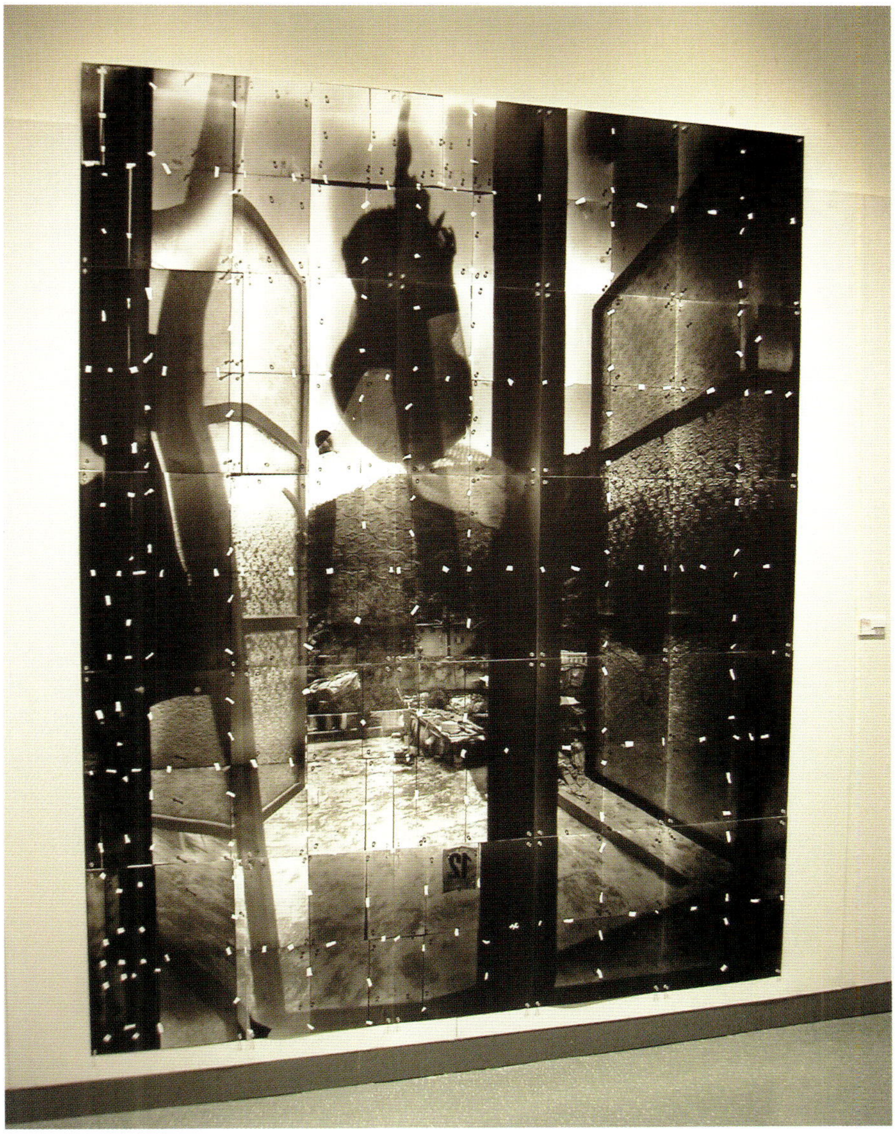

Room as Pinhole Camera Series
Photo, 1999-06

Yip Man-yam

Telling a Complete Life in a Half Room

By Carl Cheng

Yip Man-yam (alias 'Siu-chai') was born in Shanghai in 1949. He currently teaches in the School of Professional and Continuing Education (SPACE) of the University of Hong Kong and is the programme coordinator for Chinese art there. Yip learned Chinese calligraphy and seal engraving from Li Chu-sheng, a professional painter, calligrapher and seal engraver at the Shanghai Painting School. Yip moved to Hong Kong in 1982 and his calligraphy works were shown in major exhibitions in Hong Kong, China, Taiwan, Japan, Korea, the United States and Europe. His calligraphy and seals were awarded the Urban Council Fine Arts Award in the Contemporary Hong Kong Art Biennial of 1994 and 1996 respectively. He was also awarded the Fellowship for Artistic Development by the Arts Development Council and a number of other prizes on the mainland and in Japan. Yip's calligraphy follows in the steps of tradition but is also responsive to contemporary moods. His seal engraving is of a unique style that perfectly balances positive and negative space.

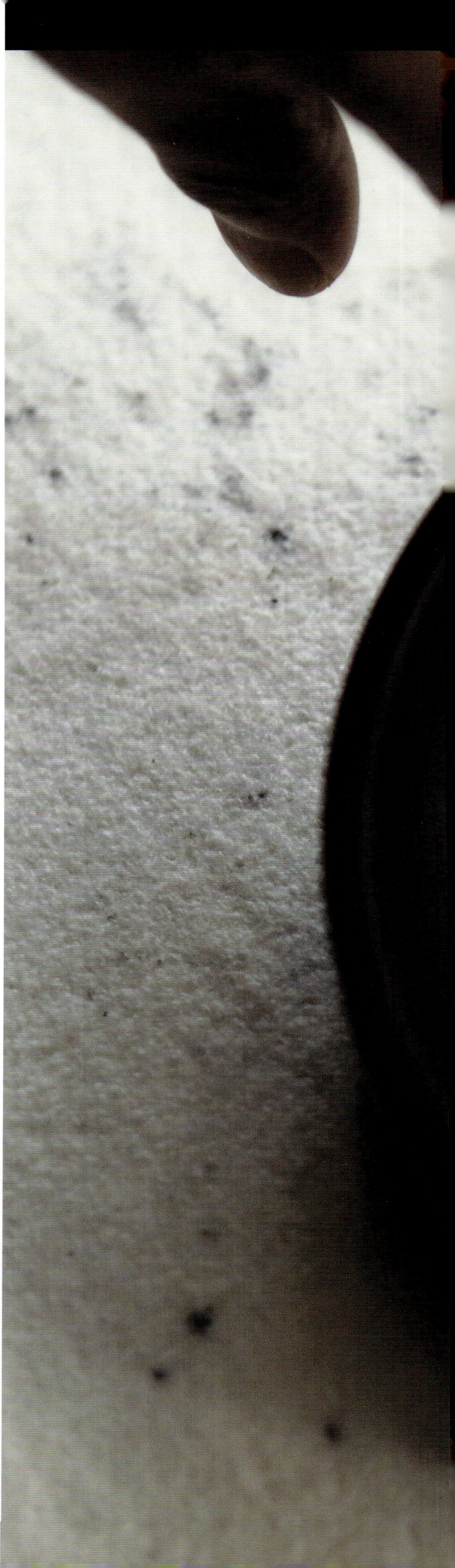

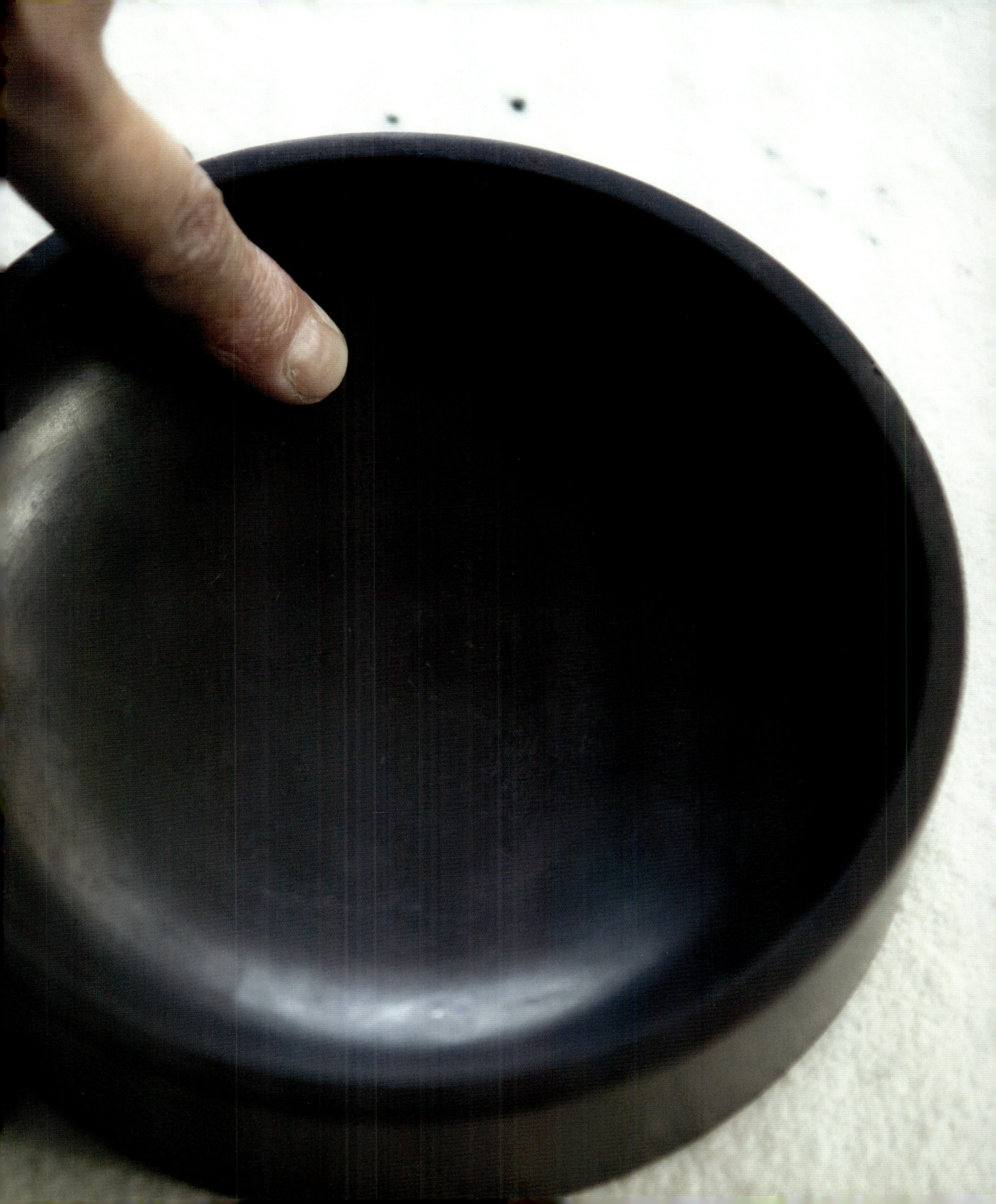

In a time of absurdity, some people may follow the trend and lead an absurd life. Some cannot bear it and break down. Still others quietly struggle against adversity and devote themselves to art. Time and people keep changing. When the years of absurdity come to an end, the world may become normal again – or even more absurd.

Yip Man-yam grew up during the Cultural Revolution. Born into a wealthy intellectual family, he started to live in constant fear when their family chemical manufacturing business founded by his grandfather was classified as belonging to the 'Five Black Categories'. He was criticised and denounced by classmates and witnessed repeated intrusions into his home by the Red Guards. It was only at night that things were peaceful. Yip started to focus his passion on calligraphy and seal engraving, deeply engaging himself with each brushstroke and each mark made by the engraving knife. Years of practice built a solid foundation in the art. Looking back, this may not be as bad as it first appeared.

When he was young, Yip considered calligraphy and seal engraving a shelter, or escape from cruel reality. He named his study 'Half Room' and told his instructor, Li Chusheng, that he had chosen the name because he only had half a life. This feeling was shared by Li, as no one could lead a normal existence in those years.

After dropping out from school Yip worked on construction sites for five years as a manual labourer. Later on he was transferred to the Jing'an district of Shanghai and spent four years in the import and export of artworks. His main duties were collecting works from artists for export to places including Japan, which had established formal diplomatic relations with China. At that time the calligraphy works and paintings he acquired did not cost much but the artists he contacted were all masters: Cheng Shifa, Lu Yanshao, Tang Yun, to name but a few. Yip had a chance to not only see the masters' artworks, but also to get guidance from them. This provided him with the basis for art appreciation in the future.

Time changes life, but life does not necessarily go as one wishes. However there is always hope for a better future. Achieving little progress on the mainland, Yip went to Hong Kong in 1982 to visit relatives from Taiwan

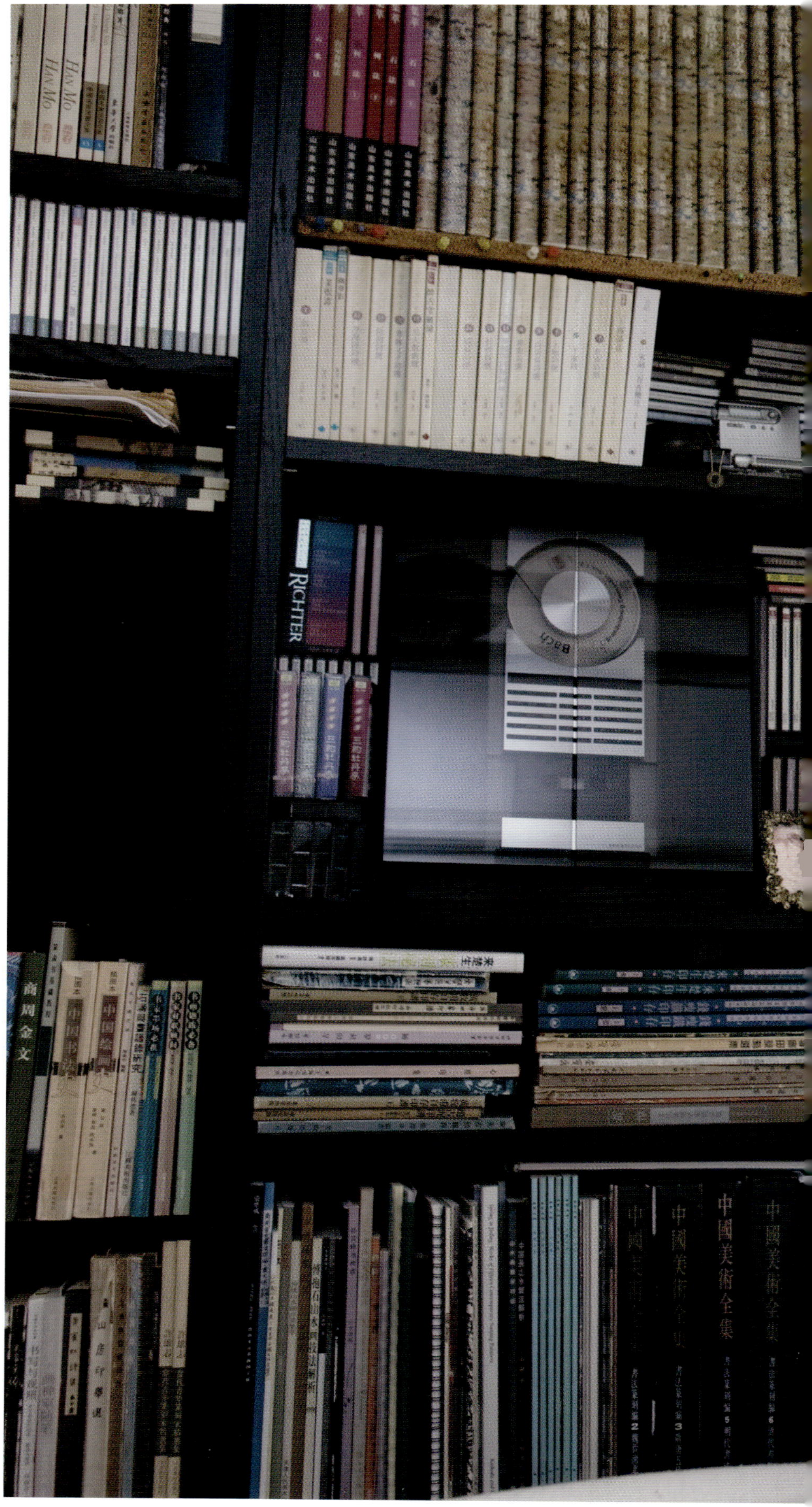

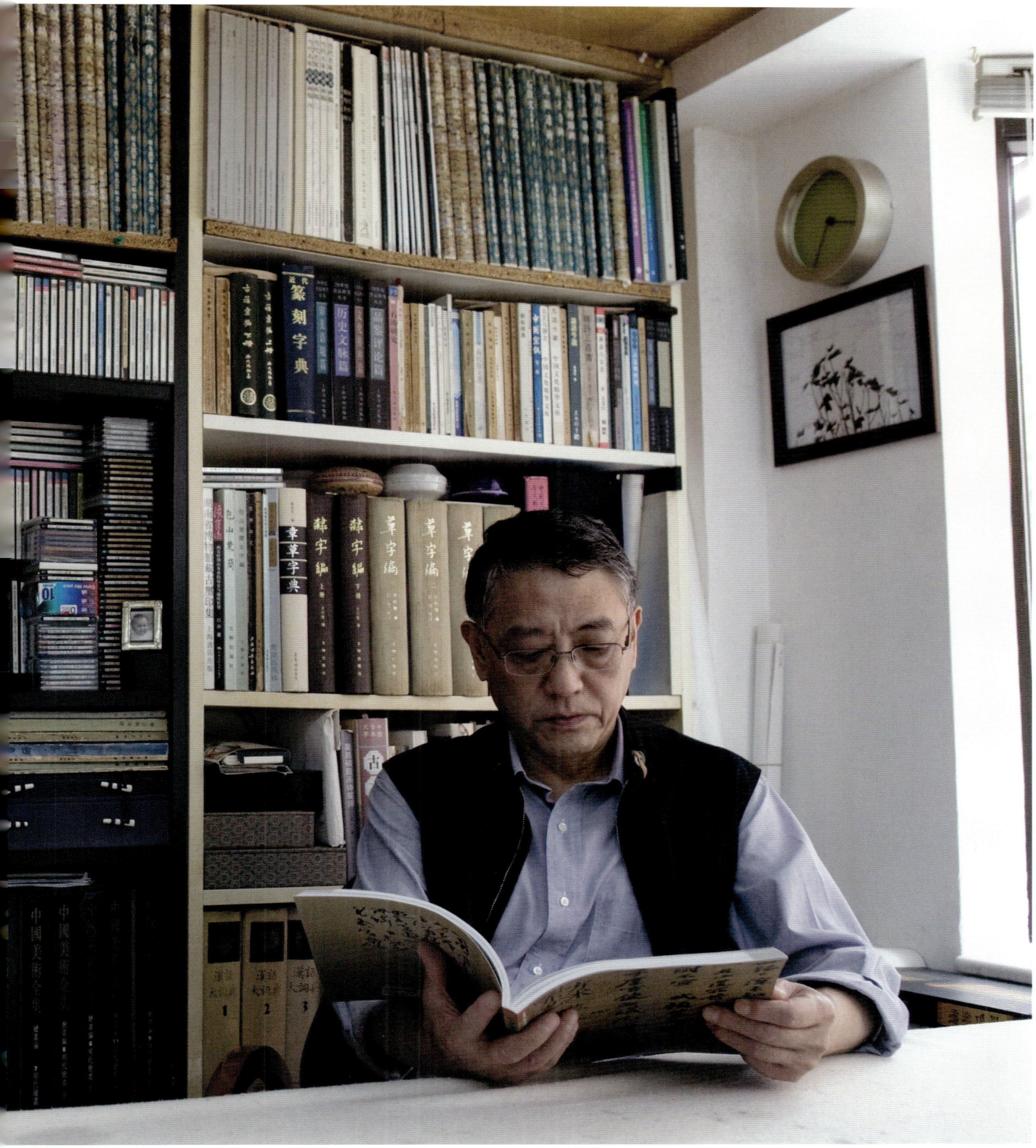
篆刻字典
历史文脉篇
品鉴评论篇
隸字編
草字編
章草字典
中國美術全集

and explore further opportunities for career development. He stayed. In an unfamiliar place and knowing little of the language, Yip's friends introduced him to a jewellery workshop where he worked as apprentice for more than half a year. Already in his thirties, Yip was a 'mature' apprentice, but his fine crafting skills were much appreciated by the workshop owner who transferred him to the jewellery design section. Yip would receive commissions to engrave seals in his spare time in order to earn more money. In less than a year, he met Leung Kui-ting, an artist and design teacher, and started to teach calligraphy and seal engraving, which is related to typography design, at the Chingying Institute of Visual Arts. Yip has since continued to teach at various educational institutions.

Yip says that he has a deep sense of belonging in Hong Kong, and is impressed by the freedom of the city. He can fully express himself here without fear of restriction, and can gain more when he pays more. In this land where the capable can reap, Yip has nearly always held down two jobs. Teaching calligraphy and seal engraving gives him a stable income and he also works hard to develop his artist career, studying intensively to perfect his skills. He does not make detailed plans for the future, but tries his best in every task. He is grateful for the chance to do what he loves and live a life that is much better than the days behind him, when everything was controlled by others. Whenever he recalls the days of the Cultural Revolution, he treasures his life in Hong Kong even more.

Looking back at the long years of artistic pursuit, Yip considers his youth to his thirties as a foundation period, for it was in his forties that he started to explore the true meaning of the art of calligraphy. He sees his fifties as the initial period of creating his calligraphy works, and his sixties will be a mature phase in the middle. He adopts Dong Qichang's[1] saying, of "adopting the tradition and turning it into something new". Reforming the spirit and method of traditional Chinese calligraphy is the direction in his art practice. Therefore his calligraphy works draw reference from the tradition, and at the same time are influenced

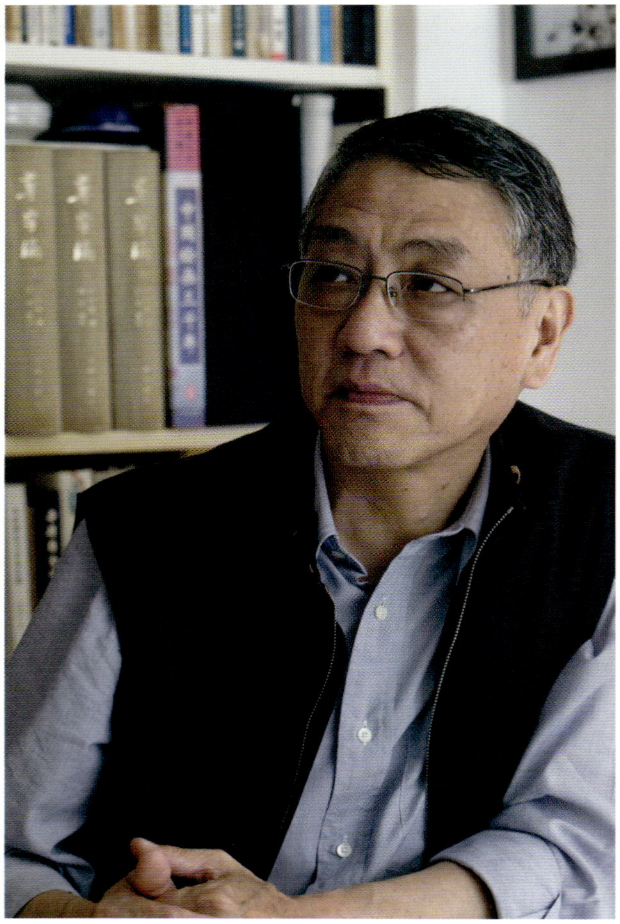

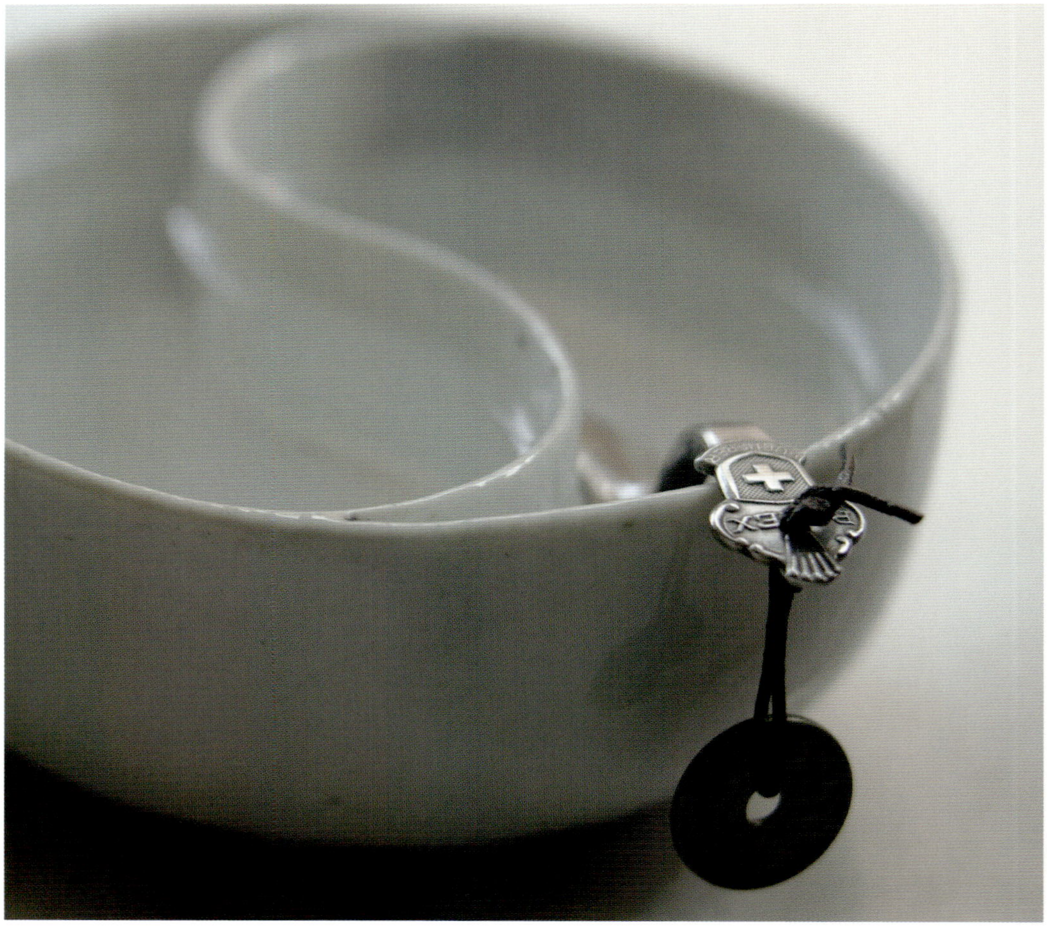

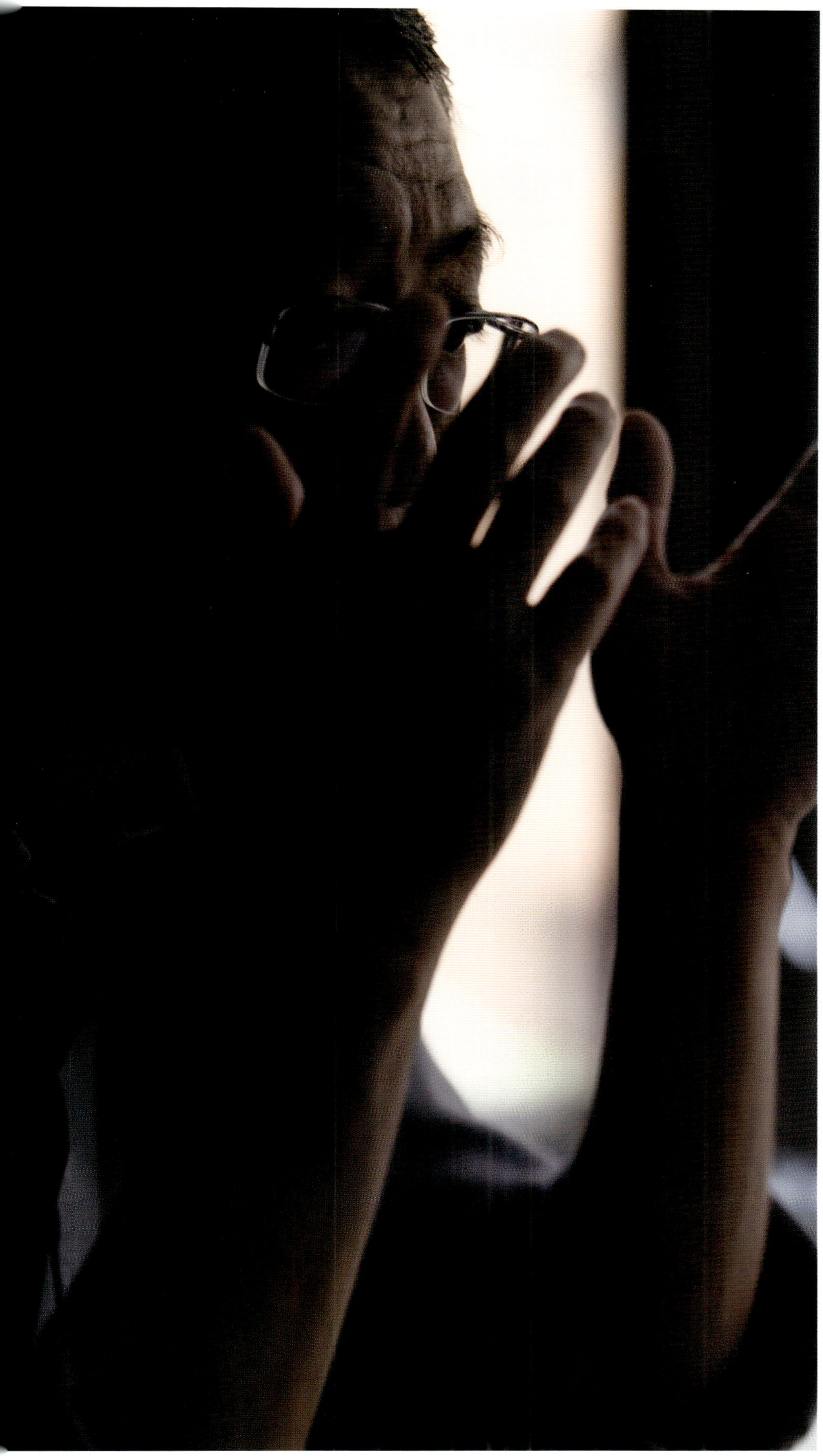

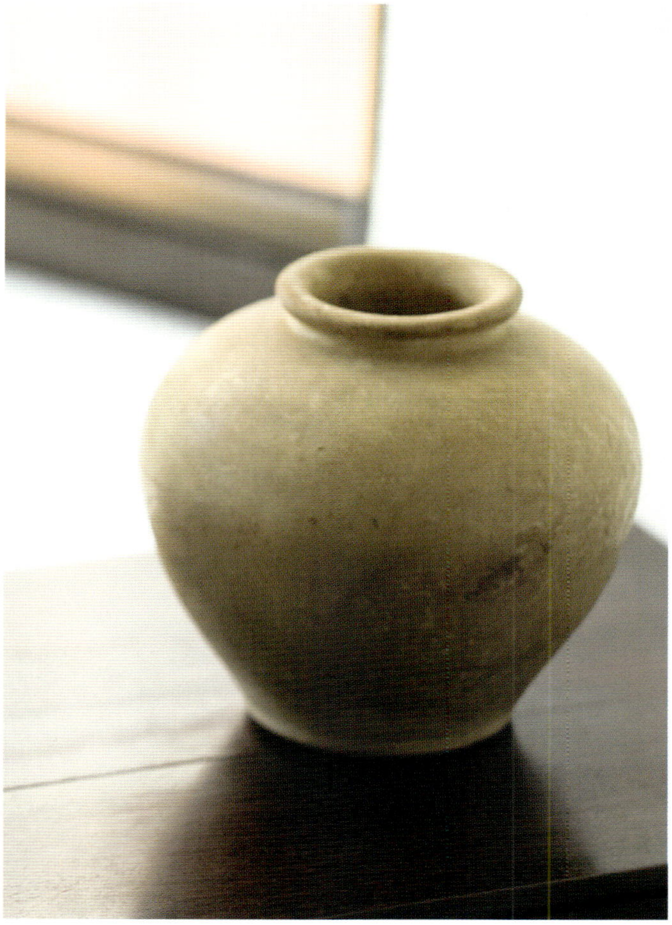

His life was spent in calligraphy and seal engraving. He named his study 'Half Room' because he only had half a life

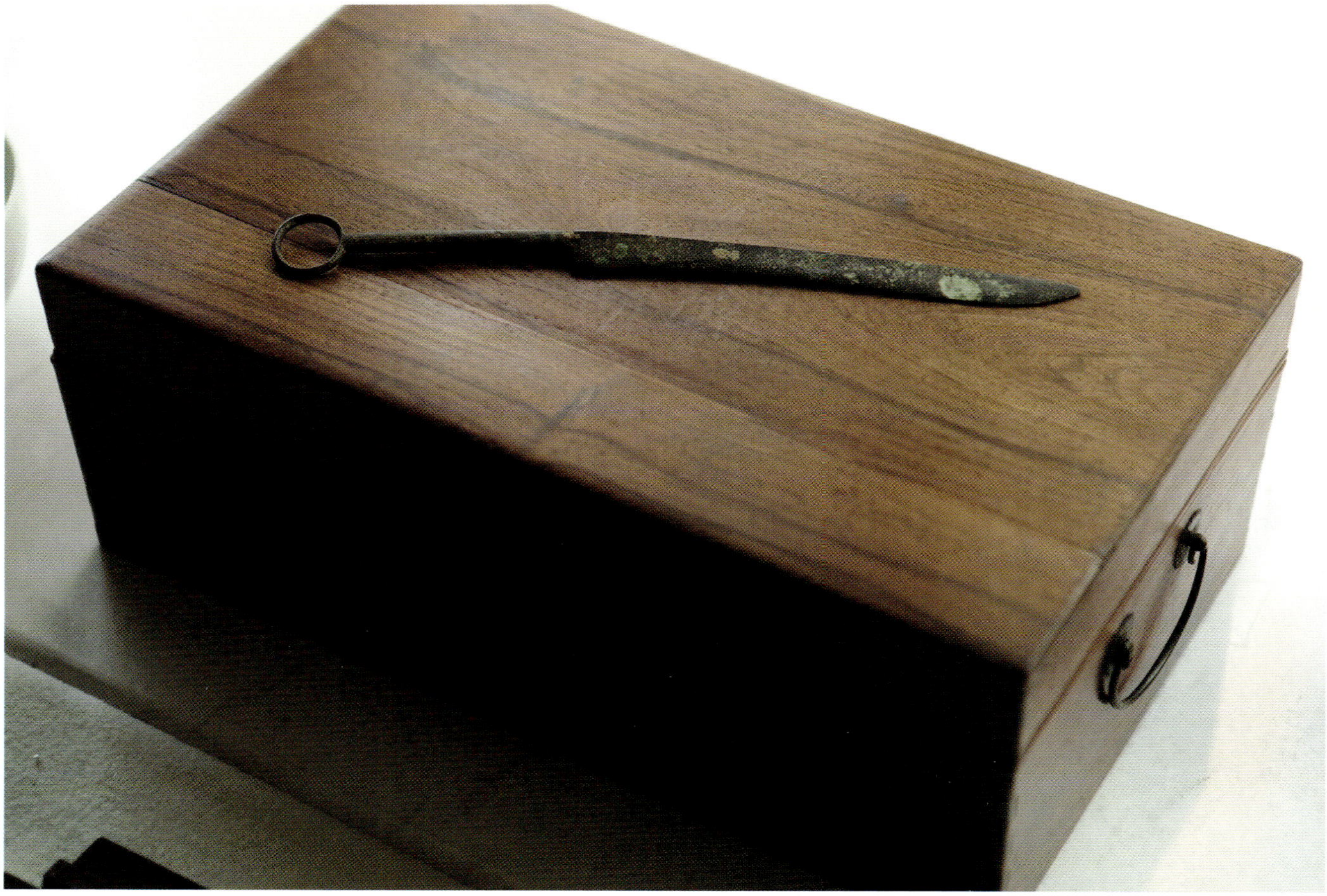

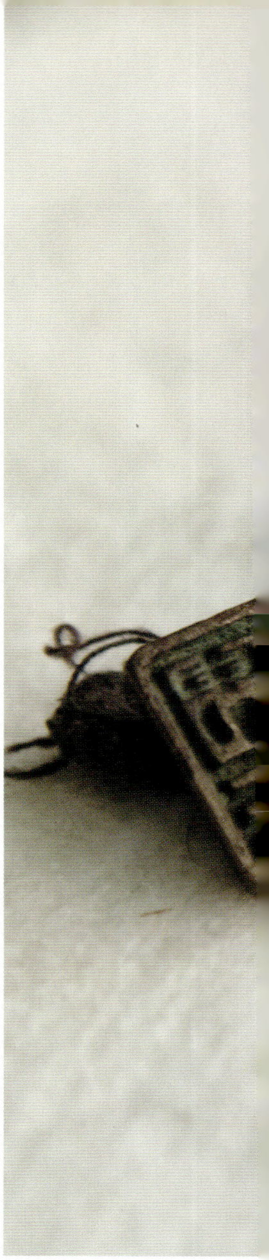

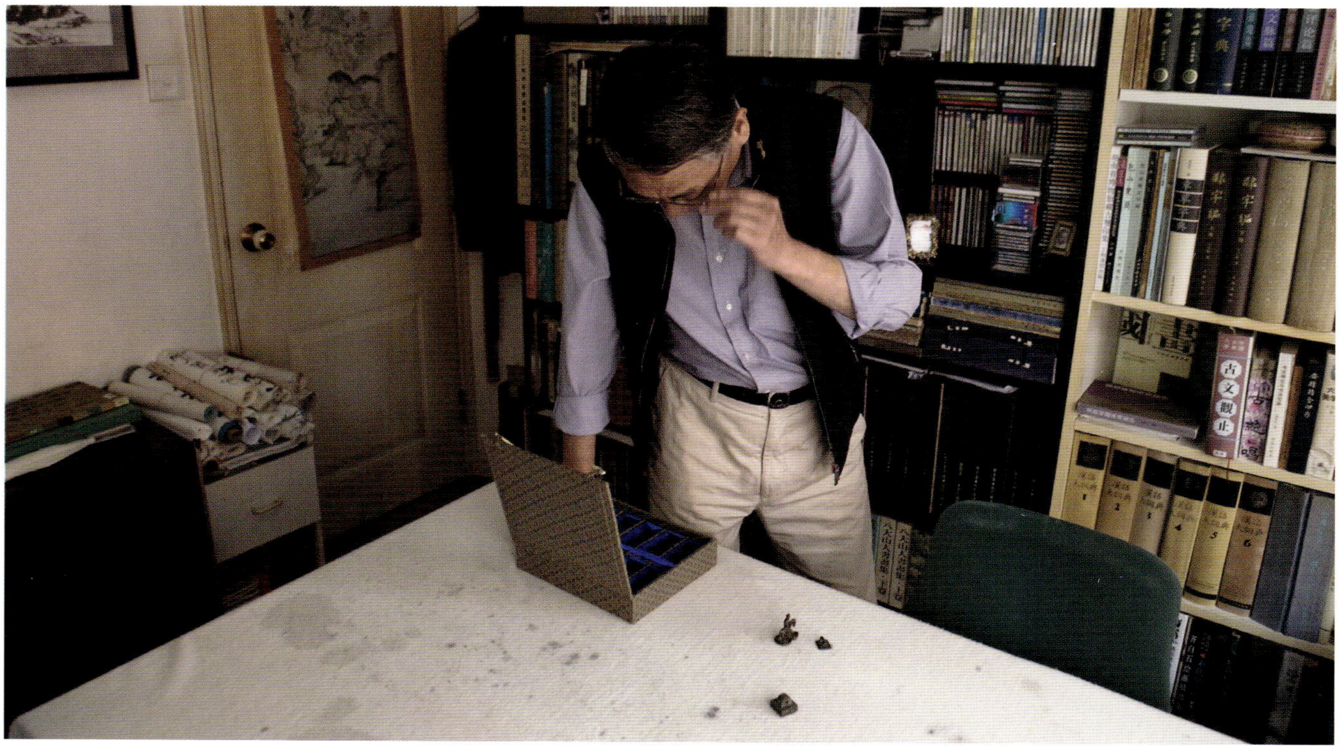

Appreciation and collection are part of art creation

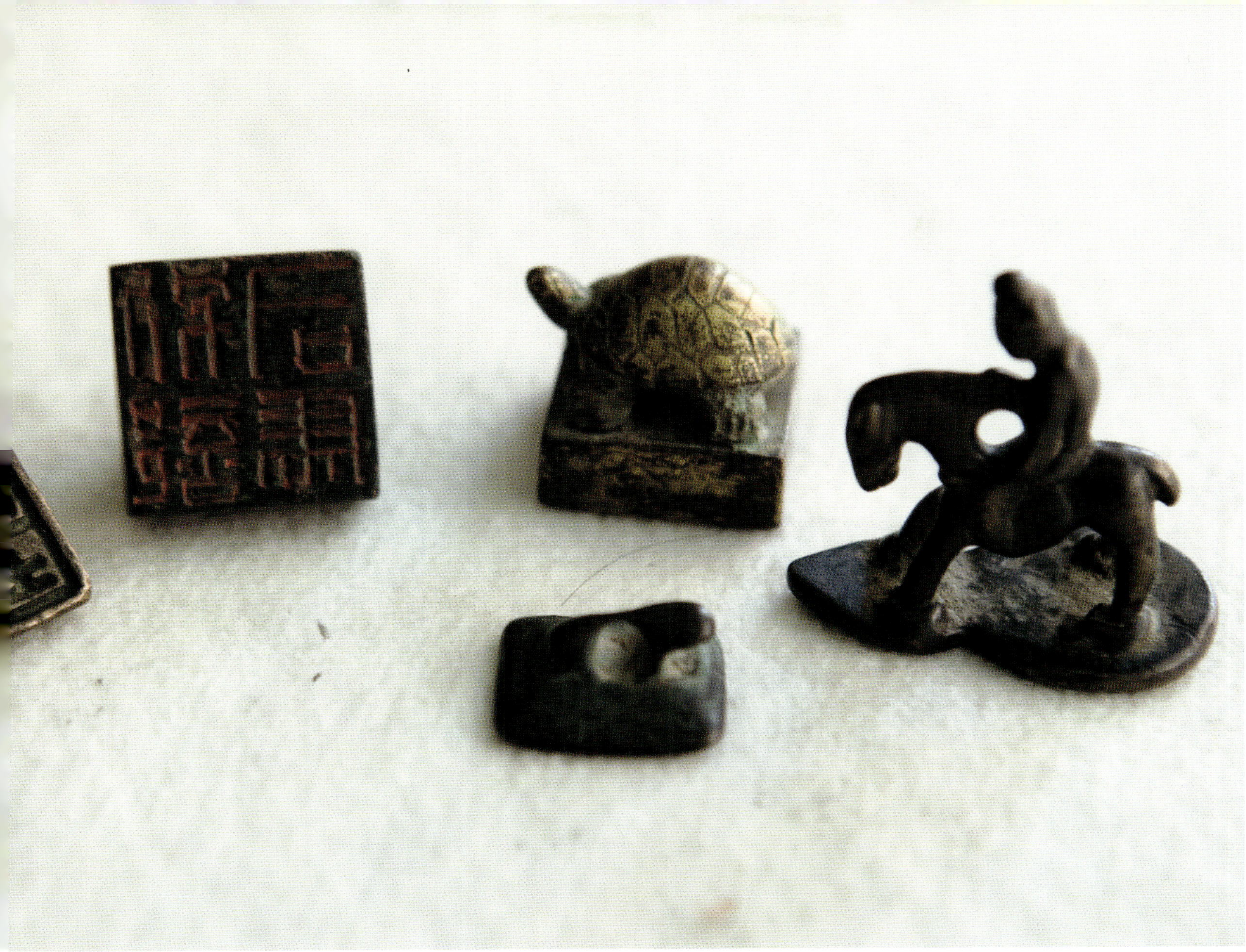

by the modern environment and spirit, showing strong characteristics of contemporary visual art. He puts much emphasis on the state attained through calligraphy, and takes it as a mirror of man's spiritual mind. That's why one's achievement in calligraphy is largely determined by mind and character.

His studio space, 'Half Room', has always been a part of his home. When he first learned calligraphy, he often practised at night while everyone else slept. Now he is largely occupied with teaching and administrative work, leaving him with little time for art. He seizes every spare hour he has. Now in his fifties, Yip can create artworks in his mind. Whenever inspiration arrives, he puts everything down, and even wakes up from his sleep. He describes this as "a destiny that one has to fulfill".

From a flat in Landale Street, Wanchai, where he lived during the 1980s, to the housing estate in mid-level North Point, where he now resides, Yip has never had strict requirements for a studio. Adequate lighting (the lamp he has used for 12 years was made in Germany, and he has got used to its light intensity) and a tabletop are the main essentials. Larger works are made in his living room. It is a bit inconvenient, as the living room in his current home is smaller than the one he had before. The storage of Chinese painting and calligraphy is relatively simple but Yip still handles it in a professional way, and records and categorises all his works in details. Yip has also started Chinese painting in recent years, echoing the Chinese saying that calligraphy and painting share the same origin.

Going through the test of the Cultural Revolution and experiencing real hardship in life has allowed Yip to know human nature. The freedom of Hong Kong has completed the half life he once led, and the support of his wife has provided him with the security he needs in an artistic career. A wooden plaque bearing the Chinese characters of 'Half Room', engraved by Yip Hoi, his first friend in Hong Kong, still hangs in his studio, reminding him of the past. Now heading into his sixties, Yip maintains the habit of making art in the quietness of the night when others have gone to sleep, expressing his life in his calligraphy, seals and paintings.

1 Translator's note: Dong Qichang (1555-1636) is a Chinese painter, scholar, calligrapher and art theorist of the late Ming dynasty.

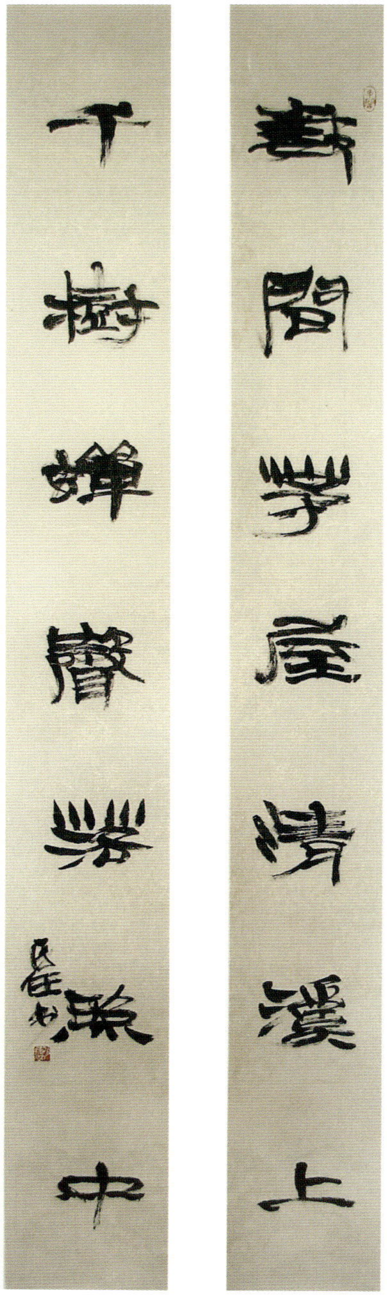

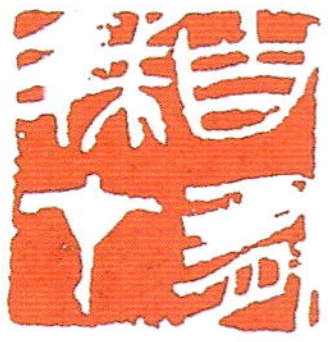

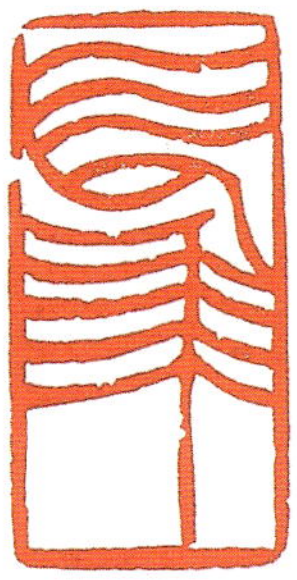

(Left) Ancient Couplet in Clerical Script
Ink on paper, 112x14x2 cm, 2006

(Middle) Seal Carving – Zi You Wo Zai (Self-presence)
White seal (intaglio), 2000

(Right) Seal Carving – Chang Nian (Long Years)
Red seal (relief), 1999

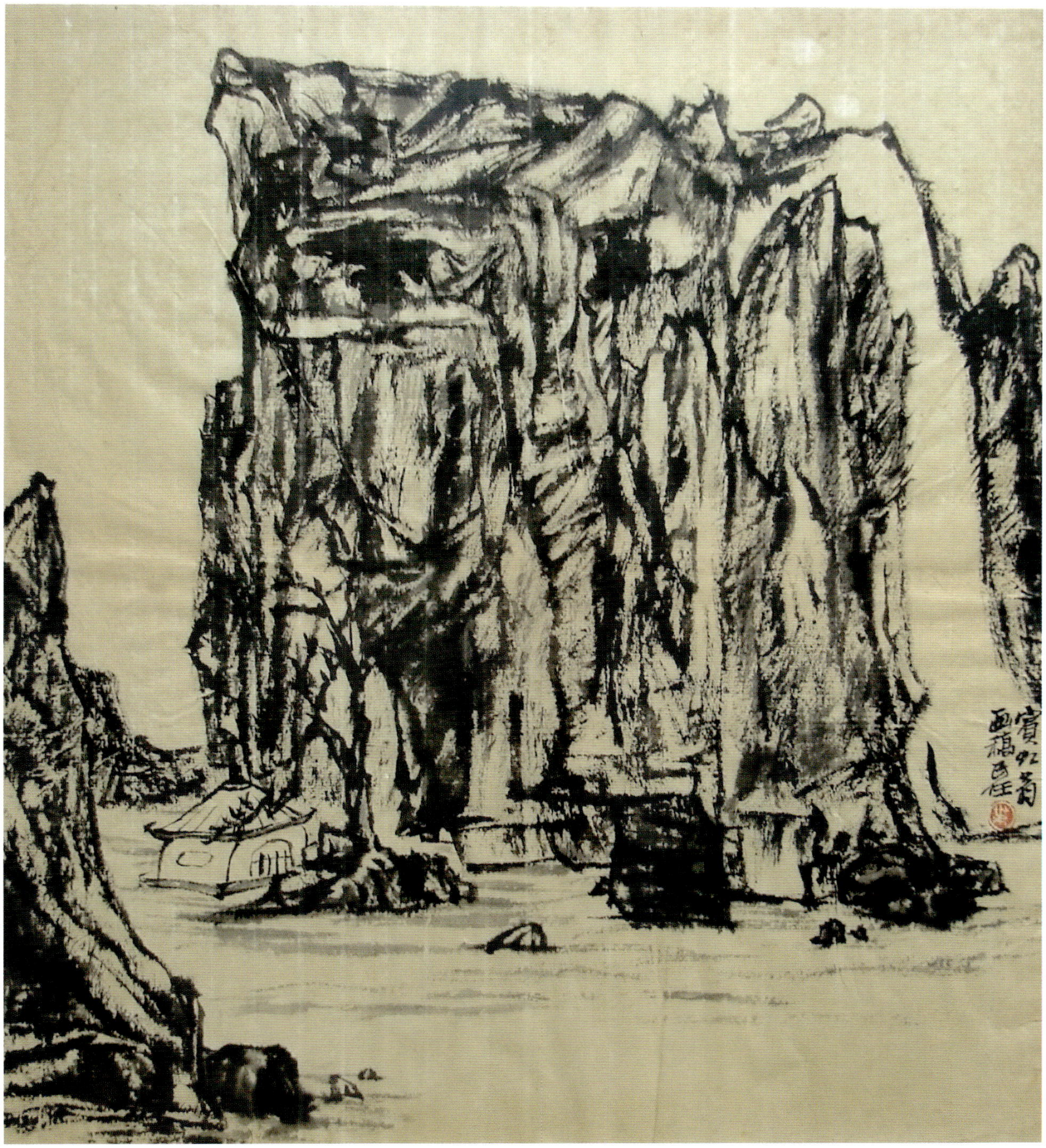

Yixie Binhong Shanshui (Bin Hong Landscape)
Ink on paper, 44x40.5 cm, 2007

Chu Hing-wah

Harvest Time

By Stephanie Cheung

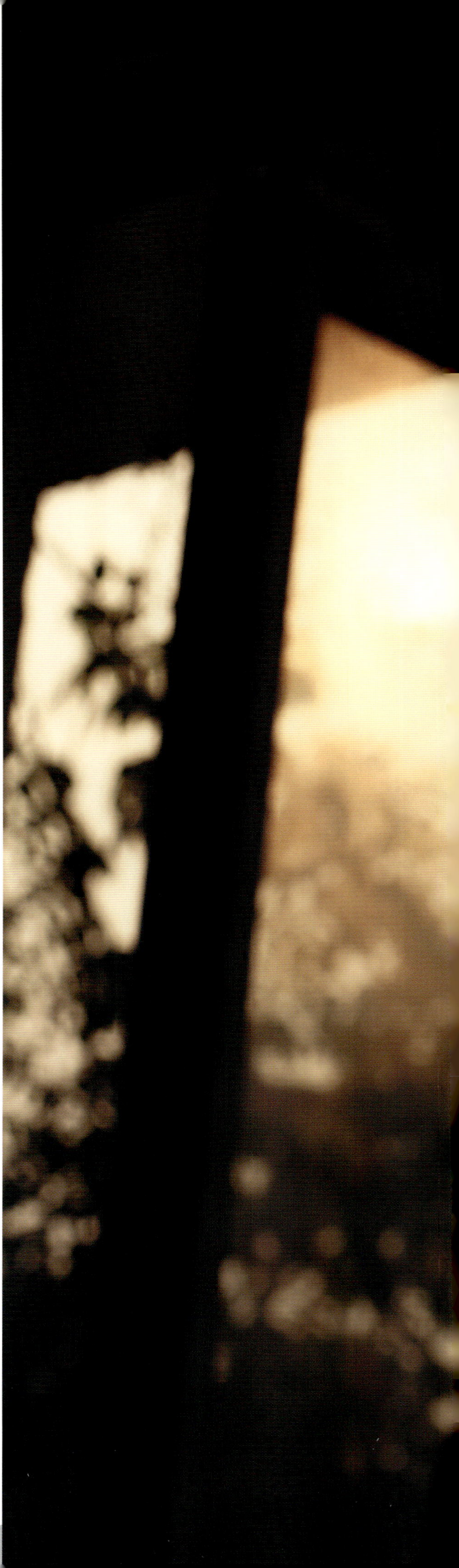

Chu Hing-wah was born in China in 1935 and has been living in Hong Kong since 1951. He has been committed to painting ever since his graduation from the Department of Extra Mural Studies at the University of Hong Kong in 1974. With their layers of ink and colour, his works show his care for the world around him. He has received the Hong Kong Urban Council Fine Art Award (1989), the Painter of the Year honour from the Hong Kong Artists' Guild Association (1992) and a scholarship for art research in the United States from the Asian Cultural Council. He is currently an Art Adviser for the Hong Kong Leisure and Cultural Services Department.

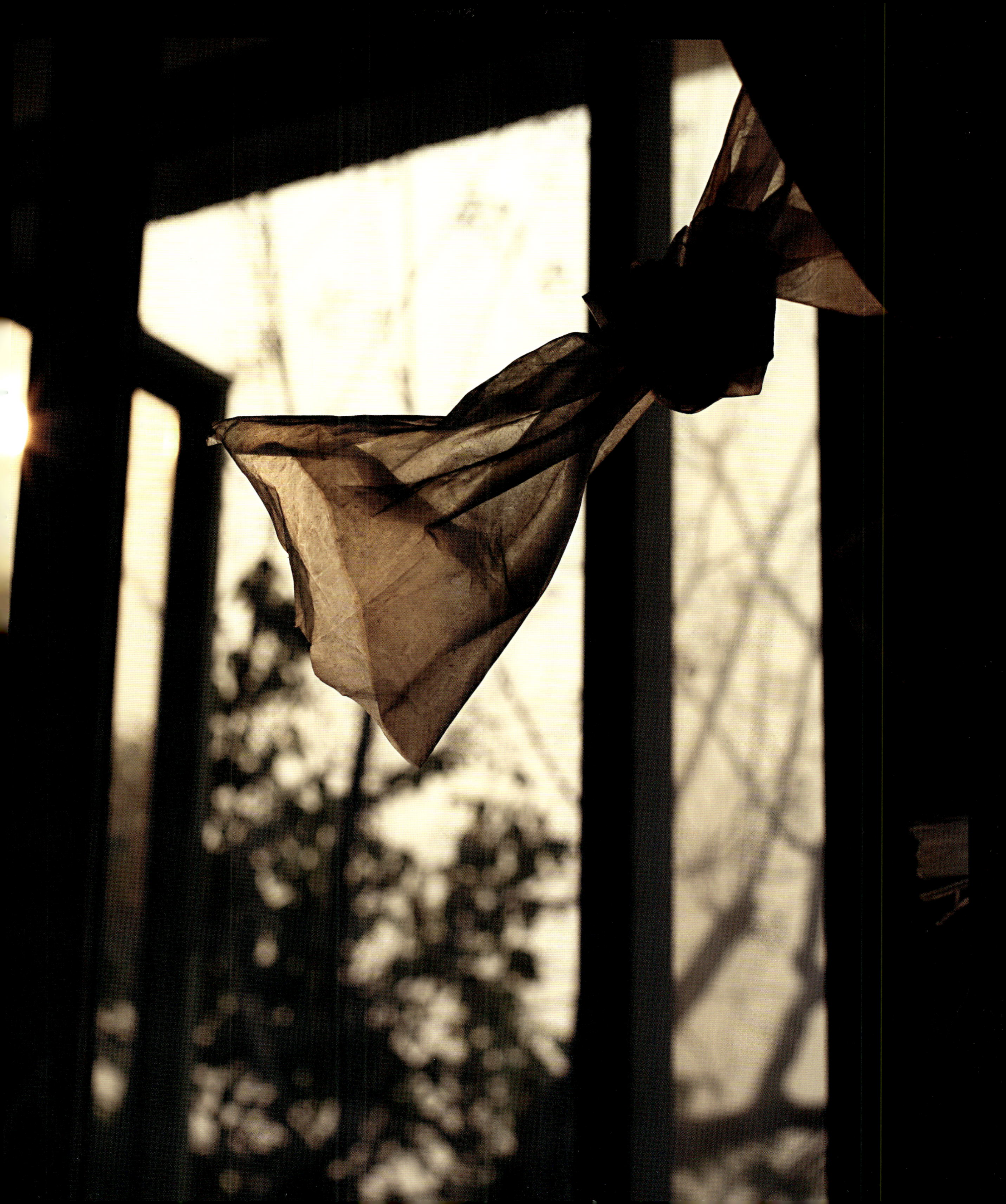

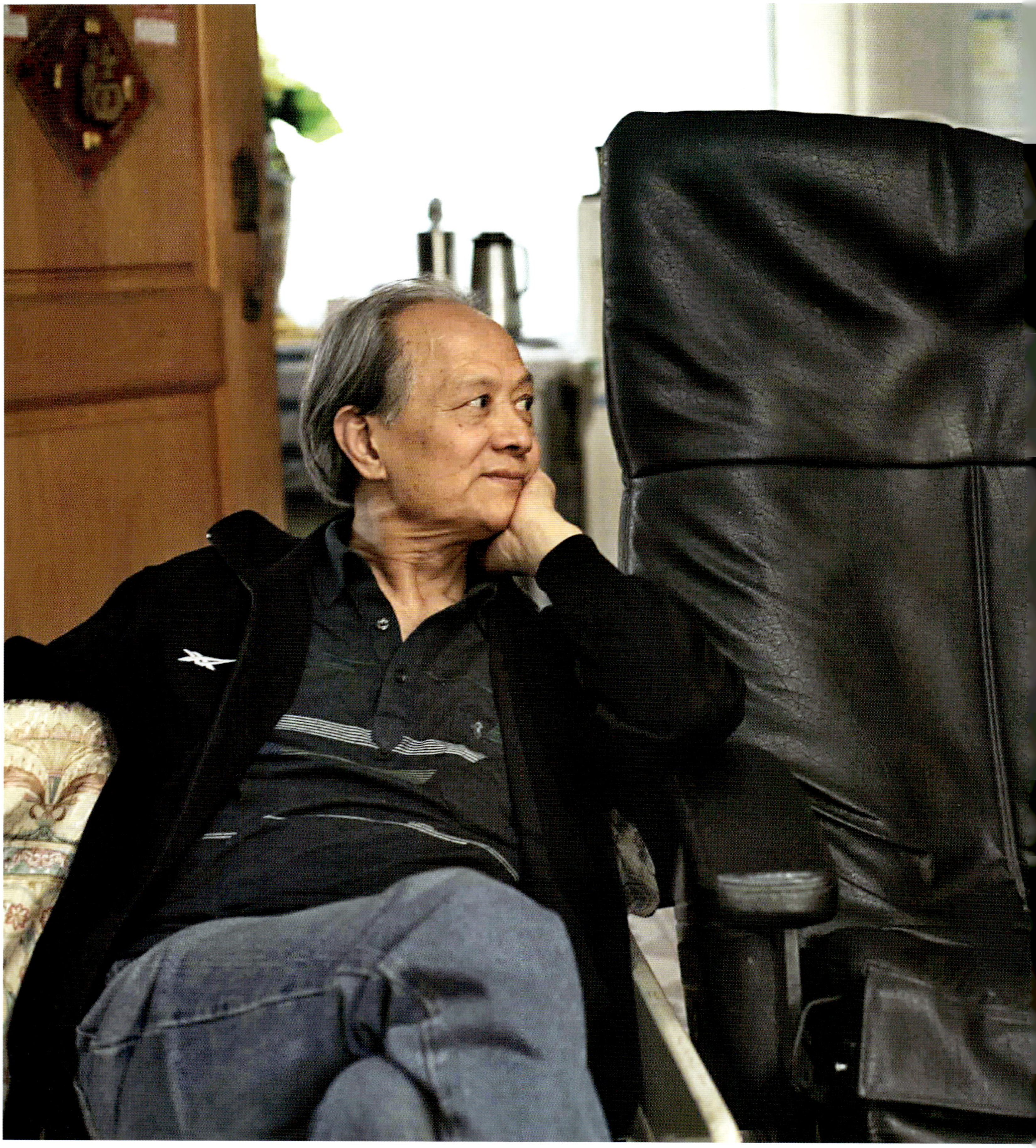

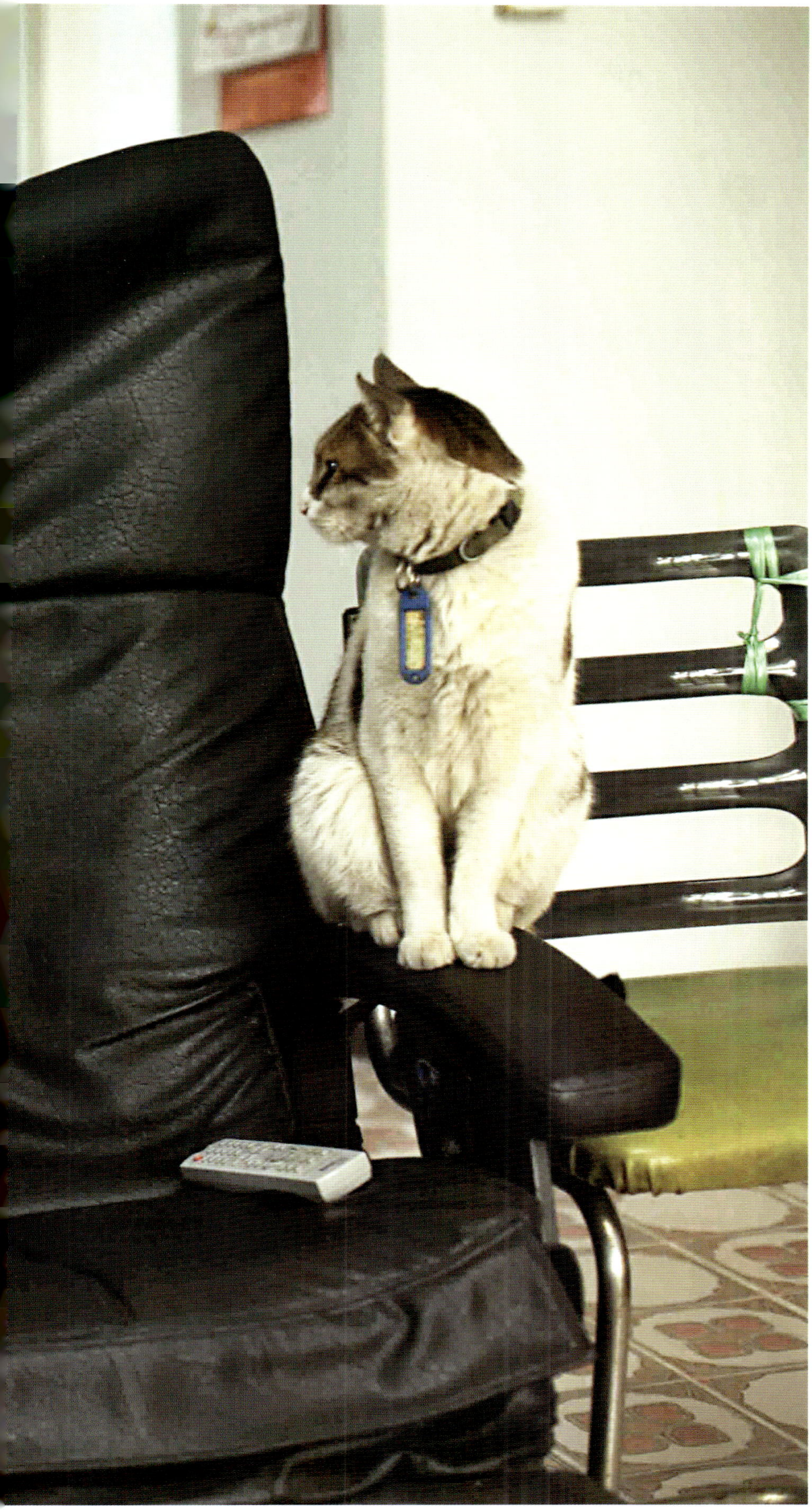

Chu Hing-wah's studio is in a suburban low-rise building that also houses his home. The studio is on the first floor, with a view of his garden. Chu works on the other side of the room, where a window lets in the morning sun. "This helps me get the colours right," says Chu, resting a hand on his desk. Close to his hand are boxes of watercolour paints, a deck of mixing dishes and clean brushes. There is not one irrelevant item.

"When did you start making art?" I begin the interview.

"Artists are born," says Chu, following with an example. "When I was young, whenever I saw a shard of chalk, I'd pick it up and carve it." With a born impulse to make images, the artist's ability to capture what was around him sprouted at a tender age. "Some 50 years ago, I was living in Temple Street. Back then, I was just a 10-year-old. But the impressions were so strong," he says. "The place is all changed now. Once in a while, I'd go back for a look — and I'd see the old days right in my eyes."

Chu had the inclinations to be an artist even before hearing the word 'art'. In the 1960s, most Hong Kong people were busy making a living. Art was virtually unheard of. "At that time, we didn't even have the City Hall. Art was a luxury, exclusive to the rich," he remembers. Born into a grassroots family, Chu reckons that such an environment is no place for artistic talent. "If I had always lived in strained circumstances, I'd not have painted even one picture."

But Chu made a move. Like most young people living in the 1950s and 1960s, Chu started working in his teens. He was in home-based manufacturing lines and eventually got a job as an usher in Queen's Theatre. At that time he had a craving for overseas immersion, but the fees were not something he could afford. He learnt that student nurses got paid, so he set his sights on nursing school.

As a young man whose formal education finished in junior secondary, Chu knew that he would have to brush up on his English. He did this by taking courses and studying the foreign movies screened in the cinema where he worked. Then he made his way to London.

In London, Chu found his nurturing ground. Stimulated by what he saw in museums and art galleries, where he spent most of his holidays, the artist finally decided to get his own paint box. He copied masterpieces, sketched outdoors and took his brushes with him whenever he travelled. As a 'Sunday artist' he was untrained; he just found it gratifying to put colours to canvas. Years later, these paintings are cherished. 'These are pretty good," the artist says smiling, as he reviews the English landscapes.

Upon the completion of his nursing training, Chu returned to Hong Kong and worked in Castle Peak Psychiatric Hospital. In his off-duty hours, he went to art school for the first time. The course was run by the Department of Extra Mural Studies at the University of Hong Kong. It was taught by first-rate artists whose expertise covered both Chinese and Western art, in theory and in practice. The whole programme lasted for three years, with a four-hour class four times a week.

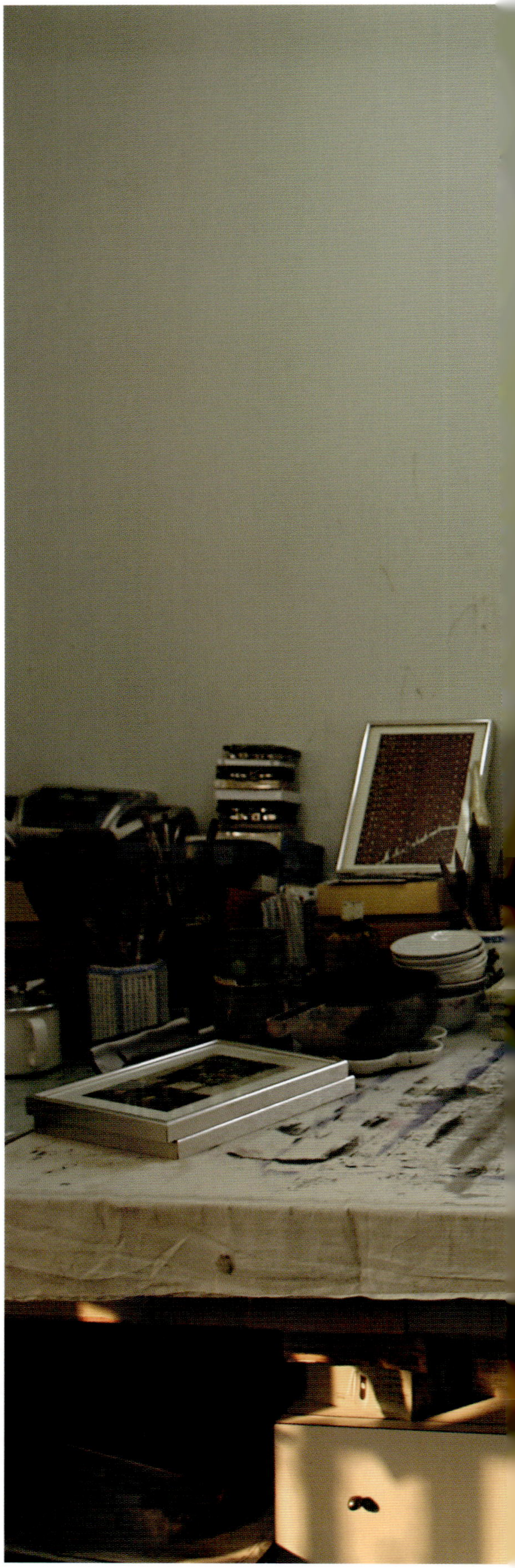

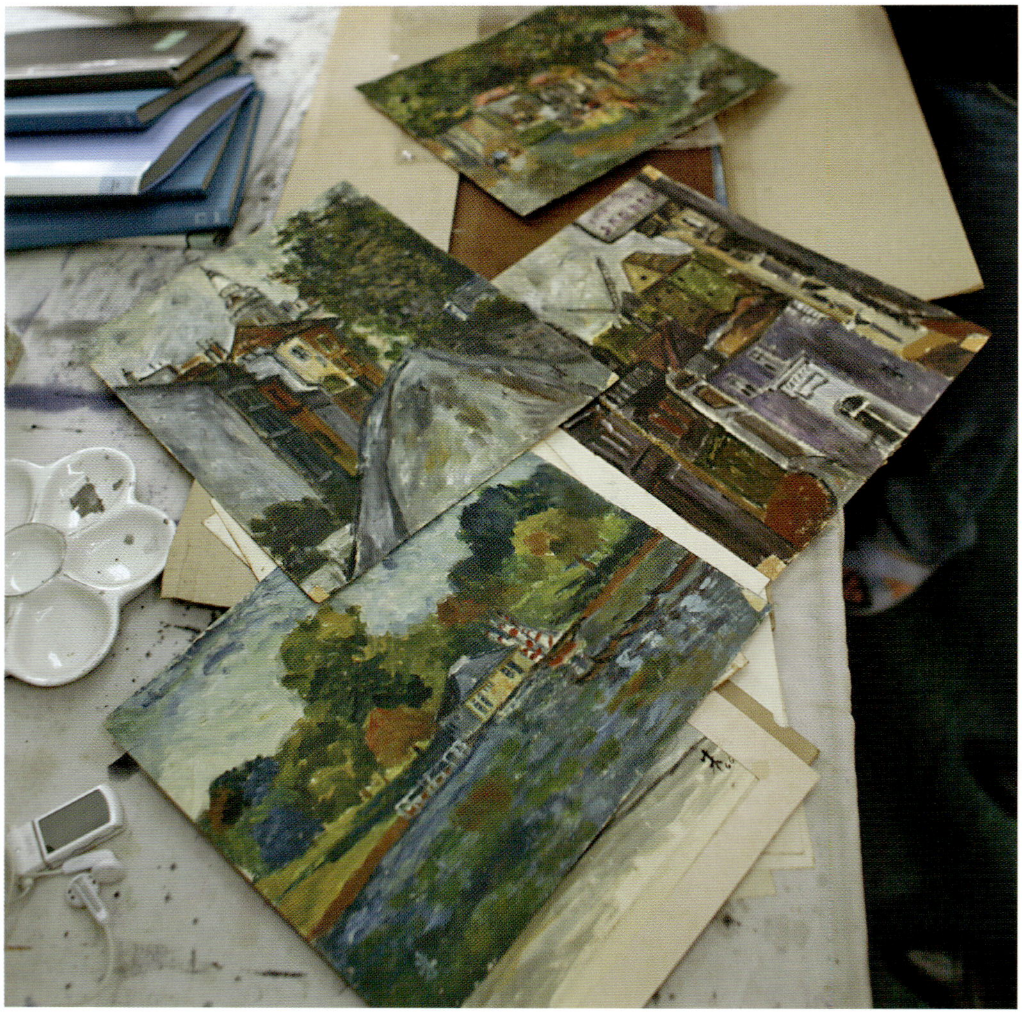

These are paintings done by the artist in his early years. "These are pretty good!" the artist says

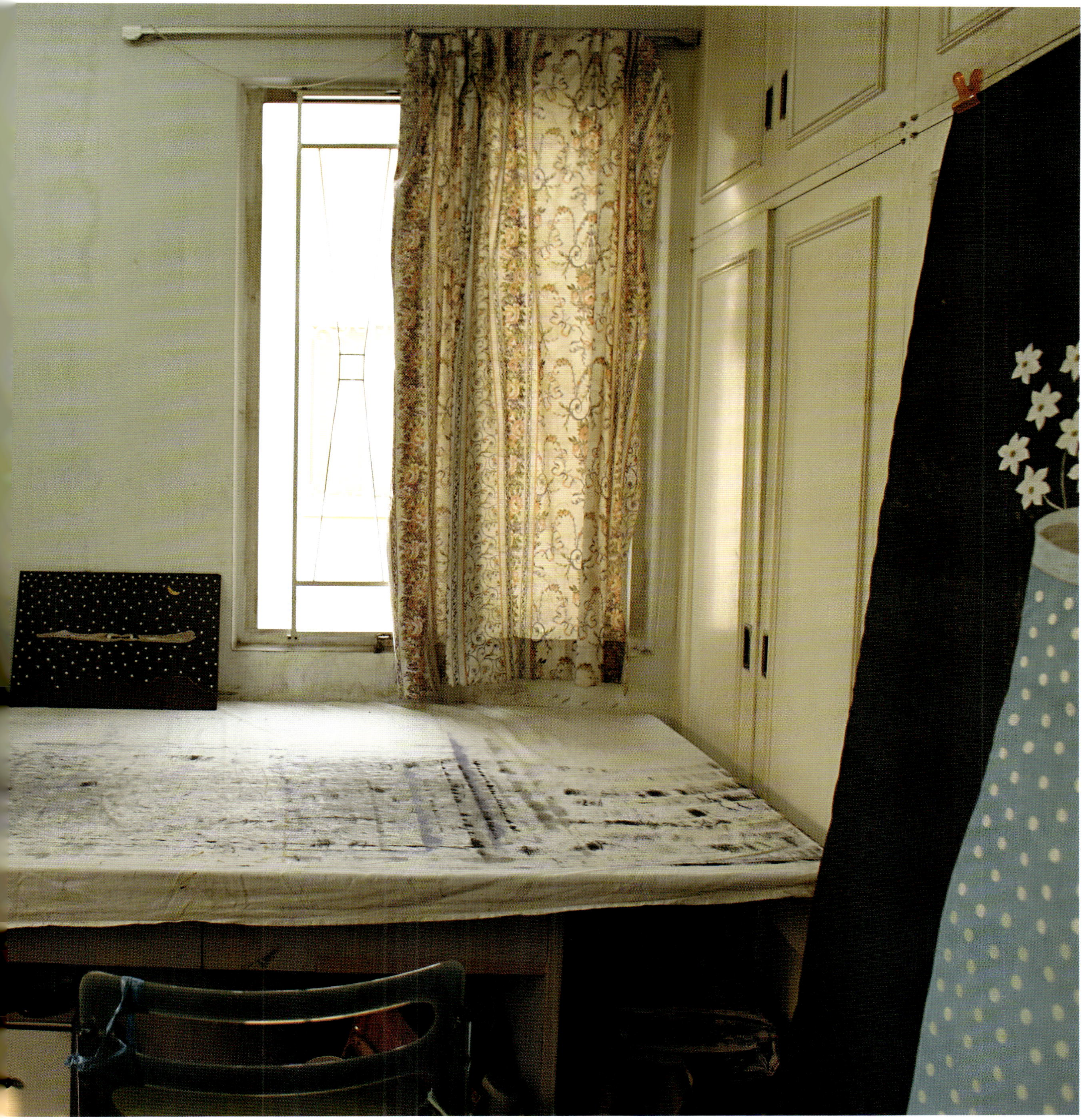

This was difficult enough for a working adult, particularly when considering the time needed for assignments. But Chu did not think this way. He devoted himself thoroughly to the love of his life and did not miss a single class. Chu considers the period formative to his artistic career.

Chu keeps frequenting museums and galleries now. "When you look at a masterpiece, don't focus on the techniques. Look for the spirit — a master's devotion and attitude inspire your own expression," he advises.

In art, Chu expresses his feelings about life. Most literature on him addresses the three phases of his career: first, his contemplation of life upon contact with inmates in Castle Peak Hospital; second, suburban vignettes painted while living in his present home after retirement; third, reactions to the social mishaps of recent years. On the whole, his work has always been connected to life. "Life is my inspiration," he says. "Some artists work on world wars, philosophy, outer space... grand themes. I live a simple life so my work is simple, but real."

In the face of life's complexity, Chu has taken a stance. Working on different subjects over the years, his approach has always been humanistic. "The stock exchange and real estate make headlines, but I am not interested," he says. His cold colours give many the impression of melancholy, but his art also celebrates the joys of life. For example, in *The Pig, Frogs & Rabbit*, one sees the sweetness of family gatherings. As he says, "My art brings joy to myself and others. Through art I connect my heart with others and share the beauty of the universe and love in life."[1] When he comes across sad moments, he depicts them with discretion. For example, *Falling* is about suicide jumpers. Represented subtly in abstract shapes, they slide across the checkered background. There are no cries of agony, but the pull of gravity is powerfully conveyed.

Chu's paintings capture real moments with a resounding presence. One hears footsteps in the neighbourhood of *The Unchanging Yau Ma Tei*, ducks quacking in *Toward Night* and leaves falling in *Autumn*. The echoes dwell in a hush. Chu insists that painting is a world of its own and should not be bothered by worldly hustle. "When one paints, there should only

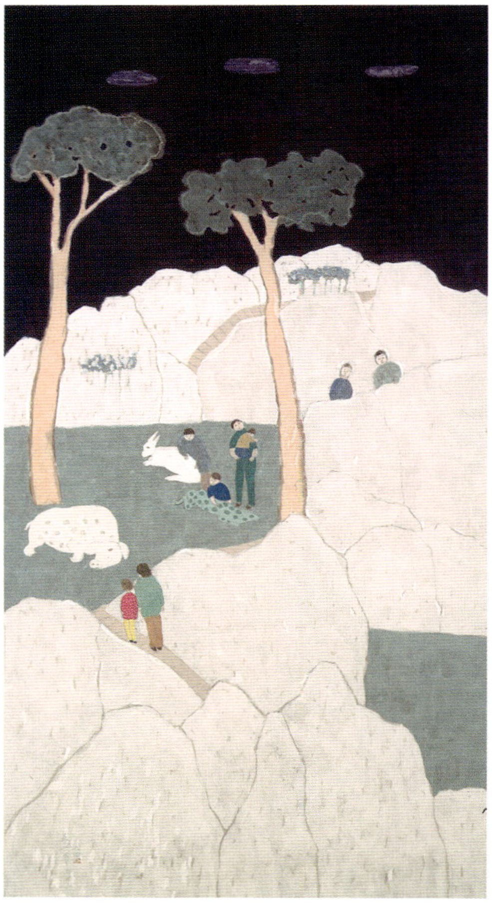

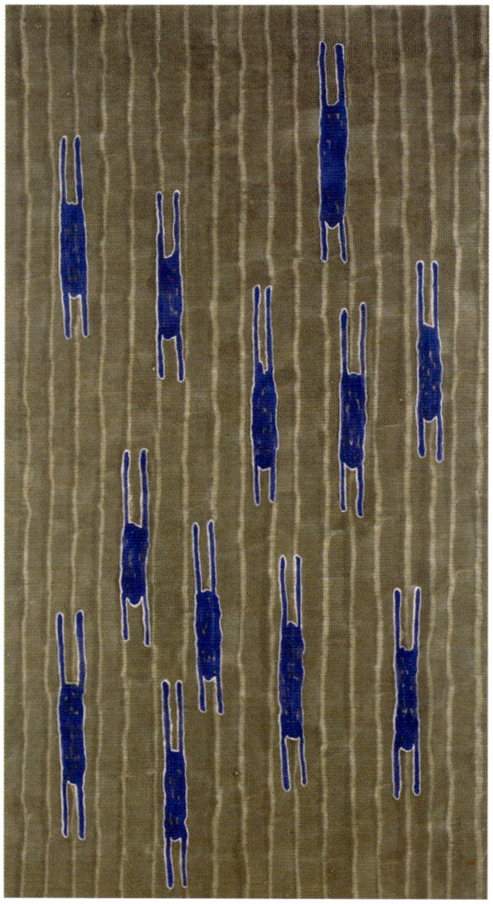

(Left) The Pig, Frogs & Rabbit
Ink and colour on paper, 179x96 cm, 1994

(Right) Falling
Ink and colour on paper, 180x97 cm, 2001

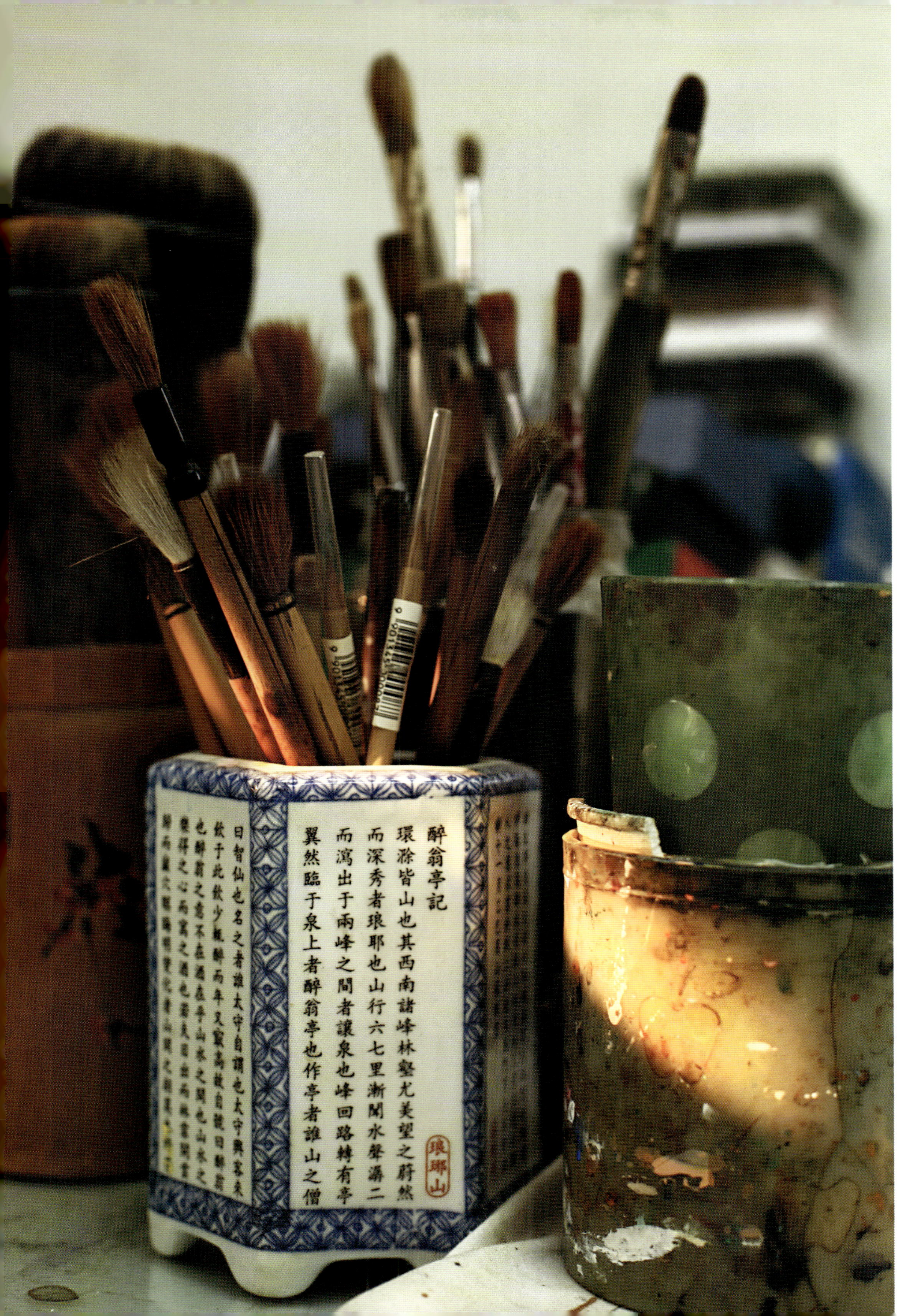
醉翁亭記
環滁皆山也其西南諸峰林壑尤美望之蔚然
而深秀者琅耶也山行六七里漸聞水聲潺二
而瀉出于兩峰之間者讓泉也峰回路轉有亭
翼然臨于泉上者醉翁亭也作亭者誰山之僧
琅琊山

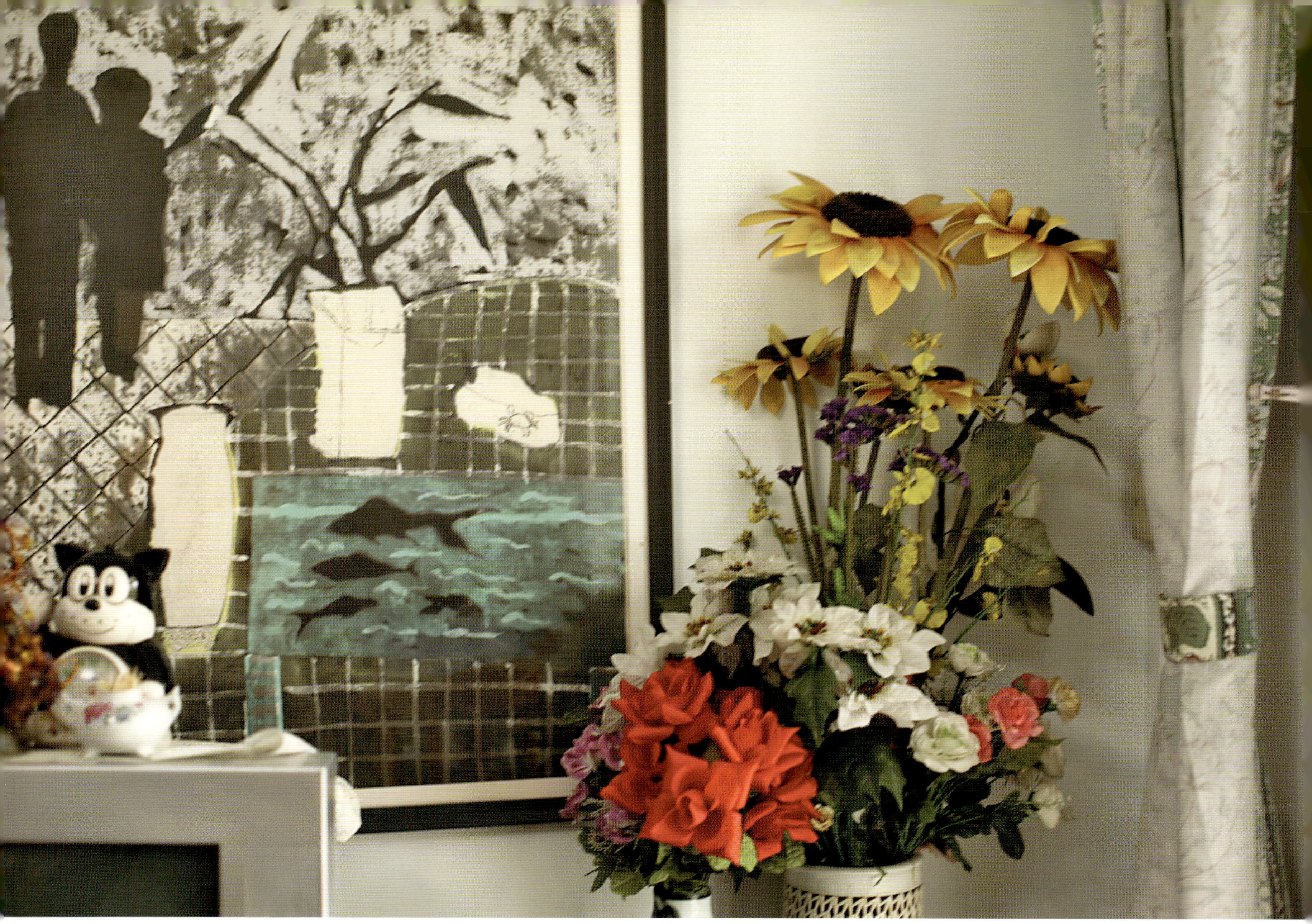

"My art brings joy to myself and others. Through art I connect my heart with others and share the beauty of the universe and love in life"

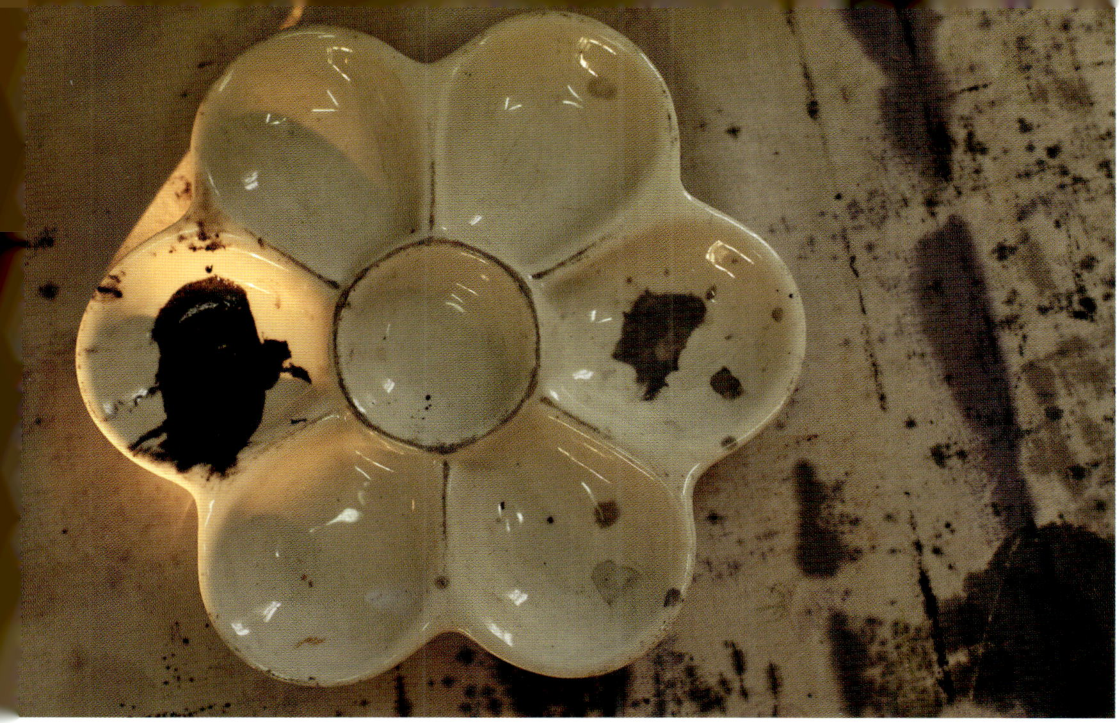

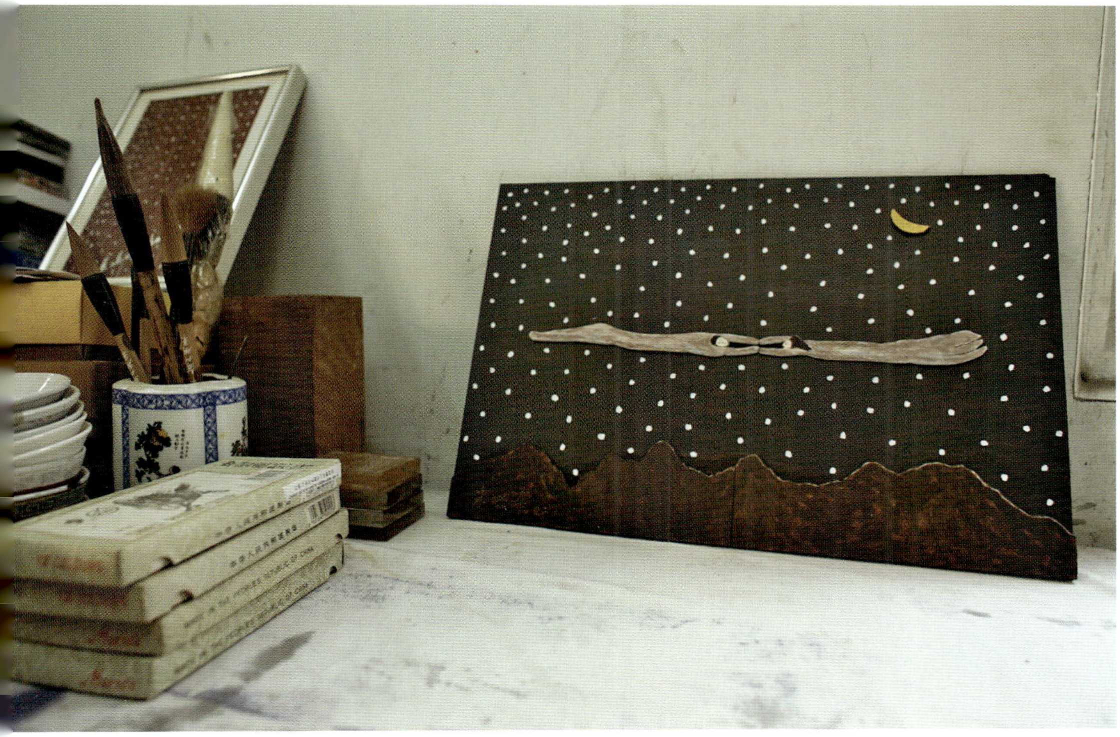

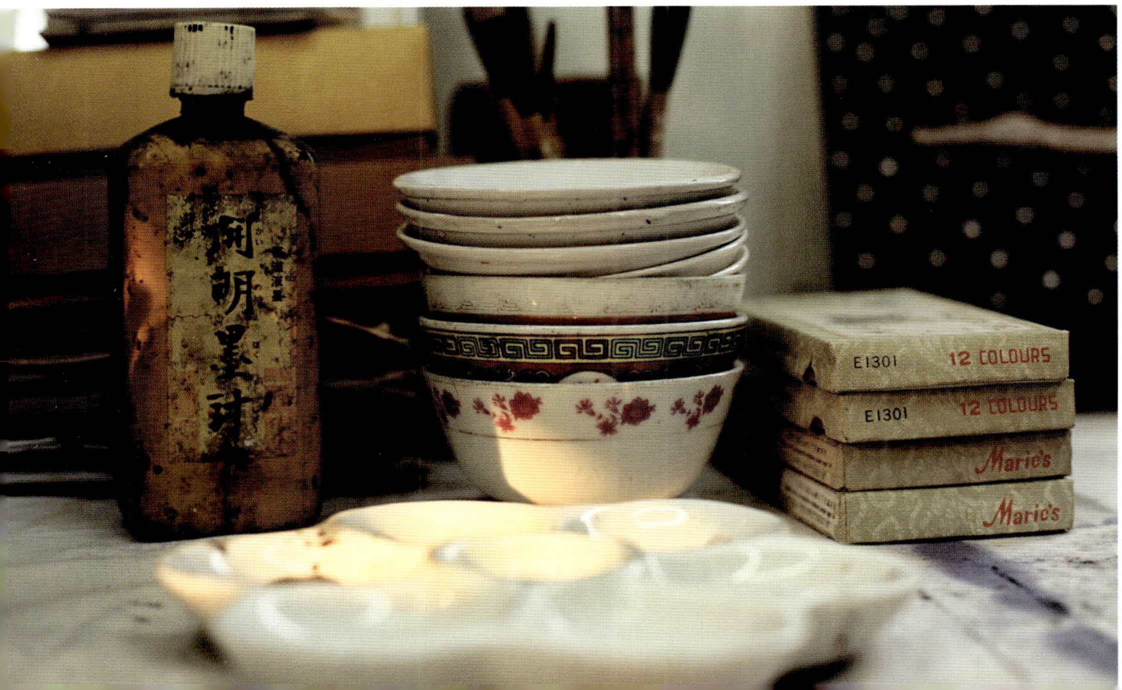

be four things: the painting, the eye, the mind and the hand. Anything else should be out of the way," he says.

This brings to mind his own workplace, filled with his passion for art and his interest in life. There is nothing irrelevant there. The window lets in the afternoon sun; the colours look so right.

In 2008 a collection of Chu's paintings was printed on a calendar. On the very last page, Chu confesses: "Somewhere in Guangdong on 12 November 1935, a boy was born. He is destined to be poor, because he is an artist. He is also destined to be happy, because he is an artist".[2] Artists are not necessarily poor, nor are they always happy. To Chu however, the statement summarises what he is about.

At the end of the interview, Mrs Chu brought in a plateful of sliced star fruit. "This is from our trees," says Mrs Chu. "He takes care of them every day." Chu has worked conscientiously in his garden for years. Watered with perseverance and diligence, the sprouts have grown into big trees. It is now time for the harvest.

1. See Works by Chu Hing-wah, calendar printed by Sino Group in 2008.

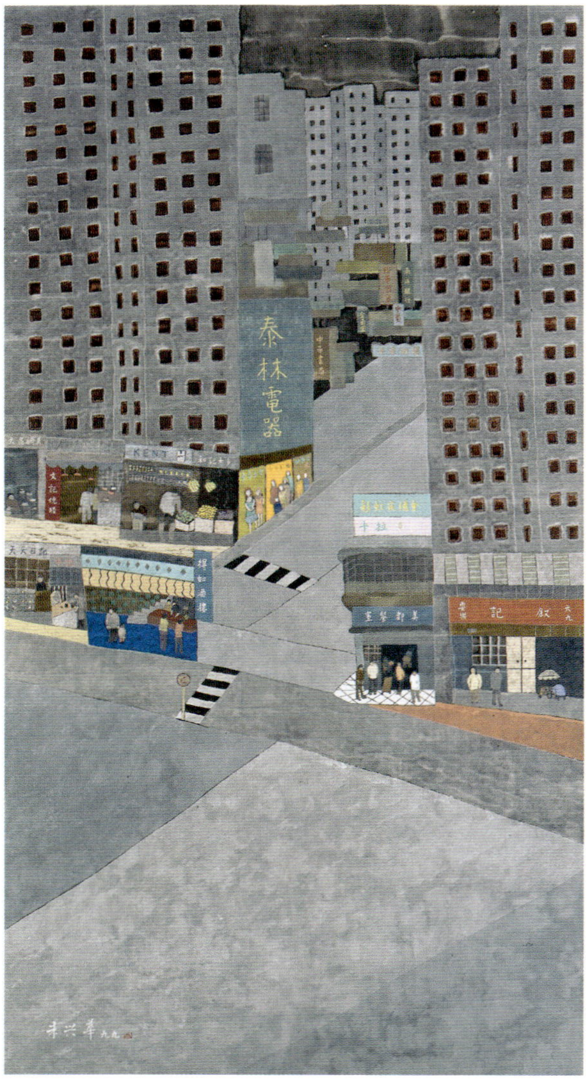

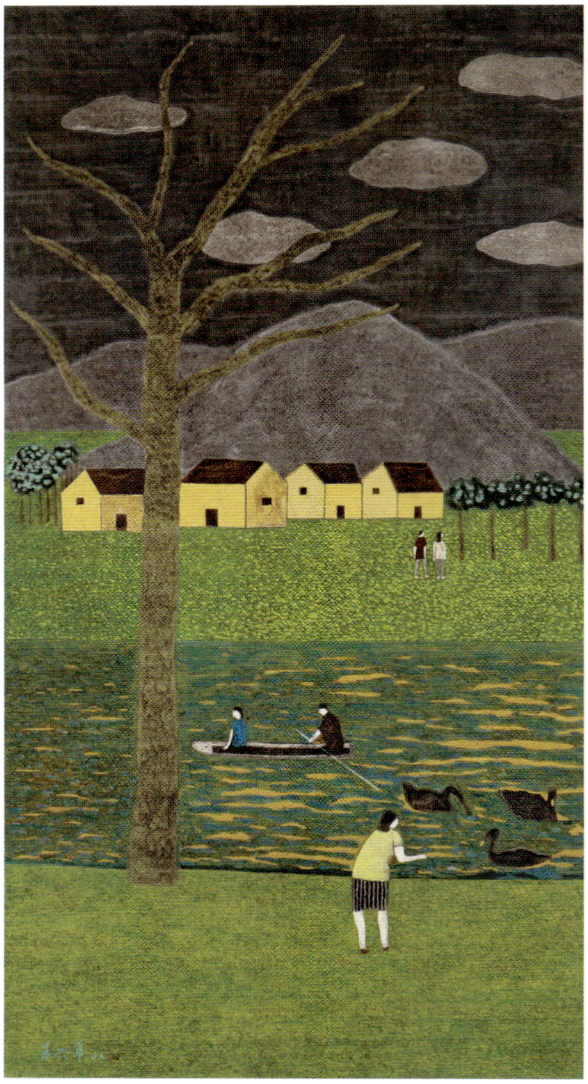

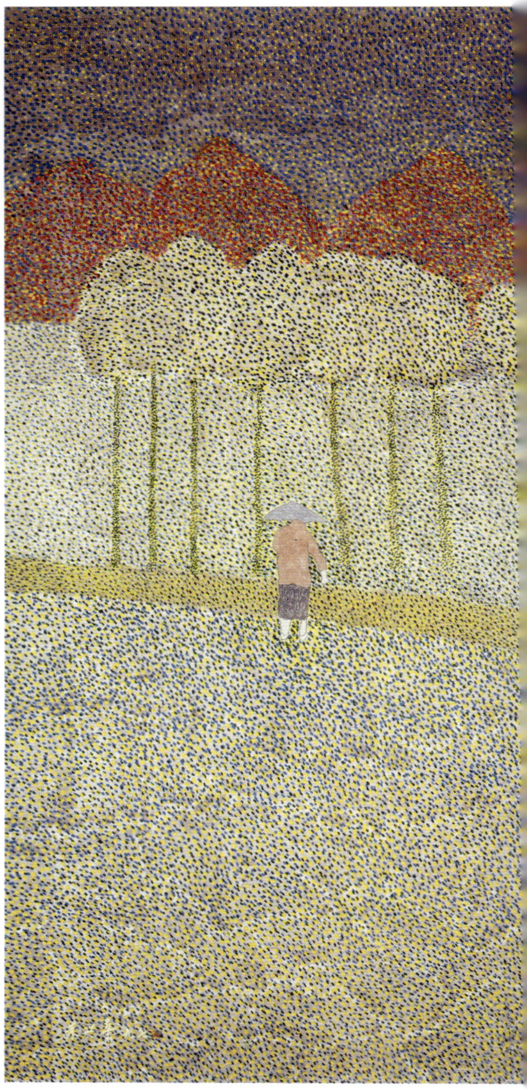

(Left above) The Unchanging Yau Ma Tei
Ink and colour on paper, 179x97 cm, 1999

(Middle above) Toward Night
Ink and colour on paper, 161x97 cm, 2007

(Right above) Autumn
Ink and colour on paper, 176x94 cm, 1997

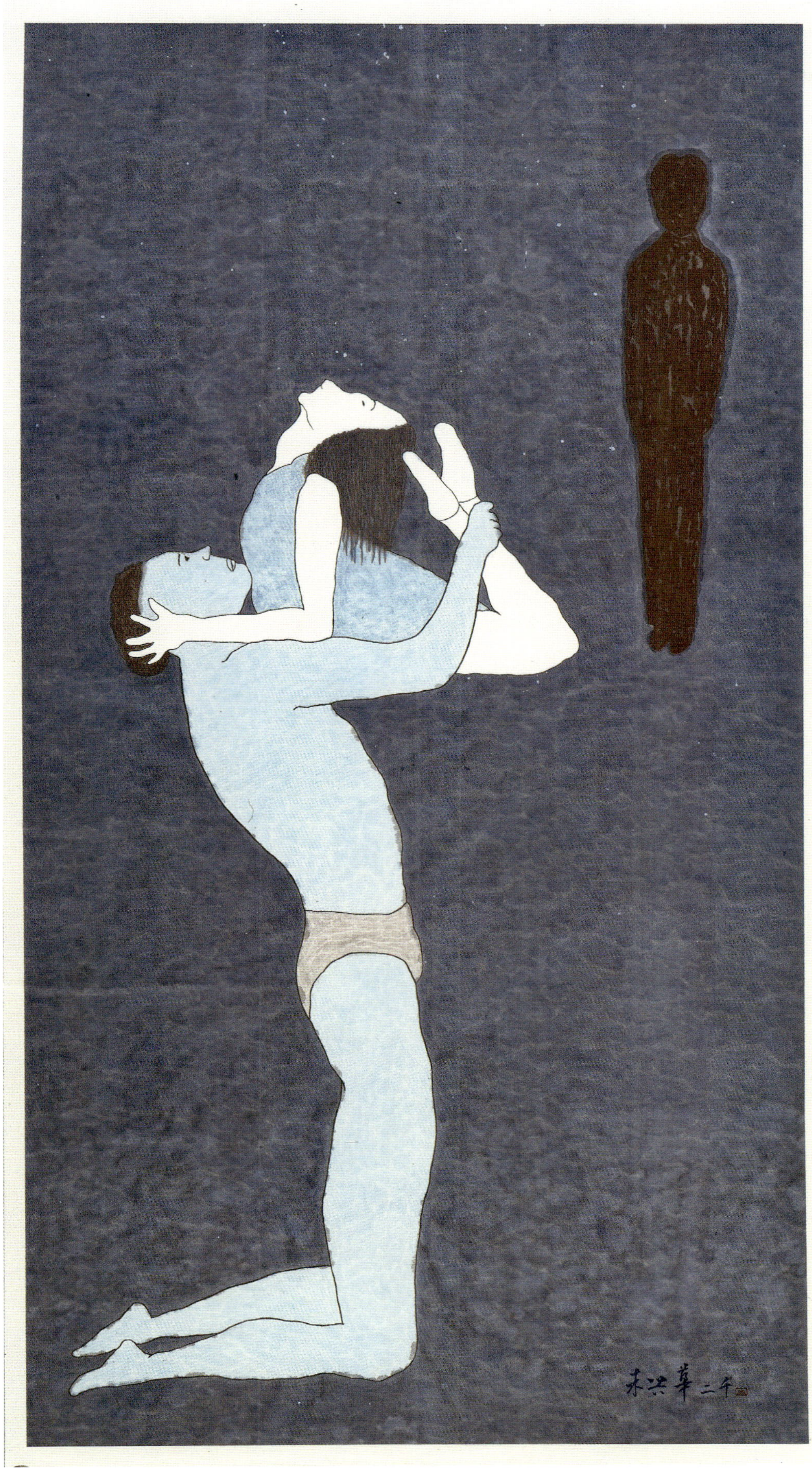

Dream Ballet
Ink and colour on paper, 83x149 cm, 2001

Kan Tai-keung

Advance Courageously despite Hardships and Dangers. Hip, Hip, Hurray!

By Carl Cheng

Kan Tai-keung is a renowned designer worldwide. His achievements in design over the past 40 years were appraised by the China Central Television (CCTV) for a feature story, and he was awarded the title of World's Outstanding Chinese Designer in 2004. Kan takes an active role in design education and promotion, and gives lectures frequently to local and international tertiary institutions. His dedication to promoting education and the reform of modern Chinese design as a profession was furthered when he was appointed as Dean of the Cheung Kong School of Art and Design at Shantou University in 2003. His art and design career are both lauded. In 1970 he developed his Chinese ink paintings, which soon brought him the Urban Council Fine Arts Award. In 2008 he organised his solo exhibition, Feelings of the Brush: Paintings by Kan Tai-keung, at the University Museum and Art Gallery of the University of Hong Kong. His works are collected in museums worldwide.

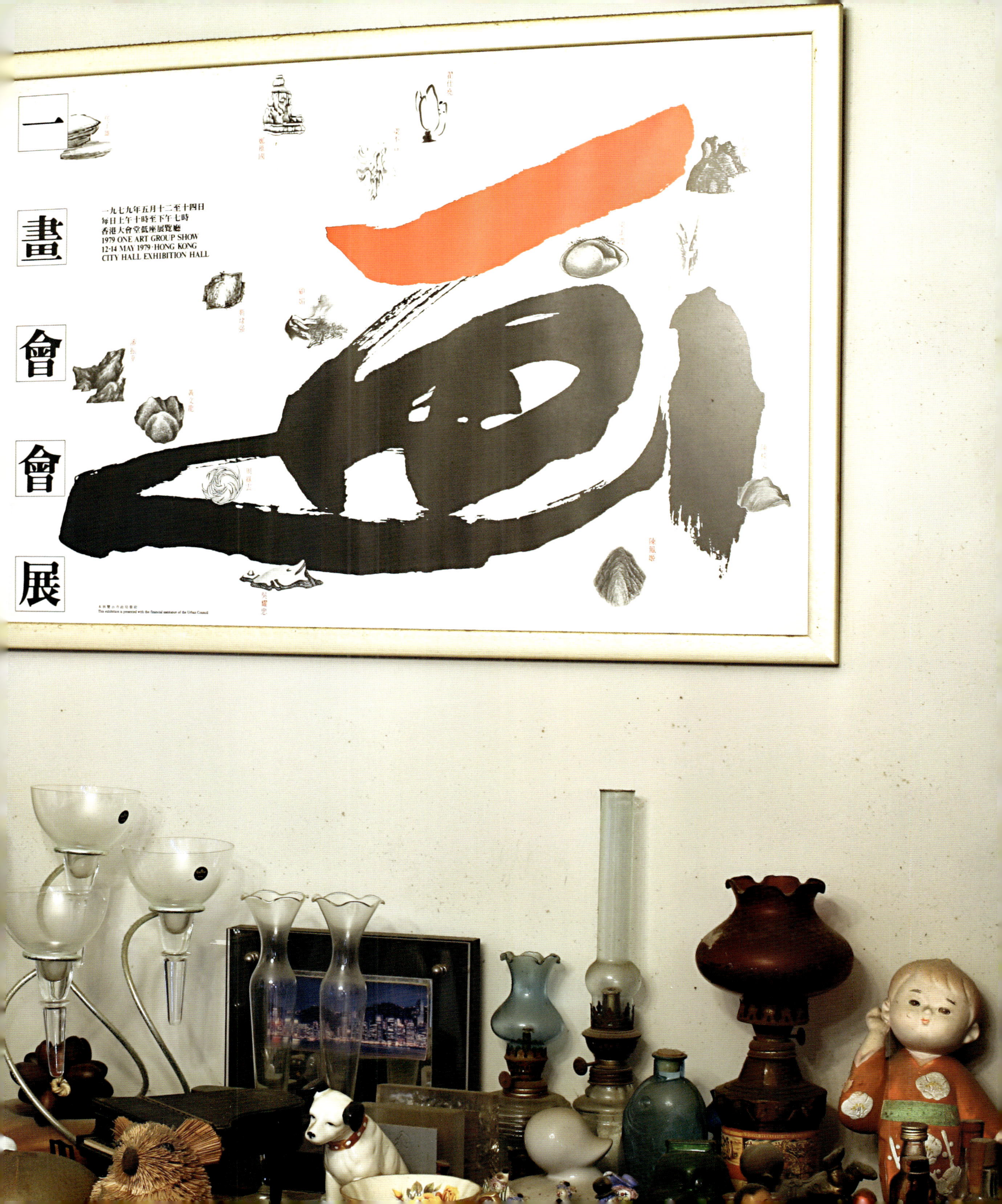
一畫會會展
一九七九年五月十二至十四日
每日上午十時至下午七時
香港大會堂低座展覽廳
1979 ONE ART GROUP SHOW
12-14 MAY 1979 · HONG KONG
CITY HALL EXHIBITION HALL

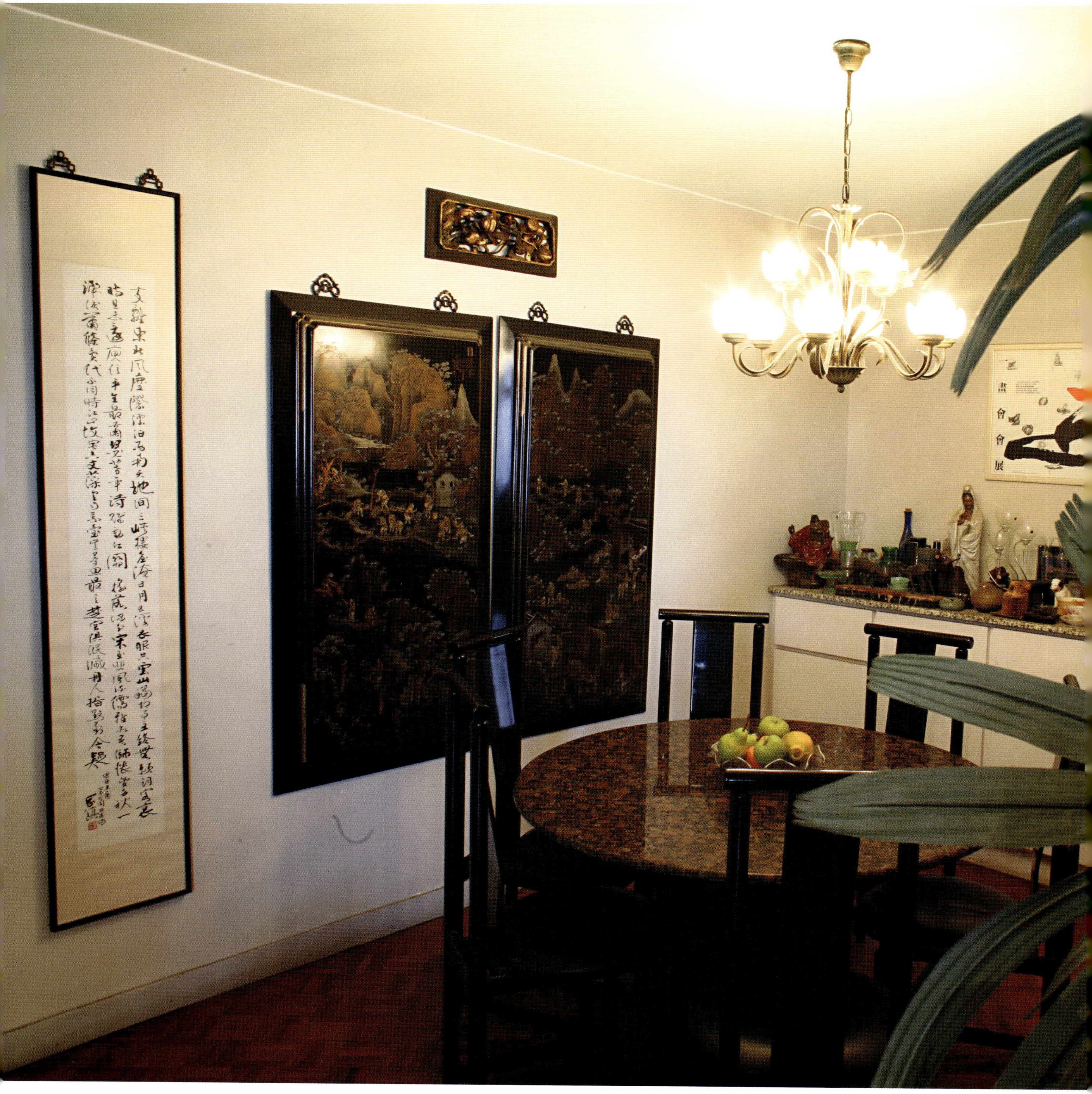

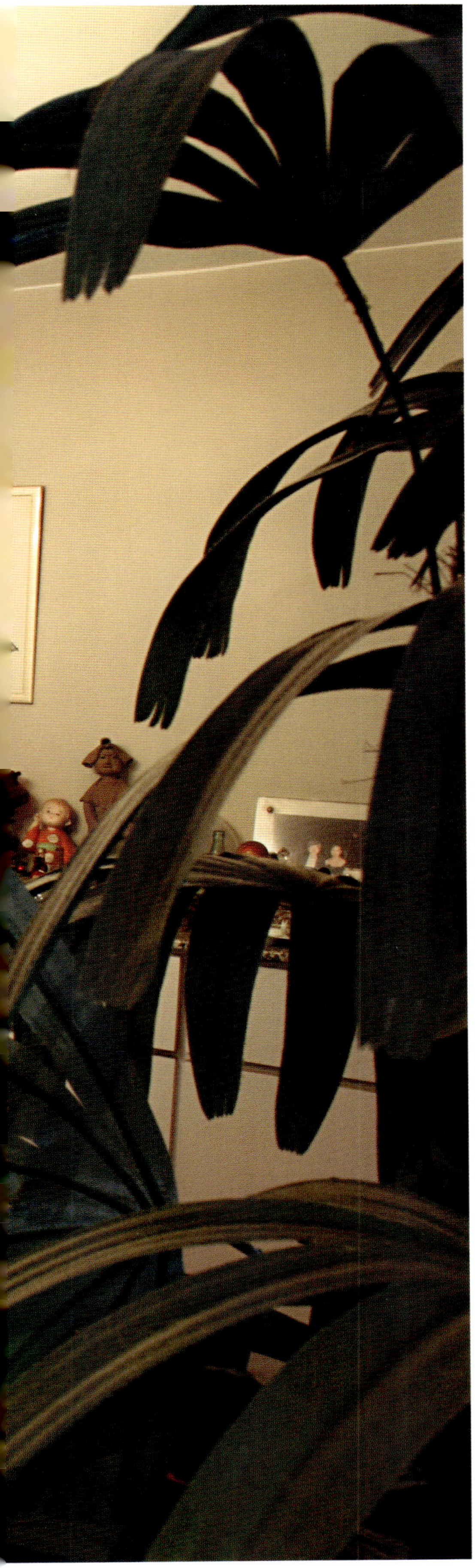

Post-war Hong Kong was in a state of desolation awaiting redevelopment. Yet the stoic people in Hong Kong were not easily discouraged by adversity; they faced hardships with optimism. The influx of immigrants from the mainland in the 1950s brought new blood to the labour force in Hong Kong, which later became the driving force for the economic boom of the '70s and '80s.

Kan grew up in such an era. In 1957 Kan came to Hong Kong with his younger brother Kan Kit-keung to reunite with his parents. Yet the family reunion did not last long owing to poverty. To earn his living, Kan left home to work as an apprentice to a tailor for three years, where he spent his youth. The difficulty of this livelihood forced Kan to give up his beloved paintings. As a lover of literature, Kan read widely and listened to classical music. At the age of 22 he learnt drawing and watercolour painting from his uncle Kan May-tin, who brought him back to his artistic endeavors.

The turning point of his life occurred when he took up design studies with Wucius Wong and studied Chinese ink painting with Lui Shou-kwan (Lu Shoukun) at the Department of Extra-mural Studies of the Chinese University of Hong Kong. Outside his mundane job

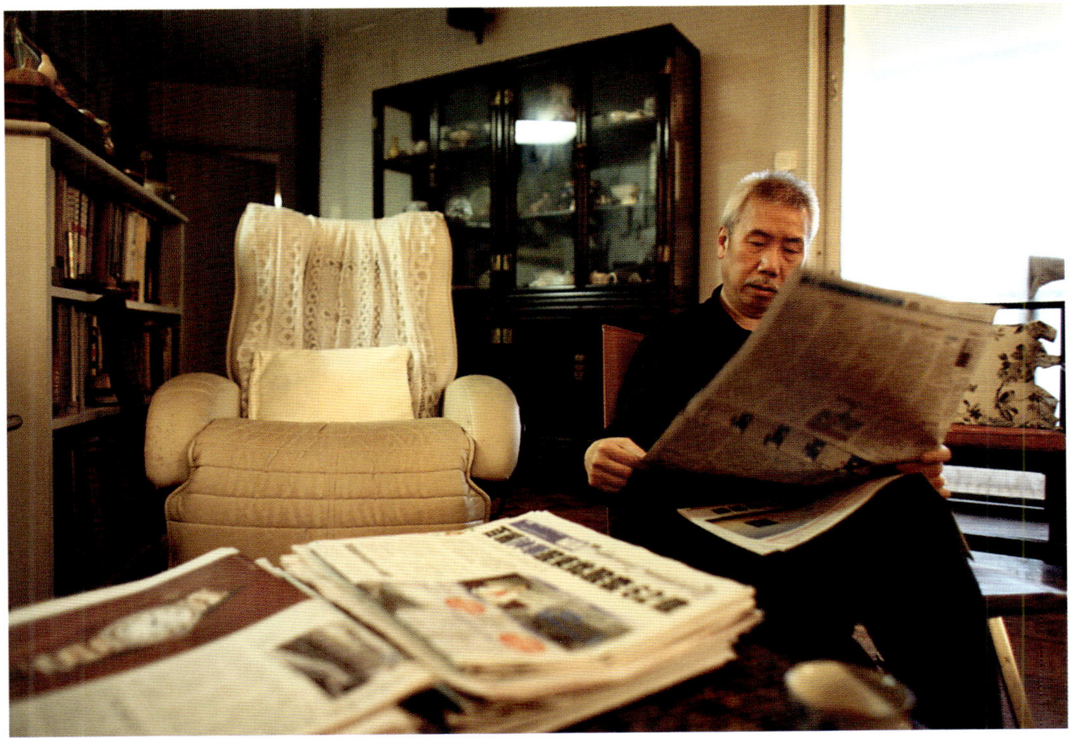

“I am not a genius, but I have been striving for my art”

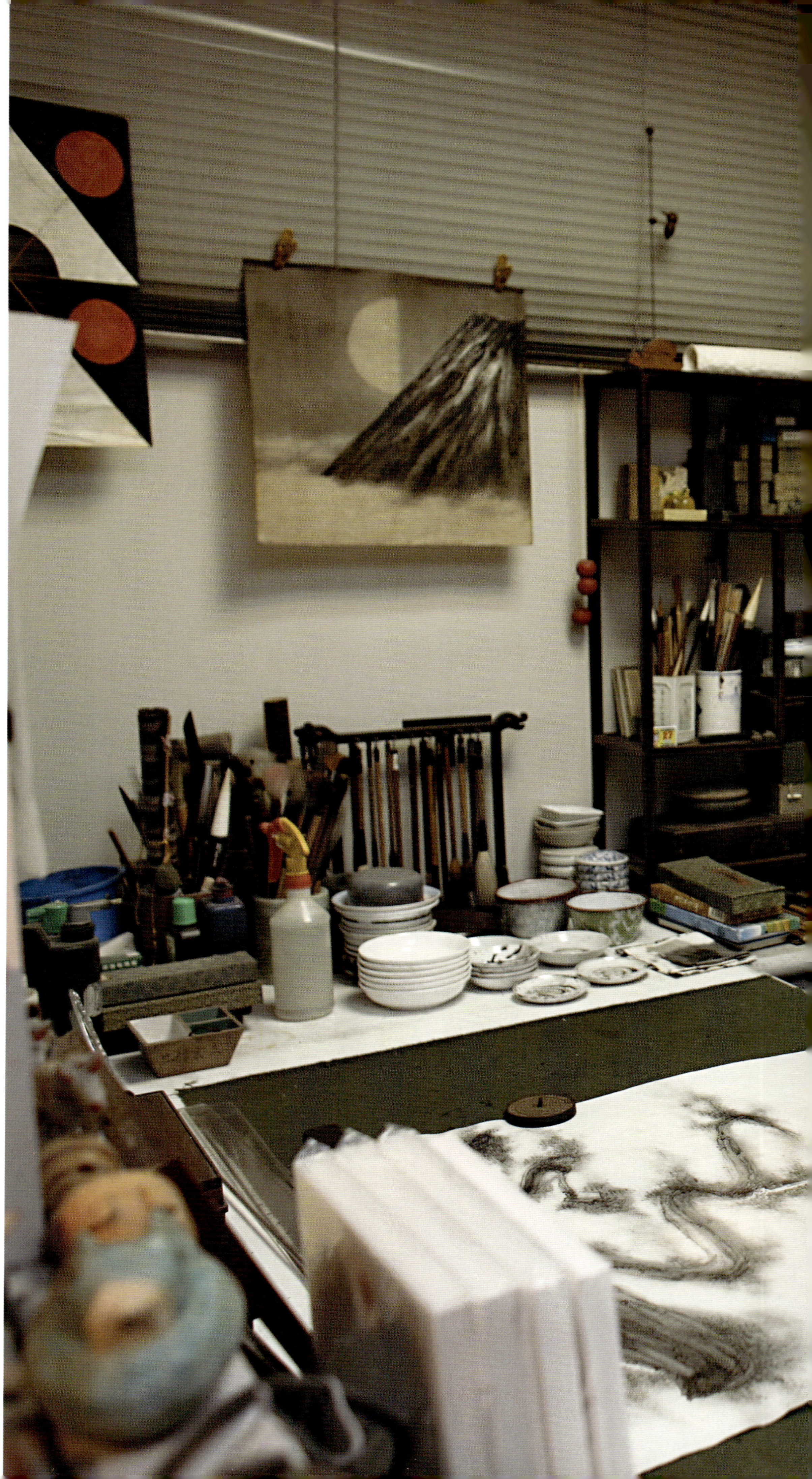

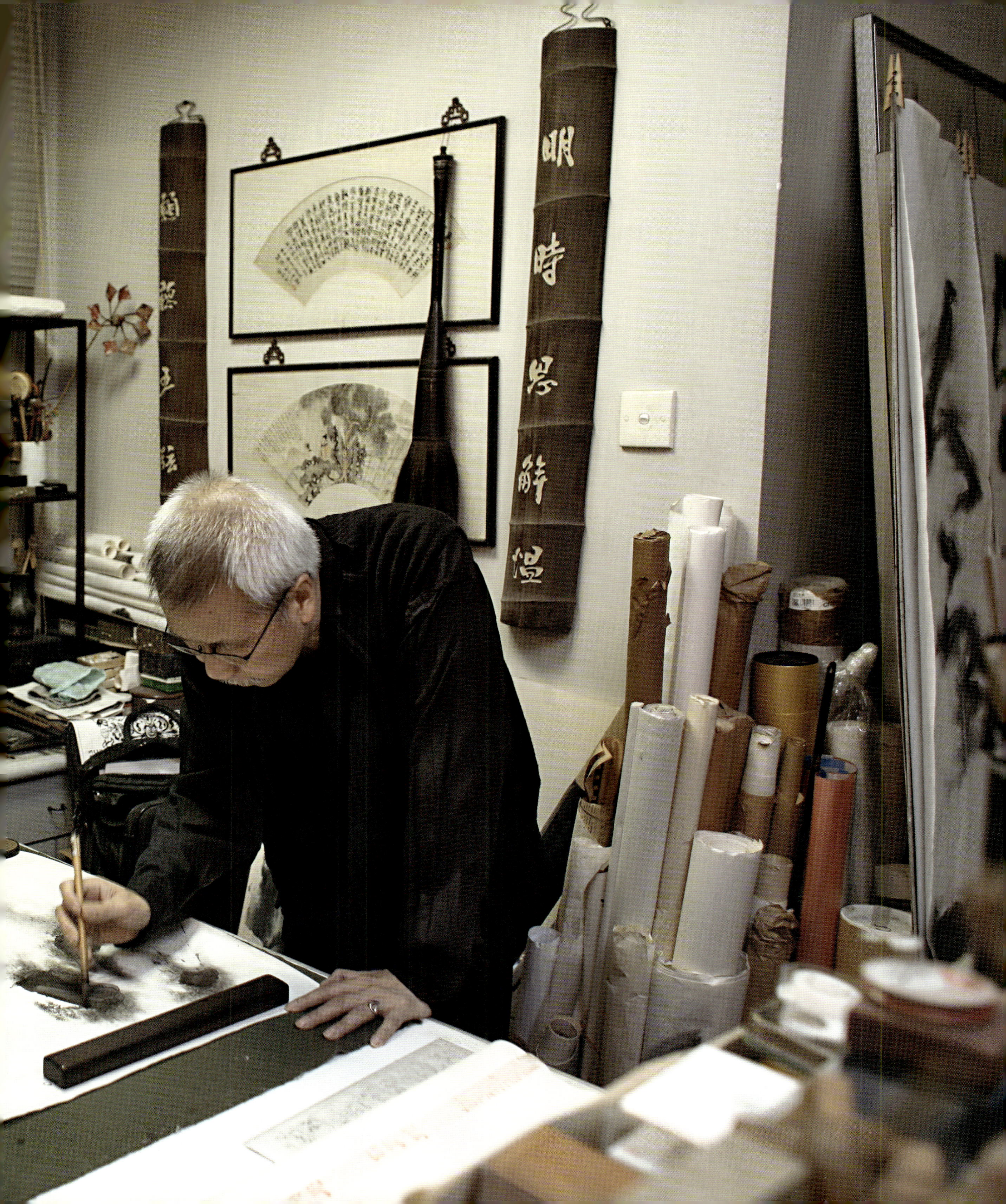
明時思解愠

he proactively pursued his knowledge to explore another side of his life. Kan recalls, "I love listening to grand music composition. Beethoven was my role model. He was not a genius and his achievements were attributed to his strong will and nurture. I am not a genius, but I have been striving for my art."

It is this unyielding spirit that has realised his dream. Though deprived of the opportunity to study, and having a job that was not his chosen way of life in youth, he overcame those adversities with his strong will. Fortunately Hong Kong was a place of freedom and opportunity, where he could develop his artistic career.

An opportunity in his life emerged in 1967. Through his design classmate Lui Lap-fun, Kan got a job as a designer at a department store. A year later, he worked as an art manager in another design company while studying commercial design part-time. Kan found that he could finally master his own life and move towards his goal. Awards from competitions, positive comments on his exhibitions and outstanding work performance have since brought him to prominence. His young heart was on fire, and his passion for creativity 40 years ago has lasted until today.

Kan used to live with his parents and siblings at Sai Wan Estate, a public housing estate in Hong Kong. Very often he did his artworks in the small living room there, but the rest of the time he worked on his bed by putting a board over it, as a tabletop. This flexible and painstaking spirit has never changed. Even nowadays he is still doing his artworks on a large piece of wood in a corner at home.

When he was learning western painting in the past, he used calico to mount his canvas, and acrylics to explore paintings in different styles, such as abstraction, constructivism, and hardedge paintings. Since he was studying part-time, he painted late at night. In those days of youth when he had boldness and grand ideas, he craved creativity, and sometimes even disregarded practical issues of transportation and storage. He once spent almost a month's salary to pay a carpenter to make him the sculpture *Work No.1* to the dimensions of 150x300x150 cm.

Kan was rebellious and idealistic when he was young. He was teased about his appearance, for with long hair he looked like a bad boy. When he tried to leave his family to live on his own, no landlord was willing to rent a place to him. Not until 1972, when he got married and spent HK$50,000 on a 300-sq-ft apartment in Sai Wan, did he have his own studio at home, by converting two small rooms into one.

Kan later also had his own studio in an 800-sq-ft apartment in Taikoo Shing. At that time he had another studio and a design desk, but he wanted to create larger works, and so he bought the opposite apartment as well. Yet owing to his busy schedule, he only visited the new studio twice in one year. Eventually he sold both apartments and moved back home.

"Apart from my busy work, I need to spare time for design education as well. If I did not paint at home, I would have no time for my family." He says this with a smile but

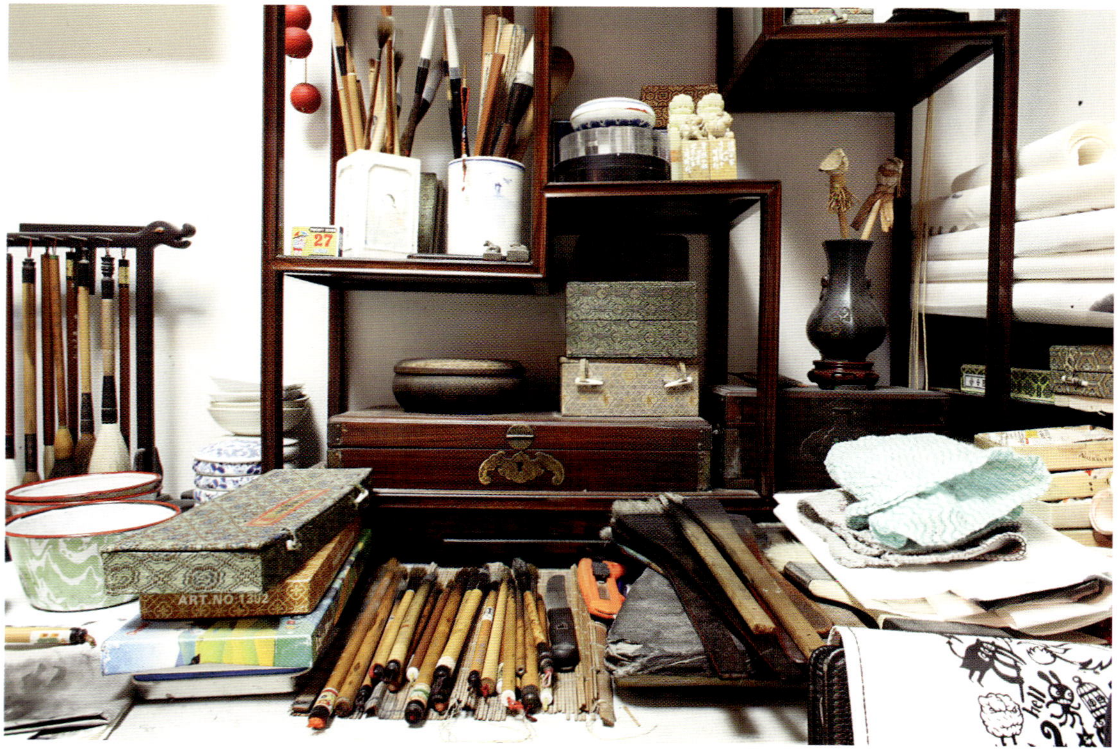

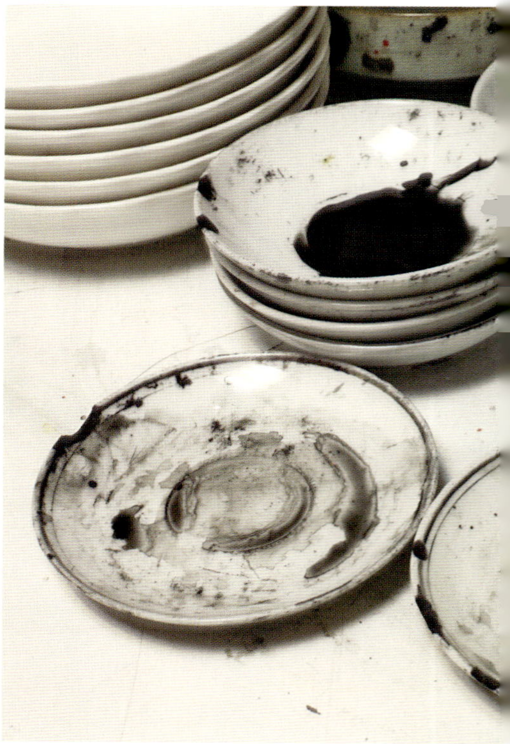

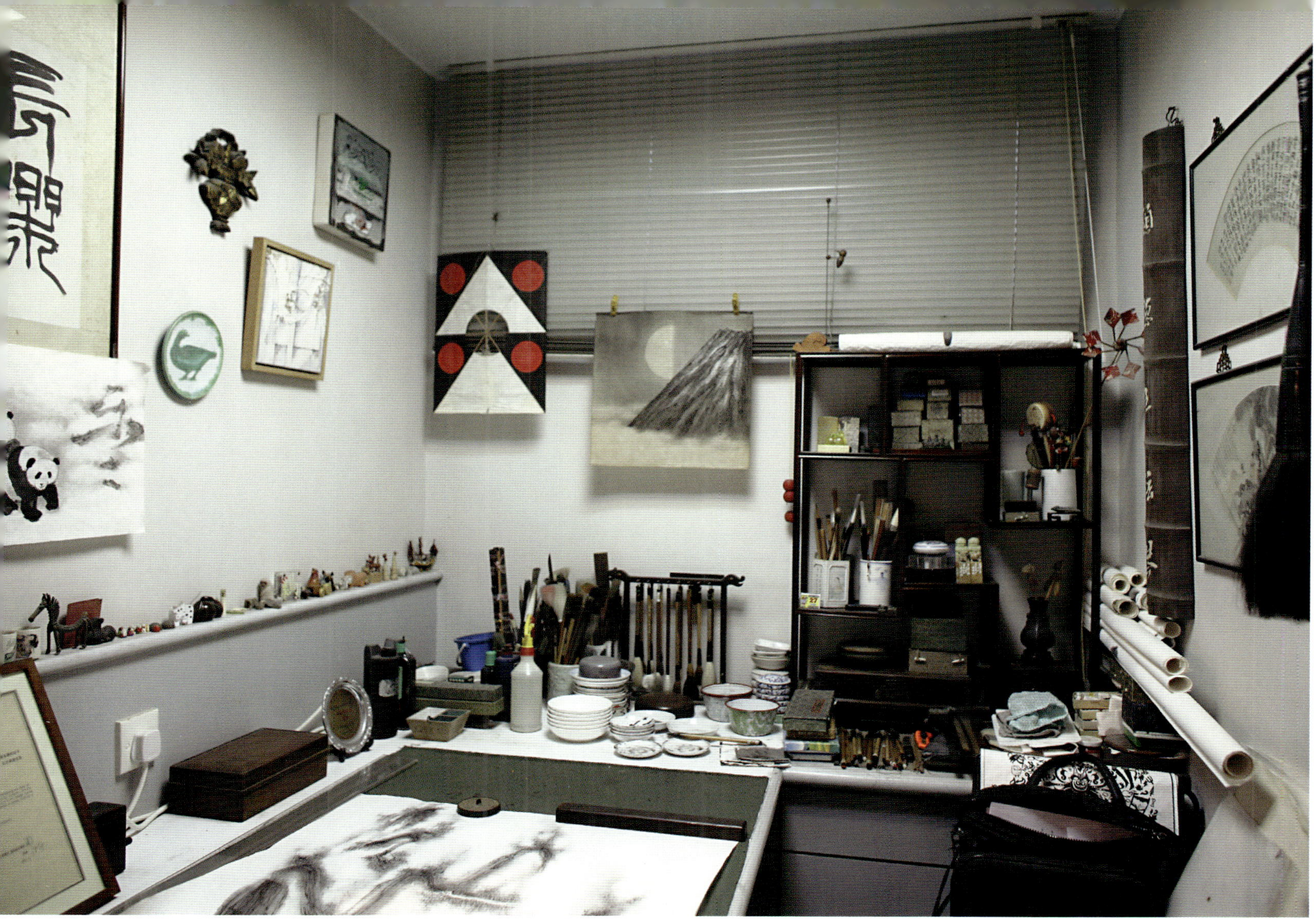

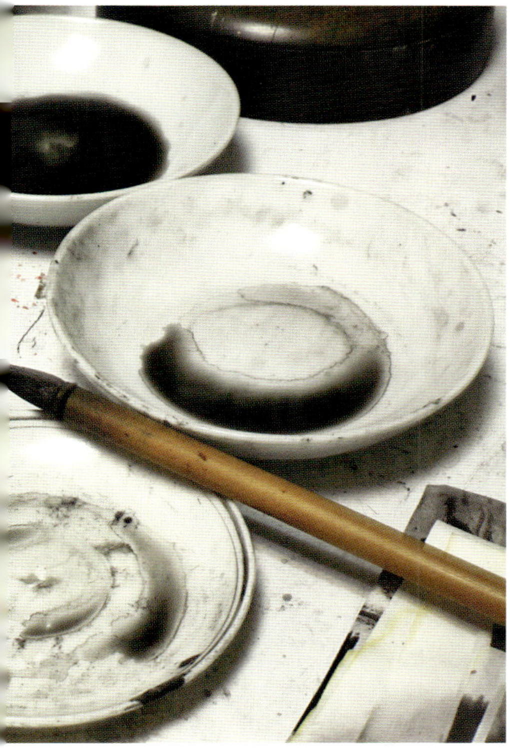

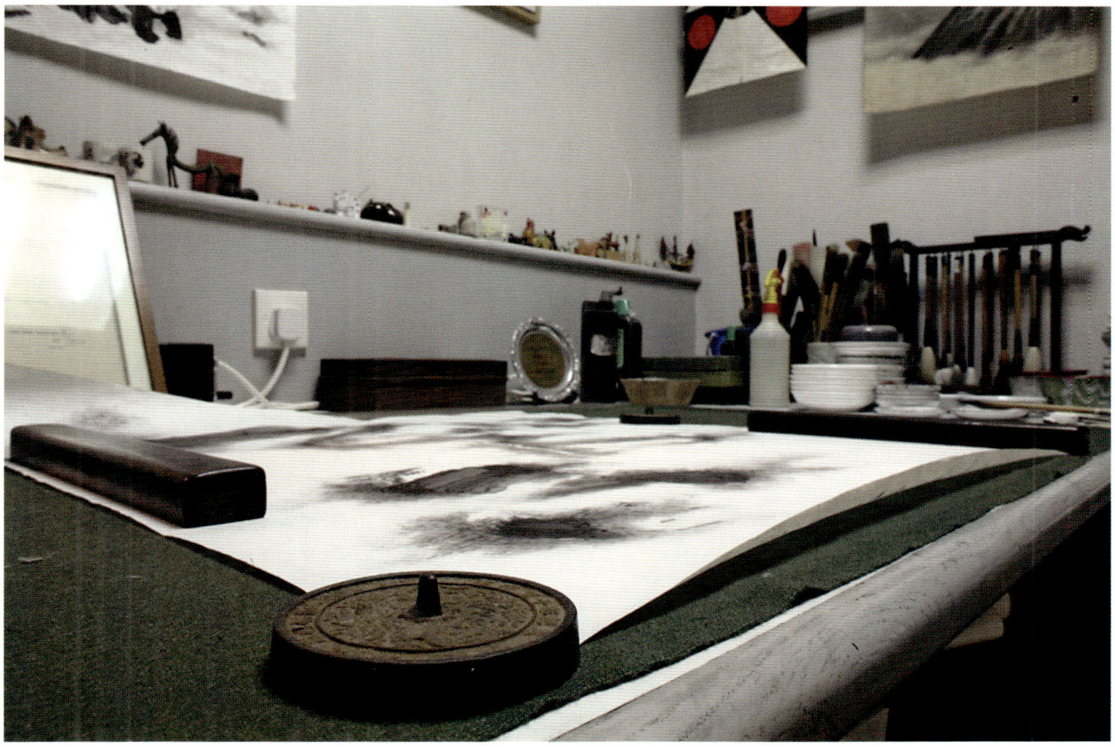

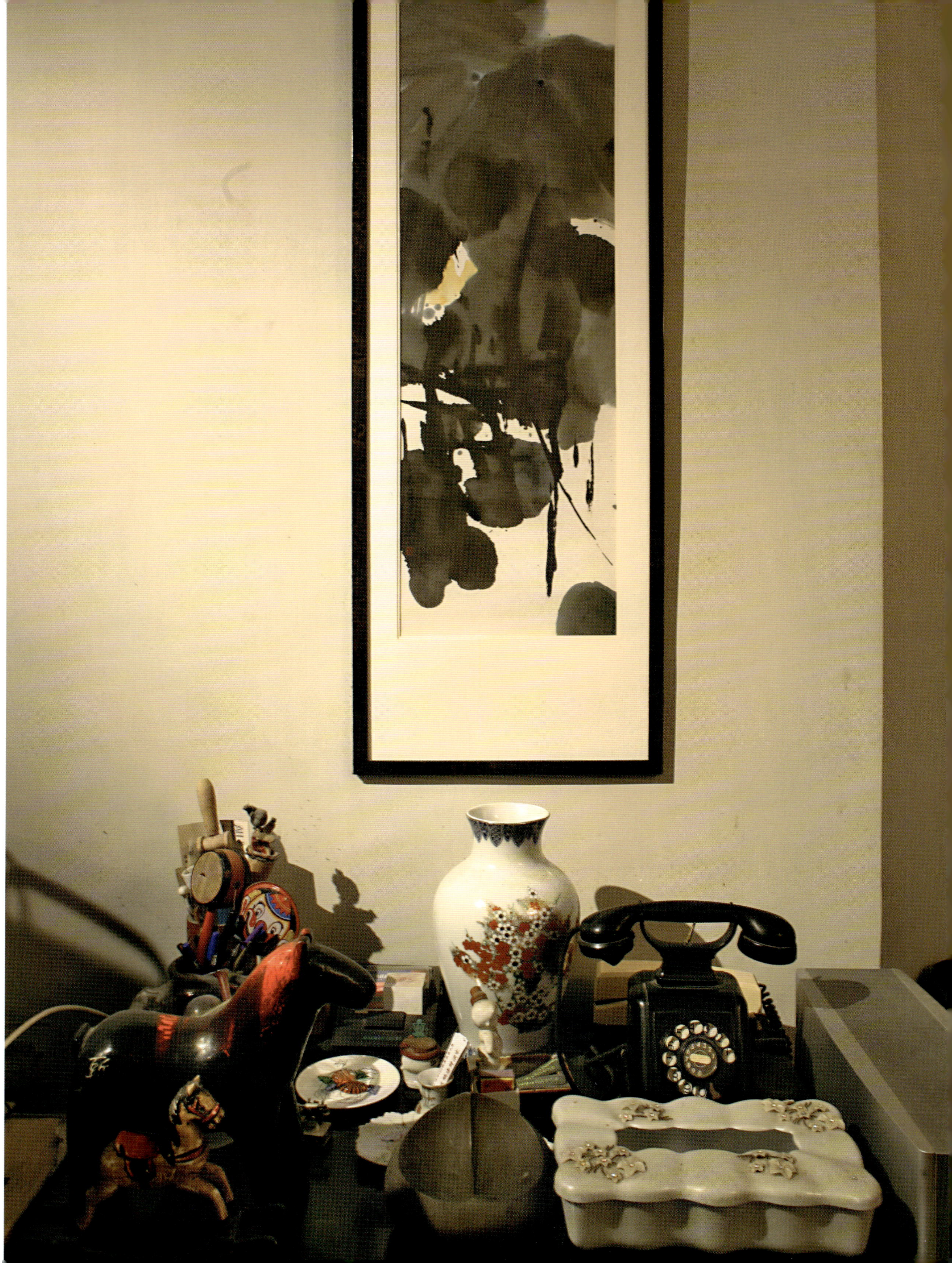

the arrangement is out of serious practical consideration. On the one hand, his diligence has kept him busy at work, on the other hand he insists on his pursuit of Chinese ink painting. Painting at home enables him to strike a balance between his work and family. While he is concentrating on his paintings at home without disturbance, his family members can still enjoy his presence, as the studio is an open space linked to the living room.

Kan was one of the active members of the New Ink Movement launched by Lui Shou-kwan in the '70s. Still, Kan had only attended Lui's lectures at the Extra-mural Department, and never learnt how to paint from him. But Lui's lectures definitely enhanced Kan's understanding of Chinese culture and painting. He was inspired to explore issues like Chinese culture, Western art, design and modernism, and to express an artist's 'mind' and 'soul' with Chinese brush and ink. It is amazing that for the past 40 years Kan has kept his habit of doing such an energy-consuming kind of painting after a day of busy work.

Kan once thought of retirement, but soon discarded such an idea. He plans to spend his whole life on design and education. His passion for artistic creation has only been increasing over the years. He even has a plan to completely renovate the apartment he has been living in for 18 years, to turn the dining room into a painting studio where he can have more space, and even teach private classes to pass on his experience to the next generation.

Kan has lived a life of aspirations. The essence of Neo-Confucianism is in his life-long career in art and design, inspiring numerous young people from Hong Kong and China. As written in the lyrics of the New Asia College anthem by Dr Ch'ien Mu, one of the founders of the New Asia College of the Chinese University of Hong Kong:

> *Advance courageously despite hardships and dangers, abundant in passion despite weariness and poverty! Hurray! Hurray!*

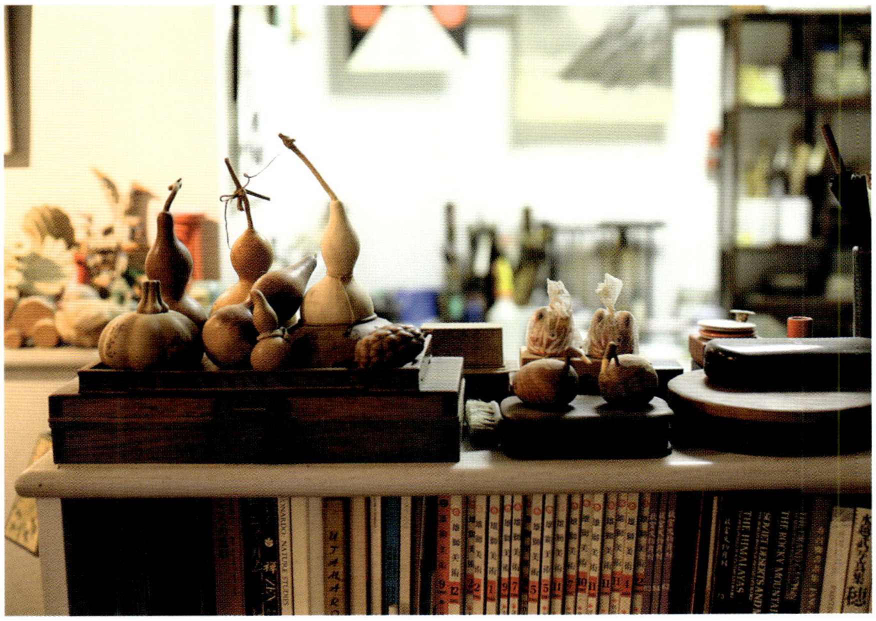

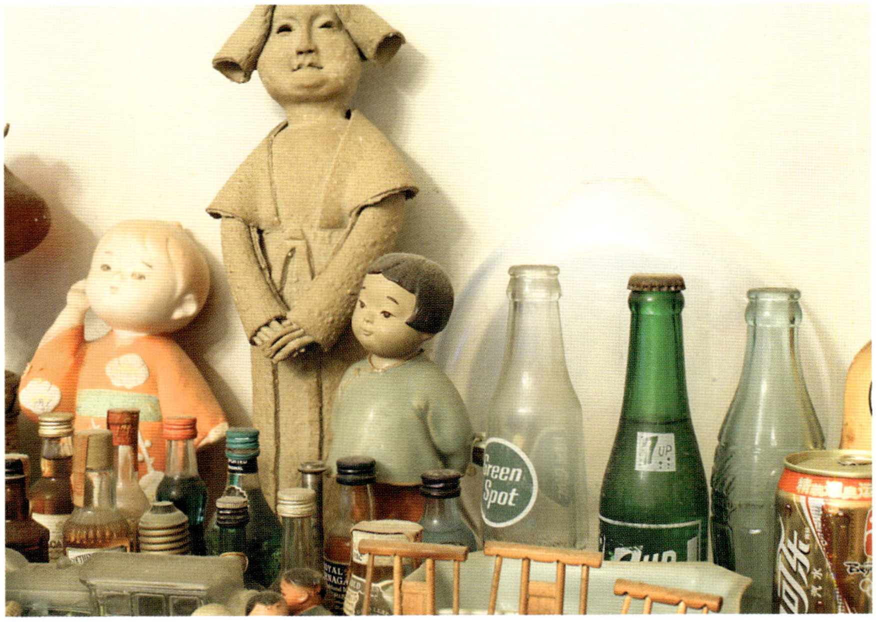

A variety of collections serve as Kan Tai-keung's sources of inspiration

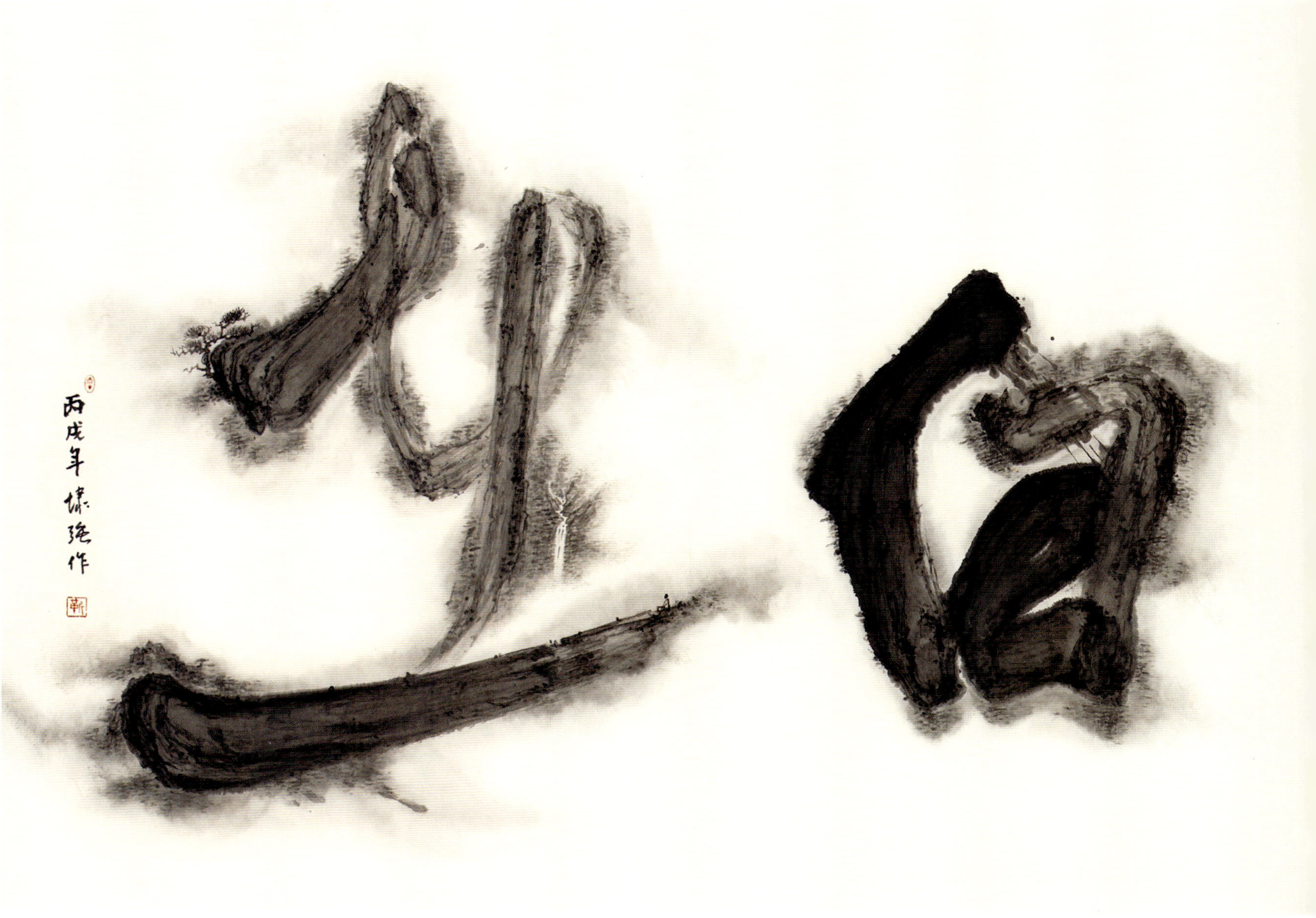
丙戌年

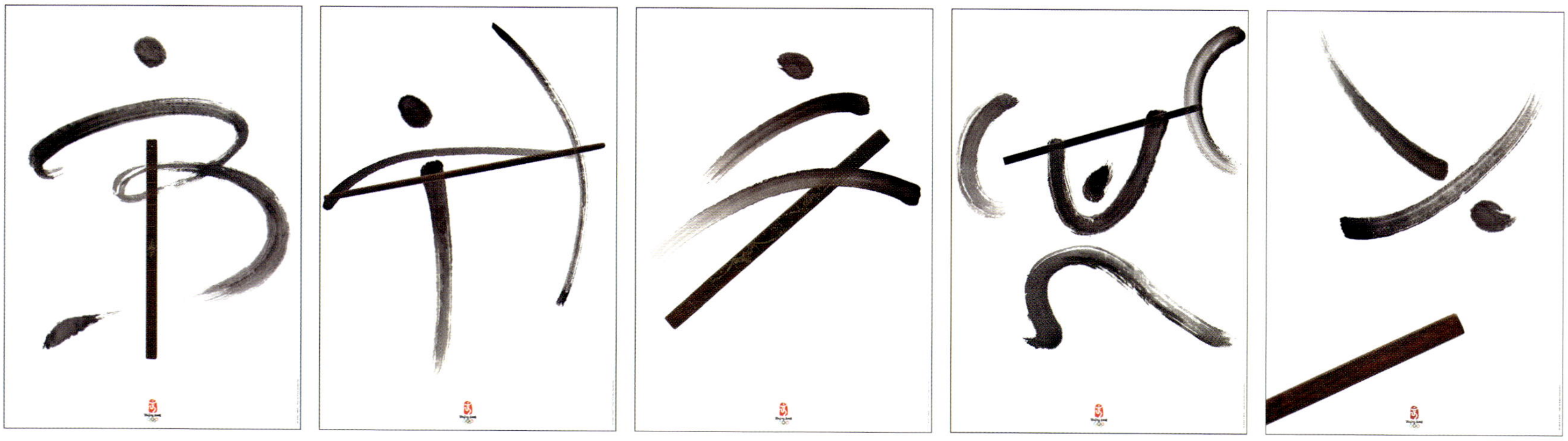

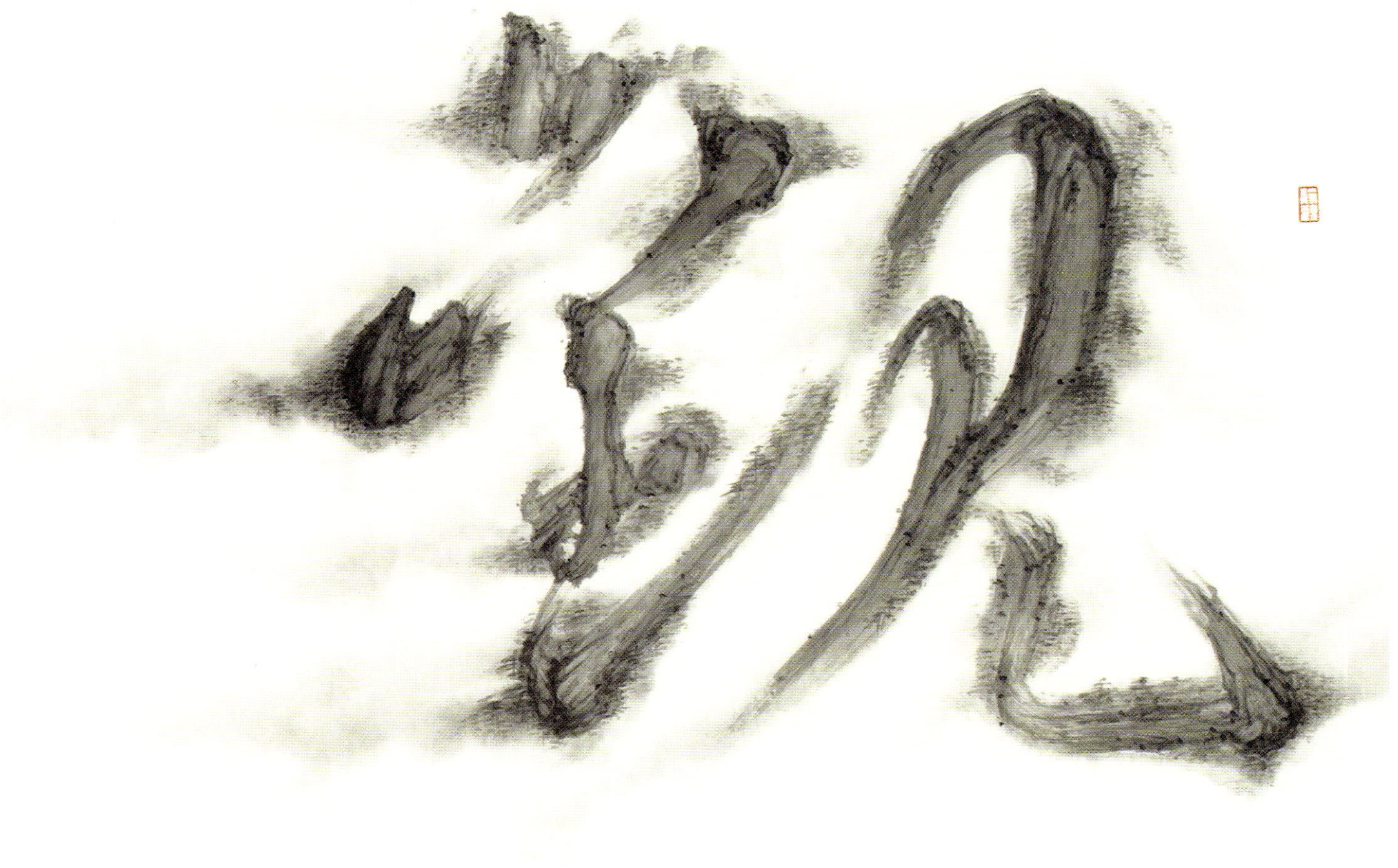

(Above) View Freedom
Ink on paper, 70x212 cm, 2006

(Bottom) Beijing 2008 Olympic Games
Poster series, dimensions variable, 2006

Academic Essays

Curators and Translators as 'Passeurs'

By Frank Vigneron

Assistant Professor, Department of Fine Arts
The Chinese University of Hong Kong

A few days ago, by chance, I met one of my colleagues in the subway. An American, he had lived in Hong Kong for just a few years and was quick to tell me that there "was no counter culture" here, whereas there was "a vibrant and lively music scene in Singapore". He found it ironic that such a thing could exist in a non-democratic, vaguely totalitarian state while he could not recognise the same thing in a more open society like Hong Kong. Needless to say I disagreed totally with this view, but then my wife is from here, I have lived in Hong Kong much longer and, although my Cantonese is not very good, I can read Chinese. I therefore have a much better knowledge of the local culture than my colleague who could not, of his own admission, read the language. Because of his very quick, ill-informed conclusion I was again reminded of the need for 'passeurs' of culture (a French term that could simply be translated as 'ferryman', ie someone who transports people, goods and ideas over borders that are considered difficult to cross) to avoid the production of such negative images — about local cultures in general and the local culture of Hong Kong in particular.

What can be said about Hong Kong culture can, in fact, be said about a number of other cultures that have been made more visible over the last decades. However Hong Kong's clear geographical limits — obtained from the historical conditions of its founding — could probably make its identification and portrait easier than in other places, where geographical limits are non-existent. I have explained elsewhere that if it is possible to identify supra-national narratives — ie the type of cultural elements and symbols used to create an identity that grows beyond old national borders — it might also be possible to acknowledge the existence of 'infra-national cultures'. This is a much better term than 'local culture' because several of these identifiable cultures are not associated with a place and can therefore not be dubbed 'local'. On the other hand, the culture of a place like Hong Kong cannot be called 'national', for it was never a nation and all of its inhabitants more easily identify with other nationalities. It had better be given another name: either 'local' or 'infra-national', as I have just explained.

In today's world, where the speed and the intensity of international exchanges have created the notion of 'global', it is within the always-renewed definitions of infra-national, national and supra-national cultures that infra-national cultures can exist and grow more visible. In fact they can only exist if they define themselves inside a narrative of oppositions. The reason 'Hong Kong people' are still seen as 'non-mainlanders', ie not Chinese from the People's Republic, is because they both need one another to define who and what they are. The creation of supra-national narratives, with the establishment of the European Union for instance, reinforces infra-national cultures. For these cultures to blossom again, and hopefully revive individuals' confidence in their own cultural makeup, there is a need for the old national cultures to somehow shrink a little. Ideally if national cultures do shrink, they leave more room in the infra-national cultures for essential elements to take back some former significance.

But this resizing of national cultures can only take place in an environment that accommodates other supra-national narratives, which, in the European Union for instance, are already in place in the form of heroes like the Eurostar and the new currency. In that new context, where infra-national and national cultures share an equal amount of cultural space in individuals, the reasons for the construed legitimacy of Hong Kong culture — even inside the national culture of China as a whole — become quite clear. But if globalisation leads to infra-national cultures becoming more visible — since old national frontiers tend to vanish or their meanings weaken (which explains why many states desire to reinforce them: states do not like the idea of seeing frontiers, a potent symbol of their legitimacy, disappear) – this also creates another need. The active presence of people is required to introduce these infra-national cultures to active members of other cultures, who do not have access to the information that can give them the richest understanding of their cultural products.

That would obviously be the role of these 'passeurs': people who are savvy to the background of these infra-national cultures' cultural products, and who are capable of making sense of them for an audience living in, or hailing from, another culture. Translators are a perfect example of the 'passeur'. It has long been my dream, for instance, to translate, with many footnotes, explanations and much background information, the texts written by Chinese painters and calligraphers over the centuries. They would make a perfect companion to the artworks themselves, allowing viewers to better understand where the works come from and how different or how similar they are from the art of their own cultures. Apart from translators, curators, the already familiar figure in the practice of contemporary art, are another kind of 'passeur'.

In contemporary art the difference between curator and artist is often a question of time, as the same person that organises shows can, at another time, be found involved in the making of artworks. The curator-as-artist creates interesting problems of authorship, as an exhibition put together by a curator is made up of works created by other people; there is therefore a sort of layering of authorship that is quite fascinating, as it can also fit the figure of the Deleuzian 'rhizome'. If the artist is connecting different points of the cultural rhizome, the curator-as-artist is connecting entire nodes on the rhizome. All the same, if contemporary artists can make installations of their own work, they are not considered curators of their own shows, whereas the curator, in essence, makes installations of the work of others. In that troubling context, the author becomes a kind of multi-dimensional being, since both the artist and the curator-as-artist can be considered authors of some kind: one creating works for different contexts while the other creates contexts for different artworks.

But beyond these questions, the curator as 'passeur' would also be required to clarify the context of the artwork's creation, hence playing a very obvious pedagogical role. The time when artists were happy to leave the meaning of their work unexplained has passed and it is an increasingly accepted fact that a contemporary work of art will not make sense, except to the happy few who have been privy to the thought process and explanations of the artist. Reading the brochure or the accompanying publication of an exhibition has become a part of understanding artworks, and the role of writing the text has become the responsibility of both artist and curator. A recent example is the curatorial work of Sally Lai, an independent curator who recently co-organised a show with Hong Kong and UK Chinese artists. In *Arrivals and Departures: New Perspectives of Hong Kong* (Urbis, Manchester, UK, from January 18 to July 8, 2007[1]), all of the works were carefully selected to illustrate the many aspects of what it means to be a Hong Kong artist and a 'diaspora' artist. In particular, I will focus on *Made in Hong Kong* (2007) by Leung Mee-ping, another founder of the Para/Site art space. As Lai explains:

> *... [it] is an expansive series of over 70 trade-paintings produced by the artist and her instructor in Shenzhen with an accompanying video documenting the artist learning the technique of production line painting. Trade-paintings were traditionally produced as tourist souvenirs that captured a clichéd Hong Kong of popular Western imagination... Leung's series presents a twist on the traditional form of trade-paintings, which instead presents a current view of Hong Kong ideals, referencing in particular the new tourist market in Hong Kong... Following the model of manufacturing relations that exists between Hong Kong and China, the 'Hong Kong' in Leung's works is constructed in Shenzhen, re-presented in Hong Kong and (while remaining unsold) is intended for mainland Chinese consumption. Leung's series foregrounds the question of who such representations are created by and for.* [2]

By just looking at the fairly pedestrian images that make up Leung Mee-ping's wall of oil paintings, one would be hard pressed to see any artistic merit in them. But that would be missing the point completely. The conceptual framework created by the artist, and the choice and explanations provided by the curator, are absolutely necessary to the understanding of the multifaceted implications of this work. Without the prior knowledge of all these elements there is no possibility for even the most cultivated viewer — who may only be familiar with the contemporary art of Europe — to understand the implications and the extraordinary value of this piece by an established Hong Kong artist.

At the Shanghai art fair, ShContemporary, in September 2007, I heard Zheng Shengtian, the managing editor of the now very popular *Yishu: Journal of Contemporary Chinese Art*, say that the art world necessitated three things to be viable: active artists, an active market and active art critics. Considering that the role of art critic has been taken on by many curators (and vice-versa), this statement could also be used to illustrate the necessity of these 'passeurs'. They would not only be introducing artworks and their context to the 'general' audience, ie those viewers who simply enjoy the art and do not think of making some themselves, but also creating the conditions for dialogues between artworks and art-makers that would take the shape of the deleuzian rhizome. In view of the works made by artists all around the world and by the way that they manage to be used and reused in different contexts, it is appears that artworks from varied cultural backgrounds do speak to other cultures, but with a multitude of voices to a multitude of different viewers. To make these passages from one culture to another is, of course, the role of our 'passeurs'. Today there is also a question of venue. Apart from the need for more 'passeurs', there is the need for more places where interactions between artworks and discourse between makers and viewers of different backgrounds, can be given free reign. Just as there is a need for publications on art, there is the need for more art spaces to show and install the artworks where writers, translators and curators can become 'passeurs' in complete freedom.

Art criticism in China only had to be given a shred of opportunity to blossom again. Even though the conditions are getting better on the mainland, to ensure a truly free discussion on the conditions of contemporary art there, a very open and well informed specialised press is appearing wherever there are Chinese artists and Chinese scholars. The Chinese world as a whole has been opened to all the new ideas about art that have been produced during the 20th century in Europe and America, and this created a measure of confusion for a while. It was largely born out of the mistaken notion that Euro-America had more to offer in terms of art theory than China. A more balanced situation is starting to emerge in which both Chinese and Euro-American 'passeurs' of all kinds are realising how much China and other regions have to bring to the art production and art discourse fields. From this more balanced situation a whole new domain of aesthetic thinking is emerging, and international Chinese curators and art critics are already writing criticism in which many ideas find their place, further enriched by the writers' Chinese backgrounds. But I believe that it is on the level of infra-national culture that the most interesting exchanges will be made.

In that sense Hong Kong and its artists and 'passeurs' might have a very important role to play, by which the idea of being a 'Chinese artist' can become richer and replete with meaning more varied than that attributed by those simply interested in the trade of 'Chinese art'. However the situation is changing quickly, like everything that concerns this art market. Even so, until recently the 'Chinese art market' has had a regrettable tendency to focus almost exclusively on mainland Chinese artists, and even more so on Beijing artists, ignoring and often even rejecting an important portion of the art made elsewhere in the 'Chinese world' — an expression that includes all art made by people who consider themselves Chinese (a complex problem well represented by the multi-faceted notion of 'Chineseness'). Just like there is no such thing as 'Chinese cuisine' (as there is no such thing as 'European cuisine'), there is no such thing as a 'Chinese artist', as all Chinese come from different regions and different cultural backgrounds, both in China and in the rest of the world.

1. Curated by Sally Lai and Yuen Fong Ling in collaboration with Hong Kong curatorial partners Howard Chan and Siu King-chung, the artists were: Leung Mee-ping, Pak Sheung-chuen, Stella So, Tam Wai-ping, Gordon Cheung, Community Museum Project, Yuen Fong Ling, Kwong Lee, Anthony Key and Mayling To. A publication on the project is forthcoming.

2. Lai, Sally: 'Up Close and From Afar: Curating Hong Kong from Dual Perspectives', in Journal of Visual Culture, 2007; 6; p.355.

Hong Kong Art – To Buy or Not To Buy?

Victor Lai Ming-hoi
Associate Professor,
Department of Creative Arts and Physical Education
The Hong Kong Institute of Education

The slow-going development of Hong Kong art has always been attributed to a lack of local talent and government support. However flipping through the two volumes of *Oasis*, one sees that there is actually a pool of talented artists. Some of them are industriously self-taught; some are from local or overseas academies and are well trained in both theory and practice. They work in a variety of media, ranging from Chinese to western painting, printmaking, sculpture, installation, video and conceptual art; their works are of an international standard.

In addition, a sum of over HK$20 billion is spent on the arts by the government every year. This is comparable to the budget of many cosmopolitan artistic hubs (although there are critics who say that the money is mostly spent on recreational activities). Other kinds of support and facilities, such as project-based and long-term subsidies granted by the Hong Kong Arts Development Council and state of the art museums and exhibition halls, also prove that the development of Hong Kong art is not hindered by a lack of talent or support. Instead, to accelerate the development of art in Hong Kong, a cultivated audience is needed. This kind of audience should include members of the general public who enjoy art, and collectors who, with varying backgrounds and personal tastes, invest in and support artists and art-related activities.

In November 2006 a silkscreened print titled *Mao Zedong* by celebrated Pop artist Andy Warhol was won with a bid of US$17 million (approximately HK$130 million) by Hong Kong tycoon Lau Luen-hung in a Sotheby's auction. Months later in October 2007, a bid for Execution by Chinese artist Yue Minjun hit the record books at £2.9 million (approximately HK$45 million) at Sotheby's in London. Works of other artists from the same generation, such as Zhang Xiaogang's *Bloodline: Big Family No. 3* and Liu Xiaodong's *Battlefield Realism: The Eighteen Arhats*, which ended up going for HK$47.36 million and HK$61.97 million respectively in an auction in April 2008, also made record prices and headlines (though there have been questions about whether auction commissions were rigged to boost lot prices).

Along with stock and real estate, the art market has become an option for Hong Kong speculators. Collecting has become chic — 'collector' sounding so much classier than 'speculator' However like foreign exchange, stock and properties, works of art have their ups and downs in the market. In 2008 China overtook France to become the third largest art market in the world, ranking behind only the United States and the United Kingdom. Since 2002 Chinese art sales have been rocketing at an annual rate of 30 percent. In 2007 auctions on the mainland and in Hong Kong, Macau and Taiwan totalled RMB23.69 billion (approximately HK$26 billion). Art investment has become a hot issue.

However collecting art is different from investing in it and the latter, as the term suggests, is just a means of investment. Investors buy works for their financial potential. They may speculate on whom they think is leading current trends and capitalise on works that promise a good return.

Studies by the big 'brand names' are good for quick deals, though forgeries must be avoided. To an art investor, market know-how and connoisseurship (the ability to tell a fake from a genuine masterpiece) are more important than personal taste. When investment is the aim, increasing turnover and maximizing profit is of more significance than art promotion and preservation. Thus real collectors are a rarity and speculative collecting never truly promotes the development of art. Collecting Hong Kong art, with its miniscule market value, is almost an idiosyncrasy.

Collecting, in contrast, is an expression of personal taste. While one always works with a limited budget, collecting involves selection. It starts with pleasing the self, and personal preferences are priceless. To be willing to spend a great sum on one's likes is a prerequisite for a collector, who should never just follow trends.

To build a collection one can start with a theme. The art market is like the fashion world. It is ever-changing, with different standards of beauty, and it is always directed by what is 'in'. For example, after the ''85 New wave' (or 85 Yishu Xinchao), which adopted the vocabulary of Western modernism — abstract ink painting manifesting traditional beliefs (such as that of Laozi and Chuangzi) took over the scene. Vernacular oil painting, which shares roots with scar literature, was overtaken by portraits of ladies in Qing-dynasty dress accompanied by bands of Chinese musicians. Later, Tibetan painting, references to the Cultural Revolution, the Mao suit, family portraiture, etc, became the new chic. The hippies of post-89 Political Pop ushered in hybrid images of the Cultural Revolution and symbols of American consumerism. These works guarantee good sales at auctions.

The above outlines the trends in the Chinese art market over the past 20 years and Hong Kong art has gone through a similar situation. For example in the 1970s 'modern ink painting' — which was much indebted to the style of Abstract Expressionism and principles of design — almost monopolised the local art scene. In the years approaching Hong Kong's return to China in 1997, conceptual art exploring the issue of identity became fashionable. When the interest in politics cooled down, the bird cages and sunken ships, once loaded with political content, resumed their original material state. Probably, they no longer make an exciting collection. Other than enriching speculators' pockets as they leverage on promotional projects, or boosting the bubble of artists' self-fashioned fame, such trendy works have little value for collection.

Collectors just follow their likes. They make critical and forward-looking selections, keeping their eyes on works with humanistic concern and innovative value. Hong Kong's niche has always been in its intermediary position; equally attuned to the cultures of China and the West, it looks at traditional Chinese culture at a critical distance. This gap gives room for a subtle blend.

Commerce and ethics also go hand-in-hand. Driven by these synergies, the art of Hong Kong is unique. This can be the starting point for a thematic collection. Readers of the two volumes of *Oasis* can browse through the listed artists and see if they can spot the masters of tomorrow and, with an eye for quality but not quantity, develop a sense for collecting 'presentable' works. To be able to amass a 'presentable' collection is a testimony to personal taste. For example, as with the Peggy Guggenheim Museum in Venice the owner shares her collection of works, in this case, by Surrealists and works from the New York School. Collections reflect a person's knowledge of art, their vision and their taste.

Wealth is another prerequisite for the collector. In general, collecting is a luxury beyond everyday consumption. According to statistics an average GDP of US$10,000 is required to support a healthy collecting institution. By this standard the people of Hong Kong are qualified. However if you are not a billionaire and are collecting with a limited budget, more preparation, such as reading related articles, websites and magazines, is needed. One has to study hard and be analytical when gathering information. Collecting art brings together scholarly work and market information, and theoretical knowledge must be complemented with fieldwork. Visiting art exhibitions, auction previews and seminars and meeting with artists comprise a collector's routine, and through this independent views and a good eye can be developed. Hard work and experience make one a connoisseur and contributes to the preservation of civilisation.

Collecting art is not speculation. It is not a way to show off one's wealth. It bears testimony to one's knowledge, taste and vision.

Art, and Inventing Ones Own Value

Choi Yan-chi
Assistant Professor, Academy of Visual Arts
Hong Kong Baptist University

China is shaking. The wave has spread to Hong Kong.

At the beginning of the year, the world was watching the riots in Tibet and the Olympic torch relay. Around that time, an article entitled *Zuihou Yidai Xianggang Wenhuaren De Gaobai* (Confession by the Last Generation of Hong Intellectuals) by cultural critic Leung Man-to was published as an editorial piece in Ming Pao and as the preface to Bono Lee's new book *Chic China Chic*. The article caused quite a stir. Discussing his recent experience in China and the decline of creativity in Hong Kong, Leung questions whether this is a place for cultured people. With China becoming chic, Hong Kong is arguably becoming a backwater, and it seems that one era is ending as another begins.

Chic China Chic and Leung's article convey the same unspoken question: what is going to happen to Hong Kong?

I trust that the wheel will still go round in Hong Kong. It may not go forward, but to the side, or on a winding course. Or it may self-rotate. Even though this is not a forward movement, it does not mean that things are stagnating or going backwards. Self-rotation reaches new depths.

The development of culture and creativity does not follow a regular pattern. What's chic in China and what's in or out in Hong Kong are always determined by human factors. They are always the outcome of people's interaction with a place. Hong Kong art has always been seen as cacti in a desert. It survives under unfavourable circumstances and has evolved into a particular, peculiar shape. Among other reasons, this has inspired me to explore Hong Kong art.

Hong Kong art has existed under adverse circumstances ever since the mid 1990s. At around the time of the handover, there was a change in the art market. Major galleries left Hong Kong due to a political premonition at first, and were attracted by the mainland's booming market. Although they are still geographically based in Hong Kong, they do not promote Hong Kong art. Art here lacks the auspices of buyers, but artists persevere. On pure soil, their works are as good as those of their predecessors. Not being driven by the market, Hong Kong art has invented its own value — coloured by artists' personal pursuits in this intricate melting point.

The first volume of *Oasis* is a delight to read. What impresses readers is not the book's design or its editing work, but its showcasing of Hong Kong's amazing art scene, comprising firstly of the presence of a group of artists who, without substantial support and despite the city's expensive land prices, have found the space to fulfil themselves; secondly, the recognition of these artists; and thirdly, the plurality, professionalism and confidence they demonstrate that surpasses the last generation.

The lack of space is a constant constraint on the development of art in Hong Kong, but artists have managed to find a way. The period between 1998 and 2002 was troubled by a slumping economy and SARS, but it saw the opening of many art spaces. The first, which opened in 1998, was the Oil Street Artists' Village which housed 1a space, Z+, Artist Commune, Videotage and other workshops in North Point. The premises were originally used for a public school and were then transformed into government warehouses. Built in the 1960s, the buildings had high ceilings and spacious rooms. Like loft spaces, which are also usually deserted warehouses, the Oil Street venue was the hottest creative space for contemporary art. It sparked a series of spatial transformations. In 2000 the Cattle Depot Artists' Village was set up, followed by similar colonies in Chai Wan, Kwun Tong, Fo Tan and Quarry Bay. With these newly found spaces Hong Kong art has never been more lively. Occupants of the art spaces in Fotan call themselves Fotanians. The place has become a new landmark of Hong Kong art.

When one examines Hong Kong culture, one finds a lot of oddities and contradictions. In a concrete jungle domineered by a 'Central value', art is not supported by the market, but still it thrives. The work of Hong Kong artists is uninhibited, autonomous, self-oriented and pure. Up-and-coming artists emerging at the beginning of the 21st century are young graduates from local and overseas institutions. Compared to their predecessors they are better trained, both academically and technically. They also have good organisation skills and are keen on expression in different ways. They make use of the media, shopping malls, alternative spaces and their own workshops to publicise their works. Critical issues for the last generation, such as cultural identity and the tension between tradition and modernity, have eventually faded out. Now everybody is concerned about cultural policy, the preservation of heritage, the role of the museum in the future, etc. Dematerialised and conceptual works are taken seriously.

The Hong Kong art scene is tiny. There is a lot of noise but a central theme is still lacking. A theoretical framework, which is vital for artistic development, is yet to be founded. This has been limiting the growth of Hong Kong art for the last 50 years.

The ability to invent one's own value, and the eagerness to pursue art for its own sake are invigorating. If all the voices join together, the plurality will arouse genuine concern for culture. Hong Kong can then become a nurturing ground for creativity.

In response to Leung's article, I think that Hong Kong is at a critical moment of change. A number of large-scale galleries have been set up in the last few months; local talents are stepping into limelight. Together with the founding of various art programmes, more new faces and ideas will emerge in the coming two years. Under such favourable circumstances, a renaissance is not far away.

Learn from the Past, Innovate for the Present

Daniel Lau Chak-kwong
Assistant Professor, Academy of Visual Arts
Hong Kong Baptist University

As a form of Chinese art, calligraphy is full of national character. In calligraphy the beautiful lines and spacing of Chinese characters are matched with literary substance. Refined imagery and profundity tends to characterise this form of visual culture, which has long been celebrated by traditional literati and cultural elites. In the past 100 years, although Hong Kong has been constantly challenged by Western influences, calligraphers have always seen it as their duty to preserve this national treasure.

In the early 20th century, political turmoil on the mainland caused many scholars to migrate from Guangdong to Hong Kong. They brought a stock of calligraphic treasures to shops, schools and temples, and a legacy for the subsequent development of calligraphy in Hong Kong. Their contribution is of extreme significance to the history of Chinese calligraphy.[1]

In the face of modernisation, Westernisation and globalisation, today's calligraphers find themselves faced with a critical challenge. However Hong Kong calligraphy, rooted in tradition, has received unanimous encomium from historians. For example, when comparing Hong Kong calligraphy to the mainland's 'modern calligraphy', Lang Shaojun is sceptical about the latter's shaky foundation and praises Hong Kong calligraphy for it adherence to traditions. "In the last few decades 'modern calligraphy' emerged in the mainland," he says. "It tries to get rid of traditional regulations and turn calligraphy into a merely formal or conceptual pursuit. Some even break away from character formation and words' meanings, dissolving the boundary between calligraphy and abstract painting. Such quests may be 'modern', but I doubt whether they make 'calligraphy'. Traditional calligraphy requires technical competence, talent, style, resonance and classiness... if these, together with the characters, are all abandoned, everything is heroically 'transcended', but is it still calligraphy? As such, I consider Hong Kong calligraphers' insistence on traditions with deepest respect."[2]

Wan Qingli shares the view. Agreeing that, on the whole, Hong Kong calligraphy is closer to traditional calligraphy, he points out its merits, noting "When compared to [that of] the mainland, Hong Kong calligraphy is generally more composed and has preserved more traditional values."[3] Harold Mok, noting the emergence of transformative currents, such as neoclassical calligraphy, modernist calligraphy, academic calligraphy, etc, in mainland China, observes that "there have been no revolutionary tides in Hong Kong calligraphy. There have also been no heated debates."[4] In his survey on and analysis of the selected calligraphic entries in the past Hong Kong Art Biennials, he reckons that "in the past 30 years, Hong Kong calligraphy has always been rooted in traditions. Besides embracing classical contents, it also follows traditional aesthetics. There is a high regard for the use of the brush, character structure, the spirited flow of the lines and compositional vigour."[5] He also suggests that "it is exceptional that Hong Kong, even though it is such an international city, can preserve more traditional elements."[6]

The traditional roots of Hong Kong calligraphy are clearly visible in Inheritance and Innovation at the Friends of Seal Stone Studio Calligraphy Exhibition held at the City Hall in 2007. Democratic Wall of Calligraphy (Fig. 1) is a spectacular piece of collaboration. Works contributed by 57 participating calligraphers are mounted in identical mirror frames. They line up neatly in two rows, in the middle of the widest wall. The work fully illustrates the ideas and endeavours of Hong Kong calligraphers who, while exploring the issue of innovation, have never forgotten the value of tradition. Among the 57 participants there are veterans and up-and-coming calligraphers and I am honoured to have taken part in this meaningful collaboration.[7]

The composite of different individual works shows a variety of scripts and styles. For example, the works of Su Shuhui (*first from the left, lower row*) and Tang Jinteng (*first from the left, upper row*) feature different scripts and styles. Combining the clerical, running and regular scripts, the former stresses the contrast of ink colour. The characters 'chengchuan' (heritage) are scribbled on the right of the work in qifeng (across the page) format, so only half of the characters are visible. This gives viewers the feeling of spontaneity and experimentation. On the contrary, the latter shows a symmetrical composition of rubbing and seal scripts. It looks more gentle and classic. Both calligraphers experiment on the composition and their superb calligraphic skills manifest themselves. Although the 57 Hong Kong calligraphers are all innovative, on the whole their practice is still rooted in tradition. All of them endeavour to learn through copying masterpieces. To them, the use of the brush, character structure and the spirited flow of the lines are of utmost importance.

As a student of calligraphy, I also study art history. As far as I know, the profundity of Chinese calligraphy lies in its philosophy and its evolution — calligraphers learn from the past in order to innovate. Therefore, the art is historicist. In the sediments of history, calligraphic traditions have nurtured numerous immortal pieces. As Dong Qicheng, calligrapher and theorist of the Ming dynasty, notes in *Huachanshi suibi* (writings in the painting studio), "The use of the brush and ink is crucial for exquisite characters. But if one has not seen a lot of actual works by ancient masters, one cannot understand this." He also states that "Calligraphers never just learn about the past and stick to it." Dong's view of 'learning from the past and innovating for the present' clearly summarises the attitude of earlier masters.

In fact, this is the path pursued by most Hong Kong calligraphers. The meaning of 'learning from the past and innovating for the present' is deeply felt by the author. I have been a pupil of Master Han Yunsha for years. He always stresses that copying is the foundation for learning calligraphy. He recommends starting with Han steles, while it is also good to touch upon Han bamboo scrolls and works on silk. Through copying all kinds of masterpieces, I have learnt to consolidate everything for transformation and have created a variety of styles. For example, *Happy-Go-Lucky Studio* (Fig. 2) is a seal, but it is not done in seal script. It is my first attempt to use this format on a square seal. The script is in the middle of clerical and regular scripts, showing features of many clerical and regular texts, carved in a spontaneous manner.

In the *Beginning was the Word* (Fig. 3), with the ground in black and characters in white, is in sinuous seal script (a script used frequently in seals). The work imitates 'black tiger' calligraphy of stone carvings and emphasises the unique texture created by brushing a Chinese brush on paper. Traces of erosion, characteristic of ancient steles, also feature in the work. These two works exemplify my own experience in 'learning from the past and innovating for the present.' This has also been pursued and achieved by many other Hong Kong calligraphers. Their work can be the subject for another paper.

I have also gained some insight into teaching calligraphy. Teaching students at different ages, I feel positive about the importance of learning through copying masterpieces, but am also aware that this is not the only way to learn. Copying is an entry point. Guided by an understanding of the history of calligraphy, students can appreciate how the scripts have evolved over time. This cultivates reverence for cultural heritage and is undoubtedly a kind of civil education.

As a way to learn, copying should not be mechanical. It has to be flexible. While students are encouraged to learn through copying, they find it more interesting if they are sensitive to their environments and bring in elements from their lives. For example, Fang Yunzhi is a student at the Academy of Visual Arts, Hong Kong Baptist University. She was in my calligraphy class and started with the Diamond Sutra of Mount Tai. She has created a rather special work, in which she conveys the feeling of *Penetrating the Woods*, a seven-word poem by her friend, Wu Yunjing, on the two little trunks, broken into halves. She sees in her friend's poem "transition from a state of drifting", and a sense of "the same old confusion." The work departs from the tradition of writing on paper or silk. It also breaks away from the conventional two-dimensionality and crosses over with three-dimensionality. The work is innovative and refreshing.

Two other examples are by my nephew, Lin Luoxi, who is five years old. He has copied a selection of hieroglyphs from many oracle bone scripts and bronze ware scripts. *Horse* is a single-character work. Although the character is not the same as the original, the spontaneous use of the brush enlivens the lines and creates varying contrasts of wetness and dryness. I think that children should be praised and encouraged. Their merits should receive more attention than their imprecision. I try to encourage him to depict things around him with a brush and create his own 'neo-hieroglyph'. *High Heel Shoe* (Fig. 4) is one such adorable work. Combining simple drawing and regular script, it is a manifestation of innocence. The lively lines and simple form shows the child's observation and confidence.

To conclude, if teachers encourage students to be imaginative, flexible and lively as they build their foundation through copying masterpieces, students can definitely 'learn from the past and innovate for the present.'

1. For the contribution to Hong Kong calligraphy by late Qing masters and scholars, please refer to 'Yueji Yilao Shufajia Yu Ershi Shiji Chuqi Xianggang Shutan' ('Cantonese Left-over Calligraphers and the Early Twentieth Century Hong Kong Calligraphy Scene'), Cheung, Wai-yee, in Lingnan Shuxue Yanjiu Lunwenji (Collected Theses on Lingnan Calligraphy) 2004, pp. 108-129; 'Xianggang Zaoqi Shufa — Yi Wenhua Wei Shijiao' ('Early Hong Kong Calligraphy — Culture as Perspective), Chen, Yafei, in Hong Kong Visual Arts Yearbook 2004 2005, pp.42-63.

For early Hong Kong calligraphy please refer to 'Xianggang Xianxian Moji — Wenhua Chengchuan Yu Shufa' ('Ink Work by Early Hong Kong Masters — Heritage and Calligraphy'), Mok, Harold, in Xianggang Xianxian Moji (Ink Work by Early Hong Kong Masters) 2006, pp.15-24.

2. 'Wokan Xianggang Dangdai Yishu' ('My View of Hong Kong Contemporary Art'), Lang, Shaojun, in Hong Kong Contemporary Art Biennial 1998 1998, p.33.

3. See Dibajie Guoji Shufa Lianzhan Tekan (The 8th International Calligraphy Exhibition Catalogue), by the Hong Kong International Calligraphy Alliance, 1999, p.3.

4. Chuancheng Yu Xinyi: Erlinglingqi Shizhaizhiyou Shufazhan Xu Yi (Heritage and Innovation: Shizhaizhiyou Calligraphy Exhibition — Preface 1]), Mok, Harold, 2007. For calligraphy on the mainland in the past 20 years please refer to Zhongguo Shufa Ershinian (20 years of Chinese calligraphy) Wu, Yuohua, 2001; Dangdai Shufa Chuangzuo Moshi Yu Liupai Yanjiu (Study on the Creative Models and Schools of Contemporary Calligraphy), Chen, Dazhong, 2005.

5. 'Cong Chuantong Dao Xiandai — Xianggang Yishu Shuangnianzhan Shufa De Sikao' ('From Traditions to Modernity — Thoughts on Calligraphy in the Hong Kong Art Biennial'), Mok, Harold in Hong Kong Visual Arts Yearbook 2005 2006, p.76. For other discussions on the Hong Kong Art Biennial and Hong Kong calligraphy, please refer to 'Cong Shuangnianzhan Dejiangzhe Guankui Sanshinian Lai De Xianggang Shufa' ('Looking into 30 Years of Hong Kong Calligraphy from the Biennial Awardees'), Tang, Hoi-chiu, in the Hong Kong Visual Arts Yearbook 1999 2000, pp.40-47; 'Xianggang Yishu Shuangnianzhan He Xianggang Shufa' ('Hong Kong Art Biennial and Hong Kong Calligraphy'), Tang, Hoi-chiu, in Shuyuan Duouing — Dangdai Xianggang Bairen Shufazhan (Calligraphic Excellence — 100-man Exhibition of Contemporary Hong Kong Calligraphy), 2003, pp. 6-7.

6. Chuancheng Yu Xinyi: Erlinglingqi Shizhaizhiyou Shufazhan Xu Yi (Heritage and Innovation: Shizhaizhiyou Calligraphy Exhibition — Preface 1], Mok, Harold

7. Participants include: Fang Zhiyong, Ren Guanzhong, Li Jixin, Li Jianqiu, Li Guoming, Li Debao, Li Zewen, Li Jinxian, Li Yingping, Yu Deguang, Lin Demao, Fan Chengzhong, Xu Peizhi, Rong Haoran, Ma Runxian, Tang Jinteng, Qu Erlian, Chen Wenyan, Chen Yong, Chen Shiliang, Chen Gengxin, Chen Ruohai, Chen Huayu, Liang Quibai, Liang Guoquan, Liang Qiming, Zhang Lizhen, Zhang Yaoping, Xu Mingzhi, Xu Baoxun, Feng Yifeng, Huang Junshi, Huang Lingyu, Huang Bozheng, Ceng Guangcai, Ye Minren, Ye Kai, Ye Rongzhi, Ye Qinghua, Zhao Yongjin, Zhao Yulan, Zhao Qijiao, Yang Zongyao, Yang Qixia, Lei Shaohua, Di Shiyao, Liu Yongyao, Danial Lau, Xiao Zi, Qian Kaiwen, Xuan Shaocan, Han Yunshan, Guan Zhenwen, Guan Zhanji, Guan Yingliang, Su Sidi and Su Shuhui (list in the order of Li Jixin, ed., Chuancheng Yu Xinyi: Erlinglingqi Shizhaizhiyou Shufazhan (Heritage and Innovation: Shizhaizhiyou calligraphy exhibition. The artists' biographies are listed in the section on 'biographies').

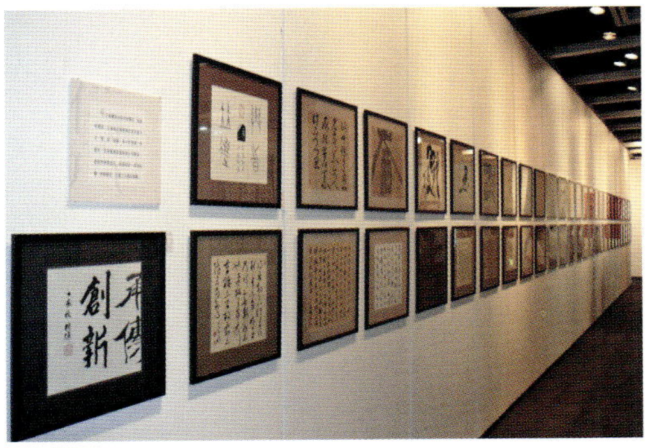

Fig. 1

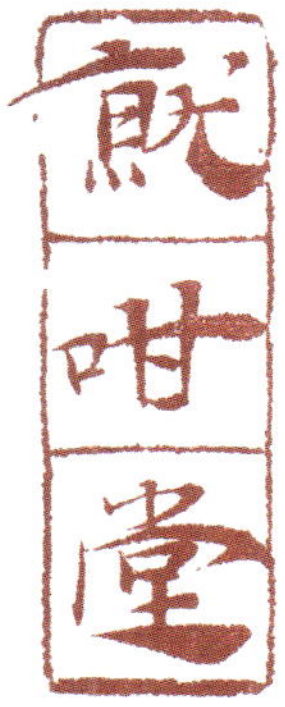

Fig. 2

Fig. 3

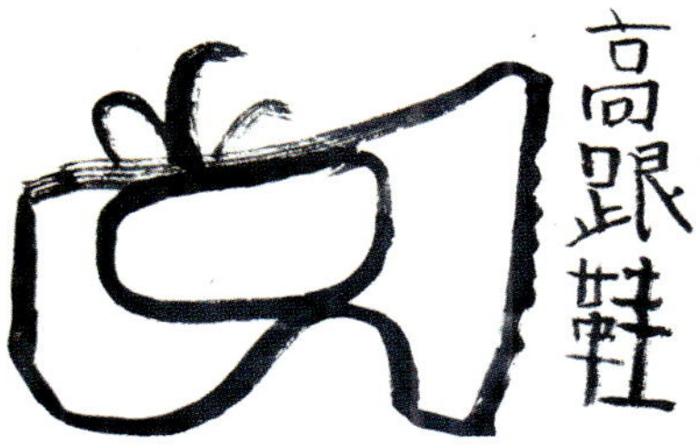

Fig. 4

Epilogue

Living with a Difference

Here are some keywords from the year: Beijing Olympics, Sichuan earthquake, Taiwan presidential election, Burma typhoon, European Cup, the United States presidential election, soaring oil prices, snowstorm, Philippine hurricane, subprime mortgage crisis...

This is a one-dimensional world. Advanced technology has drawn distant places closer. The more we know about things happening on the other side of the globe or right next to us, the less we are certain about them. One can never identify the true story.

A lot of things happened in 2008. It has been a year of immense world events, natural disasters, man-made calamities and local gossip. Have these touched us — or have they numbed us?

We now live in a hyper-busy world and are constantly being bombarded by all kinds of sensual stimulation. We can hardly spare a moment to think. We want immediate sensation. In such a world is there room for art that demands real thought?

In a world that is monotonous and indifferent, art is especially cherished for its critical capacity and its ability to inspire. Contemporary artists can no longer live in their own utopia. They must be sensitive to social developments and strive to enlighten people. Art is at the forefront of social progress.

To promote art and culture, we need not just one or two extraordinary avant-garde pieces, but a holistic institution comprising artists, museums, galleries, exhibition venues, curators, patrons, collectors, auction houses, archives, art historians, critics, art administrators, publishers, journals and a willing audience. All these are indispensable. The fatal problem with art promotion in Hong Kong is the unsupportive market. The audience base is too small to support a healthy institution. Major stakeholders, such as artists, curators, critics, galleries and museums, just mind their own respective businesses and have never synergised into a long-lasting institution. What is immediately needed is communication between the various parties. Mediators, whose roles can be fulfilled by well-trained art administrators, are urgently needed for the job.

In one of the articles collected in this volume professor Frank Vigneron raises the idea of 'passeurs'. These are among the pivotal figures that can direct the development of art and culture. How can we find 'passeurs'? In a general sense, they can be found everywhere and in everyone. First of all, we need a reflective understanding of our own cultural character. With such an understanding, members of the audience, collectors, curators and artists can all promote art as 'passeurs.' The value of Hong Kong art is discussed by professor Choi Yan-chi in her essay.

Many patrons and collectors — ranging from the Medici family, whose members have been enthusiastic supporters of the arts since the Renaissance, to the Guggenheim family, JP Morgan and JD Rockefeller — have made their names in art history. We now know about them for their wealth and also for their contribution to art. With exceptional taste, knowledge and farsightedness, they have amassed collections that have become the Uffizi Gallery, the Guggenheim Museums and the Metropolitan Museum of Art. Here is the story of another collector: the global bestseller, *Reader's Digest*, has earned its founders, DeWitt and Lila Wallace, a great fortune. Wallace, an avid art lover, has a very good eye for modern art. Since the 1940s she has been collecting works by modernists — such as the post-impressionists, surrealists and abstract expressionists — even before they came to fame.[1] The only reason for her to collect these works was that she had "fallen in love with them". She once said, "Great works of art are not only for solitary contemplation. They are equally enjoyable in hectic days."[2] Obviously Wallace has not been collecting for monetary return. She collects art because she loves it. She is a 'passeur'.

As professor Victor Lai Ming-hoi suggests, collecting is different from investing. Buying and collecting are not synonymous. Collecting serves sentimental and critical aims. It is about the desire to own things and knowledge. With their love of knowledge, genuine collectors are also promoters of culture. I hope that Hong Kong art will be recognised and collected by the city's tycoons and corporations, which will then help promote culture as 'passeurs' themselves.

The crew of *Oasis* is another group of 'passeurs'. Within 14 months we have completed two volumes. They include more than a hundred thousand words, over 10,000 photographs, visits to 50 studios and interviews with 75 artists. These artists — some of them internationally renowned, some fresh graduates — are definitely the simplest and purest group of artists in the world. Like most pragmatic Hongkongers, they have regular jobs. They spent their holidays creating art. Some even work overnight. Their works are of a professional standard but they do not necessarily aim for an artistic profession. Most of them do not make a living by selling their works. The market is not their concern. Their motivation is simple. They just want to pursue their own creative paths. Eventually, those who persevere find their own way. Together, this group of 'pure' artists tells the story of contemporary Hong Kong art.

This story is not epic, but it is real. In 2008 the Hong Kong art scene lost Tong King-sum and Jerry Kwan. In loving memory, their stories encourage us to persevere and overcome difficulties. Tong worked till the very end and was still preparing for an exhibition shortly before he passed away. In the 1980s Kwan made a great effort to go to New York for his dream. Their spirit and contribution to Hong Kong art shall always be remembered. Like these two forerunners, Hong Kong artists — because of art — live with a difference.

1. The Reader's Digest Collection of Modern Masters exhibition was held at the Hong Kong Museum of Art in 1988, showing 40 masterpieces from the company's extensive collection.

2. The display of works at Reader's Digest headquarters in Pleasantville, New York, is always open to employees and visitors.

Carl Cheng Chi-ming
Conceptual Director

Appendix

Artists' Biographies

This book introduces 25 studios and 36 artists who have each in their own way influenced the history of contemporary art in Hong Kong. The appendix contains information about their careers which may give readers a more rounded understanding of the artists' backgrounds.

Chan Hiu-ting, Winnie

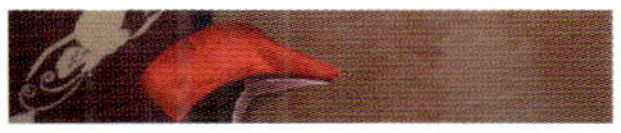

winniechan714@yahoo.com.hk
www.winniechan714.net

Winnie Chan Hiu-ting received her BA (Fine Art) in painting from the Royal Melbourne Institute of Technology (RMIT) University programme co-presented with the Hong Kong Art School in 2005. She then completed the fundamental certificate in arts management organised by the Hong Kong University School of Professional and Continuing Education in 2006. Currently she is an undergraduate at the Chinese University of Hong Kong, majoring in cultural studies and concentrating on gender studies.

Selected group exhibitions

2006 *BA (Fine Art) Graduation Show 2006 – Paradigm Shift,* Hong Kong Arts Centre, *Hong Kong*
2005 *Art Fair '05, White Tube,* Hong Kong
2005 *751 – Corporate Exhibition of Year 3 Painting (Day) students,* Hong Kong Arts Centre, Hong Kong
2004 *Art Fair '04, Hong Kong Arts Centre,* Hong Kong
2004 *Gonna Crazy – Corporate exhibition of Winnie Chan and Sunny Tam,* White Tube, Hong Kong
2004 *White Tube Opening Exhibition,* White Tube, Hong Kong

Chan, Gaylord

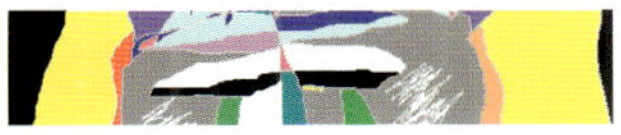

ccstudio@netvigator.com

Gaylord Chan was born in 1925 and received his certificate in art and design from the Department of Extra-mural Studies at the University of Hong Kong in 1970. He then was a founding member of the Hong Kong Visual Arts Society and the Artmatch Group in 1974 and 1995 respectively, and chaired the groups for the first four years. In 1986 he was awarded an MBE by Her Majesty the Queen and was the recipient of several arts awards including the Urban Council Fine Art Award (1983) and the Hong Kong Visual Arts Society Silver Jubilee Award (1998). Chan is now an Honorary Adviser to the Leisure and Cultural Services Department, and jointly established Culture Corner Art Academy with Josephine Chow Suk-fan, dedicated to art education emphasising visual communication.

Selected solo exhibitions

2005 *Gaylord Chan at 80,* Hanart T Z Gallery, Hong Kong
2005 *Gaylord Chan Miniature Show,* Hong Kong Arts Centre, Hong Kong
2003 *IVphase@gaylord,* The Chinese University of Hong Kong, Hong Kong
2003 *Future in the Past,* The Hong Kong Institute of Education, Hong Kong
2002 *Twin Solo Exhibition,* Hanart T Z Gallery, Hong Kong
1999 *Gaylord Chan in Black and White,* Hanart T Z Gallery, Hong Kong

Selected group exhibitions

2008 *Artmatch Exhibition 2008 – Reality,* The Hong Kong Institute of Education, Hong Kong
2008 *Artists in the Neighborhood Scheme IV,* Hong Kong City Hall Lower Block Exhibition Hall Crystal Atrium, Metroplaza, Kwai Fong, Hong Kong
2007 *The Hong Kong Visual Arts Society's 34th Annual Exhibition,* University Museum and Art Gallery, The University of Hong Kong, Hong Kong
2007 *Reversing Horizons,* Museum of Contemporary Art, Shanghai, Shanghai, China
2007 *Fotanian 2007 Open Studio,* Fotan, Hong Kong
2006 *HKU SPACE 50th Anniversary Exhibition – Creative Spirit,* Hong Kong Cultural Centre, Hong Kong
2006 *The Hong Kong Visual Arts Society's 33rd Annual Exhibition,* Hong Kong Visual Arts Centre, Hong Kong
2005 *The Hong Kong Visual Arts Society's 32nd Annual Exhibition – VAS Culture, The Chinese University Hong Kong, Hong Kong*
2003-2004 *The Hong Kong Visual Arts Society's 30th Annual Exhibition,* Hong Kong Central Libraries, Exhibition Galleries, Hong Kong
2003 *Artmatch Exhibition 2003 – Impact,* University Museum and Art Gallery, the University of Hong Kong, Hong Kong
2003 *Joint Exhibition of Artworks by Hong Kong Artists (1),* The Hong Kong Institute of Education, Hong Kong
2002 *FIRST CHOICE,* Kwang Hwa Cultural Center Gallery, Hong Kong

Selected curatorial exhibitions

2000 *L 'art de Vivre la Difference,* United Nations Educational, Scientific and Cultural Organization, Paris, France
1995 *Artmatch Inaugural Exhibition,* Hong Kong Visual Arts Centre, Hong Kong
1993 *The Hong Kong Visual Arts Society's 20th Anniversary Exhibition,* Hong Kong Arts Centre, Hong Kong
1974 *The Hong Kong Visual Arts Society's Inaugural Exhibition,* Exhibition Gallery, City Hall High Block, Hong Kong

Chen Hui-lien, Denise

denise@dollarsaver.com.hk

Denise Chen Hui-lien received her BA (Fine Art) majoring in ceramics from the Royal Melbourne Institute of Technology (RMIT) University and then completed the MFA programme co-presented by RMIT University and the Hong Kong Art School. She mainly uses ceramic and mixed media in her art practice. Chan's present DFA studies focus on how minority arts and artefacts fit into mainstream culture.

Selected solo exhibitions

2005 *Brink,* Chai Wan Industrial Centre, Hong Kong

Selected group exhibitions

2008 *Wall Piece,* JL Workshop, Hong Kong
2007 *Complex Number,* Too Art, Hong Kong
2006 *Cracker,* Hong Kong Visual Arts Centre, Hong Kong
2004 *In Progress,* White Tube, Hong Kong
2004 *Happy Works,* Hong Kong Visual Arts Centre, Hong Kong
2003 *Traces,* Shanghai Street Art Space, Hong Kong
2001 *Teapot Gala,* Cobo Ceramics Workshop, Hong Kong
1991 *JL Workshop Group Exhibition,* Hong Kong Art Centre, Hong Kong

Cheung Chung-chu

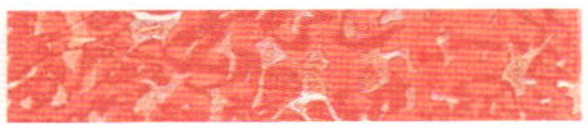

ccc@open-printshop.org.hk
http://www.open-printshop.org.hk

Cheung Chung-chu is a co-founder of the Hong Kong Open Printshop. He is in the executive committee responsible for education and community projects. Cheung's works have been shown in numerous national and international exhibitions, including in Belgium, Shanghai and France. His works are collected by Hong Kong and international museums, and private collectors.

Selected group exhibitions

2007 *Print Tokyo 2007,* Sakimi Art Museum, Okinawa, Japan
2007 *Crossing Boundaries – The Hong Kong Graphic Art Fiesta 2007,* Hong Kong Graphic Art Fiesta 2007, Tsuen Wan Town Hall, Hong Kong
2006 *The 12th International Biennial Print and Drawing Exhibition 2006,* R.O.C., National Taiwan Museum of Fine Art, Taichung, Taiwan
2005 *In Your Dreams,* Hong Kong, Shanghai, China; Paris, France and Sydney, Australia
2003 *Hong Kong Art Biennial 2003,* Hong Kong Museum of Art, Hong Kong
2003 *Detached Weapon – the 3rd International Postcard Print Exchange,* Iowa State University Ames, Iowa, USA
2002 *Virtually /Reality International Exchange of Prints and Digital Images,* Estampe Charleroi, Belgium
2002 *Grand Opening Exhibition,* Peninsula Arts Centre, Shanghai, China
1999 *The 9th International Biennial Print and Drawing Exhibition 1999,* R.C.C., Taipei Fine Arts Museum, Taipei, Taiwan
2000 *Qingdao International Biennial Print Exhibition,* Qingdao Art Museum, China
1997 *4e Triennale Mondiale Destmpes Petit Format,* Paris, France
1989 *New Wave: Chinese Ink Painting in Australia,* Museum of Chinese and Australian History, Melbourne, Australia

Selected curatorial exhibitions

2007 *Hong Kong Graphics Art Fiesta 2007,* Tsuen Wan Town Hall; Hong Kong Visual Arts Centre; SD Gallery; Hong Kong Polytechnic University, Hong Kong

Ching Chin-wai, Luke

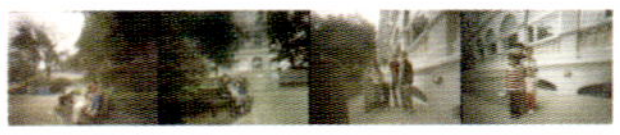

sunnyside.hk@gmail.com
www.lukeching.blogspot.com

Luke Ching Chin-wai was born in Hong Kong in 1972. He received his MFA degree from the Chinese University of Hong Kong in 1998. His major works include *Folk Art Series: Cockroach*, a work concerning city life and craftsmanship, *Easy to Learn Cantonese, Chapter 1-6*, concerning the language learning process, *Public Sculpture: Dog Footprint, Wet Print: Rainbow, and Room as Pin-hole Camera,* a close examination of public space.

Selected solo exhibitions

2007 *2 IN 1 works by Luke Ching,* Hong Kong Visual Arts Centre, Hong Kong
2006 *Language Center,* Fukuoka Asian Art Museum, Fukuoka, Japan
2006 *Two Associations in Vermont,* Vermont Studio Center, Vermont, USA
2005 *Shanghai Street Photo Studio: Photo Installation by Luke Ching,* Shanghai Street Artspace, Hong Kong
2002 *A Good Idea is a Smile,* Muse Gallery, Hong Kong
1998 *Vanishing Point,* Hui's Gallery, The Chinese University of Hong Kong, Hong Kong

Selected group exhibitions

2008 *Everyday Anomalies,* Phoenix Gallery , Brighton, UK
2007 *Reversing Horizons,* Museum of Contemporary Art, Shanghai, Shanghai, China
2007 *Chinglish,* Hong Kong Museum of Art, Hong Kong
2007 *The Pivotal Decade,* Chinese Arts Centre, Manchester, UK
2007 *HK.CityU.HK,* City University of Hong Kong, Hong Kong
2005 *Hong Kong Art Biennial Exhibition 2005,* Hong Kong Museum of Art, Hong Kong
2004 *Re-wanchai,* AiR Corner House, Hong Kong
2003 *Cheng Ming in All Directions: 40 Years of Art at the Chinese University of Hong Kong,* Hong Kong Arts Centre, Hong Kong
2003 *Wanakio 2003: Urban Art Exhibition,* Noren Market, Okinawa, Japan
2003 *A Strange Heaven: Contemporary Chinese Photography,* Galerie Rudolfinum, Prague, Czech Republic
2003 *Exercise one,* Shanghai Street Artspace, Hong Kong
1999 *Materia Prima,* West Space Gallery, Melbourne, Australia

Choi Yan-chi

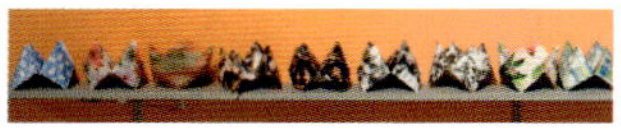

Choi Yan Chi was born in 1949 in Hong Kong. She received her BFA and MFA from the School of the Art Institute of Chicago in 1976 and 1978 respectively. Currently she is an assistant professor at the Hong Kong Baptist University. Choi has been an active participant in Hong Kong art since the 1980s. Her works have been exhibited in USA, Canada, Germany and Australia, Hong Kong, and Taiwan. In 1998 she started 1a space, in the same year she was named Artist of the Year by the Hong Kong Arts Development Council. Her works were collected by the Hong Kong Museum of Art and the Hong Kong Heritage Museum.

Selected solo exhibitions

2007 *Revision,* 1a space, Hong Kong
2007 *Re-fabrication,* Para/Site Art Space, Hong Kong
1993 *Raumfarben,* Haus der Kultren der Welt, Berlin, Germany
1985 *An Extension into Space,* Hong Kong Arts Centre, Hong Kong
1979 *From the Wall to the Floor,* Hong Kong Arts Centre, Hong Kong

Selected group exhibitions

2007 *97+10,* Museum of Contemporary Art Shanghai, Shanghai, China
2006 *Exhibition for the 50th Anniversary of Hong Kong University,* Hong Kong Cultural Centre, Hong Kong
2006 *Stained the Eclipsed Pattern,* UMA G, Hong Kong
2006 *Creative Spirit: Hong Kong Visual Arts,* Hong Kong Cultural Centre, Hong Kong
2000 *Landscape Show,* Hong Kong Cultural Centre, Hong Kong
2000 *Contemporary Hong Kong Art,* Hong Kong Museum of Art, Hong Kong
1999 *Home Affairs,* 1a space, Hong Kong
1998 *Bad Rice,* Span Gallery, Melbourne and Sydney, Australia
1997 *Hong Kong Art Festival,* Goethe Institute Munich, Munich, Germany
1997 *Journey to the East,* Centre for the Arts, Hong Kong University of Science and Technology, Hong Kong
1995 *The "OO" Show,* Red Head Gallery, Toronto, Canada
1994 *Festival Banquet,* York Quay Gallery, *Toronto, Canada*

Selected curatorial exhibitions

2003 *Tree-Man: retrospectives of Danny Yung,* 1a space, Hong Kong
2002 *Behind the Eyeball,* 1a space, Hong Kong
1998 *Painting Hong Kong,* 1a space, Hong Kong

Chow Suk-fan, Josephine

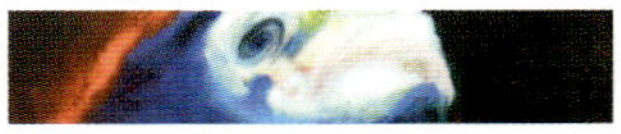

ccstudio@netvigator.com

Josephine Chow Suk Fan was born in Hong Kong. She graduated from the Chinese University of Hong Kong in 1989. In the same year, she jointly established the Culture Corner Art Academy with Gaylord Chan. Since 1991 Chow has actively joined various art organisations including the Hong Kong Female Contemporary Art Association, the Hong Kong Artists' Guild, the Hong Kong Artists' Association and the Hong Kong Visual Arts Society, and acted as Vice Chairperson of the 13th Executive Committee. She frequently served as adjudicator for art competitions, and conducted art workshops and talks.

Selected solo exhibitions

2002 *Twin Solo Exhibition,* Hanart T Z Gallery, Hong Kong
1995 *Paintings by Josephine Chow,* The Artland Gallery, Hong Kong

Selected group exhibitions

2008 *Artmatch Exhibition 2008 – Reality,* The Hong Kong Institute of Education, Hong Kong
2008 *Artists in the Neighborhood Scheme IV,* Exhibition Hall, City Hall Lower Block, Hong Kong
2007 *The Hong Kong Visual Arts Society's 34th Annual Exhibition,* University Museum and Art Gallery, The University of Hong Kong, Hong Kong
2007 *Artmatch Exhibition 2007,* Hong Kong Visual Arts Centre, Hong Kong
2006 *The Hong Kong Visual Arts Society's 33th Annual Exhibition,* Hong Kong Visual Arts Centre, Hong Kong
2006 *Artmatch Exhibition 2006,* Hong Kong Teachers' Centre, Hong Kong
2005 *Artmatch Exhibition 2005,* The Art Gallery, The Hong Kong Institute of Education, Hong Kong
2005 *The Hong Kong Visual Arts Society's 32nd Annual Exhibition – VAS Culture, The Chinese University Hong Kong, Hong Kong*
2003-04 *The Hong Kong Visual Arts Society's 30th Annual Exhibition,* Exhibition Galleries, Hong Kong Central Libraries, Hong Kong
2003 *Artmatch Exhibition 2003 – Impact,* The University Museum and Art Gallery, The University of Hong Kong, Hong Kong
2000-2007 *Art-On-Wheels,* Castle Peak Hospital, Hong Kong
1999-2000 *Artmatch Astride Millennium Show,* Museum of Site, Hong Kong

Selected curatorial exhibitions

2004 *The Community Art Exhibition – Culture Corner Art Academy 15th Anniversary Exhibition,* Tai Po Plaza Level 2 Podium, Hong Kong
2001 *Culture Corner Art Club – Parent and Child Art Exhibition 2001,* The Art Gallery, Hong Kong Institute of Education, Hong Kong
1996 *Growing with Art - Children and Youth Acrylic Painting Exhibition,* The Artland Gallery, Hong Kong
1995 *Artmatch Inaugural Exhibition,* Hong Kong Visual Arts Centre, Hong Kong

Chu Hing-wah

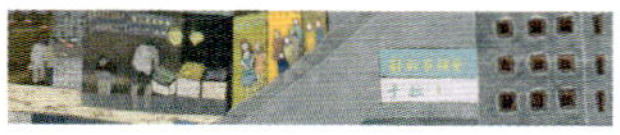

Chu Hing-wah was born in 1935 and moved to Hong Kong in 1951. He graduated from the Department of Extra-mural studies at the University of Hong Kong. He then worked as a psychiatric nurse until his retirement in 1992. Chu is now an Art Advisor of the Hong Kong Leisure and Cultural Services Department. Chu was a recipient of several art awards including the Hong Kong Urban Council Fine Art Award (1989) and the Asia Cultural Council Fellowship (1994). His work painted the emotions and the inner world of the mentally ill, the countryside and city people's lives.

Selected solo exhibitions

2006 *Chu's 50 years of Hong Kong,* Hanart TZ Gallery, Hong Kong
2003 *My Third Page,* Hanart TZ Gallery, Hong Kong
2000 *Painting and Sculpture Exhibition,* The Chinese University of Hong Kong, Hong Kong
1998 *Suspended Stage,* Hanart TZ Gallery, Hong Kong
1989 *Painting and Sculpture Exhibition,* Castle Peak Hospital, Hong Kong
1988 *Painting and Sculpture Exhibition,* The Hong Kong Institute for Promotion of Chinese Culture, Hong Kong

Selected group exhibitions

2008 *Inheritance,* Hong Kong City Hall, Hong Kong

2008 *Made in Hong Kong,* Hong Kong Museum of Art, Hong Kong

2007 *Hong Kong Visual Arts Society Annual Exhibition,* University Museum and Art Gallery, The University of Hong Kong, Hong Kong

2007 *The New Face of Ink Painting,* Central Plaza, Hong Kong

2006 *Contemporary Hong Kong Ink Painting Exhibition,* Hong Kong Central Library, Hong Kong

2004 *Neither East Nor West,* Honolulu East-West Centre, Honolulu, USA

2003 *Asian Contemporary Arts Exhibition,* Hong Kong Heritage Museum, Hong Kong

2003 *Natural Expression,* Macao Museum of Art, Macau

1992 *City Vibrance,* Hong Kong Museum of Art, Hong Kong

1992 *Memory and Resonance,* Hanart gallery,Taipei, Taiwan

1990 *Hong Kong Urban Council Fine Art Winners Exhibition,* Hong Kong Museum of Art, Hong Kong

1989 *Hong Kong Urban Biennial Exhibition,* Hong Kong Museum of Art, Hong Kong

Fung Ho-yin

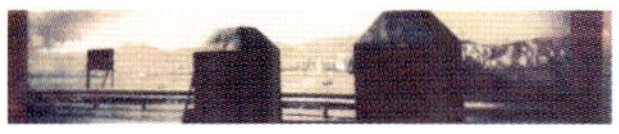

hoyin@open-printsop.org.hk
www.open-printshop.org.hk

Fung Hoi Yin was born in Hong Kong. He is one of the founders of the Hong Kong Open Printshop. Currently he is an assistant professor at the School of Design of the Hong Kong Polytechnic University. Fung's works were selected by the National Prints Exhibition of China (2002, 2005, 2007) and he was a finalist of the 75th Annual International Competition: Printmaking (2001). His works are collected by local and overseas museums.

Selected solo exhibitions

2007 *Shared Journey,* The Design Gallery, University of Sunderland, Sunderland, UK

Selected group exhibitions

2007 *Crossing Boundaries – The Hong Kong Graphic Art Fiesta 2007,* Exhibition Gallery, Tsuen Wan Town Hall, Hong Kong

2007 *18th National Prints Exhibition, China,* Shanghai Art Museum, Shanghai, China

2005 *17th National Prints Exhibition, China,* Guiyang Art Museum, Guiyang , China

2005 *In Your Dreams – An International Travelling Group Exhibition,* Fringe Club, Hong Kong; Studio Gallery at Griffith University, Brisbane, Australia; Peninsula Art Centre, Shanghai, China and Espace Accattone, Paris, France

2003 *Joint Prints Exhibition: A Heilongjiang Hong Kong Graphics Art Exchange Programme,* Heilongjiang Provincial Museum, Heilongjiang, China

2003 *Searching for Clues – An International Group Exhibition, A touring exhibition,* Fringe Club, Hong Kong; Studio Gallery at Griffith University, Brisbane, Australia; Peninsula Art Centre, Shanghai, China; Espace Accattone, Paris, France and Art Gallery of University of Pittsburgh, Philadelphia, USA

2002 *Lost and Found – An International Travelling Exhibition,* Fringe Club, Hong Kong; Gallery of the Institute of Art, Brisbane, Australia; Warwick Gallery; Redcliff Gallery; Caloundra Gallery and Logan Gallery, Queensland, Australia

2002 *16th National Prints Exhibition,* China, Anhui Provincial Museum, Anhui, China

2002 *Japan – China International Print Exhibition,* Shaanxi Provincial Museum, Xian, China

2001 *Kyoto Print 2001: Japan – China International Print Exhibition,* Kyoto Museum of Art, Kyoto, Japan

2001 *Exhibition of the 75th Annual International Competition: Printmaking,* The Print Center Philadelphia, USA

2000 *15th National Prints Exhibition, China,* Guangdong Museum of Art, Guangzhou, China

Selected curatorial exhibitions

2007 *Crossing Boundaries – The Hong Kong Graphic Art Fiesta 2007,* Exhibition Gallery, Tsuen Wan Town Hall, Hong Kong

Fung Kwok-hai, Cyrus

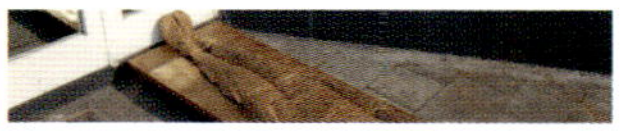

fungkwokhai@hotmail.com.hk

Cyrus Fung Kwok Hai completed his art and design foundation course and BA (Honours) in product design at the Kingston University London (UK) in 1999 and 2003 respectively. He received a BA (Fine Art) majoring in painting from the Royal Melbourne Institute of Technology (RMIT) University co-presented with the Hong Kong Art School in 2007. His works are mainly mixed media.

Selected group exhibitions

2008 *Juxtaposition – Bachelor of Arts (Fine Art) Graduation Show 2008,* Hong Kong Arts Centre, Hong Kong

2007 *Acts,* White Tube, Hong Kong

Ho Sze-man, Jasmine

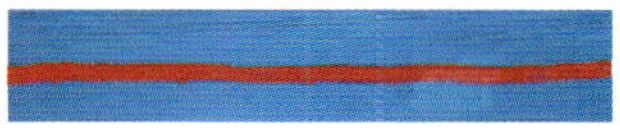

brushwood_hk@yahoo.co.uk
http://fotologue.jp/onefphotography

Jasmine Ho Sze-man completed her foundation in design studies at Ravensbourne College of Design and Communication in the United Kingdom in 2005 and received her BA (Fine Art) majoring in painting from the Royal Melbourne Institute of Technology (RMIT) University, co-presented with the Hong Kong Art School in 2007. Her works are mainly painted in acrylic.

Selected group exhibitions

2008 *Juxtaposition – Bachelor of Arts (Fine Art) Graduation Show 2008,* Hong Kong Arts Center, Hong Kong

2007 *Acts,* White Tube, Hong Kong

Selected curatorial exhibitions

2007 *Acts,* White Tube, Hong Kong

Hon Chi-fun

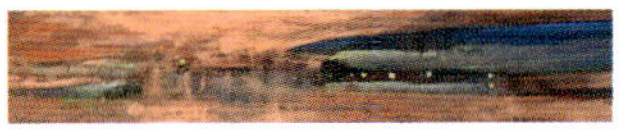

Hon Chi-fun was born in Hong Kong in 1922. He worked at the General Post Office and the Department of Extra-mural Studies at The University of Hong Kong. Hon received the Gold Medal at the 3rd Hong Kong International Salon of Paintings in 1984, and received the British Council Official Vistiorship to the UK and the International Visitorship to Germany from DAAD in 1969. His publications include *Secret Codes – The Art of Hon Chi-fun* (2005) and *Over and Yonder – Paintings by Hon Chi-fun* (1988). Hon moved to Canada in 1992, then returned to Hong Kong with his family in 2000. His works are collected by local and overseas museums and private collectors.

Selected solo exhibitions

2005 *Secret Codes – The Art of Hon Chi-fun,* Hong Kong Museum of Art, Hong Kong

1999 *Recent Journeys and Interludes by Hon Chi-fun,* University Museum and Art Gallery, The University of Hong Kong, Hong Kong

1988 *Over and Yonder – Paintings by Hon Chi-fun,* Fung Ping Shan Museum, The University of Hong Kong, Hong Kong

1981 *Exhibition of Paintings by Hon Chi-fun,* Hong Kong Arts Centre, Hong Kong

1975 *Prints by Hon Chi-fun, Department of Extra-mural Studies,* The Chinese University of Hong Kong, Hong Kong

1974 *Hon Chi-fun: Paintings and Prints 1968 – 1974,* City Museum and Art Gallery (now the Hong Kong Museum of Art), Hong Kong

Selected group exhibitions

2000 *Golden Age,* Trigram Gallery, Hong Kong

1992 *City Vibrance,* Hong Kong Museum of Art, Hong Kong

1990 *Drawing and Sketches by Contemporary Artists,* Cherng Piin Gallery, Taipei, Taiwan

1987 *Contemporary Chinese Painting,* Rotunda, Exchange Square, Hong Kong

1987 *Hong Kong Art 10 Years,* Hong Kong Arts Centre, Hong Kong

1986 *Art'86,* Fung Ping Shan Museum, The University of Hong Kong, Hong Kong

1986 *Asian Contemporary Art Exhibition,* National Museum of Singapore, Singapore

1986 *Contemporary Art 10 Years,* City Gallery, Taipei, Taiwan

1984 *Art'84,* Fung Ping Shan Museum, The University of Hong Kong, Hong Kong

1984 *Overseas Chinese Artists Exhibition, Taipei Fine Arts Museum, Taipei, Taiwan*
1984 *Into the Eighties, Hong Kong Arts Centre, Hong Kong*
1982 *Hong Kong Art, Metropolitan Museum of Manila, Manila, Philippines*

Kan Tai–keung

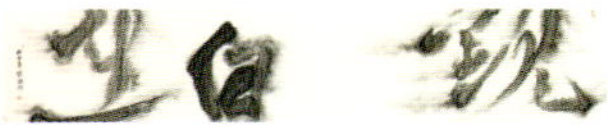

kan@kanandlau.com
www.kanandlau.com

Kan Tai Keung was awarded an honorary doctorate of design from the Hong Kong Polytechnic University in 2005. He has been creating ink paintings and working in art and design since 1970. He has received a number of significant design awards, including the Hong Kong Ten Outstanding Young Persons (1979), Artist of the Year Award – Designer of the Year (1991), Bronze Bauhinia Star (1999), Outstanding Artists and Designers of the 20th Century (2000) and World's Outstanding Chinese Designer (2004). Recently Kan has taken an active role in educating about and promoting art and design. He lectures frequently in local and overseas institutions, acting as adviser for associations and adjudicator at competitions. In 2003 Kan was appointed as Dean of the Cheung Kong School of Art and Design in Shantou University. His publications include Sentiments and Harmony, Selected Posters By Kan Tai-Keung and Applied Visual Communication Design. Kan's works have earned him international publicity and are collected by local and international museums.

Selected solo exhibitions
2008 *Feelings of the Brush,* University Museum and Art Gallery, The University of Hong Kong, Hong Kong
2003-2004 *From Life to Mind: Kan Tai-keung's Design and Art,* Alliance Francais de Singapour, HaKaren Art Gallery, Singapore
2002 *From Life to Mind: Kan Tai-keung's Design and Art,* Hong Kong Heritage Museum, Hong Kong
1995 *Rhythm From My Mind,* Asian Arts Centre, Towson State University, Maryland, USA
1988 *Mountains and Beyond: One-Man Show of Kan Tai-keung's 20 years of Painting,* Museum Luis de Campos, Leal Seuado Gallery, Macau
1985 *A Visual Trio: Pine, Mountain and Cloud,* Alisan Fine Arts, Hong Kong

Selected group exhibitions
2008 *Dialogue: Erhard Gruettner and Kan Tai-keung,* Poster Exhibition, Hong Kong City Hall, Hong Kong
2007 *Exhibitions: Graphic Messages from ggg and ddd 1986-2006,* Ginza Graphic Gallery (ggg) /DDD Gallery, Tokyo, Japan
2007 *Hong Kong Contemporary Chinese Ink Painting Exhibition 2007,* Artist Commune, Hong Kong
2007 *The New Face of Ink Paintings – Modern Ink Painting Group Exhibition and Symposium,* Central Plaza and OC Gallery, Hong Kong
2006 *Sentiments of Ink – Recent Works by Kan Tai-keung and Kan Kit-keung,* Shenzhen Fine Art Institute Exhibition Hall, Shenzhen, China
2006 *A Classic Decade – Commemorating the Tenth Anniversary of Hakaren Art Gallery,* Hakaren Art Gallery of Singapore, Singapore and Beijing Museum of Art, Beijing, China
2005 *The Act of Writing and of Non-Writing: The Open Space for Chinese Calligraphy,* International Exhibition of Modern Calligraphy, China Academy of Art, Hangzhou, China
2003 *The 119th Exhibition of Ink and Chairs: The Art and Design Exhibition of Kan Tai-keung + Freeman Lau,* DDD Gallery, Osaka, Japan and Shizuoka University of Art and Culture, Shizuoka, Japan
2003 *X-Power Design Festival 2003,* School of Design of Southern Yangtze University, Southern Yangtze, China
2002 *Hong Kong Cityscapes – Ink Painting in Transition,* Brunei Gallery, School of Oriental and African Studies, University of London, London, UK
1999 *The 9th Chinese National Art Exhibition,* Beijing Museum of Art, Beijing, China
1998 *Festival of the Applied Arts of Northern Germany,* Museum fur Kunst und Gewerbe, Hamburg, Germany

Ko Tin-yan, Celia

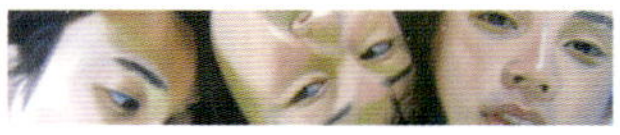

celiagogo@gmail.com
www.celiako.com

Celia Ko Tin-yan graduated from California State University, Long Beach, majoring in drawing and painting. Ko has been giving lectures at different art institutes since 1992 and passed Southern Californian mural traditions and techniques to the public. Her mural paintings can be found in Long Beach, Los Angeles, local housing estates, hospitals, schools and public places. Now she is a visiting lecturer at Hong Kong Polytechnic University, Hong Kong Art School, City University of Hong Kong and HKU SPACE. Ko received the Freeman Foundation Asia Artist Fellowship at the Vermont Studio Center (2000-01), USA. Her works are collected by the Hong Kong Museum of Art and private collectors both local and overseas.

Selected solo exhibitions
2008 *Faces and Places,* American Chamber of Commerce, Hong Kong
2006 *Objets d'amour,* Fringe Club, Hong Kong
2001 *Lost in the Woods,* Red Mill Gallery, Vermont, USA
2000 *The Essence,* City Hall, Hong Kong
1997 *Detours to Paradise,* Fringe Club, Hong Kong
1995 *Paradise,* Hong Kong Visual Arts Centre, Hong Kong

Selected group exhibitions
2008 *20C Debut – Eclectic Visions,* Hong Kong Visual Arts Centre, Hong Kong
2005 *Gan Guan – Observing the senses,* Counihan Gallery, Moreland City Council, Melbourne, Australia
2003 *SPACE 2003,* Hong Kong Cultural Centre, Hong Kong
2002 *Embark-Disembark,* Mass Gallery, Melbourne, Australia
2000 *Under the Bed,* Fringe Club, Hong Kong
1998 *Wall To Window,* Para/Site Art Space, Hong Kong
1998 *Works on Paper,* John Batten Gallery, Hong Kong
1997 *Visions of Hong Kong,* Taikoo Place, Hong Kong
1997 *The Bad Art Show,* Fringe Club, Hong Kong
1996 *Ink Momentum,* Hong Kong City Hall, Hong Kong
1995 *HKG-SYD-HKG,* Fringe Club, Hong Kong
1991 *Vagabonds – 3 people show,* Gallery B, California State University Long Beach, Long Beach, USA

Selected curatorial exhibitions
2008 *20C Debut – Eclectic Visions,* Hong Kong Visual Arts Centre, Hong Kong

Kong Khong-chang (Kongkee)

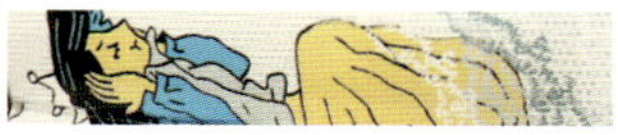

kongkee@gmail.com
www.shiningsummer.com

Kongkee is a comic artist. He is the founding member of creative group, 29s. Kongkee's first comic was called *Imperfect Shoes*, and is a dark fairy tale of the city. in 2005, his video *Name of Wu Mei* received a Special Mention at the ifva Short Film Festival, and was selected by the Hong Kong Art Biennial. In 2007 he worked with another comic artist, Chihoi to produce the comic album, *Hijacking*. In 2007 he used cartoons stickers to protest the commercials booming from train broadcast systems. In 2008 his comic series *Rice-gas* was published after positive feedback and support from readers over the internet.

Selected Solo Exhibitions
2001 *Home Safety,* Goethe-Institut, Hong Kong
1999 *Elatine (animal origin),* Hanart TZ Gallery, Hong Kong

Selected Group Exhibitions
2008 *From bee to bee,* hulahoop gallery, Hong Kong
2007 *70/ 80 Hong Kong New Designers Exhibition,* Hangzhou, Shanghai Chongqing, Shengzhen and Changshai, China
2007 *Comix Magneto – Singapore Version,* Singapore
2006 *The Inner, Outer Sphere,* KX (gallery), Hamburg, Germany
2006 *Exchanging Tools,* The Chinese University of Hong Kong, Hong Kong
2005 *Take a ST/Roll,* Para/Site Art Space, Hong Kong
2005 *Three Pieces of Thousand Layers Pudding,* 1a space, Hong Kong
2003 *People/Sea/Street,* ARTMAP, Hong Kong
2002 *Material World,* Grotto Fine Art Ltd., Hong Kong
2000 *Die Umbibalenz,* Goethe-Institut, Hong Kong Arts Centre, Hong Kong

Lam Laam, Jaffa

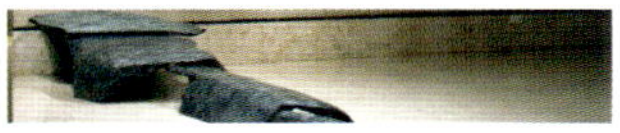

lamjaffa@gmail.com
www.jaffa.net

Jaffa Lam Laam received her BFA, MFA and diploma in education from the Chinese University of Hong Kong. After graduation she was invited to take part in many important exhibitions, both in Hong Kong and overseas. In the Artists in Neighborhood Scheme II 2003 held by the Hong Kong Art Promotion Office, she was chosen as one of the highlighted artists. She was also the Asia Cultural Council 2006 grantee, the New York Urban Glass visiting artist fellow 2007-2008, and invited artist for 10th anniversary of the Tree Museum in Toronto, Canada. Lam has participated in a number of exchange/artist-in-residence projects in different places like Kenya, Taiwan, Bangladesh, Shanghai and New York. She is teaching sculpture at the Hong Kong Art School and is active in projects related to art in public and community. Lam's works are mainly mixed media sculptural installations.

Selected solo exhibitions

2007 *Exchange Knowledge,* Dinersty Chinese Restaurant, 411 Eighth Avenue, New York City, USA
2005 *Travel with Rickshaw,* Alliance Francaise, Dhaka, Bangladesh
2004 *Twins,* Pottery Workshop, Shanghai, China
2003 *Murmur,* Shatin Town Hall, Hong Kong
2001 *Playground,* Goethe-Institut, Hong Kong
1999 *Signmotion,* Department of Fine Arts , The Chinese University of Hong Kong

Selected group exhibitions

2007 *The Tree Museum 10th Anniversary Exhibition,* The Tree Museum, Muskoka, Canada
2007 *Echoes and Reflections,* China Square Gallery, New York, USA
2007 *Prison Museum,* Victoria Prison, Hong Kong, China
2006 *Contemporary Chinese Glass Art,* Festival Hall, Navy Pier, Chicago, USA
2006 *Between Obstruction and Crossover: 2006 International Windbreak Forest Environment Arts Exhibition,* Windbreak Forest, Tainan, Taiwan
2005 *Hong Kong Art Biennial 2005,* Hong Kong Museum of Art,Hong Kong
2005 *Collation ARTtube@mtr,* Central Station, Hong Kong
2005 *Hong Kong Sculpture,* Artist Commune, Cattle Depot, Hong Kong
2004 *Wasanii International Artists' Workshop,* Lamu Fort, Lamu, Kenya
2004 *Hong Kong Wood Sculpture,* University Museum and Art Gallery, *The University of Hong Kong, Hong Kong*
2003 *Hong Kong Art Biennial 2003,* Hong Kong Museum of Art, Hong Kong
2003 *Hualien International Artists' Workshop,* Pine Garden, Hua Lien, Taiwan
2001 *Hong Kong Art Biennial 2001*
1996 *Contemporary Hong Kong Art Biennial Exhibition*

Selected curatorial exhibitions

2008 *The Preview of West Kowloon Exhibition Venue,* C and G Apartment Gallery, Hong Kong
2007 *14QK/GOD,* Para/Site Art Space, Hong Kong
2000 *Behind the Eyeballs,* Hong Kong Visual Arts Centre, Hong Kong
1998 *Made in Hong Kong,* George Fraser Gallery, University of Auckland, Auckland, New Zealand

Lam Yuk-lin, Pauline

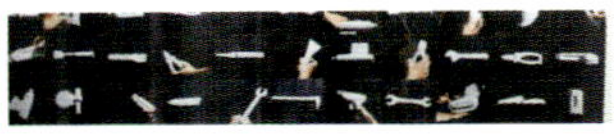

artpauline@yahoo.com
http://www.geocities.com/artpauline

Pauline Lam Yuk Lin received her BA from the Chinese University of Hong Kong and MFA from the Royal Melbourne Institute of Technology (RMIT) University. She is now teaching art at the Hong Kong Institute of Education. Lam held a number of solo sculpture and installation exhibitions and was invited to take part in various exhibitions in Hong Kong and overseas. In 2001 she was invited to participate in the Asian art project Up-ricing and staged touring art performance in various Asian cities. In the same year, she started her research art project Cultivating Civilisation. Lam has been the recipient of several art awards including the new vision award (2001) and first prize at the Philippe Charriol Foundation Art Competition (Sculpture category in 1997 and painting category in 1996). Her work was selected for the Hong Kong Art Biennial in 1995 and 2005 respectively and the Artists in the Neighbourhood Scheme IV (2008). Her works in recent years are mainly influenced by the relationship between cultural development and human activities.

Selected solo exhibitions

2003 *Drifting Sky,* the VIP lounge of triple-deck ferry Xin Guo, Hong Kong
2001 *Cultivating Civilization,* No.115, 5th Lane, Kat Hing Wai, Kam Tin, Yuen Long, Hong Kong
1999 *Sight-read – 24 hrs non-stop Installation Exhibition,* Para/Site Art Space, Hong Kong
1998 *The New Renascent Bronze Age,* Goethe-Institut, Hong Kong
1995 *Test of Rebirth, Exhibition Hall,* Hong Kong Cultural Centre, Hong Kong

Selected group exhibitions

2008 *Horse across Hong Kong, Yuen Long District,* The Hong Kong Jockey Club Archives and Museum Hong Kong, Hong Kong
2008 *Artist in Neighborhood IV Launching Exhibition,* Exhibition Hall, City Hall Lower Block. Hong Kong
2007 *Asian Video Art Exhibition Series 8 – Primitive Contemporary,* Artist Commune, Hong Kong
2007 *CHANEL – The essence of White,* Pacific Place Garden Court, Hong Kong
2007 *Visual Arts Thematic Exhibition 07/08: HarmoNow 3D and Installation Art Exhibition,* Artist Commune, Hong Kong
2006 *Dear chocolate art exhibition,* Foyer, Times Square, Hong Kong
2006 *1 M Sculpture Exhibition,* Artists Commune, Hong Kong; Guangzhou Museum of Art, Guangzhou, China
2005 *If Hong Kong, A Woman Traveler,* 1a space, Hong Kong
2004 *Environment Art Expo Korea 2004 – the 1st Exhibition of Int'l Art Expo,* COEX Convention and Exhibition Center, Seoul, Korea
2004 *Siemens Fine Art Scholarship Exhibition,* RMIT University Gallery/Siemens Headquarter, Melbourne/Melbourne, Australia/Australia
2003 *Mapping Asia,* Hong Kong Heritage Museum, Hong Kong
2002 *The 17th Asian International Art Exhibition,* Daejeon Municipal Museum of Art, Daejeon, Korea

Selected curatorial exhibitions

2007 *Taste of Hong Kong: artist-in-residence 2007 – anothermountainman@HKIED,* The Hong Kong Institute of Education Art Gallery, Hong Kong
2001 *Hong Kong Art Teacher Festival 2001: Teacher – Student Interactive Art Exhibition,* Exhibition Hall, Kwai Ching Theatre, Hong Kong

Lau Hok-shing, Hanison

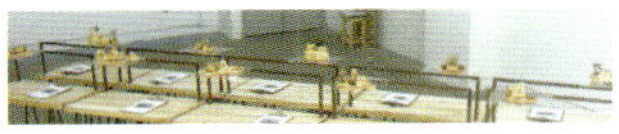

Hanison_lau2004@yahoo.com.hk

Hanison Lau Hok Shing received his BA (Fine Art) in 2005 and a MFA in 2008 from the Royal Melbourne Institute of Technology (RMIT) University co-presented with Hong Kong Art School. Lau has actively participated in a number of joint exhibitions since 2003. He held two solo exhibitions, Order—Recordation of Personal Action and Poem · Imagine in 2006, and his works were selected by the Philippe Charriol Art Competition for two consecutive years in 2004 and 2005. Lau is now a teaching assistant at the Hong Kong Art School. He has a keen interest in history and literature and assembles ready-made objects into installations in his art practice.

Selected solo exhibitions

2006 *Order – recordation of personal action by Hanison Lau,* White Tube, Hong Kong
2006 *Poem · Imagine,* Too Art, Hong Kong

Selected group exhibitions

2008 *Artists in the Neighborhood Scheme IV Launching Exhibition,* Exhibition Hall, City Hall, Lower Block,Hong Kong
2007 *The Preview of New West Kowloon Exhibition Venue,* C and G Artpartment, Hong Kong
2007 *Think After Ink – A new interpretation of brush and ink by Hong Kong artists,* Blue Lotus Gallery, Hong Kong
2007 *In · visible,* White Tube, Hong Kong
2007 *Variances in Singular,* Too Art, Hong Kong
2006 *Almost 18, Too Art, Hong Kong*
2006 *Episode II – Read Difference,* Mr. 221, Hong Kong
2006 *Paradigm Shift – Bachelor of Arts (Fine Art) Graduation Show 2006 ,* Hong Kong Arts Centre, Hong Kong
2006 *Away,* 1a space, Hong Kong
2005 *In-Between Meals,* ART Tube@mtr, Hong Kong
2005 *POKH MORF FROM HKOP,* Habitus, Hong Kong
2004 *Bodily Life,* White Tube, Hong Kong

Lee Chin-fai, Danny

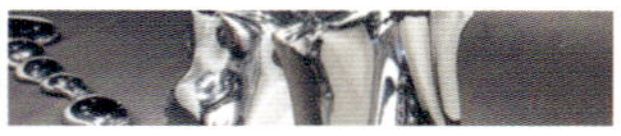

dannyart_lee@hotmail.com

Danny Lee Chin-fai graduated from the Swire School of Design of the former Hong Kong Polytechnic in 1980 and completed the Modern Sculpture Certificate Course organised by the Department of Extra-mural Studies at the University of Hong Kong in 1993. Lee established Creative Sculptors Hong Kong and became its founder and chairperson in the same year. Now he is a full-time sculptor. Lee's works are collected by the Hong Kong Museum of Art, Hong Kong Heritage Museum, Hong Kong Hospital Authority, Hong Kong Housing Department, Hong Kong Airport Authority, MTR Corporation, corporate and private collectors.

Selected solo exhibitions

2006	*Urban Karma: Sculpture by Danny Lee,* Grotto Fine Art Ltd, Hong Kong
2006	*City • Landscape – Karma, Sculpture by Lee Chin-fai ,* Exhibition Hall, Hong Kong City Hall, Hong Kong
2005	*Moving Scenery – Exhibition by Danny Lee Chin Fai,* Korkos Gallery, Hong Kong
2004	*Life and Art – Exhibition by Danny Lee Chin Fai,* Mcv Asia, Hong Kong
1999	*Art and Life – Exhibition by Danny Lee Chin Fai,* Hong Kong Visual Arts Centre, Hong Kong

Selected group exhibitions

2008	*Inheritance – 35th Anniversary Exhibition of Hong Kong Visual Arts Society,* Exhibition Hall, Hong Kong City Hall, Hong Kong
2007	*The Hong Kong Visual Art Society 34th Annual Exhibition,* University Museum and Art Gallery, The University of Hong Kong, Hong Kong
2007	*The Contemporary Sculptors Invitational Exhibition,* Cheng Du Art Museum, China
2004	*VAS 30th Annual Exhibition,* Exhibition Gallery of the Hong Kong Central Library, Hong Kong
2004	*International Ice Sculpture Exhibition,* Canada
2003	*Hong Kong Art Biennial 2003,* Hong Kong Museum of Art, Hong Kong
2001	*Hong Kong Art Biennial 2001,* Hong Kong Museum of Art, Hong Kong
2000	*Hong Kong Art in Paris,* UNSECO Headquarters, Paris, France
1999	*Volume and Form,* Singapore Sculpture Fair '99, Singapore
1997	*Reunion and Vision – Contemporary Hong Kong Art 1997,* Hong Kong Museum of Art, Hong Kong
1996	*Contemporary Hong Kong Art Biennial Exhibition,* Hong Kong Museum of Art, Hong Kong

Lee Chi-hoi (Chihoi)

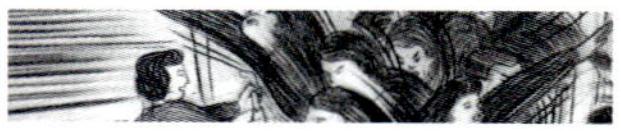

chihoilee@gmail.com
www.chihoi.net

Chihoi was born in Hong Kong in 1977. He has published comics, illustrations and writings in both local and overseas press media since 1996. His comic albums include *The Writer, Piece of Mind, The Train* (co-authored by Hung Hung) and *Hijacking – Comic Hong Kong Literature* (co-authored by Kongkee). He has also co-edited the interview archival *The Road Has Been Long – 25 Years of Independent Comics* in Hong Kong with Craig Au Yeung. In recent years Chihoi has written reviews to introduce contemporary European comics to local audience, and engaged in visual art education.

Selected solo exhibitions

2007	*Hochaaa! Chihoi's Comic, 10-Year Retrospective!,* Hong Kong Arts Centre; Hulahoop Gallery; Joint Publishing Jonathan Shop, Hong Kong
2002	*Reminiscence of Solitude,* Club 64, Hong Kong

Selected group exhibitions

2008	*Chine(s),* Centre Culturale Una Volta, Bastia, France
2008	*Sinfonia – Chihoi and Hok Tak Yeung,* Museo Morandi, Bologna, Italy
2007	*Poetry and Comics in Taipei Poetry Festival,* NTUE Nanhai Gallery, Taipei, Taiwan
2007	*Autobibliophiles – Artists who make or use books,* Studio Bibliotheque, Fotan, Hong Kong
2007	*34th International Comic Festival of Angoulême – Comix World Expo No.1 – Alone in the Crowd,* Place Champ de Mars, Angoulême, France
2006	*The Inner, Outer Sphere – Hong Kong Contemporary Arts Exhibition,* KX Gallery, Hamburg, Germany
2006	*District Borders (with Chihoi and Tsang Kin Wah),* Shanghai Street Artspace, Hong Kong
2006	*15th Fumetto Comix Festival – Hong Kong Springrollllll – Past Continuous Tense,* Hi. Geist-Kapelle, Luzern, Switzerland
2006	*Comix Homebase – Comix Magneto,* Hong Kong Arts Centre, Hong Kong, China
2005	*Three thousand-layer puddings,* 1a space, Hong Kong
2000	*9th Fumetto Comix Festival – Windows of Hong Kong,* Warehouse Luzern, Luzern, Switzerland
1999	*Cell C: Technicolor Comix Series,* Z+, Hong Kong

Leung Mee-ping

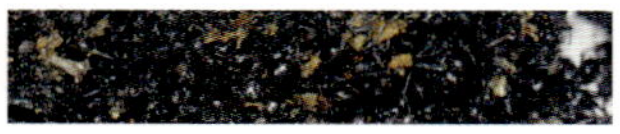

meepingleung@yahoo.com.hk
www.mpleung.com

Leung Mee-ping was born in Hong Kong. She graduated from L'Ecole Nationale Superieure des Beaux-Arts in Paris, France in 1991, and received her Master's in fine art from the Californian Institute of the Arts, USA in 2000. Her art genres include mixed media, video, multimedia installation and site-specific projects.

Selected solo exhibitions

2006	*Room with View,* Centre de Reflexion sur l'image et ses Contexts, Sierre, Switzerland
2005	*In Search of Insomnious Sheep,* 1a Space, Hong Kong
2003	*Hong Kong Contemporary – Water Tone: Leung Mee-ping 1992-2003,* Kaoshsiung Fine Art Museum, Kaoshsiung, Taiwan
2002	*Memorize the Future,* Hong Kong City Hall, Hong Kong

Selected group exhibitions

2008	*The Art Container Project,* West Kowloon Cultural District, Hong Kong
2008	*New World Order,* Groningen Art Museum, Groningen, Netherlands
2008	*Realms of Myth,* Shanghai Gallery of Art, Three on the Bund, Shanghai, China
2007	*Soft Power, Zendai MOCA,* Shanghai, *China*
2007	*Asian – Europe Mediation,* IF Museum, Pozan, Poland
2007	*Arrivals and Departures,* Manchester Urbis Center, Manchester, United Kingdom
2006	*City in Progress/Live from Zhang Jiang,* Zhang Jiang High Technology Park, Shanghai, China
2006	*Hair Dialogue – Installation Art Exhibition,* Hong Kong Museum of Art, Hong Kong
2006	*Indiana International Video Art Festival,* Kokomo Art Gallery, Indiana University, Indiana, USA
2006	*Digital and Video Art Festival,* Novosibirsk State Art Museum, Saint Petersburg, Russia
2004	*Technique of the Visible – Shanghai Biennale,* Shanghai Art Museum, Shanghai, China
2004	*Past in Reverse: Contemporary Art of East Asia,* San Diego Museum of Art, San Diego, USA

Li Tung-keung, John

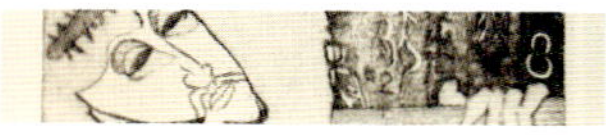

John Li Tung-keung was born in Hong Kong. He obtained his BA from The Chinese University of Hong Kong and an MA and MFA from The University of Iowa, USA. After that he proceeded to study in the Pratt Institute, New York, USA and Brighton University, UK. Li is also an educator who has been working with Hong Kong's universities for many years, with the aim of promoting art. Since the '60s he has been leaving his mark at different solo and joint exhibitions in Hong Kong and overseas. His exhibits are mainly figure paintings with a unique combination of Chinese and Western art. Li was awarded the Artistic Development Fellowship in 2000 by the Hong Kong Arts Development Council.

Selected solo exhibitions

2007	*One Man Show,* Atelier Art Institute, Seattle, USA
2006	*One Man Show,* Iowa City Gallery, Iowa, USA
2004	*Ink Painting by John Li,* Hui Gallery, New Asia College, The Chinese University of Hong Kong, Hong Kong
1999	*Art Exhibition by John Li,* Provisional Regional Council, Hong Kong
1981	*One Man Show,* Sir Run Run Shaw Hall, The Chinese University of Hong Kong, Hong Kong
1974	*One Man Show,* Arnot Art Museum, New York, USA

Selected group exhibitions

2008 *Contemporary Artistic Hong Kong,* University Museum and Art Gallery, The University of Hong Kong, Hong Kong

2005 *Art Works of Alumni of Fine Arts Department,* The Chinese University of Hong Kong, Hong Kong

2003 *40 Years of Art,* The Chinese University of Hong Kong, Hong Kong

2002 *Exhibition of 16th National Printmaking,* China

2001 *The Art of Printmaking,* Hong Kong Heritage Museum, Hong Kong

2001 *Group show,* Er Dongqiang Art Gallery, Shanghai, China

2001 *Group show,* Hong Kong Visual Arts Centre, Hong Kong

1981 *Benson and Hedges Selection of Hong Kong Art,* Hong Kong Arts Centre, Hong Kong

1979 *Printmaking Specialist Group Exhibitions,* Brighton Polytechnic, UK

1977 *Contemporary Hong Kong Art,* Hong Kong Museum of Art, Hong Kong

1974 *New Talent in Printmaking,* Gimpel Weitzenhoffer Gallery, New York, USA

Liew Come-tong

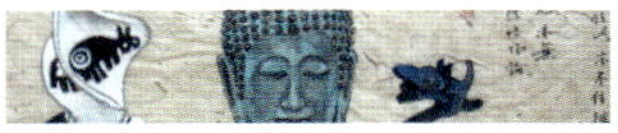

liewcometong@yahoo.com.hk
http://lcwsk.sinaman.com

Liew Come-tong was born in Malaysia in 1949. He graduated from the fine arts department of the National Taiwan Normal University in 1971. He is now teaching at the Hong Kong University School of Continuing and Professional Studies and the Hong Kong Institute of Education. Liew held a number of solo exhibitions and has been invited to take part in more than 100 important exhibitions overseas. His publications include *Ink Painting by Liew Come-tong* (1991), Watercolour *Paintings and Drawings by Liew Come-tong* (1997), *Lyrical Vision: Paintings by Liew Come-tong* (1999) and *Art appreciation, Criticism and Education* (2001) (co-author: Lai Ming-hoi and Tam Cheung-on). A biography of Liew has been included in the *Collectors' Dictionary of Contemporary Artists of Chinese Painting, Encyclopedia of Achievements by Chinese Artists in the World,* and World VIP Center. His works have been collected by the Hong Kong Heritage Museum, Hong Kong Museum of Art, overseas art institutions and private collectors.

Selected solo exhibitions

2005 *Lyrical Painting by Liew Come Tong,* Galeri MAWAR, Johor Bahru, Malaysia

2000 *Ink Painting by Liew Come Tong,* City Hall of Schorndorf and City Hall of Althütte, Schorndorf Althütte, Germany

1997 *Lyrical Vision: Paintings by Liew Come Tong,* University Museum and Art Gallery, the University of Hong Kong, Hong Kong

1996 *Ink Painting by Liew Come Tong,* Ontario Gallery of Chinese Arts Gallery, Ontario, Canada

1993 *Art of Liew Come Tong,* Shatin Town Hall, Exhibition Gallery and Tsuen Wan Town Hall, Exhibition Gallery, Hong Kong

1992 *Ink Painting by Liew Come Tong,* Foon Yew High School, Exhibition Gallery, Johor Bahru, Malaysia

Selected group exhibitions

2007-2008 *Fine Chinese Paintings Autumn – Spring Auction '07/'08,* City Hall, Exhibition Hall Central, Hong Kong

2005 *Art Exhibition Celebration of the 40th Anniversary of the School of Continuing and Professional Studies,* The Chinese University of Hong Kong, Exhibition Gallery, Hong Kong Central Library, Hong Kong

1994 *International Chinese Brush Painting Exhibition,* National Gallery, Kuala Lumpur, Malaysia

1989 *Art Exhibition by Hong Kong Major Artists,* Isetan Gallery, Tokyo, Japan

1987 *Collection of Works of Beijing International Ink Paintings Exhibition,* China Art Museum, Beijing, China

1986 *Tokyo – Asia Art Exhibition,* Fine Arts Museum, Tokyo, Japan

1986 *Modern Asian Ink and Color Paintings Exhibition '86,* Fine Arts Museum, Seoul, Korea

1984 *Contemporary Trends in Chinese Art Overseas,* Chinese Artists Exhibition, Taipei Fine Arts Museum, Taipei, Taiwan

1983 *Exhibition of Works by Extramural Art Instructors of the Chinese University of Hong Kong,* Exhibition Gallery, City Hall, Hong Kong

1980 *The 9th National Art Exhibition,* National Historical Museum, Taipei, Taiwan

1977 *Contemporary Hong Kong Art Biennial Exhibition,* Hong Kong Museum of Art, Hong Kong

1975 *Contemporary Ink Painting of Hong Kong Artists,* National Historical Museum, Taipei, Taiwan

1972 *The Chinese Culture Exhibition,* Philadelphia Museum, Philadelphia, USA

Selected curatorial exhibitions

2000 *The retrospective exhibition of art works by Liao Shiou-ping,* Hong Kong Art Centre, Hong Kong

Ma, Ivy

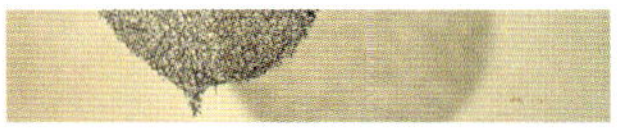

Ivymelt@gmail.com
http://www.ivyma.net

Ivy Ma received her BA in Fine Art from the Royal Melbourne Institute of Technology (RMIT) University co-presented with the Hong Kong Art School in 2001. She was awarded the Hong Kong Arts Development Council and the University of Leeds Scholarships in the same year, and received her MA in Feminist Theory and Practice in Visual Art in 2002. She has widely exhibited her works both in Hong Kong and overseas. Her work was collected by the Hong Kong Heritage Museum. Ma has taken part in artist workshops and artist-in-residence projects held in Bangladesh, Finland, Åland Archipelago and Hong Kong. She served as art administrator/manager of 1a space from 2003 to 2005 and she was also a part-time teacher at the Hong Kong Art School and at the Lee Shau Kee School of Creativity during 2005 and 2006. As a recipient of the Lee Hysan Foundation Fellowship from the Asia Cultural Council, Ma will take part in a residency programme, attend courses and observe developments in contemporary visual arts in the United States in 2008.

Selected solo exhibitions

2007 *Perhaps Solitude,* Jerry Kwan Loft 21 Studio, Hong Kong

Selected group exhibitions

2007 *October Contemporary,* Cattle Depot Artists Village, Hong Kong

2007 *A Separate Domain,* Hui Gallery, Cheng Ming Building, New Asia College, The Chinese University of Hong Kong, Hong Kong

2006 *Lianzhou International Photo Festival – Between the Observer and the Observed,* Shoe Factory, Lianzhou, China

2006 *Stained, the eclipsed pattern,* UMA G, Hong Kong

2005 *Re:wanchi,* AiR Corner House, Hong Kong

2005 *Curiosities,* Para/site Art Space, Hong Kong

2005 *Britto International Artists' Workshop, Nikera Kori Center,* Nungola, Bora, Bangladesh

2004 *Dream Garden,* Kadoorie Farm and Botanic Garden (KFBG), Hong Kong

2003 *Meat,* 1a space, Hong Kong

2002 *Articulation (Graduation Show),* Lifton Place Studio, Leeds, UK

2001 *Wo-Man,* Old Ladies' House, Art Space, Macau

Selected curatorial exhibitions

2005 *Woman/Traveler,* Bilateral Cultural Exchange Programme, 1a space, Hong Kong

Ng Kwun-lun, Tony

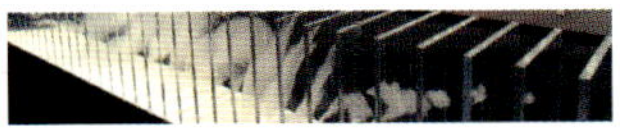

topedge2004@yahoo.com.hk
http://www.20cstudio.com

Tony Ng Kwun-lun was born in Hong Kong and received a diploma in Chinese ink painting from the former Department of Extra-mural Studies at the Chinese University of Hong Kong in 1986. Ng teaches Chinese painting at the Department of Extra-mural Studies at different universities, several art and design institutions as course instructor, and also occasionally at local secondary schools as an invited artist. He has participated in more than 50 local and overseas exhibitions. Ng was the recipient of several arts awards, including the Urban Council Fine Arts Award (1994) and the Special Award from the Tenth National Exhibition of Arts, China (2004). His works were selected for the Contemporary Hong Kong Art Biennial Exhibition several times. Ng's works are collected by the Hong Kong Heritage Museum, Hong Kong Museum of Art, overseas art institutions and private collectors.

Selected solo exhibitions

2004 *Works by Ng Kwun-lun, Tony,* Hong Kong Cultural Centre, Hong Kong

1999 *Un Peintre,* Alliance Francaise Gallery, Hong Kong

1997 *Self,* Trigram Gallery, Hong Kong
1997 *Let Stone Takes Over,* John Batten Gallery, Hong Kong
1993 *An Image,* Hong Kong Arts Centre, Hong Kong
1989 *The April Exhibition,* Galerie Du Monde, Hong Kong

Selected group exhibitions
2007 *The New Face of Ink Paintings – Modern Ink Painting Group Exhibition and Symposium,* Hong Kong Central Plaza, Hong Kong
2006 *Contemporary Hong Kong Ink Painting Exhibition 2006,* Hong Kong Central Library, Hong Kong
2004 *The 10th National Art Exhibition,* National Art Museum of China, Beijing, China
2002 *Artists In The Neighborhood Scheme II Launching Exhibition,* Hong Kong Central Library, Hong Kong
2000 *Contemporary Hong Kong Art 2000,* Hong Kong Museum of Art, Hong Kong
1999 *Earth,* Span Galleries, Melbourne, Australia
1997 *Hong Kong Art 1997 China Tour,* National Art Museum of China, Beijing, China
1996 *Out of Hong Kong,* Merging One Gallery, Los Angeles, USA
1995 *Contemporary Hong Kong Painting Exhibition,* Fukuoka Art Museum, Fukuoka, Japan
1995 *Urban Council Fine Arts Award Winners Exhibition 1995,* Hong Kong Museum of Art, Hong Kong
1994 *The 8th National Art Exhibition,* National Art Museum of China, Beijing, China
1994 *Hong Kong Art Show In LA,* Santa Monica Old Mall, Santa Monica, Los Angeles, USA
1993 *Where the Streams Became a River: Contemporary Works From Hong Kong Museum of Art,* Vancouver Art Gallery, Vancouver, Canada

Pau, Ellen

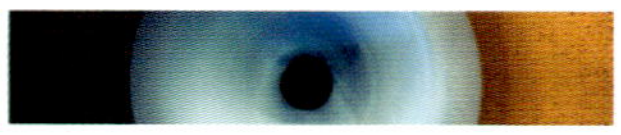

ellenpau.hk@gmail.com
http://www.ellenpau.com

Ellen Pau graduated from the Hong Kong Polytechnic in 1985. She was a member of Phoenix Cine Club and Zuni Icosahedron. A co-founder of the Videotage in 1987 and the Microwave International New Media Art Festival in 1995. Ellen travelled to the USA in 1992 for a six-month study trip sponsored by the Asia Cultural Council. In 1996 Pau was invited to Australia for an artist-in-residence project. She was awarded a Fellowship for Artistic Development (1998) by the Arts Development Council. Pau was the director of photography in Barbara Wong's film *Woman Private Parts* which won the best International Feature in the New York Independent Film and Video Festival in 2002. She acts as the consultant for a number of local culture organisations and art projects, such as Headland Centre for the Arts, Hong Kong Arts Development Council and Leisure and Cultural Services Department. She was adjudicator for the Independent Film and Video Awards of the Hong Kong Art Centre and Berlin's Transmedial. Besides artistic production and curatorial work, Pau teaches film and video in Hong Kong and is also a full time hospital radiographer. Her monograph, *Dye-a-di-a-logue with Ellen Pau* was published in 2004.

Selected solo exhibitions
2006 *The Lab: Hong Kong Video artist/filmmaker Series – Ellen Pau,* Hong Kong Art Centre, Agnès b.Cinema, Hong Kong
2003 *Heavy Head Drama,* Play Gallery for Still and Motion Pictures, Berlin, Germany
1998 *Pledge,* Spacex Gallery, Exeter, UK
1995 *The Great Movement,* Goethe-Institut, Hong Kong

Selected group exhibitions
2008 *Hong Kong and Shenzhen Bi-City Biennale of Urbanism\Architecture,* Central Police Complex and Victoria Prison, Hong Kong
2005 *Metropolis Strip(p)ed,* The Substation, Singapore
2004 *Shanghai Biennial,* Shanghai Art Museum, Shanghai, China
2003 *Mapping Asia – The 18th Asian International Art Exhibition,* Hong Kong Heritage Museum, Hong Kong
2002 *Liverpool Biennial,* FACT (the Foundation for Art and Creative Technology), Liverpool, UK
2002 *How Big is the World?,* O.K. Contemporary Art Centre, Linz, Austria
2001 *49th Biennale di Venezia,* China-Hong Kong Pavillion, Venice, Italy
2000 *The 5th International Video Art Festival,* ATA, Alta Tecnologia Andina, Lima, Peru
1999 *Internationale Medien Kunst Festival,* Podewil, Berlin, Germany
1998-1999 *Cities on the Move,* Secession, Vienna, Austria; CAPC Musee, Bordeaux, France; PS1 Contemporary Art Center, New York, USA; Louisiana, Denmark; Hayward Gallery, London, UK

1998 *Fast>>Forward, New Chinese Video Art,* Macau Contemporary Art Centre, Macau
1997 *Johannesburg Biennale,* Johannesburg, South Africa
1996 *The 2nd Asia-Pacific Triennial of Contemporary Art,* Queensland Art Gallery, Brisbane, Australia

Selected curatorial exhibitions:
2008 *Digit@logue,* Hong Kong Museum of Art, Hong Kong
2006 *International Symposium on Electronic Art Exhibition – Container Show,* South Hall, San Jose, USA
2000 *Hot Pot: Chinese Contemporary Art,* Kunstnernes Hus, Oslo, Norway
1996-2008 *Microwave International New Media Art Festival,* City Hall, Hong Kong

Shek Chun-yin, Stanthony

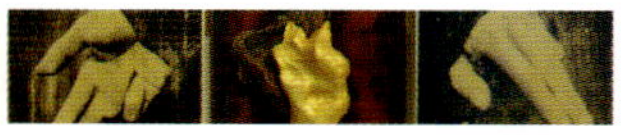

shekcy@gmail.com
www.shekcy.com

Stanthony Shek Chun-yin has recently completed a BA (Fine Art) majoring in painting from the Royal Melbourne Institute of Technology (RMIT) University, co-presented by the Hong Kong Art School in 2007. He completed a diploma in fine arts (concentrating on photography), organised by Hong Kong Art School in 2004, and completed the Certificate in Arts Studies (Visual and Applied Arts) organised by Hong Kong Art School in 2003.

Selected group exhibitions
2008 *Juxtaposition - Bachelor of Arts (Fine Art) Graduation Show 2008 ,* Hong Kong Arts Centre, Hong Kong
2007 *Holiday mood,* YY9 Gallery, Hong Kong
2007 *Merry Artists,* Too Art, Hong Kong
2007 *Little Things,* YY9 Gallery, Hong Kong
2007 *Sik7,* White Tube, Hong Kong
2007 *Variances in Singular,* Too Art, Hong Kong
2006 *On the Way,* RMIT Faculty Gallery, Melbourne, Australia
2005 *View Finder"s",* White Tube, Hong Kong
2005 *Diploma in Fine Arts Graduation Show 2005,* Hong Kong Arts Centre, Hong Kong
2004 *Arts Biennial,* White Tube, Hong Kong

Sin Long-yee, Stephanie

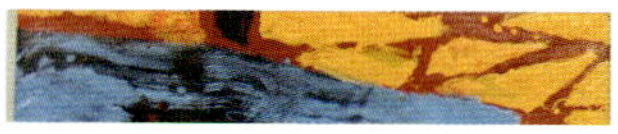

stephdonsin@yahoo.co.uk

Stephanie Sin Long-yee has recently completed a BA (Fine Art) majoring in painting from the Royal Melbourne Institute of Technology (RMIT) University programme, co-presented with the Hong Kong Art School in 2007. Sin likes to use paint to produce abstract and psychological works.

Selected group exhibitions
2008 *Juxtaposition – Bachelor of Arts (Fine Art) Graduation Show 2008,* Hong Kong Arts Centre, Hong Kong
2007 *Ning-gan,* White Tube, Hong Kong
2006 *Kong Jian,* White Tube, Hong Kong
2006 *On The Way,* RMIT Faculty Gallery, Melbourne, Australia

Selected curatorial exhibitions
2007 *Dialogue,* White Tube, Hong Kong Arts Centre, Hong Kong, China

So Yan-kei

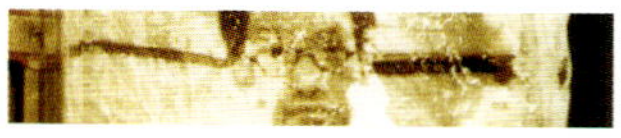

yankeiso@hotmail.com
soyankei@gmail.com

So Yan-kei received her MFA from the University of California in the USA. In 1999 she represented Hong Kong in the artist-in-residence scheme held by the PS1 Contemporary Art Center in New York City. So specialises in the application of various media to create an atmosphere that stimulates the audience to think about issues such as time, space and identity. She has received several awards and scholarships including the Hong Kong Ten Outstanding Young Persons Award (The Junior Chamber International Hong Kong, 2006), the Rising Artist Award (Hong Kong Arts Development Council, 2003), Asian Cultural Council Fellowship (New

York, USA, 2001), Freeman Foundation Asian Artist Followship (Vermont, USA, 1999), and first place at the Contemporary Hong Kong Art Biennial Exhibition.(1998).

Selected solo exhibitions

2006 *The Book's Cover,* Hong Kong Central Library, Hong Kong
2005 *6° 5' 53",* Hong Kong Arts Centre, Hong Kong
2002 *11,* Franklin D. Murphy Sculpture Garden, Los Angeles, USA
2000 *Can You Hear Me?,* Maastricht Central Station, Maastricht, Netherlands
2000 *White Ink Installation Works by So Yan-kei,* Para/site Art Space, Hong Kong
1999 *Installation by So Yan-kei,* Red Mill Gallery, Vermont, USA

Selected group exhibitions

2007 *Fine line,* Senko, Viborg, Denmark
2006 *Belgrade Triennial,* Exhibition Hall 2 of the Belgrade Fair, Belgrade, Serbia
2003 *OCEM,* West space, Melbourne, Australia
2003 *Battery Operated Car,* Track 16, Los Angeles, USA
2001 *Open 2001,* Venice Biennial, Venice Lido, Italy
2000 *Atopie,* Voormalig Bonnefanten Museum, Maastricht, Netherlands
2000 *Hide and Seek,* Mizuma Art Gallery, Tokyo, Japan
1999 *PS1 International Studio Programme Exhibition,* Clocktower Gallery, New York City, USA
1998 *Urban Council Fine Arts Award Winners Exhibition 1999,* Hong Kong Museum of Art, Hong Kong
1997 *Le French May - Perfect Tense,* Fringe Studio, Hong Kong
1997 *The Bad Art Show,* Fringe Gallery, Hong Kong
1996 *Peep Show,* Goethe-institut, Hong Kong

Van Lau

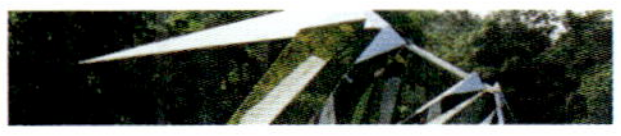

Van Lau was born in 1933. He graduated from the Fine Arts Department of the National Taiwan Normal University in 1990. He resettled in Hong Kong in 1960. He has been invited to take part in a number of international and local exhibitions. With different materials such as bronze, stainless steel and stone, Van creates works in geometric abstract forms, and his distinctive style is a fusion of Eastern and Western artistic influence. In 1999 he was awarded the Bronze Bauhinia star of The Government of Hong Kong and the Achievement Fellowship by the Hong Kong Art Development Council.

Selected solo exhibitions

1996 *Van Lau Recent Art Works Exhibitions,* Trigram Gallery, Hong Kong
1996 *Van Lau Sculptures Paintings,* Regional Council, Hong Kong
1993 *Van Lau Sculptures Exhibition ,* Szechwan Art Museum, Chengdu, China
1992 *The Exhibition of Sculptures by Van Lau – Bamboo series,* Hsiung Shih Gallery, Taipei, Taiwan
1979 *Sculpture works by Van Lau,* Hong Kong Arts Centre, Hong Kong

Selected group exhibitions

2000 *Album of Guangdong Contemporary Oil Paintings,* Guangdong Museum of Art, Guangzhou, China
2000 *Celebration of Macao's Return to the Motherland Exhibition of Chinese Art,* Macao Museum of Art, Macau
1997 *Contemporary Hong Kong Art 1997,* Beijing National Museum of Fine, Beijing, China
1997 *Reunion and Vision – Contemporary Hong Kong Art 1997,* Hong Kong Museum of Art, Hong Kong
1988 *Hong Kong Modern Art,* Beijing National Museum of Fine, Beijing, China
1972 *Vienna Prints Biennial,* Vienna, Austria
1970 *The 1st Korea International Prints Biennial,* Seoul, Korea

Wan Qingli

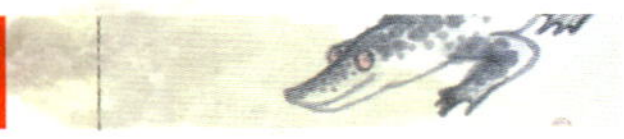

qlwan@hkucc.hku.hk

Wan Qingli was born in Beijing in 1945. He gained both his BA in art history and an MFA in Chinese painting from the Central Academy of Fine Arts in 1968 and 1981 respectively. Then he went to the United States in 1984 and received his MA and PhD from the Kress Foundation Department of Art History at the University of Kansas. From 1973 to 1983 Wan was an artist at the Beijing Painting Academy and a Research Fellow at the National Institute of Chinese Painting. He has taught Chinese art history at the University of Hong Kong for 17 years. Now he is the founding director and chair professor of the Academy of Visual Arts, the Hong Kong Baptist University and honorary professor at the Faculty of Arts, at the University of Hong Kong. Wan has published a number of books and more than 130 journal articles. Wan has hosted many solo art exhibitions around the world. His paintings are collected by noted museums and art galleries in China, Taiwan, Hong Kong and Europe.

Selected solo exhibitions

2006 *A Brush with Irony: Wan Qingli's Painting,* University of Museum and Art Gallery, The University of Hong Kong, Hong Kong
2003 *Paintings by Wan Qingli,* The Art Gallery of The Central Academy of Fine Arts, Beijing, China, Beijing, China
2002 *The Writings of My Mind,* E and J Frankel, New York, USA
1987 *The Scholar Artist in Modern China: Wan Qingli,* Wichita Art Museum, USA
1986 *A Cultural Taste from China: Paintings by Wan Qingli,* Missouri University Art Museum, Columbia, Missouri, USA
1985 *Precious Brush – Living Characters: Painting and Calligraphy by Wan Qingli,* E and J Frankel, New York, USA

Selected group exhibitions

2008 *Made in Hong Kong,* Hong Kong Museum of Art, Hong Kong
2007 *Tradition Redefined,* Harford University Art Museum, Boston, USA
2007 *The Third National Chinese Painting Exhibition,* National Art Museum, Beijing, China
2007 *20th Century Chinese Painting,* Seattle Asia Art Museum, Seattle, USA
2007 *Hong Kong art Collection,* University Museum and Art Gallery, The University of Hong Kong, Hong Kong
2006 *Modern Chinese Painting,* Phoenix Art Museum, Phoenix, USA
2005 *The 80th Anniversary of Palace Museum,* Beijing Palace Museum, China
2004 *National Landscape Painting Exhibition,* National Art Museum, Beijing, China
2004 *The 10th National Art Exhibition,* National Art museum, Beijing, China
2001 *M and K Sullivan collection of Chinese art,* Oxford University Art Museum, Oxford, UK
2000 *The 2nd international Art Biennial at Shenzhen,* Guan Shanyue Art Museum, Shenzhen, China
2000 *Chinese Painting: 1900-2000,* National Art Museum, Beijing, China

Wong Yan-kwai, Yank

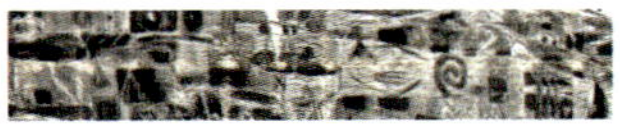

Yank Wong Yan-kwai was born in 1955. He studied art in France during the '70s then he returned to Hong Kong. He was appointed as art director for *City Magazine.* Wong has started his career as movie art director in 1980, and his works include *The Autumn's Tale* (1987) and *Summer Snow* (1995). In recent years he has been keen on writing, with articles published in *Wah Kiu Yat Po, Hong Kong Daily News, Today Daily News* and *Sing Tao Daily.* Currently, he is a columnist at *Ming Pao Weekly.*

Selected solo exhibitions

2006 *Visible Air: An Almost Transparent Landscape,* Hermes Store, Hong Kong International Airport, Hong Kong
2004 *Paintings and Painting – Yan Kwai Wong,* Shanghai Street Artspace, Hong Kong
1996 *Horizon II,* Gallery 7, Hong Kong
1995 *Horizon,* Gallery 7, Hong Kong
1993 *Balance,* Gallery 7, Hong Kong
1989 *Central Heating System,* University Museum Art and Gallery, The University of Hong Kong, Hong Kong

Selected group exhibitions

2005 *Dowda Happening: An Evening with Artists and Events without THE CANOPY Dowda Soy Sauce,* Sheung Shui, Hong Kong
2005 *Inspired by Jean Cocteau,* Hong Kong Film Archive, Hong Kong
2003 *Paysage-portage Exhibition,* Old Ladies' House Art Space, Macau
2000 *Sketch Extension 1,* Old Ladies' House Art Space, Macua
1998 *New Voices: Contemporary Art Dialogue Among Taipei,* Hong Kong and Shanghai, National Taiwan Arts Education Institute, Taiwan
1996 *Cultural Chop Shui 2,* Fringe Club, Hong Kong
1996 *Exhibition 6.30,* Hanart TZ Gallery, Hong Kong
1996 *Panoramic Visions – The 1st International Group Show,* Fringe Club, Hong Kong
1995 *Ac. Cul.tu.rat.tion: Art in Time of Change,* Low Block Exhibition Hall, City Hall, Hong

Kong
1995 *Contemporary Hong Kong Art 95,* Trigram Gallery, Hong Kong
1994 *A Festival of Installation Art: Documentary Exhibition,* Hanart TZ Gallery, Hong Kong
1994 *The Enigma Variations,* Gallery 7, Hong Kong

Wong, Wucius (Chung Ki)

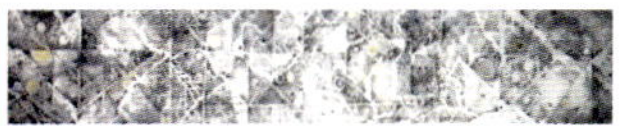

wuciuswong@hotmail.com

Wucius Wong was born in 1936. He has been creating ink painting since 1958. He received his BFA and MFA degrees in the United States. He has worked variously as assistant curator at the City Museum and Art Gallery and principal lecturer at the School of Design of the Hong Kong Polytechnic. Wong has held a number of solo exhibitions and was invited to take part in various important exhibitions in Hong Kong and overseas. He was awarded Emeritus Fellowship for distinctive achievement in the visual arts by the Hong Kong Arts Development Council (1998) and the Bronze Bauhinia Star Medal by the HKSAR Government (2007). His writings on art and design have been published in Hong Kong, Taipei, New York, Barcelona and Indonesia. His works are also collected by local and international museums. Wong is now serving as honorary adviser for the Leisure and Culture Department and adjunct professor of the Department of Fine Arts at the Chinese University of Hong Kong.

Selected solo exhibitions
2006 *At the East-West Crossroads,* Hong Kong Museum of Art, Hong Kong
2006 *Pleasures of the Brush,* Hanart TZ Gallery, Hong Kong
2002 *City Dreams,* Hanart TZ Gallery, Hong Kong
2000 *Recent Works,* Goedhuis Contemporary, London, UK
1998 *Ring of Fire,* Kaikodo Gallery, New York, USA
1987 *Mountain Thoughts,* Minneapolis Institute of Arts, Minneapolis, USA

Selected group exhibitions
2007 *China Onward,* Louisiana Museum of Modern Art, Copenhagen, Denmark
2002 *Hong Kong Cityscapes: Ink Painting in Transition,* Hong Kong Festival in London, London, UK
2001 *Beyond Boundaries,* Goedhuis Contemporary, New York, USA
2000 *International Chinese Ink Painting Exhibition,* Changzhou Art Museum, Jiangsu, China
2000 *Contemporary Guangdong Oil Painting,* Guangdong Art Museum, Guangzhou, China
1998 *China: 5000 years,* Guggenheim Museum, New York, USA
1998 *Shanghai Art Biennial,* Shanghai Art Museum, Shanghai, China
1998 *International Ink Painting Biennial,* Guangshanyue Art Museum, Shenzhen, China
1997 *Asia Traditions Modern Expressions,* Rutgers State University of New Jersey, New Brunswick, USA
1997 *The Chinese Root: Overseas Chinese Artists,* Shanghai Art Museum, Shanghai, China
1996 *Twentieth Century Chinese Painting,* Hong Kong Museum of Art, Hong Kong
1994 *Beyond the Borders,* Bronx Museum of the Arts, New York, USA
1993 *Summer Exhibition,* Royal Academy of Art, London, UK

Selected curatorial exhibitions
2000 *Solitary Peaks – Hong Kong Art,* Hong Kong Museum of Art, Hong Kong
1996 *Mutation of Ink and Paper,* Taipei Gallery of Chinese Information Center, New York, USA

Yim Wai-wai, Florence

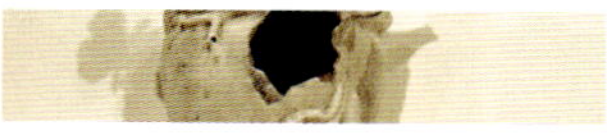

yimwaiwaihk@yahoo.com.hk

Florence Yim Wai-wai was born in Hong Kong, and graduated from the Department of Fire Arts of the Chinese University of Hong Kong in 1982 and obtained a higher certificate in Studio Ceramics from the former Hong Kong Polytechnic in 1991. She worked as an assistant curator at the Hong Kong Museum of Art, and course coordinator of the art specialist course (Ceramics) at the Art Promotion Office. She is one of the founders of the Art Farm creative art studio. In 2007 she participated in the artists-in-residence programme of the Shigaraki Ceramic Cultural Park, Japan. Her works are represented in the collections of the Hong Kong Museum of Art, the Hong Kong Heritage Museum and in private collections. She adopts ceramics, sculpture and mixed media in her art making, which reflects her strong interest in the forms of human body parts, biological structures and chemical reactions in the physical body.

Selected solo exhibitions
2001 *A Dialogue Between the Body and the Soul – Ceramic and Mixed Media Works by Yim Wai Wai,* O Café Gallery, Hong Kong.
2001 *A Limbo Between Sleep and Wake – Works by Yim Wai Wai,* Designfirst Gallery, Designfirst Institute, Hong Kong

Selected group exhibitions
2008 *Inside the Artist's World,* Art Gallery, The Hong Kong Institute of Education, Hong Kong
2007 *Works by 9 Resident Artists of the Shigaraki Ceramic Cultural Park,* The Museum of Contemporary Ceramic Art, Shigaraki, Japan
2007 *Visual Arts Thematic Exhibition 07/08 – HarmoNow 3D and Installation Art Exhibition,* Hong Kong Central Library Exhibition Gallery and Central Plaza, Hong Kong
2007 *Living with the Locale – Exhibition by Members of the Contemporary Ceramic Society (HK),* Exhibition Hall, City Hall Low Block, Exhibition Gallery, Tsuen Wan Town Hall and Tsuen Wan Plaza, Hong Kong
2006 *Creative Ceramics – Works by Contemporary Artists from Macao and Hong Kong,* Tap Seac Gallery, Instituto Cultural do Governo da R.A.E. de Macau
2003 *Yuanyang : An Exhibition on Coffee and Tea Vessels,* Flagstaff House Museum of Teaware, Hong Kong
2003 *Hong Kong Art Biennial Exhibition 2003: Trifling Skill – Works by Members of the Contemporary Ceramics Society (HK),* Exhibition Gallery, Hong Kong Cultural Centre, Hong Kong
2002 *Contemporary Ceramics Society (HK) 10th Anniversary Exhibition,* Exhibition Gallery No.4 and 5, Hong Kong Central Library, Hong Kong
2000 *Contemporary Chinese and Hong Kong Ceramics Exchange Exhibition,* Hong Kong Visual Arts Centre, Hong Kong
2000 *Clay · Form · Content,* The Hong Kong Institute of Education Art gallery and Hong Kong Arts Centre, Hong Kong
1999 *Seen / Unseen,* Hong Kong Visual Arts Centre, Hong Kong
1998 *More Than Utensils,* Hong Kong Arts Centre, Hong Kong

Yip Man-yam

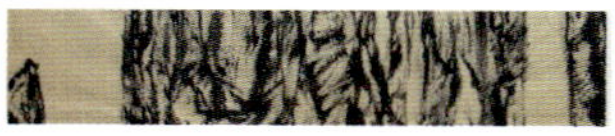

Yip Man-yam was born in 1949. He was a member of the Visual Arts Committee of the Hong Kong Art Development Council between 1999 and 2007 and is now a lecturer at the School of Professional and Continuing Education, the University of Hong Kong. His works have featured in important exhibitions in Hong Kong, China and overseas. Yip was presented with the Award for Calligraphy and Seal Engraving at the Contemporary Hong Kong Art Biennial Exhibition in 1994 and 1996 respectively.

Selected solo exhibitions
1999 *Chinese Seal Cutting Exhibition by Yip Man-yam,* Hong Kong
1992 *Chinese Seal Cutting Exhibition by Yip Man-yam,* Hong Kong
1988 *Chinese Seal Cutting Exhibition by Yip Man-yam,* Hong Kong
1986 *Chinese Seal Cutting Exhibition by Yip Man-yam,* Hong Kong

Selected group exhibitions
2007 *The Harmonization of Philosophical Ways and Calligraphy,* Hong Kong
2007 *Tradition and Idea,* Hong Kong
2006 *Life in Masterstrokes,* Hong Kong
2006 *Chinese Calligraphers Association Hong Kong Exchange Exhibition,* Hong Kong
2005 *Canghai Lienbo,* Hong Kong
2005 *Xiling Seal Association's Member Exhibition,* Hong Kong
2003 *Hong Kong Art Biennial 2003,* Hong Kong Museum of Art, Hong Kong

1997 *Contemporary Hong Kong Art 1997,* Hong Kong Museum of Art, Hong Kong
1995 *The 6th National Chinese Seal Cutting Exhibition,* Beijing, China
1995 *Dragon's Home,* Kobenhavn, Denmark
1994 *Hong Kong Art,* Kagoshima, Japan
1994 *Hong Kong Contemporary Art Exhibition,* Loa Angeles, USA

Yung Sau-mui

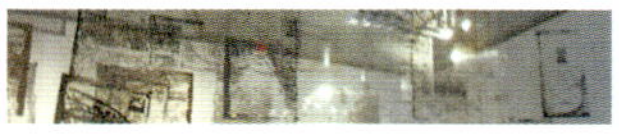

yung@open-printshop.org.hk
http://www.open-printshop.org.hk

Yung Sau-mui studied printmaking at the Hong Kong Polytechnic University, the University of Alabama, the Tamarind Institute and the University of New Mexico. In 2000, she founded the Hong Kong Open Printshop with her fellow printmakers and she is in the executive committee responsible for its project management. Yung was the recipient of several international arts awards including the Second Award of Macau Printmaking (1992) from the Instituto Cultural De Macau, the Tamarind Institute Scholarship (1995) from Tamarind Institute, the University of New Mexico, Albuquerque, USA and Making Art Safety (1999) from the Hong Kong Arts Development Council. In 2006 she was the artist-in-residence of the City Museum of Gyor in Hungary. Her works are collected by international art institutions.

Selected group exhibitions

2007 *Footprints: International Women in Printmaking,* Hyatt Crown Center Exhibit Hall, The 2007 Southern Graphic Conference, Kansas City, USA
2007 *Crossing Boundaries – The Hong Kong Graphic Art Fiesta 2007,* Hong Kong Graphic Art Fiesta 2007, Tsuen Wan Town Hall, Hong Kong
2006 *Footprints: International Women in Printmaking,* Bhasha Research and Publication Centre, Gujarat, India
2006 *Light Field,* Henric Petri Street 9-11, Basel, Switzerland
2006 *The 38th International Symposium of Artists,* Municipal Museum of Art, Gyor, Hungary
2004 *The 13th Tallinn Print Triennial,* Rotermann's Salt Storage Art Centre, Tallinn, Estonia
2003 *Prozess Skulptur,* Städtische Galerie Iserlohn, Germany
2002 *Virtually /Reality International Exchange of Prints and Digital Images,* Estampe Charleroi, Belgium
2001 *Impressed Dimensions – The Art of Printmaking,* Hong Kong Heritage Museum, Hong Kong
2000 *Reveal: Harmonise – The Macau International Exhibition of Prints,* Macau Museum of Art, Macau
2000 *Y2K International Exhibition and Symposium of Prints,* Chung-Cheng Gallery, Taipei, Taiwan and Yokohama Museum of Art, Yokohama, Japan.
2000 *Quingdao International Biennial Print Exhibition 2000,* Quingdao Museum of Arts, Quingdao, China

Selected curatorial exhibitions

2007 *The Graphics Art Fiesta 2007,* Tsuen Wan Town Hall; Hong Kong Visual Arts Centre and SD Gallery, Hong Kong Polytechnic University, Hong Kong
2001 *Contemporary European Graphic Arts in the New Millennium,* Exhibition Hall, City Hall, Hong Kong and Er's Graphic Art Center, Shanghai, China
2001 *New Vision: The Beauty of Miniature Prints in Hong Kong,* Hong Kong Cultural Centre, Hong Kong

Contributors

This book's precious record of Hong Kong contemporary art exists in no small part due to the immense collective effort of our contributors. We thank the young artists, writers and photographers who worked tirelessly over a six-month period to conduct the interviews, write up the articles and shoot the photos contained in *Oasis Vol.2*.

About Lumenvisum

Lumenvisum is the first photo resource centre in Hong Kong that aims to promote photography as a communication tool among individuals and communities, through education and exchange. It provides a platform for photographic institutes in Hong Kong, on the mainland and overseas. Despite their different backgrounds, which range from art creation and photojournalism to education, founders Dick Chan Kwong Yuen, Raymond Chan Wai Man, Leon Suen Shu Kwan and Tse Ming Chong share a similar vision. They believe people should be free to express their experiences, thoughts and feelings through visual images.

Dick Chan Kwong-yuen

Chan received his Master's degree in international communication from the University of Leeds in the UK in 2001. Starting his career as a journalist, Chan later became chief of photography departments at various Chinese newspapers. His humanitarianism led him to work as a project coordinator for the Salvation Army, which gave him a first-hand look at poverty, disaster relief work and various social issues in China and south Asian countries. His works focus on people, society and the environment, with topics covering child cancer and environmental protection.

Raymond Chan Wai-man

Chan has racked up three decades of work in the media industry. He studied photography in France after working as a sports journalist, and has also worked for *Wenweipo, Contemporary Magazine, Hong Kong Daily News, Today Daily News, Next Magazine* and *East Week*.

Leon Suen Shu-kwan

A veteran journalist and photo editor, Suen has worked for numerous local and overseas media and was chairperson of the Hong Kong Journalists Association for two consecutive terms. As curator of the exhibitions In The Eyes Of The Press and One Day in Hong Kong, Suen encouraged people to use images to record the changing face of Hong Kong as it was returned to China. He was also guest speaker for a photography exchange programme called Three Photographic Perspectives – Hong Kong, Mainland, Taiwan, presented by the Hong Kong Arts Centre. Suen is currently a lecturer for the Department of Journalism at the Hong Kong Baptist University and a part-time lecturer at the Hong Kong Art School.

Tse Ming-chong

Tse graduated in Chinese Journalism from the Hong Kong Baptist University and received his Master's degree in imaging and communication from Goldsmiths College at the University of London in 2004. He received The British Chevening Scholarship from the British Council, Hong Kong in 2003, and a Fellowship for Artistic Development, granted by the Hong Kong Arts Development Council in 1997, among other awards. His photo installation, Hong Kong Daily '94, exhibited in '-ism '95: The 1st Tokyo International Photo-Biennale at the Tokyo Metropolitan Museum of Photography in 1995. Tse currently works as programme coordinator and lecturer at the Hong Kong Art School. His works focus on how individuals behave in relation to history and society.

Teresa Chan

Teresa Chan was born in Hong Kong and completed a Bachelor's degree in fine arts at the Royal Melbourne Institute of Technology University (co-presented with the Hong Kong Art School) in 2007. Chan has taken part in a number of joint exhibitions, including *Absence* (2008), *Merry Artists* (2007), *In . visible* (2007), *Sik7* (2007) and *Quartet* (2006), and she staged her first solo show, *re-Place*, in 2008. Her work was chosen for the finalists' exhibition of the Siemens-RMIT Fine Art Scholarship Award in 2007. Chan works as a translator and continues to work in the art field by writing, translating and editing art-related projects and publications.

Stephanie Cheung

Stephanie Cheung is a graduate of the Department of Fine Arts at the University of Hong Kong. She has taught art history and art appreciation at a number of tertiary institutes. She is also a freelance writer, translator and editor.

Alice Choi

Alice Choi obtained her Bachelor's in social science from the Chinese University of Hong Kong, and earned a Bachelor's degree in fine arts from the Royal Melbourne Institute of Technology University (co-presented with the Hong Kong Art School) in 2007. She also obtained an instructor qualification from Mr Brian Bomeisler (the son of Dr Betty Edwards) in New York in 2008. Choi has contributed to various local art publications as editor, translator and feature writer, including *White Text*, *Oasis: Artists' Studios in Hong Kong*, and art exhibition catalogues. She has participated in a number of group exhibitions since 2006, and had her first solo exhibition, *Rereading*, in 2008. She was a finalist of the Philippe Charriol Foundation 2006 Art Competition.

Livia B Garcia

Livia B Garcia earned her Bachelor's degree in fine arts from the Royal Melbourne Institute of Technology University (co-presented with the Hong Kong Art School) in 2007, and currently works as a civil engineer. She has taken part in a number of exhibitions, including *Ten Years of Images — A Gift to Hong Kong* (2007) and *Fotan Artists Open Studios 2008*. Garcia exhibited as a finalist of the Siemens-RMIT Fine Art Scholarship Award in Australia in 2007. She is assistant curator of the *Art Container Departure Exhibition* (2008) and participates in other writing and editing projects.

Ronny Leung

Ronny Leung graduated from the Chinese University of Hong Kong with a Bachelor's degree in environmental science, and has worked as an art administrator and graphic designer. She currently works as an executive officer in the higher education sector. Leung was involved in the writing of *Oasis – Artists' Studios in Hong Kong* and is currently studying for a Master's degree in cultural management at the Chinese University of Hong Kong.

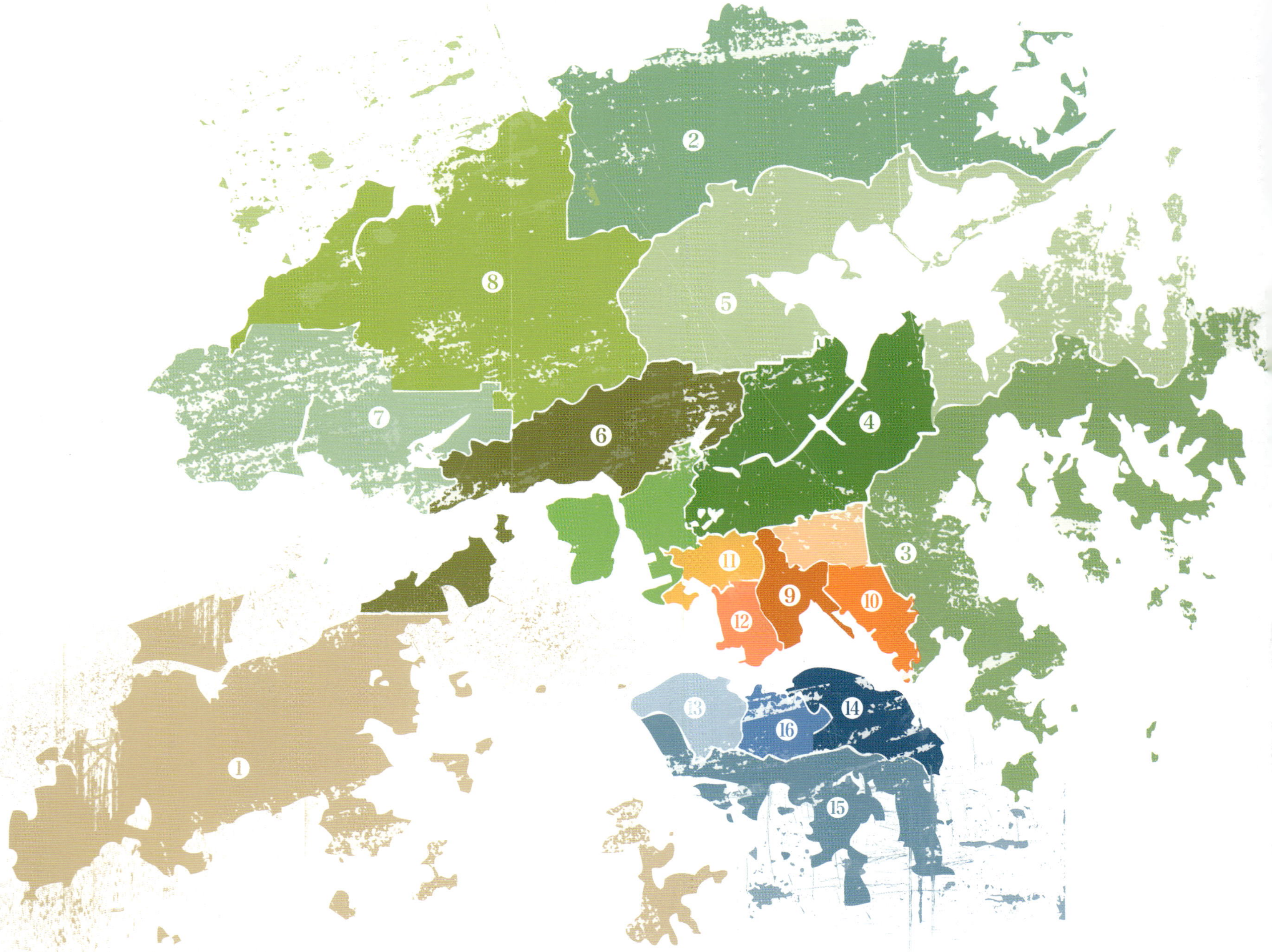

1 Lantau Island

Lantau Island

Tam Wai-ping, Lukas
Mixed-media, site-specific work
ltam@hkac.org.hk

Peng Chau

Lee, Winus
Ceramics
winuslee@gmail.com

Li, Conrad
Ceramics
conradlwy@yahoo.com.hk

Tung Chung

Sin Ying-suet, Joanne
Painting
andyjoanne@yahoo.com.hk

2 North District

Fanling

Ah 3
Painting, text-based art
ah3@hkbobby.com

Chau, Christopher
Ceramics
chris.chau.012@hotmail.com

Sheung Shui

Lai Wai-yi, Monti
Mixed-media
montilai@yahoo.com.hk

3 Sai Kung District

Clearwater Bay

Boon, Simone
Multimedia, photography, ceramics
simoneboon@hotmail.com
www.simoneboon.com

4 Sha Tin District

Fo Tan

Au Hoi-lam
Painting
au_hoilam@yahoo.com.hk
www.auhoilam.com

Chan Hiu-ting, Winnie
Oil painting
winniechan714@yahoo.com.hk
www.winniechan714.net

Chan Hon-mei
Painting, photography, mixed-media, installation
weibchan@yahoo.com.hk

Chan, Nichole
Mixed-media, ceramics
nichole_chan@yahoo.com

Cheung Yiu-wah
Painting
cheungyiuwah@hotmail.com

Chow Chun-fai
Painting, mixed-media
chowchunfai@chowchunfai.com
www.chowchunfai.com

Culp, Samantha
Sculpture, installation, performance, film/video, interdisciplinary projects
samanthaculp@gmail.com
www.embassyprojects.org

Fung Kwok-hai, Cyrus
Sculpture, installation
fungkwokhai@hotmail.com

Garcia, Livia B.
Painting, photography, objects
livialingsum@yahoo.com.hk

Acknowledgments

Unless otherwise stated, all photographs in this publication have been taken by Lumenvisum.

Special thanks to the following parties for providing images for publication:

20-21: Wucius Wong
32-33: Danny Lee Chin-fai
44-45: Jaffa Lam Laam
56-57: Ellen Pau
68-69: Ivy Ma
80-81: Pauline Lam Yuk-lin
92-93: Yank Wong Yan-kwai, Sin Sin Fine Art Gallery
104-105: Denise Chen Hui-lien
116-117: Florence Yim Wai-wai
130-131: Hon Chi-fun
132-133: Choi Yan-chi
144-145: Gaylord Chan
146-147: Josephine Chow Suk-fan
158-159: Tony Ng Kwun-lun
160-161: Celia Ko Tin-yan
172-173: Fung Ho-yin
174: Cheung Chung-chu
175: Yung Sau-mui
188-189: Kong Khong-chang
186-187: Lee Chi-hoi
202: Hanison Lau Hok-shing
203: Cyrus Fung Kwok-hai
204: Stanthony Shek Chun-yin
205: Stephanie Sin Long-yee
206: Jasmine Ho Sze-man
207: Winnie Chan Hiu-ting
220-221: Van Lau
232-233: Wan Qingli, University Museum and Art Gallery, The University of Hong Kong
241-243: John Li Tung-keung
254-255: Liew Come-tong
264-265: Leung Mee-ping
274-275: So Yan-kei
286-287: Luke Ching Chin-wai
296-297: Yip Man-yam
304, 308-309: Chu Hing-wah, Hanart TZ Gallery
320-321: Kan Tai-keung
329: Daniel Lau Chak-kwong

Heung Kin-fung, Alex
Painting
aheung@netvigator.com

Ho Chor-sze, Phiean
Painting, small sculpture, mixed-media
phieanho@netvigator.com

Ho Po-yung, Carmen
Painting
carmenh@gmail.com

Ho Sze-man, Jasmine
Painting
brushwood_hk@yahoo.co.uk

Ho, Jessica
Mixed-media
hojessica@netvigator.com

Hung Sau-lai, Jane
Painting, mixed-media
Janehung827@yahoo.com.hk

Ku Mun-chiu, Christopher
Painting
chrisku@netvigator.com

Kwan Sheung-chi
Mixed-media
artist@kwansheungchi.com
www.kwansheungchi.com

Kwan, Jacqueline
Painting
jacquekwan@gmail.com

Lai Cheuk-wah, Sarah
Painting
sasasarah_310@yahoo.com.hk

Lam Tung-pang
Mixed-media, painting
tinlamsky@yahoo.com.hk
www.lamtungpang.com

Lam Woo-cheung, Steven
Painting
stevenlamstudiohongkong@gmail.com

Lau Hok-shing, Hanison
Sculpture
hanison_lau@yahoo.com.hk

Law Yuk-mui
Photography, mixed-media
ar_mui2003@yahoo.com.hk

Lee Chin-fai, Danny
Mixed-media
dannyart_lee@hotmail.com
www.danny-leechinfai.com

Lee Ho-wing, Michelle
Painting, drawing, mixed-media, installation
howinglee@gmail.com

Lee Wai-bing, Iris
Painting
irislee@willygroup.com

Lee Kit
Painting
thrrough@yahoo.com.hk

Leung Chin-fung, Jeff
Mixed-media
read.jeff@gmail.com

Leung Ka-yin, Joey
Painting
kyljoey@yahoo.com.hk
www.hk.myblog.yahoo.com/joey-farmland

Leung, Marc
Installation, sculpture, drawing, performance
x1line@yahoo.com.hk

Leung, Teresa
Photography, installation, sculpture
twm_leung@yahoo.com

Li Tin-lun
Painting, sculpture, mixed-media
litinlun@yahoo.com
www.litinlun.com

Liew Come-tong
Painting
liewcometong@yahoo.com.hk

Liu Siu Jane
Printmaking, painting
ahjane_liu@yahoo.com.hk

Lo Ka-yin, Gordon
Painting, mixed-media
kylo221@yahoo.com.hk

Lo Lai-lai, Natalie
Painting, mixed-media
getupnat@gmail.com
http://lolailai.com

Louie, Karen
Paper, mixed-media
hamui@hotmail.com

Lui Chun-kwong
Painting
chunkwonglui@cuhk.edu.hk

Lui Long-ting
Sculpture, installation
squallingsoul@yahoo.com.hk

Lui So-kau
Painting
luikau@yahoo.com.hk

Ma Kwai-shun
Printmaking, painting
ksma@ied.edu.hk

Ng Choi-hung, Rainbow
Painting
ngbowrain@hotmail.com
www.bowbowrain.wordpress.com

Ng, Pauline
Painting, photography
paulinen@netvigator.com

Ngan, Clement
Painting
clementngan@yahoo.com.hk

Sham, Sam
Painting
i997@hotmail.com

Shek Chun-yin, Stanthony
Sculpture, installation
shekcy@gmail.com

Shieh Ka-ho, Wilson
Chinese ink painting
chengshieh@hotmail.com

Sin, Stephanie
Painting
stephdonsin@yahoo.co.uk

Tam, Tommy
Painting, computer graphics
artistoktam_ls14@yahoo.com.hk

Tang Kwok-hin
Mixed-media
hinyanhinyan0522@sinaman.com
www.flickr.com/photos/hinyantang

Tong Wai-kit, Damon
Painting, mixed-media
damon.tong@gmail.com

Tse Suk-ting, Sara
Ceramics
sara_tse@hotmail.com

Winnie Davies
Sculpture, oil painting, Chinese painting, Chinese calligraphy
wdavies@netvigator.com
www.winniedavies.com/

Wong Kit-yi
Mixed-media
wongkityi@gmail.com
www.wongkityi.com

Wong Tin-yan
Sculpture
tinyantinyan@yahoo.com.hk

Wong Wai-yin, Doris
Mixed-media
coffeedrinkme@yahoo.com.hk

Wong, Andrin
Sculpture, installation, performance, film/video, interdisciplinary projects
samanthaculp@gmail.com
www.embassyprojects.org

Wong, Antonio
Ceramics
mail@antoniowong.com

Yeung Yu-ling, Yolanda
Painting
ziziyo@gmail.com
hk.myblog.yahoo.com/iam-yo

Yim Sui-fong
Sculpture, mixed-media
yimsui@yahoo.com.hk

Yip Lai-man
Sculpture painting
laiman.yip@gmail.com

Ma Liu Shui

Van Lau
Sculpture

Ma On Shan

Cheung Wai-lok
Photography
lokvicki@yahoo.com.hk

Sha Tin

Chan Yuk-keung, Kurt
Mixed-media
kurt@cuhk.edu.hk

Wong Wing-tong
Painting, mixed-media
hunterwwt@yahoo.com.hk

5 Tai Po District

Chan, Gaylord
Acrylic painting, printmaking
ccstudio@netvigator.com

Ching Chin-wai, Luke
Mixed-media
sunnyside.hk@gmail.com
www.lukeching.blogspot.com

Chow Suk-fan, Josephine
Acrylic painting, printmaking
ccstudio@netvigator.com

Fung Ching-ping, Ivy
Multimedia
ivyphone@yahoo.com.hk
www.ivyfung.com

Yu Kei-kei
Mixed-media
keikeiyu@gmail.com

6 Tsuen Wan District

A Yip
Painting
mayipo@gmail.com
www.ayip.hk

Lai Ming-hoi, Victor
Painting
vlai@ied.edu.hk

Wong Sau-ching
Painting

7 Tuen Mun District

Yuen Mei-po
Mixed-media
po.yuen@gmail.com

8 Yuen Long District

Chu Hing-wah
Modern ink painting, Chinese painting

Leung, Bendick
Photography
bendick@netvigator.com
www.bendickleung.blogspot.com

Wong Mei-yi
Painting
meiyi1127@yahoo.com

Wong, Milton
Acrylic, digital painting, sculpture
milton99@netvigator.com
www.milmil.hk

9 Kowloon City District

Hung Hom

Fong So
Painting (Chinese ink and color), woodcut and linocut
fong@fong-yeung.com
www.fong-yeung.com

Li Wei-han, Rosanna
Ceramics
sdrosan@polyu.edu.hk

Kowloon Tong

anothermountainman
Photography, installation
0001@anothermountainman.com

Wan Qhingli
Chinese painting
qlwan@hkbu.edu.hk

To Kwa Wan
Cattle Depot Artists Village

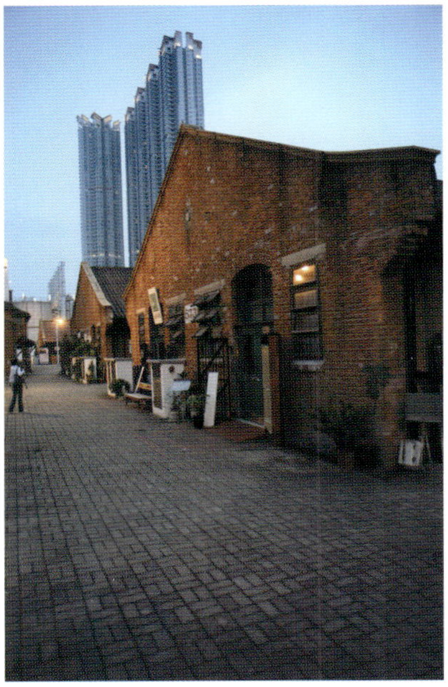

Kum Chi-keung
Mixed-media
kumchikeungkum@yahoo.com.hk

Lam Yuk-lin, Pauline
Installation, sculpture, performance, conceptual art
artpauline@yahoo.com
www.geocities.com/artpauline

Poon, Man
Painting, drawing, mixed-media
man@thinkbig.hk

10 Kwun Tong District

Kowloon Bay

Ng Kwan-to, Eric
Drawing, oil painting
ericng64@hotmail.com

Yiu Chu-tung
Drawing
afroady@yahoo.com.hk

Kwun Tong

Chung Wai-lun
Sculpture
wlchung433243@hotmail.com

Hui Wai-keung
Sculpture, installation, digital, interactive, video art
adam@huiwaikeung.org
www.art.huiwaikeung.org/

Lam Laam, Jaffa
Sculpture
lamjaffa@gmail.com
www.jaffa.net

Lee Pik-wai, Louise
Drawing, installation
pwlouiselee@yahoo.com.hk

Luk Tsing-yuen
Sculpture
luktsingyuen@gmail.com

Tat
Graphic design, illustration, street art
mail@graphicairlines.com
www.graphicairlines.com

Vi
Graphic design, illustration, street art
mail@graphicairlines.com
www.graphicairlines.com

Yu, Solomon
Painting
sawfishu@yahoo.com.hk

11 Sham Shui Po District

Lai Chi Kwok

Fong Wai-chung, Peony
Painting , video art
wc36vw@hotmail.com

Shek Kip Mei
Jockey Club Creative Arts Centre

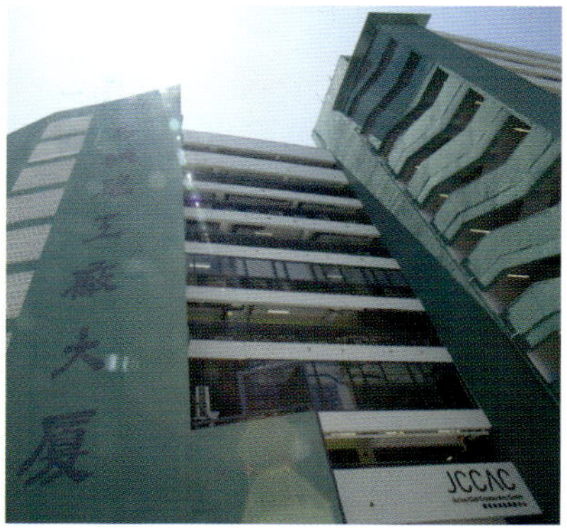

Chan Kam-shing, Chris
Sculpture
chrisvy@netvigator.com

Chan Mei-hin
Mixed-media
meihin@yahoo.com.hk
www.chanmeihin.com

Chen, Movana
Mixed-media, sculpture, performance, installation
info@movanachen.com
www.movanachen.com

Cheung Chung-chu
Graphic art
ccc@open-printshop.org.hk

Fung Ho-yin
Photography, gum bichromate printing, installation
hoyin@open-printshop.org.hk

Fung Suk-ha, Yvette
Painting
yvettefung2003@yahoo.com.hk

Ho Siu-kee
Sculpture
getkee@yahoo.com

Lee Chi-man, Paul
Action art
man_lee_hk@yahoo.com

Leung Mei
Oil painting, mosaic
mleung@edb.gov.hk
www.mail.am.npgps.edu.hk/~mleung/artroom

Lo Wai-hang
Painting, print making
lowaihang@gmail.com

Lo Wai-shan, Claire
Drawing, installation
winclaire@gmail.com

Lui Wai-yee, Ceci
Photography
play_work@yahoo.com.hk
www.luiwaiyee.com

Shum Ka-wai, Violet
Painting
violetshum@yahoo.com.hk

Tam Tat-keung, Andy
Performance, site-specific installation
andytam96@yahoo.com

Tang Ying-chi, Stella
Painting, fabric installation, mixed-media
yingchitang@yahoo.com.hk
http://tangyingchi.com

Tang Ying-mui, Grace
Installation
hkwindow@yahoo.com
http://hk.geocities.com/hkwindow

Tsang Chui-mei
Painting
info@tsangchuimei.com
www.tsangchuimei.com

Yung Sau-mui
Graphic art
ccc@open-printshop.org.hk

Tse, Laurence
Video, digital media
laurencetse@yahoo.com.hk
www.lztsework.blogspot.com/

Tse Ming-chong
Photography
mingchongtse@yahoo.com.hk

Yuen Yuen-ho
Painting
hopperyy@hotmail.com
www.hopperyy.blogspot.com/

12 Yau Tsim Mong District

Mongkok

Man Chi-loy
Acrylic painting
info@brokenbiscuit.com

Leung Mee-ping
Installation, mixed-media, performance, painting
meepingleung@hotmail.com
www.mpleung.com

Choi Yan-chi
Installation, painting
choiyanchi@netvigator.com

Hon Chi-fun
Painting
choiyanchi@netvigator.com

Tsim Sha Tsui

Yu Wai-luen, Francis
Painting
fyu@hkac.org.hk

Yau Ma Tei

Lau, Roger
Multimedia
roger@rogerlau.com

Studio Navigator

Central & Western District

al

ng Kai-sun, Suzy
ics
u@netvigator.com

gelo Costadimas
graphy
ks@mac.com
ecworks.com

ık-yin, Lucille
ing, installation
eshen@yahoo.com

hung
ainting, sculpture
222006@yahoo.com.hk

uen-wa
graph, painting
enwa@ngsartschod.com.hk

nedy Town
Celia
d-media, new genre
agogo@gmail.com

Tony
d-media, new genre
dge2004@yahoo.com.hk

Wan
w Ho-lam
amics
mou@hotmail.com

n, Sunny
nting
nflowersunny@hotmail.com

Ying Pun
ng Lai-ching, Fiona
amics
ng@hkac.org.hk

Eastern District

ai Wan
an, Cal
inting
lden_cd@hotmail.com

en Hui-lien, Denise
ramics, mixed-media
nise@dollarsaver.com.hk

how Yuet-wa, Emily
ixed-media
chow999@yahoo.com.hk

hu, Almond
otography
fo@almondchu.com
ww.almondchu.com

o, Carol
il painting, drawing
carol_@hotmail.com

Lam Lui-kong
Photography
jumpkonglam@yahoo.com.hk

Lam, Anthony
Multimedia installation
lamanthony@hkia.net
www.anthonylam.info/

Lau Pui-yiu, Alice
Painting
clio_alice@yahoo.com.hk

Lee Mei-kuen, Carol
Mixed-media
carolleemk@yahoo.com
www.carolleemk.com

Lee Suet-ying
Mixed-media
lelynnia@yahoo.com.hk

Ng Chui-ling
Mixed-media
whywhyamy@yahoo.com.hk

Tam Kar-wing
Painting
tkwingwing009@yahoo.com.hk

Wong Chun-yam
Mixed-media
leowong85@yahoo.com.hk

Yang Mei-ching, Circle
Painting
circleyang331@yahoo.com.hk

Yim Wai-wai, Florence
Mixed-media, ceramics
yimwaiwaihk@yahoo.com.hk

North Point

Hung Hoi
Chinese painting
hunghoi@netvigator.com

Ou Da-wei
Chinese calligraphy, Chinese painting

Yip Man-yam
Chinese painting, Chinese calligraphy

Taikoo

Kan Tai-keung
Drawing, poster design, public art
kan@kanandlau.com

So Yan-kei
Mixed-media
soyankei@hotmail.com

15 Southern District

Aberdeen

Wong, Wucius
Painting
wuciuswong@hotmail.com

Ap Lei Chau

Birch, Simon
Painting
info@simon-birch.com
www.simon-birch.com

Wong Kwok-choi, Kacey
Mixed-media
kacey_wong@hotmail.com
www.kaceywong.com

Wong Chuk Hang

Liang Yee-woo, Evelyna
Chinese painitng, installation
yiwoo@netvigator.com
www.2-woo.com

16 Wanchai District

Causeway Bay

Ma Ho-yin, Florian
Painting, photography, multimedia
florianma@gmail.com

Wong Mei-han, Yokky
Ceramics
yac@netvigator.com

Wanchai

Chan Wai-sze, Teresa
Mixed-media
ccteresachan@gmail.com

Cheng Chi-ming, Carl
Installation, mixed-media
chengchimingcarl@yahoo.com.hk

Cheung Wai-sze, Rachel
Ceramics
rachel_ws_cheung@yahoo.com

Choi Wing-sze, Alice
Installation, mixed-media
alice.ws.choi@gmail.com

Lai, Firenze
Painting
info@hulahoop.hk
www.hulahoop.hk

Lau, Sindy
Painting
sindy@sindylau.com

Lee, Chi-hoi (Chihoi)
Comics
chihoilee@gmail.com

Liao, Linda
Multimedia painting
lindaliao@hkpainter.com

Ngie, Lulu
Painting
info@hulahoop.hk
www.hulahoop.hk

Wan Lai-kuen, Annie
Ceramics
wan123a@hotmail.com

Wong Yan-kwai, Yank
Painting
yanksu@netvigator.com

Yuen, Steve
Mixed-media
steve@steveyuen.com

Foo Tak Building

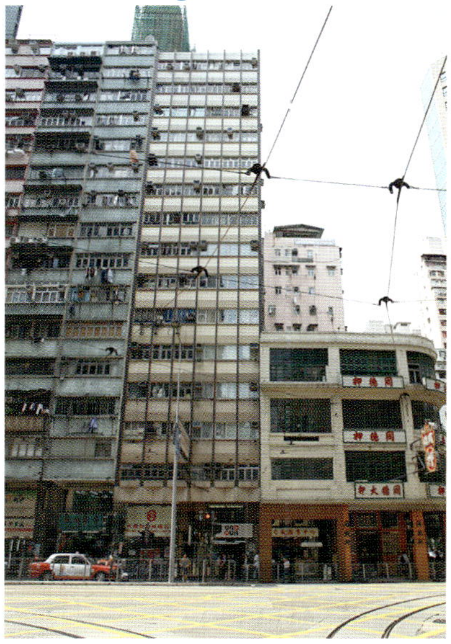

Cheung Hong-sang, Enoch
Video, interactive installation
enocheung@gmail.com
www.enocheung.net

Choi Chi-hau, Thickest
Video, photography
thickestchoi@gmail.com
www.thickestchoi.net

Hung Keung + imhk lab
Video art, interactive art
hk@hungkeung.hk

Fangönei
Photography
fansangonei@yahoo.com.hk

Kong Khong-chang (Kongkee)
Mixed-media
kongkee@gmail.com
www.shiningsummer.com

Ma, Ivy
Installation, mixed-media, painting
ivymelt@gmail.com
www.ivyma.net

Pau, Ellen
Film, video, installation, new media
ellenpau@hkstar.com
www.ellenpau.com

All data in this Studio Navigator is drawn from the best information available in 2008 and appears with the permission of the artists involved. For practical reasons, not all art studios in Hong Kong appear on this map. If you wish to recommend an artist or an art studio for our publications, or if you wish to take part in producing an upcoming Asia One Product and Publishing book, please email us at *aopp@asiaone.com.hk*.